THE ECONOMICS OF SPORTS

The sports industry provides a seemingly endless set of examples from every area of microeconomics, giving students the opportunity to study economics in a context that holds their interest. Thoroughly updated to reflect the current sports landscape, *The Economics of Sports* introduces core economic concepts and theories and applies them to American and international sports.

Updates for this sixth edition include:

- More coverage of international sports, including European football;
- A revised chapter on competitive balance, reflecting new techniques;
- A brand-new chapter on mega-events such as the Olympics and World Cup;
- New material on umpire bias;
- A completely redesigned chapter on amateur competition that focuses exclusively on intercollegiate sports. This chapter is also now modular, enabling instructors who wish to intersperse it with the other chapters to do so with greater ease.

This accessible text is accompanied by a companion website which includes resources for students and instructors. It is the perfect text for advanced undergraduate and graduate courses on sports economics.

Michael A. Leeds is Professor and Department Chair of Economics at Temple University, Philadelphia, PA, USA, and a research associate at IZA, USA. He has published numerous articles in labor economics and the economics of sports, and was co-editor of the *Handbook on the Economics of Women in Sports*. He has won departmental, college, and university awards for his teaching. From 2007 to 2009, he was an Assistant Dean at Temple University, Japan.

Peter von Allmen is Professor at the Department of Economics, Skidmore College, Saratoga Springs, NY, USA. He previously served as the president of the North American Association of Sports Economics, and his primary research area is sports economics, with a particular focus on compensation schemes, incentives, and monopsony power.

Victor A. Matheson is Professor of Economics at the College of the Holy Cross, Worcester, MA, USA. He is co-editor of the *Journal of Sports Economics* and has written over 80 journal articles and book chapters. In addition, he worked as a soccer referee for 30 years and has officiated matches in Major League Soccer as well as over 400 Division 1 college games.

THE ECONOMICS OF SPORTS

Sixth Edition

Michael A. Leeds, Peter von Allmen
and Victor A. Matheson

Routledge
Taylor & Francis Group

NEW YORK AND LONDON

Sixth edition published 2018
by Routledge
711 Third Avenue, New York, NY 10017

and by Routledge
2 Park Square, Milton Park, Abingdon, Oxon, OX14 4RN

Routledge is an imprint of the Taylor & Francis Group, an informa business

First edition published by Pearson Education 2001
Fifth edition published by Pearson 2014

Library of Congress Cataloging-in-Publication Data
A catalog record for this book has been requested

ISBN: 978-1-138-05216-1 (hbk)
ISBN: 978-1-315-16794-7 (ebk)

Typeset in Corbel and Myriad Pro
by Apex CoVantage, LLC

Visit the companion website: www.routledge.com/cw/Leeds

Printed in Canada

BRIEF CONTENTS

DETAILED CONTENTS

FIGURES

TABLES

PREFACE

As always seems to be the case, much has happened in the world of sports since the publication of the previous edition. From the doping scandals that rocked the most recent Olympics to the movement of not one but two NFL franchises to Los Angeles and the $200 million NCAA settlement over the cost of attendance, the economic landscape of professional and amateur sports is constantly changing. As a reflection of the dynamic nature of the field, the sixth edition of *The Economics of Sports* includes several major changes since the fifth edition.

Perhaps the most notable change is the addition of Victor A. Matheson from the College of the Holy Cross to the author team. Victor is an internationally recognized expert in the field of sports economics, most notably in the economic impact of franchises and mega-events. A second major change for this edition is a direct result of Victor's influence on the book: the addition of a new chapter devoted to mega-events, such as the World Cup and the Olympics. Separating mega-events from the analysis of franchise location and the costs and benefits of stadium funding allows us to analyze the public finance of sport more clearly and completely.

In addition to adding a new author, we have a new publisher. We are very excited to join Taylor & Francis. From our first meeting, we were impressed with their ability to see our vision for a comprehensive approach to learning sports economics that includes not only the text but also a full complement of online resources, including an author blog, mini-lectures from the authors, and enhanced lecture support materials and instructor resources.

From its modest beginnings as something of a novelty, sports economics has become a vibrant sub-discipline within the larger field of applied microeconomics, fully recognized by the American Economic Association as a stand-alone field with its own JEL classification code. Researchers tend to be drawn to the field for two reasons: the wide variety of interesting economic questions one can ask about the industry itself and the extraordinary availability of data that allow economists to use sport to answer broader questions about economic relationships.

As the research field has developed, the number of sports economics courses has grown as well. Throughout this growth and change, sports economics continues to serve as both a mirror and a lens; reflecting our broader culture and values, while bringing into focus such fundamental issues as fairness and the legitimacy of free markets. With the passing of each season, new events unfold in professional and amateur sports that call out for analysis. Finally, in the context of this book, sports economics remains a vital and interesting area of study for students of economics. Sports provides a seemingly endless set of examples from every area of microeconomics, giving students the opportunity to study public finance, industrial organization, and labor markets in a context that holds student interest like no other.

Over the many years that we have worked on this project, we have enjoyed continuous help and support from students and colleagues at colleges and universities across the United States and around the world. Our colleagues continue to offer encouragement, share classroom experiences, and suggest new and different coverage as the industry evolves. For all this support and help, we are most grateful. We hope that our own enthusiasm, as well as the enthusiasm others have shared with us, is reflected in the text.

New to This Edition

The sixth edition contains several meaningful changes that are reflected throughout the book. These changes enhance the features from previous editions that have made learning about sports economics meaningful as well as enjoyable:

- We have added significant coverage of sports outside North America, most notably, European soccer. While you will find discussion of leagues and events outside North America throughout the text, this new material is most evident in Chapters 3, 4, and 8.
- As noted above, Chapter 8 is new to the book. This chapter covers the economics of mega-events such as the Olympics, the World Cup, and the Super Bowl.
- Because we now devote significant attention to the Olympics in the chapter on mega-events, Chapter 12 now deals solely with intercollegiate sports in the US.
- The material on intercollegiate sports in Chapter 12 has been significantly modified to reflect the different ways in which people teach this material. Those who wish to treat intercollegiate sports separately from professional sports may continue to use Chapter 12 as a stand-alone chapter. However, the material in Chapter 12 now parallels the coverage of the preceding chapters. This allows instructors who wish to use intercollegiate sports to illustrate earlier concepts to "cut and paste" these sections into earlier chapters.
- We have added significant discussion of empirical findings of economists throughout the text.
- All tables and figures have been updated to reflect the most recently available information.
- We have substantially increased the volume and types of online support materials to include an author blog, mini-lectures from the authors, periodic updates of tables, and additional material that we were not able to include in the text.

As with the previous editions, our goal is to keep the text comprehensive yet accessible. The text is designed to serve as the foundation for undergraduate courses in sports economics. The nature of the subject matter makes this a unique challenge. Unlike area courses such as industrial organization or labor economics, which are self-contained fields in the broader area of economics, sports economics cuts across a wide array of economic disciplines. To deal with this problem, we have split the text into five parts, three of which are devoted to illustrating prominent areas of economics: industrial organization, public finance, and labor economics. We hope that this division provides students with an overview of much of economics and inspires them to pursue each individual field.

Intended Audience

Balancing accessibility against an economist's desire for theoretical rigor remains a challenge. Economics of sports classes are taught at a variety of levels, ranging from undergraduate courses with principles of economics as the only prerequisites, to the graduate level. This text is designed to provide the instructor a great deal of flexibility. All the material in the main body of the text should be accessible to students with a single semester of microeconomics principles. To enrich courses taught at a higher level, we have included appendices containing intermediate-level material at the end of several chapters. The online resources provide additional opportunities to add depth and rigor.

To ensure that all students begin the course with a common background, we provide a substantial review of principles-level material in Chapter 2. This material can be covered explicitly in class or left to the students to read on their own, as needed. For instructors interested in presenting econometric research, Chapter 2 contains an appendix on the fundamentals of regression. In advanced undergraduate- and graduate-level courses, the text can serve as a foundation for readings from primary source materials.

Organization of the Text and Coverage Options

As stated previously, the text is divided into five parts. The first two chapters introduce students to sports economics, review principles-level tools, and illustrate how economic principles apply to the sports industry. Chapters 3, 4, and 5 cover the industrial organization of the sports industry. Here, we discuss the competitive landscape, the implications of monopoly power, profit maximization, and competitive balance. Chapter 4 focuses on antitrust and regulation and how they have impacted the formation, success, and, sometimes, the failure of leagues. Chapter 5 explains why leagues worry about competitive balance, how to measure competitive balance, and how leagues attempt to alter competitive balance. Chapters 6, 7, and 8 focus on public finance. In Chapters 6 and 7, students learn the benefits and costs of providing public support for stadiums and events, why teams seem to have so much power over municipalities, and why municipalities fight so hard to keep the teams they have or court new ones. Chapter 8 presents the economics of mega-events, including why nations strive to win the right to host them and why the benefits rarely outweigh the costs. Chapters 9 through 11 focus on labor issues in sports. Chapter 9 introduces the fundamental theories of labor markets, including human capital theory and tournament theory. Chapter 10 covers monopoly unions and monopsony leagues, two labor market imperfections that profoundly impact the functioning of most sports labor markets. Chapter 11 discusses discrimination in sports. Finally, Chapter 12 focuses on the economics of intercollegiate sports. Because major college sports is an industry in itself, this chapter serves as a capstone to the text, incorporating the theories and concepts from many of the previous chapters.

Acknowledgments

In a project such as this, the list of people who contributed to its completion extends far beyond those whose names appear on the cover. We owe personal and professional debts of sincere gratitude to a great many people. First, we thank our editorial team at Routledge: Emily Kindleysides, Natalie Tomlinson, and Laura Johnson. We also are grateful for the advice, encouragement, and suggestions from the ever-growing community of sports economists who use this book. Their input and support serve as a continuing source of motivation and assistance. We would particularly like to thank all of those who read and reviewed the manuscript as we prepared the sixth edition. Their suggestions for improvements were excellent, and we tried our best to incorporate them wherever possible. A special thanks to Eva Marikova Leeds for her diligent review of the manuscript during the revision process. Finally, as always, we thank our families: Eva, Daniel, Melanie, Heather, Daniel, Thomas, Eric, Jolie, Lara, and Aly, all of whom provided unwavering support.

Michael A. Leeds
Peter von Allmen
Victor A. Matheson

Part One

INTRODUCTION AND REVIEW
OF ECONOMIC CONCEPTS

1

ECONOMICS AND SPORTS

All I remember about my wedding day in 1967 is that the Cubs dropped a double-header.

—GEORGE WILL[1]

Introduction

On May 3, 2016, the seemingly impossible came to pass: Leicester City F.C. had won the English Premier League title after beginning the season as a 5,000 to 1 underdog. This was their first championship season since their founding in 1884. Soccer fans the world over followed the team's run to the title and the victory set off wild celebration in Leicester.

Almost exactly six months later, the Chicago Cubs defeated the Cleveland Indians to capture their first World Series in over 100 years. While the Cubs' championship was less improbable than that of Leicester City, it was celebrated with the same intensity. Chicagoans could finally say that "The Curse of the Billy Goat" had been lifted. In 1945, William "Billy Goat" Sianis and his goat were denied entry to Wrigley Field to see the Cubs play in game four of the World Series. He reportedly said, "You are going to lose this World Series and you are never going to win another World Series again."[2]

Sports occupy a unique position in the human psyche. Athletic contests around the world have long been a way for individuals, institutions, cities, and nations to define themselves. Sports can bring out the best and the worst in people. As early as the 19th century, universities used football to give their students a sense of identity. Cities feel that they have achieved "big-time" status when they attract a major league franchise. At the national level, Japan's performance in the 2011 Women's World Cup provided a much-needed lift to a country devastated by the earthquake and tsunami and shaken by a near nuclear disaster. At the same time, police have had to quell riots on campuses in the wake of heartbreaking losses—or big victories. Reports of domestic violence rise in cities when "their" team is upset in the Super Bowl. In their pursuit of national pride, countries have sometimes sacrificed the physical well-being of their young athletes by giving them performance-enhancing drugs that have dire side-effects.[3]

Sports can also serve as tools by which nations conduct foreign policy. They have brought people together, as was the case in 1971 when a team of American table-tennis players and their "ping-pong diplomacy" marked the first step in the reopening of relations between the United States and China. They have also kept people apart, as demonstrated by the boycotts that disrupted the 1976, 1980, and 1984 Olympics.

The clamor over sports might lead one to think that the sports industry dominates the world economy. In fact, compared to many firms, let alone industries, it is relatively small. According to *Forbes.com*, the total revenues generated by the four largest North American sports leagues (basketball, baseball, football, and hockey) totaled about $32.15 billion in 2017, which would rank 89th among the *Fortune 500* list of largest revenue-generating companies (ironically one place behind Nike). The four sports' combined revenues are about one-sixteenth of those of Walmart and half those of PepsiCo, yet, unlike sports, Walmart does not have its own section in any newspaper, and PepsiCo is not routinely featured on "all cola, all the time" cable networks.[4]

This book harnesses our enthusiasm for sports and uses it to introduce a variety of economic concepts. These concepts frequently have applications beyond the business of sports. For example, understanding how sports leagues exercise monopoly power provides deeper insight into the policies followed by the Organization of the Petroleum Exporting Countries (OPEC) or Google, and learning about the impact of free agency on team payrolls shows how free markets affect the distribution of incomes in an economy. Studying sports economics thus provides more than an appreciation for the sports industry. It also demonstrates how economic reasoning helps us understand the world around us. This text emphasizes economic concepts rather than providing encyclopedic coverage of professional and amateur sports and athletes. As a result, we do not explain the particulars of every sport in each chapter, and some sports receive much more attention than others. The book includes significant coverage of the four major sports in North America as well as European soccer. As part of your course, your instructor may ask you to apply the lessons learned here to other leagues, events, or athletes, giving you the opportunity to apply the principles learned here.

1.1   The Organization of the Text

The text is divided into five parts. The remainder of this part provides an extensive review of basic economic tools, particularly supply and demand, the basics of production theory, and models of perfect competition and monopoly. The tools introduced in Chapter 2 are used throughout the text to inform a wide variety of questions in the broader sports industry.

The next three parts of the text are devoted to showing how three areas of economics provide insight into how sports function. Part Two presents the industrial organization of sports. **Industrial organization** is the study of firm strategy, such as how firms set prices to maximize profit, as well as the regulatory response of government when firms' interests conflict with broad societal goals. In Chapter 3, we discuss the purpose and structure of professional leagues by studying the largest leagues in North America and Europe. We also review competitive and monopoly markets and discuss the implications for profit maximization in each case. In Chapter 4, we extend the discussion of monopoly and analyze the challenges that concentrated markets create for consumers and would-be competitors. In Chapter 5, we investigate the desirability of competitive balance, how it can be measured, how it has changed over time, and how leagues have dealt with unbalanced competition.

Part Three contains three chapters on the public finance of sports. **Public finance** asks how and why governments provide goods and services, and how they raise the funds to pay for them. In Chapter 6, we discuss the potential benefits of new arenas for teams and the cities in which they play, and describe how the size and shape of facilities have evolved. In Chapter 7, we turn to the cost of these facilities, including an analysis of why local governments might view some or all of these costs as an investment and how to fund such an investment. In Chapter 8, we discuss the economics of mega-events, such as the Olympics and World Cup.

Part Four covers the labor economics of professional sports. **Labor economics** analyzes how markets determine the level of employment and compensation. In Chapter 9, we use labor markets to explain why professional athletes receive such high salaries. In doing so, we introduce labor market concepts, such as human capital and rank-order tournaments. Chapter 10 explores the monopsony power of teams and leagues and the countervailing power of player unions. We show how the two institutions set pay and working conditions. We also explore the causes and implications of work stoppages when leagues and players fail to reach an agreement. In Chapter 11, we discuss the history and implications of discrimination in professional sports. From the informal yet strictly enforced "color lines" that marked the National Football League (NFL) and Major League Baseball (MLB) until 1946 and 1947, respectively, to the limits that leagues such as Nippon Professional Baseball still place on how many foreign players are permitted on team rosters, sports provide many examples of discriminatory behavior.

Finally, in Part Five (Chapter 12), we broaden our study of sports to include amateur athletics in the form of major college sports. We begin with a brief history of the National Collegiate Athletic Association (NCAA). We go on to examine how the principles explored earlier in the textbook—industrial organization, public finance, and labor economics—apply in the context of intercollegiate sports.

Special Features and Additional Resources

At the conclusion of each chapter, you will find biographical sketches. The world of sports is filled with colorful personalities that add to our enjoyment of the game. Some of these people are well-known to even the casual sports fan. Others are less known, but all have played vital roles in the evolution of the economics of sports. These biographical sketches, the first of which appears in this chapter, highlight both their accomplishments in the context of the chapter and their character as individuals.

As you progress through the course, we encourage you to make full use of the internet as a powerful and easy-to-use source of information. First and foremost, the publisher of this text, Routledge, maintains a website specifically designed to support the book. Log on to www.routledge.com/cw/Leeds and you will find data, a set of interesting links, and supplementary material designed to enhance your learning. The site is updated regularly so that it contains links to sites and stories that are sure to be of interest.

In addition to the sites we provide, virtually every major (and almost every minor) league team, sports league, and association has its own website. These sites contain news (including economic events) from around the league. One caution: Beware of "fake news" or inaccurate, poorly maintained datasets that are rampant on noncommercial, individual blogs and private websites. The information they convey is often based on opinion rather than on fact and is of little or no value.

1.2   Babe Ruth and Comparative Advantage

Economics can often help to resolve what at first glance seems to be puzzling behavior. As we will see throughout the text, this is also true in sports economics. For example, consider how comparative advantage, a model normally used to explain international trade, can explain why the Boston Red Sox stopped using the best left-handed pitcher in baseball in 1918.

Opportunity Costs

In 1915, a young left-hander for the Boston Red Sox emerged as one of the dominant pitchers in the game, helping the Red Sox to World Series championships in 1916 and 1918. In the 1918 World Series, he won two games and set a record for consecutive scoreless innings that stood until 1961. From 1915 through 1918, he won 78 games and lost only 40, and he allowed slightly over 2 runs per game. In 1919, he pitched in only 17 games and won only 16 more games in the rest of his career, yet no fans complained. The reason was that the young pitcher was none other than George Herman "Babe" Ruth, who went on to redefine baseball as a power-hitting right fielder for the Red Sox and later for the New York Yankees.

Babe Ruth confronted the Red Sox with the classic economic problem of opportunity costs. An **opportunity cost** is the value of the best forgone alternative. We all face opportunity costs in our everyday lives. Our limited time, income, and energy constantly force us to choose between alternative actions. When we go to the movies on Saturday night, we no longer have the time or the money to go to a concert that evening. When the Red Sox used Babe Ruth as a right fielder, they gave up the chance to use him as a pitcher. (Because the main contribution of a right fielder is as a hitter, we will use the term "hitter" rather than right fielder from now on.) If the goal of a team is to win as many games as possible (an objective we will explore later in this text), then the opportunity cost of using a player at one position is the wins that the team sacrifices by not using him at another position. When the Red Sox used Babe Ruth as an outfielder, they sacrificed wins by not having a great pitcher in their rotation. If they had kept Ruth as a pitcher, they would have sacrificed wins by not having a great hitter in their lineup.

Absolute and Comparative Advantage

It is usually easy to decide where to use a player, as only a few players make good pitchers, and pitchers are typically bad hitters. Babe Ruth, however, was an exception. He was the best pitcher *and* the best hitter on the team. Being the best at everything meant that Babe Ruth had an absolute advantage at both pitching and hitting. A person or country has an **absolute advantage** in an activity when it is more efficient at that activity than another person or country. If the United States can make cancer drugs using fewer resources than Japan can, it has an absolute advantage in making cancer drugs. Because Babe Ruth was a better pitcher and hitter than any other player on the Red Sox, he had an absolute advantage over all his teammates in both pitching and hitting.

The Red Sox used Babe Ruth as a hitter because, although he had an absolute advantage as both a hitter and as a pitcher, his absolute advantage as a hitter was much larger than his absolute advantage as a pitcher. This meant that Babe Ruth had a comparative advantage as a hitter. A person or country has a **comparative advantage** when the opportunity cost of an activity is lower than it is for another person or country. Because Babe Ruth was such a good hitter, the opportunity cost of using him as a pitcher (the number of wins the team would sacrifice) was extremely high, much higher than for other players on the team. This meant that, even though Babe Ruth had an *absolute* advantage over his teammates as a pitcher, he did not have a *comparative* advantage as a pitcher.[5]

To see the gains from moving Babe Ruth from the pitcher's mound to the out-field more clearly, we compare the opportunity cost of using Babe Ruth at each position in 1918. The opportunity cost of using Ruth as an outfielder was the additional runs given up by Red Sox pitchers, which might have led to more losses. The opportunity cost of using Ruth as a pitcher was the reduction in runs scored by the Red Sox, which also might have led to more losses. Ruth's switch from pitcher to outfielder probably displaced Tilly Walker, arguably the worst of the Red Sox starting outfielders in 1917, and made room for Dutch Leonard, who had the highest earned run average (ERA) among the regular starting pitchers in 1918.[6] Ruth's last year as a full-time pitcher—1917—was an amazing one; he won 24 games, lost 13, and gave up about 2 runs per game. The first year that Ruth played mostly in the outfield was even more amazing. He led the league in slug-ging percentage (the average number of bases advanced per at bat), and his 11 home runs not only led the league, they were almost twice as much as the 6 hit by the entire Red Sox starting outfield in 1917.

Table 1.1 shows that replacing Ruth, who had a 2.01 ERA in 1917, with Leon-ard, who had a (still low) 2.72, meant that the Sox gave up 0.71 more runs per 9 innings than they would have if Ruth had had an identical year in 1918. Over the 14 games that Leonard pitched, that meant that the Red Sox' opportunity cost of using Babe Ruth in the field was about 10 runs in the 1918 season.[7] Using the formula for runs produced (runs scored + runs batted in − home runs) shows that Ruth produced 29 more runs in 1918 than Walker produced in 1917. Thus, the Red Sox came out 19 runs ahead from the switch.

At this point, one might ask why the Red Sox did not use Babe Ruth as a pitcher every four or five days and as a hitter every day in between. In baseball, the skills of pitching and hitting are so different that one cannot develop both at the same time. No American player has ever managed to play every day and pitch every fourth or fifth day, as acquiring the skills needed to become an elite hitter or pitcher demands a great deal of intensive practice.[8] This pre-commitment gen-erally does not leave enough time or energy to develop other skills.

More generally, one of the most important conclusions of the theory of com-parative advantage is that developing specific skills and specializing in activities

Table 1.1 The Gain and Loss from Moving Babe Ruth

Player	Runs Sacrificed	Runs Produced
Babe Ruth	2.01 per game	105 per season
Dutch Leonard	2.72 per game	—
Tilly Walker	—	76 per season
Net change	+9.94 per season[a]	+29 per season

[a]Uses 14 starts for the 1918 season.

Source: Baseball Almanac, at http://www.baseball-almanac.com.

that use these skills make individuals, firms, and nations better off. Professors employ research assistants and working parents hire day care providers because trying to do everything would take them away from the activities that they perform best. It is cheaper (more efficient) for them to pay other people to provide the goods or services than to try to do everything themselves.

At the national level, if the United States has a comparative advantage in producing cancer drugs, it is better off specializing in cancer drugs than in TVs, even if it has an absolute advantage over Japan in both products. The opportunity cost of our sacrificing cancer drugs to make TVs is higher than the cost of sending cancer drugs to Japan in exchange for TVs. Like Babe Ruth, we are better off specializing in what we are relatively best at and leaving the rest to others.

Biographical Sketch

Babe Didrikson Zaharias
(1911–1956)

> I knew exactly what I wanted to be when I grew up. My goal was to be the greatest athlete that ever lived.
> —Babe Didrikson Zaharias[9]

The theory of comparative advantage tells us that athletes are better off when they specialize. A quick look at athletes from the professional ranks to middle schools seems to bear this hypothesis out. "Two-way" football players have become a rarity, and athletes who play more than one sport have all but disappeared. It is thus unlikely that the athletic world will ever see another Babe Didrikson Zaharias. Zaharias dominated women's sports like no athlete before or since, achieving star status in the disparate worlds of basketball, track and field, and golf.

Mildred Ella Didriksen was born in 1911 to impoverished Norwegian immigrants in Port Arthur, Texas. The sixth of seven children and the youngest girl, Mildred got the nickname "Babe" while a young girl and still the "baby" of the family, though she later attributed the nickname to comparisons with baseball hero Babe Ruth. Her last name was changed to "Didrikson" because of a spelling error in her school records.

As a youth, Zaharias was drawn to sports at a time when sexual stereo-types still discouraged women from participating in "manly" sports, but Zaharias' working-class upbringing freed her from many of the restrictions that would have constrained her development as an athlete. She did not participate in organized sports, however, until she left high school in 1930 to play basketball for the Employers Casualty Insurance Company.

It may seem odd today for an athlete to advance her career by taking a job as a secretary for an insurance company, but at that time, many colleges did not offer athletic programs for women, and the fledging NCAA was openly disdainful of women's athletics. Employers Casualty played in the 45-member Women's National Basketball League, which played under the auspices of the Amateur Athletic Union (AAU). The AAU was then the dominant athletic body; it oversaw competitions by a few schools and by companies that sponsored teams.

The Employers Casualty "Golden Cyclones" were one of the best amateur teams in the nation. When the first All-American women's basketball team was announced in 1929, eight of its members were from Employers Casualty. Zaharias quickly established herself as a star among stars, being named an All-American for three straight years.

As good as she was on the basketball court, Zaharias had her greatest success in track and field. It was here that she recorded the greatest single performance in the history of track and field, and perhaps of any athletic competition. At the 1932 National Track and Field Competition, which was the trials for the 1932 Los Angeles Olympic Games, Zaharias was the sole representative of the Employers Casualty team. In one afternoon, she ensured that Employers Casualty won the team championship by winning the shot put, the baseball throw, the javelin throw, the 80-meter hurdles, and the broad jump. She also tied for first in the high jump and finished fourth in the discus, an event in which she normally did not compete. In all, she won six gold medals and broke four world records in about three hours. Zaharias hardly skipped a beat in the Olympics, setting world records in the javelin throw and the 80-meter hurdles. She also tied for first in the high jump, but some judges objected to her then-unorthodox style (the so-called Western Roll, which soon became the dominant style). As a compromise, she was declared the second-place finisher and won the only half-gold-half-silver medal in the history of the Olympics.

As the dominant performer and personality of the 1932 "Hollywood Games," Zaharias quickly became a national celebrity. Her publicity, however, came at a considerable cost. The public did not know what to make of a woman who defied sexual stereotypes. Zaharias seemed destined to fade from public view when the AAU stripped her of her amateur status for appearing in an automobile advertisement (even though, apparently, she had not given permission for the firm to use her likeness). After a year or so of stunts and exhibition tours, she returned to work for Employers Casualty.

Over the next several years, Zaharias reconstructed her personal and athletic lives. Stung by her treatment in the press, she strove to develop a more feminine image, playing up her role as a wife following her marriage to professional wrestler (and later sports promoter) George Zaharias in 1938, but she was anything but a typical housewife. Having picked up golf as a teenager, Zaharias threw herself into her new, more socially acceptable sport. In 1935, she won the Texas State Women's Golf Championship and was ready to enter full-time competition when the United States Golf Association banned her from amateur competition because of her appearance in the automobile advertisement. She responded by turning pro, but she quickly realized that professional golf provided neither adequate competition nor adequate pay. She succeeded in having her amateur status reinstated in 1943. Though she would have to wait until the end of World War II to enter the next stage of her athletic career, it was worth the wait.

Zaharias burst onto the women's golf tour in 1945, winning the Texas Women's Open and the Western Open, and being named "Woman Athlete of the Year" by the Associated Press (an award she had won 13 years earlier for her Olympic exploits). This proved merely a warm-up for 1946, when she won 14 straight tournaments. In 1947, Zaharias became the first American to win the British Women's Amateur golf championship in the 55-year history of the event.

After her victory in the British Amateur event, Zaharias again turned pro and a year later became a charter member of the newly formed Ladies Professional Golf Association (LPGA—it chose the term "Ladies" to avoid conflict with the unsuccessful Women's PGA). Her talents led her to be a dominant figure in the LPGA—she won about two of every three events she entered in 1950 and 1951—and her showmanship, while not always appreciated by her competitors, helped market the new tour.

In 1953, Zaharias was diagnosed with cancer, and doctors told her family and friends (but not Zaharias herself) that she had less than a year to live. Within four months, however, she was back on the tour, finishing as the sixth-highest money winner for 1953. She did even better in 1954, winning five tournaments and having the lowest average on the tour. The cancer reappeared in 1955, and Babe Didrikson Zaharias, arguably the greatest athlete of the 20th century, died in 1956.

Source: Susan Cayleff, *Babe: The Life and Legend of Babe Didrikson Zaharias* (Urbana: University of Illinois Press, 1995).

Summary

Sports occupy a unique place in the public psyche. Although sports generate less revenue than many other industries, sports results are predicted, reported, and analyzed in newspapers, magazines, books, and on TV and radio programs. This text presents economic models from industrial organization, public finance, and labor economics to provide insight into the economics of sports. As you read the text, you will learn about the largest sports leagues in North America and Europe, as well as mega-events like the Olympics and their power to illuminate economic theory. For example, one of the most important economic models is that of comparative advantage. Despite having an absolute advantage as both a pitcher and an outfielder and hitter, Babe Ruth specialized in playing the outfield because he had a comparative advantage at hitting over pitching.

Discussion Questions

1 Why do sports generate so much more news coverage than other industries that are much larger in financial terms?
2 Why do some countries prefer particular sports over others? What factors might lead us to follow different sports?
3 The theory of comparative advantage predicts that athletes perform better when they specialize. Studies show that young athletes are increasingly focusing on a single sport. Do you think this is a good idea?

Problems

1.1 Use an appropriate economic theory to explain why LeBron James might employ someone to answer his fan mail even if he can read the letters and type the responses more quickly than the person he employs.
1.2 Is the following statement true or false? Explain your reasoning. "I am attending college on a full athletic scholarship, so the opportunity cost of attending college is zero for me."
1.3 From 1946 through 1967, the placekicker and offensive lineman for the Cleveland Browns, Lou Groza, was successful on 54.9 percent of his field goal attempts. From 1999 through 2012, the Browns' kicker was Phil Dawson, who was successful on 84.0 percent of his attempts. Use the theory of comparative advantage to explain the massive improvement in the Browns' kicking game.
1.4 The term "figure skating" refers to the shapes that skaters used to trace in the ice as part of skating competitions. In the 1970s, this aspect of the sport was deemphasized and eventually eliminated. Use the theory of comparative advantage to show why eliminating this part of the competition has led skaters to perform much more difficult and sophisticated jumps and spins.
1.5 Carly Lloyd is arguably the best central midfielder in international women's soccer. She is also an effective attacker, scoring three goals in the Women's World Cup Final in 2015. Based on the theory of comparative advantage, what position should Lloyd play?
1.6 In 2012, the Indianapolis Colts released future Hall of Fame quarterback Peyton Manning despite the fact he potentially had several more years as an elite quarterback ahead of him. Explain why the Colts did this using the concept of opportunity costs.

Notes

1 George F. Will. 1998. *Bunts* (New York: Scribner): 22.
2 A.J. Perez. 2016. "The Chicago Cubs' Billy Goat Curse, Explained," *USA Today Sports*, October 25, at http://www.usatoday.com/story/sports/mlb/2016/10/25/chicago-cubs-billy-goat-curse-explained/92715898/. Accessed March 15, 2017.
3 See Katie Kindelain. 2012. "Kentucky Students Riot after NCAA Championship Win," *abcnews.com*, April 3, at http://abcnews.go.com/blogs/headlines/2012/04/

kentucky-students-riot-after-ncaa-championship-win; David Card and Gordon B. Dahl. 2011. "Family Violence and Football: The Effect of Unexpected Emotional Cues on Violent Behavior," *Quarterly Journal of Economics*, 126(1), February: 103–143; Steven Ungerleider. 2001. *Faust's Gold: Inside the East German Doping Machine* (New York: Thomas Dunne Books).

4   "Fortune 500," at http://beta.fortune.com/fortune500/list/. Accessed March 15, 2017. Forbes data are from *Forbes.com*, Business of Hockey, Basketball, Football, and Basketball lists. Revenue data are from the 2017 lists except for the NHL, which is 2016. Accessed October 21, 2017.

5   For a more complete explanation of Babe Ruth's comparative advantage during his career with the New York Yankees, see Edward Scahill. 1990. "Did Babe Ruth Have a Comparative Advantage as a Pitcher?" *Journal of Economic Education*, 21(4), Fall: 402–410.

6   The earned run average is the average number of runs a pitcher gives up per nine innings, the normal length of a ballgame.

7   The Boston Red Sox played only 126 games in 1918 because the season was terminated on September 1 due to the United States' entry into World War I.

8   Shohei Otani of Japan's Nippon Ham Fighters is doing just this. In 2016, he hit 22 home runs and had a 0.588 slugging average. As a pitcher, he went 10–4 with a 1.86 ERA.

9   Susan Cayleff. 1995. *Babe: The Life and Legend of Babe Didrikson Zaharias* (Urbana: University of Illinois Press): 46.

2

REVIEW OF THE ECONOMIST'S ARSENAL

To be a sports fan these days is to be taking a course in economics.

—ALLEN BARRA[1]

Introduction

As noted in Chapter 1, many aspects of sports business are hard to explain from a casual fan's perspective. In this chapter, we review some of the basic economic models that allow us to formalize our analysis and, in turn, explain why sports markets behave as they do.

Learning Objectives

- Use the basic model of supply and demand to explain the relationship between prices and quantity, such as why collectors pay much more for Mickey Mantle baseball cards than for Hank Aaron baseball cards, even though Aaron had better career statistics.
- Describe how teams use their most fundamental input—player talent—to generate wins, and how the law of diminishing marginal returns impacts teams' decisions on how to allocate that talent.
- Distinguish the various market structures that are present in the sports industry and apply the appropriate model to analyze such questions as why the Chicago White Sox do not lower their ticket prices when doing so would allow them to sell out like their neighbors, the Chicago Blackhawks.
- Explain why the era of professional sports began at the same time in two different countries with two different sports.

2.1 The Supply and Demand Model

The model of supply and demand is one of the simplest yet most powerful in all of economics. Recall that a **model** is a simplification of reality that allows economists to isolate particular economic forces. A good model allows economists to make predictions and provide explanations about the world quickly and easily. When the assumptions that underlie the supply and demand model are met, this model does just that.

Unlike physicists and chemists, economists and other social scientists find it difficult to conduct experiments. After all, it is far more difficult to control what people do than it is to control substances in a test tube. Even if economists were physically able to control what people do, ethical and legal considerations would make most experiments unfeasible. For example, it would be very hard—and certainly undesirable—for an economist studying bankruptcy to force a person or firm to go bankrupt. Instead, economists rely on theoretical and statistical models of market structure to make reliable predictions about behavior.

For all its simplicity, the supply and demand model has remarkable power to explain the world around us. At the same time, we must be careful to use the model under the appropriate circumstances. The supply and demand model is most suitable when there are many buyers and sellers of a homogeneous good (i.e., all suppliers are selling the same product), and consumers have good information about available prices across sellers.

Supply and demand show us how producers and consumers respond to price changes. Together, they determine how much of a good or service is produced and what value society places on it. In a different course, we might use these tools to analyze the UK's decision to exit the European Union or the impact of a higher minimum wage on employment. In this section, we introduce the concepts of supply and demand and use them to show why Mickey Mantle cards cost so much more than Hank Aaron cards.

Demand, Supply, and Equilibrium

An individual consumer's **demand** for baseball cards (or for any good or service) is the relationship between the price of those cards and the number of cards that he or she is willing and able to buy. It is a sequence of answers to the question, "If baseball cards cost this much, how many of them would you buy?" Or, from the firm's perspective, "How many would we be able to sell?" We compute the **market demand**, which shows the quantity that all consumers combined purchase at each price, by summing the individual demand curves, that is, by adding the quantity that each consumer purchases at each price. Figure 2.1 shows the **market demand curve** for a specific player's baseball card. Note that the curve is downward sloping, as the price–quantity relationship is invariably negative. As the price of cards falls, the number of cards that consumers buy rises. Economists call the negative relationship between price and quantity the **law of demand**. A change in a good's price causes a **change in quantity demanded**, moving quantity up along the demand curve when the price rises and down the demand curve when the price falls.

The **supply** of baseball cards relates price to the number of cards that sellers are willing and able to provide. Unlike consumers, who view the price of an item as the sacrifice they must make, producers view the price as a reward. As a result, higher prices encourage producers (sellers) to offer more cards. For existing cards, an increase in the price gives more card owners an incentive to offer their

Figure 2.1
The Demand for Baseball Cards

As the price of baseball cards falls, the quantity demanded rises.

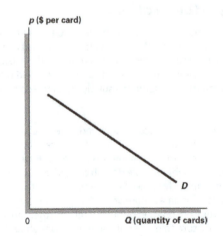

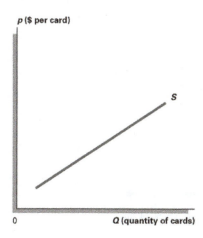

p ($ per card)

S

0   *Q* (quantity of cards)

Figure 2.2
The Supply of Baseball Cards

As the price of baseball cards rises,
the quantity supplied also rises.

cards for sale. In addition, sellers have an incentive to produce more new cards as the price rises. At the same time, other producers have an incentive to stop what they are doing and start producing cards. Some economists call the positive relationship between price and quantity the **law of supply.**

Similar to market demand, the **market supply curve** is the sum of the individual supply curves. The market supply curve is typically upward sloping, as seen in Figure 2.2. Again, if the price of cards changes, the quantity moves along the supply curve, a movement that economists call a **change in quantity supplied.**

Taken separately, demand and supply say nothing about the price of an item or how much of it is bought and sold. To find out what happens in the marketplace, one must look at supply and demand together. Figures 2.3a and 2.3b show that the two curves cross at the point labeled *e*. Economists call *e* the **equilibrium point** because, at that point, the actions of consumers and producers are in balance. Consumers are willing and able to buy Q_e cards at the price p_e, which is exactly the quantity that producers are willing and able to sell at that price. As a result, neither consumers nor producers have any desire to alter their actions, the price stays at p_e, and the quantity at Q_e.

Figure 2.3a shows that, at a price higher than p_e (such as p_h), **disequilibrium** occurs because producers want to sell Q_s while consumers want to buy only Q_d. Unable to sell all the cards they want, producers face a **surplus** or **excess supply**. Frustrated producers lower their prices in order to attract more customers. The lower price encourages consumers to buy more cards and discourages producers from selling them. As Q_d rises and Q_s falls, the excess supply falls until it equals zero, and equilibrium is restored at p_e.

Figure 2.3b shows that, at a price below the equilibrium $\left(p_l\right)$, buyers want to purchase Q_d cards while sellers want to sell only Q_s. The **shortage** or **excess demand** for cards at p_l drives the price upward until the shortage disappears at p_e.

We cannot actually see the supply and demand curves of the products we consume. We do, however, observe equilibrium prices. For example, baseball trading card prices are published regularly in price guides. In 1955, the Bowman Company produced a set of cards known as the "TV set," with pictures of players

Figure 2.3
Equilibrium in the Baseball Card Market

Equilibrium occurs at price p_e, where the supply and demand curves meet.

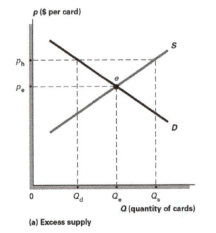

(a) Excess supply

A price of p_h results in excess supply

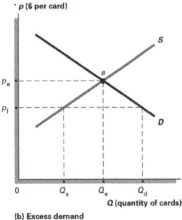

(b) Excess demand

A price of p_l results in excess demand

Table 2.1 Career Statistics of Hank Aaron and Mickey Mantle

	AB	H	R	HR	RBI	Avg.	Card Price
Hank Aaron	12,364	3,771	2,174	755	2,297	.305	$250
Mickey Mantle	8,102	2,415	1,677	536	1,509	.298	$800

Sources: Player statistics are from MLB.com; card prices are from *Beckett Baseball Card Price Guide,* 2016, p. 37.

appearing on the face of the card bordered by what appears to be a television set. Included in that set are the cards of Mickey Mantle, perhaps the greatest switch-hitting power hitter ever, and Hank Aaron, who was MLB's all-time home run leader from 1974 to 2007.

According to the *Beckett Baseball Card Price Guide,* which tracks card values, the 2016 prices of Mantle and Aaron cards from the 1955 Bowman set were $800 and $250, respectively.[2] Such a large difference in price is difficult to justify, given that Hank Aaron had more home runs (HR), hits (H), runs scored (R), runs batted in (RBI), and a higher batting average (Avg.) than Mantle (see Table 2.1). We can use the simple supply and demand model as an analytical tool to investigate the difference in prices. Because the forces of supply and demand determine prices, the explanation must lie in differences in supply, in demand, or in both.

Changes in Supply and Demand

The supply and demand relationships are not permanently fixed. They can change for many different reasons. This section reviews why the supply or demand curve might shift, and the effects that shifts have on the equilibrium price and quantity.

Factors That Affect the Location of the Demand Curve

Economists call a shift of the demand curve a **change in demand**. A change in demand stems from a change in any of five underlying factors: consumer income, the prices of substitutes or complements, consumer tastes, the number of consumers in the market, and the expectations that consumers hold.

We have seen that consumers typically buy more of a good if their incomes increase, but frequent exceptions exist. If a hockey fan living in Providence, RI, gets a raise, he might buy more hockey cards of the Providence Bruins, the local minor league team. Alternatively, he might buy fewer cards of the Providence Bruins and more cards of the National Hockey League's (NHL's) Boston Bruins. If he buys more cards of the Providence Bruins as his income rises, then the cards are normal goods. **Normal goods** get their name because consumers normally buy more of a good or service when their incomes rise. If the fan buys fewer cards, then the cards are inferior goods. **Inferior goods** need not be undesirable or poorly made. One simply buys fewer of them as one's income rises.

If hockey fans buy fewer Providence Bruins cards when their incomes fall, it seems reasonable to conclude that they would go to fewer hockey games as well. We can also ask whether the recession of 2008–2009 had a negative impact on professional sports, or if sports are "recession-proof." The evidence is mixed. Attendance at the four major sports in 2008 and early 2009 was not significantly below previous levels, but all else was not held equal as incomes fell. Some National Basketball Association (NBA) teams sold tickets at significant discounts to prop up attendance. According to ESPN.com, the Memphis Grizzlies drew about as many fans in 2008–2009 (about 12,600 per game) as they did in 2007–2008 (12,770), but they sold their tickets so cheaply that the team's gross revenue per game was only $300,000, an average of less than $24 per fan.[3] Similarly, some MLB teams discounted 2009 season tickets by up to 25 percent, and the New York Yankees had to cut the prices of some premium seats in the new ballpark by half.[4]

The major North American sports leagues have a safety net in the form of long-term TV contracts. As long as recessions do not outlast these contracts, the guaranteed income of these contracts helps to sustain teams. Sports and athletes that rely heavily on year-to-year sponsorships, such as golf and tennis, are more vulnerable. Formula 1 and the National Association for Stock Car Auto Racing (NASCAR) were particularly hard-hit by the downturn, as they rely heavily on sponsorships by car manufacturers that were devastated by the recession.[5] Similarly, the LPGA reduced its tournament schedule from 34 events in 2008 to 31 in 2009, and total prize money fell by about $5 million.[6]

When the price of a substitute good increases, the demand curve shifts to the right. If a card collector views Mickey Mantle cards and Yogi Berra cards as reasonable substitutes, an increase in the price of Yogi Berra cards causes the demand curve for Mickey Mantle cards to shift to the right.

The opposite effect occurs when the price of a complement increases. For example, older cards need protection from bending and other mishaps that reduce the value of the card. The best way to prevent such accidents is to keep the cards in protective sleeves. If the price of the sleeves rises, the demand for cards falls. This occurs because collectors use the two products together and think of them as a single commodity. When the price of sleeves rises, the price of a card with a sleeve also rises, reducing demand for cards. Figure 2.4a shows the impact of an increase in income and a reduction in the price of a substitute good on the demand curve.

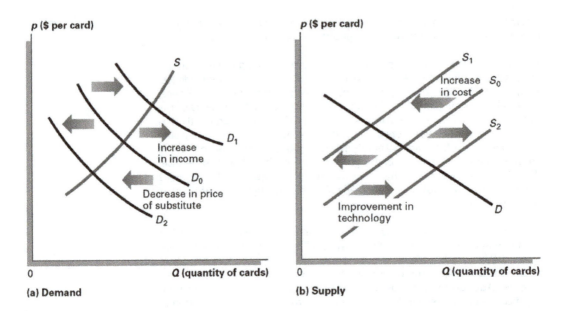

(a) Demand

(b) Supply

Figure 2.4
Changes in the Demand for and Supply of Baseball Cards

Demand and supply curves may shift to the left or right as market conditions change.

Changes in tastes and preferences can also shift the demand curve. In his book *The Blind Side*, Michael Lewis provides an interesting example of how tastes can affect the demand for a specific service.[7] Lewis notes that, until the 1980s, offensive linemen were regarded largely as interchangeable units and were among the lowest-paid players on a football team. Today, left tackles are highly sought-after specialists and are among the most highly paid players on the team. The premium paid to left tackles represents a change in tastes by football teams that have increasingly emphasized the forward pass.

The growing emphasis on the forward pass has made quarterbacks the stars of their teams and made protecting them a priority. It has become particularly important to protect quarterbacks from behind, their "blind side," where they cannot see oncoming defenders. This required players big enough to stand up to defensive ends but fast enough to move over to block linebackers. Left tackle (which protects a right-handed quarterback's blind side) thus became a unique—and highly paid—position.

Another example of the impact of tastes on prices can be found in ticket prices charged by MLB teams. Traditionally, teams have charged a fixed price for a given seat location, regardless of the opponent. Recently, they have started to behave more like European soccer teams or Japanese baseball teams by charging higher prices when more popular teams, such as the New York Yankees or the Boston Red Sox, come to town in a strategy known as variable ticket pricing. Some teams, such as the San Francisco Giants, even change ticket prices based on pitching matchups. The practice of altering ticket prices after the season begins is known as dynamic pricing. We will return to this concept in Chapter 4, but even with our simple model of supply and demand, we can predict that, because the supply of seats is the same regardless of who the visiting team is, differences in price must reflect changes in the demand curve. The demand curve for teams like the Red Sox and Yankees is farther to the right than for most other teams because of the greater taste of fans for seeing these teams play.[8]

The number of consumers in the market can also affect demand. For example, all else equal, the demand for Houston Astros tickets is likely to be greater than the demand for Atlanta Braves tickets because, with a population of well over 2 million, Houston is more than four times the size of Atlanta.

Finally, expectations of future prices can affect demand. A collector who believes that the prices of cards will rise in the near future is willing to buy more cards at any given price than a collector who believes that prices will remain stable. The expectation of a price increase shifts the collector's demand curve to the right. Similarly, if the collector believes that prices will fall, his demand curve shifts to the left.

Factors That Affect the Location of the Supply Curve

As was the case for demand, the position of the supply curve also depends on several underlying factors. A **change in supply** results from a change in input prices, technology, taxes, expectations held by producers, and natural events that destroy or promote products or resources.

An increase in input prices shifts the supply curve leftward. In the case of baseball cards, if the price of paper products rises, the cost of producing each baseball card rises as well. At any given price, the net return to making and selling cards is lower than before, and the incentive to provide cards falls. Card manufacturers produce fewer cards at any given price, and the supply curve shifts to the left from S_0 to S_1 in Figure 2.4b.

A technological innovation that reduces the cost of making cards increases the profitability of making cards and encourages producers to make and sell more cards. The technological advance shifts the supply curve rightward to S_2.

A sales tax on cards introduces a wedge between the price the consumer pays and the price the producer receives and results in a second supply curve. Figure 2.5 shows that the vertical difference between the two supply curves equals the amount of the per-unit tax. For example, a $0.10 per card tax on producers results in a new supply curve that lies $0.10 above the original. The price that consumers must pay (p_t) is determined by the intersection of the demand curve with the supply curve that includes the tax. Quantity decreases to Q_t because consumers are willing to purchase fewer cards at the higher price. The price that sellers receive is the price for Q_t cards on the original supply curve and is equal to the price that consumers pay minus the tax $(p_t - t)$. The difference between the price that consumers pay and the price that sellers receive is the per-unit tax, t. Multiplying the per-unit tax by the number of cards sold, Q_t, yields the tax revenue collected by the government. In Figure 2.5, this area is shaded gray.

Natural disasters also affect the location of the supply curve. If a hurricane damaged the card factory, it would temporarily reduce the availability of new cards. The world saw stark evidence of this type of event when a major earthquake struck Japan in 2011. The quake damaged many factories and a major nuclear energy facility, temporarily disrupting the production of such products as autos worldwide, as even non-Japanese automakers scrambled to find alternative suppliers of parts normally produced in Japan.[9] Closer to home, the New Orleans Saints were unable to play any home games during the 2005 season due to the damage to their home stadium caused by Hurricane Katrina, reducing the supply of NFL games in New Orleans to zero for the season.[10]

Figure 2.5
**A Change in Supply Due
to a Tax**

A tax causes consumers to see
the supply curve $S_0 +$ tax while
producers still act along S_0.

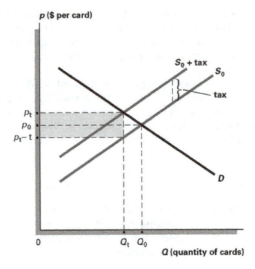

Finally, if producers expect prices to rise in the future, they have an incentive
to wait until prices rise before selling their product. At any price, producers are
willing to provide less today, if they think that they will be able to sell for more
tomorrow, and the supply curve shifts to the left.

Elasticity of Supply

Economists are often less interested in how much producers produce than in
how sensitive their production decisions are to changes in price. If the card producer has a steep supply curve, such as S_0 in Figure 2.6, then it appears that
firms do not respond very much to an increase in price. As price rises from p_0
to p_1 output grows from Q_0 cards to only Q_1. If the supply curve is relatively flat
(S_1), producers respond to the price increase by expanding output from Q'_0 to Q'_1.
Slope, however, is a misleading measure of sensitivity.

Suppose, for example, that the price of a pack of baseball cards rises from $0.10
to $0.11 and that firms respond by printing 200 more packs of cards. The slope
of the supply curve is the change in price divided by the change in quantity, or
$0.01/200 packs. The problem is that 200 packs can represent a big change in
the number of packs produced or a very small change, depending on how many
packs firms had been printing to begin with. Increasing production by 200 packs
means much more to producers if they expand from 1,000 packs to 1,200 than
if they expand from 10,000 packs to 10,200. As a result, slope cannot tell us how
meaningful the increase of 200 packs really is.

Economists account for the producers' starting point by using percentage
changes in price and output rather than absolute changes.[11] They use these percentage changes to measure the sensitivity of production to changes in price.
We call this measure the elasticity of supply (which we denote as ε_s). The **elasticity of supply** is the percentage change in quantity that results from a given
percentage change in price:

$$\varepsilon_s = \frac{\%\Delta Q^s}{\%\Delta p}$$

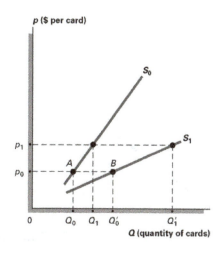

Figure 2.6
Relatively Elastic versus Inelastic Supply

Elasticity depends on more than just the slope of the curve.

In the above example, the $0.01 increase in the price of a pack of cards corresponds to a percentage change of $0.01/$0.10 = 0.10, or 10 percent. If firms originally produced 1,000 packs of cards, then the percentage change in quantity is $(1,200 - 1,000)/1,000 = 0.2$, or 20 percent, and the elasticity of supply is $\varepsilon_s = 0.2/0.1 = 2.0$. When the price of a pack of cards rises by 10 percent, producers increase their output by 20 percent. The percentage increase in output is twice the percentage rise in price.

Although the supply curve's location and elasticity are important for many of the issues we deal with later in the book, they cannot resolve our question about the relative prices of Mantle and Aaron cards. To simplify the analysis, we will make two weak assumptions and one strong assumption. A **weak assumption** is likely to be true in real life, while a **strong assumption** is often not true. Strong assumptions can be valuable, however, as long as the conclusions we draw are valid even when the assumption is not strictly true. In this case, our weak assumptions are that the Bowman Company produced the same number of Mickey Mantle and Hank Aaron cards and that the same number of Mantle and Aaron cards have survived in perfect (mint) condition. Our strong assumption is that the owners of these cards are willing and able to sell the same number of each player's cards at every price, making the supply curves identical. Figure 2.7 shows the supply curves for Hank Aaron (S_A) and Mickey Mantle (S_M) cards.

Elasticity of Demand

As with supply, we are often interested in the sensitivity of demand to changes in price rather than absolute levels of price and quantity. The **elasticity of demand** (ε_d) is the percentage change in quantity demanded for a given percentage change in price. The only difference between the elasticity of demand and the elasticity of supply is that the elasticity of demand measures movement along the demand curve rather than the supply curve:

$$\varepsilon_d = \frac{\%\Delta Q^d}{\%\Delta p}$$

Figure 2.7
**The Supply of Mickey Mantle
and Hank Aaron Cards**

The supply curves of the two
cards are identical, making the
elasticity of supply the same at
every price.

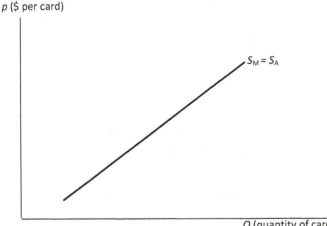

p ($ per card)

$S_M = S_A$

Q (quantity of cards)

For example, if the price of a card increases from $0.10 to $0.11 and the quantity demanded falls from 1,000 to 750 cards, the elasticity of demand[12] is:

$$\frac{(1000 - 750)/1000}{(0.10 - 0.11)/0.10} = -2.5$$

Elasticities of demand fall between zero (perfectly inelastic) and minus infinity (infinitely elastic).[13] When the elasticity lies between 0 and −1, we say that demand is **inelastic**, because the percentage change in quantity is less than the percentage change in price. When the elasticity is less than −1, we say that demand is **elastic**.

Explaining the Difference in Card Prices

We now use the simple supply and demand model to explain the difference in value between Mickey Mantle and Hank Aaron baseball cards. We previously noted that there is no reason to believe that the supply curves of Mantle and Aaron cards differ from each other. As a result, differences in price must be the result of differences in demand.

Mickey Mantle spent his entire career in New York, while Aaron spent his career in Milwaukee and Atlanta, which are much smaller cities. Even if Aaron and Mantle are equally popular with their hometown fans, the difference in population causes the demand curve for Mickey Mantle cards to lie far to the right of the demand curve for Hank Aaron cards. To see why, assume that a typical fan prefers players and memorabilia for his hometown team. The market demand curve for cards is the sum of the individual demand curves, as seen in Figure 2.8. We want to know how many cards all Braves fans combined and all Yankee fans combined buy at each price. Because the market demand curve is the sum of the individual demand curves and New York is a much larger city, the market demand curve for Mickey Mantle cards is farther to the right than the demand curve for Hank Aaron cards, increasing the relative price of Mickey Mantle cards.

In addition to having more people, the New York metropolitan area has fans who are, on average, wealthier than Braves fans in either Milwaukee or Atlanta. If baseball cards are normal goods, the higher level of income causes the demand curve for Mickey Mantle cards to shift out still farther relative to the demand for Hank Aaron cards.

Finally, one must account for the unfortunate possibility that the tastes of baseball fans for baseball cards reflect the prejudices of the population at large. As we shall see in Chapter 11, most economists regard discrimination as a taste or distaste for members of a particular group. If some card collectors prefer Mickey Mantle, who was white, to Hank Aaron, who is black, simply because of their races, the demand for Mantle cards would be greater than the demand for Aaron cards.

Figure 2.9 shows that the combined effects of the differences in market size and income and prejudice (tastes and preferences) result in greater demand for Mantle cards than for Aaron cards. The differences in demand coupled with the identical, perfectly inelastic supply curves create the difference in equilibrium price. Several studies of trading card prices have established that race plays a significant role in determining the price of playing cards. Nardinelli and Simon (1990) were the first to establish such a link. More recently, L.J. Van Scyoc and N.J. Burnett also found evidence of discrimination but concluded that it had declined over time.[14]

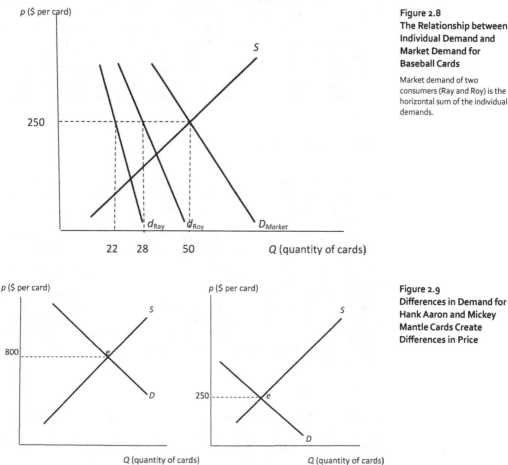

Figure 2.8
The Relationship between Individual Demand and Market Demand for Baseball Cards

Market demand of two consumers (Ray and Roy) is the horizontal sum of the individual demands.

Figure 2.9
Differences in Demand for Hank Aaron and Mickey Mantle Cards Create Differences in Price

(a) The market for Mickey Mantle cards   (b) The market for Hank Aaron cards

2.2   Output and the Production Function

In economics, production refers to the transformation of inputs into output. In this text, we discuss production of sporting events in many different contexts. In this section, we review the basics of production theory, including why these concepts are so important to the study of team sports and the special nature of sports relative to other goods and services.

A Note on the Definition of Output

Before analyzing a market, economists must determine how to measure output. In some markets, such as the pizza market, defining output (Q) is easy. It is the number of pizzas produced in a given time period. In sports markets, defining and measuring output are more complicated. If we think of output as what a firm sells in order to obtain revenue, we could measure output as attendance or television viewership. Sometimes, it may be more useful to measure output as games, because the team must combine inputs to produce games throughout the course of the season. Finally, if a team's popularity, and hence its revenue, depend on its performance, the appropriate output is wins or winning percentage rather than simply games played. Our problem resembles that facing those who study higher education. From the standpoint of revenue, a college or university may define output as the number of students enrolled. From the standpoint of input utilization, it may define output as the amount that its students learn, perhaps measured by their future incomes. Unfortunately, there is no simple resolution to this issue. To force a universal definition of output would cloud the issue as often as it would clarify it. In this text, we address this thorny issue by defining output according to the actions under consideration. For the remainder of this section, we consider output to be the number of wins produced per season.

The Production Function

Production transforms inputs into output. A **production function** shows the relationship between the quantity of inputs used and the quantity of output produced. This relationship expresses the technology of production and typically includes labor and capital as inputs. Economists divide the analysis of production into two distinct time periods: the short run and the long run. The **short run** is that time period in which at least one input, typically capital, is fixed while the other input, typically labor, is variable. In the **long run**, all inputs are variable. It is useful to think of the long run not as a day on the calendar but as a planning horizon, when firms can consider all production possibilities. In sports however, both capital (the field of play, for example) and the number of players are fixed. Thus, as we consider a team's attempt to produce wins (Q), it makes more sense to speak in terms of units of talent. The more talent a team has on the roster, the more games it can expect to win. We can show a short-run production function in which a football team can invest in either offensive talent (T_O) or defensive talent (T_D) as:

$$Q = f(T_O, T_D)$$

Another term for Q is the **total product of labor**. To evaluate the impact of increases in either input on the number of wins, we must hold the other input constant. Figure 2.10a shows the typical relationship between one variable

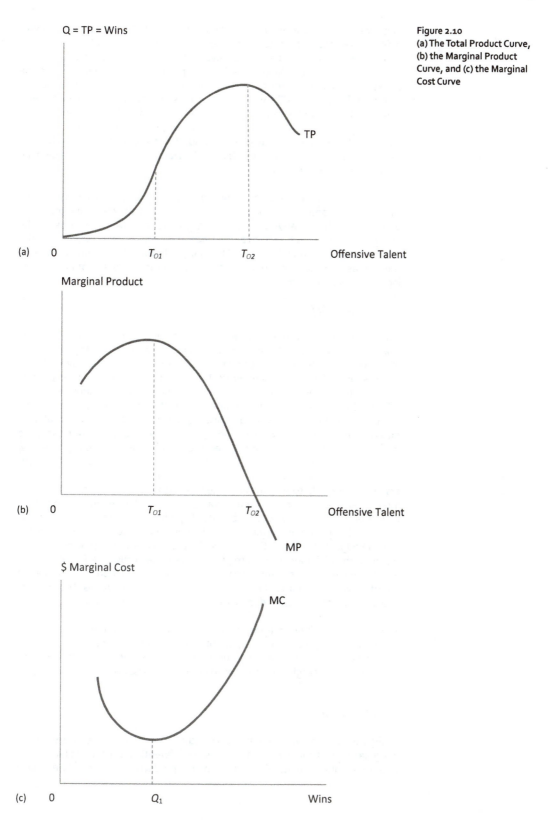

Figure 2.10
(a) The Total Product Curve,
(b) the Marginal Product
Curve, and (c) the Marginal
Cost Curve

input, offensive talent in this case, and output while holding the quantity of defensive talent constant. As T_O rises from 0 to T_{O1}, the number of wins increases at an increasing rate, as each successive unit of talent adds more to wins than the last. The intuition behind this is fairly simple. If a football team only has one or two talented players, the team will benefit enormously from additional talent on the field. From T_{O1} to T_{O2}, wins continue to rise but at a decreasing rate. These players still improve the team but not as much as the first few talented players. Beyond T_{O2}, additional talent might actually cause the team to win less. Is this possible? Perhaps you have heard the saying, "there's only one ball" in reference to the fact that having too many players who want to carry the ball can damage team chemistry and reduce wins.

When coaches and general managers consider adding talent to a roster, they think like economists—by focusing on the margin. If they add one more talented player, how many more games might the team win? To focus on the change in output resulting from a small increase in one input, economists evaluate the player's marginal product. The **marginal product** of an input indicates the increase in output that results from a one-unit increase in that input, holding the other input constant:

$$MP_{TO} = \Delta Q / \Delta T_O$$

Figure 2.10b shows the marginal product of offensive talent. From 0 to T_{O1}, as the slope of the total product curve is positive and increasing, the marginal product increases. Again, the number of games the team wins increases quickly as the coach adds talent to the roster. From T_{O1} to T_{O2}, the slope of the total product curve decreases, and marginal product falls. The decline in marginal product reflects the law of diminishing returns, one of the most important concepts in all of economics. The **law of diminishing marginal returns** states that, as a firm (team) continually increases one input while holding the others fixed, the marginal product of that input must eventually fall. This concept explains why, for example, a baseball team with five good starting pitchers does not sign yet another starter and why the Green Bay Packers do not sign both Aaron Rodgers and Tom Brady to play in the same year. Other than for a few trick plays, a team can use only one quarterback at a time, and, barring injury, additional quarterbacks rarely play. Finally, beyond T_{O2}, where the total product curve is downward sloping, the marginal product curve is negative.[15] If the Packers had signed Rodgers, Brady, and Drew Brees, the tension created over who plays how much (or the difficulty in trying to play all three) may cause the Packers to win fewer rather than more games. We use the theory of production, in particular the law of diminishing marginal returns, later in the text as we discuss the need for salary caps, roster limits, and teams' profit-maximizing strategies.

The law of diminishing marginal returns has direct implications for a firm's costs. As the marginal product of an input falls, the firm must use more of that input to achieve a given increase in output. Thus, as the marginal product falls, marginal cost rises. **Marginal cost** is the additional cost associated with an increase in output:

$$MC = \Delta C / \Delta Q$$

As Figure 2.10c shows, the marginal cost curve is essentially the inverse of the marginal product curve (though the axes are different). Marginal cost falls at first because additional units of talent are highly productive. Beyond Q_1, marginal costs begin to rise as the input is now subject to diminishing returns. The concept of marginal cost is critical to economic theories of firm decision making as we will see later in this chapter and throughout Chapters 3 and 4.

Price Ceilings and the Economics of Scalping

Sometimes outside forces in the form of rules or laws disrupt market equilibria in ways that are unintended and even bizarre. Such may be the case with price ceilings. Today, fans wanting to buy or sell tickets to sporting events at the last minute can easily do so by accessing websites such as StubHub. In the past, a University of Michigan football fan who wanted to see the Wolverines play arch-rivals Ohio State or Michigan State often had to participate in a strange ritual. Students with tickets to the game could be found walking in front of the Michigan Student Union with their tickets in one hand and a pencil in the other. When someone offered to buy the ticket, the student would agree to do so—but only if the potential buyer also bought a pencil.

The key to understanding such an odd sales arrangement lies in the state of Michigan's anti-scalping laws. According to the law, no one can sell tickets for more than the value printed on the ticket (its *face value*). The face value of the ticket, however, was well below what a free market would dictate. In economic terms, the law placed a **price ceiling** on tickets, keeping their price far below equilibrium. If the face value of a ticket is $15, and no sales are permitted above this price, the price ceiling (p^c) is $15. Such a ceiling is shown in Figure 2.11.

A price ceiling creates two problems for buyers and sellers. First, the price ceiling ($p^c = \$15$ in Figure 2.11) creates excess demand for tickets, since the quantity of tickets demanded (Q_d) is much greater than the quantity of tickets supplied (Q_s). To make matters worse, there is no guarantee that the people who place the greatest value on tickets will be able to get them. By limiting price to p^c, we know only that all buyers are willing and able to pay at least p^c to see a Michigan football game. If price does not serve as an allocation mechanism, someone who is just willing to pay the face value for a ticket might get one while someone who values it far more highly might not. Many colleges and universities have a

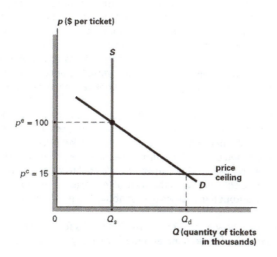

p ($ per ticket)

S

$p^e = 100$

$p^c = 15$

price ceiling

D

0   Q_s Q_d

Q (quantity of tickets in thousands)

Figure 2.11
The Effect of a Price Ceiling

A price ceiling creates excess supply of $Q_d - Q_s$.

persistent excess demand for tickets. This frequently leads to scenes of students camped outside the ticket office for days at a time to be sure that they have a seat for the big game. Thus, when prices do not ration tickets, some other limited resource, in this case time, typically does.

Universities set low prices for several reasons. For example, they might do so out of a sense of fairness to students of limited incomes. Recognizing that athletics are a student activity, athletic departments might want to ensure that all (or at least most) students can afford to see "their" team play.

When those with tickets can sell freely to those without, a mutually beneficial trade could be arranged. Suppose, for example, that Daniel is a rabid Michigan fan who is willing to pay $100 for a ticket to see Michigan play Michigan State. Melanie—the lucky recipient of a ticket—thinks a ticket is worth only $15. If Daniel pays Melanie $70 for the ticket, he would pay $30 less than the ticket is worth to him while Melanie would receive $55 more than the ticket is worth to her. Daniel and Melanie would both benefit from such an exchange, yet the law prohibits it. That is why Melanie could be found on State Street in Ann Arbor, offering her ticket for the face value of $15, but only to those who are willing to pay $55 for her pencil—and why Daniel is happy to pay so much for a pencil![16]

2.3   Market Structures: From Perfect Competition to Monopoly

So far, we have implicitly made the unrealistic assumption that all goods are bought and sold in **competitive markets.** While this assumption works for some goods, such as strawberries purchased at a local farmers' market, it is not always accurate. As we will see in Chapters 3 and 4, it is usually inaccurate for professional and elite amateur sports markets. In this section, we review both competitive and monopolistic market structures. We then use these simple models to see why the Chicago White Sox do not lower their ticket prices even though they regularly fail to sell out. We also use them to explain why teams often raise ticket prices when they sign new stars to lucrative guaranteed contracts.

Perfect Competition

Competitive markets have many producers and consumers, all buying and selling a homogeneous product. Buyers and sellers are small relative to the overall size of the market, so no single firm or consumer can alter the market price unilaterally. In addition, buyers and sellers have good information about prices. As a result, competitive firms have no market power. **Market power** is the ability to influence prices. If a competitive firm tries to raise the price it charges, consumers will purchase an equivalent product elsewhere at the market price.

Although the *market* demand curve for a good sold in a competitive market is downward sloping, each *individual* competitive firm faces an L-shaped demand curve. The horizontal part of the curve shows the market price that is determined by market supply and demand. If a firm raises its price above that charged by its rivals in a perfectly competitive market, its sales fall to zero. The vertical part of the demand curve coincides with the vertical (price) axis and shows that the firm will not sell any output if it charges a price above the prevailing market price.

Figure 2.12 shows how a competitive market works for strawberries at a large farmer's market. Market demand and market supply yield an equilibrium price

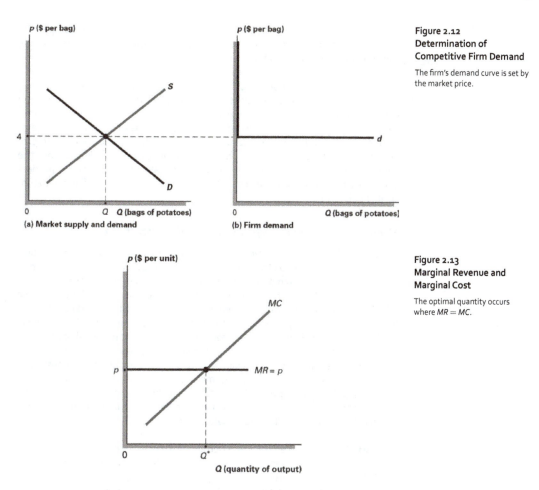

Figure 2.12
Determination of
Competitive Firm Demand

The firm's demand curve is set by the market price.

Figure 2.13
Marginal Revenue and
Marginal Cost

The optimal quantity occurs where $MR = MC$.

of $4/pint in Figure 2.12a. Each farmer faces a demand curve that is horizontal at $p = \$4$ in Figure 2.12b. If a farmer charges more than $4, her sales fall to zero. Since each farmer is so small relative to the size of the entire market, she can sell all the strawberries she wants at the market price without causing the market price to fall. Economists call firms in this position **price-takers**.

Because a farmer can sell each additional pint of strawberries for $4, the extra revenue she receives from selling an additional bag—her **marginal revenue** (*MR*)—equals the price she charges for that pint ($MR = p$). A farmer weighs the additional revenue received against the additional cost endured to produce an additional pint of strawberries, her **marginal cost** (*MC*). She maximizes profits by producing and selling additional strawberries until the extra revenue earned from selling the last pint equals the cost of producing it (*MC*), as seen in Figure 2.13.

Finally, economists assume that competitive firms can freely enter and exit the market in the long run. Thus, if strawberry farmers are making large profits, more farmers will plant strawberries. The increase in the number of farmers growing strawberries shifts the market supply curve to the right. The rightward shift of the supply curve causes prices to fall, reducing individual firms' profits.

This result is probably the single most important outcome of the competitive market. When firms in a competitive industry are profitable, other firms enter, causing price and profits to fall.

Free entry by producers benefits consumers in two important ways. It ensures that firms in the industry cannot restrict output in order to drive up prices and earn excessive profits. More importantly, competitive markets are **economically efficient.** An economically efficient outcome maximizes society's gains from exchange. In this context, profits attract new farmers and stimulate production by existing farmers until the demand for strawberries is satisfied. The competitive pressure exerted by the new farmers also forces inefficient producers to exit the industry. We discuss the concept of economic efficiency extensively in Chapter 4.

Monopoly and Other Imperfectly Competitive Market Structures

Most goods have characteristics that distinguish them from other commodities. Consumers may have no clear preferences over which farm grew the strawberries they buy, but they may prefer buying tickets to see the Colorado Rockies play baseball to buying tickets to see the Denver Broncos play football. If we measure output as the number of fans in attendance, and if sports fans in Denver feel that there are no perfect substitutes for a Rockies game, the Rockies have market power, which enables them to raise prices without losing all of their customers. As a result, the demand curve for Rockies games is downward sloping rather than L-shaped. If the Rockies had no competitors at all and consumers had the choice of seeing a Rockies game or seeing nothing, the Rockies would be a monopoly. A **monopoly** exists when a single firm is the sole producer in the market. The demand curve faced by a monopoly is the market demand curve, because the firm does not compete with any other firms.

All sports franchises exercise some degree of market power. This power stems from several sources. Baseball fans' preference for watching baseball games gives the Rockies a degree of market power. Moreover, potential competitors (i.e., other forms of entertainment) often face substantial barriers to entry, such as access to playing facilities or a television contract. These barriers prevent new entrants from providing a reasonable alternative.

Like a competitive firm, a monopoly maximizes profit when marginal revenue equals marginal cost. Unlike a competitive firm, a monopolist does not passively accept the price and quantity that are dictated by the intersection of supply and demand. The monopolist can set the price at the level that maximizes its profits.

As a monopoly, the Rockies face a downward-sloping market demand curve and must lower their ticket prices if they want to sell more tickets than they did last year. Since the Rockies cannot easily identify all the fans who bought tickets at a higher price last year, they have to reduce the price of all the tickets they sell next year.[17] The extra revenue they receive from selling an additional ticket changes for two reasons. First, the Rockies gain revenue from selling more tickets. Second, they lose revenue because they must lower the price of all tickets in order to sell more of them. For example, suppose the Rockies sold 2 million tickets last year at $30 each and want to sell 3 million this year. If they attract the additional fans by charging $25 for all 3 million tickets, they gain $25 million in revenue from selling 1 million extra tickets at $25 apiece and lose $5 on each of the 2 million tickets they could have sold for $30 each. As a result, the additional revenue from increasing sales by 1 million tickets is $15 million ($25 x 3 less $30 x 2), not

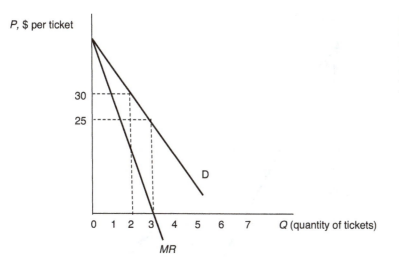

**Figure 2.14
Demand and Marginal
Revenue from Ticket Sales**

Marginal revenue, the extra
revenue from selling one more
ticket, is less than the price of
that ticket.

$30 million, and the monopolist's marginal revenue curve lies below the demand curve, as seen in Figure 2.14.

As long as a team is not at capacity, the marginal cost of accommodating an extra spectator is close to zero. It costs the team relatively little to sell one more ticket and to admit and clean up after one more fan. As a result, economic analyses of ticket sales typically assume that the marginal cost of admitting an extra spectator equals zero. When ticket sales reach the capacity of the stadium, the marginal cost effectively becomes infinite since the team cannot sell any more seats at any price. Figure 2.15 illustrates the capacity constraint with a marginal cost curve that is effectively zero until 50,381 fans (the capacity of Coors Field) are admitted and then becomes vertical.

Figure 2.15 shows that market power allows the monopoly to charge a higher price than would a competitive industry. A perfectly competitive industry operates where the market demand curve cuts the MC curve. It sells Q^c and charges $p^c = \$20$. A monopolist produces $Q^m < Q^c$ because the MR curve cuts the horizontal axis at a much lower level of output.

To find the highest price the team can charge and still sell Q^m (37,000 tickets per game in this example), we look at the demand curve. In addition to telling us how much people are willing and able to buy at a given set of prices, the demand curve tells us the maximum amount consumers are willing and able to pay for a given quantity. The demand curve in Figure 2.15 tells us that the Rockies can sell 37,000 tickets per game if they charge no more than $30 per ticket.

We can use this simple model of monopoly behavior to determine whether the Chicago White Sox or Chicago Blackhawks are irrational in their ticket policy. On the surface, it appears that someone is doing something wrong. After all, the Blackhawks regularly sell out the United Center, averaging over 110 percent of capacity in 2015–2016, while the White Sox rarely sell out Guaranteed Rate Field.

In fact, both teams may be following optimal strategies. Having at least a degree of market power, both the White Sox and the Blackhawks face downward-sloping demand and marginal revenue curves. We continue to assume that marginal costs are zero, so their marginal cost curves lie along the

Figure 2.15
Rockies Attendance and Prices

The optimal quantity of tickets, Q^m, occurs where $MR = MC$, and the optimal price lies on the demand curve, directly above Q^m.

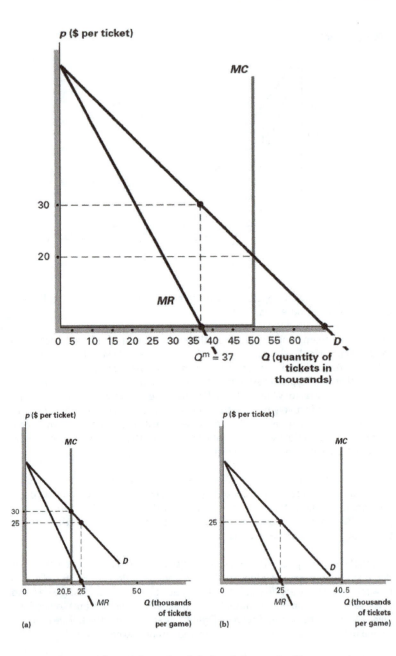

Figure 2.16
(a) Blackhawks Attendance and Prices, (b) White Sox Attendance and Prices

Stadium size dictates different policies.

horizontal axis at all attendance levels below full capacity. However, the teams reach full capacity at very different points. The White Sox home games at Guaranteed Rate Field can accommodate slightly over 40,500 fans. Blackhawk games at the United Center, however, can hold only 20,500 per game. Because the United Center is so much smaller, the marginal cost curve for Blackhawks games becomes vertical much earlier than the marginal cost curve for the White Sox, as seen in Figure 2.16.

The different MC curves mean that the White Sox and the Blackhawks follow different pricing policies even if they have identical demand curves. Because the

MC curve for the White Sox is horizontal over such a large range of attendance, the marginal revenue curve probably crosses the marginal cost curve along the horizontal axis, as seen in Figure 2.16b. This means that the White Sox were maximizing their profits from attendance even though they played in a stadium that was 40 percent empty. By contrast, the Blackhawks' marginal revenue curve is far more likely to cross the marginal cost curve on its vertical segment. The Blackhawks maximize their profits from attendance by charging a relatively high price and selling out the United Center.

The Impact of an Increase in Costs

We have shown that teams determine how many tickets to sell—and how much to charge for their tickets—by equating the marginal revenue and marginal cost of selling an additional ticket. We have also shown that the marginal cost of providing an extra seat is generally very low until the team approaches the seating capacity of its venue. Perhaps surprisingly, the model completely ignores the cost of guaranteed player contracts. That is because such contracts are fixed costs. As the term suggests, **fixed costs** do not vary with output, which we measure in this example as the number of fans attending a game. Because player contracts do not affect marginal costs, they have no bearing on ticket prices.

To see why Jason Heyward's $15 million salary represents a fixed cost to the Chicago Cubs, just ask how much the Cubs must pay him if the team draws only 1 million fans and how much they must pay him if the team draws 4 million fans. A player's salary—like any fixed cost—does not change as output rises. The $15 million that the Cubs paid Heyward in 2016 has the same impact that a $15 million legal judgment against the team might have. All else equal (or, as economists say, *ceteris paribus*), the price and quantity of tickets that maximized profits before the payment still do so after the payment. The only difference is that profits are lower than before. Why, then, might a team raise ticket prices after signing free agents?

The key can be found on the demand side of the ledger. Teams raise ticket prices when they sign a *new* free agent if they feel that the new player makes fans willing to pay higher prices than before. Teams charge higher ticket prices because the demand curve (and hence the marginal revenue curve) shifts outward, as seen in Figure 2.17. The higher demand and marginal revenue curves lead to a

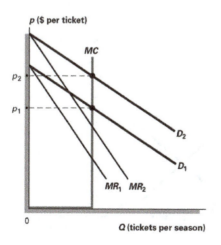

Figure 2.17
A Change in Demand Due to the Addition of a Marquee Player

Ticket prices rise because the demand for tickets rises, not because the team faces higher costs.

higher equilibrium price and (subject to capacity) quantity than before. In short, teams charge higher prices when they sign free agents because they *can* do so, not because they *must*.

2.4   The Rise of Professional Sports

While "ball sports" date back to antiquity, baseball and soccer were the first sports to become widely popular, professional national pastimes.[18] Both sports developed and flourished when and where they did as the result of broad-based economic phenomena. Historians have drawn a link between the prosperity that accompanied the Industrial Revolution in the mid-19th century and the development of sport.[19] For a society to have a pastime, it first must have time to pass.

To see why, we use the same marginal analysis that we used earlier in the chapter. The same basic principle holds for consumers who want to maximize their well-being. In this section, we apply marginal analysis to the growth of leisure activity and then use this reasoning to show why spectator sports arose in the latter portion of the 19th century in England and the United States.

Similar to a firm, a person spends an additional hour at an activity, whether it is work, studying, or leisure, until the benefit of an additional hour spent on that activity equals the cost of an additional hour. With a firm, benefits and costs are easy to understand and easy to measure. For an individual, the concepts can be more abstract. While the reward for work might be easily measured in terms of wages and salaries, the reward for many activities is the utility we gain from them, where **utility** is another word for pleasure. We call the extra happiness we get from a little more of a good or an activity the marginal utility we receive from it. The marginal cost of engaging in a little more of an activity might be monetary: the dollars we could have earned had we not studied economics or gone to a movie. It could also be the happiness we would have experienced by making a different choice.

Figure 2.18 shows typical marginal utility and marginal cost curves. The marginal utility curve slopes down, indicating that the more we engage in an activity to begin with, the less a little more means to us. The marginal cost curve slopes up, showing that, as we engage more in an activity, we have to give up increasingly valuable alternatives.

Figure 2.18
The Marginal Utility and Marginal Cost of Leisure Time

As the marginal cost of leisure fell, the time devoted to leisure rose.

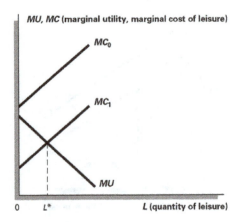

To see how this applies to the rise of spectator sports, consider what life was like prior to the Industrial Revolution. Most people toiled in subsistence, agricultural economies, meaning they spent all their waking hours growing enough food to survive. Anyone who did otherwise endangered his life and the lives of those around him. As Figure 2.18 shows, the marginal cost of leisure (MC_o) was extremely high for most people. That meant that most people devoted no time to leisure. While a few 18th-century French aristocrats enjoyed playing *jeu de pomme*, an early form of tennis, a poor peasant had no time for such a luxury.

Starting in the late 18th century, the Industrial Revolution significantly raised the living standards of large numbers of people in England. With higher incomes, people could spend time away from work without risking their lives. In terms of Figure 2.18, this meant that the marginal cost curve shifted down from MC_o to MC_1. As a result, people could spend time pursuing non-labor activities, such as schooling or leisure—or both at once.

The modern version of soccer developed in the elite "public schools" of England (e.g., Eton, Charterhouse, Westminster, Harrow, and Rugby). Starting from a vaguely defined primitive sport, soccer evolved at each of the public schools in much the same way that different species of animals evolve from a common ancestor when they live on separate islands. Each school developed its own version of soccer based on the unique characteristics of the terrain on which it was played. At most schools, rough or muddy grounds made violent contact impractical. Schools that had large, open fields, such as Rugby School, developed much rougher versions of the sport. Soccer's popularity soon spread to Cambridge University and Oxford University and to clubs formed by public school and university graduates. It is no coincidence that one of the most popular of the early clubs called itself "The Old Etonians."

In the United States, baseball also first appeared among the more prosperous elements of society. An early form of baseball was an adaptation of English games played by the Puritan upper-middle class in New England in the late 18th century. The first organized game did not appear until 1842, with the formation of the New York Knickerbocker Club.

Though they lacked the social imprimatur of the British public school, baseball clubs also strove to establish or maintain the social positions of their members. Games between baseball clubs in the pre-Civil War era were less a competition than an exercise in "manly upright fellowship, harmony, and decorum. For them, excellence in performance meant exhibiting character as well as skill. . . ."[20]

In the second half of the 19th century, the benefits of the Industrial Revolution began to spread to all segments of society in England and in the United States. The higher standard of living of working-class families led to a broader pursuit of leisure activities. As a result, soccer spread northward from the public schools around London into the industrial heartland of England and Scotland, and baseball spread south and west from New York. In addition, playing baseball became a way for members of immigrant communities to assert their "Americanness." Thus, by the turn of the 20th century, in England, soccer clubs of working-class people had largely displaced "Old Etonians," while in America, first-generation Americans of German and Irish descent had largely displaced "Yankee" baseball players.

The growing popularity of soccer and baseball among the working class led directly to the professionalization of the games. Working-class athletes lacked the independent means of earlier participants, so they could not afford to play regularly without being compensated for the opportunity cost of their time. The upper-class sportsmen on both sides of the Atlantic saw their roles change from amateur participants to financial backers of professional teams. While they remained firmly in charge of the management and financing of the clubs, the old guard roundly condemned the "moral declension" that accompanied both the increasing professionalism of sports and the participation of working-class athletes. Their concern did not keep them from recognizing that they could profit from marketing a superior, professional product to a public that now had the money and leisure time to attend sporting events regularly. We will return to the discussion of the spread of sports activities to the working class in Chapter 12 in the context of the history of amateurism.

Biographical Sketch

Mark Cuban
(1958–)

I love to compete. To me, business is the ultimate sport. It's always on. There is always someone trying to beat me.

—*Mark Cuban*[21]

The son of an auto upholsterer and grandson of a Russian immigrant, Mark Cuban learned the value of hard work early. His first foray into the business world was at the age of 12, selling garbage bags door to door. After graduating from high school in just three years and working his way through Indiana University, he started and then subsequently sold two internet firms. The first was MicroSolutions, a computer consulting company, which he sold for $6 million. In 1995, he launched the second firm, AudioNet (subsequently renamed Broadcast.com), with fellow Indiana alum Todd Wagner out of a desire to follow Indiana basketball broadcasts online. Just four years later, they sold the firm for $5.6 billion.

In 2000, he brought his passion for sports and success to the NBA. Cuban bought the sad-sack Dallas Mavericks, a team that had not had a winning record since 1993–1994, for $285 million. Although the deal included a share of the American Airlines Center, it must have seemed outlandish to many. At the time, it was the most ever paid for an NBA franchise.

Cuban's management style paid dividends almost immediately. He made a few personnel changes, but much of the roster remained unchanged.

Instead, he focused on changing the team culture and adding advanced statistical analytics similar to those made famous in baseball by Billy Beane. Cuban was an instant hit with the players. He came to a practice session at the arena after purchasing the team and challenged Dirk Nowitzki to a game of one-on-one. After realizing he was serious, Nowitzki dunked on Cuban, marking the beginning of a long-standing friendship. Cuban moved players to better hotels while on the road, sent limousines to the players' homes to make sure they could get to games safely in bad weather, purchased a new team plane, and cheered raucously from the stands rather than the owner's box. The team responded by going 53–29 in 2000–2001 and made the playoffs in 15 of the next 16 seasons. As of 2016, the Mavericks had increased in value to $1.4 billion, slightly above the league average. Clearly Cuban's investment has paid enormous dividends.

While he enjoys rock star status with fans, his relationship with the league has been uneven. The league has fined him 19 times totaling about $2 million, 10 percent of all fines levied in the league between 2000 and 2016. Eleven of those fines have been for criticizing referees. After one particularly frustrating loss in 2002, Cuban said that NBA Director of Officials Ed Rush "might have been a great ref, but I wouldn't hire him to manage a Dairy Queen."[22] This statement resulted in both a $500,000 fine and a brief stint working at a Dairy Queen.

Cuban has leveraged his celebrity status into a wide variety of ventures, ranging from television appearances on *Dancing with the Stars* and a regular role on *Shark Tank* to the motion picture industry, again partnering with Todd Wagner to purchase a chain of theaters and Magnolia Pictures in 2003. Despite Cuban's diverse interests, it is unlikely he will leave the ranks of NBA owners anytime soon. In a 2016 interview on the sports program *Any Given Wednesday*, host Bill Simmons asked Cuban if he would refuse to sell the Mavericks for $3 billion (more than twice the team's value). Cuban replied, "Yeah, what do I need $3 billion for?"[23]

Sources: "#204 Mark Cuban, Forbes 400," *Forbes.com*, at http://www.forbes.com/profile/mark-cuban/. Accessed October 31, 2016.

Dallas Mavericks. "The Business of Basketball," *Forbes.com*, at http://www.forbes.com/teams/dallas-mavericks/. Accessed October 31, 2016.

Richard Feloni. 2015. "How Mark Cuban Turned the Dallas Mavericks Franchise around by Treating It Like a Startup," *Business Insider*, at http://www.businessinsider.com/how-mark-cuban-turned-around-dallas-mavericks-2015-4. Accessed October 31, 2016.

"Mark's Bio," at http://markcubancompanies.com/about.html. Accessed October 31, 2016.

"Mark Cuban," *Bio.com*, at http://www.biography.com/people/mark-cuban-562656. Accessed October 31, 2016.

"Mark Cuban Won't Sell the Mavericks for Any Amount of Money," *SI.com*, June 30, 2016, at http://www.si.com/nba/2016/06/30/mark-cuban-dallas-mavericks-wont-sell-any-amount. Accessed October 31, 2016.

Andrew Powell-Morse. 2013. "Mark Cuban: King of NBA Fines," *Bleacher Report.com*, April 25, at http://bleacherreport.com/articles/1614812-mark-cuban-king-of-nba-fines. Accessed October 29, 2016.

Dwain Price. 2015. "Fifteen Years Ago, Mark Cuban Came to Mavericks' Rescue," *Star Telegram*, January 3, at http://www.star-telegram.com/sports/nba/dallas-mavericks/article5390883.html. Accessed October 31, 2016.

Summary

Supply and demand are among the simplest but most powerful tools in the economist's arsenal. Understanding most economic relationships requires a solid grasp of this framework. If you have a clear understanding of which external forces affect demand and supply, then you can make accurate predictions regarding the direction of change in prices and output.

Firms produce output by combining inputs. If one input is held fixed, increases in the other input are eventually subject to the law of diminishing marginal returns. The marginal productivity of that input declines and in turn, marginal costs rise.

When markets are competitive, prices are lower and output is higher than if a firm has market power. Market power gives a firm the ability to set prices rather than simply accept the price as determined by the market. In most sports markets, teams have substantial market power. By setting ticket prices, teams can control attendance, subject to the capacity of their building.

Costs and the distinction between fixed and variable costs play a vital role in the determination of output and prices. For professional sports teams, players' salaries are often best treated as fixed costs, because they are unrelated to the number of games played.

Individuals use marginal benefit and marginal cost when making decisions. People weigh the extra happiness, or marginal utility, that they get from leisure time and the marginal cost of an extra hour of leisure (the earnings forgone) when deciding how to allocate their time. The high marginal cost of leisure time prior to the Industrial Revolution explains why professional sports did not arise until the mid-19th century.

Discussion Questions

1   What factors determine the location of the demand curve for basketball at your college or university? Which of those factors might the school be able to influence and which are beyond its control?
2   Who is made better off by sites such as StubHub? What reason do you have for your answer?
3   Explain why the marginal cost of winning increases even if players of equal talent are available at a fixed salary (say, $500,000 each).
4   Given the law of diminishing marginal returns, why might rules that limit the size of a team's roster be unnecessary in professional basketball?
5   Under what circumstances does the presence of a nearby minor league baseball team decrease the monopoly power of a major league team? Could it make the major league team even more profitable? How?

Problems

2.1   Some cities in England have several teams in the Premier League (the country's top soccer league). Explain how the presence of multiple teams affects the monopoly power of those teams.
2.2   The marginal cost of admitting an additional fan to watch the Sacramento Kings play basketball is close to zero, but the average price of a ticket to a Kings game is about $60. What do these facts tell you about the market in which the Kings operate? Use a graph to justify your answer.

2.3   During the 2016 NFL season, television ratings suffered until the November elections, after which they rebounded. Use the supply and demand model to explain why this may have occurred.

2.4   Use supply and demand to show why teams that win championships typically raise their ticket prices the next season.

2.5   Use a graph with attendance on the horizontal axis and the price of tickets on the vertical axis to show the effect of the following on the market for tickets to see the Vancouver Canucks play hockey.
   a. The quality of play falls, as European players are attracted to play in rival hockey leagues in their home countries.
   b. Vancouver places a C$1 tax on all tickets sold.
   c. A recession reduces the average income in Vancouver and the surrounding area.
   d. The NBA puts a new basketball franchise in Vancouver.

2.6   Use the concepts of production and cost from section 2.2 to explain why NASCAR teams might have to spend far more to move up from an average finish of 2nd to 1st than from 20th to 19th.

2.7   Use a graph to show how the marginal product of offensive labor in the NFL might change if wide receivers in the NFL are no longer allowed to use gloves that make it easier to catch the ball on cold days.

2.8   Suppose that the WNBA's Los Angeles Sparks raise ticket prices from $50 to $60 per seat and experience a 5 percent decline in tickets sold. What is the elasticity of demand for tickets?

2.9   Since the 1990s, many MLB teams have moved to new stadiums that are far smaller than the ones they have replaced. Assuming no change in demand, use an appropriate graph to show how such a change impacts ticket prices.

2.10 Suppose the Tampa Bay Rays baseball team charges $10 for bleacher seats (poor seats in the outfield) and sells 250,000 of them over the course of the season. The next season, the Rays increase the price to $12 and sell 200,000 tickets.
   a. What is the elasticity of demand for bleacher seats at Rays games using the point method?
   b. What is the elasticity of demand for bleacher seats at Rays games using the arc method?
   c. Assuming the marginal cost of admitting one more fan is zero, is the price increase a good idea?

APPENDIX 2A

Utility Functions, Indifference Curves, and Budget Constraints

This appendix reviews the basics of consumer theory. It contains an introduction to the use of indifference curves and budget constraints. It then uses these tools to provide a more sophisticated account of the rise of spectator sports.

2A.1 Constrained Maximization

Sandy is a graduate student who loves to go to baseball games and read economics textbooks. In fact, tickets and books are the only things she buys.[24] Economists evaluate Sandy's feelings toward baseball and economics books using her utility function. Sandy's **utility function** is a mathematical representation of the happiness Sandy gets from her consumption decisions. In this example, Sandy's utility function contains only baseball tickets (T) and economics books (B), so we can write her utility function as:

$$U = u(B, T)$$

Since Sandy wants both books and tickets (they are "goods," as opposed to "bads" that she does *not* want), whenever the number of either books or tickets increases, Sandy's **total utility** increases as well.

Economists, like Freudian psychologists, believe that people are motivated by a desire for pleasure. Freudians call the pleasure impulse "the id." Economists call it "utility maximization." In this example, Sandy would maximize her utility by buying an infinite number of tickets and books.

Also like psychologists, economists see forces that hold the pleasure impulse in check. Rather than the internal, psychological barrier of Freud's superego, economists see external constraints in the limited resources that people have at their disposal. People have only so much money, time, and energy with which to satisfy their desires. As a result, they cannot have all the things or engage in all the activities that make them happy. Put simply, they have to make choices. They do not, however, choose randomly. Economists assume that people maximize their utility subject to constraint by making rational choices, the economic analogue to Freud's ego. Sandy makes a **rational choice** when she uses all available information to make the decision that maximizes her happiness.

Many noneconomists have seized on the idea of rational choice to claim that economists view people as walking calculators who carefully weigh all options and have no room for emotions of any kind. Such a characterization is unfair. In fact, rationality need not connote careful decision making—or even sanity. To an economist, actions that most people would regard as heinous or bizarre would still be rational as long as they maximized the decision maker's utility.

Indifference curves allow us to illustrate people's preferences in a world that contains two goods. Recall that Sandy likes to watch baseball games and buy economics texts. Sandy enjoys a certain amount of happiness from seeing ten baseball games and buying four economics textbooks (a combination illustrated by point *A* in Figure 2A.1). If someone took away one of Sandy's books (moving her to point *A'*), she would not feel as happy as before. Sandy would not feel so bad, however, if the person who took away her book gave her a ticket to a ballgame in exchange. In fact, if the person gave her enough tickets (say three tickets, putting her at point *B* in Figure 2A.1), Sandy might feel just as happy as she did to begin with.

If Sandy feels exactly the same about the two combinations of ballgames and books, we say that she is **indifferent** between points *A* and *B*. There are typically many combinations of ballgames and books that make Sandy equally happy. Combining all these points yields an indifference curve, like the ones shown in Figure 2A.2.

Because every combination of ballgames and textbooks yields some level of utility, every point in Figure 2A.1 is on *some* indifference curve. As a result, drawing all of Sandy's indifference curves would require filling in the entire area of

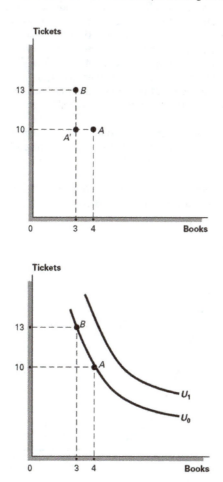

Figure 2A.1
Consumer Preferences

Sandy feels worse off at *A'* than at *A*, but she feels indifferent between *A* and *B*.

Figure 2A.2
Indifference Curves

Sandy feels the same everywhere along U_o, but she would be better off on U_1.

the graph. We therefore draw only a sampling of her indifference curves. While indifference curves can come in many different shapes, most look like those in Figure 2A.2: They are downward sloping, convex, and cannot intersect.

Indifference curves slope downward any time we consider two products that the consumer likes. If we give Sandy more of a product that she likes, she is happier. To restore her initial utility level—and keep her on her original indifference curve—we have to take away some of something else that she values. More of one good means less of the other, so the indifference curve slopes down. Having more of both goods makes Sandy happier, increasing her utility, shown by her being on a higher indifference curve in Figure 2A.2.

A convex indifference curve is typically very steep at first but becomes steadily flatter as one moves down and to the right. To see why, note that when Sandy sees many ballgames and reads few books, seeing one less game means very little to her, but reading one more book has a great impact on her happiness. As a result, she is willing to give up seeing a large number of ballgames in order to get only a few more books, as shown by the movement from point A to A' in Figure 2A.3. In this range, the indifference curve is steep. The same logic results in an almost flat indifference curve when Sandy has many books but sees only a few ballgames, as in the movement from B to B' in Figure 2A.3. Economists typically attribute Sandy's behavior to the principle of diminishing marginal rate of substitution. A **diminishing marginal rate of substitution** implies that, as consumers give up each successive unit of one good, they need increasing quantities of the other good to maintain the same level of utility. It is closely related to the law of diminishing marginal utility, which states that as a person consumes increasing quantities of one good, holding the consumption of all other goods constant, the marginal utility of the additional units consumed will eventually fall.

If indifference curves intersected, we would have to make some rather bizarre conclusions about how people behave. Figure 2A.4 shows what happens if two of Sandy's indifference curves, U_1 and U_2, cross at point A. Above point A, indifference curve U_2 lies to the right of indifference curve U_1. That means that Sandy can have more books without giving up any ballgames, leaving her better off. As a result, Sandy prefers all points on U_2 to all points on U_1. However, below point

Figure 2A.3
Diminishing Marginal Rate of Substitution

Sandy values books relatively highly and tickets relatively little at A, but she feels just the opposite at B.

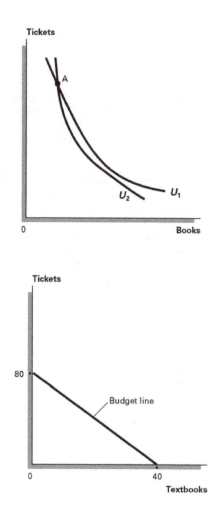

Figure 2A.4
The Impossibility of
Intersecting Indifference
Curves

If indifference curves cross,
consumers' preferences become
inconsistent.

Figure 2A.5
Budget Constraint

Sandy's budget constraint shows
the combinations of goods that
she can afford.

A, the positions of the indifference curves are reversed, meaning Sandy prefers all points on U_1 to all points on U_2. To make matters still more confusing, since the two curves have point A in common, Sandy must get the same level of utility from both curves.

To maximize her utility, Sandy wants to be on the highest possible indifference curve. She is limited, however, by the amount of time, energy, and income at her disposal. For simplicity, assume that Sandy is constrained only by her income (I) of $800 and that tickets to a ballgame cost $10 while economics texts cost $20. Figure 2A.5 shows that she can buy 80 tickets if she buys only tickets and 40 textbooks if she buys only books. Since books cost twice as much as tickets, Sandy must give up two tickets to buy one more book. As a result, her budget constraint is a straight line with slope -2 that connects the points corresponding to 80 games and 0 books, and 0 games and 40 books.

We can write Sandy's constraint algebraically as:

$$20B + 10T = 800$$

More generally, if p_b is the price of books and p_t is the price of tickets:

$$p_b B + p_t T = I$$

To see how changes in income and prices affect the constraint, consider what happens when we change the two. If the price of a ballgame doubles to $20, Sandy's opportunities fall. She can now see only 40 games if she spends all her money on tickets. Figure 2A.6 shows that the vertical intercept slides down to 40 games, and the budget constraint becomes flatter. Since ballgames and textbooks now cost the same amount, Sandy can get one more book by sacrificing one ballgame, and the slope of the constraint becomes −1. If the price of a ballgame falls to $5, Sandy can see 160 games, her opportunities expand, and the slope of her constraint becomes −4.

If Sandy gets a raise so that she now has $1,000 at her disposal (and all prices stay at their original levels), her opportunities again expand. If she buys only tickets, she can go to 100 games. If she buys only textbooks, she can buy 50 books. Both intercepts in Figure 2A.7 increase, and the constraint shifts outward. Since

Figure 2A.6
The Effect of Changes in Price on the Budget Constraint

Sandy's constraint swivels out if the price of tickets falls, and swivels in if the price of tickets rises.

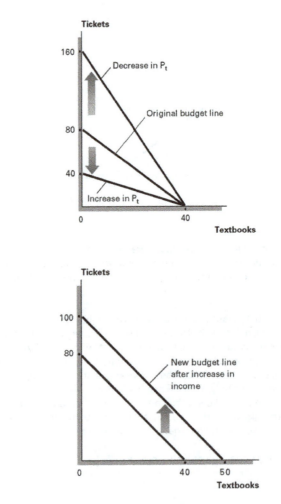

Figure 2A.7
The Effect of an Increase in Income

If Sandy's income rises, her constraint shifts out, but the slope does not change.

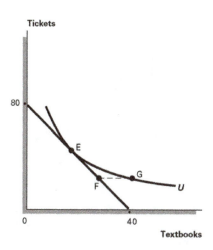

Figure 2A.8
The Utility-Maximizing
Bundle

The best possible combination
of tickets and textbooks occurs
where an indifference curve is
tangent to Sandy's constraint.

the two prices have not changed, Sandy must still give up two ballgames to buy another book, and the slope of her constraint remains -2.

Sandy's best possible choice of ballgames and economics texts comes on the highest indifference curve that satisfies her budget constraint. This occurs where the indifference curve and the budget constraint are tangent, at point E in Figure 2A.8. To see that E is the best possible point, consider any other possible point on the budget constraint (e.g., point F in Figure 2A.8). You can draw a horizontal line from the combination of games and books represented by point F to combination G, which lies on the indifference curve. This means that Sandy can have more books without sacrificing any ballgames by moving from point F to point G, leaving her better off. We also know Sandy likes points G and E equally because they lie on the same indifference curve. Since we can do this for *any* other possible point, no other attainable combination of ballgames and textbooks provides as much utility as E. In addition, Sandy cannot afford a better combination of books and ballgames because any higher indifference curve lies outside her constraint.

2A.2   Using Indifference Curves and Budget Constraints: The Rise of Soccer and Baseball

We can use the concepts discussed above to analyze the development of spectator sports and other leisure activities. Figure 2A.9 shows Sandy's indifference curves for two goods: leisure time and the consumption of goods and services. Sandy, however, cannot have all the leisure time she wants and consume all she wants. She can afford to buy goods and services only by sacrificing leisure time to work and earn income.[25] If, for example, Sandy earns $10 per hour, each hour of leisure that she sacrifices brings her $10 in added consumption. In this case, her budget constraint in Figure 2A.10 is a downward-sloping line connecting T hours, her maximal amount of leisure, with $10 \cdot T$, her maximal amount of consumption. As before, Sandy is best off at the point of tangency between an indifference curve and her constraint.

As noted in the chapter, prior to the Industrial Revolution, most societies had subsistence economies in which people spent all their time generating goods they needed to survive. If Sandy must consume at least C_o to survive, then she

Sandy can also have a preference
over goods and leisure time.

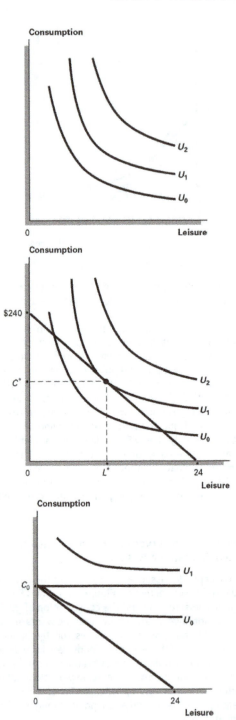

Figure 2A.10
The Utility-Maximizing
Combination of Goods and
Leisure

Sandy's optimal combination
of goods and leisure time also
comes at the tangency of an
indifference curve and her budget
constraint.

Figure 2A.11
Subsistence Level of
Income Allows No Leisure

When people live at subsistence
level, the optimal quantity of
leisure is zero.

has an additional constraint. Her survival constraint is the horizontal line through
C_0 in Figure 2A.11. Sandy cannot consume less and survive.

As an economy industrializes, workers become more productive, and their
wages rise. A higher wage allows Sandy to generate more consumption for every

Consumption

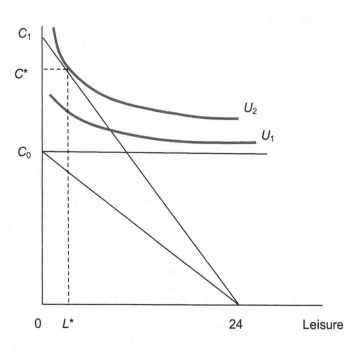

Figure 2A.12
An Increase in Income
Allows for Some Leisure

As people become more
productive, they can devote an
increasing amount of time to
leisure.

hour of leisure she sacrifices. Her budget constraint swivels outward, and her maximum possible consumption rises from C_0 to C_1 in Figure 2A.12. Sandy now has several combinations of leisure and consumption that lie above her survival constraint. She can afford to consume both goods and services and leisure time. The advent of leisure time allows Sandy to pursue nonproductive activities such as the participation in and attendance at athletic events.

APPENDIX 2B

Regression Analysis in Brief[26]

Regression analysis is an extremely powerful and useful statistical technique. Sports economists use regression-based models to analyze statistical relationships between player productivity and wins, between stadium spending and employment, and many others. While we cannot make you an expert econometrician in a few short pages, our goal here is much more modest. In this appendix, we explain the basics of how regression models work and show through example how sports economists use them to uncover statistical relationships. Throughout the text, we discuss the results of empirical models used by prominent sports economists to solidify our understanding of the theoretical models we present. Your professor may assign additional readings that contain results of empirical models. This appendix will help you to understand and interpret such models.

Suppose that a team or league wants to know which factors are most important in determining attendance at MLB games. While we might use a single variable such as the average crowd size to measure how many fans typically attend a game, such simple measures are not useful for learning the relationship *between* variables.

At the simplest level, we might expect that the more a team wins, the more fans will attend its games. Mathematically, we would say that attendance (ATT) is the dependent variable, and winning percentage (WPCT) is the independent variable. We refer to ATT as the **dependent variable** because it depends on the winning percentage. We refer to WPCT as the **independent variable** because it does not depend on the other variable in the equation (ATT):

$$ATT = f(WPCT) \tag{2B.1}$$

To use this relationship to make strategic decisions, such as whether to increase team payroll in an effort to win more games, teams need to know the nature of the relationship as precisely as possible. That is, by how much will attendance increase if, for example, a team could increase its winning percentage from .500 to .510? A very simple way to get a sense of the relationship is to simply plot the attendance figures and winning percentages for every team for a given season. Such a diagram is known as a **scatterplot**. By convention, we place the dependent variable on the vertical or y-axis and the independent variable on the horizontal or x-axis. Figure 2B.1 shows the scatterplot of attendance, measured in thousands of fans, as a function of winning percentage for Major League Baseball (MLB) for the 2016 season.

We can see from the scatterplot that attendance is generally higher for teams with higher winning percentages, but such an imprecise conclusion is not very useful for making strategy. Regression analysis estimates the relationship between the dependent variable and one or more independent variables. In this case, it estimates the line that best fits the data as shown in Figure 2B.1. Clearly,

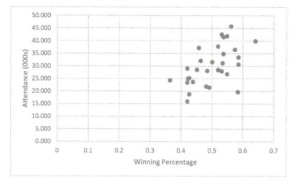

Figure 2B.1
Scatterplot of Attendance
and Winning Percentage in
MLB, 2016

we cannot draw a single straight line through every point in the scatterplot, and if we had a group of analysts draw their best guess of how the line should look, we would have a different estimate from each. Regression analysis uses a very specific criterion, minimizing errors (the distance between our estimated line and the actual point), to determine the best line. More precisely, the algorithm known as ordinary least squares or OLS minimizes the sum of squared errors. We square each error to avoid the problem of positive and negative errors canceling one another out when we add them together. The equation for this line is shown in equation 2B.2. In this equation, −2.4536 is the **intercept term**, or the value of ATT if WPCT is 0. While a negative number for attendance makes no sense, we need not be too concerned, as even the worst teams in baseball win about one-third of their games. 65.23 is the **slope term,** which tells us the increase in ATT for a one-unit increase (+0.001) in WPCT. One interesting fact about regression lines is that they pass through the mean values of our variables. Thus if we insert the average of WPCT (.500) into the equation, we get 30.163 or 30,163 fans, which is the average attendance for the year:

$$ATT = -2.4536 + 65.23WPCT \qquad (2B.2)$$

Figure 2B.2 shows the original scatterplot with the regression line. Even though it is the best line based on the OLS criteria, our line misses most points. Without some measure of the quality of the fit, teams would not know how confident they should be in the relationship and would be wary of using it to make strategic decisions. Fortunately, all statistical packages have several such measures. We describe two such measures here: the coefficient of determination (R^2) and the standard error.

The **coefficient of determination** is the proportion of variation in the dependent variable that is explained by the independent variables. It varies between 0 and 1. If $R^2 = 1.0$, the line describes the relationship exactly, and all points fall exactly on the line. The closer R^2 is to 0, the less precise is the relationship. Statisticians measure their confidence in the individual regression coefficients (65.23 in this case) using the standard error. The **standard error** is a statistical measure of our uncertainty over the value of the coefficient. The closer the standard error is to zero, the more confident we are that our estimate of the coefficient tells us the real relationship between the independent and dependent variables. Though standard errors are difficult to interpret in isolation, all widely used statistical packages also report t-statistics. The **_t_-statistic** is the ratio of the estimated coefficient to the standard error of the coefficient estimate. For us to say that an estimate is statistically significant, that is, that the true coefficient is positive (negative) given a positive (negative) estimate, we want the t-statistic to be about 2 or more. For equation 2B.2, the t-statistic for the WPCT coefficient

Figure 2B.2
The Regression Line

The regression line is the one that
"fits" the data best.

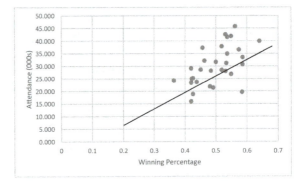

is 3.55, so we can be confident that a higher winning percentage increases attendance.

Even though the estimate of the coefficient on WPCT in equation 2B.2 is statistically significant, the R^2 for our equation above is just .311, meaning that 31.1% of the variation in attendance can be explained by variation in winning percentage. While winning percentage of the home team certainly matters, most of the variation in attendance is explained by other factors, and our estimated relationship is a weak tool for strategic decision-making. We should not be too surprised, as a host of other factors help to determine the popularity of a team. For example, major league teams are located in cities with populations as high as 8.4 million (New York) and as low as 298,000 (Cincinnati). To control for variation in attendance that results from differences in market size, we include the population variable, POP. There may also be systematic differences in attendance between the American and National Leagues, which make up MLB. If we omit important determinants of attendance from our regression equation, it creates a bias in the results, which makes our estimate of the line unusable. The solution to our problem is to include all relevant independent variables in the same equation in a process known as multiple regression. **Multiple regression** estimates the relationship between a dependent variable and several independent variables. Equation 2B.3 shows the results of estimating attendance as a function of winning percentage, population, and league. The interpretation of the coefficients depends on the nature of the variable. Population and winning percentage are both continuous variables. A **continuous variable** is one that can take on any value within a broad range. For example, winning percentage could be .500, .510, .520, and so on. The league in which a team plays, however, takes only two values. By assigning a value of 1 to all teams in the American League and a value of 0 to all teams in the National League, we create a discrete variable LEAGUE, also known as a **dummy variable**. Dummy variables have one of two values and indicate the presence or absence of a specific condition.

With multiple regression, coefficients of continuous variables are interpreted as the change in ATT that results from a one-unit change in the independent variable, holding the other independent variables constant. The coefficient of a dummy variable shifts the entire regression line, depending on its value. Table 2B.1 shows the results of our multiple regression that includes POP, WPCT, and LEAGUE in a format that we might see from a statistical package. Equation 2B.3 shows the same coefficients written in equation form:

$$ATT = -.421 + 1.174POP + 59.31WPCT - 2.014LEAGUE \qquad (2B.3)$$

Table 2B.1 Multiple regression results

Number of obs = 30
R-squared = 0.4245
Adj R-squared = 0.358
Dependent variable is Attendance (in thousands)

Variable	Coefficient	Std. error	t-statistic	p-value
POP (in millions)	1.174	.5602	2.10	.046
WPCT	59.310	17.939	3.31	.003
LEAGUE	−2.014	2.283	−0.88	.386
Constant	−.421	8.83	−.05	.962

The results show that adding population and league improves our ability to explain attendance. The adjusted R^2, which includes a small penalty for adding variables, increases from .311 in our simple regression to .358. The table also shows that population is a significant determinant of attendance—the t-statistics for both POP and WPCT exceed 2.0—but the league in which a team plays is not.

Another statistic in the table also allows us to say whether a coefficient is statistically significant. A p-value provides the same information about significance as a t-statistic for the same coefficient but can be evaluated more easily. The p-values shown in the far right column tell us the probability that we would observe a coefficient of this size or larger in our sample regression if the actual coefficient is zero. Economists look for values of less than .05 or .01 to claim that the coefficient is significant. Again, the information is always consistent with the information from a t-statistic. Notice that the t-statistic for POP is just over 2.0 and the p-value is just under .05.

As you read the sports economics literature, you will encounter the results of regression-based models covering a variety of topics. While the specifics of the models differ, the interpretation of the coefficients is very similar.

Notes

1 Allen Barra. 2000. "In Anti-Trust We Trust," *Salon Magazine*, May 19, at http://www.salon.com/news/feature/2000/05/19/antitrust/index.html.
2 *Beckett Baseball Card Price Guide*, 2016: 37.
3 Bill Simmons. 2009. "Welcome to the No Benjamins Association," *Grantland.com*, February 27, at http://grantland.com/features/welcome-to-the-no-benjamins-association/.
4 Jon Birger. 2009. "Baseball Battles the Slump," *CNNMoney.com*, February 19, at http://money.cnn.com/2009/02/18/magazines/fortune/birger_baseball.fortune/index.htm; and Richard Sandomir. 2009. "Yankees Slash the Price of Top Tickets," *New York Times*, April 28, at http://www.nytimes.com/2009/04/29/sports/baseball/29tickets.html.
5 Sean Gregory and Steve Goldberg. 2009. "Daytona Drag: NASCAR Tries to Out-race the Recession," *Time*, February 12, at http://www.time.com/time/business/article/0,8599,1879136,00.html.
6 Ron Sirak. 2008. "LPGA Facing Economic Realities," *Golf Digest*, November 18, at http://www.golfdigest.com/golf-tours-news/2008-11/20081119sirak. Accessed April 30, 2012.
7 Michael Lewis. 2006. *The Blind Side: Evolution of a Game* (New York: W.W. Norton).
8 Joshua Brustein. 2010. "Star Pitchers in a Duel? Tickets Will Cost More," *New York Times*, June 27, at http://www.nytimes.com/2010/06/28/technology/28tickets.html. Accessed February 23, 2012.

9   "Japan's Earthquake and Tsunami Hit Parts Supplies." 2011. *Motor Trend*, June, at http://www.motortrend.com/features/auto_news/2011/1106_japan_earthquake_tsunami_hit_parts_supplies/viewall.html. Accessed February 23, 2011.

10 Associated Press. 2005. "Saints' Home Games: 4 at LSU, 3 in Alamodome." September 12, at http://sports.espn.go.com/nfl/news/story?id=2159595. Accessed April 30, 2012.

11 We define the percentage change of the variable %ΔX as $\Delta X / X = (X_1 - X_0)/X_0$. We show point elasticity rather than arc elasticity here. Arc elasticity replaces the denominator with the mean of X_0 and X_1. If X_0 and X_1 are close together, the difference is negligible.

12 The arc elasticity of demand in this example is $\dfrac{(1000-750)/\left(\dfrac{1000+750}{2}\right)}{(0.10-0.11)/\left(\dfrac{0.10+0.11}{2}\right)} = -3.0$.

13 Some microeconomics textbooks eliminate the negative sign by taking the absolute value of the elasticity formula. We use the negative number because it reinforces the notion that price and quantity move in opposite directions along the demand curve.

14 Clark Nardinelli and Curtis Simon. 1990. "Customer Racial Discrimination in the Market for Memorabilia: The Case of Baseball," *Quarterly Journal of Economics*, 105(3): 575–595; and L.J. Van Scyoc and N.J. Burnett. 2013. "How Times Have Changed: Racial Discrimination in the Market for Sports Memorabilia (Baseball Cards)," *Applied Economics Letters*, 20(7–9), June: 875–878.

15 Notice that the formula for marginal product is identical to the formula one would use to compute the slope of the total product ($\Delta Q/\Delta L$).

16 Michigan house bill HB4015 would repeal the existing anti-scalping laws, which have been in effect since 1931. As of this writing, the law had yet to be considered by the State Senate or signed into law.

17 For now we ignore the complication raised by season tickets and by price discrimination. We also assume that there are no changes in anything but the price of Rockies tickets.

18 The ancient sports were typically associated with religious festivals, whereas movements such as the *Turnverein* in the early 19th-century German states were more expressions of nationalism than entertainment.

19 For a good historical overview, see William Baker. 1982. *Sports in the Western World* (Totowa, NJ: Rowman & Littlefield); and Robert Burk. 1994. *Never Just a Game: Players, Owners, and American Baseball to 1920* (Chapel Hill: University of North Carolina Press).

20 Burk. 1994. *Never Just a Game*: 6. For an excellent summary and comparison of the origins of baseball and soccer, see Stefan Szymanski and Andrew Zimbalist. 2005. *National Pastime: How Americans Play Baseball and the Rest of the World Plays Soccer* (Washington, DC: Brookings Institution Press).

21 Peter Economy. 2015. "Mark Cuban: 19 Inspiring Power Quotes for Success," *Inc.com*, at http://www.inc.com/peter-economy/mark-cuban-19-inspiring-power-quotes-for-success.html. Accessed October 29, 2016.

22 Andrew Powell-Morse. 2013. "Mark Cuban: King of NBA Fines," *BleacherReport.com*, April 25, at http://bleacherreport.com/articles/1614812-mark-cuban-king-of-nba-fines. Accessed October 29, 2016.

23 "Mark Cuban Won't Sell the Mavericks for Any Amount of Money." 2016. *SI.com*, at http://www.si.com/nba/2016/06/30/mark-cuban-dallas-mavericks-wont-sell-any-amount. Accessed October 31, 2016.

24 Sandy surely buys more than just two items, but this simplification allows us to use two-dimensional pictures rather than multivariate calculus.

25 Economists acknowledge that people can allocate their time in other ways. One example is "home production," the unpaid work that goes into cooking, cleaning, and similar household activities.

26 Data for this section are drawn from "MLB Attendance Report—2016," 2017, at http://www.espn.com/mlb/attendance/_/year/2016; "Standings," 2017, *MLB.com*, at http://mlb.mlb.com/mlb/standings/index.jsp#20161002; World Population Review, 2017, "Toronto Population 2016," at http://worldpopulationreview.com/world-cities/toronto-population/; Ballotpedia. "Largest Cities in the United States by Population," at https://ballotpedia.org/Largest_cities_in_the_United_States_by_population. Accessed May 16, 2017.

Part Two

THE INDUSTRIAL
ORGANIZATION OF SPORTS

3

SPORTS LEAGUES AND FRANCHISES

For almost twenty years I owned and ran a National Football League team, the San Diego Chargers. When I bought the Chargers I believed I could apply to professional football the same principles of good business management that had enabled me to succeed in the corporate world. There was also a time when I believed in Santa Claus, the Easter Bunny, and the Tooth Fairy.

—GENE KLEIN[1]

Introduction

As the 2015–2016 NBA season drew to a close, the Philadelphia 76ers limped into their last five games needing one more win to avoid tying the record for the worst NBA season ever. In achieving that modest goal, they finished with a record of 10–72, seven fewer wins than the second worst team in the league. With no consequences for their failure—and perhaps the reward of a high draft pick—there was little reason for panic or excitement. At the end of the same season in the English Premier League (EPL), Sunderland managed three draws and a win in their last seven games to stave off relegation (being dropped from the EPL). While Philadelphia fans had largely forgotten about the 76ers long before the end of the season, Sunderland fans cheered their team on to the very end, knowing that even one more defeat might spell the end of the team's membership in the league.

In this chapter, we focus on the economics of teams and the leagues in which they play. Around the world, virtually all professional sports compete in highly organized leagues. Leagues provide the basic structure required for competition, such as scheduling, setting rules, and organizing championships. Though early leagues in both North America and Europe were explicitly not-for-profit, today the most important function of leagues may be to create economic conditions that allow member teams to flourish economically. In this role, they perform important functions, such as league-wide marketing to promote the sport, collective bargaining with player associations, organizing revenue-sharing arrangements that promote financial stability, and controlling entry to maintain monopoly power.

Because it is impossible to discuss every league in every sport, we focus on the five largest North American Leagues and the largest European soccer leagues. For North America, we discuss Major League Baseball (MLB), Major League Soccer (MLS), the National Football League (NFL), the National Hockey League (NHL), and the National Basketball Association (NBA). For Europe, we focus on the EPL in England and Wales, though we also discuss Germany's Bundesliga and Spain's La Liga. By studying how these leagues operate, we can analyze the structure of both open and closed leagues leagues, and the economic implications for the teams that play under these two regimes.

Learning Objectives

- Understand the difference between open and closed leagues.
- Describe the various possible team goals and how those goals influence team behavior.
- Analyze team demand, revenue, and cost in closed leagues in North America.
- Understand the differences in revenue, cost, and profits in open European soccer leagues.

3.1   Open versus Closed Leagues

In this section, we describe the two most common league structures in professional sports: open and closed leagues. Closed leagues are common to all North American sports and in such settings as Japan's Nippon Professional Baseball and the Australian Football League. The open structure is common outside the United States and can be found in all European soccer leagues.

The teams that make up a closed league do not change from season to season, except when changes are approved by the existing owners. Teams generally cannot relocate without the permission of the league. For example, the NFL currently has 32 teams, each located in a fixed home city. The Houston Texans are the newest NFL team. They joined the league after the existing Houston franchise (the Oilers) moved to Tennessee to become the Titans. Both the Oilers' move to Tennessee and the Texans' entry were approved by the other NFL owners. Only rarely have teams moved without the league's permission.

The NFL, NBA, NHL, and MLB have all been in existence for at least 70 years. In contrast, professional soccer is relatively new to North America. Although there had been several previous attempts at professional men's soccer in the US, beginning with the North American Soccer League (NASL) in 1967, MLS appears to be the first sustainable league. Beginning play in 1996 with ten teams, MLS has added, shut down, and relocated several franchises. By 2017, MLS had more than doubled in size to a 22-team league. Since 1996, three franchises have closed down and one moved from San Jose to Houston.

Closed leagues, like MLB, often have affiliated minor leagues. An **affiliated minor league** is a lower league with which the major league teams have an explicit contractual relationship. For example, each major league team in MLB has affiliated teams at several levels from AAA (the highest) to A (the lowest). Each NHL team is affiliated with a team in the American Hockey League (AHL), and the NBA maintains the Gatorade League or "G-League." The most important element of this relationship is the contractual relationship with the players, as the rights of minor league players are usually held by the major league team. Players may be promoted or demoted several times between the major and minor leagues during their careers. Although affiliated teams operate under the umbrella of the major league, they cannot enter the major league. The prohibition on movement between leagues is in stark contrast to an open league.

At first glance, the structure of open leagues seems similar to that of closed leagues. The English Football League System,[2] also called the *football pyramid*, features multiple leagues, from the EPL at the top down to semi-pro leagues at the bottom. In reality, the differences far outweigh the similarities. In an open league, lower-division teams are potential competitors of teams in higher divisions because teams regularly switch leagues through promotion and relegation. Under **promotion and relegation**, at the conclusion of every season, the worst teams in each league change places with the best teams in the league below. This system gives teams a chance to move up from even the lowest minor league all the way to the highest league. In the EPL, three teams change place every year. After the 2015–2016 season, Burnley, Hull City, and Middlesbrough were all promoted from the Championship League to the Pre-mier League, replacing Aston Villa, Newcastle United, and Norwich, which had been relegated. This process frequently results in a single city's hosting multiple teams in a given league. For example, the 2016–2017 season featured six teams in the immediate London area. Having several teams in one city significantly reduces the monopoly power of each individual team. For this reason, most closed leagues typically do not locate multiple teams in one city.

Open leagues create very different incentives for the weakest teams near the end of the season. While a bad team in a closed league may prefer to finish with the worst record to enhance its draft position, teams near the bottom of the "table" or standings in an open league must continue to win to avoid relegation.[3] We will continue our discussion of the promotion and relegation system's effects on team behavior in section 3.4.

3.2   The Economics of Team Behavior

In this section, we analyze the economics of sports teams. It is useful to think of a team as we would a franchise in other industries, such as chain restaurants. Each team is an independent economic entity, but it is affiliated with the larger brand (the league). Although a team's behavior is strongly influenced by the league in which it plays, teams in most leagues are independently owned and make their own strategic decisions regarding factors that impact their revenue and cost. Thus, while teams do their best to defeat their opponents on the field, off the field, competition for players, wins, and championships must be tempered with cooperation for the good of the league. Such cooperation includes setting rules for play, scheduling, and organizing championships. Thus, while a pizza shop in your town would be better off if it could drive a competitor out of business and would never consider sharing revenue with its rival, teams in professional leagues are almost always worse off when their competitors go bankrupt, and they share significant revenues to ensure that does not happen.

There is another, potentially vital difference between a single competitive firm in most other industries and a professional sports franchise. Economists assume that the goal of most firms is to maximize profits. A professional sports team's goal may not be so simple. For some owners, winning a championship game may outweigh the bottom line. In the next section, we discuss the possibility that an owner maximizes wins rather than profits.

Maximizing Profits or Maximizing Wins?

As with firms in most industries, professional sports teams have both long-run and short-run goals. While over the long run, teams must remain profitable to stay in business, they may pursue wins over profits in the short run. As an example, consider the changing fortunes of the Phillies, Yankees, Indians, and

Table 3.1 Performance Measures for the Phillies, Yankees, Indians, and Royals, 2011–2016

Team	Winning Percentage	Attendance	Revenue[a]	Operating Income[a]
Phillies	0.630	3,680,718	249	−11.6
Yankees	0.599	3,653,680	439	10
Indians	0.494	1,840,835	178	30.1
Royals	0.438	1,724,450	161	28.5

[a] In millions of dollars.

Source: Forbes data on revenue and operating income are compiled by Kurt Badenhausen, Michael K. Ozanian, and Christina Settimi. 2011. "MLB Team Values," March 22, at http://www.forbes.com/lists/2011/33/baseball-valuations-11_land.html; winning percentages are from "MLB Standings—2011," *ESPN.com*, at http://www.espn.com/mlb/standings/_/seasontype/2/season/2011; attendance data are from "MLB Attendance Report—2011," *ESPN.com*, at http://www.espn.com/mlb/attendance/_/year/2011.

Royals between 2011 and 2016. For most of the summer of 2011, the Philadelphia Phillies dominated the National League, while the New York Yankees led the American League. The Phillies had MLB's best regular season record and topped MLB in per-game attendance, while the Yankees were a close second in both categories. The Yankees took a back seat to no one when it came to revenues, earning over $439 million in 2011. The Phillies were also among the league leaders at $249 million. Table 3.1 contrasts these impressive figures with those of the Cleveland Indians and Kansas City Royals. In 2011, neither of these teams matched the Phillies or the Yankees in wins on the field, fans in the seats, or revenues on the books. In fact, the total attendance of the Indians and Royals combined did not equal that of either the Phillies or the Yankees, while their combined revenues fell short of the Yankees. However, when it comes to operating income, the two weaklings looked more like bullies. In 2011, the Indians led MLB with $30.1 million in operating income, with the Royals close behind at $28.5 million. The Yankees were 22nd of 30 clubs with only $10 million in operating income, and the Phillies staggered home in 29th place, with $11.6 million in losses. While it is possible that the Indians and Royals were simply more efficiently run organizations than the Phillies and the Yankees, it is more likely that the Phillies and the Yankees won more games because they spent a greater fraction of their revenues to secure the best possible players. In other words, at least in the short run, they valued wins over profits.

The short-run nature of the strategies of these teams is all the more apparent if we consider more recent history. The Royals won the 2015 World Series and the 2016 Indians came within one game of winning it all, though both teams had lower operating income in their championship year than in 2011.

Such behavior is not limited to baseball. If we judged Dallas Mavericks owner Mark Cuban solely according to the bottom line, he would be one of the worst owners in professional sports. Though Cuban is one of the most successful businessmen in the United States, his Mavericks lost money in every season between 2007 and 2012. Data from *Forbes*, shown in Table 3.2, indicate that the Mavericks lost more than $60 million in operating income over those six seasons. While the economic losses made the Mavericks a poor performer off the court, they produced a winning product on the court, with an average winning percentage of .667, appearances in the NBA playoffs over the six seasons, and the NBA championship in 2011. While the Mavericks were winning on the court and losing

Table 3.2 Dallas Mavericks' and Toronto Raptors' winning percentage and operating income, 2007–2012

Year	Dallas Mavericks		Toronto Raptors	
	WPCT	Operating Income (in millions)	WPCT	Operating Income (in millions)
2007	.817	−24.4	.573	8.4
2008	.662	−1.6	.500	28.8
2009	.610	−13.6	.402	27.7
2010	.671	−17.4	.488	18
2011	.695	−7.8	.268	25.3
2012	.545	−3.9	.348	7.4

Sources: Financial data are from *Forbes.com* at http://www.forbes.com/teams/dallas-mavericks/; winning percentages are from basketball-reference.com, at http://www.basketball-reference.com/teams/DAL/2007.html. Accessed December 6, 2016.

at the bank, the Toronto Raptors were doing just the opposite. Despite logging just one winning season during this period, the Raptors had operating income of over $100 million.

It would be easier to explain these differences in profits and losses if the most profitable teams were in more desirable markets with higher numbers of fans who followed the sport regardless of team quality. But the Phillies and Yankees are in two of the largest markets in North America, while the Royals and Indians are in two of the smallest. While both Dallas and Toronto are much smaller than New York or Los Angeles, the population of the Dallas metro area is slightly larger than that of Toronto. It seems clear that these owners valued wins and profits differently.

In the EPL and other European soccer leagues, the relationship between wins and profits is even cloudier. There are at least three reasons why European football clubs are more likely than North American teams to pursue win maximization over profits. First, many teams, such as Real Madrid, are still operated by football clubs owned by fans.[4] While the members of these clubs are investors, they are first and foremost fans, who much prefer celebrating a championship to receiving a small dividend check at the end of the year. Second, teams in open leagues do not have the luxury of earning profits year after year by fielding poor teams with low payrolls. If they played in Europe, teams like the 76ers would quickly be relegated to lower divisions and lose revenue, fans, and prestige. Teams in jeopardy of relegation often spend whatever they can on players to avoid that fate. Finally, some teams have the good fortune to have very deep-pocketed owners who for reasons of personal ego, love of the game, or commitment to winning, are willing to sustain financial losses to earn championships. Well-known examples include Russian billionaire Roman Abramovich, owner of the Chelsea club in the EPL, and Sheikh Mansour bin Zayed Al Nahyan, owner of the EPL's Manchester City (as well as NYCFC in MLS). These owners subsidize the teams that they own by transferring personal wealth to the teams' coffers.

While such financial support benefits the team that receives it, it can seriously alter the competitive landscape and overall financial stability of the league (recall that teams are worse off if their rivals go out of business). To address these concerns, the Union of European Football Associations (UEFA) adopted the "Financial Fair Play" (FFP) rules in 2010. The FFP rules promote financial solvency by limiting team spending and limiting the amount of debt a club can assume. Clubs are allowed to spend no more than €5 million more than they earn over each three-year cycle unless those losses are entirely covered by the club owner or another third party. UEFA even limits covered losses. For 2015/16 through 2017/18, UEFA restricts those losses to €30 million.[5]

Below, we present a simple model of team behavior that shows the consequences of pursuing wins versus profits. The model also establishes a basic framework that will guide us through much of the rest of the book.

Maximizing Profit

Profits are the difference between revenues (R) and costs (C). For a profit-maximizing team, this relationship dictates its decision-making. As in Chapter 2, we also assume that a team's total revenue and total cost are functions of its quality. In other words, better teams attract more fans but cost more to assemble. We can write the profit function of a typical team as:

$$\pi_i = R(w_i) - C(w_i),$$

where w_i is the winning percentage of team i. For simplicity, we make two additional assumptions about the team's revenues and costs. First, we assume that revenues increase with winning percentage but at a decreasing rate. This assumption makes sense because, as we will see in Chapter 5, fans can be turned off by a team that wins too many games as well as by a team that wins too few. Second, we assume that teams can "buy wins" by hiring better players at a constant price, c_w. These assumptions yield the total revenue and total cost curves shown in Figure 3.1a.

A profit-maximizing team acquires talent until it maximizes the difference between revenue and cost. In terms of Figure 3.1a, the team increases w until the total revenue curve is as far above the total cost curve as possible. Because this point is difficult to discern with the naked eye, it is easier to recall that the distance between total revenue and total cost is greatest when the slopes of the two curves—marginal revenue and marginal cost—are equal. Figure 3.1b shows this to be at the point w^*_1.

Figure 3.1a
Total Revenue and Total Cost Curves

The firm maximizes profit when TR is as far as possible above TC.

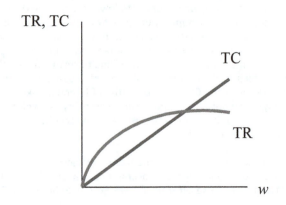

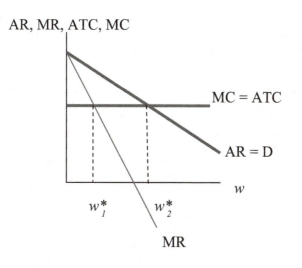

AR, MR, ATC, MC

Figure 3.1b
Profit-Maximizing and Win-Maximizing Behavior

The profit-maximizing team wins w^*_1 games, and the win-maximizing team wins w^*_2 games.

Maximizing Wins

To analyze the behavior of a win-maximizer, we assume that teams cannot simply maximize wins without regard to costs. The NHL's Ottawa Senators discovered this sad fact in 2002–2003 when they compiled the league's best record and then went bankrupt. Maximizing wins is sustainable as long as the team does not lose more money than the owner can tolerate. For simplicity, we assume that the team's profits cannot be negative ($\pi \geq 0$).[6] Saying that profits cannot be negative means total revenue is at least as great as total cost ($TR \geq TC$) or that average revenue is at least as great as average total cost ($AR \geq ATC$). Thus, a win-maximizing team acquires talent until the AR and ATC curves cross at w^*_2.

Comparing the optimal actions of the profit- and win-maximizing teams in Figure 3.1b yields the conclusion that, all else equal, win-maximizing teams win more often than profit-maximizing teams ($w^*_2 > w^*_1$) while profit-maximizing teams earn higher profits. The value of this simple model comes from seeing how other factors shift the curves in Figure 3.1 and alter the behavior of teams. In later chapters, we use this model to analyze such issues as competitive balance and salary structures in professional sports. In the remainder of this chapter, we take a closer look at the revenue and cost functions that teams face.

3.3 Closed Leagues: Revenue and Cost in North American Sports

Revenue and Cost

In the preceding section, we saw that, regardless of whether a team maximizes profits or wins, the relationship between its revenues and costs strongly influences its actions. In this section, we take a closer look at the individual components of teams' revenues and costs.

Revenue Is Determined by Demand

Firm revenue is a function of the demand for its product. In its simplest form, we compute total revenue as the product of price x quantity. For now, we focus on attendance rather than the demand for television broadcasts or live streaming. As with any product, demand for attendance is driven by six basic factors. The first factor moves us along a demand curve. The next five shift the demand curve to a new location:

- The price of the good. In the case of attendance, this is the price of a ticket.
- The price (and availability) of substitutes. For an NFL team, this could be a major college football team nearby. Increases in the cost of seeing a college game increase the demand for NFL games, and the demand curve for NFL games shifts to the right.
- The price (and availability) of complements. For an individual attending a game, this could be the price of parking and concessions. As the price of concessions increases, the demand for tickets decreases and the demand curve shifts to the left.
- Consumer income. If professional sports are normal goods, an increase in income increases ticket demand.
- The number of consumers (fans) in the market. As the size of the market increases, demand for tickets increases and the demand curve shifts to the right.
- Tastes and preferences. These reflect a wide variety of game and team characteristics, such as the day of the week, the quality of the home team, the quality of the visiting team, the importance of the game, whether fans anticipate a close game, weather, and the presence of star players. It can also reflect a general increase in the popularity of the sport as we have seen with professional soccer in the United States, or regional preferences such as the high demand for hockey in Canada.

Costs Are Driven by the Cost of Talent

As with all firms, we can divide costs for a professional team into fixed and variable costs. Teams must pay fixed costs regardless of how much they sell; variable costs increase as output increases. Team fixed costs include advertising, travel, venue-related costs, and most administrative costs, such as the cost of a community relations program, which the team has to pay whether it attracts a small crowd or a sold-out stadium. In contrast to most firms, for which labor is a variable cost, labor costs are mostly fixed for professional teams. This is because players' contracts do not depend on the number of tickets sold, and teams rarely change their payroll significantly over the course of the season because of attendance. For most teams, the only variable costs are those related to gameday staffing, like ushers or food vendors. Since staging a game involves mostly labor (players), labor costs are the most prominent component of total cost. While the proportions vary across both teams and sports, labor costs tend to be between half and three-fourths of total costs (see Table 3.3 for examples). We discuss many aspects of cost later in this chapter and throughout the text.

Comparing Revenue and Cost

Table 3.3 shows *Forbes* magazine's estimates of the revenue, operating income, and market value of selected franchises from the five major North American sports leagues in 2016.[7] It also shows the teams' payroll estimates for that season. We show the teams with the largest, smallest, and median operating income in each category.

Table 3.3 **Market Value, Revenue, Payroll, Gate Revenue, and Operating Income, 2016 ($ Millions)**

League	Team	Market Value	Revenue	Payroll	Gate Revenue	Operating Income
MLB						
Top 2	San Francisco	2,250	409	198	172	72.6
	Houston	1,100	270	107	73	66.6
Middle 2	Chi. White Sox	1,300	293	135	46	22.5
	Minn. Twins	1,050	240	125	73	20.2
Bottom 2	Phillies	1,235	263	164	72	−8.9
	Dodgers	2,500	438	346	130	−73.2
NBA						
Top 2	LA Lakers	2,700	304	76	98	133.4
	NY Knicks	3,000	307	88	128	108.9
Middle 2	Oklahoma City	950	157	87	48	20.9
	Miami	1,300	180	89	67	20.8
Bottom 2	Washington	960	146	89	31	2.9
	NY Nets	1,700	220	99	63	−5.7
NHL						
Top 2	Montreal	1,120	202	75	76	76.9
	NY Rangers	1,250	219	82	92	74.5
Middle 2	Ottawa	355	118	68	36	6.3
	Colorado	360	115	66	33	6.3
Bottom 2	Carolina	230	99	63	22	−15
	Florida	235	100	67	16	−15.4
NFL						
Top 2	Dallas	4,200	700	190	98	300
	New England	3,400	523	182	99	212
Middle 2	New Orleans	1,750	358	191	62	77
	Tampa Bay	1,800	341	171	49	75
Bottom 2	Oakland	2,100	301	169	40	46
	Buffalo	1,560	326	206	50	26
MLS						
Top 2	Seattle	285	52	10.7	N/A	N/A
	Los Angeles	265	58	18.1	N/A	N/A
Middle 2	San Jose	180	31	6.4	N/A	N/A
	NY Red Bulls	178	23	5.8	N/A	N/A
Bottom 2	Columbus	123	24	5.5	N/A	N/A
	Colorado	110	16	8.4	N/A	N/A

Revenue figures reflect revenue sharing by teams.

Sources: Financial valuation is as of 2016. All other data are as of December 2016. *Forbes.com.* "The Business of Baseball," at http://www.forbes.com/mlb-valuations/list/; *Forbes.com.* "The Business of Hockey," at http://www.forbes.com/nhl-valuations/list/; *Forbes.com.* "The Business of Basketball," at http://www.forbes.com/nba-valuations/list/; *Forbes.com.* "The Business of Football," at http://www.forbes.com/nfl-valuations/list/; MLS market value and revenue data are from Chris Smith. 2016. "Major League Soccer's Most Valuable Teams 2016: New York, Orlando Thrive in First Seasons," *Forbes.com*, September 7, at https://www.forbes.com/sites/chrissmith/2016/09/07/major-league-soccers-most-valuable-teams-2016-new-york-orlando-thrive-in-first-seasons/. Payroll data are from Daniel Boniface. 2016. "MLS Player Salaries 2016 Released by Major League Soccer Players Union," *The Denver Post: The Terrace,* May 19, at http://blogs.denverpost.com/rapids/2016/05/19/mls-player-salaries-2016-released-major-league-soccer-players-union/27671/. MLS data accessed October 22, 2017.

The revenue and cost figures require a bit of perspective. On the cost side, payroll costs give a sense of total cost. In the NFL, NHL, and NBA, payroll expenses are remarkably similar across teams, while in MLB, the highest-spending teams have payrolls that exceed the total revenue of others. We discuss the reasons for these differences across leagues later in this chapter as well as in Chapter 10, but such differences inevitably influence team profitability. Differences in revenue, and hence in value and profitability, are driven by both the demand in the team's home market, and the revenue-sharing rules that allow teams to profit from demand for other teams in the league.

Table 3.3 reveals three important features of sports leagues. First, the data generally support the view that profit maximization is a reasonable approximation of team behavior in North American leagues. With a few notable exceptions, such as the Dodgers, teams with high revenue also have high operating income, our measure of day-to-day profit. Thus, while profit maximization does not apply at all times to all teams, we use it as our rule of thumb for most of this book.

Second, the data in Table 3.3 suggest that the most profitable teams enjoy strong demand. Revenue generally rises with the number of potential consumers, so teams in large cities tend to have higher revenue and profit. We can show this relationship on a graph similar to Figure 3.1a. Figure 3.2 shows that small increases in team quality add more to the revenue of a team from a large city (TR_L) than to the revenue of a team from a small city (TR_S). As a result, "big-market" teams naturally tend to be more successful both on and off the field than "small-market" teams, a point to which we return in Chapters 4 and 5.

Third, tastes and preferences among local consumers matter. MLS, the newest of the leagues shown here, is still in its infancy as a major sports attraction. Despite the extraordinary popularity of soccer outside North America, the revenue of even the most popular MLS teams is dwarfed by the least popular teams in the other leagues. We can see the influence of regional tastes for some sports, as in the case of football in Texas, soccer in Seattle, and hockey in Canada. The financial strength of the Canadiens is even more stark if we compare it to the

Figure 3.2
Revenue, Cost, and City Size

The total revenue curve is steeper for teams in large cities, so they tend to win more games.

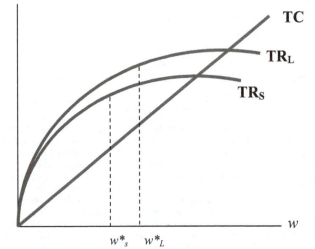

Florida Panthers, who play in a warm location without a hockey tradition. The Canadiens' gate revenue is nearly five times that of the Panthers. In other sports, we see that team quality increases fans' desire to see the home team play. In addition to being perennial Super Bowl contenders, the New England Patriots are an economic powerhouse off the field. The same is true for the San Francisco Giants, winners of the 2010, 2012, and 2014 World Series.

Some leagues are clearly more profitable than others. The median football team had operating income of $76 million, almost four times that of the median baseball team (about $21 million). The least profitable NFL team had higher operating income than the median NBA, NHL, or MLB team. The Phillies and the Dodgers had negative operating income, but the Dodgers' massive losses stand alone in professional baseball. Some of this loss is likely due to the Dodgers' pursuing wins over profits but much of it stems from questionable personnel decisions. Their 2015 payroll, the first ever to top $300 million, included payments of $95 million (more than the payroll of some entire teams) to players no longer on the roster.[8]

A Detailed Look at Revenue

Professional teams generate revenue from six principal sources: ticket sales or gate receipts (R_G); local and national broadcasting rights (R_B); advanced media such as live streaming (R_M); licensing income (R_L); other venue-related revenues including luxury boxes, concessions, and stadium-naming rights (R_V); and transfers from other teams in the league (R_T):

$$TR = R_G + R_B + R_M + R_L + R_V + R_T$$

The size and variation of each of these revenue streams differ substantially from sport to sport, which helps to explain why some sports are more profitable and why profits in some leagues are more equal than in others.

Gate Revenue

Gate revenue is an important source of income for all professional teams. Figure 3.3 shows the gate revenue for all teams in the four major North American leagues in 2016 (or 2015–2016). As expected, the most popular baseball teams, with their 81 home games per season, generate the most gate revenue. This revenue drops off fairly quickly, however, and less popular MLB teams do not generate as much gate revenue as many NFL teams, which play only eight home games per season. In 2015, seven MLB teams had gate revenue that was less than 20 percent of the Yankees' $259 million. For example, the Tampa Bay Rays averaged about 20,000 fewer fans per game than the Yankees. Lower revenue also resulted from lower ticket prices, as the average ticket in Tampa Bay in 2015 was just $21.90 compared to $51.55 for the Yankees.[9]

While baseball has the largest variation in gate revenue, the NFL has the smallest, with the Patriots having only 2.5 times the ticket revenue of the Oakland Raiders. This is partly because most football teams generally draw close to capacity crowds. As with MLB, differences are also partly driven by differences in ticket prices, as the average Patriots ticket in 2015 was $122 compared to $64.80 for the Raiders.[10]

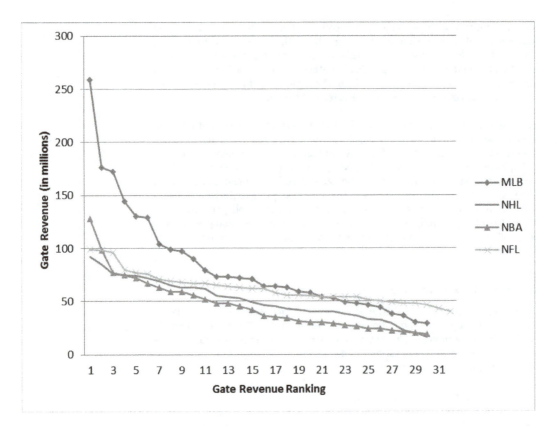

Figure 3.3
Gate Revenue for the NBA, NFL, NHL, and MLB

Gate revenue in MLB is far more variable across teams than in the other sports.

Sources: Forbes.com, Business of Baseball, Business of Hockey, Business of Basketball, Business of Football, 2016. http://www. forbes.com/mlb-valuations/ list/; http://www.forbes.com/ nfl-valuations/list/#tab:overall; http://www.forbes.com/nhl-valuations/list/#tab:overall; http://www.forbes.com/nba-valuations/list/#tab:overall. Accessed January 2, 2017.

Broadcast Revenue

Few events have changed the finances of professional sports as much as the advent of television. As Table 3.4 shows, the value of national television rights varies enormously from sport to sport. Major league baseball, basketball, and football all enjoy annual revenue streams in the billions of dollars from their league-wide, national broadcasting rights. Annual NHL rights exceed $500 million. The much smaller and newer MLS has league-wide television rights worth just $90 million per year, about the same as goes to each team in the NBA. These differences have important implications for the overall prosperity of the leagues and the disparities of operating income within each league.

The prosperity of the NFL stems directly from its huge network contracts. Recall from Table 3.2 that even the least profitable of NFL teams had operating profits of $26 million. To see the difference that TV can make, consider what would happen if the NFL and NHL had equivalent TV contracts. Table 3.4 shows that each NFL team gets about $200 million more per year than each NHL team. If both leagues had equal TV contracts (adding $100 million to NHL teams' revenues and subtracting $100 million from NFL teams' revenues in Table 3.3), almost every NHL team would have *higher* annual income than the equivalently ranked NFL team.

The structure of NFL television contracts ensures that prosperity spreads to all teams. Because all NFL games are part of the national broadcast packages,

Table 3.4 Current US Major League Television Broadcasting Deals

Sport	Years	Stations	Total Annual Fees ($M)	Annual Fees Per Team ($M)
MLB	2014-21	Fox, TBS, ESPN	1,500	50
NBA	2016-25	ESPN (ABC), TNT	2,660	88.67
NFL	2011-19/2014-22	ESPN/Fox, CBS, NBC/DirecTV	6,850	214.06
	2011-21	NBC		
NHL*	2014-26	Rogers Comm. (CA)	520	16.77
MLS	2015-22	ESPN, Fox, Univision	90	4.5

*NHL Rogers communication contract converted to American dollars at $0.74US = $1CAD.

Sources: ESPN. 2012. "MLB Completes New TV Deals," *ESPN.com,* October 2, at http://www. espn.com/mlb/story/_/id/8453054/major-league-baseball-completes-eight-year-deal-fox-turner-sports; ESPN. 2016. "NBA Extends Television Deals," *ESPN.com,* February 14, at http:// www.espn.com/nba/story/_/id/11652297/nba-extends-television-deals-espn-tnt; Bob Condor. 2011. "NHL, NBC Sign Record-Setting 10-Year TV Deal," *NHL.com,* April 19, at https://www. nhl.com/news/nhl-nbc-sign-record-setting-10-year-tv-deal/c-560238; Dan Rosen. 2013. "NHL, Rogers Announce Landmark 12-Year Deal," *NHL.com,* November 26, at https://www.nhl. com/news/nhl-rogers-announce-landmark-12-year-deal/c-693152; Kurt Badenhausen. 2011. "The NFL Signs TV Deal Worth $27 billion," *Forbes.com,* December 14, at https://www.forbes. com/sites/kurtbadenhausen/2011/12/14/the-nfl-signs-tv-deals-worth-26-billion/; *Forbes.com.* 2014. "DirecTV Extends Its Deal with NFL for $12 Billion," October 8, at https://www.forbes. com/sites/greatspeculations/2014/10/08/directv-extends-its-deal-with-nfl-for-12-billion/; Frank Pallotta and Brian Stelter. 2016. "NFL Makes Enormous 'Thursday Night Football' Deal with NBC and CBS," *CNN.com,* February 1, at http://money.cnn.com/2016/02/01/media/ thursday-night-football-nbc-cbs-deal/; Jonathan Tannenwald. 2015. "MLS, U.S. Soccer Officially Announce New TV Deal with ESPN, Fox, Univision," December 13, at http://www.philly.com/ philly/blogs/thegoalkeeper/Live-MLS-US-Soccer-officially-announce-new-TV-deal-with-ESPN-Fox-Univision.html.

virtually all of its television revenue is shared equally (the exception being local preseason broadcasts). As a result, the Green Bay Packers, who play in a city that is smaller than any city hosting an MLB team, have TV revenue that is roughly equal to that of NFL teams playing in New York or Chicago.

Local Television Revenue in MLB, NHL, and the NBA

MLB's network contract for national broadcasts is far less lucrative than football's, but unlike the NFL, baseball teams have another major source of TV revenue: TV contracts with local or regional broadcasters. This is particularly true in large markets. For example, in addition to the $50 million that the Dodgers receive from the league-wide contract, they receive an astounding $204 million per year in local broadcast revenue. The Yankees and Angels also have local revenue of $98 million or more. In contrast, the Marlins, Rockies, and Rays receive only $20 million per year. To make matters worse for small-market teams, many teams have a significant ownership stake in the regional sports networks (RSNs) that broadcast their games, and revenues earned as part of such ownership shares are exempt from local revenue sharing, which we describe below.[11] Such disparities create differences in teams' ability to compete for talent.

The NBA's current agreement with ABC/ESPN and TNT provides the league with $2.66 billion per year, which respresents a significant share of each team's total revenue. As is the case for baseball, local broadcast revenue plays an important role in team finances, though the current revenue-sharing agreement helps to even out the disparities in revenues from local television contracts.

As with the NBA, much of the disparity in revenue among NHL teams stems from large differences in local TV revenue. These differences have even more serious consequences in hockey because the NHL receives far less network revenue than the other leagues, with each team receiving less than one-fourth what NBA teams receive, about $20 million per year. In the absence of revenue sharing, teams in small markets struggle to compete with large market teams.

Television and Attendance—Exposure versus Substitution

Broadcasting games may be a double-edged sword to teams. If fans prefer watching games on television to going to the stadium, televised games are a substitute for live attendance. This reduces gate receipts by shifting the demand curve for attendance to the left. The impact of TV on attendance was first documented in 1948, when the Philadelphia Eagles saw attendance drop by 50 percent when they televised all their home games. This decline led the NFL to "black out" (forbid networks from showing in the local market) games that were not sold out. Blacking out the home team's game may not stimulate ticket sales if a New England Patriots fan in Boston prefers watching a televised game between the Cowboys and Dolphins to shivering at Gillette Stadium on a cold December day. However, if television stimulates fans' interest in the game, broadcasts may increase attendance. The NFL owes much of its popularity to its focus on nationally broadcast games and the "Sunday doubleheader," which allows fans to watch popular teams from other cities. Conversely, if fans can inexpensively watch a game live, attending a game may substitute for watching it on TV. If so, decreasing the price of live attendance reduces television ratings.

Babatunde Buraimo investigated the extent to which live attendance and television are substitutes with surprising results. He created two models, one for stadium attendance and one for television viewership, for Tier Two English football (soccer). In the attendance model, the three primary independent variables indicate various formats of television broadcasting. Buraimo controlled for other factors that might influence demand, such as the availability of other, perhaps more interesting, Champions League games on television, the quality of the game as measured by recent performances in home and away games, whether the game was a local rivalry, and whether it was played midweek or on a bank (national) holiday. He found that broadcasting games on television negatively impacted attendance. Thus, in the case of second-division English football, consumers regard watching a game on TV as a substitute for attendance. The television demand model yielded the interesting result that games with greater attendance had significantly *higher* television ratings. He concludes that watching a game on television is more entertaining when the stadium is full. As Buraimo notes, this leaves teams and leagues in the difficult position of attempting to maximize two variables that cause each other to move in opposite directions.[12]

Advanced Media

No component of team revenue has changed faster than advanced media—revenue derived from online services, such as live streaming on Twitter. All major leagues now have a significant online presence as consumers, especially younger consumers, increasingly move away from traditional cable or pay television. *Forbes.com* reports that more than three-fourths of millennials plan to give up pay television to some extent in favor of advanced media content.[13] No organization has positioned itself better here than MLB and its partners. BAMTech, a division of Major League Baseball Advanced Media (MLBAM), leads the way in providing streamed content. MLBAM is owned by MLB, the Disney Corporation, and the NHL, which exchanged its digital media rights for a minority equity stake (about 10 percent) in the firm. BAMTech offers a wide range of sports content, including MLB, the NHL, the Professional Golfers' Association (PGA), and, more recently, content from Europe with the formation of BAMTech Europe. Content is delivered across multiple platforms. For example, in 2016, MLBAM reached an agreement with Twitter to livestream MLB and NHL games. MLBAM had 2016 revenues of just over $1 billion. This dramatically changes the professional sports revenue landscape, as MLBAM accounted for 10 percent of MLB's total revenues in 2016 and, unlike cable revenue, this revenue stream is equally shared by teams.[14] As this segment of the industry grows, it will be interesting to see whether increases in advanced media revenue represent new revenue or just replace broadcast revenue. If most of the revenue from advanced media represents new demand, overall revenues will increase. The more that one form of delivery substitutes for another, the more decreases in R_B offset increases in R_M, mitigating the increase in total revenue.

Licensing Agreements

All four major North American leagues have created licensing arms—MLB Properties, NBA Properties, NFL Properties, and NHL Enterprises—to oversee the sale of official team paraphernalia to fans. This centralization has two consequences. First, as with league-wide TV contracts, league-wide licensing agreements prevent teams from competing with one another and give the teams greater market power when dealing with both manufacturers and retailers. Second, because the teams share licensing revenue (R_L), the agreements level the financial playing field. Figures are not publicly available for all leagues, but MLB's licensing revenue in 2015 was about $3.4 billion, which is split equally among all teams.[15]

Licensing is one area in which the NFL has moved away from equalizing revenue streams. Shortly after Jerry Jones bought the Dallas Cowboys in 1989, he signed licensing deals with Pepsi Cola and Nike, neither of which had an agreement with NFL Properties at the time. The NFL tried unsuccessfully to block the deal, so, while the Cowboys remain part of NFL Properties, they are the only NFL team allowed to sign their own licensing deals. The Cowboys have gone on to sign apparel deals with groups ranging from the University of Southern California to Victoria's Secret.

Venue and Sponsorship Revenue

Venue revenue, or nonticket revenue from the stadium (R_V), includes revenue from parking and concessions. More importantly, it includes revenue from luxury suites and other special seating, only a small portion of which counts as ticket revenue. Venue revenue helps explain why, according to *Forbes*, the Dallas Cowboys are the most valuable professional franchise in the United States.[16] At first, it is hard to see why the Cowboys are so valuable. While the Cowboys have long been one of the most successful teams in the NFL—only the Pittsburgh Steelers have won more Super Bowls—the NFL's policy for sharing gate and television revenue does not appear to allow them to monetize this success.

The key to the Cowboys' financial success has been its extraordinarily profitable stadium configuration and the NFL rules on the treatment of premium seating revenue. AT&T Stadium has 300 luxury boxes, which rent for $224,000 to $900,000 per season. Part of the revenue from luxury and other premium seating counts toward ticket revenue (shared revenue) and part counts toward concessions, which is not shared (known as retained revenue). For example, suppose a luxury suite in AT&T Stadium with 20 seats rents for $500,000 per year. If the Cowboys claim the value of the seats to be $50 each, they share only $3,200 ($0.4 \times 20 \times 50 \times 8$ games), and they keep the remaining $496,800. Thus, *Forbes* attributes more than $1.04 billion of the Cowboys' value to their stadium. Even in other leagues, where revenue sharing includes all local revenues, more luxury boxes means more local revenue, not all of which is shared with other teams. We revisit this strategy in Chapters 6 and 7 in our discussion of the costs and benefits of stadiums.

Concessions and parking revenue vary widely across teams and leagues. There is no standard formula for determining how much revenue teams earn from concessions, in part because not all teams own the venues in which they play and in part because of differences in the number of games and the prices of concessions and parking.

Sponsorships are another important source of revenue in professional sports. When watching a NASCAR race, a European soccer match, or even a golf tournament, fans can see the lengths to which companies go to associate their brands with a team, a player, or an event. Corporate names and logos adorn uniforms and equipment. All but two WNBA teams now bear the logo of the Boost Mobile phone company, with the Seattle Storm and the San Antonio Silver Stars receiving an exemption only because they had earlier deals with rival phone companies.[17] One enterprising boxer even had an advertisement temporarily tattooed on his body.

Sponsorship agreements occur both at the league and at the team level. Sponsoring firms pay fees to the team in exchange for publicity. These include firms of all sorts, from DraftKings to General Motors, and are negotiated at both the league and team levels. League-level sponsorships even out revenue disparities caused by variation in other sources, but team-level sponsorships exacerbate these differences, as sponsors typically offer more lucrative arrangements in large markets than small ones. The NFL led the way with total sponsorship revenue of $1.2 billion for 2015. MLB and the NBA were close behind, with $750 million and $739 million, respectively. The NHL had the least revenue, with $447 million.[18]

Perhaps the most prominent form of sponsorship is the sale of stadium naming rights. Rich Products, Inc. was the first company to purchase naming rights to a stadium when it bought the right to put its name on the Buffalo Bills' new stadium in 1973 for $1.5 million over 25 years. For the next 20 years, professional sports in America largely ignored the revenue possibilities of naming rights. In 1990, only a handful of teams had sold such rights. Today, virtually all stadiums and arenas bear corporate names.

Table 3.5 identifies the ten most lucrative naming rights deals as of 2016. It shows that companies spend up to $20 million per year to put their names on sports facilities. However, evidence suggests that, while naming rights add millions each year to many teams' coffers, the purchases add little to a sponsor's profitability. One study of 54 stadiums and arenas showed that only a handful of purchases had any impact on the company's profitability and that the effect was as likely to be negative as it was positive.[19]

Table 3.5 The Ten Most Lucrative US Naming Rights Deals (in $ Millions)

Stadium	Team	Sponsor	Total Value ($Mil)	Length of Deal (Years)	Ave. Rev./Yr. ($Mil)
MetLife Stadium	NY Jets/Giants	MetLife	450	25	18
AT&T Stadium	Dallas Cowboys	AT&T	400	20	20
Citi Field	NY Mets	Citigroup	400	20	20
Mercedes-Benz Stadium	Atlanta Falcons	Mercedes-Benz	310	27	11.48
NRG Stadium	Houston Texans	NRG Energy	300	30	10
SunTrust Park	Atlanta Braves	SunTrust Banks	240+	30	8
Gillette Stadium	New England Patriots	Gillette	220	20	11
Levi's Stadium	San Francisco 49ers	Levi Strauss	205	27	7.59
FedEx Field	Washington Redskins	FedEx	200	20	10
Barclay's Center	Brooklyn Nets	Barclay's	200	20	10

Source: Kurt Badenhausen. 2016. "Warriors, Chase Tie-Up Ranks among Biggest Stadium Naming Deals Ever," *Forbes.com*, January 28, at http://www.forbes.com/sites/kurtbadenhausen/2016/01/28/warriors-chase-tie-up-joins-ranks-of-biggest-stadium-naming-rights-deals/. Accessed January 4, 2017.

While many North American leagues have impressive sponsorship arrangements, these amounts do not come close to what some European soccer clubs earn. Chevrolet pays Manchester United $80 million per year for the right to put its logo on the front of ManU jerseys. Real Madrid will take in $28 million per year for renaming Santiago Bernabeu in a deal with the United Arab Emirates that begins once the stadium has been renovated.[20]

Revenue Transfers

Teams in all North American leagues share a substantial fraction of their revenue. While revenue sharing is frequently justified as a mechanism to increase competitive balance, a claim we address in detail in Chapter 5, revenue sharing is at least as important for the financial stability of the league. If not for this important source of funds, teams in many small markets might fold. The extent of and mechanism for sharing revenue vary by league, but none can match the NFL.

One major reason why revenue in the NFL is so evenly distributed comes from the league's generous gate-sharing policy, which reduces R_G for some teams and adds to R_T for others. Initially, this policy was not the result of a carefully thought-out business plan. Instead, it was born of desperation in the NFL's early years. For the first 16 years of its existence, 1920 through 1935, the NFL did not field the same set of teams in two consecutive years, and 43 of the 50 teams that played in at least one season had moved or gone out of business by the end of that era.[21] Faced with such extreme instability, the NFL instituted a generous gate revenue-sharing policy. Today, home teams in the NFL keep only 60 percent of all net gate revenue. The remaining 40 percent goes into a common pool that is distributed among all teams.[22] This arrangement means that an NFL team's gate revenue is actually:

$$R_G = 0.6 * R_{G,H} + 0.4 * (R_{G,P}/32)$$

where $R_{G,H}$ is a team's gate revenue from home games and $R_{G,P}$ is the total gate revenue generated by all 32 NFL teams. Gate sharing enabled the league to survive its lean, early years and helps to explain why operating incomes and market values today are so much closer in the NFL than in other leagues. It also set the stage for other revenue-sharing policies that would help make the NFL the most uniformly profitable of all the major North American leagues. NFL teams receive an equal share of all television (R_B), advanced media (R_M), and licensing revenue (R_L). Thus, only differences in other venue revenues from sources such as luxury boxes separate the highest-earning teams from the lowest.

Though the NHL does share national television and other league-wide revenues, unlike the NFL, much of the revenue generated by NHL teams is at the local level. In the absence of local revenue sharing, this could create vast disparities between the highest- and lowest-earning teams. To address this issue, the league has implemented a complex revenue-sharing system in the collective bargaining agreement with its Players' Association (the union that represents the players). Article 49 of the current agreement, spanning more than 20 pages, explains the rules that stipulate the circumstances under which a team would either contribute to or receive from the revenue-sharing system.[23] Briefly, the system creates a pool of available funds, computed as a percentage of total hockey related-revenue. Contributions to this pool come from three sources. Fifty percent is paid by the ten highest-revenue clubs. Playoff clubs contribute 35 percent of their playoff gate receipts. This portion of the pool is essentially a tax on the gate revenue of the best teams. If necessary, the league completes the funding pool from league-generated revenues (i.e., not from a particular team). These funds are distributed to lower-revenue teams so that they can afford to pay a pre-determined target payroll. The league can also redistribute revenue through an industry growth fund designed to assist low-revenue teams with long-term improvements.

The NBA has recently instituted a large-scale revenue-sharing plan to address differences in local revenues. Each team now contributes 50 percent of its total revenue (less certain allowable expenses) into a central pool and receives a share equal to the average team payroll.[24] Teams whose revenue is less than twice the average payroll are net recipients from this pool, while teams whose revenue is more than twice the average payroll are net payers. As a result, R_T is negative for high-income teams and negative for low-income teams.

MLB teams also share a substantial portion of their local revenue. According to MLB's collective bargaining agreement, teams must place 31 percent of all "net local revenue" in a pool, from which all 30 teams draw equally. Thus, teams that earn higher than average local revenue, such as the Yankees, effectively transfer some of that revenue to less well-off teams, such as the Athletics, so R_G falls for popular teams and R_T rises for less popular teams. Similar to the revenue-sharing arrangements of the NHL and NBA, MLB's largest market teams are disqualified from revenue sharing after 2016. The impact of this rule may be minimal, however, as large market teams are typically payers rather than recipients of revenue-sharing funds.[25]

Costs

Like revenues, a firm's costs come in a variety of forms. Recall that variable costs change as a firm's output changes, while fixed costs remain constant no matter how much the firm produces. Most models of firm behavior treat the cost of labor as a variable cost, since the firm must hire more labor to produce more output and can change the number of workers that it hires relatively easily. In professional sports, labor costs and most other costs are fixed (or variable over only a narrow range) in a given season. At the team level, the NBA, NFL, and NHL all designate a relatively narrow band within which a team's payroll must fall. Baseball is the only major North American sport that does not directly limit a team's payroll. At the individual level, the team cannot reduce a player's salary if the team draws fewer fans than expected. Thus, individual salaries and overall payrolls do not change significantly with output, as measured in the number of fans, over the course of a season.

The data in Table 3.3 show that players' salaries figure prominently in the total costs of professional franchises. Salaries, which include deferred payments, bonuses, workers' compensation expenses, and pension contributions, make up over half a team's costs in every major sport.

Teams must also pay for travel, advertising, administration (both team and league), and venue expenses. Travel expenses increase with the size of the team, the number of away games, and the distances traveled. Teams incur advertising and administrative costs at two levels. Each team advertises in its own market, and each team has its own administrative costs, which include everything from office supplies to the salaries of team executives. Advertising and administrative costs also occur at the league level. These costs range from broad-based ad campaigns designed to increase demand for the sport to the salaries of the referees.

Total venue costs differ significantly across teams. Many teams pay rent to local governments that own the venues in which they play. Those rents might be close to market value or far below it. Some teams that own their own venues receive millions of dollars in public subsidies, while others receive little or no public support. We explore these issues in detail in Chapters 6 and 7.

In MLB and, to a lesser extent, the NBA and NHL, teams pay a portion of player development costs for players in their minor league systems. Each MLB team operates six minor league teams (in AAA, AA, and three single A leagues). Income statements for six major league teams that were leaked to the website Deadspin.com in 2008 showed player development costs that ranged from $15.5 million for the Seattle Mariners to $23.2 million for the Pittsburgh Pirates.[26] Because each minor league system generates only a few major league players per year, developing a major league player costs millions of dollars.

League Size, Opportunity Cost, and Team Movement

Opportunity cost never appears on a team's balance sheet, yet it figures in all teams' decision making. When franchises move from one city to another, they are driven by the prospect of higher profits in the new city. The opportunity costs of staying in a given city are the profits forgone by not moving to the new city. When a team contemplates a move, its owner usually cites the need for more skyboxes, lower lease payments, and better practice facilities. The implied threat in such statements is that another city is offering such facilities. We discuss franchise moves in detail in Chapters 6 and 7.

While many teams move because they are suffering losses in their current city, not all teams that move are losing money. When the Dodgers moved to Los

Angeles in 1957, they ended a remarkably successful run in Brooklyn. In the decade before they moved west, the Dodgers were the most profitable team in baseball, accounting for 47 percent of the profits of the entire National League. Similarly, in their last season before sneaking off to Indianapolis, the Baltimore Colts had an operating profit of $5.1 million, the third highest in the NFL.[27]

Entry as Cooperative Behavior

The number of teams in a closed league is fixed. In North America, MLB and the NBA restrict themselves to 30 teams. The NFL has 32 teams, and, with the addition of Las Vegas, the NHL has 31. In contrast, the Australian Football League has 18 teams and Nippon Professional Baseball (NPB) has just 12. The forces that determine how large a league becomes can be found in the work of Nobel laureate James Buchanan.[28] Buchanan reasoned that admitting a new member to a club brings costs and benefits. In the case of a sports league, existing teams benefit from the admission fees that new teams pay to join the league and from the additional fan base and media outlets new teams bring.[29] Additional members also bring a cost. For example, admitting new teams to the league spreads any shared revenue over more members and reduces the ability of existing members to use the threat of moving to the new city as a bargaining chip when negotiating with their current home cities.

If the revenue from admitting one more team declines as the league grows—as one might expect if leagues admit teams from the most profitable cities first and then admit teams from less profitable cities—the marginal revenue curve slopes downward, as in Figure 3.4. Similarly, if the cost of admitting one more team rises, the marginal cost curve slopes upward. The equilibrium point occurs where the marginal revenue and marginal cost curves meet (e_0), which leads to optimal league size Q_0.

Figure 3.4 also shows the dangers that face professional leagues when they limit the number of teams. At the turn of the 20th century, the National League, then

Figure 3.4
Determining the Optimal Size of a Closed League

The optimal size of the league is set where the marginal revenue meets marginal cost.

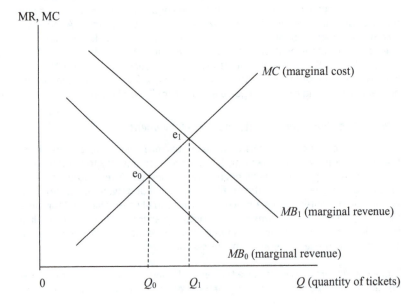

Table 3.6 Ten Most Populous Metropolitan Statistical Areas and Their Sports Teams, 2017

City (Population)[a]	MLB	NBA	NFL	NHL	MLS	WNBA
New York (18.9)	2	2	2	3	2	1
Los Angeles (12.8)	2	2	2	1	1	1
Chicago (9.5)	2	1	1	1	1	1
Dallas (6.4)	1	1	1	1	1	1
Philadelphia (6.0)	1	1	1	1	1	0
Houston (6.0)	1	1	1	0	1	0
Washington, DC (5.6)	1	1	1	1	1	1
Miami (5.6)	1	1	1	1	0	0
Atlanta (5.3)	1	1	1	0	1	1
Boston (4.6)	1	1	1	1	1	0

[a]2010 Population in millions.

Source: U.S. Census Bureau, "Population and Housing Occupancy Status: 2010—United States—Metropolitan Statistical Areas," *American FactFinder*, at http://factfinder2.census.gov/faces/tableservices/jsf/pages/productview.xhtml?pid=DEC_10_NSRD_GCTPL2.US24PR&prodType=table, viewed April 4, 2012.

the only major professional league in North America, restricted itself to only eight teams. It failed to recognize, however, that rising populations and incomes in urban centers had shifted the marginal revenue curve rightward from MB_0 to MB_1. The shift caused the equilibrium point to shift to e_1 and the optimal league size to grow from Q_0 to Q_1. The failure of the National League to expand led Ban Johnson to found the American League in 1901.

Leagues also dictate *where* entry can occur. Table 3.6 shows that each of the ten largest metropolitan areas has several professional franchises. As expected, New York, the largest market, has the most franchises, with 11. Los Angeles and Chicago, the second and third most populous metropolitan areas, have nine and seven. MLB, the NFL, and the NBA have at least one franchise in all of the 10 largest metropolitan areas. The NHL is in every area except Houston and Atlanta, both southern cities with no tradition of professional ice hockey. The WNBA has entered 6 of the 10 largest metropolitan areas, while MLS is in 9, with 2 teams in New York.

Placing franchises in the largest cities has important implications for the individual teams, as it ensures that each team has a large fan base to which it can appeal. On the other hand, adding teams to a market dissipates the monopoly power of the existing teams. As the number of available substitutes increases, the demand curve facing the incumbent team becomes more elastic. In Figure 3.5, adding a nearby team shifts the demand curve from D_0 to D_1, reducing the profit-maximizing price from p_0 to p_1. The more teams that occupy any given area, the more vigorously they must compete with one another to generate revenue.

Placing teams in all the most desirable cities also helps to keep out competing leagues in much the same way that controlling access to a key input limits entry in other markets. The lack of profitable markets dogged the American Basketball

Figure 3.5
The Effect of Entry on Demand

When a new team enters an existing market, the demand curve for the existing team shifts leftward and becomes more elastic.

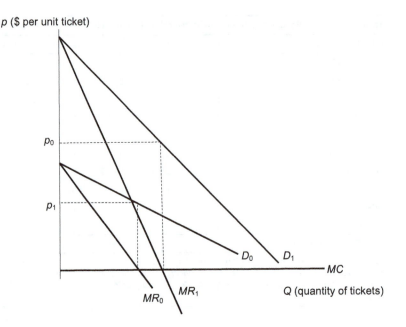

Association (ABA), which competed with the NBA from 1967 to 1976. To avoid direct competition with the NBA, the ABA chose mostly midsized cities for its franchises. In part because of its weak locations, the ABA eventually folded, with only the Denver, New Jersey, San Antonio, and Indiana franchises surviving to join the NBA. The same fate awaited the World Hockey Association (WHA), which played from 1972 through 1979. Four of its teams joined the NHL, two were compensated for not joining the NHL, and the remaining teams disbanded. All teams that attempted to compete head to head with NHL teams in the same market failed. The only teams to survive played in midsized markets where no other team already existed.

Some analysts regard leagues as multiplant monopolies. According to this view, a season of games is a "peculiar mixture: it comes in divisible parts, each of which can be sold separately, but it is also a joint and multiple yet divisible product."[30] After all, part of the excitement of attending a single game comes from how the outcome relates to league standings, which involve all teams in the league and all games in the season.

Closed leagues carefully coordinate the output (here measured as games played) and prices charged to broadcasters or licensees by member teams for the betterment of the league, even if such restrictions reduce the profits of some teams. Major network television contracts are negotiated at the league level rather than by individual teams. Cooperative behavior allows the most popular games to be aired on national television, and it prevents teams from competing with each other for broadcast rights, thereby keeping prices high.

Restricting the number of teams (and the geographic locations they occupy) gives owners a guaranteed source of ticket and media revenue as well as a restricted market for apparel and other team-related enterprises. Leagues enforce territorial rights by setting a radius within which no other member of the league may relocate. For example, in the NFL, each team is given exclusive rights to an area with a radius of 75 miles from its home stadium. A team that moves into another's territory must compensate the existing team. Similar rules exist in baseball. When MLB, which had taken over the Montreal Expos, moved the team to Washington, DC, it paid the Baltimore Orioles $75 million. In keeping with the changing economic landscape of sports, the payment brought the Nationals a stake in the Mid-Atlantic Sports Network, of which the Orioles had owned 90 percent.[31] A dispute with the San Francisco Giants over territorial rights has prevented the Oakland A's from moving to San Jose.

The Limits of Leagues

In the often-surprising world of sports law, few lawsuits had as many twists as *American Needle v. NFL.* In 2009, the NFL asked the Supreme Court to reconsider a decision that it had won, and, a year later, it snatched defeat from the jaws of victory. As part of the brief it submitted to the US Court of Appeals, the NFL claimed that it was taking a "nuanced economics-based approach," which brought a stinging response from several of the nation's top sports economists.[32] Finally, in losing the case, the NFL may have turned what some had derided as "American Needle management's sour grapes over being snubbed by the league" into the event that saved the 2011–2012 football season.[33]

Few could have foreseen the chain of events that would follow when, in 2000, NFL Properties terminated its licensing agreement with a variety of manufacturers to sign an exclusive deal with Reebok (now a part of Adidas).[34] Upset over the loss of a lucrative contract, American Needle sued, claiming that NFL teams had violated antitrust laws by acting as a single entity rather than as individual firms. American Needle lost its suit and multiple appeals, as the courts ruled that the NFL was entitled to negotiate apparel contracts as a single entity. Then, to everyone's surprise, the NFL joined American Needle in asking the US Supreme Court to take up the issue.

While American Needle just wanted its contract back, the NFL saw an opportunity to expand the concept of a league. We have seen that leagues necessarily involve collusion by the teams they comprise and that, when the collusion involves core activities, such as rules of play or scheduling, this collusion is desirable, even necessary. The question is how far that collusion can go. Court rulings and acts of Congress had extended the NFL's core activities to negotiating broadcast rights and licensing agreements, but now the NFL wanted to push the boundary still further. In its appeal, the NFL claimed that the league was not 32 separate operations, but in effect one large firm.

If the Supreme Court had agreed with this argument, then *any* action the NFL took, from deciding where franchises located to setting limits on salaries, would be within the normal operation of one single entity. With the NFL embroiled in contentious negotiations with its players' union, a favorable ruling would have greatly strengthened its hand and encouraged it, in the words of one observer, to "really go for the jugular."[35] As it turns out, the Supreme Court agreed with the economists rather than the NFL and refused to extend the lower court ruling beyond the apparel agreement. Chastened by this ruling, the NFL finally reached an agreement with the players, and the 2011–2012 season was saved.

3.4   Open Leagues: Revenue and Cost in European Soccer

Every four years, Americans are reminded that most of the world pays little attention to baseball or American football and that hockey and basketball are distinctly secondary diversions. Soccer dominates the world stage. UEFA, the European soccer governing body, oversees a dizzying array of teams from the best in the world to semi-professional ones. The top teams in Spain, England, Germany, Italy, and France are economic giants as well. As Table 3.6 shows, Real Madrid, Barcelona, and Manchester United have operating incomes and market values that exceed those of every team in the NBA, NHL, and MLB and all but the most profitable NFL teams. Team revenues are also higher than virtually all North American teams. Tottenham Hotspur, which ranks tenth, has revenues that are greater than any team in the NHL or NBA.

In this section, we take a closer look at the economics of open leagues. Recall that the number of teams in each division of an open league is fixed, but the teams that make up each division change every year through promotion and relegation. Before we explore the details of revenues, costs, and profits, we develop an understanding of how a typical open league is structured. We focus mostly on England, but soccer leagues across Europe are organized along the same principles.

As Table 3.8 shows, professional soccer around the world is governed hierarchically, a model that often leads to controversy. Continental organizations, such

Table 3.7 Top Ten European Soccer Club Values and Revenues, 2016 ($ Millions)

Team	Country	Value	Revenue	Operating Income
Real Madrid	Spain	3,465	694	162
Barcelona	Spain	3,549	675	108
Manchester Utd.	England	3,317	625	190
Bayern Munich	Germany	2,678	570	60
Arsenal	England	2,017	524	122
Manchester City	England	1,921	558	131
Chelsea	England	1,661	505	25
Liverpool	England	1,548	471	115
Juventus	Italy	1,299	390	81
Tottenham Hotspur	England	1,017	310	73

Source: Forbes.com. "The Business of Soccer 2016," at http://www.forbes.com/soccer-valuations/list/#tab:overall. Accessed January 5, 2017.

Table 3.8 Organizational Structure of English Soccer

Organization	Jurisdiction
Premier League	20 best teams
Football League	72 teams in next 3 leagues
Football Association	500+ teams in all leagues
UEFA	Football clubs throughout Europe
FIFA	Football clubs worldwide

Table 3.9 The Hierarchy of English Soccer Competition

Champions League	The top 81 teams in UEFA—top 4 English teams
Europa League	The next best 158 teams in UEFA—next 3 English teams
Premier League	Best 20 teams in England and Wales
FL Championship League	Next 24 teams after the Premier League
FL League One	Next 24 teams after the Championship League
FL League Two	Next 24 teams after League One
FA Leagues below League Two	Hundreds of teams spread across many divisions

as UEFA, answer to the Fédération Internationale de Football Association (FIFA). FIFA is best known for the World Cup championship it stages every four years. In the World Cup competition, players return from their club teams to their home countries to compete as a nation.

Under the umbrella of FIFA, UEFA governs competition in Europe. Within England, the Football Association (FA) oversees soccer at all levels, including the English Premier League (EPL) and the Football League (FL), which represent the top four divisions.

Table 3.9 shows these leagues ranked in order of the level of competition. The Premier League contains the best 20 teams in England and Wales. The Championship League, League One, and League Two are the next three divisions, in order. While in any given season, teams in the Premier League do not compete against teams in the lower divisions (with the exception of the FA Cup and the EFL Cup),[36] the promotion and relegation system means that a Premier League club could one day play against a team currently in League Two, as recently happened when Bournemouth moved from the brink of relegation to semi-pro status to the Premier League.

There are two additional leagues in Table 3.9, the Champions League and the Europa League. These are not really leagues but pan-European tournaments in which the top teams from national leagues compete. As its name suggests, the Champions League pits the champions of each of UEFA's 55 national associations against one another. In addition, the strongest leagues in Europe, as measured by their performance in previous editions of the tournament, are allowed up to three additional entrants, and their teams are exempt from playing in the earliest rounds of playoffs.[37] For example, the top four teams in the EPL, which was ranked the 3rd best league in Europe after Spain's La Liga and Germany's Bundesliga in 2016–2017, will earn a place in the Champions League in 2017–2018. The top three teams from the EPL will enter at the Group Stage consisting of the final 32 teams, while the fourth-place EPL team will have to earn its way into the Group Stage by winning its games in the final playoff round. Conversely, lowly Lithuania, ranked 48th in UEFA, earns but a single spot in the Champions League, and its representative has to play its way through four playoff rounds in order to make its way into the Group Stage, a feat no team from Lithuania has ever accomplished. Indeed, the tournament has been dominated by clubs from the Big Four European Leagues—Germany, England, Spain, and Italy—who have combined for 48 of the 62 championships in the competition's history including 21 of the past 22 through 2017.[38]

The Europa League operates in a similar manner. With minor exceptions, each country sends its best three teams that did not qualify for the Champions League to the Europa League. As in the Champions League, stronger countries enter into the event later in the tournament. In addition, a number of teams from the Champions League join in the later stages of the Europa League after they have been eliminated from the Champions League. As in the Champions League, the strongest national associations have dominated the Europa Cup with the Big Four winning 32 out of 45 titles through 2016.

The seasons of the various European leagues and these two tournaments typically overlap, so a team may be playing matches in its home country at the same time that it competes in the Champions or Europa League. The Champions League and to a lesser extent, the Europa League, provide access to large revenue streams. Thus, they play an important role in teams' decision making. As we shall see, if and how the most successful teams in a national league share revenues with other teams in that league impacts the overall economic health of the league.

Profit Maximization in Soccer

As we saw earlier in this chapter, profit maximization is one of several possible objectives for a team owner. The Russian oligarch Roman Abramovich did not have profits in mind when he bought a controlling interest in Chelsea of England's Premier League. His motivation was probably closer to Mark Cuban's reasons for owning the Dallas Mavericks. Abramovich once remarked: "No, it's not about making money. I have many much less risky ways of making money than this. I don't want to throw my money away, but it's really about having fun and that means success and trophies."[39]

Broad social forces have limited profit seeking by soccer team owners. In England, the limits were remnants of the social hierarchy that surrounded the origins of the sport. As recently as 1982, the Football League, which then oversaw the four top divisions of soccer in England, prohibited teams from paying salaries to club directors.[40] One example of the odd decisions that resulted from the lack of professional management came in 1967, when what is now the Premier League "rejected a BBC proposal of a million pounds for live broadcast of championship matches."[41] This is tantamount to the NFL refusing to allow the networks to broadcast the Super Bowl.

In some countries, outside authorities limit the activities of teams. In France, the national soccer association strictly limits the teams' ability to borrow and spend. In Germany, a controlling share of every team must be held by the football club's member association. Both limits have restricted teams' ability to take on massive debt.

Sources of Revenue

Like teams in North American leagues, European soccer clubs derive revenues from a variety of sources, though there are some differences. Teams in the EPL and other major European leagues derive the majority of their revenue from attendance, broadcasting, sponsorship, and participation in the Champions and Europa Leagues. As we shall see, differences in revenue sharing in the EPL, Serie A, La Liga, Ligue1, and the Bundesliga have a dramatic impact on the financial health of weaker teams across these national leagues.

Table 3.10 summarizes the revenues of the five largest European leagues for the 2014–2015 season. The data show that the Premier League is clearly the most

Table 3.10 Revenue Distributions for the EPL, the Bundesliga, La Liga, Serie A, and Ligue1, 2014–2015

	EPL (England)	Bundesliga (Germany)	La Liga (Spain)	Serie A (Italy)	Ligue1 (France)
Total revenue (€m)	4,400	2,392	2,053	1,792	1,418
Attendance (€m)	768	521	435	210	165
Broadcasting (€m)	2,337	731	975	1,099	628
Sponsorship (€m)	1,295	673	643	483	307
Other (€m)	—	467	—	—	318
Average club revenue (€m)	220	133	103	90	71
Average attendance	36,163	42,685	25,734	21,586	22,329

Source: Deloitte Sports Business Group. June 2016. "Annual Review of Football Finance 2016," ed. Dan Jones, at https://www2.deloitte.com/content/dam/Deloitte/uk/Documents/sports-business-group/deloitte-uk-annual-review-of-football-finance-2016.pdf. Accessed January 9, 2017.

prosperous European league. Other than attendance, where the Bundesliga tops all others with an average of over 42,000, the Premier League dominates every category, most notably broadcast revenue. In this category, the Premier League's dominance will only increase with time, as its revenue from non-UK markets will soon be more than twice that of every other UEFA league. According to Deloitte's Sport Business Group, the Premier League is set to earn £1.1 billion per season from international rights fees. Broadcast rights also figure prominently in the revenue of Italian clubs, representing over 60 percent of their total revenue. In contrast, teams in the Bundesliga derive over half of their revenue from sponsorship and other commercial arrangements. Such an enormous financial advantage in broadcasting (and hence total) revenue will serve the Premier League teams well as they vie for spots in the lucrative Champions League.

There are stark revenue disparities across clubs within leagues. Deloitte reports that even in the EPL, where revenues are distributed relatively evenly by UEFA standards, Manchester United, Manchester City, Arsenal, and Chelsea all had revenues that were at least four times those of Burnley. Even Southampton, which was 10th highest, had revenues that were less than one-third of those of the top three teams. Such large revenue differences make for similar disparities in profits. More than in North American leagues, European football teams' payrolls can make profits elusive. Payrolls of the top 5 EPL teams exceed the total revenue of 14 of the 15 remaining teams.[42]

The impacts of three forces in particular on revenues are worth noting. First, teams with a longer history of success and those in larger cities clearly prosper at the gate. For example, in the EPL, Manchester United's gate revenue was £108m and Arsenal's was just over £100m, but Crystal Palace had just £11m and Burnley fared even worse, at £3.9m.[43] Second, some teams receive revenue from participating in the Champions or Europa League. In the 2015/16 Champions League, the 32 clubs in the group stage all earned at least €16.7 million. Teams that reached the round of 16 earned at least €27 million. The finalists, Real Madrid and Atletico Madrid, earned €80m and €69.7m, respectively. Such revenues can destabilize leagues, as the Champions League payments to Real Madrid equal almost 80 percent of the total revenue earned by an average La Liga team. While Europa League revenues are lower, they are far from trivial, as Liverpool earned almost €38 million in total prize money for winning the 2015/16 championship.[44] In addition, the winner of the Europa League is guaranteed entry into the next Champions League, resulting in even more revenue.

One last source of revenue for soccer teams stems from the promotion and relegation system. Many soccer teams keep themselves financially afloat by developing talented young players and then selling their rights to wealthier teams. A wealthy team such as Manchester United might purchase the rights to players from small "provincial" English teams, from teams in relatively poor countries such as Ukraine or Brazil, or from financially conservative teams such as Olympique Lyonnais in France's Ligue1.

Baroncelli and Lago refer to this process as the "virtuous circle." They actually describe two circles. Large market teams use their financial resources to obtain and pay star players. Their success on the field increases revenue, which they use to purchase the rights to more top players, and the cycle begins again. For small-market teams, the cycle begins with selecting and training young players who generate wins and revenue. While such results increase revenue, in lower divisions or poorer leagues, the increases are modest. To further increase revenue, these teams sell the contracts of promising players to wealthier teams, which allows them to select and develop young players, starting the cycle again. While such teams may survive financially, they are trapped in this circular flow, which seldom allows them to rise through the ranks.[45]

Revenue Sharing in European Football

As we saw with the NFL, revenue sharing can be a powerful tool to mitigate financial differences among teams. There are two primary forms of revenue sharing in European football: broadcast revenues and Champions/Europa League revenues. Historically, most European leagues have not shared much of their broadcast revenues, placing small-market teams at an enormous disadvantage. Recent agreements have reversed this trend, providing a much larger share of the revenue pool to small-market teams.

The EPL distinguishes international television revenue from revenue earned within the UK. All international broadcast revenues are shared equally. National broadcast revenues are shared as well. Domestic television revenue is broken down into one part that is shared equally and another that is divided using both a "merit" system that provides more revenue to teams based on performance and a "facility fee" based on the number of times each team appears in live telecasts within the UK.

Prior to 2016, La Liga teams negotiated individual television contracts. This gave the most popular teams, Real Madrid and FC Barcelona, an enormous revenue advantage. Since 2016, a radically different system has been in place. Ten percent of the total broadcast revenue is shared among teams in the second division. Of the remaining 90 percent, half is shared equally among teams in the top division, 25 percent is based on performance in the last five seasons, and the remaining 25 percent is based on the popularity of the teams.[46] The Bundesliga television agreement that runs through 2021 shares 65 percent of revenues equally and the remaining 35 percent based on performance over the previous five years.[47] The Italian Serie A agreement that runs through 2018 is less egalitarian. Forty percent of domestic revenues are divided equally, 30 percent are based on the club's popularity in Italy, and the remaining 30 percent are based on a multi-season merit formula. Forty percent of international revenues are shared equally, while the remaining 60 percent are shared among the top 10 teams based on performance.[48]

Because teams in the top league have access to higher revenue streams, relegation can jeopardize the financial health of a team. As a result, teams in the top division of open leagues share revenue with teams in lower divisions, particularly those teams that have been most recently relegated. These payments, known as **parachute payments**, soften the financial blow of relegation, especially since those teams may have player contracts that would be unsustainable with lower division revenues. Parachute payments are made on a declining scale over three seasons, with clubs receiving 55 percent of the broadcasting revenue payout to each Premier League club in the first year. Below the top division, revenues drop off very steeply, as teams rely on matchday revenue and solidarity payments. For example, Deloitte reports that the Championship League's (the division below the Premier League) total revenues were only about one-eighth of the Premier League's, and of those, a significant fraction were in the form of parachute payments made to ten different teams. Similarly, UEFA distributes **solidarity payments** to UEFA member teams that do not participate in the Champions or Europa League in an effort to distribute the wealth generated by these tournaments. For the 2016 season, 183 clubs shared €77 million. While these revenues are welcome, they average less than €500,000 per club and pale in comparison to the millions of euros received by teams that made it far into the competition.

In sum, while television and other revenues have increased dramatically in European football, wide disparities remain across nations and, more importantly, within the top divisions of individual leagues. Thomas Peeters and Stefan Szymanski cite a UEFA report that more than 60 percent of European clubs suffered an operating loss in 2012.[49] While the FFP regulations may help to level the playing field, they contain numerous loopholes that reduce their effectiveness. The open league system, the Champions and Europa Leagues, and the "virtuous circles" driven by the sale of player contracts, success on the field, and on the bottom line will tend to keep the winners on top and the losers on the bottom. As a result, the tension between soccer's enormous popularity and the unequal ability of teams to profit from the game will likely persist.

3.5   Single-Entity Ownership

All of the leagues we have discussed so far have one thing in common: They are based on a franchise model. Each team is owned by a different individual, group, or corporation and is free to pursue its own goals, within limits imposed by the league. Although this model of ownership is popular, especially among long-established sports, some newer leagues in sports that do not have large followings have adopted a different ownership model: the single-entity league.

In a single-entity league, investors purchase a share of the league itself rather than an individual team or a share of a team. All league operations, including the negotiation of player contracts, the allocation of players to teams, marketing, and advertising are made by the central office.[50] The advantage of this structure is that it manages costs across all teams, reducing disparities between large and small markets.[51] The challenge for single-entity leagues is to respond to demand differences across local markets. The advantage of the franchise system is that individual team owners can make decisions that they believe are best for their own teams rather than bowing to a single decision that is good for some teams, but not for others.

Some leagues, such as MLS and the WNBA, are transitioning from the single-entity model to a franchise model as they grow in popularity and individual franchises become more stable. Thus, while it seems clear that established leagues in well-known sports prefer the franchise model, there is no single answer as to which league structure is best for emerging sports.

Biographical Sketch

Bill Veeck
(1914–1986)

> *People need people (who else is there to take advantage of?)*
> *—Bill Veeck*[52]

Many owners have won more games than Bill Veeck did with the Cleveland Indians (1946–1949), St. Louis Browns (1951–1953), and Chicago White Sox (which he owned twice, 1959–1961 and 1975–1980), but it is safe to say that no owner in the history of the game had nearly as much fun. Veeck was literally born into baseball—his father was president of the Chicago Cubs—and he never left. In the 1920s, young Bill helped plant the ivy that now covers the wall at Wrigley Field.

A self-described hustler, Veeck was a showman *nonpareil* who gave baseball such attractions as bat day and the exploding scoreboard, and such disasters as "disco demolition night," at which a sellout Chicago crowd ran amok after thousands of disco records were blown up. Veeck also proposed many innovations that baseball adopted only after he had passed from the scene. In his 1969 memoir, *The Hustler's Handbook,* for example, Veeck proposed using the scoreboard to do a variety of things—to review disputed plays or to inform the fans about the type and speed of a pitch that had just been thrown—that teams took decades to implement.

Veeck had an innate sense of how the market and social justice come together. Between 1947 and 1964, only two American League teams other than the New York Yankees—the Cleveland Indians and the Chicago White Sox—won pennants, and only one won a World Series. Veeck was the owner of the Cleveland Indians when they won the 1948 World Series, and he built the team that appeared in the 1954 World Series. He was later the owner of the Chicago White Sox when they made it to the 1959 World Series, their first appearance since the Black Sox scandal of 1919. It was no coincidence that these teams were among the leaders in integrating the American League. Veeck brought Larry Doby to the Indians in 1947, a few weeks after Jackie Robinson broke the color line with the Brooklyn Dodgers. In 1943, the Philadelphia Phillies were one of the worst teams in baseball and one of the least popular. Veeck tried to integrate baseball when he sought to buy the sad sack Phillies and stock the team with players from the Negro Leagues. Veeck had long opposed baseball's color line on moral grounds, but he also felt that integrating the game made good business sense. He thought that bringing in star players from the Negro Leagues would build a talented, exciting team that fans would want to see. According to Veeck, MLB Commissioner Kenesaw Mountain Landis stepped in at the last minute and found another buyer for the Phillies, preventing his purchase of the team.

Veeck also showed a sense of fairness as an outspoken critic of baseball's reserve clause, which effectively bound a player to a team for life. He was the only owner to testify against the reserve clause in Curt Flood's lawsuit against baseball in the 1970s.[53]

Veeck's unorthodox beliefs and promotions did little to endear him to the other owners. They went so far as to block his attempt to move the Browns from St. Louis to Baltimore, allowing the move only after Veeck had sold the team. In St. Louis, the Browns were poor relations of the Cardinals. In an attempt to boost interest in his team, Veeck tried such stunts as sending 3'7" Eddie Gaedel to the plate as a pinch hitter (he walked) and holding "You Be the Manager Day," in which fans were given the opportunity to make substitutions and determine strategy. Predictably, some owners attempted to block Veeck's attempt to get back into baseball in the 1970s.

Veeck's last go-round as an owner—his second stint with the Chicago White Sox—was not as successful as his previous efforts. The advent of free agency and the growing importance of TV and venue revenue did not fit his limited means and hustler mentality. He was forced to sell the team after seven years. Fortunately, Bill's son Michael, the part-owner of several minor league teams, has kept the Veeck legacy alive. As owner of the St. Paul Saints, Michael Veeck staged such stunts as "Mime-O-Vision," in which mimes acted out the action on the field as a sort of living instant replay. The fans responded by pelting the mimes with hot dogs, a travesty trumpeted by headlines in all the local papers. Michael's father would have been proud.

Sources: Bill Veeck with Ed Linn, *The Hustler's Handbook* (Durham, NC: Baseball America Classic Books, 1996); and John Helyar, *Lords of the Realm* (New York: Ballantine Books, 1994).

Summary

Unlike most firms, sports teams do not necessarily maximize profit. Pursuing a different goal, such as maximizing wins, can lead to very different behavior by a team, but even if teams do not maximize their profits, they cannot afford to ignore them entirely. Teams derive their revenue from ticket sales, the sale of broadcast rights, licensing income, advanced media, other venue-related income, and the transfer of funds from other teams. The degree to which revenues are shared among teams varies from league to league, with the greatest sharing occurring in the NFL.

In the sports industry, most sources of cost are fixed over the period of a single season. Primary sources of costs are player salaries, stadium leases, and administrative costs. In the NHL and MLB, subsidies to minor league affiliates for player development also add significantly to team total cost.

Leagues regulate the behavior of teams on the field and off it. Financially, leagues attempt to keep revenue imbalances in check and control costs. In some cases, it is more useful to view the league as the monopoly and teams as producers of a joint product.

European soccer teams face a very different business climate than do North American sports teams. While some teams are highly profitable, most struggle financially. This is partly due to the club ownership model, the existence of deep-pocketed owners willing to place wins above profits, and the relegation and promotion system.

Discussion Questions

1   Are the New York Yankees correct when they claim that revenue sharing simply rewards teams that do not try to win?
2   Would teams operate differently if they had corporate affiliations (e.g., the IBM Lions) rather than city or state affiliations?
3   Should the NBA or NHL switch to a promotion and relegation system?
4   If you were CEO of a company, would you spend $15 million per year to put your company's name on a stadium?
5   "From each according to his ability, to each according to his need" is a familiar Marxist slogan. Is the NFL's revenue-sharing policy incompatible with a market economy?

Problems

3.1   Suppose that you are the owner of a professional baseball team in a major city, and MLB allows a second team to locate in your city. Describe and show using a graph the potential impact on your attendance.
3.2   Draw a graph that shows the demand for attendance at a given game at an NFL stadium. Show how this demand would be affected if:
     a. The prices of parking and food at the games increase.
     b. Televised games switch from free TV to pay-per-view only.
     c. A new league forms with a team that plays nearby.
     d. The quality of the team decreases dramatically.
     e. The length of the season is increased.
3.3   True or false; explain your answer: "If all teams are of equal quality, it doesn't matter whether they share gate receipts—revenue will remain unchanged."
3.4   Some researchers argue that revenue sharing is like socialism in that it removes the incentive to outperform rivals. Do you agree with this statement? Why or why not?
3.5   Suppose that each team in a league has a demand curve for a league-wide, non-team-specific campaign equal to $Q=1,000-5p$. If there are

20 teams in the league, and the price of an ad is $175, how many ads will teams want to purchase as a group?

3.6 Use the marginal revenue and marginal cost curves from the theory of clubs to explain why the NFL has 32 teams, while Bundesliga-1, the top German soccer league, has only 20.

3.7 How can it be that the weakest teams in the National League from a wins/ losses perspective are among the most profitable?

3.8 Suppose that teams in the major European leagues shared all revenue equally (less a contribution to parachute payments). How might this impact the quality of teams? Explain the likely impact on the teams from that league that qualify for the Champions League. Would they be more or less successful?

3.9 Why might a league favor a single-entity ownership model? Explain the differences in the risks and rewards of such a system compared to a franchise owner system.

Notes

1 Eugene Klein. 1987. *First Down and a Billion: The Funny Business of Pro Football* (New York: Morrow): 12.

2 As you read, keep in mind that, outside the US, soccer is known as football.

3 During the 2014–2015 and 2015–2016 seasons, the Philadelphia 76ers were widely believed to be losing on purpose, or "tanking," to enhance their draft position. We return to the economics of the player entry draft in Chapter 5.

4 Many clubs are more general athletic clubs that sponsor teams in several sports, though soccer is generally the dominant sport. See, for example, Stefan Szymanski. 2015. *Money and Soccer* (New York: Nation Books).

5 UEFA.com. 2015. "Financial Fair Play: All You Need to Know," June 30, at http://www.uefa.com/community/news/newsid=2064391.html. Accessed January 2, 2017.

6 Short-run losses might be part of a strategy that maximizes long-run profits, but we ignore that possibility here.

7 The *Forbes* estimates are just that—estimates based on the best publicly available information. Nevertheless, they are widely used by economists as the best data available.

8 Forbes.com. 2017. "Business of Baseball," at http://www.forbes.com/teams/los-angeles-dodgers/. Accessed December 10, 2016.

9 Figures are from Team Marketing report—April 2015, at https://www.teammarketing.com/public/uploadedPDFs/2015%20mlb%20fci%20%281%29.pdf. Accessed January 2, 2017.

10 Team Marketing Report—September 2015, at https://www.teammarketing.com/public/uploadedPDFs/FINAL_%20NFL_FCI_2015.pdf. Accessed January 2, 2015.

11 Craig Edwards. 2016. "Estimated TV Revenues for All 30 MLB Teams," *FanGraphs*, April 25, at http://www.fangraphs.com/blogs/estimated-tv-revenues-for-all-30-mlb-teams/. Accessed January 3, 2017.

12 Babatunde Buraimo. 2008. "Stadium Attendance and Television Audience Demand in English League Football," *Managerial and Decision Economics*, 29(6): 513–523.

13 Maury Brown. 2016. "How Major League Baseball Continues Massive Growth with the Addition of BAMTech Europe," *Forbes.com*, November 1, at http://www.forbes.com/sites/maurybrown/2016/11/01/how-major-league-baseball-continues-massive-growth-with-addition-of-bamtech-europe/. Accessed January 4, 2017.

14 Maury Brown. 2016. "2016 MLB Advanced Media Revenues Projected to Reach $1.1-$1.2 Billion," *Forbes.com*, March, at https://www.forbes.com/sites/maurybrown/2016/03/03/mlb-advanced-media-projected-revenues-to-be-1-1-1-2-billion-in-2016/.

15 Matt Perez. 2016. "Where MLB Receives Its Revenue," *Camden Depot*, January 26, at http://camdendepot.blogspot.com/2016/01/where-mlb-receives-its-revenue.html. Accessed May 8, 2017.

16   Forbes.com. 2016. "Business of Football," at http://www.forbes.com/teams/dallas-cowboys/. Accessed January 3, 2017.

17   Ken Belson. 2011. "New Sponsor on WNBA Uniforms," *New York Times*, August 22, at http://www.nytimes.com/2011/08/22/sports/basketball/wnba-makes-sponsorship-deal-with-boost-mobile.html, viewed April 27, 2017.

18   MLB: IEGSR. 2015. "Sponsorship Spending on MLB Totals $778 Million in 2015 Season," *Sponsorship.com*, November 9, at http://www.sponsorship.com/iegsr/2015/11/09/Sponsorship-Spending-On-MLB-Totals-$778-Million-In.aspx; NBA: Statista.com. 2017. "National Basketball Association (League and Teams) Sponsorship Revenue from 2010 to 2017 (in Million U.S. Dollars)," at https://www.statista.com/statistics/380270/nba-sponsorship-revenue/; NFL: Statista.com. 2017. "NFL League and Team Sponsorship Revenue Worldwide 2010 to 2016 (in Million U.S. Dollars)," at https://www.statista.com/statistics/456355/nfl-league-team-sponsorship-revenue-worldwide/; NHL: Statista.com. 2017. "NHL League and Team Sponsorship Revenue Worldwide 2011 to 2016 (in Million U.S. Dollars)," at https://www.statista.com/statistics/456365/nhl-league-team-sponsorship-spending-worldwide/. Accessed January 4, 2017.

19   Eva Marikova Leeds, Michael A. Leeds, and Irina Pistolet. 2007. "A Stadium by Any Other Name," *Journal of Sports Economics*, 8(6), December: 581–595.

20   Chris Smith. 2016. "The Most Valuable Sponsorship Deals in Soccer," *Forbes.com*, May 11, at http://www.forbes.com/sites/chrissmith/2016/05/11/the-most-valuable-sponsorship-deals-in-soccer/, viewed January 26, 2017.

21   Victor Matheson. 2005. "Professional Sports," in *Encyclopedia of American Business History*, ed. Charles Geisst (New York: Facts on File).

22   The NFL dates its founding from when the initial body, the "American Professional Football Association," took the name "National Football League" in 1922. See David Harris. 1986. *The League: The Rise and Decline of the NFL* (New York: Bantam Books): 12; and Eric M. Leifer. 1995. *Making the Majors: The Transformation of Team Sports in America* (Cambridge, MA: Harvard University Press): 98–109.

23   NHLPA. 2013. "Collective Bargaining Agreement between National Hockey League and National Hockey League Players' Association," Article 49, at http://cdn.agilitycms.com/nhlpacom/PDF/NHL_NHLPA_2013_CBA.pdf. Accessed January 3, 2017.

24   John Lombardo. 2012. "Inside NBA's Revenue Sharing: How Complex Plan Will Shift $140 Million to Needy Teams," *Street & Smith's Sports Business Journal*, January 23, at http://www.sportsbusinessdaily.com/Journal/Issues/2012/01/23/Leagues-and-Governing-Bodies/NBA-revenue.aspx. Accessed January 3, 2017.

25   See for example, Ronald Blum. 2016. "Dodgers, Latin American Players Losers in MLB Labor Deal," *Associated Press*, December 1, at http://bigstory.ap.org/91335e2ae60d440d9a72ee1ed3caa14d; Evan Drellich. 2016. "MLB Changes Market Rank Formula in Revenue Sharing," *Boston Herald*, December 3, at http://www.bostonherald.com/sports/red_sox/clubhouse_insider/2016/12/mlb_changes_market_rank_formula_in_revenue_sharing.

26   The other teams were the Florida Marlins, the Tampa Bay Rays, the Los Angeles Angels of Anaheim, and the Texas Rangers. For the Pirates and Mariners figures, see "MLB Confidential: The Financial Documents MLB Doesn't Want You to See, Part 1," *Deadspin*, August 23, 2010, at http://deadspin.com/5615096, viewed April 2, 2012; and "MLB Confidential Part 2: Seattle Mariners," *Deadspin*, August 23, 2010, at http://deadspin.com/5619509, viewed April 2, 2012.

27   James Quirk and Rodney Fort. 1992. *Pay Dirt* (Princeton, NJ: Princeton University Press): 135; and Jon Morgan. 1997. *Glory for Sale: Fans, Dollars, and the New NFL* (Baltimore, MD: Bancroft Press): 106.

28   James M. Buchanan. 1965. "An Economic Theory of Clubs," *Economica*, 32(125) February: 1–14; and John Vrooman. 1997. "Franchise Free Agency in Professional Sports Leagues," *Southern Journal of Economics*, 64(1), July: 191–219.

29   More generally, Buchanan assumes that members of a club produce "club goods" that members of the club share with one another but outsiders cannot enjoy.

30   Walter C. Neale. 1964. "The Peculiar Economics of Professional Sports," *Quarterly Journal of Economics*, 78(1), February: 3.

31 Graydon Ebert, "MLSE Buy," *Offside: A Sports Law Blog,* at http://offsidesportsblog. blogspot.com/p/mlse-buy.html, viewed April 5, 2012.

32 Quoted in Craig Corbitt and Jan Yi, 2009. *"American Needle, Inc. v. National Football League, et al.*: Amicus Curiae Brief of Economists in Support of Petitioner," at http:// people.stern.nyu.edu/wgreene/entertainmentandmedia/AmericanNeedleEconomists. pdf, viewed May 1, 2012.

33 Tom Van Riper. 2010. "The NFL Vs. American Needle," *Forbes.com,* January 7, at http:// www.forbes.com/2010/01/06/american-needle-supreme-court-business-sports-nfl. html.

34 For more background on the lawsuit, see Jennifer S. Forsyth. 2009. "American Needle Throws Downfield in NFL Licensing Dispute," *Law Blog: The Wall Street Journal,* September 18, at http://blogs.wsj.com/law/2009/09/18/american-needle-throws-downfield-in-nfl-licensing-dispute/.

35 ESPN analyst John Clayton, quoted in Doug Farrar. 2010. "The NFL Loses American Needle: What It Means," *Shutdown Corner/Yahoo! Sports,* May 24, at http://sports. yahoo.com/nfl/blog/shutdown_corner/post/The-NFL-loses-American-Needle-What-it-means?urn=nfl,243282.

36 The FA Cup pits clubs of all divisions against one another. This tournament is best known for its occasional Cinderella stories, such as when Lincoln City, a 5th-division team, played its way into the quarterfinals where it lost to Arsenal in 2017. The results of FA Cup matches are not included in the win/loss records of the participating teams.

37 UEFA.com. 2016/17. "Regulations of the UEFA Champions League 2015-2018 Cycle," at http://www.uefa.com/MultimediaFiles/Download/Regulations/uefaorg/ Regulations/02/35/87/89/2358789_DOWNLOAD.pdf. Accessed May 8, 2017.

38 Paul Saffer. 2015. "How Each Nation Has Done in Champions League," UEFA.com, September 10, at http://www.uefa.com/uefachampionsleague/news/newsid=2275207. html. Accessed January 5, 2017.

39 Jeff Randle. 2003. "Chelsea Owner Seeks 'Fun and Trophies,'" *BBC News,* July 3, at http://news.bbc.co.uk/2/hi/business/3039750.stm. Accessed May 8, 2017.

40 Stefan Szymanski and Andrew Zimbalist. 2005. *National Pastime: How Americans Play Baseball and the Rest of the World Plays Soccer* (Washington, DC: Brookings Institution Press): 132.

41 Wladimir Andreff and Paul D. Staudohar. 2002. "European and US Sports Business Models," in *Transatlantic Sport: The Comparative Economics of North American and European Sport,* ed. Carlos Pestana Barros, Muradali Ibrahimo, and Stefan Szymanski (Cheltenham, UK: Edward Elgar): 25.

42 Deloitte Sports Business Group. 2016. "Annual Review of Football Finance 2016."

43 Nick Harris. 2015. "Club by Club Guide to the Premier League's Financial Health: Find Out What State Your Club Is in with Our Graphic," *Daily Mail,* March 28, at http://www. dailymail.co.uk/sport/football/article-3016432/Club-club-guide-Premier-League-s-financial-health.html. Accessed January 9, 2017.

44 UEFA.com. 2016. "2015/16 Champions League Revenue Distribution," November 1, at http://www.uefa.com/uefachampionsleague/news/newsid=2418253.html; UEFA.com. 2016. "2015/16 Europa League Revenue Distribution," November 1, at http://www.uefa. com/uefaeuropaleague/news/newsid=2418259.html. Accessed January 9, 2017.

45 Alessandro Baroncelli and Umberto Lago. 2006. "Italian Football," *Journal of Sports Economics,* 7(1): 13–28.

46 Harshit Amar. 2015. "La Liga Suspended: The Strange Case of TV Rights," *Football-target.com,* November 5, at http://www.footballtarget.com/la-liga-strange-case-tv-rights/. Accessed January 9, 2017.

47 Totalsportek2. 2016. "German Bundesliga New TV Rights Money Distribution System," June 9, at http://www.totalsportek.com/money/bundesliga-tv-rights/. Accessed January 9, 2017.

48 Totalsportek2. 2016. "Italian Serie A TV Rights & Prize Money Distribution for 2016 (Explained)," February 17, at http://www.totalsportek.com/football/italian-serie-a-tv-rights-money-distribution/. Accessed January 9, 2017.

49 Thomas Peeters and Stefan Szymanski. 2014. "European Football," *Economic Policy*, 29(78), April: 343–390.

50 Roger G. Noll. 2003. "The Organization of Sports Leagues," *Oxford Review of Economic Policy*, 19(4), Winter: 530.

51 Tripp Mickle and Terry Lefton. 2008. "Several Leagues Later, Debate on Single Entity Model Still Lively," *Street and Smith's Sports Business Journal*, August 4, at http://www.sportsbusinessdaily.com/Journal/Issues/2008/08/20080804/This-Weeks-News/Several-Leagues-Later-Debate-On-Single-Entity-Model-Still-Lively.aspx. Accessed June 8, 2009.

52 Bill Veeck with Ed Linn, *The Hustler's Handbook*: 196.

53 We discuss Flood's lawsuit in Chapter 4 and analyze the reserve clause in Chapter 10.

4
MONOPOLY AND ANTITRUST

Gentlemen, we have the only legal monopoly in the country, and we're [messing] it up.

—TED TURNER, ATLANTA BRAVES OWNER[1]

Introduction

Major League Baseball's National League is the oldest professional sports league in the United States.[2] Founded in 1876, it rested on two basic principles:

1   Member clubs had an exclusive right to their home territory.
2   A reserve system bound players to member clubs for as long as the team wanted them.

These principles proved so profitable that many succeeding North American sports leagues adopted them for themselves, often word for word. One need not look far to see why the leagues were so successful. In a closed monopoly league, the principle of "territorial rights" gives teams **monopoly power** in their host cities that magnifies the monopoly power of the league, as it precludes the entry of competing teams who might produce output (games) that could lure consumers away. On the input side, the reserve system kept owners from bidding up salaries to lure away a rival team's players, giving each team **monopsony power** over its players. Baseball and all subsequent sports owe much of their early success to these two barriers. However, teams' financial success often came at the expense of the players whom the teams employed, the fans whom they entertained, and the cities where they played. To see how a monopoly league might not be in the best interest of fans, consider the plight of NFL fans in St. Louis and San Diego as their teams left in 2016 and 2017 for Los Angeles, or Raiders fans whose team left Oakland for Las Vegas.

Learning Objectives

- Identify the social costs of monopoly power.
- Analyze how teams apply pricing strategies that result in increased profits and reduced consumer well-being.
- Describe the circumstances under which society may be better off with a monopoly than with many competing firms.
- Recognize the importance of entry barriers for monopoly sports teams and leagues.
- Explain the importance of US antitrust law and describe the significance of MLB's exemption to these laws.

4.1   What's Wrong with Monopoly?

As we saw in Chapter 2, monopolies produce output at the level where marginal revenue equals marginal cost, while perfectly competitive firms set price equal to marginal cost. Consider the NFL as a monopoly league. Figure 4.1 illustrates the profit-maximizing attendance for a monopoly team with a marginal cost curve that coincides with the horizontal axis up to the point of stadium capacity, and downward-sloping demand and marginal revenue curves. A competitive industry would sell Q_c tickets, where price equals marginal cost.[3] The NFL's market power allows it to restrict output to Q_m, charging a higher price ($100 in this case) and selling fewer tickets. If, for example, instead of moving franchises from other cities, new franchises had simply entered the Los Angeles market, ticket prices would have fallen. With free entry, as in perfect competition, new teams could continue to enter until profit was driven to zero, large cities would have several NFL teams, and those teams would charge lower ticket prices. The NFL would never permit such entry to the league. It has also diligently protected its monopoly power to prevent new teams from competing leagues, a topic we return to later in the chapter.

Monopolists and Deadweight Loss

Most non-economists dislike monopolies because of the high prices they charge. High prices, however, are a two-edged sword. They may hurt the consumers who pay them, but they benefit the stockholders, employees, and other stakeholders in the firms that receive them. In Figure 4.1, consumers pay an amount equal to the area *EFBG* because they pay a price per unit equal to segment *EF* on *EG* units of output. While the $100 price exceeds the competitive price (zero in this

Figure 4.1
The Cost of a Monopoly to Society

When a firm charges the monopoly price of $100, it creates a deadweight loss equal to area *BCG*. Consumer surplus falls from *ACE* under competitive pricing to *ABF*.

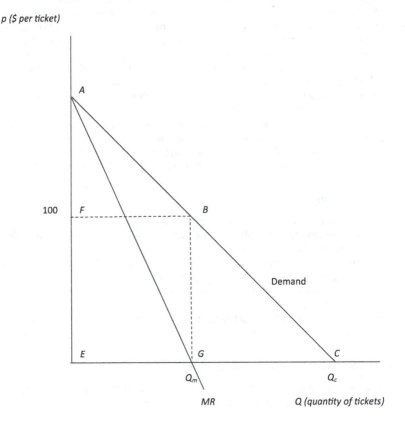

example), society—which consists of both consumers and producers—is not necessarily worse off, because producers receive *EFBG* more than if they charged
the competitive price. Thus, higher prices reshuffle some of the gains without
changing the total amount of income for society. The higher price simply transfers money from the consumer's pocket to the monopolist's. Because one cannot say whether this transfer helps producers more than it hurts consumers,
economists assume it brings no overall change in society's well-being.

Economists are much more concerned about the impact of the decline in output that accompanies monopoly. They worry about how monopoly affects the
sum of consumer surplus and producer surplus. Consumer surplus stems from
the fact that, despite our protestations to the contrary, we are never satisfied
"getting exactly what we paid for." In fact, if all we got out of an item was what
we paid for it, we would be just as happy without it. **Consumer surplus** is the net
value that flows to consumers because not all consumers are charged the maximum that they are willing to pay. **Producer surplus** is the net value that flows
to producers because not all units are sold for the minimum that the producer
would accept to sell them.[4] Measuring consumer surplus is quite easy in theory.
It equals the area that lies below the demand curve and above the price up to the
last unit sold. In Figure 4.1, at a price of $100, consumer surplus is the area *ABF*.

To see how consumer surplus arises, consider the case of four football fans. Hannah loves the Carolina Panthers and is willing and able to pay $160 for a ticket to
see them play. Ian also likes to go to Panther games, though not as much as Hannah; he is willing and able to pay $100. Juan is still less enthusiastic; he is willing
and able to pay $40. Kathleen has no interest in seeing the Panthers play; she is
willing and able to pay $0.

If consumers must pay the competitive price of $0 from Figure 4.1, all four con-
sumers buy tickets to see the Panthers, but none of them feels the same way
about his or her purchase. Since Hannah is willing and able to pay $160 for the
ticket but pays $0, she gets a bonus—or consumer surplus—of $160 (the vertical segment *YY* in Figure 4.2). Ian has a surplus of $100 (the vertical segment
ZZ), Juan has a surplus of $40 (the segment *WW*), and Kathleen has no surplus
whatever. Kathleen is the only consumer who "gets what she pays for." She is
willing and able to pay exactly what the Panthers charge her. Purchasing the
ticket leaves her no better off—and no worse off—than before. Economists refer
to a person in Kathleen's position as a **marginal consumer,** since she is indifferent between buying the ticket and not buying it.

In fact, thousands of consumers, all with their own desires and abilities to pay,
want Panthers tickets. As a result, there are thousands of vertical segments
indicating consumer surplus for the fans who buy tickets. Eventually, these segments fill up the triangle formed by the demand curve and the horizontal line
representing the market price in Figure 4.2.

Suppose instead that the price was $100. If the Panthers charged $100, Kathleen would suffer a loss if she bought the ticket because she must pay $100
more than she is willing and able to pay. As a result, she no longer buys the
ticket. Juan, too, would suffer a loss and does not buy the ticket. Bill would now
be the marginal consumer, because he pays exactly what the ticket is worth to
him. Only Hannah would enjoy a consumer surplus, though her surplus is much
smaller than it had been ($60 instead of $160). More generally, when a monopoly serves the market, consumers buy fewer tickets and consumer surplus

**Figure 4.2
Consumer Surplus for
Individual Consumers**

Consumer surplus for each
consumer is the difference
between the price ($0 in this
example) and the maximum that
they would be willing to pay. For
example, Hannah is willing to
pay $160 to see the game, and so
receives a consumer surplus of
$160. Kathleen, who values the
game at $0, receives no surplus.

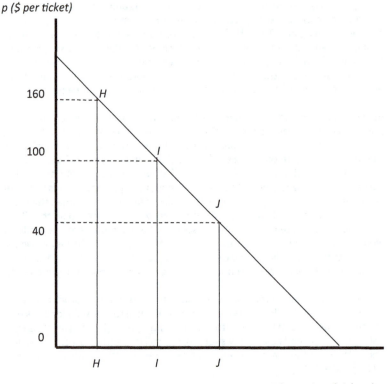

shrinks. In terms of Figure 4.1, consumer surplus is *ACE* if the market for tickets
is perfectly competitive. Because the equilibrium price in this example is zero,
consumer surplus is the entire area under the demand curve. When the same
market is a monopoly, consumers pay an amount equal to *EFBG*. As a result,
consumer surplus shrinks to *ABF*. In addition to the rectangle *EFBG*, consumers
lose the area of the triangle *BCG* because they buy less than before. This loss is
not offset by gains elsewhere. Economists call losses that do not have offsetting
gains elsewhere in the economy **deadweight losses**. The deadweight loss *BCG*
that accompanies monopoly reduces the well-being of society.

Economists who belong to a particular school of thought known as **public
choice**, believe that the social costs of monopoly exceed the deadweight loss of
triangle *BCG* in Figure 4.1. They regard the expenditure the monopolist makes
to obtain and protect its market position—behavior they call **rent seeking**—as
an unproductive expenditure that adds to society's deadweight loss. They would
claim, for example, that the $1.44 million that the NFL spent lobbying Congress
in 2016 to protect its monopoly power[5] imposed an additional cost on society,
since that money could have been spent in more productive ways. In the limit,
the monopolist is willing to spend up to the total gains from its monopoly position, the area of the rectangle *EFBG*.[6] As a result, the total cost to society could
be as large as the original deadweight loss plus the revenue of the monopolist
(BCG+EFBG).

Do Monopolies Always Charge Monopoly Prices?

Figure 4.1 shows that a monopoly team maximizes profit by setting output where the MR curve crosses the horizontal axis (point G, where MC = 0). If MC > 0, then the monopolist operates to the left of G, where MR > 0. Because we never see MC < 0, monopolists should not set output higher than G. It is easy to show that MR = 0 at the level of output where the price elasticity of demand equals –1.[7] Because the demand curve becomes less elastic as we move down and to the right, we can say that a monopolist should not operate where $0 > e_D > -1$. That is, it should never operate on the inelastic part of the demand curve. Intriguingly, economists have found that sports teams often operate in that part of the demand curve. This seems to imply that monopolists set their price too low for them to maximize profit.[8] How could this be?

Research by David Berri and Anthony Krautmann, among others, has found that this seemingly irrational strategy may maximize profit if we recognize that stadium concessions (drinks, food, and souvenirs) are complements for tickets since consumers can purchase them only in the stadium.[9] Such expenditures can be substantial. *Team Marketing Report* attempts to capture the full cost of attending a game with its **Fan Cost Index (FCI)**. The FCI includes four average-priced tickets, two small beers, four small soft drinks, four hot dogs, parking, and two hats. In 2016, the average NFL ticket was about $93 but the FCI was slightly over $500.[10] In Figure 4.1, the optimal price for a team that earns no revenue from concessions is $100. If the firm does earn profits from concessions, it should set a lower price so that more people enter the stadium and buy concessions. While the team sacrifices some revenue from attendance, the profit it earns on concessions more than makes up for this loss.

Promotion, Relegation, and Monopoly Power in Open Leagues

In Chapter 3, we saw that the promotion and relegation system causes open leagues to behave differently from closed leagues. Perhaps the most important difference lies in the consequences for monopoly power. A closed league can create local monopoly power because it is limited to a fixed set of teams. New teams can enter the league and existing teams can enter a new market only with the permission of the existing teams.

An open league has no such restriction. While the number of teams in the top division in an open league is fixed, promotion and relegation take away the top league's ability to control the geographic distribution of those teams. As we know from Chapter 3, every year, three teams from the league below (for example, the Championship League) are promoted to the league above (in this case the EPL). Thus, while the NFL permits only the Bears to play in the Chicago metropolitan area, 14 members of the Football League play in the London metropolitan area. Of these, six teams (Arsenal, Chelsea, Crystal Palace, Tottenham Hotspur, Watford, and West Ham) played in the EPL in 2016–2017. There is, moreover, no guarantee that this number could not rise even higher in the years ahead. Similarly, poor business or personnel decisions have caused some major metropolitan areas—such as Leeds or Bristol—to go without a franchise in the EPL. At the same time, dozens of teams from lower divisions compete nearby, also vying for the attention of local fans. So, while the EPL enjoys great popularity in England, its teams do not enjoy the same sustainable market dominance as teams in the closed leagues of North America. With no way to limit the entry or exit of competitors, teams' ability to charge prices above the competitive level is limited by fan loyalty (unwillingness to switch allegiance to another local competitor as the teams' various fortunes rise and fall).

While EPL teams do not have the same market exclusivity as NFL teams, they clearly have market power born of the enormous popularity of the sport and the loyalty of their fans. If English fans do not see other local teams as substitutes, their favorite team can raise prices without losing all their support. Ticket prices in the UK indicate that this market power is substantial: EPL ticket prices increased at three and a half times the rate of inflation between 1981 and 2016, while total league attendance rose from 11.4 million to 13.85 million.[11]

4.2 Strategic Pricing

We know that teams in closed leagues need not worry about new entrants. Entry occurs only with the explicit permission of existing firms. The market power of teams in such leagues allows them to set prices without regard for how other suppliers or even potential suppliers might react. Despite its powerful position, a monopoly is limited by the extent of demand in their market. Table 4.1 shows that, while there were modest increases in total attendance across the four major leagues in North America, prices in some leagues increased substantially between 2001 and 2016. This 15-year span was a boom period for the NFL and MLB, as prices rose 73.3 percent and 64.4 percent, respectively, well above the rate of inflation. Average ticket prices in the NHL increased at about the same rate as inflation. Only in the NBA did average ticket prices increase at a rate less than that of other goods during this period, though the NBA experienced the largest increase in attendance over this time period.

Table 4.1 makes clear the enormous market power of the NFL. With a fixed number of games in a stadium of fixed size, teams cannot respond to increases in demand by increasing quantity. Because the league is closed, new teams cannot enter to satisfy the additional demand as we might expect in a competitive market. Existing teams respond to higher demand by raising prices. Recall from

Table 4.1 Changes in Attendance and Average Ticket Prices 2001–2016*

League	2001 Attendance (000s)	2016 Attendance (000s)	2001 Prices	2016 Prices	Percent Price Increase
NFL	16,307	17,789	$53.64	$92.98	73.3
MLB	72,530	73,156	$18.86	$31.00	64.4
NHL	20,400	21,619	$47.70	$62.18	30.6
NBA	19,956	21,955	$51.34	$55.88	8.8
CPI	—	—	177.1	240	35.5

*NHL prices in column four are 2014–2015.

Sources: Attendance data except NFL are from ESPN.com. NFL attendance data are from *Pro Football Reference*, at http://www.pro-football-reference.com/years/2016/attendance.htm. Team average ticket prices are from Teammarketing.com, at https://www.teammarketing. com/public/uploadedPDFs/NBA-FCI-2015-16.pdf; https://www.teammarketing.com/public/ uploadedPDFs/MLB_FCI_2016.pdf; https://www.teammarketing.com/public/uploadedPDFs/ NFL_FCI_2016.pdf; https://www.teammarketing.com/public/uploadedPDFs/nhl%20fci% 2015.pdf. CPI data: "United States Consumer Price Index for All Urban Consumers (CPI-U) 1970 – 2016," at http://www.dlt.ri.gov/lmi/pdf/cpi.pdf. All accessed January 20, 2017.

Chapter 3 that all NFL teams are profitable. While extensive revenue sharing and lucrative national television contracts are strong contributing factors to this universal profitability, individual team profits would surely be lower if new teams could enter freely.

For a monopoly, market power may bring advantages beyond the ability to set a single price. In the next section, we describe advanced pricing strategies that may be available to firms with market power.

Variable and Dynamic Ticket Pricing

For a Red Sox fan, there is nothing like going to a game when the Yankees come to town. In the NHL, Chicago Blackhawk fans circle the date on the calendar when the always good (and popular) Red Wings visit. These are just two examples of what we intuitively know to be true: Some games are much more popular than others. When individual fans' desire to attend a game increases, the market demand curve shifts to the right.

The quality of the opponent and the existence of a long-standing rivalry are not the only reasons for differences in demand. Differences may arise from the presence of a star player on the opposing team, promotional events such as giveaways and fireworks nights, the day of the week, even the weather.[12] Rather than charge the same price for all games, teams can increase profits if they vary the price of tickets from game to game. **Variable ticket pricing (VTP)** sets ticket prices according to expected demand for a future game. When a team believes that demand for a given game will be lower, it can reduce the price to compensate. Conversely, it can increase the price for a game it believes will be popular. Some of the factors that affect consumer demand for a specific game, such as the day of the week, are known before the season even begins. Other factors, such as the home team's and opponent's records, may not be known until shortly before the game.

Many professional teams now change the prices of games in response to actual realized demand. Firms with significant ticketing expertise such as Ticketmaster and Qcue work closely with teams to increase revenue by adjusting ticket prices as game day approaches. Qcue's clients, which include the Montreal Canadiens of the NHL and MLB's San Francisco Giants, can adjust prices within seconds as demand for a particular game rises or falls.[13] This process, known as **dynamic ticket pricing (DTP)**, allows teams to capture additional revenue based on individual game characteristics that are unknown at the start of the season, such as a matchup of All-Star pitchers, which might produce exceptionally high demand, or, conversely, a game against a non-contender on a chilly weekday evening, which would do the opposite. For example, in 2009, the San Francisco Giants played a series against the New York Mets. For the first game, played on a cold Thursday night, upper deck prices were $1 off the usual $10, and bleacher seats were $2 off the usual $17. The next night, a weekend game with the Giants' best pitcher on the mound, those same seats went for $19 and $27, respectively. On Sunday, which featured a bobblehead doll giveaway, the Giants raised the price of a bleacher seat to $23. Some of these price adjustments were made shortly before game day.[14] Variable and dynamic ticket pricing schemes have spread quickly across MLB, the NHL, and the NBA. According to Patrick Rishe in *Forbes* magazine, by 2012, more than 30 teams in the NHL, MLS, MLB, and NBA utilized dynamic ticket pricing and had increased revenue substantially because of it.[15] The Buffalo Sabres are a good example of a team that uses both VTP and DTP. Sabres tickets are initially priced on three tiers based on the opponent, visiting marquee players, day of the week, and time of year. Within those tiers, the Sabres partner with Qcue to adjust the prices of individual tickets based on real-time changes in demand with the stipulation that the new ticket price will never fall below the season ticket price for the game.[16]

The NFL was the last of the four major North American leagues to adopt variable and dynamic ticket pricing, perhaps because, with so few home games and so many seats sold as season tickets, relatively few individual seats are available, regardless of opponent. The league began to allow variable ticket pricing in 2014 and first permitted dynamic ticket pricing in 2015. Despite the relatively small number of available seats, at least half the teams use variable ticket pricing, dynamic pricing, or both. The NFL reports that teams earned additional revenue measured in the millions from just the first few games of the 2015 season. If such revenue enhancements are possible for the NFL, it is highly likely that others will follow suit.[17]

Variable ticket pricing is widely used in the EPL as well. In 2017–2018, the best seating for a Tottenham Hotspur match against a traditional power like Liverpool or a local rival like West Ham United cost £95 (about $125). The same seat for a match against the far less popular Burnley cost only about £70 ($92).[18]

From the team's perspective, differences in demand across games present an opportunity to increase profits. With the marginal cost of attendance essentially zero, costs are about the same no matter how many fans attend. But, up to a point, revenues increase as more fans buy tickets at lower prices. We can see the impact of variable vs. constant pricing in Figure 4.3. As usual, we assume that marginal cost is zero up to the point of stadium capacity (40,000). Demand for a less popular game is D_0 and demand for a more popular game is D_1.[19] A team using variable ticket pricing sets marginal revenue equal to marginal cost for each game ($MC = MR_0$ and $MC = MR_1$), resulting in prices of $60 and $80,

Figure 4.3
Variable Ticket Pricing

A team using differential demand for its games (D_0 and D_1) maximizes profits by charging $80 per seat for the more popular game and $60 per seat for the less popular game, as opposed to a single price of $70 for both games.

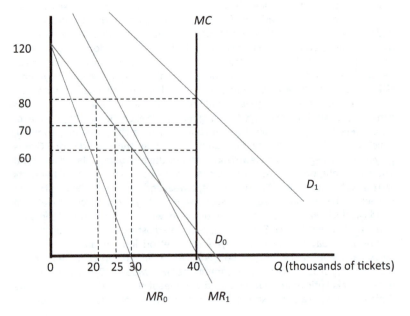

respectively. The team will sell out the popular game and sell 30,000 tickets to the less popular game. Total revenue for the two games is $5 million [($60 x 30,000) + ($80 x 40,000)]. The graph indicates that if the team tried to sell tickets to the less popular game for $80, half of the seats would go unfilled (and revenue would fall by $200,000). Similarly, if the team charged only $60 for the popular game, it would sell the same number of tickets as at the higher price, but revenue would fall by $800,000. Suppose that, instead of charging two prices, the team charged a single intermediate price, such as $70, for both games. We can easily show that such a strategy results in a price that is too high for the unpopular game and too low for the popular game. At a price of $70, the more popular game still sells out, but revenue falls from $3.2 million to $2.8 million. For the less popular game, attendance falls to 25,000, resulting in revenue of just $1.75 million. Thus, overall revenue from charging a single price of $70 is $4.55 million, almost half a million less than the two-price scheme. This analysis is far from a theoretical abstraction. Barry Kahn, CEO of Qcue, a firm that provides computer software that allows teams to run dynamic pricing schemes, says that teams using this strategy have increased revenue by an average of 30 percent for high-demand games and 5–10 percent for low-demand games.[20]

Bundling

In addition to charging fans for individual games, teams can increase revenue by bundling games together. With **bundling,** a consumer who wants to buy good A must also buy good B (or perhaps many more goods, as in the case of season tickets). With product bundling, firms take advantage of differing demand across products to capture some of the consumer surplus that might otherwise accrue to buyers. To illustrate this point, consider Duane, a huge Cubs fan who particularly likes to see them play their cross-town rivals, the White Sox. Because so many other Chicagoans feel the same way, tickets can be hard to find. Fortunately for Duane, he can get tickets to a White Sox game—and highly desirable games against the Cardinals and Detroit Tigers as well—by purchasing a Cubs six-game pack. The six-game pack allows Duane to buy tickets to the White Sox game as long as he also purchases tickets to five other games, including a game on a Wednesday afternoon against the Pittsburgh Pirates, for which demand is likely much lower than for the White Sox game.[21]

To see how this pricing scheme benefits both Duane and the Cubs, let's assume that a ticket for the White Sox game costs $30. Duane is willing to pay $100 to see a Cubs–White Sox game, but he would pay only $25 to see any other Cubs game. If the tickets were sold separately for $30, he would go to the White Sox game and receive a surplus of $70, but would not buy a ticket to the other games. Suppose now that Duane can see the Cubs–White Sox game only if he buys a six-pack of tickets. Unlike variable ticket pricing, bundling does not rely on setting different prices for each game. Instead, it relies on the large surplus consumers would receive from seeing a specific game. If all tickets cost $30 but must be purchased in a group of six, tickets to the hypothetical six-game set cost $180 (6 x $30). Duane values the six tickets at $225 ($100 for the White Sox game and $25 each for the other five games). At a price of $180, he is better off making the purchase because he still receives a surplus of $45. Even though he experiences a loss of $5 on the five less popular games, the loss is more than offset by the surplus he receives from seeing the White Sox game. The Cubs are better off as well because they sell tickets to six games instead of only one. With the marginal cost of Duane's attendance at these extra games at or close to zero, the Cubs' profits also increase.

Price Discrimination and Two-Part Pricing

In our discussion of variable ticket pricing, dynamic pricing, and bundling, teams used advanced pricing strategies based on differences in the perceived quality of the games by a given consumer. We now move on to a different strategy that relies on teams' identifying differences in willingness to pay *for the same game.*

Recall that in Figure 4.1, a single monopoly price led to a deadweight loss of area *BCG*, and left consumers with a surplus of area *ABF*. We know that consumer surplus is the extra benefit that consumers receive because the firm charges a single profit-maximizing price for all units it sells. Often, firms charge a single price to all consumers because they have no way to determine which consumers are willing to pay more. If a monopolist could sort consumers by their willingness and ability to pay and set prices accordingly, it could capture some or even all of the consumer surplus. As we will see, such a pricing strategy reduces or eliminates the deadweight loss associated with a single monopoly price.

Economists call charging different prices to different consumers based on their willingness and ability to pay **price discrimination**. Unlike the common use of the word *discrimination*, which refers to actions based on prejudice, price discrimination has nothing to do with dislike for a particular demographic group. Instead, a firm price discriminates when it charges more to customers who are willing and able to pay more. On the surface, charging a higher price to wealthy customers than to poor consumers sounds like the fair thing to do. We shall see, however, that firms that price discriminate seldom have such altruistic motives, and that price discrimination does not leave consumers better off.

Perfect Price Discrimination

In Figure 4.1, if the Panthers know exactly how much Hannah, Ian, Juan, and Kathleen are willing and able to pay, they can extract their consumer surplus by charging each person exactly what he or she thinks the ticket is worth. By charging Hannah $160, Ian $100, and Juan $40, the Panthers turn all their consumers into marginal consumers.[22] All the consumers are now just willing to pay for the tickets because what was once their consumer surplus is now additional revenue for the Panthers.

By treating each additional consumer like the marginal consumer, the Panthers no longer have to reduce the price for everyone when they want to sell more tickets. Charging each consumer the maximum that he or she is willing to pay is known as **perfect (first-degree) price discrimination**. When the Panthers perfectly price discriminate, their marginal revenue is the price of the cheapest ticket that they sell. The marginal revenue of selling a ticket to Ian is thus $100, while the marginal revenue of selling a ticket to Juan is $40. In terms of Figure 4.1, if the Panthers can perfectly price discriminate, their *MR* curve coincides with their demand curve. The Panthers now sell the same number of tickets as a perfectly competitive industry, and total surplus grows to *ACE*. Social well-being is once again maximized, as the perfectly price-discriminating monopolist acts in an economically efficient manner. Consumers, however, do not receive any of the increase in social well-being. By charging all consumers exactly what the ticket is worth to them, the Panthers claim Hannah and Ian's consumer surplus for themselves. If the Panthers could perfectly price discriminate, they would charge all their fans exactly what they are willing and able to pay. This would enable the Panthers to capture all of the area *ACE* in Figure 4.1 as revenue.

Quantity Discounts[23]

Another way for firms to increase profit is to offer a menu of price–quantity combinations and to let consumers choose the combination they most prefer. As with perfect price discrimination, this allows producers to charge prices that reflect the intensity of the consumers' desire. Teams often offer an array of choices based on quantity.

Quantity discounts take advantage of the team's knowledge that—assuming a given quality of games—fans' marginal utility from consuming a sporting event declines with the quantity of games they attend. While the team does not know exactly what the fan is willing and able to pay for each game, the team knows that the fifth hockey game is worth less than the first and the twenty-fifth is worth less still. Many teams, particularly those with longer seasons, offer a variety of partial- and full-season ticket plans in which the cost per game is lower than the cost of buying a ticket to each game individually. A common example of this pricing strategy is the ubiquitous BOGO (buy one get one). If a team offers tickets at a "buy one get one 50 percent off," the consumer can purchase the discounted ticket only if she first buys the more expensive full-priced ticket.

Segmented Markets

Sometimes, the Panthers may know nothing about specific individuals, but they know that some groups are less willing or able to pay. For example, the Panthers may know that most students have little disposable income and as a result are more sensitive to changes in price than are middle-aged adults.[24] If the Panthers can separate the student market from the adult market (e.g., by requiring students to show their university ID cards), they can practice third-degree price discrimination by charging a higher price to adults than to students. **Segmented market (third-degree) price discrimination** occurs when a firm charges different prices for the same good in different segments of a market. Figure 4.4

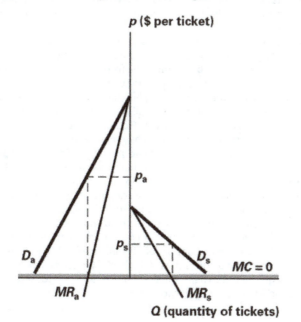

p ($ per ticket)

p_a

p_s

D_a

D_s

$MC = 0$

MR_a

MR_s

Q (quantity of tickets)

**Figure 4.4
Segmented Market Price Discrimination**

If student demand is lower than adult demand, the team can charge students p_s and charge adults p_a.

shows what the Panthers can do if they can separate the demand by adults for Panthers tickets from the demand by students. Ignoring capacity constraints, if the marginal cost of providing seats is approximately zero, the Panthers maximize profit when the marginal revenue from selling to students and the marginal revenue from selling to adults both equal zero. Figure 4.4 shows that setting $MR_s = MR_a = MC$ results in a lower price for students than for adults. In effect, the Panthers maximize profits by charging a lower price to consumers whose demand is more elastic and a higher price to those with less elastic demand. To practice this type of price discrimination, the firm (in this case the team) must be able to prevent consumers from switching from the higher-priced market to the lower-priced market and must prevent reselling between markets. In the case of student discounts, the team can easily require that students present ID to purchase a cheaper ticket. Preventing resale may be more difficult as the team would have to print different tickets for students and require that attendees present student IDs with the student tickets to gain entry.

Personal Seat Licenses

In general, firms do not have enough information to extract all the consumer surplus. Few firms know exactly how much each consumer is willing and able to pay for an item. However, firms have other ways to extract at least part of the consumer surplus. One such method is two-part pricing. As its name indicates, **two-part pricing** involves two distinct segments—a fixed component and a variable component that changes with the amount the consumer purchases. Personal seat licenses (PSLs) are a form of two-part pricing that has become particularly popular in the NFL. They were first introduced by the Carolina Panthers to help finance the construction of Ericsson Stadium (now Bank of America Stadium) in 1993.[25]

The idea of a PSL is very simple. A person pays a fixed fee for the right to buy season tickets for a given period. This allows teams to claim the deadweight loss that ordinarily results from a monopoly. The Panthers could eliminate the deadweight loss by charging the competitive price for season tickets and selling the competitive quantity. The lower price and higher quantity restore consumer and producer surplus to their competitive levels. The Panthers then exert their monopoly power by charging the fixed PSL fee. The fee allows them to claim some of the consumer surplus that their fans enjoy. If the Panthers know exactly how much consumer surplus the typical fan enjoyed, they can charge a PSL fee that extracts almost all his or her surplus. This leaves the fan just willing to buy the season ticket. Figure 4.5 shows the demand curve for a typical fan (consumer). Instead of charging the monopoly price (P_m), the team can increase profits by utilizing a two-part price. The variable portion of the two-part price is zero, as the Panthers charge the competitive price for the ticket (which is $0 if MC = 0). The fixed portion of the price is the cost of the PSL. If all fans have the preferences described by the demand curve in Figure 4.5, the team sets the PSL fee equal to the shaded area, and consumer surplus falls to nearly zero. The Panthers could thus keep all the benefits of a competitive market for themselves. If consumers do not all have the same preferences, the task of the team is more complicated. A low PSL leaves some surplus for high-demand consumers. A high PSL fee leads low-demand consumers to forgo the PSL. The optimal PSL maximizes the total revenue (PSL fee plus per ticket price) from attendance.[26]

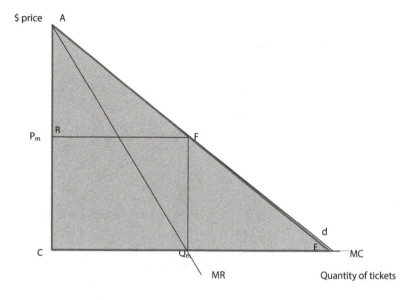

Figure 4.5
Representative Demand Curve for a Consumer and Two-Part Pricing

A two-part price consists of a fixed fee and a per-unit fee. In this case, the firm attempts to set the fixed fee equal to the shaded area *ACE* and the per-unit price is zero. Deadweight loss is eliminated but the consumer surplus falls from *BAF* in the single-price case to zero.

4.3 What's Right with Monopoly?

While monopolies often impose deadweight losses on society, the case against them is not always as straightforward as it may appear. First, it is not always easy to identify a monopoly. For example, since Detroit has only one football team, the Lions, one might logically conclude that the Lions are a monopoly. The Lions, however, could plausibly claim that they are not a monopoly and that they actually operate in a very competitive environment. The key to this difference of opinion lies in the definition of the market in which the Lions operate. If the market is defined as one for an NFL team in the Detroit area, then the Lions are clearly a monopoly. The Lions could respond that such a definition is far too narrow. In the sports industry alone, the Lions must compete for attention with professional baseball, basketball, and hockey teams in and around Detroit. They also must contend with major college football programs, such as the University of Michigan and Michigan State University. If the market expands still further to include all possible leisure and cultural activities in the area, the market becomes very crowded, and the Lions begin to look like very small cats in a large jungle.

Even if the Lions fail to convince you that they are not a monopoly, they may be able to persuade you that their monopoly power arose from the natural functioning of the market, not from immoral or illegal actions on their part. In short, the Lions may claim that they are a **natural monopoly**. Natural monopolies result when large firms operate more efficiently than small firms. **Minimum efficient scale** is the point at which long-run average cost is minimized. If the firm's minimum efficient scale is sufficiently large compared with the number of customers, there may be no room for competing firms to enter. This generally results when firms face high start-up costs and low marginal costs.[27]

Figure 4.6a shows that a professional sports team may be a natural monopoly. As we showed in Chapter 2, a team's payroll is a fixed cost because the cost to the team is the same regardless of its output, as measured in tickets sold. Except

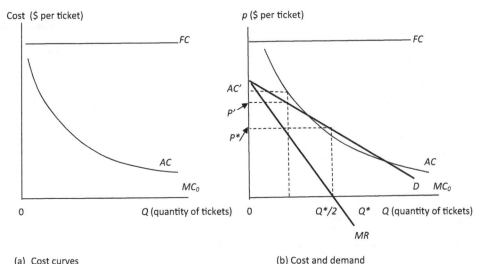

(a) Cost curves   (b) Cost and demand

Figure 4.6
Profit-Maximizing Output for a Natural Monopoly

Part (a) shows the cost curves for a natural monopoly. Average cost declines continuously. In part (b), the firm maximizes profits by setting price $p*$ and selling $Q*$. If the firm were broken into two equal-size smaller firms, each selling $Q*/2$, both firms would suffer losses, as average cost (AC') would exceed price (p').

for that part of rent that is tied to attendance, the expense of renting or building a stadium also adds to fixed costs. Because the marginal cost of accommodating an additional fan is effectively zero, the Lions' costs do not rise very much beyond this fixed amount until they reach the capacity of their stadium. Using these assumptions, we can approximate the **average cost,** or per-unit cost, of the Lions as:

$$\text{Average cost} = \frac{\text{Total costs}}{\text{Quantity}} = \frac{\text{Fixed costs}}{\text{Number of tickets sold}}$$

As the number of tickets the Lions sell rises, their average cost gets closer and closer to MC_0. As a result, "bigger is better" to the Lions, since they can charge a lower price and still cover their costs as their output rises. Figure 4.6b again shows the cost curves for the monopolist and adds the demand and marginal revenue curves. The monopolist produces $Q*$ and charges $p*$. Note that if another firm enters the market, and output is divided equally, neither firm makes a profit, as price (p') is less than average cost (AC'). In such cases, as the term implies, the market structure naturally evolves to a single seller. In this case, the scale economies create a natural entry barrier.

Leagues may also claim that, while perfectly competitive markets produce more and charge a lower price, a league's monopoly power delivers other benefits to fans. One of the major benefits that MLB's monopoly power has conferred on baseball fans has been the relative stability of franchises. MLB owners who want to move their teams must have the approval of the other owners. The failure of MLB's Pittsburgh Pirates and Chicago White Sox to secure approval was instrumental in preventing their moves to St. Petersburg. Leagues use these aborted moves as evidence that the monopoly power of leagues protects the interests of the hometown fans.

4.4 Strategic Barriers to Entry

Not all monopolies stem from the natural working of the market or from explicit government policy. Some entry barriers are part of a firm's strategy to increase profits. Sports leagues have become experts at erecting barriers to entry, and—when the barriers have failed to keep out competitors—at co-opting the opposition.

In the 1960s, the battle lines in professional football reflected network battle lines. Fans of the National Football League tuned in to CBS, while devotees of the American Football League watched ABC and then NBC. Today, the NFL licenses its broadcasts to an alphabet soup of networks. In addition to providing a great source of revenue for the NFL, the variety of networks creates a crucial barrier to entry. Rival football leagues have long recognized that their livelihood depended on forming a lasting and profitable link with a television partner. The AFL owed its survival in the 1960s to the willingness of ABC and later NBC to pay for broadcast rights. The infusion of cash from network TV helped the AFL hang on through years of relatively low attendance. Much of the blame for the failure of the WFL in the 1970s and the USFL in the 1980s can be traced to their failure to get sufficient support from major television networks. The collapse of the XFL after only one season in 2002 stemmed largely from its steadily declining TV viewership and the imminent loss of its TV contract.

As noted in Chapter 3, leagues can create barriers and forestall entry by locating franchises in the appropriate cities. In baseball, the American League found sufficient markets to enter thanks to the dogged refusal of the National League to admit more than eight franchises. The AFL tried to exploit the NFL's refusal to expand in the late 1950s by planning flagship franchises for the rapidly growing cities of Dallas and Minneapolis. When the NFL got wind of these plans, it quickly convened an expansion meeting and awarded franchises to those same cities. This successfully prevented the AFL from entering Minneapolis and doomed the Dallas entry to failure. The AFL sued, claiming that the NFL had awarded these franchises solely to monopolize professional football. Despite the admission by Redskins' owner George Preston Marshall that the NFL had awarded the franchises just to prevent the AFL from penetrating the markets, the AFL lost a bench verdict.[28] In some cases, legal disputes have arisen within leagues when teams relocate without the permission of the league and invade the protected market of another team. Such was the case when the San Diego Clippers of the NBA moved to Los Angeles without league approval.

The NBA's Clippers have not always called Los Angeles home. In 1978, they moved from Buffalo, where they played as the Braves, to San Diego (which had previously hosted the Rockets). The Clippers suffered from poor attendance in San Diego, so when Donald Sterling purchased the team in 1984, he moved the franchise to Los Angeles without first obtaining league permission. Sterling likely assumed he would prevail in a legal battle because Al Davis had just successfully sued the NFL on antitrust grounds when it attempted to block his moving the Raiders from Oakland to Los Angeles (see Chapter 7 for more information on the Raiders' suit).

Not surprisingly, the Lakers did sue the Clippers for invading their territory. Like the Raiders, the Clippers argued that any attempt by the league to block their move would violate antitrust law. While the case (NBA v. San Diego Clippers Basketball Club) was in process, the Clippers played in Los Angeles. With the Clippers already in Los Angeles (interestingly, with the permission of the Lakers) the league changed the rules on relocation to require any moving franchise to secure a majority vote of all other franchises. In the initial trial, the District Court granted a summary judgment in favor of the Clippers, which the league promptly appealed. In the Ninth Circuit Court of Appeals, the court rejected the Clippers' assertion that "a restriction on franchise movement in and of itself violates antitrust laws"; found that, since the District Court had not employed the correct standard, the decision should be reversed; and remanded the case for trial.[29] Though the Clippers were ultimately allowed to stay in Los Angeles—in fact, the two teams now share the Staples Center—the Clippers had to pay $6 million to the Lakers for invading their territory.[30]

4.5   Society's Response to Monopoly: Antitrust Laws

In 1890, the United States made its first concerted effort to combat monopolies and monopsonies with the Sherman Antitrust Act. The Sherman Act was later supplemented by the Clayton Act, which allowed private lawsuits to recover three times the damages caused by subversion of the free market. The Sherman Act has two main clauses. They say (in part):

1   Every contract, combination in the form of trust or otherwise, or conspiracy, in restraint of trade or commerce among the several States, or with foreign nations, is declared to be illegal.
2   Every person who shall monopolize, or attempt to monopolize, or combine or conspire with any other person or persons, to monopolize any part of the trade or commerce among the several States, or with foreign nations, shall be deemed guilty of a felony.[31]

At first glance, the two clauses seem almost identical. The differences, while subtle, have been crucial in determining the course of antitrust suits against professional sports teams and leagues.

The first clause prohibits "independent entities that *ought* to be competing against one another from agreeing *not* to compete."[32] It prevents firms from joining together to form **cartels**, also known as *trusts* (hence the name of the act).

The second clause attacks monopolies themselves, regardless of how they are formed. It outlaws "conduct by a firm which creates, protects, or entrenches a dominant position in some relevant market."[33] Lawsuits brought under the second section, while well-publicized, have generally had little impact on the sports industry.

The courts use two different standards when considering potential violations of the Sherman Act, which place very different demands on the litigants. The *per se* standard applies when there are what the courts have called "naked restraints" to competition, such as price fixing. Under this standard, the restraints on competition are inherently bad and no further information regarding damage to consumers or competitors is needed. One need only establish that a prohibited activity took place for the *per se* standard to apply. The *rule of reason* standard takes a more nuanced view of monopolies and cooperative activities among firms. According to this standard, each case must be judged on its own merits. Some cooperative activities may be permitted or even encouraged, and some monopolies may be left intact. For example, a monopoly whose production is characterized by significant scale economies may be able to produce at lower average costs than several small firms. Rather than break up such a firm, governments try to **regulate** natural monopolies, requiring that they receive the approval of an oversight board before raising price. Those who feel that professional sports leagues are natural monopolies advocate regulating the sports industry to prevent it from earning monopoly profits.[34]

The rule of reason is particularly important in professional sports because, on the surface, all leagues appear to violate antitrust legislation under the *per se* standard. By their very nature, leagues coordinate the actions of their member teams. The coordination can be relatively innocent, as when they establish and enforce a common set of rules or arrange a commonly respected schedule. However, coordination can also result in harmful **collusion** that restricts or eliminates competition.

An Important Anomaly: Baseball's Antitrust Exemption

Baseball occupies a unique place in the American economy. Unlike all other industries, it has long enjoyed an absolute exemption from all federal antitrust laws with no time limits, no governmental oversight, and no regulation of its pricing policies. Oddly, the courts and legislative branch recognize that baseball's exemption defies all legal and economic logic, yet they have done nothing to terminate it for 90 years. Recent changes have been merely cosmetic, with no real effect.

Baseball owes its exemption to the last serious challenge to its monopoly position, the attempt by the Federal League to form a third major league in 1914 and 1915. The outlook for a third league seemed promising at the time. The successful entry by the American League to major league status in 1901 showed that a rival league could succeed. In addition, the Federal League felt it could attract players from the American and National Leagues, as salaries had been steadily falling since the two leagues had stopped competing for players in 1903.[35]

As part of its assault on the two existing leagues, the Federal League filed an antitrust lawsuit against the 16 owners as well as the three members of the "National Commission" that oversaw the two major leagues. The lawsuit was based on both sections of the Sherman Act, charging the major leagues "with being a combination, conspiracy and monopoly."[36]

The Federal League filed its suit in the US District Court of Northern Illinois before Judge Kenesaw Mountain Landis because Landis had a reputation as a trustbuster. Unfortunately for the Federal League, he was also a rabid baseball fan. Landis scolded the Federal League's lawyers, saying that attacks on baseball "would be regarded by this court as a blow to a national institution."[37] After hearing the arguments, Landis refused to issue a ruling for over a year, by which time the Major Leagues had reached an agreement with all but one of the Federal League owners, driving the Federal League out of business.[38]

The one holdout was Ned Hanlon, the owner of the Federal League's Baltimore Terrapins. Hanlon was upset that his buyout offer of $50,000 was well below that offered to owners whose teams competed in cities with major league franchises.[39] He was also offended because Charles Comiskey, the owner of the Chicago White Sox, had called Baltimore a "minor league city, and not a hell of a good one at that," and that Charles Ebbets, owner of the Brooklyn Dodgers, had said that Baltimore was unfit to have a team because "you have too many colored population [*sic*]. ··· " Hanlon filed his own antitrust suit—*Federal Baseball Club of Baltimore, Inc. v. National League of Professional Baseball Clubs* (hereafter *Federal Baseball*)—and won an $80,000 settlement (trebled under the provisions of the Clayton Act to $240,000) in a Washington, DC, Federal District Court. The judgment was overturned on appeal, whereupon Hanlon took his suit to the Supreme Court.[40]

In 1922, the Supreme Court ruled unanimously that baseball was not subject to antitrust laws. In his opinion for the court, Justice Oliver Wendell Holmes Jr. wrote that baseball was a "public exhibition, not commerce" and that the interstate travel, which would have made baseball subject to federal legislation, was purely incidental to staging these exhibitions.

The rationale for this ruling has never been clear. Some claim that the Court feared that ruling against MLB would do irreparable damage in the wake of the "Black Sox" scandal in which eight members of the Chicago White Sox had been accused of conspiring with gamblers to throw the 1919 World Series. Others point out that Chief Justice William Howard Taft had played third base for Yale University's baseball team and was related to Philip Wrigley, the owner of the Chicago Cubs.[41]

Subsequent court decisions made baseball's exemption increasingly difficult to justify. The Supreme Court consistently denied other industries, particularly other sports, the right to use the *Federal Baseball* ruling as a precedent. Somehow, the Court maintained that other sports were interstate commerce while baseball was not.

The Supreme Court's 1955 ruling in an antitrust lawsuit that the US government had brought against the International Boxing Club is a prime example. The Supreme Court ruled that, while boxing matches occurred in a specific place and did not involve moving across state lines, deals for TV, radio, and motion picture rights did cross state boundaries. The Court acknowledged that this judgment contradicted previous rulings regarding baseball but declared that those rulings were "not authority for exempting other businesses merely because of the circumstance that they are also based on the performance of local exhibitions."[42]

The tortured logic required to justify baseball's exemption from the antitrust laws was never more evident than in the early 1950s, when George Toolson, a player in the New York Yankees' farm system, resisted being sent back to the minor leagues. He then sued the Yankees, claiming that the reserve clause violated the antitrust laws. The reserve clause, which was a part of all player contracts until the advent of free agency in 1975, allowed teams to maintain the rights to players for their entire careers. This prevented players from soliciting competing wage offers. We discuss the reserve clause extensively in Chapter 10. As Toolson's suit worked its way through the courts, the House Subcommittee on the Study of Monopoly Power (chaired by Rep. Emmanuel Cellar and hence called the "Cellar Committee") began to hold hearings on baseball's antitrust exemption. When it became obvious that the Toolson case was going to the Supreme Court, the Cellar Committee postponed further action under the assumption that the courts would settle the matter. The Supreme Court seized upon this inaction, saying that Congress had signaled its approval of baseball's antitrust exemption by refusing to take any action against it. The "approval" granted by the Cellar Committee formed the basis of the Supreme Court's ruling in favor of the Yankees.[43]

Perhaps the most misunderstood legal case surrounding the reserve clause is Curt Flood's antitrust suit of the early 1970s. Most people incorrectly think of

Flood as the man who single-handedly overthrew the reserve clause in base-ball. In fact, Flood lost his case as well as his career. After the ruling against him, baseball players had to wait another four years before their union overturned the reserve clause.

In the late 1960s, Curt Flood was a star outfielder for the St. Louis Cardinals. In 1968, after a particularly good season, Flood asked the team for a $30,000 raise. Not one inclined to tolerate such demands, Cardinals owner Augustus Busch traded Flood to the Philadelphia Phillies after the 1969 season. Curt Flood had many reasons for objecting to this trade. It sent him from a team that had won a World Series in 1967 and had come within one game of another in 1968 to a team that was a perennial also-ran. It also sent him away from friends, family, and developing business interests in St. Louis to a town that had a history of bad relations with black ballplayers.[44] Because of the reserve clause and baseball's exemption from antitrust regulations, Flood had no say in his own destiny. As a black man who had endured severe discrimination early in his career, Flood saw a parallel between his own position and that of enslaved blacks in America barely 100 years earlier. In asking Commissioner Bowie Kuhn to repeal the trade, Flood used words that Frederick Douglass might have used: "I do not feel I am a piece of property to be bought and sold irrespective of my wishes."[45]

In 1970, with the support of the Major League Baseball Players Association (MLBPA), Flood filed suit in US Federal District Court against the commission-er's office, asking for $3 million (to be trebled) and for free agency. In language reminiscent of Kenesaw Landis's rhapsodies to baseball in the Federal League suit, the trial judge ruled in Kuhn's favor, arguing that baseball was on "higher ground" than mere commerce. An appeals court also ruled in Kuhn's favor, citing Congress's failure to act against the reserve clause, as the Supreme Court had argued almost 20 years earlier in its *Toolson* ruling.

The Supreme Court's decision, written by Harry Blackmun, was even more curious. Blackmun denied the basis for baseball's exemption by acknowledging that base-ball was a business that engaged in interstate commerce. He called the exemption "an exception and an anomaly" and referred to the *Federal Baseball* and *Toolson* rulings as "aberration[s] confined to baseball." Despite these stinging condemna-tions of the reserve clause and of baseball's exemption from the antitrust laws, the Supreme Court ruled 6–2 (with one abstention) in Kuhn's favor in 1972. The Court based its decision on the principle of *stare decisis* ("let the old decision stand"), effectively saying that the original antitrust ruling was wrong but that too much now rested on the original decision for the Court to overturn it.[46]

In 1998, Congress finally placed limits on baseball's antitrust exemption by pass-ing the "Curt Flood Act." The legislation, however, does little to change the status quo. It limits baseball's powers only in the area of labor relations, granting players the right to file antitrust suits to resolve labor disputes. For example, MLB can still limit the number of teams and restrict their ability to relocate. In addition, the legislation is likely to have no impact on labor markets, as the players' right to sue is highly limited. US courts have long ruled that collective bargaining agree-ments between unions and management are not subject to antitrust laws, and the Supreme Court's 1996 *Brown v. Pro Football, Inc.* ruling effectively states that the players' association must decertify itself before a player can sue on antitrust grounds.[47] Given the baseball players' association's history as the most effective of all sports unions, it is a highly unlikely event that it would ever be decertified.

Leagues That Lack an Antitrust Exemption

Baseball's exemption from the antitrust laws has given it a greater ability to protect both its monopoly power and its monopsony power in the marketplace. It is no coincidence that the Federal League, whose antitrust suit was the basis for the antitrust exemption, was the last league to pose a serious challenge to Major League Baseball. Since then, baseball has faced only the feeble attempt to form a rival Mexican League in the 1940s and the stillborn attempts to form the Continental League in the late 1950s and the United Baseball League in the mid-1990s.

Unlike baseball, all the other major professional leagues have endured serious challenges to their monopoly power. The existing league has sometimes had to absorb teams from a rival league and—in one case—to merge with a rival entrant. Forty of the 123 franchises in the 4 major North American leagues "began life as members of rival leagues, and 7 or 8 were created in direct response to the threats posed by rival leagues."[48] In 1976, the NBA ended a costly 10-year war with the American Basketball Association by allowing the Denver Nuggets, Indiana Pacers, New Jersey Nets, and San Antonio Spurs to join the NBA. Three years later, the NHL ended its own costly war with the World Hockey Association by absorbing the surviving WHA teams: the Edmonton Oilers, Hartford Whalers (now Carolina Hurricanes), Quebec Nordiques (now Colorado Avalanche), and the original Winnipeg Jets (now Phoenix Coyotes).[49]

Perhaps because it has been the most consistently profitable, the NFL has faced the most frequent and the most successful challenges. In the midst of a war with the second of four challengers to call itself the "American Football League," the NFL persuaded the Cleveland Rams to join the NFL as a pseudo-expansion team in 1937. The AAFC, while it survived only from 1946 through 1949, had several lasting impacts on professional football. Of the four teams absorbed into the NFL in 1950—the Baltimore Colts, Cleveland Browns, New York Yankees, and San Francisco 49ers—two (the Browns and Colts) went on to become the dominant teams of the 1950s.[50] More importantly, by allowing teams to employ black players, the AAFC helped force an end to the NFL's short-lived color line.

The most successful attack on the NFL's monopoly came from the fourth incarnation of the American Football League. After battling each other from 1960 through 1965, the two leagues agreed to a merger that was completed after the 1969 season.[51] In the 1980s, an antitrust suit by the rival USFL alleged that the NFL had denied rival leagues access to television by contracting with all three major networks. A jury found the NFL guilty but assessed damages of $1 (trebled to $3). Some say that the jury mistakenly assumed that the trial judge could later increase the fine.[52] Others claim that it felt the USFL's demise resulted from its decision to compete directly with the NFL and college football by moving its season from the spring to the fall, a move championed by the owner of the USFL's New Jersey Generals, future US President Donald Trump, who said, "If God wanted football in the spring, he wouldn't have created baseball."

Limited Exemptions: The NFL and Television

When Alvin "Pete" Rozelle became commissioner of the NFL following the death of longtime commissioner Bert Bell in 1959, professional football still lagged badly behind baseball and college football in the nation's consciousness. The NFL now generates more broadcast revenue than any league in the history of

North American professional sports, an agreement that pays each team over $230 million per year. While we all take "the NFL on Fox" or "the NBA on ABC" for granted, professional sports—and Rozelle in particular—had to overcome serious obstacles to obtaining a league-wide contract.

The most significant obstacle was that such contracts were illegal. The NFL had been under an injunction since 1953 that expressly prohibited a league-wide con-tract.[53] Faced with a legal system that would not permit such "restraint of trade," Rozelle actively lobbied Congress to grant a limited exemption from antitrust laws to football, basketball, and hockey. The exemption would apply solely to these leagues' ability to negotiate league-wide broadcast rights. In 1961, Con-gress passed the Sports Broadcasting Act, granting the exemption.[54]

The exemption had an immediate impact on the market for broadcast rights. NFL teams no longer had to negotiate local contracts (often in markets that overlapped one another, further depressing prices). By 1969, a mere seven years after the exemption was granted, the revenue from broadcast rights had risen by a factor of 5 for the "big-market" New York Giants and by a factor of 13 for the "small-market" Green Bay Packers. The merger of the NFL with the rival AFL in the late 1960s further increased the monopoly power of professional football, giving yet another upward boost to broadcast revenues.

Biographical Sketch

Larry C. Morris/*The New York Times*
Alvin "Pete" Rozelle
(1926–1996)

> *If he were in private business and accomplished what he had with the NFL, he'd be worth one hundred million dollars.*
> —*Anonymous corporate executive*[55]

Paul Tagliabue and Roger Goodell, the NFL's last two commissioners, may have brought the NFL's broadcast revenue to its current stratospheric heights, but none of the magic they have worked would have been pos-sible without the efforts of Alvin Ray "Pete" Rozelle. As the NFL's com-missioner from 1960 to 1989, Rozelle transformed football from an afterthought on the American sports scene to the most popular of its major team sports. He also laid the groundwork on which the future success of other sports could be built.

Growing up just outside of Los Angeles, little about Rozelle's early life presaged a career in football. Rozelle joined the navy upon graduating from Compton High School in 1944 and entered Compton Junior College after being discharged in 1946. In one of the remarkable coincidences that seemed to guide his career, the Cleveland Rams moved to Los Angeles that same year and selected Compton Junior College as their training camp. Rozelle worked part-time in the Rams' publicity department until he left to attend the University of San Francisco (USF), which he chose after a chance meeting with USF's legendary basketball coach Pete Newell, who promised him a part-time job as athletic news director. When Rozelle graduated in 1950, he became USF's full-time news director. Thanks to the high profile of USF sports at that time (an undefeated football team and a basketball team that won the then-prestigious National Invitational Tournament), Rozelle had the opportunity to meet many prominent sports figures, including Tex Schramm, the general manager (GM) of the Los Angeles Rams. When the Rams' public relations director abruptly left for another team in 1952, Schramm offered Rozelle the chance to come back to Los Angeles. Rozelle worked with the Rams until 1955, when he moved back to San Francisco to become a partner in a public relations firm.

Rozelle might never have had any further contact with football had it not been for the turmoil that engulfed the Los Angeles Rams in the late 1950s. Ownership of the team was equally divided between long-time owner Dan Reeves and two partners who shared a hatred for Reeves. The result was a paralysis that drove Tex Schramm to seek a job with CBS Sports and caused NFL Commissioner Bert Bell to seek a GM who could mediate between the two factions. Bell was a friend of Rozelle's partner in the PR firm and recalled Rozelle's previous attachment to the Rams as well as the work the firm had done in marketing the 1956 Melbourne Olympic Games. In 1957, Rozelle once again headed south, to become GM of the Rams.

Two years later, fate again took a hand, when Bell died suddenly of a heart attack, leaving no clear successor. At their annual meetings the next January, the owners spent ten fruitless days trying to agree on a successor. Finally, during a break, Dan Reeves proposed his 33-year-old GM to Wellington Mara, the son of New York Giants' owner Tim Mara, as a compromise candidate. When Mara suggested the owners consider Rozelle, the ensuing discussion was almost comical.

"What do you know about him?" [Steelers owner] Art Rooney asked.

"Reeves says he's good. . ." Mara answered.

"Rozelle?" Frank McNamee of the Philadelphia Eagles blurted out. "Who's he?"[56]

Becoming "boy czar" of the NFL in 1960 was not the prize it would be today. The league had failed to capitalize on the popularity of its 1958 championship game between the Baltimore Colts and the New York

Giants, and it remained a backwater. League offices were in the back room of a bank in Bell's hometown of Bala Cynwyd, PA, and teams still struggled financially.

One of the main problems facing the NFL was the balkanized structure of its television dealings. With each team pursuing its own contracts, gross inequities in revenue resulted (the Baltimore Colts made $600,000 from television in 1959 while the Packers made only $80,000), though no team made very much. In the words of then-president of CBS Sports Bill McPhail, "Local stations made more money then by showing old movies than they did showing professional football games."[57]

Rozelle quickly responded to the challenge. To raise the profile and increase the marketability of the NFL, he immediately moved the league offices to Manhattan. He then set to work consolidating the league's tele-vision contracts. Rozelle faced two profound obstacles to his efforts. First, he had to instill a "league-think" mentality in owners who had previously had little ability or reason to look beyond their own survival. Using all the patience and marketing skills at his disposal, Rozelle convinced the own-ers of the big-city teams, such as the Giants and the Chicago Bears, to sacrifice their own short-term goals in favor of the long-term gains that would come from adopting a unified TV policy and sharing revenues equally.

Convincing the owners, however, was the easy part. Negotiating a league contract with the television networks was illegal for an entity that had lost any pretense of exemption from the antitrust laws with the *Radovich* deci-sion of 1957. Rozelle spent the summer of 1961 lobbying Congress for a limited exemption that would allow the NFL to negotiate a single league-wide TV contract. His efforts were rewarded that September with the Sports Broadcasting Act, which allowed football, hockey, and basketball leagues to pool their revenues from television.

Even then, Rozelle's work was not over. Unlike the lords of baseball, who steadily put obstacles in the way of television coverage, Rozelle actively courted the networks and their affiliates. The results of Rozelle's league-think mentality became readily apparent. In 1962–1963, the NFL's first contract with CBS paid approximately $330,000 per franchise per year. By 1964–1965, the payments had risen to about $1 million per franchise per year.

While such figures are far below current contracts, they broke new ground at the time and induced a sense of unity among the owners. This unity allowed Rozelle to create NFL Properties, which pooled the revenues from league licensing agreements. It also allowed the owners to with-stand conflict with a restive players' union far better than the fractious lords of baseball.

In later years, Rozelle would see much of this unity of purpose fracture. The first major setback came with Al Davis's successful antitrust suit over the NFL's attempt to prevent his Oakland Raiders from moving to Los Angeles in 1980. The second came with the entry of a new breed of owners, best exemplified by the Cowboys' Jerry Jones, who—having paid huge sums for their franchises—were determined to maximize their own revenues, even if that meant scrapping the old league-think mentality. Still, the continued prosperity of the NFL and of all professional sports is a testament to the work of the one-time gofer for the Los Angeles Rams.

Sources: David Harris. 1986. *The League: The Rise and Decline of the NFL* (New York: Bantam Books); John Hilyar. 1994. *Lords of the Realm* (New York: Villard Books).

Summary

Monopolies maximize profit by raising prices and reducing output. Their ability to do so depends on having entry barriers to prevent the entry of new competition. In a closed league, existing firms prevent competition by only allowing new teams when it can increase the profits of all and place strong restrictions on the existence of multiple-team markets. The reduction in output increases profits but creates a deadweight loss that does reduce social well-being. Teams may be able to increase profits with variable ticket pricing, dynamic ticket pricing, bundling, and various forms of price discrimination. Teams also use multi-part pricing in the form of personal seat licenses to extract consumer surplus and increase profits.

Unlike North American leagues, soccer leagues in Europe have limited ability to exert monopoly power. The promotion/relegation system can undermine a team's local monopoly power or even remove it from a specific market.

Since the late 19th century, the US government has opposed monopoly. The basis of antitrust policy is the Sherman Antitrust Act, which has been applied against professional sports and the NCAA with varying degrees of success. Due to a series of bizarre court rulings early in the 20th century, baseball has enjoyed a blanket exemption from antitrust laws. It used the exemption to great effect, exerting monopsony power thanks to the reserve clause long after the clause was ruled illegal for other sports.

Discussion Questions

1   With two teams in the NFL, NBA, and MLB, what percentage of sports fans in Los Angeles change their rooting interest from year to year?
2   Is it fair to fans when teams create a bundle of more popular games and less popular games that must be purchased together?
3   What strategy would you follow if you were trying to create a rival basketball league?
4   Why do you think that antitrust lawsuits brought under the second clause of the Sherman Antitrust Act have generally been so unsuccessful?
5   How would professional baseball change for both teams and fans if it practiced promotion and relegation?

Problems

4.1   Use a standard monopoly firm graph to show and explain how the monopoly power of a team is changed when another team locates nearby.
4.2   You are the commissioner of the NHL. You have been called to testify at an antitrust case against the NHL. Argue that:
a. The NHL is not a monopoly.
b. Even if it is a monopoly, it is a natural monopoly.

4.3 Why can't EPL teams like Arsenal exert as much monopoly power as the NFL's Chicago Bears?

4.4 Suppose that the demand curve for tickets to see a football team is given by $Q = 100,000 - 100p$ and marginal cost is zero.

a. How many tickets would the team be able to sell (ignoring capacity constraints) if it behaved competitively and set $p = MC$?

b. How many tickets would it sell—and what price would it charge—if it behaved like a monopoly? (*Hint:* In this case the marginal revenue curve is given by $MR = 1,000 - .02Q$.)

c. Which strategy generates more revenue?

4.5 Why was the limited exemption from antitrust laws so crucial to the development of the NFL?

4.6 Suppose that all Los Angeles Rams fans feel the same as Jane, who values every game at $28, regardless of the opponent. Can the Rams increase profits by bundling the Rams–Bears game with three others? Why or why not?

4.7 Suppose most fans prefer Sunday afternoon baseball games (regardless of opponent) to all other types of games. Describe two pricing strategies that a team could use to increase profits based on this difference in demand.

4.8 Suppose you were granted the next MLS expansion franchise and the right to locate the team anywhere in North America. Explain the factors you should consider in choosing a profit-maximizing location. What would be the costs and benefits of choosing a city that already has a team?

4.9 Suppose that Mahesh is a typical Buffalo Bills fan, and his demand curve for Bills football games is: $P = 120 - 10G$ where G is the number of games the fan attends.

a. If the Bills want to sell him a ticket to all eight home games, what price must they charge? What are their revenues?

b. Suppose that there are 30,000 Bills fans with demand equivalent to Mahesh's. What would total revenue be at a price that sells all eight games to every fan? How would your answer change if, instead of charging a single price, the Bills perfectly price discriminate and charge the maximum that each fan would pay for the first game, second game, and so on through game eight?

4.10 Suppose that instead of price discriminating, the Bills are able to charge a two-part price including a fixed fee for entry and a price per game. If the marginal cost of attendance is $0, what is the optimal fixed fee per fan (again assuming that all have the same demand curve)?

4.11 Suppose that, in order to protect Cristiano Ronaldo from his adoring fans, soccer teams that host Real Madrid must hire extra security, and security costs go up as the number of fans at the game goes up. When a team such as Arsenal host Real Madrid, how do these extra costs affect the price of a ticket for that game compared with the price of a ticket when they host any other team? Is this price discrimination by Arsenal? Why or why not?

Notes

1 Quoted in John Helyar. 1994. *Lords of the Realm* (New York: Villard Books): 268.

2 The fact that it predates the American League by about 25 years has led to its nickname, "the senior circuit."

3 Strictly speaking, the industry supply curve is the horizontal sum of all the individual marginal cost curves. For our purposes here, we ignore any complication raised by capacity constraints.

4 Producer surplus is the extra revenue that a firm receives beyond what it requires to sell a given level of output. It is related to—but not identical to—profit. Economists calculate producer surplus as the area between the supply (or marginal cost) curve and the market price.

5 "Annual Lobbying by the National Football League," *OpenSecrets.org*, January 25, 2017, at https://www.opensecrets.org/lobby/clientsum.php?id=D000027847, viewed February 1, 2017.

6 See, for example, Richard Posner. 1975. "The Social Costs of Monopoly and Regulation," *Journal of Political Economy*, 83(4), August: 807–827; Robert Tollison. 1997. "Rent Seeking," in *Perspectives on Public Choice: A Handbook*, ed. Dennis Mueller (Cambridge, UK: Cambridge University Press); Associated Press. 2002. "Commissioner Spent $1.2 Million on Lobbying in 2001," *ESPN.com*, May 15, at http://a.espncdn.com/mlb/news/2002/0515/1382924.html.

7 This is because MR = $P*(1+1/\varepsilon_D)$, where ε_D is the price elasticity of demand.

8 See, for example, Roger Noll. 1974. "Attendance and Price Setting," in *Government and the Sports Business*, ed. Roger Noll (Washington, DC: Brookings Institution); Rodney Fort and Robert Rosenman. 1999. "Streak Management," in *Sports Economics: Current Research*, ed. J. Fizel, E. Gustafson, and L. Hadley (Westport, CT: Praeger); and Jason Winfree, Jill McCluskey, Ron Mittelhammer, and Rodney Fort. 2004. "Location and Attendance in Major League Baseball," *Applied Economics*, 36(19), October: 2117–2124.

9 For a discussion of the previous literature on pricing decisions related to demand elasticity as well as the empirical results described here, see: Anthony C. Krautmann and David C. Berri. 2007. "Can We Find It in the Concessions: Understanding Price Elasticity in Professional Sports," *Journal of Sports Economics*, 8(2), May: 183–191.

10 Team Marketing Report—NFL 2016, at https://www.teammarketing.com/public/uploadedPDFs/NFL_FCI_2016.pdf. Accessed January 20, 2017.

11 David Dubas-Fisher. 2016. "How Much Should Chelsea Season Tickets Cost Based on the Rate of Inflation?" *getwestlondon*, February 9, at http://www.getwestlondon.co.uk/sport/football/football-news/how-much-should-chelsea-season-10864543. Attendance figures are from "Premier League 2015/16 Attendance," *worldfootball.net*, At http://www.worldfootball.net/attendance/eng-premier-league-2015-2016/1/. Accessed January 26, 2017.

12 Daniel A. Rascher, Chad D. McEvoy, Mark S. Nagel, and Matthew T. Brown. 2007. "Variable Ticket Pricing in Major League Baseball," *Journal of Sport Management*, 21(3): 407–437.

13 "Price Better," *Qcue*, at http://www.qcue.com/#price-better. Accessed January 21, 2017.

14 Ken Belson. 2009. "Tickets Cost Too Much? Check Back Tomorrow," *The New York Times*, May 18: D-2.

15 Patrick Rishe. 2012. "Dynamic Pricing: The Future of Ticket Pricing in Sports," *Forbes.com*, January 6, at https://www.forbes.com/sites/prishe/2012/01/06/dynamic-pricing-the-future-of-ticket-pricing-in-sports/. Accessed March 16, 2012.

16 Staff Writer. 2016. "Sabres Announce New Dynamic Ticket Pricing Structure," *NHL.com*, August 24, at https://www.nhl.com/sabres/news/sabres-announce-new-dynamic-ticket-pricing-structure/c-891524. Accessed January 21, 2017.

17 Daniel Kaplan. 2015. "Dynamic Ticket Pricing Makes Successful Debut in NFL," *Street and Smith's Sports Business Journal*, October 26, at http://www.sportsbusinessdaily.com/Journal/Issues/2015/10/26/Leagues-and-Governing-Bodies/NFL-dynamic.aspx. Accessed January 21, 2017; Associated Press. 2015. "NFL Teams That Use Variable or Dynamic Ticket Pricing," *ESPN.com*, July 11, at http://www.espn.com/espn/wire?id=13237217&section=nfl. Accessed January 21, 2017.

18 Tottenham Hotspur. "Match Day Prices 2017/2018," at http://www.tottenhamhotspur.com/tickets/ticket-prices/. Accessed October 23, 2017.

19 The equation for D_0 is P = 120 − 2Q. The equation for D_1 is P = 160 − 2Q.

20 Rishe. 2012. "Dynamic Pricing."

21 Cubs.com, "Six Game Pack," example given is "Pack B" for 2012. At http://chicago.cubs.mlb.com/chc/ticketing/sixpacks.jsp. Accessed March 20, 2012.

22 Technically, the Panthers would have to charge $159.99, $99.99, and $39.99 to be sure that Hannah, Ian, and Juan buy tickets, respectively. We round off for ease of exposition.

23 Quantity discounting is also known as second-degree price discrimination or block pricing.

24 Senior citizens comprise another group that firms frequently feel is more sensitive to price.

25 The argument that follows is based on Roger Noll and Andrew Zimbalist. 1997. "Build the Stadium—Create the Jobs!" in *Sports, Jobs, and Taxes*, ed. Roger Noll and Andrew Zimbalist (Washington, DC: Brookings Institution Press): 20–25.

26 For more on the role of PSLs in stadium funding, see for example, Robert Baade and Victor Matheson. 2006. "Have Public Finance Principles Been Shut Out of Financing New Stadiums for the NFL?" *Public Finance and Management*, 6(3): 284–320.

27 For a good discussion of natural monopoly and the general issue of antitrust policy as it applies to the NFL see Robert Heintel. 1996. "The Need for an Alternative to Antitrust Regulation of the National Football League," *Case Western Reserve Law Review*, 46(4), Summer: 1033–1069.

28 The AFL's Dallas Texans moved to Kansas City in 1963 to achieve great success as the Chiefs. See Gary R. Roberts. 1992. "Antitrust Issues in Professional Sports," in *Law of Professional and Amateur Sports*, ed. Gary Uberstine (Deerfield, IL: Clark, Boardman, and Callaghan): 19-8, 19-9; and James Quirk and Rodney Fort. 1992. *Pay Dirt* (Princeton, NJ: Princeton University Press): 346–347.

29 Ronald J. Shingler. 1988. "Antitrust Law and the Sports League Relocation Rules." *Golden State University Law Review*. 18(1), article 5. At http://digitalcommons.law.ggu.edu/ggulrev/vol18/iss1/5. Accessed April 4, 2012.

30 Daniel A. Rascher, 2008. "Franchise Relocation, Expansions, and Mergers in Professional Sports Leagues," in *The Business of Sports Volume 2: Economic Perspectives on Sport*, ed. B.H. Humphreys and D.R. Howard (Westport, CT: Praeger); Gerald W. Scully, 1995. *The Market Structure of Sports* (Chicago, IL: University of Chicago Press); Shingler. 1988. "Antitrust Law."

31 Legal Information Institute. Cornell University Law School, at https://www.law.cornell.edu/uscode/text/15/1. Accessed January 26, 2017.

32 Roberts. 1992. "Antitrust Issues": 19-9. Emphasis in original.

33 Roberts. 1992. "Antitrust Issues": 19-4.

34 See, for example, Gary R. Roberts in G.R. Roberts, S.F. Ross, and R.A. Baade. 1996. "Should Congress Stop the Bidding War for Sports Franchises?" Hearing before the Subcommittee on Antitrust, Business Rights, and Competition. Senate Committee on the Judiciary. August 1. *Heartland Policy*, at https://www.heartland.org/_template-assets/documents/publications/3924.pdf: 4–5.

35 Roger Abrams. 1998. *Legal Bases: Baseball and the Law* (Philadelphia, PA: Temple University Press): 53–60.

36 The commission consisted of Ban Johnson, the president of the American League; John Tener, the president of the National League; and August Hermann, the owner of the Cincinnati (NL) team, who had been instrumental in brokering the peace between the National and American Leagues. See Harold Seymour. 1960. *Baseball: The Early Years* (New York: Oxford University Press): 212.

37 Harold Seymour. 1971. *Baseball: The Golden Age* (New York: Oxford University Press): 212; and Abrams. 1998. *Legal Bases:* 55.

38 Seymour. 1971. *The Golden Age*: 212–213; and Andrew Zimbalist. 1992. *Baseball and Billions* (New York: Basic Books): 9.

39 Some Federal League owners bought the Major League teams with which they competed. Wrigley Field was originally built for the Federal League's Chicago Whales. See

Seymour. 1971. *Baseball: The Golden Age*: 215–243; and Zimbalist, 1992. *Baseball and Billions*: 9.

40   Abrams. 1998. *Legal Bases*: 56; Seymour. 1971. *The Golden Age*: 243; and John Johnson. 1996. "When a Professional Sport Is Not a Business: Baseball's Infamous Antitrust Exemption," in *Sports and the Law,* ed. Charles Quirk (New York: Garland Publishers): 151.

41   Abrams. 1998. *Legal Bases*: 57; and Johnson. 1996. "Baseball's Infamous Antitrust Exemption": 151.

42   Earl Warren writing for the majority. Cited in *U.S. v. International Boxing Club of N.Y.* Justia US Supreme Court. United States *v.* International Boxing Club. 348 U.S. 236 (1955), at https://supreme.justia.com/cases/federal/us/348/236/case.html#241. Accessed October 22, 2017.

43   See Abrams. 1998. *Legal Bases*: 62; Quirk and Fort. 1992. *Pay Dirt*: 188–189; Roberts. 1992. "Antitrust Issues": 19-33–19-36; and Zimbalist. 1992. *Baseball and Billions*: 12–15.

44   Personal communication with Andrew Zimbalist, 2012.

45   While playing for a minor league town in the deep South early in his career, Flood was not allowed to mix his dirty laundry with that of his white teammates. White clubhouse attendants would not even handle his uniform. Flood's reference to slavery was not lost on Supreme Court Justice Thurgood Marshall, who also drew an analogy to slavery in his minority opinion.

46   Blackmun's decision included the poems "He Never Heard of Casey," by Grantland Rice, and "Baseball's Sad Lexicon," by Franklin Pierre Adams. See Abrams. 1998. *Legal Bases:* 62; Quirk and Fort. 1992. *Pay Dirt:* 188–189; Roberts. 1992. "Antitrust Issues": 19-33–19-36; and Zimbalist. 1992. *Baseball and Billions:* 12–15.

47   Gary R. Roberts. 1997. "Brown v. Pro Football, Inc.: The Supreme Court Gets It Right for the Wrong Reasons," *Antitrust Bulletin,* 42(3), Fall: 595–639.

48   Quirk and Fort. 1992. *Pay Dirt*: 297.

49   Interestingly, one man, a lawyer named Gary Davidson, was instrumental in the formation of both the ABA and the WHA.

50   The NFL's Yankees lasted for only a few years and played in Yankee Stadium.

51   One sidelight to the agreement was the institution of an AFL–NFL Championship Game, later renamed the Super Bowl.

52   See Jim Byrne. 1986. *The $1 League: The Rise and Fall of the USFL* (New York: Prentice Hall): 346; Roberts, "Antitrust Issues": 1992; and Eric Leifer. 1995. *Making the Majors: The Transformation of Team Sports in America* (Cambridge, MA: Harvard University Press): 142.

53   Due to its exemption from antitrust laws, baseball faced no such prohibition, though it did little in the 1950s to exploit this advantage.

54   One of the concessions that the NFL had to grant Congress in order to get its limited exemption was a promise not to compete with college or high school football. As a result, the NFL does not play Saturday games until the high school and college seasons end in early December.

55   David Harris. 1986. *The League: The Rise and Decline of the NFL* (New York: Bantam Books): 13.

56   Quoted in Harris. 1986. The League: 11.

57   Quoted in Harris. 1986. The League: 13.

5

COMPETITIVE BALANCE

You're doing all right . . . We're ahead but you just can't tell what those Cumberland players have up their sleeves. They may spring a surprise. Be alert, men!
—GEORGIA TECH COACH JOHN HEISMAN, speaking to his team at halftime with his team up by 18 touchdowns in the worst blowout in college football history (222–0).[1]

Introduction

One of the oldest adages in professional football is that on any given Sunday, each team has a chance to beat the other. But what if, year after year, a few teams regularly win, while the rest almost always lose? No doubt, the games would be less interesting. As early as 1956, economists noted that successful leagues must be based on relatively even competition,[2] but the degree of parity within a sports league can mean different things to different people. To some, it means close competition every year, with the difference between the best and worst teams being relatively small. To others, it means regular turnover in the winner of the league's championship. Whatever the measure, we call the degree of parity within a league **competitive balance**. This chapter discusses competitive balance from the perspectives of the fan and the owner. In addition, it explores how economists measure competitive balance, how leagues try to alter competitive balance in a league, and why such efforts might not be successful.

Learning Objectives

- Understand why owners and fans may care about competitive balance.
- Master the use and interpretation of the different measures of competitive balance.
- Be able to compare the tools that leagues use to promote competitive balance and the limitations of those tools.

5.1 Why Study Competitive Balance?

Fans and owners alike have a conflicted relationship with competitive balance. No Bears fan enjoys losing to the Packers, but each recognizes that an occasional loss makes the games more interesting. Similarly, the McCaskey family, which owns the Bears, gets a greater financial return—and greater satisfaction— if the team is successful but does not always win. Thus, whether competitive balance is a good thing depends on one's perspective. On any given day, hometown fans want to see wins, so owners want to provide them. Over longer stretches of time, the viability of the league may depend on some uncertainty of outcome. In this section, we look more deeply at the value of competitive balance to fans and owners.

The Fans' Perspective

Suppose you grew up in Wyoming without much exposure to professional sports. On a visit to your uncle in Texas, you go to your first MLB game, one between the Texas Rangers and the Minnesota Twins. The Rangers quickly build a commanding lead, scoring on the overmatched Twins in almost every inning. While the Rangers' fans seem to enjoy the rout, as a casual fan, you quickly become bored because the talent on the two teams is very uneven. If that were your only exposure to baseball, you would probably leave the game thinking it is all a waste of time. Your uncle, however, feels great about the big win for the home team. On the way home, he says, "I'm glad the Rangers won. A close game might have been more fun, but a Rangers loss would have been awful." Even this short example shows that fans view competitive balance differently from casual observers.

From the fan's perspective, an uncertain outcome in a game may be more interesting than a foregone conclusion, but, as we discuss below, fans may prefer an easy win to seeing their team lose in an upset. Historically, fans have shown their displeasure with unbalanced competition, even when their own team did most of the winning. The Cleveland Browns of the late 1940s were so dominant in the All-American Football Conference that they became less popular with their home fans.[3] In baseball, the New York Yankees may have dampened attendance at their own games and across the American League when they won eight league pennants and six World Series between 1950 and 1958. Table 5.1 shows that between 1950 and 1958, a period generally marked by prosperity and economic growth, attendance for both Yankee games and the American League as a whole either stagnated or fell as the Yankees dominated the league. In contrast, in the National League, which had four different champions (Phillies, Giants, Dodgers, and Braves), attendance grew substantially. This relationship between competitive balance and attendance requires that we look more deeply into the question of the desirability of competitive balance.

Studies of fan behavior show interesting asymmetries in the benefits (utility gained) of winning versus the costs (utility lost) of losing. Several empirical

Table 5.1 New York Yankees' Success and American League and National League Attendance, 1950–1958

Year	AL Champion	World Series Champion	Yankees Attendance	AL Attendance	NL Attendance
1950	Yankees	Yankees	2,081,380	9,142,361	8,320,616
1951	Yankees	Yankees	1,950,107	8,888,614	7,244,002
1952	Yankees	Yankees	1,629,665	8,293,896	6,339,148
1953	Yankees	Yankees	1,531,811	6,964,076	7,419,721
1954	Cleveland	NY Giants	1,475,171	7,922,364	8,013,519
1955	Yankees	Brooklyn	1,490,138	8,942,971	7,674,412
1956	Yankees	Yankees	1,491,784	7,893,683	8,649,567
1957	Yankees	Milwaukee	1,497,134	8,169,218	8,819,601
1958	Yankees	Yankees	1,428,438	7,296,034	10,164,596

Source: Attendance data are from Rodney Fort and James Quirk, *Pay Dirt* (1992). Performance data are from *MLB.com*, "World Series History: Championships by Club," at http://mlb.mlb.com/mlb/history/postseason/mlb_ws.jsp?feature=club_champs. Accessed May 17, 2017.

studies show that fans enjoy an uncertain outcome and are most likely to attend games in which the home team has a 60 to 70 percent chance of winning.[4] Fans do not want their teams to lose 30 to 40 percent of the time, but the chance of losing makes the game more interesting and stimulates demand. This is known as the **uncertainty of outcome hypothesis (UOH)**.

Recent research by Dennis Coates, Brad Humphreys, and Li Zhou casts doubt on the universal applicability of the UOH. They use concepts from behavioral economics to investigate whether the UOH applies in some circumstances but not others. Behavioral economics incorporates elements of psychology in analyzing decision-making. Though elements of behavioral economics were developed over 40 years ago, its power as an economic tool was popularized by the work of Daniel Kahneman and Amos Tversky in the 1980s. More recently, economists have found widespread applicability to their theories regarding human behavior and economic action.

One of the most important concepts of behavioral economics is prospect theory. **Prospect theory** was developed by Kahneman and Tversky to analyze settings in which individuals treat gains and losses differently. Rather than acting in accordance with the strict predictions of economic rationality, individuals tend to show greater aversion to losses than desire for gains, a concept known as loss aversion.[5]

Coates et al. construct a model that incorporates these elements of behavioral economics. Unlike the strict UOH model, which posits an optimal probability of winning, with increasing and decreasing probabilities having a symmetric effect on a fan's expected pleasure from attending a game, Coates et al. present a more complex set of motives. They begin by claiming that, consistent with reference-dependent preferences (i.e., preferences that may differ depending on how the spectators feel about their team's chances going into a match), fans prefer a win of any kind to a loss. They then posit a variation of the UOH by saying that unexpected wins are sweeter than expected wins and that unexpected losses are worse than expected losses. Finally, they incorporate loss aversion by hypothesizing that *being* upset reduces utility more than *staging* an equally improbable upset increases utility. Their estimates using game-level data for the 2005–2010 baseball seasons support their hypotheses.[6]

The Owners' Perspective

Perhaps the briefest explanation of why competitive balance matters to owners and the leagues in which they compete is that, as seen in Table 5.1, it matters to fans. This is particularly true for teams that rarely win. Overall American League attendance fell by about 2 million during the era of Yankee dominance in the 1950s, while National League attendance rose by 2 million. While all owners would rather win than lose any given game (and so may also be loss-averse), they are also concerned with the health of the league. If the same team wins every game or every championship, fans may lose interest. In Chapter 3, we saw that owners may have a variety of objectives, such as maximizing profits or maximizing wins. No matter what objective individual team owners have, consistently unbalanced competition alienates fans and is not in the best interest of the league.

Recall that leagues perform functions that individual teams either cannot do or have no incentive to do. Hence, leagues often adopt policies to promote competitive balance because individual teams lack the means or the motivation to do so. As we will see later in the chapter, the concern with unbalanced competition and the will to adopt rules designed to increase competitive balance vary greatly across leagues and national borders. In particular, we shall see that European soccer leagues, such as La Liga, have long been characterized by highly unbalanced competition.

One challenge of maintaining competitive balance is that it may not be the natural state of the league. Leagues and professional associations do not need to take specific action if they tend naturally toward equal strength. If, in the absence of intervention, a few teams flourish while most teams languish, the league must create a more competitive environment. For example, in auto racing, NASCAR goes to great lengths to promote equal competition among cars. It measures each car in a Sprint Cup race with a device known as "the claw," to ensure the dimensions of the car bodies comply with regulations that prevent cars from having an aerodynamic advantage. Engines must meet an exacting set of criteria and are even restricted to lower horsepower on larger tracks, where speeds are greatest. To further ensure even competition, some cars are retested at the conclusion of the race. NASCAR places so many restrictions on cars to promote close competitions decided by the skills of the drivers and their teams.

Intervention might be necessary in team sports for two reasons: the motivation of team owners and market size.[7] If some owners maximize wins while others maximize profits, competitive balance can suffer, harming all teams financially. Even if all owners have the same motivation, in the absence of revenue sharing, the financial return to investing in talented players is likely greater for teams from large cities. As the attendance data in Table 5.1 show, actions that maximize individual team profits or wins may be detrimental to competitive balance.

The Effect of Market Size

There is considerable disagreement among those who have studied the impact of market size on competitive balance. There appear to be three primary sources of contention: what to use as a measure of success, how to characterize market size, and how to measure the impact of policies designed to alter competitiveness, such as revenue sharing. Studies that use different measures of success or market size come to very different conclusions. For example, MLB's Blue Ribbon Panel reported in 2000 that low-payroll teams (their measure of market size) rarely succeeded in the playoffs (their measure of success) from 1995 to 1999. However, Berri, Schmidt, and Brook (*Wages of Wins*, 2006) note that success in the playoffs is different from success in the regular season, and, using a longer data-set, find only a weak correlation between payroll and wins.[8] Other work by Schmidt and Berri tests several measures of market size and concludes that team quality is not strongly related to population or per capita income.[9]

Determining market size is particularly complex, in part because the way in which markets are defined continues to evolve. Before the television era, teams relied almost solely on gate revenue, so attendance was most relevant and the financial advantage of large cities was limited. The growth of regional sports networks (RSNs) (and the revenue they provide) has created an income differential that is not limited by the size of a stadium. As a result, teams in large markets can now generate much more revenue for each additional win than teams in small ones can.[10] The impact of their greater revenue on competitive balance, however, remains a point of debate.

To further complicate matters, even if fans desire some level of uncertainty, our conclusions regarding how to best distribute success change when we change our unit of analysis from the team to the fan. Because teams in large markets (such as the New York Yankees) have many more fans than teams in small markets (such as the Milwaukee Brewers), a profit-maximizing league prefers that the teams in the largest markets win more often than teams elsewhere.[11] In a 30-team league, perfect parity means that the Yankees and Dodgers—teams in the two largest markets—win the World Series only once every 30 years on average. If championships were allocated so that they were distributed equally on a per capita (per fan) basis, rather than a per-team basis, the Yankees would win about once every 9 years, the Dodgers once every 14 years, and the Milwaukee Brewers almost once a century. Over the 100 World Series from 1917 to 2016, the Yankees have won more than twice as often as they would if wins were allocated evenly by population (26 v. 11), the Dodgers come up a little short (6 v. 7), and the Brewers are still waiting, with no World Series wins in their 48 years of existence.

To see why big-market teams gain more from winning than small-market teams do, assume that each team gets its revenue only from tickets and local television revenue, and that teams benefit from having a higher winning percentage, but the additional benefits of increasing the winning percentage become smaller as it approaches 1.000. Thus, the marginal revenue curve from additional wins is positive but downward sloping. Because teams in large cities enjoy greater increases in fan support from an additional win than teams in small cities, an additional win generates more gate revenue, more media revenue, and more venue revenue for a team in Los Angeles than it does for a team in Indianapolis. Figure 5.1 illustrates the greater value of wins for a team in a large market. It shows the additional (marginal) revenue from one more win for a team in a small market (MR_s) and a team in a large market (MR_L)[12]

If all firms maximize profits then they operate where the marginal revenue of wins equals the marginal cost of wins. To keep the focus on revenue, assume that the marginal cost of a win is constant and equal for all teams. For a small-market

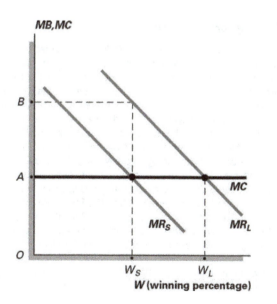

Figure 5.1
The Benefit of Improving the Team Depends on Market Size

Because winning is more valuable to a big-market team, it pursues winning more avidly than a small-market team does.

team, MR = MC occurs at W_S wins. A large-market team has an incentive to acquire more talent and wins $W_L > W_S$ games. Thus, even in a world without Mark Cubans or Jerry Joneses, where all teams maximize profit, the model predicts that, all else equal, teams from big cities win more frequently than teams from small cities.

The Influence of Diminishing Returns

While teams from large cities may have a greater incentive to acquire talent and win games than teams from small cities, there is still a limit to how far they go in pursuit of wins because of the law of diminishing marginal returns. Diminishing returns to labor are found in every industry. In the short run, as a firm adds units of labor, the marginal product (the additional output) of the last unit of labor must eventually fall, even if labor is homogeneous. The reason is straightforward: In the short run, capital is fixed, so the additional workers eventually have less capital to work with and are less productive.

In the context of sports, diminishing returns may set in very quickly, especially in basketball, where only five teammates play at a time, and, as the saying goes, "there is only one ball." The same logic applies across all team sports. With rare exceptions, professional football teams have only one quarterback on the field at a time. The New England Patriots would not dispute that Cam Newton is a great player, but his value to the Patriots is surely less than the salary that a team without a top quarterback would offer, given that the Patriots already have Tom Brady.

Diminishing returns act as a brake on team behavior because they reduce the incentive any one team has to stockpile talent. It does not make economic sense for a team to spend large sums of money acquiring all the best players at each position when some, perhaps many, of them will contribute very little. As we will learn later in the chapter, even with the influence of diminishing returns, variations in market size and owner motivations have led leagues to seek additional ways to equalize team quality.

A Brief History of Competitive Balance

In MLB, five different teams won the five World Series played between 2012 and 2016. But the league has also seen long periods of dominance by the New York Yankees. The Yankees have been a dominant franchise since the 1920s, when they won six American League championships between 1921 (the year after they acquired Babe Ruth) and 1928. It was even more pronounced when they won five straight World Series between 1949 and 1953. Two of the three other major sports have similar instances of a single team dominating the league over many seasons. The Boston Celtics won every NBA championship but one between 1959 and 1969. Between 1965 and 1979, the Montreal Canadiens won the NHL's Stanley Cup ten times. The Canadiens' dynasty was followed by that of the New York Islanders, who won the Cup the next four years in a row. Only in the NFL has no team ever won the league championship (the Super Bowl) more than twice in a row, but even there, the Steelers, Cowboys, Patriots, and 49ers have each won at least five times while two teams—the Browns and the Lions—have never appeared in a Super Bowl, despite being in the NFL for all 51 of them.[13]

Internationally, unbalanced competition is the norm in the elite European soccer leagues. A few dominant teams have long runs of championships. For example, from the 2000–2001 season through the 2015–2016 season, FC Barcelona and Real Madrid combined to win 13 of 16 La Liga championships in Spain, and Bayern Munich and Borussia Dortmund won 13 of 16 Bundesliga championships. The EPL in England and Serie A in Italy show similar patterns of dominance by one or two teams over many seasons.

Competitive imbalance also appears at the amateur level. For example, since the formation of college football's Big 10 Conference in 1896, the University of Michigan has won or shared 42 titles, more than one-third of the total. In contrast, Indiana University has won only two titles, five fewer than the University of Chicago, which gave up football in 1939.

Changes in the relative importance of the various revenue sources and the growth of the sports industry in general have increased the concerns that the financial consequences of unbalanced competition are becoming more severe. Before we analyze the potential implications of unbalanced competition, we first need to consider the various ways in which it is measured.

5.2   Measuring Competitive Balance

There are two approaches to measuring competitive balance.[14] The first focuses on team performance over the course of a given season. A wide dispersion in winning percentages means that some teams are much better than others in that season. The second approach looks across several seasons. It measures the concentration of championships or turnover in the league's standings over a given period. Leagues with a high concentration of championships have a small set of teams winning year after year. No single approach is necessarily better than the other. To fully evaluate competitive balance in a league, one should use both measures. While fans may prefer lopsided wins to unexpected losses in individual games, fans and owners are likely to desire both tightly contested seasonal competition and regular turnover in champions.

Within-Season Variation

In a way, sports fans resemble opera or classic rock buffs. Both are attracted by the absolute quality of the performers. A serious music fan would much rather see Eric Clapton than even the best local band. Similarly, the demand to see a big-time college football game between Texas and Oklahoma far outstrips the demand to see a game between Ivy League powers Harvard and Penn. However, absolute quality is not the only factor; relative quality matters too. As seen in Table 5.1, a tight race for the conference championship will generate more demand for games than a season in which the winner is a foregone conclusion. Within-season variation in winning percentage focuses on the evenness of competition over the course of a season.

Measures of within-season variation start with the standard deviation of winning percentage. The **standard deviation** is the distance of the typical observation from the sample mean. In the case of a professional sports league, ignoring ties, there is a loser for every winner, so the mean winning percentage for a league must be 0.5.[15]

The formula for the standard deviation of winning percentages within a single season is:

$$\sigma_{w,t} = \sqrt{\frac{\sum_{i=1}^{N}\left(WPCT_{i,t} - .500\right)^2}{N}},$$

where $WPCT_{i,t}$ is the winning percentage of the ith team in the league in year t, .500 is the average winning percentage of all teams for the year, and N is the number of teams in the league. The larger the standard deviation, the greater the dispersion of the winning percentages. For example, consider the final standings for MLB's 1996 season. We use this season because it was before inter-league play began in 1997, ensuring that the mean winning percentage in each league is exactly 0.500. Table 5.2 shows the final standings for both the American and National Leagues. One can get an impression of how balanced the two leagues were by looking at the highest and lowest winning percentages. In the American League, the Cleveland Indians had the highest winning percentage (.615), while the .327 winning percentage of the Detroit Tigers was the lowest. The Atlanta Braves led the National League with a .593 winning percentage—with three fewer wins than the Indians. At the bottom of the standings, the last-place Phillies won 14 more games than the Tigers. Computing the standard deviation of winning percentage confirms this impression. The standard deviation in the American League was 0.067, meaning that the typical team's winning percentage varied by 0.067 from the mean. In contrast, the standard deviation in the National League was 0.054, about three-fourths that of the American League.

The standard deviation of winning percentages is a useful summary of competitive balance, but it has significant limitations. In particular, the standard

Table 5.2 Winning Percentages for the National and American Leagues, 1996

American League				National League			
Team	W	L	WPCT	Team	W	L	WPCT
Cleveland Indians	99	62	0.615	Atlanta Braves	96	66	0.593
New York Yankees	92	70	0.568	San Diego Padres	91	71	0.562
Texas Rangers	90	72	0.556	Los Angeles Dodgers	90	72	0.556
Baltimore Orioles	88	74	0.543	Montreal Expos	88	74	0.543
Seattle Mariners	85	76	0.528	St. Louis Cardinals	88	74	0.543
Boston Red Sox	85	77	0.525	Colorado Rockies	83	79	0.512
Chicago White Sox	85	77	0.525	Houston Astros	82	80	0.506
Milwaukee Brewers	80	82	0.494	Cincinnati Reds	81	81	0.500
Minnesota Twins	78	84	0.481	Florida Marlins	80	82	0.494
Oakland Athletics	78	84	0.481	Chicago Cubs	76	86	0.469
Kansas City Royals	75	86	0.466	Pittsburgh Pirates	73	89	0.451
Toronto Blue Jays	74	88	0.457	New York Mets	71	91	0.438
California Angels	70	91	0.435	San Francisco Giants	68	94	0.420
Detroit Tigers	53	109	0.327	Philadelphia Phillies	67	95	0.414
Mean			0.500				0.500
Standard deviation			0.067				0.054

Source: MLB.com, "Standings," at HTTP://MLB.MLB.COM/MLB/STANDINGS/INDEX.JSP?TCID=MM_MLB_STANDINGS#19960929. Accessed April 17, 2012.

Table 5.3 Dispersion of Winning Percentages, 2015–2016

League	Actual	Ideal	Ratio
MLB[a]	.065	.039	1.67
NFL[a]	.197	.125	1.58
NBA	.166	.056	2.96
NHL	.077	.056	1.38
English Premier League	.132	.081	1.63
Bundesliga	.149	.086	1.73
Serie A	.147	.081	1.81
La Liga	.155	.081	1.91

[a]MLB and NFL results are for the 2016 season.
[b]Because teams receive one point for overtime losses and EPL teams receive one point for draws, winning percentages in the NHL and EPL are computed as the percentage of possible points and means are not equal to 0.5.

Sources: All data are generated from the standings on the official league websites and skysports.com.

deviation of winning percentages varies with the number of games in a season. To see why, try flipping a fair coin—one with an equal chance of coming up heads or tails—four times. This is the equivalent to two equally matched teams playing one another four times, with only random factors determining the outcome. More than 12 percent of the time (about once in 8 tries), you will get an extreme outcome of all heads or all tails.[16] As you increase the number of flips to 40, 400, or 4,000, the chance of an extreme outcome becomes more and more remote. This experiment tells us that, even if a league were perfectly balanced, we might see some teams with many more wins than others in a short season. As the season gets longer, winning and losing streaks begin to offset one another, just like runs of heads and tails with coin flips.

Table 5.3 shows the standard deviation of winning percentages in the four largest North American leagues and four major European soccer leagues. If we consider only the standard deviations, it appears that the NFL has the least balanced competition. Alternatively, it might simply be that the NFL has only a 16-game season, by far the shortest of any league. Because the standard deviation is larger for sports with shorter seasons, we do not directly compare standard deviations. Instead, we first compute what the standard deviation of winning percentage would be for a league that had completely equal teams. The ratio of the actual standard deviation to this "ideal" standard deviation tells us how far out of balance the league was. Because the ratios for MLB and the NFL account for the length of the season, we use them to compare competitive balance in the two leagues.

The standard deviation that corresponds to a world in which each team has a 0.5 chance of winning each game is:

$$\sigma_I = \frac{0.5}{\sqrt{G}},$$

where 0.5 indicates that each team has a 0.5 probability of winning, and G is the number of games each team plays.[17] Because each MLB team plays 162 games per season, the ideal is 0.039. Because NFL teams play only

16 games, a randomly occurring string of wins or losses has a greater impact on a team's final winning percentage, so the ideal standard deviation is much larger, 0.125. In the NHL and NBA, whose teams play 82-game schedules, the standard deviations are 0.056. In all but the Bundesliga, which has a slightly shorter season, the ideal standard deviation in the European leagues is 0.081.

To measure competitive balance within a single season, we use the ratio (R) of the actual standard deviation of winning percentages (σ_w) to the ideal standard deviation (σ_I):[18]

$$R = \frac{\sigma_w}{\sigma_I}.$$

Thus, for the NBA in 2015–2016:

$R = 0.166/0.056 = 2.96$

Based on this result, the standard deviation of winning percentages in the NBA is close to three times what it would be in a world with absolutely balanced teams. Again, this result is consistent with our casual observation that competition appears unbalanced in the NBA, as two teams had winning percentages of over .800, five teams had winning percentages over .670, and four teams had winning percentages less than .300.

In addition to the actual standard deviations, Table 5.3 presents the ideal standard deviations for each of the eight major sports leagues and the ratio, R. In 2015–2016, the NHL was the most equally balanced North American league, with an R-value of 1.38. The NFL and MLB followed with R-values of 1.58 and 1.67. Competition in the top divisions of European soccer was less balanced than most North American sports. It is notable that the EPL was the most balanced European league as it has the most extensive revenue sharing of the European leagues, a subject we return to later in the chapter. As noted previously, the NBA, with $R = 2.96$, is by far the least balanced of the eight leagues.

In *The Wages of Wins*, Dave Berri, Martin Schmidt, and Stacey Brook discuss why competition in the NBA is so unbalanced.[19] Their theory is based on the old adage "you can't teach height." In basketball, taller players have a distinct advantage over shorter ones. There are good players who are not tall, but if we compare two players of equal skill but substantially different heights, the taller player will be more effective. The number of very tall people who are also very gifted athletes—and whose athletic skills are well suited for basketball—is extremely small. Thus, a team lucky enough to get an unusually gifted player, such as LeBron James, has a competitive advantage. The small number of players who are on the court at any one time adds a premium to rare talent in basketball. In soccer, even an extraordinarily gifted player such as Lionel Messi represents only one-eleventh of his team's resources at any one time.

Between-Season Variation

For baseball fans everywhere, spring is a special time of year that brings the promise of a new baseball season and the chance that "this could be the year" that their team wins it all. Across seasons, competitive balance implies that each team can realistically compete for the championship. This type of competitive balance is called turnover, or team-specific variation. It differs from within-season variation in that it considers the change in the relative positions of the teams in the standings each year rather than the distance between teams in each season. Brad Humphreys (2002) defines team-specific variation for a team as:

$$\sigma_{T,i} = \sqrt{\frac{\sum_{i=1}^{T}(WPCT_i - \overline{WPCT})^2}{T}},$$

where T is the number of seasons, and $\overline{WPCT}$ is the team's average winning percentage over the T seasons.[20] The larger $\sigma_{T,i}$ becomes, the more a team's fortunes change from year to year. If team i always finished with the same record, $s_{T,i}$ would be zero. If fans support only teams that have a reasonable chance of winning their division or conference, variation across seasons is vital to maintaining fan interest over long stretches of time. If $\sigma_{T,i}$ were zero for all teams, we would know how all teams would perform before the season even started. Such a situation would surely reduce demand for all teams.

One frustrating aspect of using the variation between seasons is that, unlike the within-season standard deviation, there is no obvious standard of comparison. We cannot say whether fans or owners care more about how much their team's winning percentage varies across the years or how their team's position changes relative to other teams. For example, would Philadelphia hockey fans be happier if the Flyers had a very good record instead of a mediocre record but finished second to the New Jersey Devils every year or if they won the Stanley Cup once every few years but finished in last place every other year? Though turnover is important, the absence of an absolute standard means that team-specific variation is useful only as a relative measure of dispersion (when comparing one time period with another or one sport with another).

Frequency of Championships

We can also evaluate competitive balance by looking at the frequency with which teams win successive championships. At one extreme, if the San Jose Sharks win the Stanley Cup almost every year, then the winning percentages of the teams in the league may not matter as much, since the ultimate outcome is seldom in doubt. At the other extreme, if a different team wins the Stanley Cup every year, then one can argue that competition is balanced regardless of how unequal the teams' records are. This criterion is similar to the turnover criterion discussed above, but it relates to championships rather than regular season standings.

The data in Table 5.4 provide an interesting contrast to the within-season data in Table 5.3. While the NHL appears to be the most competitive league within a single season, it is the least balanced league in North America when it comes to championships. Just 3 of the 30 teams won 70 percent of the championships in the 10-year period ending in 2016. In the NBA, the within-season competitive balance was by far the worst of any league in Table 5.3, but Table 5.4 shows no team winning more than two championships. As noted in the previous section, the distribution of championships in the European soccer leagues is highly skewed toward a few dominant teams. In all four leagues, just one team won at least half the championships over the ten-year span. In many of those championships, the runner-up is also one of the teams featured in the table. For example, in La Liga, nine of the ten championships listed in the table featured

Table 5.4 Distribution of Championships, 2006–2007 to 2015–2016

NBA	NFL	MLB	NHL
Miami 2	NY Giants 2	San Francisco 3	Chicago 3
LA Lakers 2	New England 1	St. Louis 2	Pittsburgh 2
San Antonio 2	Denver 1	Chicago Cubs 1	LA Kings 2
Cleveland 1	Seattle 1	Kansas City 1	Boston 1
Golden State 1	Baltimore 1	Boston 1	Detroit 1
Dallas 1	Green Bay 1	NY Yankees 1	Anaheim 1
Boston 1	New Orleans 1	Phillies 1	
	Pittsburgh 1		
	Indianapolis 1		
HHI = 0.16	HHI = 0.13	HHI = 0.18	HHI = 0.20
Bundesliga	La Liga	EPL	Serie A
Bayern Munich 6	Barcelona 6	Man. United 5	Juventus FL 5
Borussia Dortmund 2	Real Madrid 3	Man. City 2	Internazionale 4
Vfl Wolfsburg 1	Atletico Madrid 1	Chelsea 2	AC Milan 1
Vfb Stuttgart 1		Leicester City 1	
HHI = 0.42	HHI = 0.46	HHI = 0.34	HHI = 0.42

either Barcelona or Real Madrid as the runner-up. No matter how balanced the competition was over the course of the season, either Barcelona or Real Madrid probably won the league championship. To the extent that teams can "buy championships" because they have more revenue than their competitors, differences in market size and team popularity may be to blame. Recall from Chapter 3 that most European leagues share a much lower percentage of revenue than North American leagues. We return to the influence of revenue sharing on competitive balance later in the chapter.

The Herfindahl-Hirschman Index

Counting the number of teams that win a championship in a given period suggests that the NHL is more balanced than the NFL and that the EPL is more balanced than Serie A. Unfortunately, simply counting the number of teams that have won in a given time period does not provide a single value that measures this variation. Fortunately, there is a statistic that does. The Herfindahl-Hirschman Index (HHI) was originally developed to measure the concentration of firms in an industry, but sports economists use it to measure the concentration of league championships.

We calculate the HHI by counting the number of championships (c_i) team i won within a given period, dividing by the number of years in the period (T), squaring this fraction, and adding the fractions for all teams:

$$HHI = \sum_i \left(\frac{c_i}{T}\right)^2$$

The maximum, 1.0, indicates perfect imbalance. If the number of years exceeds the number of teams in the league or conference, then the minimum value of the HHI is $1/N$, where N is the number of teams in the league. For shorter periods of time, the minimum value is $1/T$. Thus, the value of the HHI for the NHL (0.13) is very close to the minimum possible level (0.10) for a ten-year period. The NHL could not have been much more competitive by this standard. To see this, consider two leagues, each with five teams. In one league, each team has won two championships over the last ten years. In the other league, one team has won all the championships. The HHI for each league is:

$$HHI_1 = \left[\left(\frac{2}{10}\right)^2 + \left(\frac{2}{10}\right)^2 + \left(\frac{2}{10}\right)^2 + \left(\frac{2}{10}\right)^2 + \left(\frac{2}{10}\right)^2\right] = \frac{20}{100} = \frac{1}{5}$$

$$HHI_2 = \left[\left(\frac{10}{10}\right)^2 + \left(\frac{0}{10}\right)^2 + \left(\frac{0}{10}\right)^2 + \left(\frac{0}{10}\right)^2 + \left(\frac{0}{10}\right)^2\right] = \frac{100}{100} = 1$$

The HHI for the eight leagues in Table 5.4 appears beneath each list of champions. As expected, the HHI values for the European leagues are far greater than for any North American league. This lack of competitive balance combined with the extraordinary popularity of European soccer provides additional evidence that fans may be less concerned with competitive balance than one might think.

Illustrating Competitive Imbalance

Thus far, we have measured competitive balance with purely statistical measures. In this section, we show how to express competitive balance graphically. To do so, we use an economic tool known as the Lorenz curve. Initially created to show income inequality, the Lorenz curve illustrates how evenly distributed any resource or characteristic is in a population.

The Lorenz curve is often used to show income inequality by illustrating the percentage of income earned by a given percentage of the population. For example, if the poorest 10 percent of the population earns just 3 percent of total income and the richest 10 percent of the population earns 25 percent of total income, we can see that income is highly concentrated among the wealthy. In this application, we show the cumulative winning percentage of the teams in a league, divided into deciles. In a league with perfectly equal competition, 10 percent of the teams would earn 10 percent of the wins (or points), 20 percent of the teams would earn 20 percent of the wins, and so on. The more unbalanced the competition, the smaller the percentage of wins or points earned by the weakest teams.

Consider the 2015–2016 regular season in the NHL and La Liga. Because draws are possible and NHL teams earn points for overtime losses, we analyze the number of points earned in each decile as a fraction of the total points accumulated in each league in that year rather than counting wins. We know from Table 5.3 that in 2015–2016, the NHL was the most balanced and La Liga was one of the least balanced of the eight leagues we considered. The three weakest teams (i.e. the lowest 10 percent) in the NHL combined to earn about 7.8 percent of the total points earned in the NHL that season, and the weakest 20 percent earned 16.3 percent. In La Liga, the weakest 10 percent of teams earned only about 6.5 percent of the points, and the weakest 20 percent earned just 13.8 percent, far less than the 20 percent we would observe with perfect equality. Plotting these points for each decile up to the 10th (100 percent of the wins) creates the Lorenz curve. In Figure 5.2, we see the Lorenz curves for both the NHL and La Liga. Notice that the curve for La Liga lies below that of the NHL. The less balanced the competition, the more the curve bows downwards. For comparison, Lorenz curve graphs include the line of perfect equality, a straight 45-degree line from the lower left to the upper right. Along this line, each decile of teams earns 10 percent of the wins. However, while the Lorenz curve provides an

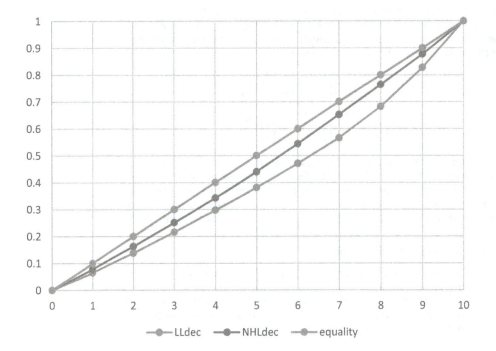

Figure 5.2
The Lorenz Curves for
La Liga and the NHL,
2015–2016

The lower Lorenz curve for La
Liga shows that competitive
balance was worse than in the
NHL in 2015–2016.

easy-to-read graphic of competitive balance, it makes no claim regarding the desirability of this outcome. As discussed earlier, the optimal distribution of wins may well favor larger-market teams.

In sum, there are many ways to measure competitive balance, and no single method should be regarded as most appropriate. To fully grasp the state of competitive balance in a league, one must consider intra-season balance—the spread of winning percentages across teams—and inter-season balance, which includes both the turnover of teams in the standings and the frequency of championships. In the next section, we discuss ways in which leagues attempt to alter competitive balance.

5.3 Attempts to Alter Competitive Balance

All major North American sports leagues have developed policies designed to promote competitive balance. In this section, we discuss three such policies: revenue sharing, salary caps and luxury taxes, and the reverse-order draft.[21] The draft is meant to equalize competition over time by allocating new talent in a systematic way toward weaker teams. Revenue sharing and salary limitations are designed to limit the advantages of big-market teams by reducing the benefits or increasing the costs that big-market teams face when pursuing talent. Whatever impact these policies have on competitive balance, many players believe that the true goal is to depress salaries. We analyze the impact of these policies on salaries in Chapter 9. In this section, we focus on their impact on competitive balance. Before we begin, we discuss an important economic principle that speaks directly to the effectiveness of such efforts.

The Invariance Principle

Many of the tools we consider in this section are designed to limit the impact of **free agency** (the right of a player to sell his services to the highest bidder) on the distribution of talent. Team owners have consistently asserted that free agency and competitive balance cannot coexist. Economic theory, however, says that free agency should have no impact on competitive balance. A basic principle of economics is that freely functioning markets distribute resources to where they are most highly valued. Changing **property rights**—the ownership or control of resources—affects who gets paid but not where the resources are employed. The fact that the allocation of resources does not vary when property rights change is known as the **invariance principle**, which was first applied to sport over 50 years ago by Simon Rottenberg.[22]

To see how the invariance principle works, consider how the International Olympic Committee (IOC) might allocate tickets for the 2020 Summer Olympics in Tokyo. Japanese officials are confident that the opening ceremonies can attract far more than the 50,000 tickets available at the new National Stadium in Tokyo. As seen in Figure 5.3, the opening ceremonies would sell out if tickets cost $150. (For simplicity, we assume that all seats are equally valuable.) Suppose the IOC decides that $150 is too much to charge and declares that tickets will cost only $10. At a price of $10, however, 500,000 people are willing and able to buy tickets. At that price, the IOC must ration the tickets. It could, for example, institute a lottery in which 50,000 people are chosen at random. Those lucky winners can buy tickets for $10.

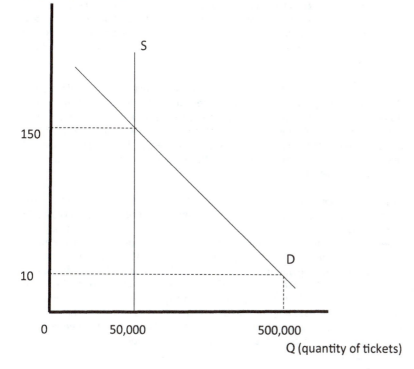

$p (price per ticket)

Figure 5.3
The Market for Tickets to the Opening Ceremonies at the 2018 Olympics

At the equilibrium price of $150, the IOC can sell exactly 50,000 seats. At a price of $10, there is an excess demand of 450,000.

The invariance principle says that, as long as people are free to transact with one another, the final allocation of tickets will be the same under both the free market and the lottery. Suppose, for example, that Barry is willing to pay $300 for a ticket, while Ann won a ticket, which she values at $20. As we saw in Chapter 2, Barry and Ann can become better off if Barry buys the ticket at a price between $20 and $300. For example, if Barry pays Ann $150, he enjoys a consumer surplus of $150 and Ann enjoys a producer surplus of $130.

More generally, if people are free to transact with one another, there are two results. First, the market price of a ticket rises from the official price of $10 to the free market price $150. Second, because the market price is $150, only consumers who place a value of at least $150 on a ticket attend the game, just as with the free market solution. By transferring the property rights to the ticket holders, the IOC has not altered the ultimate distribution of tickets. It has simply changed who gets paid for them.

In the context of professional sports, consider the case of Bryce Harper, the star outfielder for the Washington Nationals, who will be a free agent in 2018. One of the top young stars in baseball, Harper is a popular draw and would add greatly to the gate and media revenue of any team for which he plays. In a midsize city like Washington, DC, he might generate $15 million per year in additional revenue. However, in a much larger, wealthier metropolitan area, such as greater Los Angeles (which has twice the population of the Washington, DC, consolidated metropolitan area), Harper would add considerably more. As a free agent, Harper will be able to sell his services to the highest bidder, and the Nationals may well lose out to the Dodgers because they will be willing to pay Harper as much as $30 million per year.

Consider now what would happen in a world in which players are not free to move but profit-maximizing owners were free to sell the rights to players' services for cash or payment in kind. The Dodgers would still get Harper because they were willing to pay the Nationals more than he was worth to DC but less than he was worth to Los Angeles. As a result, both teams profit.

This example shows that property rights do not affect where top players like Bryce Harper play. They do, however, determine whom the Dodgers pay to obtain his services. Under free agency, the player owns the rights to his services. In such a world, the Dodgers lure Harper from DC to Los Angeles by offering him a higher salary. If Harper were unable to move freely, the Dodgers would not have to worry about enticing Harper to Los Angeles. Instead, they would have to pay the Nationals.

In some situations, the invariance principle fails to hold. For our purposes, the most important situation occurs when there are substantial transaction costs. As the term suggests, a **transaction cost** is the expense of dealing with a buyer or seller in a market *in addition to* the price one pays for the good or service. Returning to our Olympics ticket example, suppose Barry had to take out a $200 advertisement in the newspaper to find Ann. He would face a market price of $150 plus a transaction cost of $200. Because the ticket is worth only $150 to Barry, the transaction cost would discourage Barry from buying the ticket. More generally, when there are substantial transaction costs, resources might not flow to their most valued use. In this section, we analyze several ways in which leagues have imposed transaction costs that prevent the free flow of players to their most valued positions.

Revenue Sharing

As we showed in Chapter 3, revenue sharing equalizes teams' profits. Some team owners also claim that they need revenue sharing to equalize the demand for talent. As the magnitude of revenue and the variety of revenue sources continue to increase, leagues have initiated an increasingly sophisticated array of revenue-sharing mechanisms that typically treat league-wide revenue differently from local revenue. Because revenue sharing is explained in detail in Chapter 3, we review it only briefly here.

The NFL has extensive revenue sharing. Teams share equally in the large national television revenue. With very little local media revenue, this has been a strong equalizer. While less important than it used to be, the 60–40 split of gate revenue described in Chapter 3 still has a big impact.

The most recent NBA contract substantially increased the amount of revenue shared by teams.[23] In addition to sharing national television and sponsorship revenue, all teams submit up to 50 percent of their revenue, less certain expenses, to a common pool, from which they receive an amount equal to the average payroll. Teams that contribute less than the average payroll are net receivers of income, while high-revenue teams, which contribute more, are "net payers."[24]

Since the early 2000s, MLB has significantly increased the degree of revenue sharing. Beginning with the 2002 labor agreement, teams now pay 31 percent of their net local revenue (which includes gate and local broadcasting revenue) into a pool that is divided equally among the 30 teams. They also redistribute a portion of the Central Fund, which includes all non-local revenue (i.e., national television revenue), which helps to even out revenue disparities. Teams with larger local revenues receive smaller shares, while the teams with smaller local revenues receive larger shares.[25] The 2012 agreement phased in additional provisions. Teams in the 15 (later reduced to 13) largest markets are ineligible for shares even if they have low local revenues.[26] Further, teams are not allowed to use these revenues to pay down team debt (and so increase profits), and have to report how the funds increase team quality.[27] To the extent that these new restrictions induce net recipients to increase player quality, they increase competitive balance.

Following the 2004–2005 lockout, the NHL adopted a complex formula that makes transfers from high-revenue teams to low-revenue teams to equalize payrolls. In order to qualify for these revenues, a team must be among the bottom 15 in revenue and play in a city with a media base of less than approximately 2 million people.[28]

Interestingly, the model shown in Figure 5.1 predicts that if teams are profit maximizers, revenue sharing will not increase competitive balance, as shared revenue represents a tax on wins for all teams, shifting MR_L and MR_S downwards equally and leaving the distribution of wins unchanged. Research by John Solow and Anthony Krautmann supports this prediction.[29] Revenue sharing increases competitive balance if teams that receive revenue use it to improve the quality of the team (i.e., maximize wins).[30]

From a league-wide profitability standpoint, revenue sharing is problematic because the entire league benefits when large-market teams win more often. To see why, think of revenue sharing as a tax on big-market teams and a subsidy to small-market teams. At its most extreme, the tax/subsidy system equates all incomes, effectively directing all revenue to a central pool from which each team takes an equal share. Even if post-tax revenues are all equal, the central pool is larger if big-market teams win more often. If the central pool is larger, then the post-tax payment to all teams—small-market as well as big-market—is larger. Thus, all teams have a financial interest in the success of big-market teams.

Salary Caps and Luxury Taxes

Of the major North American sports leagues, only MLB does not have a salary cap. A **salary cap** restricts the amount a team is allowed to pay its players. In Chapter 9, we will see how caps affect payrolls. Here, we focus on their impact on competitive balance. The term "salary cap" is a misnomer for two reasons. First, its principal target is *payrolls*, not individual salaries. Second, salary caps are accompanied by minimum salary levels. Together, the two create a band, setting both a ceiling and a floor on what teams can spend on players. Most of the attention has focused on the ceilings, which were $155.27 million in the NFL (exclusive of carry-overs from the previous season), $71.4 million in the NHL, and $70 million in the NBA for the 2016 (2015–2016) season. The minimum payrolls are approximately $138 million in the NFL, $52.8 million in the NHL, and $63 million for the NBA.[31] While the caps restrict spending, the minimum payroll values prevent teams from substantially under-investing in talent. In contrast to most North American leagues, the major European soccer leagues do not control team salaries. In the EPL, for example, 2016–2017 payrolls varied from a high of $335 million (Manchester City) to a low of just $25 million (Hull City).[32] The disparities in other soccer leagues are similar.

The big difference between the salary restrictions in the NFL and the NBA is that NFL payrolls have a hard cap, while NBA payrolls have a soft cap. A **hard cap** is an absolute limit. NFL teams must stay within the limits of the cap. A **soft cap** has exceptions to the limits that the cap imposes. The three most important exceptions in the NBA's soft cap are the mid-level exception, the rookie exception, and the Larry Bird exception.

The mid-level exception allows each team to sign one player to the average NBA salary even if the team is already over the salary limit or if signing a player to such a contract puts the team over the limit. Under the rookie exception, a team can sign a rookie to his first contract even if doing so puts the team over its cap limit. The Larry Bird exception permits teams to re-sign players who are already on their roster even if doing so exceeds the cap limit. This rule got its name because its first use permitted the Boston Celtics to re-sign their star player in 1983. That year, the Celtics were loaded with stars, and a hard cap would have forced the Celtics to break up this very popular team to re-sign Larry Bird. To avoid this, the NBA softened the cap, permitting the Celtics to keep their team intact. The soft cap may explain why competitive balance in the NBA is so low. A soft cap makes it easier for teams to stock up on and retain talented players.

Because the exceptions have undermined the soft cap, the NBA has developed a number of supplemental measures to reinforce it. These include caps on salaries that teams can pay individual players and a luxury tax. The cap on individual salaries classifies players according to their years of experience and specifies maximum and minimum salaries that a team can pay players with a given amount of experience.

A **luxury tax** has nothing to do with luxury boxes; it is a surcharge the league imposes on teams whose payroll exceeds a specified level. The 2011 collective bargaining agreement (CBA) significantly tightened the NBA's luxury tax. Prior to 2012–2013, teams that exceeded the cap had to pay a $1 tax for every $1 by which they exceeded the cap. Now, teams must pay a tax rate that increases for every $5 million by which they exceed the cap. For example, a first-time offending team that is $15 million over the cap used to pay a $15 million tax but now must pay a $28.75 million (1.5 × $5million + 1.75 × 5million + 2.5 × $5million) tax. Penalties are greater still for teams that exceeded the cap in three of the four previous seasons.[33]

Baseball's luxury tax (now known as a "competitive balance tax") also charges teams for having a payroll above a pre-specified threshold (starting at $178 million in 2011–2013, and rising over time to $197 million in 2018, then up to $210 million by 2021). Like the NBA, MLB charges a higher tax rate to repeat offenders. Teams that exceed the threshold for the first time pay a 20 percent tax rate. Subsequent violations increase the tax rate to 30 percent for a two-time violator and then to 50 percent for teams exceeding the threshold three or more times.[34] In addition, beginning with the 2017 CBA, teams that exceed the threshold by more than $20 million pay another 12 percent in tax, while teams with payrolls more than $40 million over the maximum pay an additional 45 percent competitive balance tax. In total, a team with a large payroll and multiple violations could pay as much as a 95% tax on any payroll above the threshold. In 2016 a record-high six teams were subject to the tax: the Yankees, Tigers, Red Sox, Giants, Cubs, and Dodgers. Between 2003 and 2016, the Yankees have paid the luxury tax every year, with total payments exceeding $325 million.[35] The Yankees' continued willingness to exceed the threshold indicates that the luxury tax has had a limited impact on their behavior. Another important difference between the luxury taxes in the NBA and MLB is in the distribution of the collected tax revenues. In the NBA, luxury tax revenues are distributed to non-violators (though there is room in the contract language for the league to keep 50 percent or more for "league purposes"). These distributions increase the revenue of teams who follow the salary cap. In MLB, tax revenues are not redistributed to teams but instead go to player benefits and the Industry Growth Fund.

The Reverse-Order Entry Draft

The reverse-order entry draft allows teams to select amateur players in reverse order from their finish of the previous season. The team with the worst record chooses first, the second-worst team chooses second, and so on, until the team that won the previous season's championship chooses last. The same procedure continues through subsequent rounds. All players not chosen in the draft are free to sign contracts with any team.

The origin of the draft can be traced to 1934, when two NFL teams—the old Brooklyn Dodgers and the Philadelphia Eagles—competed for the services of Stan Kostka, an All-American player at the University of Minnesota. The resulting bidding war drove salary offers to the then-unbelievable level of $5,000 (what Bronko Nagurski—the greatest player of the era—made). At the next annual league meeting, Bert Bell, the Philadelphia Eagles owner, proposed a unique way to avoid future bidding wars. Teams would select the rights to unsigned players, with the order of selection determined by each team's performance in the previous season.

The dubious impact of the reverse draft on competitive balance and the clear limitations drafts place on the market power of drafted players have led critics to claim that the reverse-order draft is nothing more than a tool to keep players' salaries low. It might be no coincidence that Bert Bell's Eagles were a last-place team when he proposed the draft. Still, some teams gave up a considerable advantage by agreeing to the draft. The New York Giants and the Chicago Bears, two teams from the biggest markets at the time, dominated the NFL's early years. Sacrificing the right to bid against other teams was not in their immediate self-interest, as the Giants and Bears could have outbid all other teams for any player they desired. However, the owners of the Giants and Bears recognized that a larger issue was at stake. In the words of Tim Mara, the owner of the Giants at the time, "People come to see a competition. We could give them a competition only if the teams had some sort of equality."[36]

All the major North American leagues now have a reverse-order draft. Partly because NBA rosters are so small—each team has only 12 players on its active roster—the NBA draft lasts only two rounds. Because other leagues have larger squads, and because success at the professional level has traditionally been harder to predict, they have longer drafts: the NHL draft lasts 5 rounds, the NFL draft lasts 7 rounds, and the MLB draft lasts 40 rounds or until all teams decide to stop drafting players.

Evaluating the Reverse-Order Draft

In theory, reverse-order drafts promote competitive balance by allocating the best new players to the weakest teams. However, its success in equalizing talent depends on the teams' motivations—a draft is most effective if all teams are win-maximizers—and on the ability of teams to identify and develop talented players. Some teams (such as the NFL's New England Patriots) consistently find talented players despite having poor draft picks, while other teams regularly fail to find good players despite having excellent draft positions.[37]

Because the reverse-order draft rewards failure with high draft picks, it can worsen competitive balance. As teams fall out of competition, they could begin to lose deliberately so as to improve their position in a future draft.[38] In recent years, this strategy has been made somewhat famous (or infamous) by the Philadelphia 76ers, who developed a long-term strategy that became known as "the process." Unfortunately for Philadelphia fans, the process involved winning just 19 games in 2013–2014 and only 10 games in 2014–2015. During this time period, the team was widely regarded as making little effort to win in an effort to secure the top draft picks. In response to concerns that teams may be losing intentionally, the NBA and NHL have instituted lottery systems in which teams with the worst records have the best chance of securing the top draft pick but are not sure to get it. A lottery reduces the incentive to lose games intentionally, but it also reduces the possibility that the weakest teams benefit most from the draft. For example, the NBA's Orlando Magic won the 1993 draft lottery despite having the best record of any team eligible for the lottery.

Evaluating Talent: The Oakland Athletics and Moneyball

In the early 2000s, the management of the Oakland Athletics baseball team found a new way to evaluate talent. Despite being a quintessential small-market team that regularly had among the lowest revenues and payroll in MLB, the Athletics became a consistent winner. They finished first in their division four times between 2000 and 2006 and finished second the other three years.[39]

Michael Lewis analyzed the Athletics' astonishing run in the best-selling book and hit movie *Moneyball*.[40] Lewis attributes much of the Athletics' success to their GM, Billy Beane. Lewis claims that Beane stood much of the conventional wisdom regarding player evaluation on its head.[41] Teams traditionally looked for "five-tool" players who could run fast, throw far, field well, have a high batting average, and hit the ball hard. The standard yardstick for the two latter tools was slugging percentage, which measures a player's total bases per at bat. A player who hits a lot of home runs will, all else equal, have a much higher slugging percentage than a player who hits a lot of singles. Beane, a follower of baseball statistician Bill James, claimed that the key to success lay in a team's getting on base as often as possible, which is best measured by on-base percentage.[42] Lewis asserts that, while traditional scouts look for physically gifted athletes, Beane looked for players who were disciplined and received a lot of bases on balls (walks), even if they were not much to look at in a uniform.

In an economic analysis of *Moneyball*, Hakes and Sauer find evidence to support Lewis's claim that Beane found an unexploited market imperfection.[43] Applying multiple regression analysis, they show that, prior to the success of the A's, increasing a team's on-base percentage contributed more to wins than increasing its slugging percentage. Using salaries to measure the value that teams place on a player's characteristics, they also show that teams generally valued slugging percentage more highly than on-base percentage. Emphasizing on-base percentage allowed Beane to acquire players whose contribution to success had been undervalued by other teams. This gave the Athletics a competitive advantage and allowed them to win consistently with far lower payrolls than other teams.

Unfortunately, the Athletics could not translate their success in the regular season to a World Series appearance. As Beane himself admits, his strategy was better suited to a 162-game season than to a 7-game series.[44] More importantly, as in any competitive market, the first mover enjoys a relatively brief advantage. Hakes and Sauer demonstrate that the relative valuation of slugging percentage and on-base percentage had begun to shift by 2004. With wealthier teams now applying Bill James's principles, the Athletics were relegated to also-ran status by 2007.

The ability of teams in other sports to adopt and profit from the advanced analytics—*Moneyball*—approach has been widely debated. The advantage of such analysis in baseball is that performance of the players is often separable. For example, no other players directly assist a batter in hitting a home run. Bill Gerard argued that to transfer the analytical approach to what he calls "complex invasion sports," such as ice hockey, basketball, and soccer, analysts must resolve three measurement problems: tracking, attribution, and weighting. These amount to tracking the actions of various players both in and out of possession of the ball or puck, attributing productivity to those actions, and then weighting that contribution to success.[45] David Berri, Martin Schmidt, and Stacey Brook published the first significant contribution to the body of work on this subject in their well-known book *The Wages of Wins*. Similar to *Moneyball*'s view of baseball, they conclude that NBA team owners make systematic errors in signing and paying players because they are too focused on scoring totals instead of efficient use of possessions.

Schedule Adjustments in the NFL

The NFL has a unique approach to increasing parity across seasons, which is unrelated to player movement or salaries. Each team's schedule is determined in part by its performance in the previous season. Each team plays 16 games, 14 of which are independent of its prior success. It plays the other three teams in its own division twice, all four teams in another division of its conference, plus all four teams from one division in the other conference. The remaining two games are intended to increase balance and are based on the team's performance in the previous season. The first-place team in each division plays the first-place teams in the two divisions (within conference) that the team is not scheduled to play, the second-place team plays the two other second-place teams, and so on. As a result, stronger teams play tougher schedules and weaker teams play easier schedules the following year, creating a natural tendency toward parity.

Promotion and Relegation

The promotion and relegation system provides an additional incentive mechanism that may increase competitive balance. We saw that top European leagues, such as the EPL and the Bundesliga, have competitive balance ratios that are second only to the NHL, North America's most balanced league. Yet, if we use frequency of championships as the measure of balance, Table 5.3 provides strong evidence that these same leagues are among the least competitive. The promotion and relegation system helps explain this puzzle.

When a team in a closed league is having a bad season and stands to finish near the bottom of the standings, it may not have much incentive to win. Once eliminated from the playoffs, the team may use the remaining games to invest in future seasons, trying out new players from its minor league system and trading or selling off top players to playoff-bound teams in search of an edge. Thus, the winning percentage of the poor team may erode further, increasing the standard deviation of winning percentage.

In an open league, teams near the bottom of the standings have no such luxury. If they let their performance slide further, they may be relegated to a lower league. Teams that are near the bottom of the standings have an incentive to play to win right to the end. Thus, promotion and relegation may not increase turnover of the league champion, but it may decrease the standard deviation of wins within the league.

Biographical Sketch

Bud Selig
(1934–)

> *Selig listened and questioned and murmured empathetically, all of the things he did best.*
>
> —John Helyar[46]

Perhaps no person symbolizes the struggle over competitive balance more than baseball Commissioner Alan H. ("Bud") Selig. Selig served as the commissioner of Major League Baseball from 1998 to 2015. After stepping down, he was given the title of Commissioner Emeritus.

Selig's Wisconsin roots run deep. Born in Milwaukee, he graduated from the University of Wisconsin, Madison in 1956 and, after serving in the military for two years, joined his father's automobile business. Business proved so good that, when major league baseball came to Milwaukee, Selig was able to act on his love of baseball by becoming a stockholder in the Milwaukee Braves. Selig's ties, however, were to the Milwaukee Braves. When the team moved to Atlanta in 1965, Selig promptly sold his stock and formed a group dedicated to bringing a new team to Milwaukee. His efforts bore fruit when the Seattle Pilots, a badly financed expansion team, went bankrupt after the 1970 season. Selig immediately bought the team for $10.8 million and moved it to Milwaukee, renaming it the Brewers.

With Selig as their president, the Brewers gained a reputation as an exemplary organization, and the team came within a game of winning the 1982 World Series. The Brewers' performance on and off the field led Selig to play a growing role in the governance of MLB's affairs. When the owners forced Fay Vincent to resign as commissioner in 1992, Selig, as chairman of the owners' executive council, effectively took over the duties of commissioner. For the next six years, Selig walked a tightrope, serving the interests of all of baseball while working to advance the interests of his own Milwaukee Brewers. Finally, in July 1998, Selig's fellow owners elected him as commissioner. Selig then put his holdings in the Brewers into a blind trust and turned over operations of the Brewers to his daughter Wendy Selig-Preib.

Selig's popularity with his fellow owners and his insistence on consensus brought the owners unprecedented cohesion. That enabled him to introduce a variety of innovations designed to bring greater excitement to the game. Under his tenure, baseball raised the number of divisions per league from two to three, increasing the number of teams in the postseason. The number was further increased by the introduction of a "wildcard" playoff team (which has won the World Series six times since it was instituted). He also oversaw greater consolidation of the American and National Leagues, whose war of the early 1900s did not fully end until Selig brought both leagues under the authority of the commissioner's office in 2000.

Most importantly, by bringing the often-fractious owners together, Selig reversed a trend of over 20 years. All labor stoppages prior to Selig's becoming commissioner had ended with the owners capitulating. The 1994–1995 strike effectively ended in a draw, with neither side achieving its aims. In the near-strike of 2002, the owners forced the players' association to blink and to approve a revenue-sharing plan and luxury tax that it had bitterly opposed. This marked ownership's first outright victory in negotiations since labor negotiations began in 1972. Sadly, the 1994–1995 strike caused the cancellation of the 1994 World Series, something two world wars had failed to do. The willingness of owners to forgo the rest of the season severely tarnished the game's reputation.

The resurgence of baseball's popularity in the late 1990s has since been marred by allegations that many of the period's greatest stars used performance-enhancing drugs. The allegations of drug use and the weak antidrug stance by MLB led to Congressional hearings at which Selig, union representatives, and star players were subjected to embarrassing questions on national television. In response, Selig played an instrumental role in the development and enforcement of a strong anti-doping policy, including a first-ever in US professional sports policy on human growth hormones in 2010.

Selig stepped down as commissioner in 2015, turning the reins over to Robert Manfred. Because of his controversial record, some see Selig as a man who saved the game, while others feel that he was ill-suited to be anything other than the owner of a small-market team. Whatever one's opinion of him, few can deny that he has had a major impact on Major League Baseball.

Sources: Andrew Zimbalist. 2013. *In the Best Interests of Baseball? Governing the National Pastime* (Lincoln: University of Nebraska Press); *MLB.com.* "Alan H. 'Bud' Selig," Commissioners, at http://mlb.mlb.com/mlb/official_info/about_mlb/executives.jsp?bio=selig_bud. Accessed March 7, 2017.

Summary

For a league to succeed financially in the long run, it must have a semblance of even competition among teams. At the same time, recent research shows that teams' aversion to losing causes them to prefer lopsided wins to unexpected losses. Given that the value of a win is much greater in large cities, it is unlikely that leagues would maximize revenue from perfect parity across teams, and they would likely do better to have better teams in cities where demand for the sport is greatest.

Fans and owners both have an interest in competitive balance. The perception that fans are less likely to follow a league in which a few teams win most of the games or championships gives owners a financial stake in maintaining competitive balance. Policies aimed at increasing competitive balance are generated by the central league office as individual teams always prefer winning to losing.

There are several ways to measure competitive balance, no one of which is necessarily better than the others. A popular measure of within-season balance is the ratio of the standard deviation of winning percentages to the "ideal" standard deviation that would prevail if all teams were equally talented. A popular measure of cross-season balance is the Herfindahl-Hirschman index, which shows how narrowly concentrated championships have been over a given time period. By both measures, MLB is relatively competitive compared to other sports. This contradicts the claims of MLB owners that baseball has had a competitive balance crisis since the advent of free agency.

Economic theory predicts that free agency will not affect the distribution of talent in a sport as long as the team owners maximize profit, players maximize income, and transaction costs are low. Sports leagues have implemented several policies—such as revenue sharing, salary caps, luxury taxes, and the reverse-order draft—to increase transaction costs and limit the movement of players from small-market to big-market teams. These measures have met with uneven success.

Discussion Questions

1 How far should leagues go to ensure parity among teams?
2 What means more to you, occasionally winning the championship or being competitive every year?
3 Should MLB adopt a system of promotion and relegation?
4 Why do European soccer fans follow their teams with such passion even though most have little chance of winning a championship?

Problems

5.1 Suppose, as an owner, you could leave the highly competitive league (in terms of closeness of contests) that you currently play in and enter a league that assured that your team would never lose again. Would you want to do so? Why or why not?
5.2 Based on the work of Coates, Humphreys, and Zhou, it appears that hometown fans are happy to see lopsided wins. Yet at the league level, it appears that competitive balance is crucial. How can we resolve the apparent contradiction?
5.3 Explain how the law of diminishing returns provides a natural tendency toward competitive balance.
5.4 Suppose in a six-team league, the winning percentages were as follows at the end of the season—Team A: .750, Team B: .600, Team C: .500, Team D: .500, Team E: .400, Team F: .250. Compute the standard deviation of winning percentages.
5.5 In question 4, suppose each team plays a 50-game schedule. Compute the "ideal" standard deviation based on equal playing strength, and the ratio of the actual to the ideal.
5.6 If the NFL increased its schedule from 16 to 36 games, what would the new benchmark ideal standard deviation be (assuming equal playing strength)?
5.7 Why do many economists believe that free agency has not affected competitive balance?
5.8 Draw a graph that recreates the Lorenz curves from Figure 5.2. Based on what you know from this chapter, add a Lorenz curve for the NBA. Why did you place it where you did?
5.9 Suppose that over five seasons, the orders of finish for five teams (A–E) in the West League and the East League are as follows. Use the HHI to determine which league has better competitive balance across seasons.

West League Season					East League Season				
1	2	3	4	5	1	2	3	4	5
A	A	A	E	E	A	B	C	D	E
B	B	D	D	D	E	A	A	A	A
C	C	C	C	C	C	B	D	E	D
D	D	B	B	B	B	D	B	B	B
E	E	E	A	A	D	E	E	C	C

5.10 If you were a fan of Team A, which set of distributions shown in the previous question (West or East) would you prefer? Why?

5.11 Go to the NFL regular season standings for 2017 (http://www.espn.com/nfl/standings/_/season/2017) and compute the standard deviation of winning percentage and the ratio of actual to ideal standard deviation. Was competitive balance in 2017 better or worse than it was in 2016?

Notes

1   Christopher Klein. 2016. "College Football's Most Lopsided Game," *History in the Headlines*, October 7, at http://www.history.com/news/college-footballs-most-lopsided-game. Accessed February 28, 2017.

2   Simon Rottenberg. 1956. "The Baseball Players' Labor Market," *Journal of Political Economy*, 64(3), June: 242–258.

3   Over the four seasons of the AAFC's existence (1946–1949), the Browns won 47 games, lost 4, and tied 3.

4   See Glenn Knowles, Keith Sherony, and Mike Haupert. 1992. "The Demand for Major League Baseball: A Test of the Uncertainty of Outcome Hypothesis," *The American Economist*, 36(2), Fall: 73–80; and Jeffrey Borland and Robert MacDonald. 2003. "Demand for Sport," *Oxford Review of Economic Policy*, 19(4): 478–502. For a different view, see Babatunde Buraimo and Rob Simmons. 2008. "Do Sports Fans Really Value Uncertainty of Outcome? Evidence from the English Premier League," *International Journal of Sport Finance*, 3(3), August: 146–155.

5   Daniel Kahneman won the Nobel Prize in economics based on his work on behavioral economics with Amos Tversky in 2002. Kahneman's 2011 book *Thinking Fast and Slow* describes his work with Tversky, including the development of prospect theory.

6   Dennis Coates, Brad R. Humphreys, and Li Zhou. 2014. "Reference-Dependent Preferences, Loss Aversion, and Live Game Attendance," *Economic Inquiry*, 52(3), July: 959–973.

7   For an excellent discussion of the possible motivations of owners, see A. Zimbalist. 2003. "Sport as Business," *Oxford Review of Economic Policy*, 19(4): 503–511.

8   Dave Berri, Martin Schmidt, and Stacey Brook. 2006. *The Wages of Wins: Taking Measure of the Many Myths in Modern Sport* (Stanford, CA: Stanford University Press).

9   Martin B. Schmidt and David J. Berri. 2002. "Competitive Balance and Market Size in Major League Baseball." *Review of Industrial Organization*, 21(1), August: 41–54.

10 It may also be the case that players may prefer to play in large markets for endorsement reasons, but we do not assume that in the foregoing analysis.

11 Andrew Zimbalist. 2003. *May the Best Team Win: Baseball Economics and Public Policy* (Washington, DC: Brookings Institution Press): 35–36.

12 This model first appeared in Mohamed El-Hodiri and James Quirk. 1971. "An Economic Model of a Professional Sports League," *Journal of Political Economy*, 79(6), November/December: 1302–1319.

13 While no team has won three consecutive Super Bowls, the Green Bay Packers did win three consecutive NFL championships between 1965 and 1967.

14 For more sophisticated views of some of the techniques presented here, see Craig A. Depken II. 1999. "Free-agency and the Competitiveness of Major League Baseball," *Review of Industrial Organization*, 14(3), May: 205–217; Brad Humphreys. 2002. "Alternative Measures of Competitive Balance," *Journal of Sports Economics*, 3(2), May: 133–148; and P. Owen Dorian, Michael Ryan, and Clayton R. Weatherston. 2007. "Measuring Competitive Balance in Professional Team Sports Using the Herfindahl-Hirschman Index," *Journal of Industrial Organization*, 31(4), December: 289–302.

15 When computing the standard deviation of winning percentages for a subset of teams in the league such as a conference or division (as opposed to the population of the whole league), the formula for the standard deviation of a sample should be used instead. To do so, one would divide by N–1 instead of N. Also, if teams play games outside the conference, the average winning percentage may not be exactly .500, and the average winning percentage should be used instead.

16   This is a straightforward application of the binomial distribution.

17   This results from the fact that the variance of the binomial distribution is
$\sigma^2 = \dfrac{p*(1-p)}{N}$, where p is the number of successes and N is the number of trials.

18   See Gerald W. Scully. 1989. *The Business of Major League Baseball* (Chicago, IL: University of Chicago Press) for an early application of this method to professional baseball. We can use the same idea to evaluate competitive balance over many seasons by calculating the average value of the standard deviation over several years and using that value as σ_w when computing R.

19   Berri, Schmidt, and Brook. 2006. *The Wages of Wins*. The arguments presented here are based on a previous paper by David Berri, Stacey Brook, Bernd Frick, Aju Fenn, and Roberto Vicente-Mayoral. 2005. "The Short Supply of Tall People: Explaining Competitive Imbalance in the National Basketball Association," *Journal of Economic Issues*, 39(4), December: 1029–1041.

20   To learn more about the debate over which measures are appropriate and about additional measures of competitive balance see the articles by Brad R. Humphreys and E.W. Eckard in *Journal of Sports Economics*, 4(1) (February 2003).

21   For a more detailed account of how leagues use these tools to promote competitive balance, see Michael A. Leeds. 2008. "Salary Caps and Luxury Taxes in Professional Sports Leagues," in *The Business of Sports*, vol. 2, ed. Brad R. Humphreys and Dennis R. Howard (Westport, CT: Praeger): 181–206.

22   The invariance principle is sometimes attributed to 1991 Nobel Laureate Ronald Coase. However, Coase's contribution was to apply the invariance principle in the context of externalities, a concept we cover in Chapter 7. See Ronald Coase. 1960. "The Problem of Social Cost," *Journal of Law and Economics*, 3(1), October: 1–44. See also Simon Rottenberg. 1956. "The Baseball Players' Labor Market."

23   The collective bargaining agreements for all leagues are discussed in detail in Chapter 10. In this section, we limit the discussion to the portions of the agreements that relate to competitive balance.

24   John Lombardo. 2012. "Inside NBA's Revenue Sharing: How Complex Plan Will Shift $140 million to Needy Teams," *Street and Smith's Sports Business Journal*, January 23, at http://www.sportsbusinessdaily.com/Journal/Issues/2012/01/23/Leagues-and-Governing-Bodies/NBA-revenue.aspx, viewed March 13, 2017.

25   According to the collective bargaining agreement that established this process (*2007-2011 Basic Agreement*), the net result is that all teams that pay more than they receive have a "Net Transfer Value" equivalent to that which would result from a 48% straight pool plan (not including the Commissioner's Discretionary Fund). https://ipmall.law.unh.edu/sites/default/files/hosted_resources/SportsEntLaw_Institute/2012MLB_MLBPA_CBA.pdf. Accessed October 21, 2017.

26   "Summary of Major League Baseball Players Association—Major League Baseball Labor Agreement," at http://mlb.mlb.com/mlb/downloads/2011_CBA.pdf. Accessed April 25, 2012; Evan Drellich. 2016. "MLB Changes Market Rank Formula in Revenue Sharing," *The Boston Herald*, December 3, at http://www.bostonherald.com/sports/red_sox/clubhouse_insider/2016/12/mlb_changes_market_rank_formula_in_revenue_sharing. Accessed March 6, 2017.

27   Jason Stark. 2011. "How the New CBA Changes Baseball," *ESPN.com: Baseball*, November 22, at http://espn.go.com/espn/print?id=7270203&type=story. Accessed April 24, 2012.

28   Tim Campbell. 2012. "Jets Will Not Need NHL's Revenue-Sharing." *Winnipeg Free Press*, April 25, at http://www.winnipegfreepress.com/breakingnews/Jets-will-not-need-NHLs-revenue-sharing--146445605.html. Accessed April 25, 2012.

29   John L. Solow and Anthony C. Krautmann. 2007. "Leveling the Playing Field or Just Lowering Salaries? The Effects of Redistribution in Baseball," *Southern Economic Journal*, 73(4), April: 947–958.

30   For an advanced treatment of the differential outcomes resulting from profit maximization versus win maximization, see John Vrooman. 2009. "Theory of the Perfect Game: Competitive Balance in Monopoly Sports," *Review of Industrial Organization*, 34(1), February: 5–44.

31   In the NFL, teams must spend 89 percent of the cap average over four years. In the NBA, teams must spend 90 percent of the cap. Salary cap data are from: Austin Knoblauch. 2016. "NFL Salary Cap Set at $155.27 Million for 2016," *NFL.com*, February 26, at http://www.nfl.com/news/story/0ap3000000639226/article/nfl-salary-cap-set-at-15527-million-for-2016; Mike Chiari, 2015. "NHL Salary Cap Announced for 2015-16 Season," *Bleacher Report*, June 23, at http://bleacherreport.com/articles/2504174-nhl-salary-cap-announced-for-2015-16-season; NBA.com. 2015. "Salary Cap for 2015-16 Season Jumps to $70 Million," July 8, at http://www.nba.com/2015/news/07/08/nba-salary-cap-2016-official-release/. All accessed April 18, 2017.

32   Totalsportek2. 2017. "Premier League Player Salaries of 20 Clubs (Wage Bills 2016-17)," January 20, at http://www.totalsportek.com/money/english-premier-league-wage-bills-club-by-club/. Accessed March 6, 2017.

33   Larry Coon, "Larry Coon's Salary Cap FAQ," at http://www.cbafaq.com/salarycap.htm#Q2. Accessed March 6, 2017.

34   "2017–2021 Basic Agreement," at http://www.mlbplayers.com/pdf9/5450407.pdf: 107–110. Accessed October 21, 2017.

35   USA Today. 2016. "Record Six Teams to Pay Luxury Tax, Led by Dodgers," December 2016, at http://www.usatoday.com/story/sports/mlb/2016/12/16/apnewsbreak-record-6-mlb-teams-to-pay-luxury-tax/95536006/. Accessed March 6, 2017.

36   Michael MacCambridge. 2004. *America's Game: The Epic Story of How Pro Football Captured a Nation* (New York: Random House): 44.

37   Patrick Rishe. 2012, "The Best and Worst NFL Teams Regarding Drafting Proficiency," *Forbes.com*, April 25, at http://www.forbes.com/sites/prishe/2012/04/25/the-best-and-worst-nfl-teams-in-drafting-collegiate-talent/. Accessed May 11, 2012. Perhaps the best selection by the Patriots came in 2000, when they chose future Hall of Fame quarterback Tom Brady in the sixth round of the draft, meaning that all other NFL teams had five or more chances to select Brady before the Patriots chose him.

38   See Beck A. Taylor and Justin G. Trogdon. 2002. "Losing to Win: Tournament Incentives in the National Basketball Association," *Journal of Labor Economics*, 20(1), January: 23–41; and Joseph Price, Brian Soebbing, David Berri, and Brad Humphreys. 2010. "Tournament Incentives, League Policy, and NBA Team Performance Revisited," *Journal of Sports Economics*, 11(2), April: 117–135.

39   They finished second in 2001 despite winning 102 games because the Seattle Mariners won an American League record 116 games.

40   Michael Lewis. 2003. *Moneyball: The Art of Winning an Unfair Game* (New York: Norton).

41   The credit for the approach made famous by Billy Beane belongs at least in part to his predecessor as the A's GM, Sandy Alderson.

42   Slugging percentage is computed as $(1B + 2*2B + 3*3B + 4*HR)/AB$, where $1B$ is the number of singles a player hits, $2B$ is the number of doubles, $3B$ is the number of triples, HR is the number of home runs, and AB is the number of at-bats. On-base percentage equals $(H + BB + HBP)/(AB + BB + HBP + SF)$, where H is the number of hits, BB is the number of bases on balls ("walks"), HBP is the number of times the player was hit by a pitch, and SF is the number of sacrifice flies. Appearances that result in BB, HBP, or SF are not counted as an AB.

43   Jahn Hakes and Raymond Sauer. 2006. "An Economic Evaluation of the *Moneyball* Hypothesis," *Journal of Economic Perspectives*, 20(3) Summer: 173–185.

44   Berri, Schmidt, and Brook. 2006. *The Wages of Wins*.

45   Bill Gerrard. 2007. "Is the *Moneyball* Approach Transferrable to Complex Invasion Sports?" *International Journal of Sport Finance*, 2(4), November: 214–230. The NBA is making headway in this regard as they are now able to track player movement on the court.

46   John Helyar. 1994. *Lords of the Realm* (New York: Villard Books): 505.

Part Three

PUBLIC FINANCE AND SPORTS

6

THE PUBLIC FINANCE OF SPORTS

Who Benefits and How?

The pride and the presence of a professional football team is far more important than 30 libraries.

—ART MODELL, FORMER OWNER OF THE BALTIMORE RAVENS[1]

Introduction

"Build it, and they will come." The vision that worked such wonders for Kevin Costner in *Field of Dreams* has long been a mantra for sports teams at all levels.[2] To the team that occupies it, a new venue means more fans, additional luxury boxes or premium seating, and enhanced gate and venue revenue. However, teams are quick to point out that they are not the only ones to gain. Building a new stadium or attracting a new team seems to have something for everyone.

Many state and local officials see sports facilities as the anchors around which their cities can revive decaying downtown areas.[3] They have visions of tourists drawn to their towns to attend sporting events, of residents staying in central city areas for entertainment and shopping rather than heading for the suburbs, and of local merchants relocating to prosperous downtown sites.

At the same time, sports fans in cities without franchises long for the status of a "big-league" city in which they can at last root for "their" team. Fans who live in cities that already have a franchise hope that a new home will enable the home team to attract free agents that will make their team a winner. Even if they are not sports fans, local construction workers look forward to the jobs created by the extensive building project and members of the hospitality industry eagerly await the fans that will visit—and spend money in—their city.

In the next three chapters of this text, we examine the economic impact of sports venues, sports franchises, and major athletic events, such as the Olympics, Super Bowl, or World Cup. In this chapter, we focus on the benefits that new sports facilities confer on teams, fans, and cities. In Chapter 7, we turn to who pays for the facilities that the teams use and the different ways in which they pay for them. In Chapter 8, we examine the costs and benefits of major sporting events and explore the special history of FIFA and the International Olympic Committee, sponsors of the two biggest sports mega-events in the world.

Learning Objectives

- Show how a new facility can increase a team's revenue stream.
- Recognize how new facilities might make fans better off even if they never attend a game.
- Appreciate how new facilities, new teams, or new events might contribute to a local economy—and why they generally add little.

6.1   How Teams Benefit from New Facilities

Ray Kinsella may have been moved to build a baseball diamond in the middle of his corn field in the movie *Field of Dreams*, but today's sports teams want a bit more. Construction costs for football and baseball stadiums, even hockey arenas, now routinely exceed $1 billion.[4] It was not always so. Ebbets Field, a structure so extravagant that Brooklyn Dodgers' owner Charles Ebbets had to sell half his share of the team to finance it, cost $750,000 when it was built in 1913. Even accounting for inflation, that would come to only a little over $18 million in 2016. As recently as 2002 Gillette Stadium, home of the New England Patriots and the New England Revolution of Major League Soccer, cost $325 million ($432 million in 2016 dollars), one-sixth the cost of the estimated $2.6 billion price tag of the new NFL stadium in Los Angeles scheduled to open in 2020. With the costs of new facilities skyrocketing, the cities and teams that pay for them must expect the benefits to skyrocket as well.

Facilities, Attendance, and Profits

New stadiums and arenas almost invariably lead to increases in attendance in the years following their construction. The Baltimore Orioles and the Cleveland Indians, the two teams whose new stadiums in 1992 and 1994, respectively, touched off the boom in "retro" stadiums in the early 1990s, saw their average attendance rise by 40 percent and 31 percent in their first year in Oriole Park at Camden Yards and Jacobs (now Progressive) Field, respectively.

Over time, however, the novelty of a new ballpark fades. Attendances at Oriole Park and Progressive Field have fallen in recent years as the Orioles and Indians, which fielded powerful teams in the 1990s, fell back to also-ran status in the 2000s and 2010s. In 2016, attendance at Progressive Field was only 19,650 per game, barely half the 1994 figure. The Orioles did little better, drawing 26,819 fans, less than two-thirds what they drew in 1992.[5] More significantly, the Orioles and Indians drew more fans in their last year in their old ballparks than they did in 2016.

The "honeymoon effect" of a new facility on attendance has received a great deal of attention with the construction boom of the 1990s and early 2000s.[6] Studies have shown that a new facility has a greater impact on baseball teams than on teams in the other major sports, increasing attendance by about one-third. The greater impact on baseball probably stems from the fact that baseball games do not sell out as much as basketball, football, or hockey games. The lack of sellouts comes from baseball's long season—about twice the length of those of basketball and hockey and over ten times that of football—and from the large size of its facilities compared to basketball and hockey. Thus, there is typically more room for a baseball team's attendance to increase than for the three other sports.

As the experience of the Orioles and Indians suggests, the increase does not last forever. All else equal, attendance typically falls back to its original level after about ten years. Over time, a new facility cannot disguise the quality of the team that plays there, as the experience of the Milwaukee Brewers has shown. When Miller Park first opened in 2001, attendance rose by 80 percent, going from 19,427 to 34,704 per game. Attendance fell quickly, however, as fans were turned off by poor performance on the field. Just two years later, attendance had fallen to 20,992, nearly pre-Miller Park levels. Since then, attendance has risen and fallen with team performance, reaching 37,918 fans per game in 2001, when the Brewers won their division for the first time since 1982, but falling to 28,575 in 2016 after several mediocre finishes.

New hockey and basketball arenas have a smaller, shorter-lived effect on attendance. Perhaps due to the smaller capacity of such arenas, attendance rises by only 15 to 20 percent in the facility's first year. In addition, the honeymoon effect quickly diminishes. Hockey attendance falls back to previous levels within five to eight years, while basketball attendance returns to previous levels by year nine.

In a few cases, new ballparks have failed to draw additional fans. Partly because of the financial meltdown of 2008–2009, the New York Yankees drew over a half-million fewer fans in 2009—their first year in the new Yankee Stadium—than they did in 2008. Despite this decline in attendance, *Forbes* magazine states that the team's gate revenue rose by over $100 million. The reason lies in the fact that, in addition to drawing more fans, teams in new facilities put fans into different, more expensive seats. According to *Forbes*, the average ticket price in the new Yankee Stadium cost $26 more than in the old stadium.[7] The increase in revenue indicates that, at least in the case of the Yankees, the income elasticity of demand and the price elasticity of demand were low.

While new stadiums affect all ticket prices, the biggest impact is typically on the number, size, and cost of luxury boxes and other special seating. Surprisingly, until the Astrodome opened in 1965, no modern stadium had luxury boxes. Roy Hofheinz, part-owner of the Houston Astros and the moving force behind the building of the Astrodome, was inspired to create "Skyboxes" by the "high perch for noblemen in Ancient Rome's Colosseum."[8] Indeed, the whole idea for a domed stadium came from the Colosseum's use of a retractable roof.[9] Since the Astrodome was constructed, luxury boxes and other premium seating have become an indispensable part of the contemporary sports facility.

While NFL teams share much of their revenue with other teams in the league, they retain most of their revenue from luxury boxes. Luxury seating therefore provides an important source of profits for owners. When the new LA Stadium at Hollywood Park opens in 2020, NFL stadiums built since 2009 will have an average of 220 luxury boxes, about 80 more than in the remaining 24 stadiums built prior to 2009.[10]

The impact of luxury seating on a team's profit can be seen in the *Forbes* data. Table 6.1 shows financial and seating information for the five most valuable NFL teams in 2016, which—not coincidentally—also have the five highest revenue streams.

All five of these teams occupy stadiums built since 1997, and the 49ers have one of the newest facilities in the NFL. Moreover, three of the five most valuable franchises in the NFL play in the three stadiums with the most luxury boxes in the league. While the Patriots and 49ers have fewer luxury boxes, they make up for this shortfall in other ways. The Patriots' suites are among the largest in

Table 6.1 Stadium Age and Luxury Seating for the Five Most Valuable NFL Franchises

Team	Market Value[a]	Revenue	Year Stadium Opened	Number of Luxury Boxes (Rank)
Dallas Cowboys	$4,200	$700	2009	342 (1)
New England Patriots	$3,400	$523	2002	87 (26)
New York Giants	$3,100	$444	2010	218 (3)
San Francisco 49ers	$3,000	$446	2014	176 (8)
Washington Redskins	$2,555	$447	1997	243 (2)

[a]All dollar figures in millions.

Sources: Mike Ozanian. 2016. "The NFL's Most Valuable Teams 2016," *Forbes.com*, September 14, at https://www.forbes.com/sites/mikeozanian/2016/09/14/the-nfls-most-valuable-teams-2016/; Munsey and Suppes, *Ballparks.com.* 2017.

the NFL and include two "Super Suites" that seat up to 36 people. The 49ers, meanwhile, have the most expensive suites in the NFL.[11] In 2020, the Rams and the Chargers will move in together into a new stadium in Inglewood, California with a planned 275 executive suites, more than the two teams had in their old stadiums in St. Louis and San Diego combined.[12]

6.2 How Fans Benefit from a New Facility

In the next two sections, we examine how a new facility benefits fans and host cities. It might seem odd to distinguish between how a city benefits from hosting a sports franchise and how its fans benefit. After all, the population of the host city typically forms a great part of the team's fan base, and the fan base might be a large segment of the city's population. Our distinction, however, is not based on differing constituencies. Rather, it refers to the type of benefits each receives. In this section, we examine the largely intangible benefits that come from attending a game in a new stadium and from rooting for the "home team" regardless of whether one actually attends a game. In the section that follows, we evaluate the impact of teams and facilities on measures of economic activity, such as jobs, incomes, and tax revenues.

The Size and Shape of Stadiums and Arenas

One way that fans benefit from new stadiums is from having better seating arrangements. During the wave of stadium construction in the 1960s, 1970s, and early 1980s, numerous cities, including Atlanta, Oakland, New York City, Washington, DC, Houston, St. Louis, San Diego, Cincinnati, Pittsburgh, Philadelphia, Seattle, and Minneapolis, constructed large, circular, multi-purpose stadiums designed to host both football and baseball.[13] The stadiums' distinctive, round shape and their close resemblance to one another led critics to call them "cookie-cutter stadiums." The average capacity of these facilities for baseball was 52,659 fans. The capacity expanded slightly for football games, growing to an average of 60,380. In addition, several other cities including Denver and Cleveland hosted both baseball and football in the same stadiums but in facilities that pre-dated the cookie-cutter era.

Starting in the 1990s, a new era began in which baseball and football teams occupied separate facilities. No longer limited by having to share with a very different sport, the new baseball-only stadiums that replaced the multi-purpose stadiums shrank by over 10,000 seats. In contrast, the typical new football-only stadium grew by about 10,000 seats.

The reason for the changes in size can be found in the histories of the sports. Until the 1960s, most football teams were tenants in stadiums built by baseball team owners specifically to house the teams they owned.[14] By that time, football had become increasingly popular, and municipalities were paying much or all of the construction costs. In an effort to reduce costs, cities built large, multi-purpose stadiums rather than separate facilities for football and baseball. The size of the multi-purpose stadiums was thus a compromise, too large for baseball and too small for football.

Baseball and football teams did not just compromise on size, they also compromised on shape. The cookie cutter stadiums' circular shape was an attempt to meet the needs of both baseball and football. Unfortunately for the fans of both sports, the ideal seating arrangements for football and baseball look nothing alike, and these facilities presented an unavoidable conflict between what worked for one sport and what worked for the other. Football teams play on a standardized, rectangular field. Teams score by going to one end of the field or the other, but the bulk of the action takes place in the middle of the field. Seats at either end of the field give little perspective on the action and provide a poor view of what is happening for most plays. By contrast, most of the action on a baseball field takes place within the diamond that forms the infield.

Figure 6.1 shows a typical seating and field configuration for a cookie-cutter stadium which had many seats in the least desirable locations. When arranged for

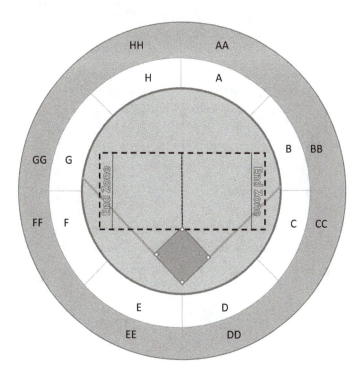

Figure 6.1
Seating and Field
Configuration for a
"Cookie-Cutter" Stadium

football, there were too many seats deep into the corners of the end zone, such as sections BB and GG, and even the best seats near midfield, like sections A and H, were far from the action. And while sections A and H were still pretty good for watching football, when arranged for baseball, these seats were deep in the outfield. In addition, choosing the angles of the seats themselves is problematic. Should seats in Section G be positioned to face toward the middle of the football field or toward home plate? As a result, fans of both sports had poor views of the action, and teams had trouble selling large blocks of tickets in these stadiums, at least at the prices the teams wished to charge. In fact, as recently as the late 1990s, the Minnesota Twins, playing in the multi-use Hubert H. Humphrey Metrodome, sold season tickets for the deepest outfield seats for as low as \$1 per game.

The move back to single-use stadiums that began in the 1980s allowed each sport to find its optimal size and shape. Figure 6.2 shows a stadium built specifically for football (or soccer) and which thus has the ideal configuration for that sport. The sections in the middle of the field, such as A and H, are brought much closer to the players, and the number of seats in the upper end zones, such as sections BB and GG, are minimized. Even the upper deck seats, especially those in the middle of the field such as sections AA and HH, provide good sightlines for the action. While a typical round stadium has only about one-third of its seats between the football goal lines and has two-thirds of the total seating in the end-zone and the corners, these percentages are essentially reversed for stadiums built specifically for football.

**Figure 6.2
Seating and Field
Configuration for a
Football-Only Stadium**

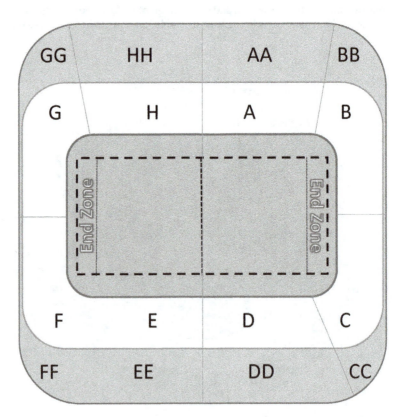

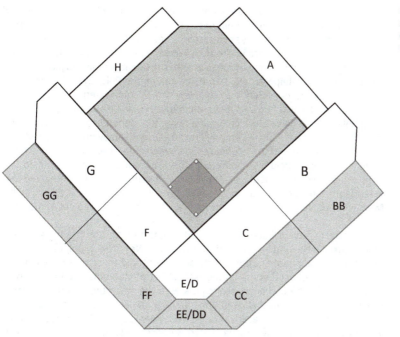

Figure 6.3
Seating and Field
Configuration for a Modern
Baseball-Only Stadium

Figure 6.3 shows a stadium designed specifically for baseball. Notice that most of its seats are near home plate and the infield, and relatively few fans sit far from the action in the outfield. Baseball stadiums built in the 19th and early 20th centuries followed a similar design consisting of grandstands that extended outward from home plate along the foul lines, and seating areas typically did not encompass the outfield. When baseball returned to single-use stadiums beginning in the 1990s, the new stadiums closely resembled the ballparks from 100 years earlier.

The cookie-cutter shape also imposed uniformity on baseball, which had previously been characterized by idiosyncratically shaped ballparks. While the size and shape of a football field and a baseball infield are carefully specified, the shape of a baseball outfield has few restrictions. As a result, stadiums built early in the 20th century came in a dizzying array of sizes and shapes. Some were designed around the particular strengths or weaknesses of the home team. Yankee Stadium may have been the "house that Ruth built," but it was also built to order for Babe Ruth, a left-handed batter who hit prodigious home runs. Yankee Stadium accommodated Ruth with a short right field fence and a left-center field so deep that it came to be known as "Death Valley." The old Baker Bowl in Philadelphia so favored left-handed hitters that Red Smith, the famed columnist, commented, "It might be exaggerating to say the outfield wall casts a shadow across the infield. But if the right fielder had eaten onions at lunch, the second baseman knew it."[15]

Other fields were shaped to fit into a pre-existing city plan. Center field in Philadelphia's Shibe Park came to a distinctive point 515 feet from home plate so that the stadium could fit in the square grid formed by city streets. Two of the most dramatic plays in baseball history—Bobby Thompson's "shot heard round the world," a dramatic ninth-inning home run that beat the Dodgers in a 1951 playoff game, and Willie Mays's miraculous catch of a mammoth drive by the Cleveland Indians' Vic Wertz in the 1954 World Series—had as much to do with the configuration of the Polo Grounds as with the talents of the two players. With one of the oddest shapes of any baseball stadium, the Polo Grounds, named for an area north of Central Park that the New York Giants shared with polo teams before moving to their home in upper Manhattan, could be a very easy place or an incredibly difficult place in which to hit a home run, depending on where one hit the ball. The left field wall was only 258 feet away, with an overhang that reduced the effective distance of the left field seats—where Thompson hit his home run—to 250 feet. Center field was a different story. The stands in left-center field and right-center field were about 450 feet away, with a cutout in dead center field that extended the distance to about 480 feet.[16] In almost any other stadium, Willie Mays would have been staring at the ball Vic Wertz hit as it sailed out of the park.

Many modern baseball stadiums have attempted to capture the idiosyncratic feel of the old ballparks. Citi Field, home of the New York Mets, has an exterior that explicitly evokes Ebbets Field and an outfield fence that bends at odd angles because of aesthetics, not necessity. "Retro" stadiums give fans the best of both worlds, the feel of a historic park with the amenities of a modern one. Newer baseball and football stadiums offer optimally placed seating and provide numerous architectural advantages over older facilities. Older stadiums like Wrigley Field and Fenway Park have narrow concourses, limited bathroom facilities, and numerous obstructed-view seats where support pillars block the view of home plate, annoying features that have been corrected in newer facilities. Most modern stadiums also allow the fans to see the field while buying concessions, encouraging fans to get out of their seats to spend money more often.

The Size and Shape of Basketball and Hockey Arenas

In the early years of professional basketball, hockey team owners often resembled MLB owners by renting their buildings to basketball teams when their teams were on the road. However, the similarity ends there. Because basketball courts and hockey rinks are similar in size and shape, multipurpose arenas can serve hockey and basketball teams with fewer constraints than stadiums that host both baseball and football teams. As a result, hockey and basketball commonly share facilities. As of the 2016–2017 season, 17 NHL and NBA teams were in the same metropolitan area, and 10 pairs of teams shared an arena. By contrast, in 2017, 26 MLB and NFL teams were in the same metropolitan area. Once the Oakland Raiders move to their new stadium in Las Vegas in 2020, no NFL and MLB teams will share a facility (other than the Buffalo Bills who play one "home" game each season in the Rogers Centre, the home field of the Toronto Blue Jays).

The main conflict between basketball and hockey teams has been financial. In recent years, NBA teams have typically been the primary tenants of the arenas that they share with NHL teams, and hence have benefited much more from their facilities. A hockey team that is a secondary tenant generally faces worse financial arrangements than the basketball team with which it shares the arena.[17] It is no surprise that the four most profitable teams in the NHL—the Toronto Maple Leafs, New York Rangers, Montreal Canadiens, and Detroit Red Wings—are all primary tenants in their facilities. The Maple Leafs and Rangers have arrangements with the Air Canada Centre and Madison Square Garden that are equal or superior to those of their co-tenants, the NBA's Knicks and Raptors, while the Canadiens and Red Wings have their own arenas.

The Size and Shape of Football and Soccer Stadiums

The most recent stadium building boom in the United States has involved Major League Soccer. At first glance, it seems odd that soccer cannot co-exist with football. The sports' playing surfaces are extremely similar in shape and size, so the ideal seats for soccer and football are nearly identical. In fact, MLS originally did use a variety of NFL and college football stadiums.

Soccer in the US is not as popular as football, however, so the ideal-size stadium for an MLS team with 17 home games each season is much smaller than for an NFL team with 8 home games. In the early days of the league, MLS teams frequently played to small crowds in enormous stadiums. Playing in stadiums filled to only 10% capacity led to a less-than-vibrant atmosphere. As in the case of the NHL and NBA, MLS teams' status as secondary tenants was also problematic. Finally, many soccer fans were turned off by the presence of football markings on a soccer field, and the damage done to the playing surface by football teams often made the grass surface uneven or necessitated the use of artificial turf, an outrage to most soccer purists.

In 1999, the Columbus Crew opened MLS's first soccer-specific stadium. The Crew increased its average attendance despite moving to a stadium with less than one-quarter of the capacity of its original home in "The Shoe" at The Ohio State University. Other teams quickly followed suit. In 1998, MLS's third season, all ten of the teams that remain in the league today played in football stadiums with an average capacity of over 70,000 seats. These teams filled their stadiums to less than 22% of capacity on average. By 2016, eight of the ten teams had built new, smaller stadiums and were filling them to nearly 90% capacity. The league had also expanded by ten teams, most of which had constructed new stadiums as a condition of entry into the league.

Table 6.2 MLS Soccer-Specific Stadiums

Team	Original Stadium	Capacity	Avg. Attendance (1998)	New Stadium	Capacity	Avg. Attendance (2016)
San Jose Earthquakes	Spartan Stadium	31,218	13,653	Avaya Stadium	18,000	19,930
Sporting Kansas City	Arrowhead Stadium	79,451	8,072	Children's Mercy Park	18,467	19,597
Colorado Rapids	Mile High Stadium	76,273	14,812	Dick's Sporting Goods Park	18,061	16,278
New England Revolution	Foxboro Stadium	60,292	19,187	Gillette Stadium	66,829	20,185
Columbus Crew SC	Ohio State Stadium	89,841	12,274	Mapfre Stadium	19,968	17,125
D.C. United	RFK Stadium	56,692	16,007	RFK Stadium	45,596	17,081
New York Red Bulls	Giants Stadium	80,242	16,519	Red Bull Arena	25,000	20,620
LA Galaxy	Rose Bowl	92,542	21,784	StubHub Center	27,000	25,147
Chicago Fire	Soldier Field	66,944	17,886	Toyota Park	20,000	15,602
FC Dallas	Cotton Bowl	68,252	10,947	Toyota Stadium	20,500	14,094

Source: mlssoccer.com and various team websites.

Do New Facilities Create Better Teams?

Team owners do not just promise that new stadiums bring better seats, they invariably claim that the increased attendance and revenue will allow them to field better teams. However, research by Hakes and Clapp and by Quinn et al. suggests that the link between new stadiums and better teams is tenuous at best.[18] Both papers assume that teams maximize profits and that both winning and playing in a new facility increase revenues. In terms of the basic profit function first presented in Chapter 3,

$$\pi_i = R\,(w_i, A_i) - C_o - C(w_i),$$

revenue (R) increases with wins, w, and decreases with the age of the team's facility, A, as fans prefer to watch games in new facilities. We assume that cost has two components, one independent of wins, C_o, and one that rises with additional wins, $C(w)$. We assume that a new stadium increases costs only with regard to the fixed cost of building the stadium. Because C_o does not change with the number of games a team wins or the number of fans it attracts, it does not influence the team's desire to win. In this simple model, a new stadium increases profit if the added revenue exceeds the fixed cost C_o, but does it also increase the number of games the team wins? The answer is "yes" if new facilities increase the impact of an additional win on revenue—that is, if fans are more attracted to a winning team when it plays in a nice, new facility. As Figure 6.4 shows, if having a new facility increases the marginal revenue of a win, then teams with new facilities have a greater incentive to acquire talented players and win games.

Quinn et al. test the relationship between facility age and winning directly by analyzing how a new stadium affects the winning percentage of teams in the four major North American sports. They find that stadium age has no impact on winning percentage in any sport except baseball, where it has only a small effect. Hakes and Clapp test whether the impact of a win on revenue and attendance for

Figure 6.4
A New Facility Might Encourage a Team to Win More Games

If a new facility shifts the marginal revenue of a win to the right, a team's optimal number of wins rises from W_o to W_1.

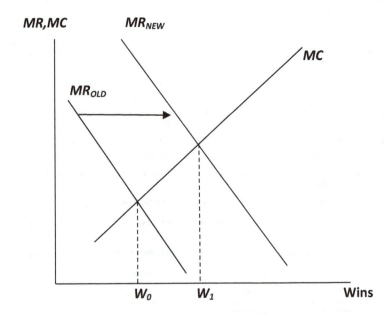

baseball teams is greater in new stadiums than in old ones. They find that both winning teams and newer stadiums bring more fans and revenue, but that winning teams do no better in new stadiums than they do in old ones. They conclude that baseball teams in new stadiums have no financial incentive to reinvest their revenue into hiring better players.[19]

Having a better team playing in a more attractive stadium does not necessarily benefit the fans who attend the games. Teams know that fans are willing to pay more for the amenities and the novelty of new facilities and will price tickets accordingly. Indeed, the rightward shift in the MR curve in Figure 6.4 results in part from teams charging higher prices for tickets. In fact, teams commonly increase ticket prices upon opening a new stadium. For example, Robert Baade and Victor Matheson find an average increase in ticket prices of nearly 30% in the first season for the 16 NFL teams that built new stadiums or significantly refurbished their existing field between 1997 and 2003.[20] Similarly, Seth Gitter and Thomas Rhoads find minor baseball ticket prices rise between 20% and 25% on average in the first season of a new stadium.[21] Fans suffering through seasons of poor teams in dilapidated stadiums might want to be careful what they wish for. New stadiums come at a steep price for fans.

Teams as Public Goods

One does not have to attend a game to benefit from the presence of a sports franchise. First, consumers may place an "option value" on a sports team. An option value is the value one places on having the ability to go to a game if one chooses, even if one rarely actually chooses to attend sporting events. Consumers value having options even if some options are rarely exercised. Furthermore, just as a nation takes pride in the accomplishments of its Olympic athletes or national teams, states, cities, and neighborhoods can feel a sense of identity from having a professional franchise in their midst.[22] A successful team, in particular, contributes to a city's self-image. As Bill Veeck said of his 1948 Cleveland Indians, "there is that feeling of reflected glory in a successful baseball team. Cleveland is winning the pennant. The eyes of the whole country are upon Cleveland, upon us, upon me and you. *We're looking pretty good, aren't we, Mac?*"[23] All the residents of a team's city can share in the goodwill and sense of community that their hometown team generates without attending a game or watching it on TV.

When teams are closely integrated into their communities, they become public goods. A **public good** is **non-excludable** and **non-rival** in consumption. Non-rivalry in consumption means that one person's consumption does not prevent another person from consuming the good; non-excludability means that once the good is available to anyone, it is available to everyone. In the context of professional sports, attending the game is not a public good because fans can be excluded from Fenway Park unless they buy a ticket. However, a citizen of "Red Sox Nation"[24] can consume the good feeling that comes from the Red Sox winning the World Series without ever having attended a game. Generally, teams are local public goods in the sense that the feelings they generate apply to a particular region. At times, the feelings could extend beyond a city's borders, particularly if the feelings of community or pride apply to a different aspect of personal identity, such as ethnicity or religion, as has long been the case with Notre Dame's so-called "subway alumni," a term first applied to the large number of Catholics in New York who devotedly followed Notre Dame football.

Residents of small to midsized cities feel they are part of a "big-league" city when their hometown has a major league franchise. Indianapolis may not be able to compete with New York in terms of economic or cultural clout, but its residents derive a sense of superiority to New York whenever *our* Indiana Pacers defeat *their* New York Knicks. It therefore comes as no surprise that a survey of residents of Indianapolis in the 1990s found that the Indiana Pacers were a close second to the city's museums as a source of civic pride, with the Indianapolis Colts placing third.[25] Of course, this also means that smaller cities may be willing to pay larger subsidies to attract professional sports teams than large cities with many other attractions. Indianapolis, one of the smallest cities with an NFL franchise, provided $620 million in taxpayer subsidies for the construction of the Lukas Oil Stadium for the Indianapolis Colts, then the largest public subsidy ever for a sports facility in the US.[26] New York City and Los Angeles, on the other hand, provided no direct subsidies for the construction of MetLife Stadium and the new Los Angeles Chargers and Rams stadium.[27]

The links between sport and society can run far deeper than good feelings about one's hometown and can have far more serious consequences than just a pride in being part of Red Sox Nation. Local sports teams sometimes reflect the aspirations of rival ethnic groups. For example, the Glasgow Rangers and Glasgow Celtic soccer teams play out the rivalry between Protestants and Catholics in Glasgow in the Scottish Football League. The Montreal Canadiens and FC Barcelona have been symbols of something even larger: the nationalist yearnings by ethnic minorities.

French Canada has long identified with the Canadiens. In fact, some historians trace the separatist movement in Quebec to the "Richard riot" of 1955. The riot ostensibly began in response to the suspension of hockey great Maurice Richard for several games at the end of the 1954–1955 NHL season and the ensuing play-offs. Richard's suspension might have simply been the last straw for Montreal's French-Canadian residents, who had long felt shut out from opportunities by the English-speaking élite.

While some French-Canadian fans speak of separation, FC Barcelona fans fought for it during the Spanish Civil War. "Barça," as the football team is called, has long been a symbol of Catalan separatist aspirations and, from 1938 to 1975, of opposition to the Fascist rule of Francisco Franco. With the Catalan language banned and the Franco regime openly supporting arch-rival Réal Madrid, "Only the Camp Nou [FC Barcelona's home field] provided Catalans a place to yell and scream against the regime in their own, banned vernacular."[28]

6.3   How Cities Benefit from Teams and Facilities

Candidates for public office often claim that government should be run like a business. If that were the case, then many stadiums and arenas would not be built. Cities would also not compete so vigorously for mega-events such as the Olympics, a topic we will explore in Chapter 8. The central question facing any private business is whether a project is profitable. By this standard, most studies find that sports facilities fall short. Without public support, most contemporary facilities fail to cover their costs of construction and operation.[29] Building a stadium (or subsidizing its construction) thus seems to be a losing proposition that cities should avoid. While cities might spend too much on stadiums and arenas, people who insist that the facilities serve as profit centers misunderstand the role of government. Economists agree that the private sector's pursuit of profit generally does a good job of allocating resources. However, they also agree that unfettered markets sometimes fail to provide the socially desired amount of a good or service. When markets fail, government intervention can lead to improved outcomes.

Market failure can occur for several reasons. For example, markets provide too little of a public good when consumers attempt to free ride, and they provide too much of a common resource, as in the tragedy of the commons. Monopolies maximize profit by producing less than the socially optimal amount of output. In this chapter, we focus on the market failure caused by externalities. An **externality** is an unintended and uncompensated cost or benefit that a firm imposes on a third party who has no say in the firm's provision of a good or service.

Governments exist in part to bring a broader perspective to the allocation of goods and services by ensuring that firms pay the full costs and receive the full benefits of their actions. When the presence of a team or a new facility brings large benefits that are not captured by the private sector, local governments can prevent market failure and improve economic well-being by providing subsidies to teams. In this section, we examine some of the benefits teams bring that the private sector does not take into consideration but that governments can and should. The focus in this section widens from just facilities to the presence of the team or event itself. This is because cities typically confront the decision to build a new facility in the context of the broader decision to attract a team or to prevent a team from leaving.

Positive and Negative Externalities

Governments subsidize facilities and mega-events because of the externalities they cause. A **positive externality** occurs when a party not directly involved in a transaction receives unintended benefits from a transaction, and a **negative externality** occurs when a party bears unintended costs from a transaction for which they do not receive compensation. If a project generates only private costs and benefits that accrue to the parties involved, then they can decide whether they should finance the project based solely on those costs and benefits. If externalities are involved, however, then the private parties may not be able to make the economically efficient decision that brings the most net benefits to society as a whole. One rationale for public funding of a stadium or arena rests on the belief that the private benefits of hosting a sports franchise do not outweigh the private costs, but that the private benefits plus the positive externalities of sports franchises outweigh the private costs plus the negative externalities. If this is so, then a subsidy will ensure that social well-being is maximized.

Consider, for example, a typical Chicago Cubs game. In addition to whatever direct costs and benefits the Cubs convey to the residents of Chicago, they also create negative externalities each time they play a game. In deciding how much to produce, the Cubs, MLB, and firms in general typically consider only the private cost of operation—how much they must spend on salaries, travel, and a host of other inputs. They do not usually consider—and may not even be aware of—the external costs of the health problems and inconvenience they create for people affected by the traffic congestion caused by those who attend the game and the resulting noise, overcrowding, and pollution. The private costs that underlie the Cubs' and MLB's profit maximization decisions understate the

Figure 6.5
Negative Externalities Shift
the Supply Curve Leftward

The socially optimal quantity
of games (Q_s) is less than the
privately optimal quantity (Q_p).

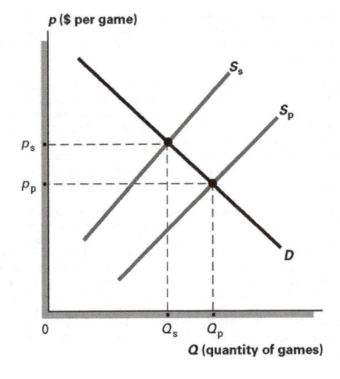

full social costs, which include both the private costs and the costs imposed on third parties.[30] If the Cubs or any firm considered all these costs, the net rewards associated with any given price—and the incentive to produce—would be lower. As a result, the "private" supply curve (S_p) in Figure 6.5, which includes only private costs experienced directly by the firm, lies to the right of the "social" supply curve (S_s), which includes all private and social costs.

The market equilibrium that results from the private decisions of producers and consumers in Figure 6.5 is Q_p games, while the socially optimal quantity is only Q_s. The difference $(Q_p - Q_s)$ shows that the negative externality causes the Cubs to schedule too many games when left to their own devices. Similarly, the difference between the price that the Cubs charge and the price that society would like them to charge $(p_p - p_s)$ shows that a negative externality causes the Cubs to charge their fans too little.

Because the Cubs do not pay for the congestion and pollution they cause, the negative externality allows the Cubs to charge a lower price, which benefits both the Cubs and the fans who attend Cubs games. Chicago residents, most of whom do not attend games, suffer from the costs that the Cubs impose on them. Residents of the neighborhoods surrounding Wrigley Field know that whenever the Cubs play night games at home, traffic will make the commute home much longer and will make parking impossible for those not fortunate enough to have private garages.

Surprisingly, Chicago does not want to eliminate the negative externalities that the Cubs impose on it. The only way to ensure that the Cubs impose no negative externalities would be for them to play no games. Ending Cubs games to get rid of the negative externality would probably leave Chicago worse off because people are worse off without the output even if it means a cleaner, safer environment. In this example, Chicagoans want to see the number of games reduced to Q_s, where the benefits and social costs of one more ballgame are equal, but they do not want to eliminate the games entirely.

The negative externalities associated with sports facilities tend to decline over time. Residents of neighborhoods where a proposed structure will be built often complain bitterly about the problems it will bring. However, residents are almost rhapsodic about long-existing structures. In the words of baseball historian Harold Seymour, a ballpark is "a landmark, an asset to city life—especially to the lives of those who live in the neighborhood."[31]

The change in attitudes does not come because the stadium or the fans change. It comes because the residents change. None of the homeowners who lived in what is now called "Wrigleyville" when the stadium was built in 1914 are still alive. Almost all the residences and businesses have been sold several times over since then. The turnover has two effects. First, Wrigleyville attracts people and businesses that enjoy having a team in the neighborhood. These gains could outweigh the losses of the negative externalities and leave residents and local merchants better off. Second, even if the stadium's negatives dominate, the turnover has internalized the externality because people who have bought homes or businesses in Wrigleyville have been compensated for any inconvenience. The compensation comes in the form of lower real estate prices. The only ones to be affected by the externality were the original homeowners and businesses. They paid full price for their locations and were not compensated for the costs imposed on them or received a windfall if the stadium increased property values. The externalities generated by newer facilities, such as Mercedes-Benz Park in Atlanta which opened in 2017, have yet to be fully internalized. People who own nearby housing may see the value of their properties change in the future.

Sports facilities also bring benefits to the neighborhoods, cities, and metropolitan areas in which they are located. Firms and households that have no direct connection to the facility see their incomes rise because of its construction. Because they do not compensate the team for locating in the city, these firms and households benefit from a positive externality.

Just as the costs imposed by a negative consumption externality cause the private supply curve to be too far to the right in Figure 6.5, the benefits brought by a positive consumption externality cause the private demand curve to be too far to the left. Figure 6.6 shows that, in the absence of government intervention, a positive externality causes the Cubs to play too few games. Chicago wants the Cubs to play Q_s games, but the Cubs want to play only Q_p. Because the Cubs' revenues understate the total benefit to Chicago residents, the city must provide an additional incentive for the Cubs to play in Chicago. In the case of professional sports franchises, these incentives often take the form of public funding of sports facilities.

Figure 6.6
Positive Consumption
Externalities Shift the
Demand Curve Outward

The socially optimal quantity
(Q_s) is greater than the privately
optimal quantity (Q_p).

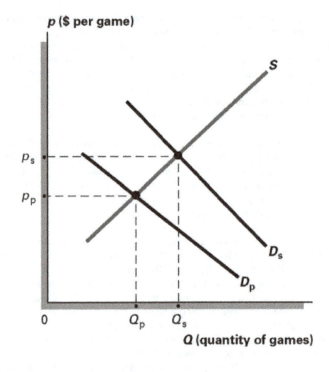

p ($ per game)

Facilities, Spending, and Tax Revenue

New facilities generate many different forms of spending. Constructing even the simplest major league facility produces hundreds of millions of dollars in spending and income. Once the facility is built, fans spend tens of millions of dollars to attend and enjoy games. From the standpoint of a team, the story ends there. Cities, however, have a broader perspective. Businesses and households that have nothing to do with the facility or the team that occupies it benefit if people who come for a game stay in the city for dinner or spend the night at a local hotel. In addition, the stadium employees or restaurant workers who earn higher incomes because of the new facility now have more money to spend, which increases the incomes of still other people in the local economy. We next examine the impact of these direct and indirect benefits to cities.

Direct Benefits

In 2014, the Chicago Cubs began a five-year, $575 million renovation of Wrigley Field and the surrounding area. From an economic standpoint, the important questions are how much impact do the Cubs have on the Chicago economy and what will the impact of the refurbished stadium be?

The direct benefit of the Cubs to Chicago is the increase in new spending that is attributable to the team and the stadium renovations. The construction phase of the plan is easiest to examine. Supporters of the plan cite the construction jobs it will create as the first of many direct benefits of the project for Chicago. However, a closer look suggests that the benefits might be smaller than they appear. First, if the city finances a portion of construction, any benefits from new construction jobs are largely offset by the reduction in economic activity that occurs as a result of the higher taxes that have to be levied to pay for the construction. Thus, most economists do not consider taxpayer expenditures on stadium construction to be a benefit to the local economy. Even if all the construction costs were privately funded, as is the case in the Wrigley Field plan, if the economy is currently operating at full capacity, then the stadium project simply **crowds out**—or displaces—other initiatives and does not increase total spending. Of course, if stadium construction coincides with an economic downturn, then publicly subsidized stadium construction could serve as an economic stimulus, but typically stadium projects require far too long a planning period to be effectively used in this manner.

A longer-term direct impact comes from the additional money that Cubs fans will spend at the newly renovated ballpark and its surroundings. New spending takes one of two forms. First, a franchise might cause Chicagoans to spend more—and save less—than they otherwise would. Second, and more importantly, the Cubs stimulate net exports by Chicago. International trade economists define **net exports** as the difference between the value of goods and services that a nation exports and the value of goods and services it imports. While Chicago and other US cities are not separate countries, we can treat them as such because they buy and sell goods from and to one another. Chicago exports the services of its sports teams to the surrounding region if the teams attract fans from the surrounding area to their games in Chicago. The teams also increase Chicago's net exports by reducing its imports from other cities. Chicago's imports fall if Chicagoans attend Cubs games rather than spend their money outside Chicago.

The Cubs generated $340 million in revenue in 2015, roughly $200 million of which was spent by fans on tickets, concessions, and other items at Wrigley Field itself. A renovated stadium might increase this figure substantially. So, should we consider the economic impact of the team on Chicago to be $200 million or $340 million or more? In fact, its annual impact is likely to be far less than $340 million. The main reason is that much of the expenditure in Wrigleyville is not additional expenditure in Chicago. Most Cubs fans are locals who would have spent much of that money elsewhere in Chicago if there had been no renovation to Wrigley Field or even if the Cubs and Wrigley Field did not exist at all. To a great extent, the team and the renovation merely induce **substitution spending**, as Chicagoans shift their spending from one local leisure activity to another without significantly increasing total spending in the economy. The crowds and congestion that occur during 81 games a year in the Wrigleyville neighborhood also **crowd out** other economic activity, as businesses, such as movie theaters and grocery stores that do not cater to baseball fans, find it difficult to attract customers during ballgames.

Of course, some fans at every game are from outside of Chicago, and their spending counts as net exports. However, even the money spent by out-of-towners in Wrigleyville is not new spending if residents of other cities decide to visit Wrigley Field rather than other attractions, such as the Chicago Art Institute, when they visit Chicago.

Finally, despite their high profile, sports franchises are rather small businesses. In the words of one expert, "the sales revenue of Fruit of the Loom exceeds that for all of Major League Baseball."[32] While the $340 million in revenue generated by the Cubs looks like a lot of money, it comes to less than one-tenth of one percent of the total income generated by the Chicago economy. The total revenue of all six Chicago franchises comes to less than one-half of one percent of all local incomes.[33] The impact of sports franchises on local economies is thus very small.

Multiplier Effects

The money spent at Cubs games also has an indirect effect on Chicago's economy, which benefits people who have nothing to do with the Cubs. The indirect benefit stems from the higher incomes of people who work at or near Cubs games. Their higher incomes lead to added spending elsewhere in Chicago. The spillover of added income and spending into the broader economy is known as the **multiplier effect**.

To envision the multiplier effect, think of Chicago's economy as a still pond. Spending additional money at a Cubs game is like throwing a pebble into the pond. The direct impact of the spending is the splash caused by the pebble hitting the water. A series of ripples quickly spreads out from the initial point of impact. As they spread out, the ripples become fainter and fainter, until they are indistinguishable from the flat pond. The multiplier effect is like those ripples, spreading the direct impact of the spending throughout the city. To illustrate this, suppose that Rachel, a Chicago resident who runs a restaurant in Wrigleyville, earns an additional $30,000 in income thanks to the increased attendance that the renovations at Wrigley Field generate. That added income is part of the direct impact of the renovation, the initial splash the pebble makes in the pond. Rachel saves some of her income and spends, say, $27,000 on a new kitchen installed by a local company. Her expenditure on the kitchen becomes part of the first ripple. Her purchase, in turn, increases the income of the contractor who works on her kitchen. The contractor saves some of his additional $27,000 and spends, say, $24,300 on a new car from a local dealer, forming yet another ripple, and so on.

The ripples get smaller because people do not spend all their additional income. Economists call the fraction of an additional dollar of income that consumers spend the **marginal propensity to consume** (MPC). They call the fraction of an additional dollar that they save the **marginal propensity to save** (MPS). Consumers must spend or save that entire additional dollar, so:

$$MPC + MPS = 1.$$

Studies indicate that Americans spend more than nine-tenths of each additional dollar that they earn. In the preceding example, Rachel's $MPC = 0.9$, so she spends:

$$(0.9)(\$30,000) = \$27,000$$

The $27,000 that Rachel spends is additional income to the contractor, who then spends nine-tenths of that income, or:

$$(0.9)[(0.9)(\$30,000)] = \$24,300$$

The process continues in steadily decreasing ripples until the additional expenditure becomes indistinguishable from zero, and the ripples effectively disappear.

The total impact of Rachel's $30,000 increase in income on Chicago's economy is:

$$T = \$30,000 + \$27,000 + \$24,300 + \$21,870 + \ldots$$

While the numbers in this sum decline steadily to zero, it is not clear what the total impact is. We can, however, find the limit of this infinite sum. Using what we know about the numbers in the sum, we can rewrite T as:

$$T = \$30,000 * M$$

where:

$$M = 1 + 0.9 + 0.9^2 + 0.9^3 + 0.9^4 + \ldots$$

It is not hard to solve for M, which in this case equals $\dfrac{1}{1-0.9}$ or 10. The total impact of Rachel's additional earnings is thus $30,000*10$, or $300,000. Because we multiply the initial expenditure by M, we call M the **multiplier**. Of course, the MPC need not equal 0.9. More generally, we compute the multiplier as:

$$M = \frac{1}{1-MPC} = \frac{1}{MPS}$$

The multiplier effect can cause a relatively small direct increase in incomes to have a large impact on the well-being of a city. For example, a multiplier of 10 means that a tourist's spending $100 in Wrigleyville brings a total impact of $1,000 on the region.

The simple multiplier, however, vastly overstates the impact of professional sports teams.[34] The most important reason for this inaccuracy is that the simple multiplier applies to a **closed economy**, one that does not engage in trade. Cities, however, are **open economies** that trade extensively with other cities as well as with foreign countries. In open economies, much of the added consumption that results from higher incomes consists of imports from other economies. In our example, that would happen if Rachel spent some of her $30,000 on a Japanese-made camera or a laptop made in California. Leakages from the local economy reduce the ripple effect in two ways. First, they cause local incomes to rise by less, as Rachel might spend only $20,000 on her new kitchen. Second, the contractor, who now receives less income, spends less of *his* additional income locally, causing the next ripple to be smaller still.

We account for the impact of leakages from the system by adding the **marginal propensity to import**, the amount of an extra dollar of income that is spent on imported goods, to the multiplier. A more accurate multiplier is therefore:

$$M = \frac{1}{(1-MPC+MPI)}$$

If we assume that 40 cents of every additional dollar of income leave Chicago, the multiplier shrinks from 10 to 2 ($1/(1-.9+.4)) = 1/.5 = 2$). In general, local multipliers are much smaller than national multipliers.

Leakages from professional sports tend to be very large since most team employees do not live in the cities where they work. Most of the total payroll of the Cubs goes to the team's athletes, relatively few of whom live year-round in Chicago. To see this in another setting, while 93 percent of average employees live near where they work, only 29 percent of NBA players do. In all, while over 58 percent of an average employee's income is injected into a local economy, only about 10 percent of an NBA player's income is.[35] Sports teams thus serve as a conduit, transferring money from local sports fans to out-of-town residents.

Leakages are also inversely related to the size and diversity of the local economy. Large cities, which provide more opportunities to buy locally made items, generally have larger multipliers than do small cities. However, the larger multiplier is at least partly offset by greater substitution spending. A larger local economy provides residents with more alternative outlets for their leisure time, reducing the likelihood that a sports franchise generates new spending that would not otherwise take place.[36]

Two additional factors further reduce the multiplier effect of professional sports franchises. First, because professional athletes' salaries are much higher than for most workers, they are taxed at a higher rate, leaving less of their income available for consumption. Second, as income increases, workers have a greater tendency to save, so the MPC falls. Because professional athletes' careers tend to be relatively short, they have an additional incentive to save, so their MPC is even smaller. In sum, the local multiplier is unlikely to be much bigger than 1.0, meaning that spending on a professional sports franchise has no multiplier effect on the local economy.

Studies of Economic Impact

Many economists have studied the impact of sports facilities, franchises, and mega-events on cities.[37] Most studies analyze measures of the increases in economic well-being (such as per capita income, tax collections, or employment) resulting from the presence of an athletic team or a new facility after controlling for other factors that are unrelated to sports. From the pathbreaking work of Robert Baade and Richard Dye to recent research by Baade, Victor Matheson and Robert Baumann, or Dennis Coates and Brad Humphreys, economists have consistently found little or no evidence that facilities and teams affect the level of employment, tax receipts, incomes, or wages in a city.[38]

A more recent strand of the literature asks whether the presence of a team makes a city more attractive even if it does not directly increase incomes or employment. If it does, then the increased demand for home and office space drives up property values. The results of this literature are mixed. Studies by Gerald Carlino and Edward Coulson and by Charles Tu find a positive impact on property values. These findings, however, might be specific to the data they use.[39] Papers by Coates and Humphreys and, more recently, by Feng and Humphreys find smaller effects that drop off rapidly with greater distance from the facility.[40] Both papers conclude that, all else equal, a professional sports franchise makes the immediate community more attractive to potential homebuyers but that it has little effect on the city as a whole.

Interest Groups and Public Choice

Even if new facilities are losing propositions, cities might still pursue them. One explanation for this seemingly irrational behavior is that specific interest groups, particularly in the construction and hospitality industries, might gain a lot. If these interest groups have disproportionate influence over the city's politicians, then the project might go forward even if a majority of the city's residents oppose it. This helps to explain how cities like Phoenix and Pittsburgh got new ballparks after the proposal had been rejected in a referendum.[41] In this section, we use an area of economic theory known as public choice to develop an economic framework for such behavior.

Public choice theory stems from the work of Nobel laureate James Buchanan, Gordon Tullock, William Niskanen, and others in the 1960s. It rests on the notion that decision makers in the public sector do not automatically act to resolve the market failures of public goods and externalities. Instead, public officials are subject to many of the same temptations and constraints facing consumers and producers in the private sector.

According to public choice theory, the interests of politicians and the owners of sports franchises dovetail neatly. Politicians want to attain, maintain, and improve their political standing. They therefore take actions designed to ensure their election or re-election to higher office. Since it is costly to determine the specific interests of large numbers of disparate voters, politicians are most responsive to organized group interests; the more highly organized the group, the more influence it wields over officeholders.[42]

Team owners, often in alliance with business and labor interests, have sought to influence the political process. By expressing the intensity of their desires, interest groups may—through a process known as **logrolling**—induce politicians to pass legislation that majority rule would deny. To see how this works, suppose a legislature consists of three equal groups, each representing one-third of the state (i.e., East, Central, and West). The state is considering building two stadiums, one each in the East and West of the state. Suppose each new stadium would greatly benefit the region in which it is located but mildly hurt—through higher taxes that everyone in the state must pay to fund the stadiums—the other two portions of the state, as seen in Table 6.3. If politicians voted according to the impact of the stadium on their constituents, they would defeat both stadium proposals, because each proposal hurts two-thirds of the state. However, according to the payoffs in Table 6.3, each proposal benefits the host constituency so much that majority rule leaves the state worse off.

Logrolling allows each group to express the intensity of its desires, thereby improving the efficiency of the political process. While residents of the East are harmed by the facility in the West and vice versa, if each agrees to support the other's proposal, the gain from their own stadium outweighs the cost of the other's stadium, leaving both better off.[43] Each proposal passes by a 2–1 margin, and the overall well-being of the state improves, despite the fact that each facility benefits only one region.[44]

Table 6.3 How Logrolling Can Improve Social Well-Being

Region	Payoff to Proposal #1	Payoff to Proposal #2
East	+$10 million	−$ 2 million
Central	−$ 2 million	−$ 2 million
West	−$ 2 million	+$ 10 million
Overall impact	+$ 6 million	+$ 6 million

Group interests do not always have a positive impact on social well-being. Sometimes they are simply an attempt to claim economic rent. **Economic rent** is the extra return received by a producer or by an input above and beyond the opportunity cost of providing the output or input. Monopoly and monopsony power and public subsidies are common sources of economic rents. With tens or hundreds of millions of dollars in public funding for a new stadium or arena at stake, teams, leagues, and other stakeholders are willing to spend heavily to influence the political process in their pursuit of economic rents.

Pro-stadium forces regularly outspend their opponents in public referenda on stadium funding. In Seattle, Paul Allen used some of the fortune he made from Microsoft to cover the $4.2 million cost of the state referendum on financing a new football stadium for his Seattle Seahawks. He went on to spend $5 million to convince voters to support the proposal. His return, $300 million in state funding for Seahawk Stadium (now CenturyLink Field), made the $9.2 million investment one of Allen's most profitable moves since joining with Bill Gates to form Microsoft.[45]

Even when the vote does not go their way, lobbyists often get what they want. Frequently, that involves getting state legislators to provide what their constituents will not. In 2012, voters in Minnesota saw their rejection of public funding overturned by the state house, which approved $498 million in funding for a new $1.1 billion home for the Minnesota Vikings.[46] Similarly, in 2003, Chicago's $800 million Soldier Field project preserved a portion of the old stadium's façade so that the city planners could designate the project as a "renovation," which did not require the consent of the voters, as opposed to a new stadium, which would have required a voter referendum.[47] The resulting mix of modern and classical architecture was not well received. In the words of University of Chicago sport economist Allen Sanderson, "If we started out to build the ugliest stadium in the country for the most money with the fewest alternative uses in the worst possible location, we're pretty much there."[48]

Location, Location, Location

The impact of a team or facility on the local economy also depends on its precise location. A city maximizes the positive externalities associated with a sports franchise if it integrates the facilities into the urban fabric.[49] To do so, a city must develop an urban plan that exploits the attractions of a ballpark. Baltimore attempted to do just that when it placed Oriole Park and Ravens Park (now M&T Bank Stadium) at Camden Yards in the Inner Harbor. Tourists could come to the Inner Harbor, spend time at other attractions such as the Baltimore Aquarium, see a ballgame, and have nearby hotels to stay in overnight. Cleveland followed a similar strategy. Jacobs (now Progressive) Field, which kept the Indians in town, and Gund (now Quicken Loans) Arena, which brought the Cavaliers back to Cleveland from suburban Richfield, were both part of a broader Gateway Project designed to revitalize downtown Cleveland.

The results of these projects have been mixed. While Cleveland experienced job growth following the construction of its sports facilities, the growth was actually lower downtown than elsewhere in the region and was slower than in the years immediately preceding the project.[50] Studies of Baltimore show that Orioles

Park created fewer than 600 jobs and left the typical household roughly $12 poorer through the taxes paid to support the construction. Estimates suggest that, if anything, Baltimore's M&T Bank Stadium did even less.[51]

The warm feeling associated with the downtown location of many of the newest stadiums is proof that nostalgia is not what it used to be. When they were first built, the old ballparks were built at the edge of town. When Shibe Park (later renamed Connie Mack Stadium) was built at 21st and Lehigh Streets in North Philadelphia in 1909, it stood near the site of a recently demolished hospital for communicable diseases. Given the state of medical knowledge at the turn of the 20th century, society tended to deal with communicable diseases by locating the patients as far from the center of town as possible. For several years after Shibe Park was built, Philadelphians complained about the distance they had to travel to reach it.[52] Similarly, Yankee Stadium in the South Bronx was not always associated with urban congestion. It was built on an empty 10-acre lot, bordered by unpaved roads, in a part of town known as "Goatville," hardly a metropolitan setting.[53] Brooklyn's Ebbets Field was not much different. By the mid-1950s, it may have come to epitomize the urban ballpark, but in 1913, the neighborhood in which it was built bore the nickname "Pigtown . . . where poor Italian immigrants lived in miserable shanties amidst goats and dandelions."[54]

As time went on, urban areas first developed and then decayed around many of the old ballparks. As the old ballparks began to decay, team owners and cities considered relocating to the outskirts of town and the suburbs for sociological, technological, and economic reasons. An increasingly suburbanized fan base was increasingly reluctant to attend games in the crumbling inner city. Suburbanization also brought a need to accommodate fans who drove to the game. Any new ballpark would have to come packaged with acres of parking lots, which vastly increased the space required for a stadium. Since fans found it inconvenient to go into town to enjoy restaurants, taverns, and other forms of entertainment, the stadium took on many of those functions itself, further isolating the stadium and its income flows from the city. In the words of Robert Baade, "in many cases the modern sports facility resembles a small walled city."[55] In moving stadiums back to the center of town, cities are expressing a willingness to spend more in order to generate greater spillovers for the community. But with greater benefits (in the form of consumer spending at local businesses) counterbalanced by higher construction costs, there is little reason to believe that the new trend in building stadiums downtown will result in substantial benefits for the cities that fund the stadiums.

We would be remiss, however, to ignore the success stories. New baseball stadiums such as Petco Park in San Diego's Gaslamp District and Coors Field in the Lower Downtown (LoDo) neighborhood of Denver are anchors to vibrant and growing entertainment districts. Still, while the Gaslamp and LoDo are thriving neighborhoods with many new bars and restaurants, there is no evidence that total economic activity in Denver and San Diego has increased because of the stadiums, and there is no reason to believe the local residents are now eating and drinking more than in the days before downtown baseball. If the goal was to relocate business activity to a new, trendy location in the city core, then the stadiums have been a clear success. If the goal was to increase total economic activity in these cities, there is less reason for cheer.

Biographical Sketch

Al Davis
(1929–2011)

> *To me, professional football is a business and an avocation. I never
> wanted to hurt anybody. To Davis, it is a war.*
>
> —*Gene Klein*[56]

For most of the 2000s, the Oakland Raiders were known as a dysfunc-
tional losing team. In the 1980s and 1990s, they were a successful but
peripatetic franchise, moving from Oakland to Los Angeles and back
again. From the late 1960s through the 1970s, all they did was win. All
three of these eras reflected the personality of their long-time owner, Al
Davis. Until his death in 2011, Al Davis *was* the Raiders. He had been their
head coach, general manager, team owner, even—briefly—the commissioner of the league in which they played. In so doing, he infuriated his
fellow team owners, as well as the residents of northern and southern California as his team moved from Oakland to Los Angeles and back again.

As an undergraduate at Syracuse University in the early 1950s, Davis
became enchanted by the innovative offensive schemes of the team's
football coach, Ben Schwartzwalder. Although he had no official position
with the team, Davis became a fixture at team practices. Never one to
let the lack of credentials get in his way, Davis talked his way into a job
as an assistant coach at Adelphi University after graduating from Syracuse. Later stops at the Citadel and the University of Southern California
confirmed Davis as a first-rate offensive mind and a brilliant recruiter.
These qualities also had a downside, as Davis constantly battled with fellow assistant coaches and never hid his desire to be head coach. To make
matters worse, his aggressive recruiting practices often ran afoul of NCAA
rules.

Tainted by scandal and unable to find a head coaching position, Davis
found himself adrift in 1960 when the fledgling AFL opened up a realm
of new opportunities. He soon found a position on the staff of the Los
Angeles (later San Diego) Chargers' head coach Sid Gillman, an acclaimed
offensive genius. With the Chargers, Davis refined the concept of an

attacking, pass-oriented offense and applied his marketing skills to stealing players from the NFL and rival AFL clubs. In 1963, Davis's success with the Chargers brought him the chance of a lifetime—though it hardly seemed so then.

When Davis arrived in Oakland, the Raiders were the laughingstock of the AFL. They were, in fact, something of an accidental franchise. The AFL had originally hoped to locate a flagship franchise in Minneapolis. Caught unprepared when the NFL hastily expanded to Minneapolis, the AFL awarded the Minnesota franchise to Oakland even though no one had expressed an interest in owning a franchise there. A group led by developer Wayne Valley eventually stepped forward, but the Raiders reflected their slapdash origins, compiling an appalling record in front of minuscule crowds. In 1963, desperate for a respectable team, the Raiders hired Davis as head coach. Within a year, Davis made the Raiders competitive, and within five years, they were playing in the Super Bowl. By that time, however, Davis had moved beyond the coaching ranks.

In 1966, the AFL's owners narrowly approved Davis as the league's second commissioner. Six months later, they negotiated a merger with the NFL behind his back. This experience confirmed Davis's low opinion of football's owners and instilled a deep dislike of NFL Commissioner Pete Rozelle, whom Davis—Rozelle's opposite in upbringing and temperament—felt had undermined him during the merger talks. Some even believe that Davis felt that he should have been named commissioner of the expanded league.

His term as commissioner quickly over, Davis again was a man without a team until Wayne Valley brought him back in 1966 as a "managing general partner" with a one-tenth interest in the team. Valley soon regretted bringing Davis back to Oakland. In 1972, Davis masterminded a coup that reduced Valley to a figurehead position and—after four years of bitter legal battles—gave Davis control of the team.

As effective owner of the Raiders, Davis quickly became a pariah among the other owners, who were deeply committed to the "league-think" approach of Commissioner Rozelle. Whether out of principle or personal animosity, Davis repeatedly challenged the rest of the league. Unlike his peers, he welcomed free agency, declaring, "Just cut all the players and make everybody a free agent." He testified on behalf of the USFL in its antitrust suit against the NFL. (In return, the USFL pointedly sued only 27 of the 28 NFL teams.) He even refused to sign over the Raiders' share of profits from NFL Properties to the NFL Charities Foundation, claiming that the Raiders did their charity work locally.

Davis's biggest challenge to Rozelle and the NFL came in March 1980, when he sought to move the Raiders to Los Angeles. Davis had long coveted a larger stage than Oakland afforded, and he was among the first owners to see that favorable stadium deals would affect the balance of power in the NFL. The other owners, however, forbade him from moving the team, citing the league's constitution, which barred a team from moving into another's home territory without the league's unanimous consent. Davis responded by filing an antitrust suit against the NFL. After a series of trials that were finally settled in 1989, the NFL dropped its objections to the move and agreed to pay the Raiders $18 million. Davis quickly became disenchanted with Los Angeles. The rush to an agreement had left much of the language open to multiple interpretations, and Davis soon saw that his move would not bring the financial benefits that he had anticipated.

The return to Oakland in 1995 was not a joyous homecoming. Perhaps because of their many moves, the Raiders were not the dominant team that they had been in the 1970s and 1980s. Almost constant litigation since the mid-1970s absorbed much of Davis's time and energy. In addition, the rest of the league finally caught on to Davis's tactics, both on the field and off. In the end, the man who had for so long been one step ahead of his colleagues found himself behind the times.

Sources: Glenn Dickey. 1991. *Just Win, Baby: Al Davis and His Raiders* (New York: Harcourt, Brace and Jovanovich); David Harris. 1986. *The League: The Rise and Decline of the NFL* (New York: Bantam Books); and Mark Ribowsky. 1991. *Slick: The Silver and Black Life of Al Davis* (New York: Macmillan).

Summary

Teams, fans, and cities all benefit from the presence of new facilities, though not in the same way or to the same degree. New facilities typically mean more fans for the teams that play in them, as a "honeymoon effect" can last for up to a decade. In addition, new facilities typically bring additional premium seating, which adds further to teams' revenues.

Baseball and football fans have benefited from the new configuration of stadiums. As teams moved from shared, multi-purpose stadiums to their own facilities, they have been able to change their size and shape to conform to their specific needs. Because basketball and hockey draw similar crowds and have similar playing areas, there has not been a similar move to separate, uniquely shaped facilities for these two sports. Soccer in the United States has also moved to create soccer-specific stadiums that are sized to accommodate the smaller crowds the sport attracts.

Cities can benefit in a variety of ways. A new facility can increase a city's net exports, increasing the amount that outsiders spend in the city and reducing what city residents spend elsewhere. This added spending could have a multiplied effect, as people earning the first round of direct spending spend more themselves, increasing the incomes of others, and so on. Unfortunately, studies have shown that the impact on net exports is relatively small, as spending on sports displaces other spending. The multiplier effect is also small. While stadiums rarely create new economic activity, they can serve to effectively relocate economic activity within a city or metropolitan area.

Discussion Questions

1   Describe the externalities associated with a football stadium compared with an amusement park. Which would have greater positive externalities? Which would have greater negative externalities?

2   Suppose your city (or the nearest city housing an NBA franchise) is deciding where to build a new arena. Think of two or three possible sites and describe the pros and cons of each. Which site do you think is best?

3   Who will benefit most from the new stadium in Minneapolis: the Vikings, their fans, or the city as a whole?

Problems

6.1 Why is the multiplier effect for the Los Angeles Lakers likely to be greater than the multiplier effect for the Sacramento Kings, when they are both teams in the NBA?

6.2 Why are the negative externalities associated with the new Barclays Centre in Brooklyn likely to be greater than the negative externalities associated with the Staples Center in Los Angeles?

6.3 If a majority of people do not want a stadium built, how can building it lead to an improvement in social well-being?

6.4 While football and baseball teams have gone from multipurpose to football- and baseball-only facilities, basketball and hockey teams continue to share arenas. Why?

6.5 If the marginal propensity to consume in a municipality is 0.8, what is the value of the simple multiplier? If a new stadium that adds $30 million in new consumption expenditures is built, what is the impact on the economy based on this multiplier? Suppose the marginal propensity to import is 0.3, what happens to the multiplier and to the impact on the economy?

6.6 How does your answer change if city residents spend 60 cents of every additional dollar on goods made in other cities or countries?

6.7 If a new baseball stadium has only a very short-term impact on a team's attendance, why do MLB teams still pursue them?

6.8 The Seattle Sounders are the most financially successful team in MLS. They attracted over 42,000 fans per game in both 2015 and 2016 to the stadium they share with the Seattle Seahawks of the NFL. Should the Sounders try to build a soccer-specific stadium? Why or why not?

Notes

1   Quoted in Joanna Cagan and Neil deMause. 1998. *Field of Schemes* (Monroe, ME: Common Cause Press): 137.

2   Students of the film or the book on which it is based, *Shoeless Joe* by W.P. Kinsella, will know that the correct quotation is "Build it and *he* will come" (emphasis added).

3   Mark Rosentraub. 1997. "Stadiums and Urban Space," in *Sports, Jobs, and Taxes,* ed. Roger Noll and Andrew Zimbalist (Washington, DC: Brookings Institution Press): 178–180.

4   According to Munsey and Suppes. 2017. *Ballparks.com*, Cowboys Stadium cost about $1.15 billion to construct, New Yankee Stadium cost $1.3 billon, and the Barclays Centre, which hosts the NBA's Brooklyn Nets, cost $1 billion.

5   Attendance figures here and later in the chapter are based on data from *Baseball Almanac*, at www.baseball-almanac.com and *ESPN.com*, viewed February 8, 2017.

6   The following discussion is taken from Christopher M. Clapp and Jahn K. Hakes. 2005. "How Long a Honeymoon? The Effect of New Stadiums on Attendance in Major League Baseball," *Journal of Sports Economics*, 6(3), August: 237–263; John C. Leadley and Zenon X. Zygmont. 2005. "When Is the Honeymoon Over? National Basketball Association Attendance 1971–2000," *Journal of Sports Economics*, 6(2), May: 203–221; John C. Leadley and Zenon X. Zygmont, 2005. "When Is the Honeymoon Over? Major League Baseball Attendance 1970–2000," *Journal of Sport Management*, 19(3), July: 278–299; and John C. Leadley and Zenon X. Zygmont. 2006. "When Is the Honeymoon

Over? National Hockey League Attendance 1970–2003," *Canadian Public Policy*, 32(2), 2006: 213–232.

7   The Yankees' attendance was 4,298,655 in 2008 and 3,719,358 in 2009. Their gate revenue was $217 million in 2008 and $319 million in 2009. Average ticket prices were $47 in 2008 and $67 in 2009. See "New York Yankees Attendance Data." 2012. *Baseball Almanac*, http://www.baseball-almanac.com/teams/yankatte.shtml, viewed May 21, 2012; Kurt Badenhausen and Michael Ozanian. 2009. "The Business of Baseball," *Forbes.com*, April 22, at http://www.forbes.com/lists/2009/33/baseball-values-09_New-York-Yankees_334613.html; and Kurt Badenhausen, Michael Ozanian, and Christina Settimi. 2010. "The Business of Baseball," *Forbes.com*, April 7, at http://www.forbes.com/lists/2010/33/baseball-valuations-10_New-York-Yankees_334613.html.

8   Peter S. Canellos. 1997. "In City with Short Memory, Astrodome May Become History," *Milwaukee Journal-Sentinel,* July 27: 26A. The Colosseum, which held 80,000 people, also had drinking fountains and elevators that allowed animals to appear in the arena as if by magic. Unlike most stadiums today, it was privately funded (by slaves and booty taken during the conquest of Jerusalem) and remained in use for 500 years. See Joe Meyer. 2009. *The Roman Colosseum*, at http://www.synthreal.com/Colosseum.htm, March 10; and Louis Feldman. 2001. "Financing the Colosseum," *Biblical Archaeology Review*, 27(4), July/August, at https://members.bib-arch.org/biblical-archaeology-review/27/4/1.

9   Edgar W. Ray. 1980. *The Grand Huckster: Houston's Judge Roy Hofheinz, Genius of the Astrodome* (Memphis, TN: Memphis State University Press); 230–231.

10 Figures are from Munsey and Suppes. 2017. *Ballparks.com*, viewed April 27, 2017.

11 Munsey and Suppes. 2017. *Ballparks.com,* viewed April 27, 2017; and Cork Gaines. 2014. "A Luxury Suite at the New 49ers Stadium Will Cost You up to $60,000," *Business Insider*, October 22, at http://www.businessinsider.com/49ers-stadium-suites-nfl-2014-10.

12 James Rufus Koren and Roger Vincent. 2017. "How Much Could the Rams and Chargers Make in their New Stadium? We Ran the Numbers," *Los Angeles Times*, February 11, at http://www.latimes.com/business/la-fi-rams-chargers-revenue-20170211-story.html.

13 Several of these stadiums also hosted soccer teams in the North American Soccer League or major soccer events, but the use of these stadiums as soccer facilities was almost certainly an afterthought.

14 NFL teams even adopted variants of the names of those MLB teams whose facilities they used (e.g., the Chicago Bears, who rented Wrigley Field from the Cubs) or took on the names of the teams themselves (e.g., the New York Giants of the NFL, who rented the Polo Grounds from MLB's Giants).

15 Quoted in Rich Westcott. 1996. *Philadelphia's Old Ballparks* (Philadelphia, PA: Temple University Press): 32.

16 Stew Thornley. 2000. *Land of the Giants: New York's Polo Grounds* (Philadelphia, PA: Temple University Press): 3.

17 See Robert La Franco. 1997. "Profits on Ice," *Forbes*, May 5: 86–89.

18 Jahn Hakes and Christopher Clapp. 2006. "The Edifice Complex: The Economics of Public Subsidization of Major League Baseball Facilities," *The International Journal of Sport Finance*, 1(2): 77–95; and Kevin Quinn, Paul Bursik, Christopher Borick, and Lisa Raethz. 2003. "Do New Digs Mean More Wins? The Relationship between a New Venue and a Professional Sports Team's Competitive Success," *Journal of Sports Economics*, 4(3), August: 167–182.

19 See Quinn et al. 2003. "Do New Digs Mean More Wins?"; and Hakes and Clapp. 2006. "The Edifice Complex."

20 Robert Baade and Victor Matheson. 2006. "Have Public Finance Principles Been Shut Out in Financing New Stadiums for the NFL?" *Public Finance and Management*, 6(3), July: 284–320.

21 Seth Gitter and Thomas Rhoads. 2014. "Stadium Construction and Minor League Baseball Attendance," *Contemporary Economic Policy*, 32(1), January: 144–154.

22 Michael Danielson. 1997. *Home Team: Professional Sport and the American Metropolis* (Princeton, NJ: Princeton University Press); Mark Rosentraub. 1997. *Major League*

Losers (New York: Basic Books): 30–73; and David Swindell and Mark Rosentraub. 1998. "Who Benefits from the Presence of Professional Sports Teams? The Implications for Public Funding of Stadiums and Arenas," *Public Administration Review*, 58(1), January/February: 11–20.

23 Bill Veeck with Ed Linn. 1962. *Veeck as in Wreck* (Chicago, IL: University of Chicago Press): 121. Emphasis in original.

24 This term is often used to denote the collective fans of the Boston Red Sox, particularly those living in New England. The term has been traced to an article about the split loyalties of Connecticut residents during the 1986 New York Mets/Boston Red Sox World Series. Nathan Cobb. 1986. "Baseball Border War: In Milford, Conn. Geography Brings Sox and Mets Fans Cheek to Jowl," *Boston Globe*, October 20: 8.

25 Mark Rosentraub, 1997. "Stadiums and Urban Space": 189–190; and Swindell and Rosentraub, 1998. "Who Benefits from the Presence of Professional Sports Teams?": 11–20.

26 The new NFL stadium planned for Las Vegas, an even smaller city than Indianapolis, proposes a $750 million public subsidy.

27 Robert Baade and Victor Matheson. 2013. "Financing Professional Sports Facilities," in *Financing Economic Development in the 21st Century*, ed. Sammis White and Zenia Kotval (Armonk, NY: M.E. Sharpe).

28 Franklin Foer. 2004. *How Soccer Explains the World: An Unlikely Theory of Globalization* (New York: Harper Collins): 195.

29 See, e.g., Hakes and Clapp. 2006. "The Edifice Complex": 78; and Judith Grant Long. 2012. *Public/Private Partnerships for Major League Sports Facilities* (New York: Routledge Research in Sport Business and Management).

30 Some teams, including the Cubs, have tried to reduce or eliminate negative externalities. The Cubs provide shuttle buses to reduce traffic, and cleanup crews to reduce litter in the surrounding community. See Christopher Hepp. 1999. "Near Fabled Park, Ambience a Lure," *Philadelphia Inquirer* (September 29): A1, A6.

31 See the Foreword to Michael Betzold and Ethan Casey. 1992. *Queen of Diamonds: The Tiger Stadium Story* (West Bloomfield, MI: Northfield Publishing).

32 Gary R. Roberts, Stephen F. Ross, and Robert A. Baade. 1995. "Should Congress Stop the Bidding War for Sports Franchises?" Hearing Before the Subcommittee on Antitrust, Business Rights, and Compensation, Senate Committee on the Judiciary, November 29, vol. 4, "Academics," *Heartland Policy*, at https://www.heartland.org/_template-assets/documents/publications/3924.pdf: 19.

33 The total revenue data come from the *Forbes* team valuations for 2015–2016. Personal income data for Cook County, Illinois come from US Department of Commerce, "Table CA1-3: Personal Income Summary," *Regional Data: GDP & Personal Income*, at http://www.bea.gov/iTable/iTable.cfm?reqid=70&step=1&isuri=1&acrdn=5, viewed March 17, 2017.

34 The following argument is based on John Siegfried and Andrew Zimbalist. 2002. "A Note on the Local Economic Impact of Sports Expenditures," *Journal of Sports Economics*, 3(4), November: 361–366.

35 John Siegfried and Andrew Zimbalist. 2000. "The Economics of Sports Facilities and Their Construction," *Journal of Economic Perspectives*, 14(3), Summer: 95–114.

36 See Roger Noll and Andrew Zimbalist. 1997. "The Economic Impact of Sports Teams and Facilities," in *Sports, Jobs, and Taxes*, ed. Roger Noll and Andrew Zimbalist (Washington, DC: Brookings Institution Press, 1997): 79–80; and Peter von Allmen. 2012. "Multiplier Effects and Local Economic Impact," in Stephen Shmanske and Leo Kahane, eds. *The Oxford Handbook of Sports Economics*, vol. 2 (Oxford: Oxford University Press).

37 For a good survey of this literature, see Dennis Coates. 2007. "Stadiums and Arenas: Economic Development or Economic Redistribution?" *Contemporary Economic Policy*, 25(4), October: 565–577.

38 Robert Baade and Richard Dye. 1988. "Sports Stadiums and Area Development: A Critical Review." *Economic Development Quarterly*, 2(3), August: 265–275; Dennis Coates and Brad R. Humphreys, "The Effect of Professional Sports on Earnings and Employment in U.S. Cities," *Regional Science and Urban Economics*, 33(2), March: 175–198;

Robert Baade, Robert Baumann, and Victor Matheson. 2008. "Selling the Game: Estimating the Economic Impact of Professional Sports through Taxable Sales," *Southern Economic Journal,* 74(3): 794–810.

39   Tu's case study of FedEx Field in Landover, MD does not account for the fact that another venue—US Airways Arena—closed at about the same time that FedEx Field opened, while Carlino and Coulson exclude a large number of low-value properties. See Gerald Carlino and N. Edward Coulson. 2004. "Compensating Differentials and the Social Benefit of the NFL," *Journal of Urban Economics,* 56(1), July: 25–50; and Charles Tu. 2005. "How Does a New Stadium Affect Housing Values? The Case of FedEx Field," *Land Economics,* 81(3), August: 379–395.

40   Dennis Coates and Brad R. Humphreys. 2003. "Professional Sports Facilities, Franchises and Urban Economic Development," *Public Finance and Management,* 3(3): 335–357; and Brad Humphreys and Xia Feng. 2012. "The Impact of Sports Facilities on Housing Values: Evidence from Census Block Group Data," *City, Culture and Society,* 3(3), September: 189–200.

41   See Kevin Delaney. 2003. *Public Dollars, Private Stadiums* (New Brunswick, NJ: Rutgers University Press); and Robert Trumpbour. 2007. *The New Cathedrals* (Syracuse, NY: Syracuse University Press).

42   See, for example, Arthur Seldon. 1987. "Public Choice and the Choices of the Public," in *Democracy and Public Choice,* ed. Charles Rowley (London: Basil Blackwell): 122–134.

43   In 2001, the Steelers and Pirates in Pittsburgh received state financing for new stadiums only after their state legislators agreed to support state subsidies for building new stadiums in Philadelphia for the Eagles and Phillies.

44   See, for example, Thomas Stratmann. 1997. "Logrolling," in *Perspectives on Public Choice: A Handbook,* ed. Dennis Mueller (Cambridge, UK: Cambridge University Press): 322–341.

45   Cagan and deMause. 1998. *Field of Schemes:* 16, 44, 166–168.

46   See Kevin Delaney. 2003. *Public Dollars, Private Stadiums;* Robert Trumpbour. 2007. *The New Cathedrals;* and Baird Helgeson and Jennifer Brooks. 2012. "After Years of Dealing and Debate, Vikings Get Their Biggest Win," *Minnesota Star-Tribune,* May 11, at http://www.startribune.com/politics/statelocal/150960525.html, viewed May 12, 2012.

47   Associated Press. 2000. "Soldier Field Referendum Rejected," December 29, 2000.

48   Steve Chapman. 2003. "A Stadium Deal That Is Hard to Bear," *Chicago Tribune,* September 14, 2003.

49   Thomas Chema. 1996. "When Professional Sports Justify the Subsidy," *Journal of Urban Affairs,* 18(1): 20; and Robert Baade and Allen Sanderson. 1997. "The Employment Effect of Teams and Sports Facilities," in *Sports, Jobs, and Taxes: The Economic Impact of Sports Teams and Stadiums,* ed. Roger G. Noll and Andrew Zimbalist (Washington, DC: Brookings Institution Press): 94–95.

50   Ziona Austrian and Mark Rosentraub. "Cleveland's Gateway to the Future," in *Sports, Jobs, and Taxes,* ed. Roger Noll and Andrew Zimbalist (Washington, DC: Brookings Institution Press, 1997): 355–384.

51   Bruce Hamilton and Peter Kahn. 1997. "Baltimore's Camden Yards Ballparks," in *Sports, Jobs, and Taxes,* ed. Roger Noll and Andrew Zimbalist (Washington, DC: Brookings Institution Press): 245–281.

52   See Bruce Kuklick. 1991. *To Everything a Season: Shibe Park and Urban Philadelphia, 1909–1976* (Princeton, NJ: Princeton University Press): 21–25; and Westcott. 1996. *Philadelphia's Old Ballparks:* 104–105.

53   William Nack. 1999. "This Old House," *Sports Illustrated,* June 7: 100–116.

54   Harold Seymour. 1971. *Baseball: The Golden Years* (New York: Oxford University Press): 52.

55   Ross Roberts and Robert Baade. 1995. "Should Congress Stop the Bidding War for Sports Franchises?", 4: 16.

56   Eugene Klein. 1987. *First Down and a Billion: The Funny Business of Professional Football* (New York: Morrow).

7

THE PUBLIC FINANCE OF SPORTS

Who Pays and Why?

Introduction

One day in the late 1950s, Jack Newfield and Pete Hamill, both reporters for New York newspapers, discussed writing an article called "The Ten Worst Human Beings Who Ever Lived." On a whim, each wrote the names of the three people he regarded as "the all-time worst" on a napkin. To their amazement, they listed the same three names: Adolf Hitler, Joseph Stalin, and Walter O'Malley.[3]

Since Newfield and Hamill lived in a nation with fresh memories of the Second World War and new worries over the Cold War, their inclusion of Hitler and Stalin was no surprise, but their both naming O'Malley, then-owner of the Los Angeles Dodgers, was. Unlike his companions on the list, O'Malley committed neither war crimes nor genocide. Instead, he forever changed the landscape of professional sports by moving the Dodgers from Brooklyn to Los Angeles. From that point on, sports franchises recognized that they had tremendous leverage in their dealings with the cities that hosted them. They were quick to exercise that market power, insisting that cities bear a much greater share of the burden of constructing and maintaining sports venues than they had in the past. In this chapter, we explain the source of the teams' market power and show how teams exercise it in their dealings with cities. In Chapter 8, we extend this reasoning to see how the sponsors of mega-events, such as the International Olympic Committee, exert similar market power in choosing a host city. Finally, we consider costs from the viewpoint of cities. We show that the cost of construction helps dictate where cities place stadiums, and we evaluate the ways cities fund the construction of facilities that now typically cost billions of dollars.

Learning Objectives

- Appreciate the connection between the mobility of sports franchises and the increase in public funding of stadiums and arenas.

- Understand the ways that sports teams, leagues, and institutions exercise monopoly power in their dealings with municipalities.
- Grasp the impact that exchange rates and stadium location have on the ability of cities to retain franchises and subsidize facilities.
- Appreciate the advantages and disadvantages of different methods of financing public support of sports facilities.

7.1   How Cities Came to Fund Stadiums

Today it seems normal for teams to threaten to look for a new home unless their current host city builds a new facility or restructures the rental agreement on the current one. It wasn't always this way. Until the 1950s, teams seldom moved, and few noticed or cared if one did. This section provides a historical context for the growing mobility of sports franchises and their consequent increase in market power.

Teams on the Move

While the Dodgers' move to Los Angeles was the most notorious relocation, the Dodgers were not the first team to change cities. Nor was baseball the only sport to experience such moves. In the 19th century, teams entered, exited, and moved so frequently that they were reluctant to erect permanent facilities. In general, they moved from small towns to large cities. The NFL likes to reminisce about its small-town Midwestern origins, but professional football did not become financially stable until teams like the Decatur Staleys and Portsmouth Spartans had moved to large cities to become the Chicago Bears and Detroit Lions.[4] Between 1920 and 1935, over 50 teams played at least one season in the NFL, 43 of which had folded or relocated by the end of that era. Unfavorable locations proved the undoing of entire leagues, as seen by the demise of baseball's American Association in the 1890s, the National Basketball League (NBL) in the 1940s, and the women's American Basketball League in the 1990s. Following the merger of the Basketball Association of America and the NBL in 1949 to form the NBA, only 8 of the original 23 teams still existed after 5 years, and 4 of the remaining teams had relocated by 1960.[5]

The "Golden Age" of baseball marked the longest period of franchise stability. Between 1903, when the Baltimore Orioles left for New York to become the Highlanders (and later the Yankees), and 1953, when the Braves left Boston for Milwaukee, no MLB team entered, left, or changed cities. Baseball's growing prosperity led to the construction of its historic ballparks, starting with Shibe Park in Philadelphia and Forbes Field in Pittsburgh in 1909 and Comiskey Park in Chicago a year later. The construction boom ended with Yankee Stadium in 1923. Over the next 30 years, only one new baseball stadium was built, Cleveland's Municipal Stadium.

The Braves' move to Milwaukee did not necessarily signal the end of MLB's Golden Age. The Boston Braves, the Philadelphia Athletics, who moved to Kansas City in 1954 (and then to Oakland in 1968), and the St. Louis Browns, who moved to Baltimore and were rechristened the Orioles in 1953, were all neglected stepsisters in cities whose hearts belonged to the Red Sox, Phillies, and Cardinals, respectively. When the Braves left Boston, few fans noticed and fewer still mourned their loss. In the Braves' first nine games in Milwaukee, they drew as many fans as they had attracted in the entire preceding year.[6]

Unlike the franchises that moved in the early 1950s, the Brooklyn Dodgers were second to none. In the 11 years prior to their move, from 1947 to 1957, the Dodgers were the most successful and most profitable team in the National League. Their value, moreover, went beyond dollars and cents. The Dodgers were "a cultural totem" for the residents of Brooklyn, a rallying point for those who felt scorned by the wealthier, more sophisticated Manhattanites.[7] It was this sense of loss—and the sense of powerlessness that accompanied it—that prompted the sportswriters to elevate O'Malley to the elite company of Hitler and Stalin.

To O'Malley, the issue was a simple matter of economic reasoning. While the Dodgers did well in Brooklyn, he realized that they would do even better if they had Los Angeles and, at the time, all southern California to themselves. O'Malley recognized the difference between accounting and economic profit. **Accounting profit** is what we typically think of as profit, the revenue a firm makes minus its explicit cost of production. **Economic profit** equals revenue minus all opportunity costs of the firm's production decisions. Opportunity costs include the explicit costs of the resources used in the production process *plus* the profit that could have been earned in the firm's best alternative activity. In this case, a major opportunity cost of O'Malley's keeping the Dodgers in Brooklyn was the revenue they could have earned had they moved to Los Angeles. Because economic profit subtracts all costs, a firm can have negative economic profit even when its accounting profit is very high. The Dodgers thus had very high accounting profits, but the profit they sacrificed by playing in front of about 1 million fans each year in Brooklyn rather than over 2 million fans in Los Angeles was too great to ignore.

The Four Eras of Stadium Construction

Building on the work of Judith Grant Long, we identify four phases of stadium funding.[8] The first phase, which Long calls the "entrepreneurial period," lasted from 1890 to 1930. During this period, the owners of baseball teams built and operated their own ballparks. The owners of several hockey teams did the same thing, though we focus here on baseball, as it was the dominant professional sport in the United States. In contrast, football teams lacked both the money and the fans to construct their own stadiums, and basketball did not even have a stable league.[9]

Almost all the facilities built during this period had two common features. First, only one facility had the word *stadium* in its title. The rest had names like Wrigley Field or Shibe Park.[10] The use of the words *Park* and *Field* reflects the pastoral origins of baseball. Prior to the enclosure of games in private structures, baseball teams played in open fields or parks. They typically built ballparks to prevent bystanders from seeing ballgames for free.[11] The term *stadium* was not used until Jacob Ruppert applied the name to his new "Yankee Stadium" in 1923 to recall the grandeur of classical architecture. (*Stadium* comes from the Greek word *stadion,* which originally meant a specific distance, later referred to a race of that distance, and eventually came to mean the seats for spectators who watched the race.) Second, most of the ballparks, with exceptions like Fenway Park, bore the name of the owner of the team for which the stadium was built.

The stability that baseball enjoyed during its "Golden Age" kept teams in the facilities they built in the early 20th century. Prior to 1950, Cleveland's Municipal Stadium and the Los Angeles Coliseum were the only major publicly built facilities, and the Coliseum was built for the Olympics, not baseball or football. The aging of the facilities, the changing face of American cities, and the growing market power of franchises led to the gradual disappearance of facilities built in the first period. Only Wrigley Field and Fenway Park still exist.

Long refers to the second period as the era of "civic infrastructure," in which cities viewed teams and stadiums as centerpieces of urban development. With franchises becoming mobile, cities often bid against one another to attract or retain them. As a result, the public sector often bore the full cost of stadium funding. The second period began in 1953, with the construction of Milwaukee's County Stadium and Baltimore's Memorial Stadium, and lasted until about 1982 with the construction of Minneapolis' Metrodome. Many of the stadiums built during this period were named for the cities or counties that funded them, such as Atlanta-Fulton County Stadium or Seattle's (King County) Kingdome. Others, such as Cincinnati's Riverfront Stadium or Pittsburgh's Three Rivers Stadium, were identified with distinctive local geographical features. Still others, such as Veterans Stadium in Philadelphia, took on patriotic names.

Long's third period, which she calls the "public–private partnership," began after 1980 and significantly accelerated with the opening of Oriole Park at Camden Yards in 1992. This lasted until at least 2007. During this period, local and state governments funded about two-thirds of the construction costs, with teams and leagues paying the rest. With the decline in public subsidies, teams sought out new sources of income. One such source is found in the names of the facilities, which bear the names of private sponsors that purchased naming rights. The sale of naming rights even extends to totally publicly financed facilities, such as the Toyota Center in Houston or the FedEx Forum in Memphis.

We denote a fourth era of stadium construction beginning in 2008 with the onset of the Great Recession. Between 1989 and 2007, North American cities initiated an average of six major stadium or arena projects every year for professional sports franchises. With the start of the most significant economic downturn since the Great Depression, state and local governments experienced major financial difficulties. Local authorities and taxpayers found it increasingly distasteful to provide lavish subsidies to millionaire players and billionaire owners while having to lay off police officers, firefighters, and teachers. While numerous stadiums and arenas that were already under construction when the downturn hit, such as Yankee Stadium and Orlando's Amway Center, were completed during the recession, other projects were delayed or cancelled, and the pace of new project proposals crawled to a halt.

While it did not rival baseball's "Golden Age," the NFL had its own period of stability in the 1960s and 1970s. For 15 years after the Chicago Cardinals moved to St. Louis in 1960, no NFL team changed cities. The first crack in the system—the New York Giants' move from Yankee Stadium in the Bronx to Giants Stadium in New Jersey in 1976—was so short that it might have gone unnoticed were it not for the flap caused by the Giants' crossing state lines but not changing their name. The move actually put the Giants closer to midtown Manhattan. Similarly, the Los Angeles Rams did not bother to change their name when they moved down the freeway to Anaheim in 1980. In addition, both team owners—Wellington Mara of the Giants and Carroll Rosenbloom of the Rams—were liked and respected by their peers. This last point was crucial, as the NFL's Board of Governors had to give unanimous approval to any move.

The next move proved harder to swallow. No sooner had the Rams left town than Al Davis moved his Oakland Raiders into the now-empty Los Angeles Memorial Coliseum. To use a baseball metaphor, this move had three strikes against it. First, the move was so far—close to 400 miles—that Davis could not argue—as Mara and Rosenbloom did—that his team was still serving its long-time fans. Second, in relocating to Los Angeles, Davis was moving within 75 miles of the Rams' new home in Anaheim. Third, Davis was as unpopular with his fellow owners as Mara and Rosenbloom were popular. The NFL board again voted unanimously, 22–0, but this time the vote was against the move.

The result was the groundbreaking lawsuit, *LA Memorial Coliseum Commission v. NFL*, in which the LA Memorial Coliseum Commission and Al Davis joined forces to claim that the NFL had violated section 1 of the Sherman Antitrust Act when it tried to prevent the Raiders from moving. The Los Angeles District Court found, using the rule of reason standard, "that the restriction on franchise movement was anti-competitive because it perpetuated local monopolies,"[12] a ruling that was upheld in 1984 by the Ninth Circuit Court. Rather than appeal the awarding of $4.6 million to the Coliseum, and $11.5 million to the Raiders—both of which would be trebled—the NFL settled out of court, agreeing to pay $18 million and to grant formal approval to the Raiders' move. (They had moved anyway in 1982.)[13]

The ruling opened the floodgates to moves by other NFL franchises. The Baltimore Colts moved to Indianapolis in 1984, the Rams moved again, this time to St. Louis in 1995, the Cleveland Browns departed for Baltimore (and became the Ravens) in 1996, and the Houston Oilers decamped for Tennessee (and became the Titans) in 1997. In a crowning irony, the Raiders returned to Oakland in 1995, leaving the Los Angeles area without a franchise for over 20 years.

Similar moves occurred in basketball and hockey, though the courts allowed leagues to block some moves, such as the Phoenix Coyotes' attempt to move to Winnipeg, if they had a reasonable relocation policy in place. Only baseball, thanks to its antitrust exemption, managed to avoid wholesale moves. The only baseball team to move since the court ruling was the Montreal Expos, who at that time were a ward of the league, to Washington, DC.

7.2 How Teams Exploit Monopoly Power

The Dodgers' move fundamentally altered the relationship between teams and the cities that host them. If the highly profitable Dodgers could be uprooted, so could any team. Teams began to exploit the monopoly power they exerted by encouraging bidding wars between cities hoping to attract a team and cities that were determined to keep "their" team. The bids have generally taken the form of new facilities that are either subsidized or entirely funded by the host city.

Leagues, Cities, and Market Power

For over 100 years, North American sports leagues have limited the number of teams to increase both competitive balance and profits. They have feared that admitting too many teams would lead to competitive imbalance, which can cause fans to lose interest and harm all teams. The fear of instability made all sports leagues reluctant to expand until the 1960s. Leagues also limit the number of teams because it allows them to raise the "price" cities will pay to attract or retain teams, thereby maximizing the profits of the members of the cartel.

As early as the 1930s, demographic changes and falling transportation costs put pressure on MLB to expand, but the Great Depression and World War II delayed any moves. By the mid-1940s, the distribution of teams made little financial sense. For example, Los Angeles had no major league teams, while Boston had two baseball teams and a hockey team.[14]

After the war, both MLB and the NFL placed teams on the West Coast, but neither league increased the number of teams. The NFL's Rams left Cleveland for Los Angeles in 1946, a move prompted by the creation of the Cleveland Browns of the new All-American Football Conference.[15] Baseball had an explicit offer to expand westward when the Pacific Coast League (PCL), a high minor league that had sent such stars as Joe DiMaggio and Ted Williams to MLB, proposed becoming a third major league. The negotiations collapsed when MLB, which regarded its own reserve clause as sacrosanct, refused to honor the PCL's contracts with its own players. Instead, MLB allowed the Giants and Dodgers to move to the West Coast, reducing the PCL to truly minor league status.[16]

MLB seemed content to respond to demographic pressures by rearranging franchises until it undertook the first systematic expansion by a professional sports league in 1961. The new policy, however, did not reflect a new business plan. Instead, it was a direct response to pressure from Congress. Seeing the controversial moves of the Dodgers and Giants, and aghast at the impending loss of the Washington Senators to Minneapolis–St. Paul (where they became the Twins), Congress had begun to investigate baseball's antitrust exemption. In addition, Branch Rickey, the man who built the great Cardinal teams of the 1930s and Dodger teams of the late 1940s and 1950s, was trying to form a new league, with two of the flagship teams planned for Houston and New York. Not surprisingly, three of MLB's first four expansion teams were in Houston, New York, and Washington, DC.[17] Creating these three teams placated Congress and prevented the rival league from forming. The fourth team, the Los Angeles Angels, gave the American League the West Coast presence that it had long coveted.

The NFL's first several expansions also came under duress. As noted in Chapter 4, the NFL had no intention of expanding in the early 1960s until it learned that the fledgling AFL planned to put teams in Dallas and Minneapolis. The AFL also spurred the NFL's second expansion in 1967. This time, however, the motive was peace, not war. The NFL and AFL recognized that their impending merger would violate antitrust laws and requested a limited exemption that would allow them to merge. In their path stood two powerful legislators from Louisiana, Representative Hale Boggs and Senator Russell Long, who could have delayed or derailed the legislation. Fortunately for the NFL, both men were keen to have an NFL franchise in New Orleans. Less than two weeks after Congress passed the legislation granting the NFL and AFL the right to merge, the NFL approved the creation of the New Orleans Saints.[18]

Cities sometimes contribute to the monopoly power of teams by committing themselves to projects despite having no corresponding guarantee from the franchise. For example, in May 1990, the residents of Cuyahoga County, which includes Cleveland, voted to approve the construction of a new baseball stadium for the Indians and a new basketball arena for the Cavaliers, who were playing in the Richfield Coliseum in a nearby suburb. Unfortunately for Cuyahoga County, neither the Indians nor the Cavaliers had agreed to lease terms or to architectural plans for the facilities before the referendum. Having committed themselves to new facilities, the civic leaders forfeited any bargaining power with the franchises. The teams then insisted on such added features as stadium suites, office complexes, and restaurants, all at no extra charge to them. These add-ons increased the cost of Jacobs Field from $127 million to $175 million and raised the cost of Gund (now Quicken Loans) Arena from $79 million to $152 million.

In recent years, some leagues may have undermined their monopoly power by creating too many teams. In 2002, faced with a failing franchise in Montreal and few serious destinations to relocate the team to, MLB seriously considered contracting the league by removing the Expos and the financially struggling Minnesota Twins. Having fewer franchises would have given the remaining teams more bargaining power than they had before. The NHL has recently faced a similar situation. The financial troubles facing several teams make them candidates to relocate, driving down teams' ability to extract large subsidies from local taxpayers.

The NFL has placed itself in the opposite situation. The league last expanded in 2002, when the Houston Texans paid $700 million to join the league. At the time, a second ownership group proposed an expansion franchise in Los Angeles, which had been without a team since the Rams and the Raiders left in the early 1990s. The NFL rejected the proposal, leaving the city without a team until the Rams returned to California in 2016. At first glance, leaving the nation's second largest media market without a team seems like a colossal mistake. In fact, having a highly desirable open market like Los Angeles served the league well as team after team could use the credible threat of moving to LA to extract large stadium subsidies from local governments. In the 20 years Los Angeles was without a team, 24 new NFL stadiums were constructed, and 5 others underwent major renovations at a cost of $14 billion, half of which was paid by taxpayers.[19] With the move of the San Diego Chargers and St. Louis Rams to LA, and the Oakland Raiders to Las Vegas, three cities have opened as potential relocation sites keeping the NFL's game of musical chairs going.

Leagues can also limit their monopoly power by locating their franchises in an unbalanced manner. Of the 18 teams in the Australian Football League (AFL), 9 are in Melbourne, with a 10th in nearby Geelong. While the fans of the Western Bulldogs might be upset if the team threatens to move to Canberra, Melbourne itself is not likely to suffer. As with baseball, bidding wars for Australian Football franchises are unlikely. On top of the geographical considerations, most clubs in the AFL are member-owned, which limits the desirability of moving a team away from its base of owners and fans.

Similarly, as we saw in Chapter 3, the promotion and relegation system of many soccer leagues reduces a team's ability to threaten to move. Every location is already likely to have a franchise either in the team's league or with the potential to be in its league. In addition, unlike the case in North America, local governments have gained some managerial control over franchises in exchange for their investment in the franchise, further reducing the chance of a move.[20]

How does a city decide how much a team, stadium, or event is worth? Objectively, it could calculate the item's present value. The **present value** (or present discounted value) of a good or service is what a stream of future benefits is worth today. To see how cities, firms, or consumers compute the present value of a stadium built to host a new team, we make three simplifying assumptions. First, all costs to build the stadium (C) are paid the moment the stadium opens. Second, the revenue the city receives from the team (e.g., rent payments, shares of concession or advertising revenue) comes in annual lump sums. Third, cities know exactly how much revenue they will receive, so expected revenue always equals actual revenue.

Under these assumptions, if the city receives benefits of B_t for each of T years after it builds the stadium, it is willing to pay the price V, where V is the value of the future stream of returns. One might expect V to equal the sum of payments the city receives $\left(B_1 + B_2 + B_3 + \cdots\right)$, but reality is a bit more complicated. Because one can save the dollar that one receives today and earn the market rate of interest, r, a dollar today equals $1 + r$ dollars a year from today, $(1 + r)^2$ dollars two years from today, and so on. The **future value** that $1 today will have in t years is thus $\$(1 + r)^t$, while the **present value** of $1 that one will receive t years from today equals $\$1/(1 + r)^t$. The present value of the stream of benefits to the city is:

$$V = \frac{B_1}{\left(1 + r\right)} + \frac{B_2}{\left(1 + r\right)^2} + \frac{B_3}{\left(1 + r\right)^3} + \cdots + \frac{B_T}{\left(1 + r\right)^T}$$

The city then compares its costs with its future stream of benefits. The project is profitable if $V > C$ and is not profitable if $C > V$.

Unfortunately, objective calculations might not reflect the subjective feelings of the city's residents. The contingent valuation method (CVM) says that one good way to determine how much a city's residents are willing to pay is to ask them.[21] **Contingent valuation** confronts individuals with a hypothetical event and asks them how much they would be willing to pay to ensure that event does or does not occur. It was originally devised by environmental economists to simulate a market for goods that have no natural market, such as clean air.

In the context of sports, a CV survey presents a scenario, such as the chance to host a major event or the possibility of losing the Minnesota Vikings to a different city. It then asks respondents to state how much they are willing to pay to ensure that the event does or does not occur in one of three ways. It can be open-ended, asking respondents the maximum they are willing to pay. It can be bracketed, asking the respondent to choose from among several options. Finally, it can be closed-ended, giving respondents one possible payment (randomly selected from several possibilities) and asking whether respondents are willing to pay that amount.

CV surveys have several potential drawbacks. The most obvious is that they are not binding. Unless respondents believe that they will be held to their responses and that the gain or loss of the team depends on their answers, they have no incentive to answer truthfully. Because people are generally more willing to spend hypothetical dollars than real dollars, CV responses are typically taken as the upper bound on what residents are willing to pay. In addition, some economists believe that respondents have difficulty understanding payments made over a period of time and typically understate the burden of a series of payments relative to a single upfront payment. Thus, CV surveys can come up with different answers depending on how they structure the payments. Still, a CV survey designed to determine the value of a new facility for the NHL's Pittsburgh Penguins closely paralleled the results of a referendum. Both found that about 40 percent of the population of Pittsburgh supported the construction of a new facility.[22]

7.3   Stadium Location and Costs

The Minnesota Vikings' new home, U.S. Bank Stadium, ultimately cost about $1.1 billion to build, an increase of over $1 billion from their old home.[23] What could have caused such an increase? The cost of sports facilities has risen for many reasons. All contemporary facilities are far more elaborate than even the fanciest stadium in the early 20th century, with sophisticated scoreboards, fine restaurants, even wireless internet connections. Accommodating all the extra amenities has also expanded the "footprint" of contemporary facilities, causing them to take up more space than they used to. In addition, the per-unit cost of urban space has risen. Because stadiums are so "space-intensive," teams and cities must account for the cost of space when they choose the precise location for the facility.

Location decisions also take place on a larger scale, when leagues cross national boundaries. From the mid-1990s to the mid-2000s, there was a steady flow of Canadian hockey franchises to the US. Even the Montreal Expos baseball team moved south to Washington, DC. In 2011, the flow reversed itself, and a US hockey franchise moved north. In this section, we explore how location affects the cost of building a facility and operating a franchise, whether one is considering a move across town or across national boundaries.

How Exchange Rates Affect Costs

When the Winnipeg Jets left Canada in 1996 to become the Phoenix Coyotes, they were just one in a steady progression of teams relocating from Canada to the US. The Quebec Nordiques had decamped for Colorado (to become the Avalanche) the year before, and there was concern that the Vancouver or Edmonton franchises might soon follow. Observers had begun to speculate that Canada might soon be left with only the Toronto Maple Leafs and Montreal Canadiens.[24] That sense of doom has long since disappeared, and in 2011 something that was once unthinkable occurred: a US-based franchise (the Atlanta Thrashers) moved to Canada, and the Winnipeg Jets were reborn.

Many changes took place between 1996 and 2011 that made such a move possible. For example, greater revenue sharing, strict salary caps, and a vastly improved US television deal made small-market Canadian cities more viable homes for franchises. However, what may have been the greatest factor in Canada's hockey renaissance had nothing to do with the NHL or local governments—it was the growing strength of the Canadian dollar.

With 7 of 30 NHL teams located in Canada, players and teams frequently move back and forth between US and Canadian currencies. The Canadian franchises must pay particular attention to the two currencies, as much of their revenue (ticket sales, venue revenue, etc.) is denominated in Canadian dollars, while their need to compete for players on a cross-national market means that their payroll—their largest single cost—is effectively in US dollars. Fluctuations in the relative value of the two currencies—their exchange rate—thus affect the ability of Canadian franchises to compete both on and off the ice.

To show the impact of exchange rates on Canadian franchises, we make the simplifying assumption that a Canadian team pays its team in US dollars. Since its revenues are all in Canadian dollars, the team must buy US dollars on a currency market before it can pay its players. **Currency markets** allow people to trade

Figure 7.1
The Currency Market Sets the Exchange Rate for Canadian and US Dollars

An increase in the supply of US dollars reduces the equilibrium exchange rate

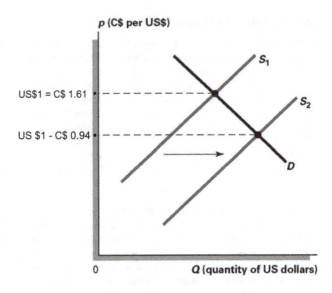

dollars, yen, or euros for any other currency. Figure 7.1 shows the market for US dollars. The "price" of US dollars is the number of Canadian dollars it takes to buy US$1. This price is called the **exchange rate**, because it determines how many Canadian dollars must be exchanged to get US$1. In January 2002, the Canadian dollar fell to its lowest point, requiring C$1.61 to buy US$1.

At this exchange rate, the Canadian hockey teams' expenses were magnified 61 percent by the exchange rate with the US dollar. This created an "exchange rate deficit" of up to C$8 million for some teams, despite tax breaks of up to C$4 million given by some Canadian provinces. Team owners could escape this burden—and lessen their tax burden as well—by moving south of the border.

Between January 2002 and February 2013, the increasing US trade deficit steadily weakened the US dollar.[25] The US supplies dollars to currency markets when it buys more from abroad than it sells abroad. This shifts the supply curve of US dollars rightward, as in Figure 7.1. The exchange rate fell, reaching C$0.94 per US$1 in July 2011, and the financial pressure on Canadian hockey teams that was such a burden in the 1990s disappeared. The Canadian dollar has since weakened relative to the US dollar, reaching $1.33 per US$1 in March 2017, placing Canadian teams back in jeopardy.

Why Most Stadiums Are Not in the Center of Town

In Chapter 6, we saw that a sports facility typically provides the greatest benefits to a city if it is integrated into the fabric of the city and not banished to the edge of town. Yet that is precisely where many facilities are located. The reason is neither incompetence nor corruption—it is economic reality.

Arenas and stadiums take up a lot of space. Even disregarding the "sea of asphalt" that accommodates the thousands of cars in which fans arrive, one can shrink a football field or basketball court only so much. As we will see, this space costs money and becomes increasingly costly as one moves toward the center of town.

Consider, for example, the case of two jewelry shops that are trying to decide where to locate in the circular city shown in Figure 7.2. If the population is evenly spread over the city, then the best place for the stores to locate is in the very center of the circle. To see why, assume that store A and store B initially consider locating at the edge of town, along the diameter AB in Figure 7.2. Since the stores are identical in every way but convenience, customers base their purchases on how close they are to each store. In this case, half the city's population is closer to store A and half is closer to store B, and each store gets an equal share of the city's business. The managers of store A understand how customers decide to shop and recognize that they can capture some of B's business by moving to a more convenient location. They can do so by moving along the diameter toward the center of the circular town. The managers at store B see this and try to do store A one better by moving still closer to the center of the circle. The process continues until both stores compete for space in the center of town. The tendency of businesses to locate in the center of a city has given rise to the term **central business district**.

The competition for space also explains why property values are so much higher near the center of town. Urban economists call the rise in property values as one moves toward the center of town the **rent gradient**. Figure 7.3 shows a

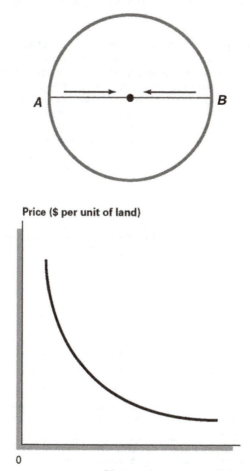

Figure 7.2
Competing Firms Move to the Center of Town

If the population is spread evenly in a circular city, rival firms locate in the central business district.

Price ($ per unit of land)

Distance from center of city

0

Figure 7.3
The Rent Gradient

Because firms want to locate in the center of town, land prices rise as one moves closer to the center.

typical rent gradient. As the price of land rises, people economize on their use of it. If the cost of land rises high enough, developers find it cheaper to build vertically—high-rise offices and apartment buildings—than to build horizontally. Buildings therefore tend to become taller as one moves toward the city center, and Figure 7.3 could illustrate the heights of buildings as well as the cost of land. A stadium surrounded by parking facilities requires so much space that the cost of land can make locating in the center of town prohibitively expensive. Thus, when cities replaced the old, urban ballparks in the 1960s and 1970s, they frequently built them on the outskirts of town. Of course, that was where team owners had put the original stadiums a half-century earlier.

7.4   Stadium Costs and Financing

Recent estimates indicate that from 1990 through 2017, which roughly spans Long's third period of stadium construction as well as the post-Great Recession slowdown, teams, leagues, and cities spent almost $49 billion on 129 major sports infrastructure projects. Of this amount, the public sector spent nearly $26 billion, over 50 percent of the total.[26] The breakdown by league appears in Table 7.1. This section examines how cities fund the construction of new facilities and shows that the actual subsidy might be far greater than the official figures indicate.

Bidding wars for sports franchises differ from normal auction markets in two important respects. First, a city's successful bid for a team does not bring ownership rights. Professional leagues have gone to considerable lengths to prevent cities from owning franchises. For example, MLB owners blocked Joan Kroc's attempt to give the Padres to San Diego after she inherited the team from her late husband. The NFL's bylaws specifically require that teams have an individual majority owner. The Green Bay Packers are frequently cited as an exception to the rule against public ownership, but, contrary to popular belief, the Packers are not owned by Green Bay; they are a publicly held corporation. Thus, in 2000, this supposedly city-owned team threatened to leave Green Bay if the city did not accede to its demands for stadium improvements.[27]

Table 7.1 Stadium Construction in North American Sports Leagues, 1990–2017

League	Number of Construction Projects	Cost[a]	Public Cost[a]	Percent Public
MLB	27	$12,959	$7,804	60%
NFL	31	$17,717	$9,899	56%
MLS	17	$2,236	$1,142	51%
NBA	31	$11,113	$4,925	44%
NHL	32	$11,217	$3,488	31%
Total	129	$48,769	$25,883	53%

[a]In millions of 2017 dollars. Shared stadiums may be counted twice. MLS figures do not include costs for new stadiums shared with NFL teams, but do include costs for stadiums shared with Canadian Football League teams.

Source: Baade and Matheson. 2013. "Financing Professional Sports Facilities," in *Financing Economic Development in the 21st Century*, ed. Sammis White and Zenia Kotval (New York: M.E. Sharpe).

Leagues oppose municipal ownership for two reasons. Because a municipally owned team is immobile, the city could provide facilities on its own terms, thereby undercutting much of the market power that teams hold over cities. In addition, city ownership would make the finances of the team a matter of public record.

The second unique characteristic of the market for teams is the way in which cities pay for "their" teams. Unlike auctions, which result in monetary payments, cities do not pay directly for the teams they have "won." They pay by providing teams with facilities.

Table 7.2 shows the total cost and public share of facilities built for major league sports teams since 2010. Adding up the figures in Table 7.2 shows that $11.34

Table 7.2 Facilities Built between 2010 and 2017

Year	League	Location	Facility	Construction Cost[a]	Percent Public
2010	NFL	New Jersey	MetLife Stadium	$1,794	0%
2010	NBA/NHL	Brooklyn	Barclays Center	$714	24%
2010	NHL	Pittsburgh	Consol Energy Center	$360	40%
2010	MLS	New Jersey	Red Bull Arena	$213	47%
2010	MLS	Philadelphia	Talen Energy Stadium	$135	64%
2010	NFL	Kansas City	Arrowhead Stadium (rehab)	$420	67%
2010	MLB	Minneapolis	Target Field	$610	72%
2010	NBA	Orlando	Amway Center	$538	90%
2011	MLS	Kansas City	Children's Mercy Park	$174	50%
2011	NFL	New Orleans	Superdome (repair and rehab)	$549	97%
2011	MLS	Portland	Providence Park	$34	100%
2011	MLS/CFL	Vancouver	BC Place Stadium	$419	100%
2012	MLS	San Jose	Avaya Stadium	$64	0%
2012	MLS	Houston	BBVA Compass Stadium	$117	45%
2012	MLB	Miami	Marlins Park	$559	70%
2013	NBA/NHL	New York	Madison Square Garden (rehab)	$1,123	0%
2015	NFL	Santa Clara	Levi's Stadium	$1,341	9%
2016	NHL	Las Vegas	T-Mobile Arena	$382	0%
2016	NHL	Edmonton	Rogers Centre	$404	42%
2016	NBA	Sacramento	Golden 1 Center	$568	46%
2016	NFL	Minneapolis	U.S. Bank Stadium	$1,081	47%
2017	MLS	Orlando	Orlando City Stadium	$155	0%
2017	MLS/CFL	Toronto	BMO Field (expansion)	$150	7%
2017	NBA/NHL	Detroit	Little Caesar's Arena	$733	39%
2017	NFL/MLS	Atlanta	Mercedes Benz Stadium	$1,600	44%
2017	MLB	Atlanta	SunTrust Park	$622	63%

[a]In millions of 2017 dollars.

Sources: Baade and Matheson. 2013. "Financing Professional Sports Facilities," in *Financing Economic Development in the 21st Century*, and authors' estimates based on various media reports.

billion has been spent since 2010 to construct new facilities for the major North American sports leagues. More than half this amount, about $6.1 billion, has come from state and local governments. Sometimes, the spending on sports facilities comes when the city has other pressing needs. In 2013, Detroit approved $283 million in construction subsidies for a new arena for the Red Wings just six days after the city filed for bankruptcy.[28] Like individuals and firms, governments face opportunity costs. They must consider the alternative uses to which public funds can be put when evaluating public policy.

The data in Table 7.2 tell only part of the story. These data alone can lead analysts to misstate the full burden of a facility on a city. Construction costs are not the only expenditure that a city makes on a sports facility. It also pays for infrastructure, such as roads and utilities, and for support services, such as police and sanitation. Some costs do not involve any expenditure by the government. For example, cities frequently donate the land on which the facility is built, thereby sacrificing revenues that could have been made from using, renting, or selling the property. As with alternative expenditures, alternative uses of public resources, such as land and police, are an opportunity cost of building and maintaining a sports facility. If the stadium is owned by the state or local authority or by a public–private partnership, the city could also lose tax revenue, as a local government cannot tax itself.

As Table 7.2 shows, the public share of the expenditure on individual facilities has ranged from 0 to 100 percent. This variation is reflected in the facilities' ownership structure. Amway Center and Marlins Park, for example, are owned and operated outright by the cities in which they are located. Levi's Stadium, Target Field, and Consol Energy Arena are run by public authorities created by the City of Santa Clara, the state of Minnesota, and Allegheny County for the express purpose of operating stadiums and arenas. Finally, MetLife Stadium, home to the New York Giants and the New York Jets, which received no state funding, is jointly operated by Giants Stadium LLC and Jets Development LLC. While these two companies are technically separate from the two football teams, they are effectively run by the teams.[29]

Because many stadium costs are indirect or unobservable, they are hard to measure, and estimates of the public share of stadium costs vary widely. For example, the Steinbrenner family paid for the entire construction cost of the new Yankee Stadium. Having spent $1.1 billion, the late George Steinbrenner felt justified in telling New Yorkers, "It's a pleasure to give this to you people."[30] But was Yankee Stadium really a gift? The city donated the land on which the stadium was built, erected parking facilities, and made a variety of improvements to transportation and other infrastructure. Mayya Komisarchik and Aju Fenn estimate the city's contribution to be about $220 million, or about 13.8 percent of total expenditure on the stadium, close to Judith Grant Long's estimate of 17 percent.[31] Munsey and Suppes go much higher on their *Ballparks.com* website; they put the figure at $430 million, about 28 percent. The *Sports Facility Report* of the National Sports Law Institute goes higher still. It says that public expenditure came to $480 million or 32 percent of the total.[32]

7.5   Paying for Stadiums

We have seen two basic motivations for publicly funding sports facilities. First, if the sports team is a public good, people can enjoy the team without paying for it by watching it on TV, following it in the newspaper, or simply discussing it around the water cooler. These consumers can free ride by letting other fans spend money on the team. Second, if sports teams provide positive externalities, people benefit from the presence of the team even if they pay no attention to it and have no say in how often or how well it plays. In both cases, the free market will provide less of the good than the economy desires.

Governments can fill this void by providing public goods and subsidizing firms whose production gives off positive externalities. The public goods aspect of sports teams is particularly difficult for governments to fund because consuming a sports team can be intangible. All we can say is far more people enjoy the team than just the fans in the arena or the residents of the city. People who gain from spillovers are easier to identify, as one can trace at least the initial beneficiaries from a team's presence, such as the construction and hospitality industries. For these reasons—and because the major North American sports leagues prohibit public ownership of franchises—we focus on subsidies rather than outright government provision.

Subsidizing a new sports facility brings a crucial question: How does the government raise the revenue to provide the subsidy? Economic theory suggests that governments maximize the well-being of their residents if they finance the subsidy by imposing taxes or fees in line with the benefits each resident or business receives. Unfortunately, one reason positive externalities are external to the market mechanism is that it is hard to identify exactly who benefits. Fortunately, we have some general principles for determining who should pay how much for a sports franchise.

One such principle—known as the **Ramsey rule**—dictates that sales taxes should be in inverse proportion to the price elasticity of demand for the good or service on which the government places the tax. Such a tax is more efficient than alternative tax schemes because it minimizes the deadweight loss. For example, suppose Minneapolis considered two ways to raise revenue for its new stadium: a tax on hotel stays and a tax on kidney dialysis.[33] Assume, for simplicity, that the local government thinks it can raise all the revenue it needs by imposing a $4 tax on either. Figure 7.4 shows the impact of a tax on

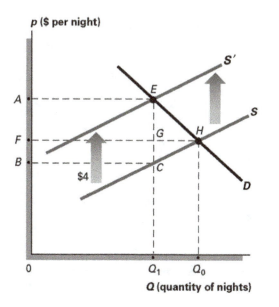

Figure 7.4
The Impact of a $4/Night Tax on Hotel Stays

The tax shifts the supply curve upward to S'. A deadweight loss of ECH results.

staying at a local hotel. As shown in Chapter 2, a $4 sales tax causes consumers to see a supply curve that is $4 higher than the supply curve without the tax.

Since the equilibrium number of nights spent at local hotels falls from Q_0 to Q_1, the deadweight loss imposed by the tax equals the area of the triangle ECH. This burden consists of lost consumer surplus for hotel guests (EGH) and lost producer surplus for hotel operators (CGH). We explore the implications of this shared burden later in the chapter.

Contrast the deadweight loss from a hotel tax with the deadweight loss from a tax on kidney dialysis, as seen in Figure 7.5. A $4 tax on dialysis shifts the supply curve (which, for simplicity, we assume to be identical to the supply curve in Figure 7.4) up by $4, just like before. Unlike hotel stays, kidney dialysis has no good substitutes. The demand for dialysis is therefore much less sensitive to changes in price than the demand for hotels. Since the demand curve is so inelastic, the quantity of dialysis hardly changes, and the price rises by almost the full amount of the tax. Because the tax on dialysis causes little loss of output, there is very little deadweight loss (the area of the triangle ECH). If the city wants to impose a tax that minimizes deadweight loss, then a tax on dialysis may be just the thing. Most people, however, would not choose to impose a greater burden on people who are unfortunate enough to require dialysis.

Society must often choose between policies that are efficient and policies that satisfy some notion of fairness or equity. Tax analysis applies two forms of equity: horizontal and vertical. A policy satisfies **vertical equity** if it falls most heavily on those with the greatest ability to pay and places a smaller burden on those with low incomes. Since hotel stays are generally either part of a vacation by relatively well-to-do households or underwritten by businesses, while dialysis is an undesired burden borne by people from a variety of income groups, a hotel tax is more vertically equitable than a dialysis tax. Minneapolis relied

Figure 7.5
A Tax on Dialysis Causes
Very Little Deadweight Loss

The demand for dialysis is highly inelastic. Here the deadweight loss is *CHE*.

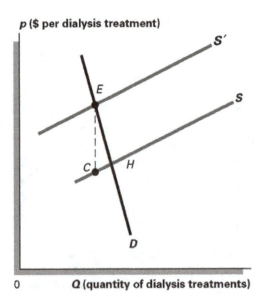

heavily on lottery sales to pay for the Vikings' stadium, a revenue source that is highly inequitable.

While vertical equity applies across income levels, horizontal equity refers to fairness at a given income level. A tax is **horizontally equitable** if it treats equals equally. Since public expenditure often confers unequal benefits on the population, the pursuit of horizontal equity leads governments to levy taxes in proportion to the benefits received from the expenditure. In this example, the tax on hotel stays seems more horizontally equitable, as staying at a local hotel is more likely to be connected to enjoying the home team than a visit to the dialysis unit.[34]

Some economists think that governments should rely on **user fees**, such as taxes on tickets, parking, or concessions, rather than public taxation to fund facilities. They claim that the public good aspects of a professional franchise are dwarfed by the private consumption that takes place. The emphasis that teams now place on luxury boxes and prime seating has made it difficult for middle- or low-income fans to attend the major professional sports games on a regular basis.[35] If this is the case, then private consumption by the wealthy few has crowded out public consumption by the broader population.

In addition to spanning the income distribution, benefits can cut across geographic boundaries. Many of the consumption benefits of a major league franchise flow out of the city to the residents of the relatively wealthy suburban ring. The suburbs disproportionately house the people who can most afford tickets to sporting events. They also disproportionately house corporate executives who use the luxury boxes and other premium seating that account for so much of the cost of a facility. In addition, as explained earlier, most cities get only a small fraction of the revenue from luxury boxes. Taxes that fall on residents of the city that houses the team therefore allow suburbanites to escape the taxes that fund the facility, while city residents, who bear the heaviest tax burden, seldom if ever attend a game.

Who Pays a Sales Tax?

In addition to creating deadweight loss, sales taxes often burden groups that the government does not wish to target, such as people who do not benefit from the new facility, thereby violating horizontal equity. We consider the merits of sales taxes on items directly related to sports facilities later in the chapter. This section explores the problem posed when the burden of a sales tax does not fall solely on the people who ostensibly pay the tax. The tax burden shifts because people respond to the world around them. Governments that impose a tax expecting people to behave the same way they did before the tax was levied are in for a rude awakening.

The Dallas Cowboys stirred up a major controversy when they proposed raising a portion of the $1.15 billion for their new stadium with a three percentage-point increase (up to 18 percent total, among the highest in the nation) in the tax on hotel stays in the Dallas–Fort Worth area. Such a tax would seem to be a very popular way to raise funds. After all, it was designed to fall on out-of-town visitors, thereby exporting the burden of paying for a new stadium to taxpayers from other states. The proposed tax, however, drew a firestorm of protest from the local Visitors Bureau and—of all groups—Mary Kay Cosmetics.[36] Mary Kay's opposition was understandable. The company holds its annual convention in the area and did not want to see its expenses rise. Why, however, did the Visitors Bureau, which represents the local hospitality industry, object to having out-of-towners pay?

To see why local hotels objected, we simplify the problem and assume that the city passes a hotel tax of $4 for each person spending an evening in a local hotel. We further assume that, before the tax is imposed, 1 million people spend an average of 5 nights each in hotels in the Dallas–Fort Worth area in a typical year. One might conclude that the tax would raise $20 million ($4 per night × 1 million people × 5 nights per person) per year. This naïve calculation, however, assumes that visitors do not respond to the higher cost of staying in a local hotel.

Recall from Figure 7.4 that the tax causes the price of a night in a hotel room to rise—though by less than $4—and the number of nights spent at hotels to fall. The higher price that people pay per night spent at a hotel (segment *AF* in Figure 7.4) is the portion of the $4 tax that they bear. Since the government has imposed a $4 tax but the price of a night at a hotel has risen by less than $4, hotel operators receive a lower price per night than they did before the tax was imposed. The drop in price that hotel operators receive (segment *FB* in Figure 7.4) is the portion of the $4 tax passed on to the local hotel industry.

The total tax burden equals the $4 tax (segment *AB* in Figure 7.5) times the number of rooms rented (segment *AE*). This product, the total tax revenue, equals the area of the rectangle *ABCE* in Figure 7.4. The portion of this rectangle that lies above the original price of the room (the rectangle *AFGE* in Figure 7.4) is the burden borne by people who stay at hotels. The rectangle below the original price (*FGCB* in Figure 7.4) is the burden borne by local hotel operators. When tourists or business travelers respond to the higher price of hotel stays by making fewer or shorter visits, local businesses are hurt—hence the opposition by the Dallas–Fort Worth Visitors Bureau—and the revenue generated by the tax falls short of its target.

The idea that having out-of-towners pay for a stadium is like getting a stadium for free is also wrong because of **opportunity costs**. Even if tourists or business travelers do pay most of the cost of a hotel tax, there is no reason to believe that these revenues are best directed toward the construction of a stadium. By using them for this purpose, this revenue stream cannot be used to fund other services in the local economy, like police officers or school teachers, requiring the local government to raise other taxes whose burdens are likely to fall on local residents.

Cleveland applied a different kind of sales tax to help fund the facilities it built. It imposed a 15-year sin tax on residents of Cuyahoga County (which consists of Cleveland and its immediate suburbs). Like most **sin taxes**, these taxes consisted of sales taxes on tobacco products and alcohol. They are popular with many citizens because they impose a burden on people who engage in or cater to "sinful" behavior. Much of the public favors sin taxes because they raise revenue by taxing other people and discourage undesirable activity. Unfortunately, sin taxes cannot achieve both goals. As shown in Figure 7.4, if a tax discourages behavior, it creates a large deadweight loss and fails to raise the anticipated amount of revenue. In contrast, if drinking and smoking are addictive behaviors, the demand for them is highly price inelastic. Figure 7.5 showed that taxes on goods for which demand is inelastic cause very little deadweight loss and come much closer to raising the desired revenue. However, because the change in quantity demanded is so small, the tax fails to discourage the sinful behavior.

Public choice theory helps to explain why Cleveland's sin taxes stirred less organized opposition than the Dallas area's proposed hotel tax. The deadweight loss of a tax adds to the burden on the group that pays the tax and hence subsidizes the publicly funded facility. A larger burden makes that group more likely to organize opposition to the tax. Since the demand for cigarettes and alcohol is far less price elastic than the demand for hotel stays, a smaller deadweight loss resulted and less opposition arose to the sin tax.[37]

Incremental Financing

San Francisco and San Diego have attempted to finance their new facilities (AT&T—originally Pacific Bell—Park and Petco Park) through a new technique that tries to avoid raising taxes. **Tax increment financing** (TIF) does not impose a new tax. Instead, it earmarks increased tax revenue to pay the city's debt to its bondholders. The idea behind this is that the new facility may stimulate tourism. The additional tourists increase hotel occupancy rates, increase patronage at local restaurants, and generally increase expenditure in the community. This added expenditure leads to higher revenues from existing sales taxes and hotel taxes without the city's having to increase tax rates. The city just commits to using this additional tax revenue to pay its bondholders. San Francisco has committed to raising $15 million through TIF, while San Diego hopes to raise $29 million.[38]

If it succeeds, incremental financing minimizes the burden on both tourists and local merchants. To succeed, however, the new facility must cause tourist expenditure to rise for a sustained period. Unfortunately, the honeymoon period for a new stadium might not be long enough. TIF appears particularly risky in San Diego. After spiking to 3 million in Petco Park's first season (2004), attendance fell dramatically, bottoming out at 1.9 million in 2009. While attendance has since recovered somewhat, it remains well below both the National League average and the Padres' average attendance in their last five years at Qualcomm Stadium. The Giants might not have such worries. Thanks in part to World Series Championships in 2010, 2012, and 2014, they have drawn over 3 million fans in 13 of the 15 years since AT&T Park opened, and their attendance has been among the highest in MLB since 2011.

Taxes That Spread the Burden

In general, taxes aimed at out-of-towners or those behaving "sinfully" do not meet the criteria set out at the beginning of this section. Some are inefficient; others fail on equity grounds. We now turn to two funding mechanisms that, while flawed, do a better job of meeting the criteria. Each tries to allocate burdens more equitably, though they do so differently.

The first mechanism thinks big, as exemplified by how the Milwaukee metropolitan area has funded Miller Park: instituting a general sales tax on Milwaukee and the surrounding five-county region. The broader geographic reach of this tax accounts for the regional impact of a stadium, reducing the vertical and horizontal inequities that result when inner-city taxpayers finance a facility that benefits wealthy suburbanites. While the sales tax does a better job of targeting the beneficiaries of the stadium, it remains a rather broad brush, as it is based on people's purchases of goods and services and not on their benefits from having the Brewers in town.[39]

The second mechanism thinks small, as demonstrated by the way that Seattle and the state of Washington have funded Safeco Field. This package of taxes targets those who benefit most from the presence of the facility. It imposes a sales tax of 0.5 percent on restaurants, bars, and taverns in King County and a tax of up to 5 percent on admissions to Safeco Field. They have also sought to export some of the burden with a 2 percent tax on rental cars. The sales tax tries to match burdens to benefits by placing the greatest tax burden on those who benefit from having the Mariners in town, though it does not get things quite right. By charging a five-star French restaurant at the opposite end of the county the same tax as a bar across the street from the stadium, the government does not match costs to benefits particularly well. The tax on admissions does a better job of matching costs and benefits. The tax on car rentals has the same imperfect impact as the hotel room tax example discussed earlier.[40]

The Benefits of Debt

If a city does not raise taxes to pay for a new stadium, it must borrow. According to economic theory, borrowing to finance a new stadium does not lessen the tax burden on a community. It simply delays the inevitable, as it substitutes taxes now for taxes later when it repays the debt. Since David Ricardo first stated the famous "equivalence theorem," economists have known that borrowing and taxation could have the same impact on residents, at least in theory.[41] State and local governments, however, face several institutional factors that lead them to prefer debt funding to direct taxation.

Individuals and small firms typically borrow money from a financial intermediary, such as a bank. Large corporations and governments typically borrow directly from financial markets by issuing bonds. A **bond** is a promise to pay its holder a fixed amount, the **face value** of the bond, at a future point in time, called **maturity**. Both the face value and maturity are stated on the bond, as is the bond's interest rate, also known as its coupon rate. The interest payment on a bond is given by its coupon rate times its face value, which is usually $1,000. Thus, a 5% coupon bond pays its holder $50 each year, usually in the form of two $25 semi-annual payments.

Bonds issued by state or local governments have an advantage over otherwise identical corporate bonds. Tax laws allow bondholders to deduct the interest they earn from state and local bonds from their federal taxes. If a $1,000 municipal bond pays 5 percent, the holder keeps $50 ($1,000*0.05) after taxes. If a corporate bond pays $50, the holder keeps less after taxes. For example, the after-tax interest payment to a person in the 28% tax bracket is only $36 ($50*[1–0.28]). The higher after-tax interest payment on municipal government bonds drives up the demand for them and causes their price to rise from p_0 to p_1, as shown in Figure 7.6. Because of their lower after-tax return, the demand for corporate bonds is also lower. This, in turn, lowers their price. In equilibrium, the after-tax interest rate on otherwise identical corporate and municipal bonds

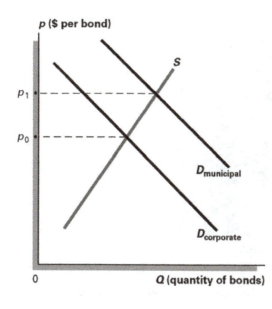

Figure 7.6
Tax Breaks Favor Municipal Bonds

Because they are tax exempt, all else equal, the demand for municipal bonds is greater than for corporate bonds.

of the same risk must be the same, otherwise no one would buy the bond with the lower return. At tax rates of 28 percent, a corporate bond must pay a pre-tax rate of 6.94 percent to have a post-tax return of 5 percent (6.94*[1–0.28] = 5.0). Thus, the interest rate on municipal bonds is lower than the rate on otherwise identical corporate bonds.

Because they pay a lower rate, municipal bonds reduce the cost of building a stadium, by reducing the cost of borrowing. According to the Brookings Institute, since 2000, the use of tax-exempt bonds have provided an effective subsidy of $2.6 to $3.3 billion for 36 professional stadium projects across the country.[42] The lower federal tax revenues mean that taxpayers in other states and municipalities must pay higher taxes, federal programs will have to be cut, or the federal government will have to borrow more and drive up interest rates in general. No matter what, the tax deductibility of interest on municipal bonds imposes costs on the rest of the nation. The Internal Revenue Service (IRS) has tried to limit the use of municipal bonds to purposes that serve public, rather than private interests.[43] States and cities must now convince the IRS that private interests receive no more than 10 percent of the proceeds of the bond issue and that no more than 10 percent of the repayment of the debt comes from private sources. This restriction did not prevent New York from issuing $240 million in bonds to pay for the new Yankee Stadium's parking garages.[44]

Even if debt does not export the burden geographically, it can export the burden intertemporally. If future generations enjoy the benefits of the new facility, then economic theory says that society is better off if they pay some of the burden. Debt financing allows a city to impose some of the burden of a new facility on future generations. Unfortunately, stadiums do not last as long as they once did, and future generations might be stuck with the bill for a facility that their teams have already abandoned. Taxpayers in St. Louis, for example, still owed over $100 million in bond debt on the Edward Jones Dome when the Rams left town for Los Angeles in 2016.[45]

Biographical Sketch

George W. Bush
(1946–)

I never dreamed about being President. I wanted to be Willie Mays.
—G.W. Bush[46]

Born into one of the most prominent political dynasties in America, George W. Bush had political ambition but little to show for a 20-year career in business and politics. Then, an opportunity in Major League Baseball opened a path for him that eventually led to his election as the 43rd President of the United States. Bush's grandfather, Prescott Bush, was a Senator from Connecticut, and his father, George H.W. Bush, held prominent governmental positions, including UN Ambassador, Director of the CIA, and Vice President under Ronald Reagan, ultimately becoming the 41st President. George W. Bush, also known as "W" or "Bush-43" to distinguish him from his father, graduated from Yale University like his father. While Bush, Sr. played baseball at Yale, Bush-43 was a cheerleader. In 1975, Bush earned an MBA at Harvard Business School, and later became the first American president with an MBA.

He started an oil exploration firm in Texas in 1977 and ran unsuccessfully for Congress in 1978. His company went through various iterations, none of which achieved any measure of success.[47] After helping his father in his winning presidential campaign in 1988, Bush set his sights on the governor's office, but he had a weak resume and little to offer other than a famous name.

In fall 1988, Eddie Chiles, the owner of the Texas Rangers, informed Bush and his business partner William DeWitt that he was interested in selling the team. Bush and DeWitt quickly assembled an ownership team with the help of MLB Commissioner Peter Ueberroth. The $86 million sale was completed in April 1989. Bush contributed only $500,000 to the purchase, earning him a 1.8% ownership stake, and even that amount had to be borrowed. He later paid an additional $106,302.[48] Despite his small stake in the team, the partnership valued Bush's celebrity and named him managing partner. Eventually Bush was awarded an extra 10% of the team ownership.

Like many MLB franchises of the day, the Rangers played in an older stadium with few amenities and no luxury boxes. Bush and the Rangers desperately wanted the higher revenue that came along with new, modern stadiums but did not want to spend their own money to get it. They used the threat of relocation to force a ballot initiative on public financing for a new stadium in Arlington, Texas. The Rangers won the vote handily, helped by the fact that the pro-stadium side outspent its opponents by a wide margin. The Ballpark in Arlington opened in 1994 at a cost of $191 million, 71% of which was provided by local taxpayers.[49] After accounting for other subsidies including property tax exemptions, the total public contribution to the stadium exceeded $200 million.

Bush profited handsomely from his Rangers deal. The team sold in 1998 at a price of $250 million, a threefold increase from nine years earlier. Thanks to his increased ownership stake, Bush walked away with $14.9 million, a 2,358% return on his $606,302 investment.[50] More importantly, his management position in a well-known local business gave him exposure and the opportunity to prove his business acumen, which he parleyed into a successful campaign for the Texas governorship in 1994 and eventually into his place as the 43rd US President.

Summary

Cities began to underwrite sports facilities in the 1950s and 1960s, after teams showed that they would move to new cities in response to economic incentives. Over the next several decades, cities came to see stadiums as part of their infrastructure and paid most or all of the expenses of new stadiums. Since the 1980s, there has been a more equal partnership, with cities paying about two-thirds of the costs of new construction until the Great Recession and closer to one-third of costs since then. Leagues specifically limit the number of franchises in order to create scarcity and increase the bargaining power of their teams when it comes to negotiating stadium deals. The precise degree of public support is often hard to measure, as many of the costs are implicit or difficult to quantify.

The cost of attracting and retaining a team is affected by its location. When leagues cross national borders, exchange rate movements can create problems for franchises located in a country whose currency is weakening. Within a city, the cost of constructing a facility depends on how close it is to the center of town.

To subsidize a facility, cities must raise funds. Economists have established standards by which they evaluate a tax's efficiency as well as its vertical and horizontal equity. Most cities' tax schemes are neither particularly efficient nor equitable. In addition, the taxes often fall on people whom the city did not intend to burden. Still, by targeting individuals and firms that benefit from the facilities, such as the fans themselves or the nearby businesses that cater to them, some cities and regions have designed taxes that are more efficient and more horizontally and vertically equitable than others.

Discussion Questions

1   Are the stadiums or arenas of your local sports franchises located downtown or on the edge of town? Do you think that is the best place for them?
2   Did the NFL make a mistake in allowing the Rams and Chargers to relocate to Los Angeles? Did the voters in San Diego and St. Louis make a mistake in letting them leave?
3   What do you believe is more important in taxing the public to provide funds for stadiums—horizontal equity or vertical equity? Why?
4   How has your city raised funds to subsidize its sports facilities? Would you use a different method? Why?

Problems

7.1 Evaluate the following taxes from the standpoint of vertical and horizontal equity:
    a. A 25-cent per-gallon tax on milk;
    b. A tax on stock market transactions;
    c. A sales tax on men's clothing;
    d. A tax on cigarettes.
7.2 Suppose the demand for toothbrushes is perfectly inelastic, at $Q_d = 3,000$. The market supply curve is perfectly elastic and is equal to $p = 2.00$. What would be the deadweight loss associated with a $0.20 tax on toothbrushes? Based on the Ramsey rule, would this be a good product to tax?
7.3 Suppose a city is laid out along a major highway, so the city is shaped like a straight-line segment rather than a circle. If the city wants to build a sports arena, where along the segment should the city build the arena? Why?
7.4 True or false; explain your answer: "The new stadium was entirely privately funded because all the city contributed was a 50-acre lot on which to build it."
7.5 Use the rent gradient to show why New York did not build a new stadium for the Yankees in midtown Manhattan.
7.6 Your city is committed to raising $100 million for a new arena. The mayor suggests putting a tax on taxicab rides since out-of-towners disproportionately use taxicabs. Evaluate the wisdom of this policy decision.
7.7 Why might a city want to go into debt as a way to fund a new stadium?
7.8 Suppose New York wants to build a new facility to replace Madison Square Garden. Assume that the cost of building a new arena in midtown Manhattan is $2 billion and that all the costs occur right away. Also assume that New York will receive annual benefits of $100 million for the next 30 years, after which the new arena becomes worthless. Does it make financial sense to build the new facility if interest rates are 5 percent?
7.9 If you are a Red Sox fan, do you want the Yankees to be able to finance a new stadium through the use of municipal bonds? Explain.

Notes

1   Quoted in Michael Danielson. 1997. *Home Team: Professional Sport and the American Metropolis* (Princeton, NJ: Princeton University Press): xvii.
2   Dave Barry. 1999. *Dave Barry Turns 50* (New York: Random House): 62.
3   Geoffrey Ward and Kenneth Burns. 1994. *Baseball: An Illustrated History* (New York: Alfred A. Knopf): 351–352.
4   See Danielson. 1997. *Home Team:* 20–24; and Charles Euchner. 1993. *Playing the Field* (Baltimore, MD: Johns Hopkins University Press): 4. The NFL Hall of Fame is in Canton, Ohio, home of the long-defunct Canton Bulldogs.

5   Victor Matheson, "Professional Sports," in *Encyclopedia of American Business History*, ed. Charles Geisst (New York: Facts on File, 2006): 403–408.

6   Neil J. Sullivan. 1987. *The Dodgers Move West* (New York: Oxford University Press): 42.

7   See Sullivan. 1987. *The Dodgers Move West*: 15; and Danielson. 1997. *Home Team*: 9. Manhattan was the home of the Dodgers' archrivals, the New York Giants, who moved to San Francisco when the Dodgers left for Los Angeles.

8   Judith Grant Long. 2004. "Public Funding for Major League Sports Facilities Data Series: A History of Public Funding, 1890 to 2005," Edward J. Bloustein School of Planning and Public Policy, Center for Urban Policy Research Working Paper Series.

9   Charles Clotfelter. 2011. *Big-Time Sports in American Universities* (Cambridge: Cambridge University Press): 47, notes that many of today's major college football stadiums were built in the 1920s.

10 Wrigley Field was originally named Weeghman Field for the owner of the Chicago Whales of the Federal League, which first occupied the stadium. When Philip Wrigley bought the team and the stadium, he renamed it for himself.

11 In 1936, Connie Mack went so far as to erect a "spite fence" behind right field of Shibe Park to prevent fans from viewing the game from the roofs of nearby apartment buildings.

12 Glenn Wong. 2010. *Essentials of Sports Law*, 4th ed. (Santa Barbara, CA: Praeger): 468.

13 See David Harris. 1986. *The League: The Rise and Decline of the NFL* (New York: Bantam Books); and Wong. 2010. *Essentials of Sport Law*.

14 See Danielson. 1997. *Home Team*: 25.

15 The Rams feared the popularity of a new team headed by the legendary Ohio State coach Paul Brown, who gave his name to the new team. See Jon Morgan. 1997. *Glory for Sale: Fans, Dollars, and the New NFL* (Baltimore, MD: Bancroft Press): 59.

16 See Sullivan. 1987. *The Dodgers Move West*: 90–94.

17 See Andrew Zimbalist. 1992. *Baseball and Billions* (New York: Basic Books, 1992): 16–17; and James Miller. 1990. *The Baseball Business: Pursuing Pennants and Profits in Baltimore* (Chapel Hill: University of North Carolina Press): 78–84.

18 Morgan. 1997. *Glory for Sale*: 89; and Harris. 1986. *The League: The Rise and Decline of the NFL*: 17.

19 Robert Baade and Victor Matheson. 2013. "Financing Professional Sports Facilities," in *Financing Economic Development in the 21st Century*, ed. Sammis White and Zenia Kotval (New York: M.E. Sharpe).

20 See Stefan Szymanski and Andrew Zimbalist. 2005. *National Pastime: How Americans Play Baseball and the Rest of the World Plays Soccer* (Washington, DC: Brookings Institution Press): 130.

21 For a good introduction to CVM, see Bruce K. Johnson and John C. Whitehead. 2012. "Contingent Valuation of Sports," in *The Oxford Handbook of Sports Economics*, ed. Stephen Shmanske and Leo Kahane (Oxford: Oxford University Press).

22 Peter Groothuis, Bruce Johnson, and John Whitehead. 2004. "Public Funding of Professional Sports Stadiums: Public Choice or Civic Pride?" *Eastern Economic Journal*, 30(4), Fall: 515–526. Pittsburgh built the Consol Energy Center anyway.

23 According to Munsey and Suppes. 2012. *Ballparks.com*, the Hubert H. Humphrey Metrodome cost $68 million to build in 1982.

24 Michael Farber. 1995. "Giant Sucking Sound," *Sports Illustrated*, March 20.

25 In 2011, the US trade deficit with Canada was $35.6 billion.

26 Mayya Komisarchik and Aju Fenn. 2010. "Trends in Stadium and Arena Construction, 1995–2015," Colorado College Working Paper, April 5, 2010.

27 The Packers are, however, the only NFL team that does not have a single managing partner. See Joanna Cagan and Neil deMause. 1998. *Field of Schemes* (Monroe, ME: Common Courage Press): 93–94, 191–192; Richard Jones and Don Walker. 2000. "Packer Boss Warns of Move if Stadium Doesn't Get Upgrade," *Milwaukee Sentinel Journal*, March 1; and Barry Lorge. 1990. "Kroc Wanted to Give Padres to City," *San Diego Union-Tribune*, July 29: H1.

28 Christine Ferretti. 2015. "John Oliver Challenges Funding of New Red Wings Arena," *The Detroit News*, July 13.

29 Giants Stadium LLC is co-owned by John Mara, who is president, CEO, and co-owner of the New York Giants. BusinessWeek. "Company Overview of Giants Stadium LLC,"

BusinessWeek.com, http://investing.businessweek.com/research/stocks/private/snapshot. asp?privcapId=36320464, viewed May 19, 2012.

30   Karen Mathews. 2006. "Yankees Break Ground on New $1 Billion Stadium," *USAToday.com*, August 16, at http://www.usatoday.com/sports/baseball/al/yankees/2006-08-16-stadium-groundbreaking_x.htm.

31   Mayya Komisarchik and Aju Fenn. 2010. "Trends in Stadium and Arena Construction, 1995-2015."

32   National Sports Law Institute, "Sports Facilities Reports," *Marquette University Law School*, at http://law.marquette.edu/national-sports-law-institute/sports-facility-reports.

33   In fact, it has imposed a 2 percent hotel tax.

34   For more on these—and other—criteria for evaluating taxes, see, for example, Harvey Rosen and Ted Gayer. 2014. *Public Finance* (New York: McGraw-Hill).

35   For interesting examples, see Andrew Flohr. 2015. "The Gentrification of Oracle Arena," *SBNation*, December 22, at https://www.goldenstateofmind.com/2015/12/22/9775912/NBA-ticket-prices-2015-golden-state-warriors-christmas; and John Siegfried and Andrew Zimbalist. 2000. "The Economics of Sports Facilities and Their Construction," *Journal of Economic Perspectives*, 14(3) Summer: 95–114.

36   See Hugh Aynsworth. 2004. "Owner of Dallas Cowboys Seeks $1 Billion in Tax Funds," *Washington Times*, February 2, at http://www.washingtontimes.com/national/20040202-120350-8901r.htm.

37   See Gary Becker. 1983. "A Theory of Competition among Pressure Groups for Political Influence," *Quarterly Journal of Economics*, 98(3), August: 371–400.

38   San Jose Redevelopment Agency. 2009. "Economic Impact Analysis: Proposed Major League Ballpark in San Jose, CA," September 22, at http://www.sjredevelopment.org/ballpark/meetings/092409/SanJosePresentation092109.pdf.

39   See Dennis Zimmerman. 1997. "Subsidizing Stadiums: Who Benefits, Who Pays?" in *Sports, Jobs, and Taxes*, ed. Roger G. Noll and Andrew Zimbalist (Washington, DC: Brookings Institution Press): 137.

40   Seattle Times. 2011. "Safeco Field Taxes: In with a Bang, Out with a Whimper," *The Seattle Times*, October 11, at https://www.seattletimes.com/opinion/safeco-field-taxes-in-with-a-bang-out-with-a-whimper/.

41   In fact, Ricardo rejected the notion that the two were equivalent.

42   Ted Gayer, Austin J. Drukker, and Alexander K. Gold. 2016. "Tax-Exempt Municipal Bonds and the Financing of Professional Sports Stadiums," Economic Studies at Brookings, September.

43   Kevin McManimon. 2006. "The House That Debt Built: Will the IRS Allow Cities to Finance Construction of Stadiums on a Tax-Exempt Basis?" *McManimon and Scotland, LLC*, May 29, at http://www.mandslaw.com/articles/the-house-that-debt-built-will-the-irs-allow-cities-to-finance-construction-of-stadiums-on-a-tax-exempt-basis/.

44   Money & Company. 2011. "Yankee Stadium's Troubled Tax-Free Financing," *LATimes. com*, June 17, at http://latimesblogs.latimes.com/money_co/2011/06/yankee-stadiums-troubled-tax-free-financing-.html.

45   Travis Waldron. 2016. "St. Louis Taxpayers Aren't Finished Paying for the Stadium the Rams Abandoned," *Huffington Post*, January 13, at http://www.huffingtonpost.com/entry/rams-los-angeles-st-louis-taxpayers_us_5696955ee4b0778f46f7c330.

46   Baseball Almanac, "President George W. Bush Baseball Related Quotations," at http://www.baseball-almanac.com/prz_qgwb.shtml, accessed April 20, 2017.

47   Molly Ivins and Lou Dubose. 2000. *Shrub: The Short but Happy Political Life of George W. Bush* (New York: Vintage Books).

48   Center for Public Integrity. 2000. "How George W. Bush Scored Big with the Texas Rangers," January 18, at https://www.publicintegrity.org/2000/01/18/3313/how-george-w-bush-scored-big-texas-rangers.

49   Baade and Matheson, 2013. "Financing Professional Sports Facilities."

50   Center for Public Integrity, 2000. "How George W. Bush Scored Big with the Texas Rangers."

8

MEGA-EVENTS

Introduction

On December 2, 2010, US Soccer President Sunil Gulati waited anxiously for the Fédération Internationale de Football Association (FIFA), soccer's world governing body, to announce the countries that would host the 2018 and 2022 World Cups. Gulati, who also teaches economics at Columbia University in New York, had good reason to be optimistic about the United States' chances. When the US last held the tournament in 1994, the event set an attendance record that still holds, with nearly 3.6 million fans attending games at 9 venues across the country. The US could also point to the exponential increase in domestic interest in soccer since it hosted the 1994 World Cup. In 2010, the number of players registered by US Youth Soccer had topped 3 million, nearly double the number involved 20 years previously,[2] and it appeared that the country finally could claim a stable and growing professional league. Major League Soccer, founded in 1996 as a 10-team league, had expanded to 18 teams, and, as we saw in Chapter 6, the increase in demand for US soccer had set off a wave of soccer-specific stadium construction across the country.

To be sure, the United States faced competition from other countries, but they could not possibly bring the same resources to the table. It was understood that a European country would be awarded the 2018 World Cup, but that Europe would not be awarded two tournaments in a row, so America's biggest potential rivals, England and Russia, would not directly compete with the US. That left only Australia and Qatar. As a wealthy nation with well-developed tourist and sports infrastructure, Australia was a real threat. It had proven itself on the world stage before, hosting Summer Olympics in Melbourne in 1956 and in Sydney in 2000. Furthermore, Australia is a country of rabid sports fans sure to fill stadiums across the country. Despite these advantages, Australia still had to be considered a long shot compared to the US. In Australia, soccer was at most the fourth or fifth favorite sport in the country behind rugby, cricket, Australian rules football, and maybe even tennis, horse racing, and Formula 1. To top it all off, Australia has only 5 major population centers to accommodate the 32 teams participating in the tournament. The US, on the other hand, provided an initial list of 70 stadiums spread across 50 cities that would be suitable for World Cup matches, and its final list of 18 potential host cities all offered stadiums with capacities of at least 65,000 fans.

The idea that Qatar might win the bid seemed far-fetched. Qatar is the size of Connecticut, with about one-tenth of Connecticut's infrastructure and a total population of only about 2 million. It had no significant soccer tradition, had never qualified for the World Cup, possessed only one of the eight stadiums minimally required for the tournament, and suffered from daytime temperatures during the usual time frame of the World Cup that routinely topped 120 degrees Fahrenheit.

Against this backdrop, FIFA President Sepp Blatter's announcement that Qatar would be the 2022 host shocked the soccer world. By winning, Qatar was obligated to spend billions of dollars to prepare for a one-month event. What motivates a country like Qatar, or the US for that matter, to bid for these events, what do they stand to gain, and what are the costs to the host region?

Learning Objectives

*   Define what constitutes a "mega-event" and describe the history of these events.
*   Describe the short-run and long-run cost and benefits of hosting a mega-event.
*   Understand the different ways to measure the economic impact of a mega-event.
*   Evaluate the potentially exaggerated claims of "mega-benefits" from mega-events.
*   Explain why cities still bid for mega-events despite their dubious benefits.

8.1   A Brief History of Mega-Events

There is no single definition of a mega-event. Mega-events are characterized by several factors that differentiate them from other sporting contests. First, they occur irregularly or infrequently. Second, they command a high level of public interest and media attention, especially at the national or international level. Finally, they attract participants or spectators from outside the local region. Because they exhibit these characteristics, they present local economies with unique opportunities and challenges, which make their study an interesting topic for economists.

Despite the common use of the term "mega-event," size is not the sole factor determining whether a sporting contest qualifies as a mega-event. The annual Honolulu Marathon attracts about 30,000 total runners, roughly half of whom travel to Hawaii from Japan. The average NFL regular season game attracts 68,400 fans, most of whom are local season ticket holders. Since the Honolulu Marathon occurs only once a year and attracts a large out-of-town contingent, the marathon is considered a mega-event while the typical NFL game is not, despite its larger size.

Some mega-events change locations regularly based on the awarding of the event by a selection committee. Examples of this type of event include international tournaments such as the Summer and Winter Olympic Games; World Cups in various sports such as soccer, rugby, and cricket; and the Champions League Final; as well as American events such as the Super Bowl, All-Star games in the major sports, the US Open golf tournament, and NCAA championships in basketball and football. Other mega-events, such as the World Series, Stanley Cup, and NBA Finals change locations based on the teams participating. Still other mega-events always take place in the same location but do so only annually. These events include the Grand Slam tennis tournaments; College Bowl games, such as the Rose Bowl in Pasadena; major marathons in locations such as Boston, New York, and Chicago; auto races, such as the Daytona 500 or Monaco Grand

Prix; and horse races like the Kentucky Derby. Finally, the study of mega-events is not confined to sports. Political events such as national political conventions and presidential inaugurations, cultural events like New Orleans' Mardi Gras or Rio de Janeiro's Carnival celebrations, major art exhibitions and music concerts, and even events like Burning Man in the Nevada desert or the Harley Davidson motorcycle rally in Sturgis, South Dakota, all fit the definition of a mega-event, and may have similar effects on the local economies.

The Original Mega-Event: The Ancient Olympics

The Olympic Games were one of four sets of Greek athletic contests, the other three being the Pythian, Nemean, and Isthmian Games. The Olympics were first held in 776 BC (the earliest recorded exact date in history) and continued every four years for over a millennium to honor the Greek god Zeus. These athletic competitions had a deeper, more spiritual role in the lives of the ancient Greeks than sporting events have in the lives of people today. Athletic contests were an integral part of religious festivals, not a sideshow like the modern Thanksgiving Day football games. The ancient Olympic Games arose "because Olympia was already an established sacred site, not the other way round."[3]

In the worldview of the ancient Greeks, people could rise above the limits of their mortality by defying death and performing heroic deeds in war. When there was no war to fight, the Greeks replaced the battlefield with the athletic field. The word *athlete* comes from the Greek word *athlos*, which means "conflict" or "struggle." In struggling against one another and against adversity, the participants came to resemble the gods they worshipped. Initially, the rewards for success at the Games were crowns of olive sprigs, which became the reward when the modern Olympic Games were revived. This practice was supposed to symbolize the pure motives of the competitors, who sought only the joy and glory of competition.

The practice of awarding an olive crown stems from the legend that surrounds the origins of the Games. It states that, in order to win the hand of the daughter of King Oenomaus and hence inherit the kingdom, Pelops, a young Greek hero, first had to beat Oenomaus in a chariot race. Having won the race—and in the process killed the king by sabotaging his chariot—Pelops tried to dispel the impression that he sought personal gain. He turned down the gold that was part of his prize for winning the race and asked instead to mark his victory with a crown made of a branch from a wild olive tree.

Even in ancient Greece, though, amateurism had little to do with reality. The olive crown given to the winners of the Olympic Games masked an array of greater rewards. Those selected to compete in the Games were regarded as heroes in their home cities. Honors, favorable marriages, and cash awaited them, especially if they returned victorious. According to Plutarch, Athenian winners at the Olympic Games were awarded 500 drachmae by their grateful city as early as 600 BC. An Athenian inscription from the 5th century BC notes that Athens rewarded citizens who won an Olympic event with a free meal every day for the rest of their lives.[4] As a result of the ever-increasing prizes for victors at the Games, athletes earned enough to train full-time. "[A] rising young sports star [could] support himself entirely by athletics. . . . Awards in Athens, for example, totaled an estimated $600,000 in today's terms."[5] They also began to specialize in certain events, further detaching the Games from their original connection to warfare.[6] After the Romans conquered Greece and took on its customs in the

2nd century BC, the Games became completely professionalized and slowly degenerated until Christian Emperor Theodosius stopped them in AD 393, when he banned all pagan practices.[7]

The British Ethic and the Rise of the Modern Olympics

By the 19th century, the Olympic Games of ancient Greece had been forgotten by all but a few historians and archaeologists. However, as the British came to dominate the economics, politics, and culture of Europe, their brand of "muscular Christianity" assumed increasing importance. The British, more than any country, took Juvenal's claim *mens sana in copore sano* ("a sound mind in a sound body") to heart. The Duke of Wellington found a practical application of this admonition when he attributed his victory over Napoleon at Waterloo to the sports his soldiers played at British public schools.[8]

For the rest of Europe, the impetus to develop sports programs sprang from defeat on the battlefield. Humiliated by Napoleon, the German states expressed their nationalism and combated the popular perception that they were physically inferior to the French through a mass gymnastics association known as the *Turnverein*, or Turner Movement.[9]

When the German States turned the tables on the French in the Franco-Prussian War of 1870–1871, the French sought a model for national revival. Pierre de Coubertin, a wealthy young Frenchman, looked to England for a way to restore French youth to the moral and physical vigor associated with the days of Napoleonic glory. Two particular items captured de Coubertin's attention: the British educational system's emphasis on athletics (probably a result of his lifelong fascination with the book *Tom Brown's School Days*) and the "Wenlock Olympian Games," a festival staged in the town of Wenlock by William P. Brookes, a physician and fitness advocate.

De Coubertin's 1892 proposal to revive the Olympic Games stems from an attempt to shame and inspire French youth to follow the example of superior athletes from elsewhere in the world, especially from England and the United States. De Coubertin's choice of the name "Olympic Games" was a mix of public relations gimmickry and his happening upon Dr. Brookes and his festival. De Coubertin found the name of Brookes's contest "more festive and potentially inspiring than any other at hand."[10]

Given the vital role of the Olympic Games in the history of competitive sports, it is worth noting that early sporting events were limited by gender. At the insistence of de Coubertin, women were prohibited from competing in early Olympic contests. Women did not compete in the Olympics at all until 1900, and did not compete in track and field events until 1928.[11]

The Modern Olympic Games

The first modern Olympic Games, held in Athens in 1896, were a small affair, encompassing only 14 nations and fewer than 250 athletes. Winners at the time were given silver medals and runners-up were awarded copper, a noticeable difference from the gold, silver, and bronze that athletes take home today. Despite its rather modest size, the event was considered a rousing success, and the main events in the Panathenaic Stadium attracted the largest crowds ever to watch a modern sporting event to that date.[12] From these rather humble origins, the

Summer Olympic Games have grown to become one of the world's premier sporting events. In 2016 in Rio, over 10,000 athletes, representing 204 countries, participated in 300 individual events in 28 different sports. Roughly 10 million tickets were sold to spectators, and a worldwide audience in the billions tuned in to watch on television.[13]

On a somewhat smaller scale, the Winter Olympics have been held since 1924. In 2014, Sochi, Russia, welcomed nearly 3,000 athletes from 88 countries to compete in 98 events in 15 disciplines.[14] Like its summer counterpart, the Winter Games generate massive ticket sales and television revenues.

At least in theory, the Olympic Games stayed true to its amateur ideals for decades, preventing professional athletes from participating in the Games until 1984. In fact, Jim Thorpe, widely considered one of the greatest athletes in US history, was stripped of the gold medals he won in the decathlon and pentathlon in 1912 when it was discovered that he had earned money playing semi-professional baseball in the years before his appearance at the Olympics. By 1984, it was clear that, due to the rise of highly organized (and lucrative) professional leagues across the globe, many of the best athletes in the world were no longer amateurs in any sense of the word. Fans had revealed that they tended to want to watch talent rather than valuing amateurism. It had also become increasingly difficult to distinguish between amateurs and professionals. The skaters on the Russian national hockey team, who were famously beaten by a rag-tag team of American collegiate skaters in the 1980 Winter Olympics in the "Miracle on Ice," were officially employed as soldiers of the Red Army so as not to jeopardize their amateur status even though they were paid to train full-time, year-round as hockey players. Today, the participation of recognized (and recognizable) professionals is both taken as given and touted as one of the attractions of the Olympics.

Location

Both the Summer and Winter Olympics take place every four years at various cities throughout the world. The International Olympic Committee (IOC) selects the host city through an extensive, costly, and occasionally corrupt bidding process roughly six years before the event. Historically, the IOC awarded the Games exclusively to large cities in the world's richest countries. Between 1896 and 1952, every Summer and Winter Games was held in either Western Europe or the US. Beginning with Melbourne, Australia in 1956, the Olympics spread its footprint to new parts of the globe, but the IOC still favored bids from communities in rich, industrialized nations. In 1968, Mexico City became the first city in the developing world to host the Games, and Eastern European countries won bids for the first time for the Summer Games in 1980 (Moscow) and Winter Games in 1984 (Sarajevo, Yugoslavia).

Over the past two decades, the IOC has encouraged bids from poorer countries, and has awarded the Games on several occasions to countries outside of the OECD.[15] Beijing hosted the 2008 Summer Games and will stage the Winter Olympics in 2022. In 2016, Rio de Janeiro became the first South American Olympic host. As seen in Table 8.1, the list of countries submitting formal bids has also dramatically changed in recent decades. Prior to 2000, 20 percent of the bids submitted for the Summer Games came from outside of Western Europe, Japan, Australia, Canada, and the US. Since 2000, over half of all bids have come from this group, including applications by Istanbul, Bangkok, Havana, Buenos Aires,

Table 8.1 Number of Bids for Summer and Winter Olympic Games

Event	Bidders			Hosts		
	Industrialized Countries	Developing Countries	Eastern European/ Former Soviet States	Industrialized Countries	Developing Countries	Eastern European/ Former Soviet States
Summer Olympics: 1896–1996	71 (82%)	9 (10%)	7 (8%)	20 (87%)	2 (9%)	1 (4%)
Summer Olympics: 2000–2020	23 (49%)	21 (44%)	4 (7%)	4 (67%)	2 (33%)	0 (0%)
Winter Olympics: 1924–1998	51 (93%)	1 (2%)	3 (5%)	17 (94%)	0 (0%)	1 (6%)
Winter Olympics: 2002–2022	21 (56%)	4 (9%)	12 (34%)	4 (67%)	1 (17%)	1 (17%)

Source: Robert Baade and Victor Matheson. 2016. "Going for the Gold: The Economics of the Olympics," *Journal of Economic Perspectives*, 30(2), April: 203.

and Cape Town, with successful bids by Beijing and Rio. The Winter Olympics has undergone a similar change. Kazakhstan was one of two finalists for the 2022 Winter Games, and several Eastern European and Central Asian countries submitted bids for the first time.

FIFA and the World Cup

The world's other major international sporting mega-event is the FIFA World Cup. Soccer's first governing body, the English Football Association, formed in 1863, and the first international soccer match was played between Scotland and England in 1872,[16] but it took over 40 years for an international organization to bring together various national soccer organizations. In 1904, officials representing seven European soccer associations met in Paris to form FIFA,[17] and the first official match under the auspices of the group was played later that year. The addition of England, Scotland, Wales, and Northern Ireland the next year cemented FIFA as the dominant body worldwide. The Olympics held international soccer competitions starting in 1900, with FIFA taking the lead role beginning in 1908. FIFA always had a different view of amateurism from the IOC, with the IOC holding it up as an ideal and FIFA arguing for the inclusion of professional players in international tournaments.

In response to soccer's growing prominence in the Olympics as well as ongoing disagreements about amateurism, FIFA inaugurated the World Cup in 1930 to be held every four years opposite the Summer Olympics.[18] Due to the number of large stadiums required to accommodate the tournament, FIFA selects a host country for the event as opposed to the IOC's tradition of choosing a single host city. For the first 60 years of the competition, the World Cup essentially alternated between the two biggest centers of soccer interest, Europe and Latin America, so, unlike the Olympics, numerous countries in Central and South America have hosted the World Cup, including Uruguay, Brazil, Chile, Argentina, and Mexico.

This rotation scheme lasted until 1994 when FIFA attempted to expand world interest in the game by awarding the World Cup to the US, a huge untapped market for the sport. Along a similar line, Japan and South Korea held the tournament in 2002, which was the first tournament co-hosted by two countries and the first World Cup played in Asia. South Africa became the first African host in 2010, and Russia will be the first Eastern European host when the teams take the field in 2018. Qatar will become the first Middle Eastern host in 2022. FIFA added a women's World Cup in 1991, which operates in a similar manner to the men's tournament.

8.2 The Short-Run Benefits of Hosting Mega-Events

Why would a country or city want to host a mega-event? An economist would typically say to follow the money, and no explanation seems more compelling than the search for an economic windfall.

Event boosters envision hordes of wealthy tourists descending on host cities with their wallets open and credit cards at the ready. It is hard to imagine while sitting in a packed stadium, surrounded by the noise of 75,000 cheering fans, that sports do not have a huge impact on local economies. Indeed, for many sporting events, ranging from mega-events like the Olympics and the World Cup down to smaller events such as All-Star Games, league championships, and even local 5K runs, consultants produce economic impact studies claiming thousands, millions, and perhaps even billions of dollars of benefits for the host economy.

Economic studies by academic economists, however, are not nearly as optimistic. The overwhelming consensus among these economists is that sporting events have little to no significant short-run economic impact on local economies. How can professional consultants and academic economists arrive at such differing conclusions for the same event?

It might seem that the biggest monetary impact on a local community is the revenues directly generated by the mega-event. One-time events generate revenue streams that are very similar to those generated by teams, which we examined in Chapter 3: ticket sales, media rights, venue-related revenues, and sponsorships. In fact, in most cases, the sanctioning body such as the NFL, IOC, or FIFA, and not the local organizing committee, controls these revenues. Every penny of the $5 million the NFL earns from every 30-second Super Bowl commercial,[19] as well as all of the ticket revenue, parking fees, and concessions money, goes straight into the NFL's pockets and not to the host city. As shown in Table 8.2, for the 2009–2012 Olympics cycle that included the London and Vancouver games, the IOC earned about $3.8 billion in television rights and another $1 billion in international sponsorships, roughly one-third of which was shared with the local organizers. The host cities kept ticket revenue, domestic sponsorships, and licensing money, totaling about $7.5 billion in Vancouver and $11.4 billion in London. As the table shows, however, revenues were not nearly large enough to cover the expense of hosting for either city.

Because, as shown above, much of the direct revenue that hosting a mega-event generates does not stay in the host city, the primary economic benefits from such events are the indirect expenditures by tourists who come to watch the games. These events attract visitors (and athletes, officials, and staff) who spend money on such items as hotels, restaurants, souvenirs, and rental cars. The impact can stretch well beyond the end of the event, especially if it leaves a

Table 8.2 Direct Revenues from Olympic Games ($ Millions)

Revenue Source	IOC 2009–2012	Vancouver 2010	London 2012
Broadcast rights	$2,723	$414	$713
International sponsors	$475	$175 (est.)	$300 (est.)
Domestic sponsors	$0	$688	$1,150
Ticketing	$0	$250	$988
Licensing	$0	$51	$119
Total	$3,198	$1,578	$3,270
Hosting costs	—	$7,556	$11,401

Source: Levi Pace. 2006. "Economic Impact of the 2002 Olympic Winter Games," Policy Brief: 07-25-2006, at http://gardner.utah.edu/_documents/publications/econ-dev/olympics-econ-impact.pdf.

legacy of infrastructure that can be used after the games are over or if the event generates a "buzz" about the host city that induces future tourists to visit the region after the athletes have departed. Measuring these benefits, however, is surprisingly difficult.

Two Types of Event Studies

Analysts typically produce two types of studies of mega-events. Consultants commonly generate *ex ante* economic impact studies that follow a fairly simple formula: estimate the number of people who will attend an event and how many days they will stay, determine the amount the average attendee will spend per day while at the event, and then apply an "economic multiplier" to account for the ripple effects of the initial round of spending through the economy. This type of impact study can also be produced in real time during an event by interviewing current attendees about their visit and their spending patterns.

The easiest way to see how an *ex ante* study works is to see one in action. The biggest annual sporting event in America is the Super Bowl. The NFL's premier event is held each year in late January or early February in a neutral site selected several years before the game. It attracts tens of thousands of visitors to the host city. Typically, the NFL or the local host committee provides an estimate of economic impact, although the details of these studies are often not made public.

One study that is publicly available is that of Super Bowl XXVIII, held in Atlanta in 1994. An economic impact analysis of the event by local economists estimated that roughly 75,000 visitors would stay an average of 4 days for a total of 306,680 visitor days. Next, it determined that a typical visitor would spend $252 per day. Multiplying the number of visitors by the daily spending results in a direct impact of $77.3 million.[20]

Of course, money spent in the local economy is likely to circulate through the city as the money is spent and re-spent. As we showed in Chapter 6, the equation for the multiplier is:

$$M = \frac{1}{(1 - MPC - MPI)}$$

where MPC is the marginal propensity to consume, and MPI is the marginal propensity to import. Numerous private companies as well as the federal government provide estimates of how much an increase in spending in one sector of the economy increases overall spending. While every city and industry is different, multipliers of roughly two are commonly applied to visitor spending so that an initial increase in direct spending leads to a similar level of indirect spending and a doubling of the total economic impact.

In the case of Atlanta in 1994, Jeffrey Humphreys, the author of the economic impact study, applied an economic multiplier of 2.148 to the original direct impact of $77.3 million for a total impact of $166 million.[21] Increases in the number of visitor days, the average daily spending amount, or the multiplier cause the resulting estimate of total economic activity to rise accordingly. While this method of calculating economic impact is straightforward and easy to understand, it can result in economic impact estimates that are wildly inaccurate. How could such a relatively simple calculation go so badly wrong?

Problems with ex ante *Economic Impact Studies*

In some cases, the problems start right at the beginning. Unrealistic projections of the number of visitors or their potential spending will clearly lead to bad estimates. To take an example from the NBA, Denver tourism officials predicted that 100,000 visitors would come to town for the 2005 National Basketball Association (NBA) All-Star Game. The fact that the game was taking place at the 18,007-seat Pepsi Center and that downtown Denver has fewer than 9,000 total hotel rooms might have tipped the city off that disappointment loomed.[22] Unlike the widely touted predictions of a $30 million windfall for the Denver economy, the event's less-than-stellar reality was acknowledged only two years after the fact, when an official explained away the failure by claiming, "Fears about traffic around downtown that weekend kept many people away and hurt the area economically."[23]

Denver should not feel too badly since many other cities have made equally implausible assumptions, leading to large overestimates of economic impact. The 2014 Super Bowl, held just outside New York City, arrived with a predicted economic impact of well over half a billion dollars. Every hotel room in town was expected to sell-out rapidly, despite the fact that the New York/New Jersey area is home to 115,000 hotel rooms and MetLife Stadium holds fewer than 83,000 fans. Some officials projected that 400,000 visitors would come to New York for the game, a number that seems highly optimistic.[24] Just four days before the big game, two-thirds of Manhattan hotels had rooms available, and prices had fallen over 30 percent from their peak.[25]

Other times, the range of predictions is enough to give one pause. According to one source, the projected impact of the 1989 NBA All-Star Game in Houston was $35 million, while the expected impact of the 1992 game in Orlando was only $3 million. Similarly, the impact of the 1997 NCAA Women's Basketball Final Four in Cincinnati was predicted to be $7 million, but just two years later projections for the same event in San Jose, California came in at $32 million.[26] Either the popularity of men's and women's basketball varies widely from year to year or the assumptions made by the consultants preparing economic impact reports have an enormous degree of subjectivity.

Even when one takes care to make reasonable assumptions, at least three prime factors might lead a typical *ex ante* economic impact study to overestimate the true economic impact of a sporting event: the substitution effect, leakages, and crowding out. These issues also face those studying the economic impact of stadiums, so we previously examined these concepts in Chapter 6. The unique way in which they affect mega-events, however, leads us to re-examine them here.

Substitution Effect

The substitution effect occurs when a sporting event attracts spending that otherwise would have been spent elsewhere in the local economy. Since most fans at a typical game are local, most spectator sports just reallocate where spending occurs in the economy rather than generating new economic activity. Many economists say economic impact studies should not include spending by locals. Mega-events, however, are characterized by the extent to which they attract fans from outside the region. For example, only 5 percent of tickets to the Super Bowl are allocated to the host team, while 70 percent are allocated to the other 31 teams in the league, with the remaining 25 percent divvied up by the NFL itself to important corporate sponsors and VIPs from across the country.[27] Thus, mega-events result in a lower substitution effect than regular season games or local sporting events.

Even spending by out-of-town visitors at a sporting event might not cause a net increase in economic activity, as sporting events can induce "time-switching." A person planning to visit a city or country may time their visit to coincide with a sporting event. Just as a summer vacation to Boston might be planned around a Red Sox home stand, a trip to Brazil might be timed to take advantage of the World Cup or Summer Olympics. In this case, mega-events do not increase the number of visits to a city; they simply alter the timing of such visits.

Crowding Out

The second reason that *ex ante* studies might exaggerate the economic impact of an event is "crowding out." The crowds and congestion associated with a sporting event may dissuade other economic activity from occurring. As Yogi Berra once said, "Nobody goes there anymore. It's too crowded."[28]

As we saw in Chapter 6, when looking at the negative externalities associated with stadiums, flooding a neighborhood with sports fans may be good for bars and souvenir shops, but it is bad for other businesses in the area. The Boston Marathon, the world's premier distance running event, is a prime example. The event attracts over 25,000 runners from around the world, as well as hundreds of thousands of spectators. It also makes the streets of downtown Boston nearly impassible every third Monday in April. Any economic benefits associated with out-of-town racers and spectators who buy goods and services relating to their running and watching the race need to be balanced with the economic costs of businesses that cannot service customers on that day due to the travel difficulties associated with shutting down 26.2 miles of major roads and every associated cross-street in the city.

Sports fans may also occupy hotel rooms that otherwise would have been used by other tourists or business travelers. Non-sports tourists may have difficulty finding affordable transportation or accommodations around the time of a mega-event. In the worst-case scenario, a tourist's fears about crowds are unfounded, but the worries alone keep her at home. Thus, the fear of crowds keeps regular tourists away but the crowds themselves never materialize. Just as in the case with the substitution effect, a good economic impact study subtracts out those who do not come from those who do. To be fair, it is much easier to count the number of people who are in town for an event than to count the number of people who are not in town due to an event. Nevertheless, in an economic sense, the person who is not there is every bit as important as the one who is.

The 2012 London Olympics provide a case in point. The UK's Office for National Statistics reported that an impressive 590,000 overseas visitors came to the UK during July and August 2012 in connection with the Olympics. Unfortunately for the English economy, despite this hefty Olympic boost, there was an overall *decline* in the number of overseas visitors to the UK, from 6.57 million in July and August 2011 to 6.17 million a year later during the Olympics, a decline of 6 percent. Put another way, the number of visitors to the UK for reasons other than the Olympics fell by nearly 1 million between the summers of 2011 and 2012.[29]

This example would just be an anecdote proving nothing general about mega-events and tourism, but the pattern has been seen over and over again in countries and cities hosting mega-events. Beijing reported a decline in tourism during its Olympic Games in 2008, and international arrivals were flat in South Korea during their stint as World Cup host in 2002. Tax receipt data suggest that the 2002 Winter Olympics in Salt Lake City, Utah, caused a surge in skier visits . . . in Colorado. Faced with high prices for lodging and crowds of people watching skiing, those folks actually wanting to ski avoided Utah and instead headed to the state next door.[30]

In 2007, Terry Lanni, CEO of MGM Mirage, the largest casino owner in Las Vegas, blamed poor first-quarter profits in part on the NBA All-Star Game, which took place in Sin City that year.[31] The game coincided with Lunar New Year, a prime gambling weekend for high-rollers from Asia, and the general rowdiness of the NBA crowds reduced pedestrian traffic on the Vegas Strip as well as in the major casinos.

Detailed academic studies of tourist arrivals also show clear evidence of regular tourists being crowded out by sports fans. Prior to the 2010 World Cup in South Africa, event promoters initially predicted that 483,000 international soccer fans would descend upon the country for the tournament. This number was later reduced to 373,000. After the event concluded, FIFA reported that 310,000 spectators had come from abroad for the World Cup. However, Thomas Peeters, Stefan Szymanski, and Victor Matheson examined monthly visitor arrivals in South Africa around the time of the 2010 World Cup and identified an increase in international arrivals of only 220,000 travelers, less than half the original estimate.[32] Stan du Plessis and Wolfgang Maennig arrive at an even lower figure of 40,000 to 90,000 new arrivals during the World Cup.[33] Assuming that South Africa accurately counted the number of soccer arrivals, one can account for the difference between the 310,000 international spectators and the actual increase of 40,000–220,000 international visitors by other tourists' avoiding the country during the chaos of the FIFA tournament.

We can also detect crowding out in events smaller than the Olympics or World Cup. A study of detailed arrival data for Hawaii shows a similar phenomenon. The two biggest sporting events of the year in the state, the Honolulu Marathon and the NFL's Pro Bowl, attract roughly 15,000 and 25,000 out-of-state visitors, annually. However, during the weeks of these events, tourist arrivals into the state increase by less than 7,000.[34] Thus, runners and football fans must be displacing up to 18,000 other tourists during the weeks of these events. Hotel occupancy data for cities hosting major events like the NCAA Men's Basketball Final Four and the Super Bowl show a similar pattern.[35]

Leakages

The third source of potential bias is related to the appropriate use of multipliers and the level of leakages that an economy experiences during a major sporting event. The use of a multiplier magnifies any errors made while estimating the direct economic impact of an event, and one can apply an unrealistically high multiplier to exaggerate the economic impact of any study. That said, the use of multipliers should not be rejected out of hand, as they have a solid base in economic theory, as we saw in Chapter 6.

The leakages associated with mega-events may be worse than those experienced during a recurring sporting event, such as a baseball game. The multipliers used in economic impact analyses are derived from a careful examination of the patterns of expenditures in various industries during the normal operation of the economy. During a mega-event, however, the economy is anything but normal. For example, during the Super Bowl or the Olympics, a city's hotels might be charging two or three times the normal room rate. The desk clerks and room cleaners, however, will not see their paychecks increase by a factor of two or three. Thus, if the hotel is part of a national chain, the extra profits the hotel generates will not make their way into the pockets of workers and owners in the local economy. Instead, they head back to corporate headquarters in some distant city and into stockholders' accounts around the world. In other words, lots of money may be spent in a city during a mega-event, but the money may not stay there.

Mega-events may also require a city to import labor to meet the demands of the event. For example, during the 2017 Super Bowl in Houston, ride-sharing company Uber issued an alert to all of its drivers in nearby cities that it expected high demand in the city during Super Bowl weekend and encouraged them to go to the city for a nice paycheck. These guest workers left town with their earnings when the event was over, eliminating any hope of this money recirculating in Houston. This case is even worse than a small multiplier effect, as the direct spending does not accrue to anyone in the local economy. Instead, it goes to someone from out of the region who benefits from the event. Capital might also be imported. To meet the demands for hotel rooms during the 2005 Jacksonville Super Bowl, the host committee arranged for three large cruise ships to dock in the Jacksonville area to provide additional accommodations.[36] Once the big game was over, the ships sailed away with the extra rooms and with most of the economic impact generated by those rooms.

Ex post *Economic Impact Studies*

At this point, all we have is two competing approaches. Sports boosters point to the packed stadiums and arenas and the hotel rooms full of visitors going to games and claim that the events are a big contributor to the local economy. Critics point to the potential flaws in *ex ante* economic impact studies and offer some anecdotes to justify their caution. Ultimately, the question must be answered using data to carefully analyze events after they occur. These analyses are called *ex post* studies. When conducted by economists with expertise in this area, such studies can provide a much clearer picture of the costs and benefits. Economists

Table 8.3 Examples of Mega-Event *ex ante* Economic Impact Studies

Event	Impact	Source
2006 World Cup, Germany	60,000 jobs, up to €10 billion	German Chamber of Commerce, reported in Deutsche Welle. 2006. "World Cup to Boost German Economy," January 2, at http://www.dw.com/en/world-cup-to-boost-german-economy/a-1842332.
2006 World Cup, Germany	3.3 million foreign tourists, 5 million hotel nights, €3.4 billion	German Federation of Hotels, reported in Swatje Allmers and Wolfgang Maennig. 2009. "Economic Impacts of the FIFA Soccer World Cups in France 1998, Germany 2006, and Outlook for South Africa 2010," *Eastern Economic Journal*, 35(4): 500–519.
2010 World Cup, South Africa	$12 billion, 483,000 visitors	Kevin Voigt. 2010. "Is There a World Cup Economic Bounce?" CNN.com, June 11, at http://edition.cnn.com/2010/BUSINESS/06/11/business.bounce.world.cup/index.html.
1996 Summer Olympics, Atlanta	$5.1 billion, 77,000 jobs	Jeffrey Humphreys and M. Plummer. 1995. *The Economic Impact on the State of Georgia of Hosting the 1996 Summer Olympic Games*. Athens: Selig Center for Economic Growth, University of Georgia.
2002 Winter Olympics, Salt Lake City	$4.8 billion, 35,000 jobs	International Olympic Committee, "Factsheet: Legacies of the Games, Update—January 2010," at http://www.olympic.org/Documents/Reference_documents_Factsheets/Legacy.pdf.
2015 Super Bowl, Glendale, Arizona	$720 million	Peter Corbett. 2015. "Report: Super Bowl Lifted Valley Economy by $720 Million," *Arizona Republic*, June 23.
2017 Super Bowl, Houston	$500 million	Steve Jansen. 2017. "The Super Bowl May Bring a $500 Million Boost to Houston, or None at All," *Houston Press*, January 31, at http://www.houstonpress.com/news/the-super-bowl-may-bring-a-500-million-boost-to-houston-or-none-at-all-9156999.

look for changes in economic variables such as personal income, employment, taxable sales, tourist arrivals, or other data that might show whether economic activity increased during a mega-event. By and large, independent studies by researchers who are not associated with the events being studied have found little or no economic impact from a broad range of spectator sporting events.

Table 8.3 shows the predicted *ex ante* economic impact from a variety of different events held across the US and around the world. If these estimates are to be believed, mega-events bring hundreds of millions of dollars for a weekend event like the Super Bowl or even billions of dollars for a month-long event like the World Cup or the Olympics.

Table 8.4 shows *ex post* economic impact studies for the same events. The differences are striking. In many cases, the event has either an observed impact that is a fraction of what was predicted or no observed impact whatsoever. One anomalous result deserves attention. Julie Hotchkiss, Robert Moore, and Stephanie Zobay (2003) examined employment data for Atlanta around the time of the 1996 Summer Games and estimated that the 1996 Games created 293,000 new jobs, a figure that not only exceeded those of Baade and Matheson (2000) by about a factor of 10 but far surpassed the estimates of the local organizing committee itself. Arne Feddersen and Wolfgang Maennig claim that the uncharacteristic finding was the result of attributing too much of the general growth

Table 8.4 Examples of Mega-Event *ex post* Economic Impact Studies

Event	Impact	Source
2006 World Cup, Germany	No overall job gains, 2,600 new jobs in the hospitality sector	Feddersen and Maennig. 2012. "Sectoral Labour Market Effects of the 2006 FIFA World Cup," *Labour Economics*, 19(6): 860–869.
2006 World Cup, Germany	100,000 tourists, 708,000 hotel nights, €570 million income	Allmers and Maennig. 2009. "Economic Impacts of the FIFA Soccer World Cups in France 1998, Germany 2006, and Outlook for South Africa 2010," *Eastern Economic Journal*, 35(4): 500–519.
2010 World Cup, South Africa	40,000–90,000 arrivals from non-neighboring countries; 220,000 additional arrivals from non-SADC (Southern African Development Community) countries	Du Plessis and Maennig. 2010. "The 2010 FIFA World Cup High Frequency Data Economics: Effects on International Tourism and Awareness for South Africa," *Development Southern Africa*, 28(3): 349–365; Peeters, Matheson, and Szymanski. 2014. "Tourism and the 2010 World Cup: Lessons for Developing Countries," *Journal of African Economies*, 23(2): 290–320.
1996 Summer Olympics, Atlanta	3,500–42,000 jobs; 29,000 jobs; 293,000 jobs	Baade and Matheson. 2002. "Bidding for the Olympics: Fool's Gold?" in *Transatlantic Sport: The Comparative Economics of North American and European Sports*, Barros, Ibrahimo, and Szymanski, eds. (London: Edward Elgar): 127–151; Feddersen and Maennig. 2013. "Mega-Events and Sectoral Employment: The Case of the 1996 Olympic Games," *Contemporary Economic Policy*, 31(3): 580–603; Hotchkiss, Moore, and Zobay. 2003. "The Impact of the 1996 Summer Olympic Games on Employment and Wages in Georgia," *Southern Economic Journal*, 69(3): 691–704.
2002 Winter Olympics, Salt Lake City	Retail sales up by $70 million at hotels and restaurants but down by $167 million at general retailers; 4,000–7,000 new jobs	Baade, Baumann, and Matheson. 2010. "Slippery Slope: Assessing the Economic Impact of the 2002 Winter Olympic Games in Salt Lake City, Utah." *Region et Développement*, 31: 81–91; Baumann, Engelhardt, and Matheson. 2012. "Employment Effects of the 2002 Winter Olympics in Salt Lake City, Utah," *Journal of Economics and Statistics*, 232(3), May: 308–317.
1996 Summer Games and 2002 Winter Games	No impact on taxable sales, hotel occupancy, or airport usage; significant increase in hotel prices	Porter and Fletcher. 2008. "The Economic Impact of the Olympic Games: Ex Ante Predictions and Ex Post Reality," *Journal of Sport Management*, 22(4): 470–486.
Super Bowl, multiple years	$124 million increase in personal income; no statistically significant increase in taxable sales	Baade and Matheson. 2006. "Padding Required: Assessing the Economic Impact of the Super Bowl," *European Sports Management Quarterly*, 6(4): 353–374; Porter. 1999. "Mega-Sporting Events as Municipal Investments: A Critique of Impact Analysis," in *Sports Economics: Current Research*, ed. John Fizel, Elizabeth Gustafson, and Larry Hadley (Westport, CT: Praeger).
2004 Super Bowl, Houston	$55 million increase in taxable sales; $4 million increase in tax revenue	Coates and Depken. 2010. "Mega-Events: Is Baylor Football to Waco What the Super Bowl Is to Houston?" *Journal of Sports Economics*, 12(6): 599–620.

of the Atlanta metropolitan area, even those counties far removed from any of the important venues of the 1996 Olympics, to the Games. After correcting for this, they found a significant but highly localized effect of just 29,000 new jobs with an obvious peak occurring only in Fulton County, encompassing the heart of downtown Atlanta. These differing results illustrate the difficulty in estimating the economic impact of sporting events in the large, diverse metropolitan areas in which they often take place.

Economists have studied many other mega-events ranging from single-week-end or short-term events, like the Champions League Final, the Daytona 500, the NCAA Men's Basketball Final Four, and MLB's All-Star Game, to longer series like the MLB or NBA playoffs, to the European Cup or the Rugby World Cup. With a few exceptions, such as the Hotchkiss et al. paper, the overwhelming consensus of these studies is again that sports boosters routinely overestimate the benefits of these events and that objective studies by neutral observers generally find that the event has little to no short-run economic effect on the host. In fact, some economists like to joke that if you really want to know what the true economic impact of a sporting event is, just take whatever number the promoters give you and then move the decimal point one place to the left.

Several recent studies have taken a prospective look at the economic impact of mega-events by using a financial technique called "event analysis." Most event analyses measure the impact of an action or incident on the profitability of a firm by evaluating the effect of the event on the company's stock price.[37] If investors make rational use of all available information—a common assumption in finance—the company's stock price should respond rapidly to an event and its impact on the future profits of the firm. Several studies have used this technique to test whether overall stock market indices change in response to the announcement that a country will host the Olympics. A rise in the indices predicts that the country will prosper as a result of its hosting the Olympics. Again, the findings are mixed. Gabrielle Berman et al. find that the announcement that Sydney would host the 2000 Summer Olympics had no impact on the Australian exchange. Nikolaos Veraros et al. find a positive overall impact on the Athens exchange from the announcement of the 2004 Summer Olympics. They also find a positive impact on indices for the industrial and construction sectors. Michael Leeds et al. find only a short-lived rise on the Shanghai exchange following the announcement that Beijing would host the 2008 Olympics. They attribute this to momentary euphoria that was quickly swept away. They also find mixed effects for sectoral indices, with some rising while others fell.[38]

Thus, whether one looks retrospectively or prospectively, at a wide range of mega-events, from Super Bowls to World Cups to Olympics, there is no clear evidence that mega-events bring large, short-run benefits to the host cities.

8.3   The Long-Run Benefits of Hosting Mega-Events

There are several potential long-run benefits of hosting a mega-event. First, they can leave a legacy of sports facilities or other infrastructure that can benefit future generations. Second, they can advertise a city as an attractive tourist or business destination. Finally, major international events like the World Cup or Olympics can promote foreign direct investment and increased international trade, as the Olympics familiarizes investors and companies worldwide with the area.

The most obvious potential legacy from a major event is also the one least likely to pay economic dividends. Cities often build new sports facilities to host mega-events, but as we learned in Chapter 6, sports facilities tend to have little or no positive impact on host communities. This is especially true for the Olympics, since many Olympic events require highly specialized sports infrastructure, such as bobsled runs or velodromes that have little use beyond the Games. These venues do not create long-run benefits, and they may burden cities with heavy on-going expenses to maintain little-used "white elephants." While Athens' dilapidated stadiums from 2004 are the best-known examples, many recent mega-events have suffered from the problem of dealing with the facilities once the Games are over. Brazil built or refurbished 12 stadiums for the 2014 World Cup at a cost of $3.6 billion.[39] Several of these stadiums were built in cities without the top-flight teams that could hope to fill the large stadiums built for World Cup crowds. Brasilia, the nation's capital and the home of the most expensive stadium built for the tournament, is using its gleaming new facility as a bus depot.[40] Similarly, Beijing's iconic "Bird's Nest" Stadium has rarely been used since 2008 and has been partially converted into apartments.

Even when sports facilities can be repurposed, converting to new uses after a mega-event can be costly. The Stadium at Queen Elizabeth Olympic Park in London was the venue for the track and field events as well as the opening and closing ceremonies for the 2012 Summer Olympics. The stadium was designed to be converted after the Games into a soccer stadium for the EPL club West Ham United. However, much like we saw in Chapter 6 with baseball and football facilities, track and field stadiums and soccer (and football) stadiums have very different optimal seating configurations. A standard 400-meter track is much wider than a typical soccer pitch, so redesigning the stadium for its new tenant was quite expensive. The Olympic stadium was originally slated to cost $360 million,

Figure 8.1
Athens' Olympic Athletic Center, the "Spiros Louis" Stadium, Built in 2004 and Fallen into Disrepair Less Than Ten Years Later

Photograph by Judith Grant Long.

but cost overruns (a common problem with stadiums built for mega-events) led to a final construction cost of over $550 million. Removing the track and preparing the facility to accommodate soccer matches cost an additional $350 million, of which West Ham United paid a mere $20 million.[41]

General Infrastructure

Spending on general infrastructure improvements clearly has much better potential for positive returns. Athletes' villages from Olympic Games in Atlanta and Los Angeles are used to this day as dormitories for students attending Georgia Tech and UCLA, and the people of Utah still benefit from the expanded highways built for the 2002 Winter Games linking Salt Lake City and the ski resorts to the east. In fact, it is sometimes argued that a primary benefit of a major event like the Olympics is that it can generate the political will required to undertake needed infrastructure investments and give a region a firm deadline by which to complete these projects. Any student knows that there is nothing like a looming deadline to motivate someone to work on a term paper, but these same deadlines can lead to shoddy work or higher costs. In addition, just because an infrastructure project built for a mega-event leads to positive net benefits does not mean that the project is the best use of public funds. Economists must always consider **opportunity cost**. As we defined them in Chapter 1, opportunity costs are the value of what we give up to get something else. If a mega-event project uses public money that could have been directed to an alternative project with a higher return, then the Olympics spending reduces national output even if the event itself runs a surplus.

This is exactly what Australian economists James Giesecke and John Madden found when they examined Sydney's 2000 Summer Olympic Games. Using a complex computer modeling technique known as Computable General Equilibrium Analysis, which corrects for problems like the substitution effect, crowding out, and leakages, they compared the current state of the Australian economy against a hypothetical world in which Sydney had never hosted the Olympics. They estimate that household consumption in Australia would have been $2.1 billion higher had the Olympics never gone to the land down under.[42]

Advertising and Branding

Much like the way a sports team can make a community a "big league city" as discussed in Chapter 6, a mega-event can "put a city on the map," increasing its profile as a major tourist or business destination. Barcelona, which is often cited as hosting one of the most economically successful Olympics, was relatively unknown prior to 1992 and received less than half the number of annual visitors of its Spanish neighbor, Madrid. The city focused its Olympic preparations on revitalizing its harbor and central business district, minimized its spending on sports facilities, and highlighted its non-sports offerings during its three weeks at the center of the sports world's attention. As a result, the city experienced the fastest tourism growth of any of Europe's major cities, rising from the 13th to the 5th most popular tourist destination in Europe.[43] Perhaps even more important to Barcelonians, by 2010 Barcelona had eclipsed Madrid, its bitter rival both on and off the soccer field, as the most popular tourist destination in Spain. Utah experienced a similar increase in the popularity of its ski resorts following the 2002 Winter Games, with its ski resorts enjoying a 20.4 percent increase in skier days between 2000–2001 and 2014–2015 compared to Colorado's 8.0 percent gain.[44]

However, most other mega-event hosts have not had the same experience as Utah and Barcelona. One explanation for their success is that they were "hidden gems," destinations that had lots to offer potential tourists but were relatively unknown compared to their more famous neighbors. Given their moment in the sun, they were ready to capitalize on the national and international exposure. However, this does not work for all cities. Some cities lack attractions that would make them desirable for future tourism once an event is over. The 2000 Super Bowl did not magically turn its host Jacksonville into Orlando with its myriad amusement parks and tourist attractions. Other cities face the opposite problem: they are already so well-known as tourist destinations that any additional advertising is unlikely to make much difference. Before the 2012 Olympics, London was already one of the world's top three tourist destinations with nearly 18 million international visitors per year. Hence, the Olympics were never likely to increase international awareness about London as a tourist destination. In sum, mega-events have the potential to raise a city's tourism profile, but they are far from a surefire way to ensure a steady stream of visitors after the event is over.

One final line of research points to a potential positive impact from the Olympics. Andrew Rose and Mark Spiegel examine 196 countries between 1950 and 2006 and find that exports increased by over 20 percent among countries that hosted the Olympics.[45] This appears to demonstrate that the Olympics have a significant positive impact on host countries. However, the same study shows that countries that bid unsuccessfully for the Olympics experienced the same bump in exports. If hosting the Olympics causes large increases in exports, it seems odd that bidding for the Olympics, but not hosting them, would produce the same result. Rose and Spiegel argue that bidding for the Olympics signals to other countries around the world that a country is opening itself to globalization and trade liberalization, an idea they dub the "Olympic Effect."

The signaling effect is not the only potential explanation. The cities that bid for the Olympics are not a random sample drawn from countries from across the world, but are in countries with stable governments, strong economies, and good prospects for the future. These are exactly the sort of countries that should experience strong rates of growth in exports. Wolfgang Maennig and Felix Richter argue that Rose and Spiegel have mixed up correlation and causation, and that bidding for the Olympics does not cause higher export growth. Instead, countries experiencing high export growth are more likely to bid for the Olympics.[46] To test for this, they compare every country that bid for the Olympics with a country that did not bid for the Olympics but is otherwise as similar as possible to the bidding country. They find that the growth in exports for Olympic bidders and otherwise similar non-bidders is the same, and the "Olympic Effect" disappears.

8.4   The Costs of Hosting Mega-Events

If the benefits of hosting are often overstated, the opposite is typically true for the costs of hosting a mega-event. The world's biggest sporting events can be extraordinarily expensive affairs. The most austere bid for the Summer Olympics runs into the billions of dollars. Even short-term events not requiring major infrastructure investments like the Super Bowl can have a price tag in the tens of millions.

The first major expense associated with hosting a mega-event is ensuring that the region has sufficient infrastructure to accommodate the anticipated wave of tourists and athletes. For example, for the Summer Olympics, the IOC requires that all prospective hosts have at least 40,000 hotel rooms and housing for 15,000 participants. In addition, the city needs transportation facilities that can welcome hundreds of thousands of international visitors and move them between hotels and sporting venues after they arrive. Rio, for example, needed to add 15,000 hotel rooms and upgrade its subway systems as a precondition of hosting the 2016 Summer Games. As noted earlier, general infrastructure investment may leave a positive legacy for the host city, but building hotels and transportation networks to meet peak demand during a mega-event may leave a city with severe excess capacity once the Games are over. Lillehammer, the site of the 1994 Winter Olympics, saw 40 percent of its luxury hotels declare bankruptcy immediately after the fans and athletes left town.[47]

Many events require the construction of competition venues. These expenses tend to be higher for the Olympics than other mega-events due to the relatively obscure sports they feature. Even large, wealthy cities with extensive existing sports infrastructure are unlikely to have a world-class velodrome, swimming pool, or bobsled run with a large seating capacity for ticket-buying fans. While single-game events like the Super Bowl or All-Star Games generally do not require new infrastructure, leagues often dangle the possibility of hosting events like these as a carrot to persuade otherwise reluctant taxpayers to provide large subsidies for stadium and arena construction. Between 2016 and 2021, each of the four newest stadiums in the NFL will have hosted the big game.

Once the construction phase is complete, hosting a mega-event still entails large expenditures for items like event management, transportation, and security. Public safety and its costs have been a particular concern for event organizers for decades. Deadly terrorist attacks occurred at the 1972 and 1996 Summer Olympics as well as the 2013 Boston Marathon, and dozens of sporting events have experienced major disasters ranging from fires to rioting to stampedes, resulting in multiple fatalities. Perhaps the most famous disaster took place at Hillsborough football stadium in Sheffield, England, in 1989 when 96 fans were killed because of overcrowding during a soccer match between Sheffield Wednesday and Liverpool. Security costs for all types of events have escalated rapidly in the post-September 11, 2001 era. For example, the security costs during the 2000 Summer Olympics in Sydney totaled roughly $250 million. Just four years later, security spending for the Athens Games shot up to $1.6 billion and it has remained near that level since then.[48]

Even smaller events can entail large expenditures. The cost to host the Super Bowl is generally a closely guarded secret between the NFL and the local host committee. However, the event places extensive demands on local organizers, including hotel space for team and NFL officials, a large convention center for the "NFL Experience," an interactive entertainment festival for fans, full use of the local stadium and its parking lots, transportation for players, volunteers, entertainers, and enhanced security. The extent of the NFL's demands became clear when the league's bid documents with Minneapolis for the 2018 Super Bowl were leaked to the public.[49] In addition to the items listed previously, the NFL demanded that if the League found the cell phone service in the hotel designated as the primary NFL headquarters unacceptable, the host committee would install temporary cell towers for the duration of the event at no cost to the NFL. In fact, the term "at no cost to the NFL" was the most common phrase in the bid document, but, as mentioned previously, the NFL shares none of the revenue generated by the Super Bowl with the city or local organizers.

It is often difficult to find accurate figures relating to the cost of hosting mega-events. One problem is that, even if mega-events receive significant public funding, they are often run by private organizations that are not required to release financial statements to the public. It can also be difficult to disentangle a region's normal expenditures and investments from those related to a mega-event. Some economists might include, for example, the cost of the highway built between Salt Lake City and the mountains as a cost of the Olympics since the Games clearly influenced the timing of the project. Others might not include the highway as an expense of the Olympics since the investment was long-planned and would have taken place at some point in the future even without the Olympics.

Sometimes, public officials and organizers are reluctant to release a full accounting of the costs because they fear a public outcry over cost overruns or corruption. For example, we will never know the true cost of the 1998 Winter Olympics in Nagano, Japan (estimated at $14 billion or more), because at the conclusion of the Games the organizing committee ordered that all records be burned.[50] Keeping these concerns in mind, Table 8.5 provides cost estimates for several recent mega-events, breaking up the costs into various components such as operations, sports infrastructure, and general infrastructure when such information is readily available.

Even when host cities work to contain costs, they are frequently unsuccessful. The Olympics, for example, have consistently come in far over budget. According to a study by Bent Flyvberg and Allison Stewart, every Olympic Games between 1968 and 2012 cost more than originally planned. The average Olympics ended up 150% over budget, and the worst offenders, Montreal in 1976 and Sarajevo in 1984, exceeded the original cost estimates by a factor of ten.[51]

Even these figures may understate the true cost overruns. London's original bid for the 2012 Summer Olympics was £2.4 billion when it was awarded the Games in 2005, a very reasonable figure compared to many recent Olympics. Within two years, however, its budget had grown to £9.3 billion, an increase of nearly 300%. When the final cost came in at "only" £8.77 billion, the organizers claimed without a trace of irony that the Olympics came in under budget.[52]

The nature of the bid selection process also tends to drive up costs, as the bid itself can be quite expensive. Andrew Zimbalist reports that Chicago spent between $70 and $100 million in its ultimately unsuccessful attempt to host the 2016 Summer Games.[53] More importantly, by pitting cities against each other, the IOC can insist on more lavish accommodations for athletes and officials and more impressive venues. Cities facing rivals not only have to present a plan to successfully host the Olympics, they must also present a plan that is lavish enough to beat out the other candidates. The story of the 1984 Los Angeles Summer Olympics illustrates this phenomenon.

Interest in hosting the Olympics waned in the 1970s due to concerns about spiraling expenses. Taxpayers in Denver, which had been awarded the 1976 Winter Olympics, rejected a $5 million bond referendum to fund part of the Games, an amount that seems small today given the figures presented in Table 8.5. Faced with a lack of funding, the IOC had to move the Games from Denver to Innsbruck, Austria. Shortly thereafter, Montreal suffered severe financial losses hosting the 1976 Summer Games. By the time the IOC awarded the 1984

Table 8.5 Costs of Hosting Mega-Events

Event	Spending (billions, $2017)	Source
2004 Summer Olympics, Athens	$14.2 (Total)	Tagaris. 2014. "Ten Years on, Athens 2004 Gives Greece Little to Cheer," *Reuters*, August 7, at http://uk.reuters.com/article/2014/08/07/uk-olympics-greece-idUKKBN0G70Y220140807.
2008 Summer Olympics, Beijing	$2.4 (Sports infrastructure) $46.0 (Total, est.)	Preuss. 2004. *Economics of the Olympic Games*. London: Edward Elgar; Fowler and Meichtry. 2008. "China Counts the Cost of Hosting the Olympics." *Wall Street Journal*, July 16.
2012 Summer Olympics, London	$11.8 (Total)	BBC. 2013. "London 2012: Olympics and Paralympics 528 Million under Budget," July 19, at http://www.bbc.com/sport/0/olympics/20041426.
2016 Summer Olympics, Rio	$13 (Total)	Rios. 2016. "These Are the Actual Costs of the Rio Olympics," *Mother Jones*, August 5, at http://www.motherjones.com/media/2016/08/true-cost-rio-summer-olympics-zika.
1998 Winter Olympics, Nagano	Over $15.7 (Total)	Longman. 1998. "Nagano 1998: Seven Days to Go—High Costs and High Expectations," *New York Times*, January 30.
2006 Winter Olympics, Torino	$4.5 (Total)	Associated Press. 2006. "A Look at Spending on Recent Winter Olympics," October 2, at http://wintergames.ap.org/article/look-spending-recent-winter-olympics.
2010 Winter Olympics, Vancouver	$0.7 (Sports infrastructure) $3.6 (General infrastructure) $7.8 (Total)	Van Wynsberghe. 2011. "Olympic Games Impact (OGI) Study for the 2010 Olympic and Paralympic Winter Games: Games-time Report," at http://cfss.sites.olt.ubc.ca/files/2011/10/The-Olympic-Games-Impact-Study-Games-time-Report-2011-11-21.pdf.
2014 Winter Olympics, Sochi	$7.0 (Sports infrastructure, est.) $51.0 (Total, est.)	Farhi. 2014. "Did the Winter Olympics in Sochi Really Cost $50 Billion? A Closer Look at that Figure," *Washington Post*, February 10.
2002 World Cup, Japan / South Korea	$3.7 (Stadiums, S. Korea) $6.2 (Stadiums, Japan)	James Brooke. 2002. "Legacy of World Cup May Be the Stadiums Left Behind," *New York Times*, June 2, at http://www.nytimes.com/2002/06/02/sports/soccer-legacy-of-world-cup-may-be-the-stadiums-left-behind.html.
2006 World Cup, Germany	$2.0 (Stadiums)	Downie. 2012. "Soccer-Brazil World Cup Stadiums on Track, but Costs Soar," *Reuters*, April 3, at http://www.reuters.com/article/2012/04/03/soccer-world-brazil-idUSL2E8F2GG820120403.
2010 World Cup, South Africa	$1.4 (Stadiums) $4.2 (Total)	Voigt. 2010. "Is There a World Cup Economic Bounce?" *CNN.com*, June 11, at http://edition.cnn.com/2010/BUSINESS/06/11/business.bounce.world.cup/index.html.
2014 World Cup, Brazil	$4.0 (Stadiums) $14.1 (Total, est.)	Downie, 2012.
2018 World Cup, Russia	$2.6 (Stadiums) $10.8 (Total)	Wall Street Journal. 2017. "Russia's 2018 World Cup Stadiums," October 2, at https://graphics.wsj.com/embeddable-carousel/?slug=russia-world-cup-2018, accessed October 24, 2017; Associated Press. 2017. "Russia Increases 2018 World Cup Budget by $325 Million," February 6, at http://www.espnfc.com/fifa-world-cup/story/3055194/russia-increases-2018-world-cup-budget-by-$325-million.
2022 World Cup, Qatar	$200 (Total, est.)	Associated Press. 2013. "Deloitte: Qatar to Spend $200 Billion for World Cup," *USA Today*, July 9, at http://www.usatoday.com/story/sports/soccer/2013/07/09/deloitte-qatar-to-spend-200-billion-world-cup/2501815/.
2014–2016 Super Bowls, New York, San Francisco, Arizona	$30–70 million (Total)	Peter. 2015. "Hosting a Super Bowl a Huge Economic Plum, and Costly," *USA Today*, January 25, at https://www.usatoday.com/story/sports/nfl/2015/01/25/super-bowl-host-cities-economic-impact/22324109/.

Summer Games, Los Angeles was the only bidder. Being the only bidder put Los Angeles in the driver's seat, and the Los Angeles Organizing Committee (LAOC) could dictate the terms of the bid to the IOC rather than the other way around. The LAOC insisted on utilizing the area's existing sports infrastructure, some of which had been used five decades earlier when Los Angeles had hosted the 1932 Olympics. Rather than building a new stadium as the centerpiece of the Games, Los Angeles utilized the 60-year-old Los Angeles Coliseum for the track and field events as well as the opening and closing ceremonies. Corporate sponsors were also used heavily for the first time to finance the Games. The LAOC kept costs down, resulting in total expenditures of only $546 million ($1.244 billion in 2015 dollars), a figure less than one-quarter that spent by Montreal eight years earlier. The 1984 Los Angeles Games also managed to become one of the only profitable Games in modern Olympic history, with a profit of $232.5 million.[54]

In the wake of Los Angeles's profitable showing, multiple cities entered the bidding process in the hopes of earning a similar economic windfall. However, the large increase in bidders shifted bargaining power back to the IOC. A successful bid no longer had to simply meet the minimum requirements set forth by the IOC; it also had to beat out the bids of the other competing cities. This situation led to an escalating "arms race" among Olympic bidders, leading to increasingly spectacular bids and serious corruption in the bidding process as detailed in the biographical sketch of Mitt Romney at the end of this chapter. Bidding cities commonly attempted to impress the IOC selection committee with architectural monuments constructed specifically for the Olympics, such as Beijing's $480 million Bird's Nest Stadium or the £269 million London Aquatics Centre. Before public outrage over spiraling costs forced cutbacks, Tokyo's planned Olympic Stadium, the centerpiece of its 2020 Summer Games, had an estimated price tag of over $2 billion, making it not only the costliest athletic facility in history but also more expensive than the entire 1984 Los Angeles Olympics, even after accounting for inflation.[55]

More recently, likely in response to what cities saw as out-of-control spending by hosts such as Sochi and Rio, the enthusiasm to bid for the Olympics has again waned. Five of seven cities originally in the running for the 2022 Winter Olympics withdrew their bids, often in response to unfavorable outcomes on voter initiatives or general public pressure. Notably, the two remaining cities were Beijing, China and Almaty, Kazakhstan, two locations not known for respecting the democratic wishes of their citizens. The competition for the 2024 Olympics went down to just two bidders as well, Los Angeles and Paris, as Hamburg, Rome, Budapest, and Boston all dropped from the running due to public concerns about costs.

8.5   Why Do Cities Continue to Bid?

If both history and economics suggest that hosting mega-events is often a fool's errand, why have so many cities vigorously competed against each other to host these events year after year? Before we explore this topic in more depth, it is important to realize that every mega-event is different, and some may offer greater potential for economic success than others. An NBA or NHL All-Star Game does not offer the worldwide audience that the Olympics or World Cup do, but they present a much easier (and less expensive) organizational challenge, utilize an existing arena, and are not as disruptive of normal economic activity. Thus, even if the economic impact of an NBA All-Star Game is less than advertised, it still may make sense for a city to pursue the event, as its net benefits could be positive simply because it is less costly to host the game.

Similarly, some regions may be better equipped than others to host these events. When the United States took on the 1994 World Cup, it spent relatively little on sports facilities because, as a large, wealthy country, it already had in place all the stadiums and general tourism infrastructure it needed to host the tournament. In fact, the 1994 World Cup generated a healthy profit that was used to endow the US Soccer Foundation, a charity that provides funding for youth soccer facilities across the country to this day. On the other hand, as seen in Table 8.5, Qatar may spend over $200 billion to hold the 2022 tournament, and both Russia and Brazil spent over $10 billion to host the 2014 and 2018 installments, largely because they had to build expensive new facilities.[56]

Distribution of Costs and Benefits

Even when the total costs of hosting an event exceed the expected benefits, some sectors of the economy stand to gain. The hospitality industry is likely to earn high profits during a mega-event. The increase in demand for hotel rooms leads to both higher prices and an increase in occupancy rates. Local transportation providers such as taxis, limo services, and Uber drivers, as well as bars and restaurants near the competition venues also are likely to see higher profits. Finally, construction companies gain from the need for new infrastructure for events like the Olympics. Boston's ultimately unsuccessful bid to host the 2024 Summer Games was spearheaded by leaders in the heavy construction and hospitality industries, the two sectors of the economy that stood to gain the most from the city hosting the Olympics.[57]

Non-Economic Rationales

In many cases, economics may not be the primary reason a city hosts an event. The bidding process may be driven by the egos of local politicians or by countries that wish to demonstrate their growing political or economic might. The 2008 Summer Olympics in Beijing were seen as a signal to the world that China had arrived as global leader. The proliferation of bids from developing countries shown in Table 8.1 can also be seen in this light. Similarly, it is nearly impossible to justify the $51 billion cost of the 2014 Winter Olympics in Sochi, Russia in economic terms, but it was an effective display of Russian President Vladimir Putin's political power.

The last decade or two has been marked by the rising economic power of the BRICS nations (an acronym for Brazil, Russia, India, China, and South Africa). This growing power has been reflected in these nations' sports profiles. If one includes the 2010 Commonwealth Games hosted by India, each of these BRICS nations will have hosted at least one of the world's top sporting events over the past decade.

Mega-events may also be worthwhile if they bring non-monetary benefits to the citizens of the host cities. Hosting a major event can generate the same sense of civic pride that a professional sports franchise brings (as discussed in Chapter 6). In fact, while the study of the 2006 World Cup in Germany by Swatje Allmers and Wolfgang Maennig (Table 8.3) found only a very small change in tourism and national income, it did find a measurable increase in the self-reported happiness of Germans following the tournament. Anecdotally, many Germans reported that the 2006 World Cup was the first time since the 1940s that large numbers of German houses could be seen flying the German flag. Similarly, Dolan et al. find that Londoners reported higher life satisfaction following the 2012 Summer Olympics, although this bump dissipated within one year.[58] Some economists liken mega-events to parents throwing a big birthday bash for their child. They are fun events for everyone involved, but no one, especially not the parents paying for the entertainment, the cake, and the goody bags, expects them to have a positive net impact on the family's finances.

The Winner's Curse

Sometimes host cities make bids that no amount of non-monetary benefits can justify. They simply seem to defy economic logic. The branch of economics known as behavioral economics provides one possible explanation. **Behavioral economics**, which combines elements of traditional economic theory and psychology, proposes that cities might be falling victim to the winner's curse.

The winner's curse occurs in auctions in which the bidders do not know the value of the prize with absolute certainty. In such a setting, the winner may overpay for what has been won. The winner's curse was first applied to oil leases, when researchers sought to explain why investments by oil companies in the oil-rich Gulf of Mexico "paid off at something less than the local credit union." Since then, it has been applied to settings as diverse as advances paid to authors and the salaries paid to baseball players.[59]

To see how the winner's curse works, consider the fact that Rio had to outbid several other cities, including Chicago, Madrid, and Tokyo, to host the 2016 Summer Olympics. Suppose all competing cities based their bids on how much they expected the Olympics to be worth and hired experts to evaluate the benefits of the Games. Based on these estimates, each city submitted bids to the IOC.[60] Rio won the auction by bidding more than any other city. It might have won the bidding for any of three reasons.

First, it might have been able to put on a more profitable Olympics than any other city. For example, Rio might have valued the ability to use the Olympics to advertise the city as a tourist destination more than other bidders, or Rio may have thought that it could host the Games at a lower cost than its competitors. In this case, Rio's winning the auction is an efficient outcome.

Second, Rio might have overestimated the benefits that the Olympics would bring. In addition to any objective advantages it may have over other cities, Rio's winning bid reflects its optimism about the uncertain value of the Olympics. If Rio mistakenly overstates the value of the Summer Games, it might submit a winning bid that exceeds the true value of the Olympics. In this case, Rio falls prey to the winner's curse because it was the most optimistic bidder.

Finally, the auction process itself might lead Rio to bid more than the Games are worth by making winning the auction more valuable than the prize itself. Rio gets caught up in trying to win the right to host the Summer Olympics, independent of the expected benefits. Empirical studies and clinical experiments of bidding behavior have shown that, on average, bidders accurately assess the value of uncertain prizes. The winning bid, however, consistently overstates the value of the prize. Moreover, the degree to which a winner overbids, and hence the degree of loss, generally rises with the number of bidders. This has led some economists to conclude that participants get caught up in the action and begin to set winning the auction as a goal in itself. As a result, bids by cities and individuals alike may reflect both the value of the prize and the desire to win the prize regardless of its inherent worth.

The All-or-Nothing Demand Curve

When the IOC seeks a host city for the Games, it does not offer cities a choice of which sports they wish to host. Cities have to host the entire Olympic Games or none at all. Similarly, a country bidding for the World Cup does not get to choose which of the games it wishes to stage but has to take all of the matches. The **all-or-nothing** choices give the IOC and FIFA an advantage that even the most powerful monopoly seldom has. While a monopoly has the power to set the price it charges or the quantity it sells, it cannot do both at once. If a monopolist sets the price of its product, consumers respond by buying as much of the good or service as they want. If it decides how much to produce, then by trial and error consumers will determine the price they will pay. The monopoly's power is thus limited by the demand curve that it faces. Even the most powerful monopolist cannot tell consumers how much to pay *and* how much to buy.

Under certain circumstances, however, a monopolist can dictate both price and quantity. Foot-long hot dogs at the ballpark or one-pound boxes of Milk Duds at the movie theater may have become something of a tradition, but they are also far bigger than most consumers want. This enables producers to extract consumer surplus by getting consumers to buy more than they wish to buy. Similarly, sports teams, sports leagues, or institutions such as the IOC or FIFA exploit their monopoly power by auctioning off teams or events to an array of eager cities. They confront cities with an all-or-nothing choice. Since a city cannot choose to host part of a franchise or event at a lower overall cost, it must pay the full price or host nothing at all.

In Figure 8.1, if the IOC had acted like a typical monopolist, it would have charged cities the monopoly price of p_1 per Olympics and let them "buy" as many of the Olympic events as they wanted. A city would choose to buy Q_1 events, and its residents would enjoy consumer surplus AEC. Figure 8.1 shows that the IOC could take some of this surplus by telling the city that if it wanted to host any event at all, it had to stage all Q_2 of them. The host city's buying more events than it wants at the price p_1 results in a loss equal to EFG, because residents must pay more than the additional quantity is worth to them. The city accepts this loss as long as the surplus that residents enjoy on the first Q_1 sports is greater than the loss residents suffer on the next $Q_2 - Q_1$. As long as consuming "too many" sports is preferable to consuming none, the city chooses to consume too much. The franchise can push the city to stage more events until the size of the loss (EFG) catches up with the size of the surplus (AEC).

Figure 8.2
A Monopolist Can Extract
Consumer Surplus by
Setting Price *and* **Quantity**

Monopolists can force consumers
to pay p_1 for Q_1 units of output,
confronting them with an all-or-
nothing choice.

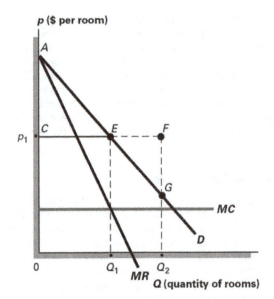

Biographical Sketch

Willard "Mitt" Romney
(1947–)

> *He felt like he was walking into an empty elevator shaft.*
> —Fraser Bullock, describing Romney's
> reaction to learning the financial state
> of the Salt Lake Organizing Committee[61]

Seldom have politics and sports been more intertwined than in the
recent career of Willard ("Mitt") Romney. Mitt Romney was born and
raised in Michigan; his father, the late George Romney, had served as
the state's governor and had once been a presidential candidate. Romney graduated with highest honors from Brigham Young University in
1971, and in 1974, he received both a JD and an MBA from Harvard.
After spending two years on a Mormon mission to France, Romney
worked at Bain and Co., a Boston management consulting firm. In
1984, he founded Bain Capital, a venture capital firm that invested in
hundreds of companies, including Staples, Domino's Pizza, and The
Sports Authority.

In 1994, Romney entered the political arena by challenging Senator Edward Kennedy's re-election bid. The election's outcome was a foregone conclusion, as Kennedy garnered 60 percent of the vote. This might have been the end of Romney's political career were it not for a surprising move he made five years later.

In late 1998, the Salt Lake Organizing Committee (SLOC), the body charged with organizing and financing the 2002 Winter Olympics, was facing a severe crisis. With the Olympics just three years off, the SLOC was almost $400 million in debt, having badly underestimated the cost of the Games. To make matters worse, fundraising was at a standstill, with no new sponsors secured in over a year. Voluntarism was also lagging, and the leadership of the SLOC was under investigation by the US Justice Department for allegedly giving bribes exceeding $1 million to IOC officials in order to secure the Games. The SLOC was in desperate need of a person who could combine business connections and savvy with unquestioned integrity and would not mind moving to Utah for the next three years. The job requirements seemed to fit Romney perfectly, and he soon showed why.

In February 1999, Romney took over as CEO and president of the SLOC and quickly put his personal stamp on the process. Recognizing that the allegations of corruption had demoralized workers and frightened off donors, Romney insisted on strict ethical standards in all SLOC's activities. He opened all meetings and records to the public. He also demanded that all employees and board members report any possible conflicts of interest and complete annual surveys of ethical conduct.

Knowing that morality alone would not balance the budget, Romney cut the Games' budget by about $200 million and vigorously pursued his political and business connections. The results were impressive. Romney's governmental contacts helped secure an estimated $1.5 billion from the federal government, almost ten times the federal support per athlete provided to the 1996 Summer Olympic Games in Atlanta. Between the government support and private sponsorships, the SLOC pulled out of its financial hole and wound up slightly in the black. The citizens of Utah were also energized, as 67,000 people volunteered for 23,000 volunteer positions.

Although the Games did little to revive the flagging business community in Salt Lake City, they were a public relations triumph. As head of the Games, Romney had become a celebrity. Less than six weeks after the Olympic flame had been extinguished, Romney had become the Republican candidate for governor of Massachusetts. This time he won, despite having spent most of the previous three years across the country. However Mitt Romney's political journey ends, his success in politics began in the afterglow of the 2002 Winter Olympics.

Sources: Donald Bartlett and James Steele. 2001. "Snow Job," *Sports Illustrated,* December 10: 79–97; Mitt Romney and Timothy Robinson. 2004. *Turnaround: Crisis, Leadership, and the Olympic Games* (Washington, DC: Regnery Publishing); Paula Parrish. 2002. "Leap of Faith: Mitt Romney Embraces Challenges, and This Might Be His Biggest One," *Rocky Mountain News,* February 4: 8S; Lewis Rice. Spring 2002. "Games Saver," *Harvard Law Bulletin,* at https://today.law.harvard.edu/feature/games-saver/.

Summary

Mega-events, such as the Olympics, World Cup, and Super Bowl, can have large effects on host regions. They bring new economic activity to a region by attracting visiting spectators and their spending. Events can also leave a lasting infrastructure or image legacy that can generate economic benefits far beyond the event's end. However, due to substitution effects, crowding out, and leakages, the true economic impact may be lower than what is predicted. The majority of economic analyses conducted after events have taken place find that mega-events have little or no economic impact on host cities or countries.

Hosting mega-events, especially the Olympics and World Cup, can be very expensive. Host cities must often build expensive new sports facilities and make significant investments in general infrastructure to handle the inflow of tourists. The costs do not stop once construction is completed. Operating costs, especially with respect to security, can seriously escalate costs.

Despite the evidence that mega-events often do not pay, cities line up to host them. In part, this is due to special interests who benefit from events at the expense of the general public but have outsized political influence. In many cases, cities and countries may be bidding for these events for prestige or civic pride rather than purely economic reasons. The economic phenomena of the winner's curse and the all-or-nothing demand curve also influence cities to make bids that ultimately make little economic sense.

Discussion Questions

1   If a city already has sports infrastructure in place, should it frequently bid for mega-events? Should relatively poor countries refrain from hosting?
2   Should the IOC choose one (or perhaps two or three) permanent location(s) and host the Olympics in the same places every few years?
3   Standard economic theory assumes that people behave rationally. The winner's curse implies that people behave irrationally by paying more for an asset than it is worth. Can we reconcile the winner's curse with rational behavior?

Problems

8.1 How does the economic impact of holding the Super Bowl in Minneapolis, Minnesota—the site of Super Bowl LII—compare with holding it in Miami or New Orleans at the same time?
8.2 Why would a Super Bowl at Ford Field in Detroit have more of an impact on Detroit than a regular season Detroit Lions game that draws the same number of fans?
8.3 If you are the mayor of a city hosting the Super Bowl, do you want the hometown team to make it to the championship game?
8.4 Use the all-or-nothing demand curve to explain why the IOC is unlikely to accept a bid by Los Angeles to host only the track and field events in its bid for the 2024 Summer Olympics.
8.5 If you had a choice, would you rather your city (or the nearest large city) host a major sports franchise or a mega-event such as the World Cup or Olympics? Why?
8.6 Suppose the IOC announced that it would hold all of its Summer Games in Athens and all of its Winter Games in Sapporo. What is the likely impact on

the monopoly power of the IOC, the IOC's ability to exploit an all-or-nothing demand curve, and the winner's curse?

8.7 Using the concepts of the substitution effect, leakages, and crowding out discussed in this chapter, discuss whether a small city like Indianapolis or a big city like Los Angeles would benefit more from hosting the NCAA Men's Final Four Basketball Tournament.

8.8 Every summer, a large number of the world's sports economists meet for a conference in a major city in the western United States. If the schedule permits, the economists always try to go to a local sporting event, such as a MLB, MLS, or National Women's Soccer League (NWSL) game while they are there. Should the economists' spending at these events count as economic impact for the city? Why or why not?

Notes

1   Canadian Broadcasting Corporation, "Montreal Says No to 'Big Owe'," http://www.cbc.ca/news/canada/montreal-says-no-to-big-owe-1.569446, October 8, 2005.

2   US Youth Soccer, "Key Statistics," http://www.usyouthsoccer.org/media_kit/keystatistics/, accessed March 31, 2017.

3   Quotation taken from Moses Finley and H.W. Pleket. 1976. *The Olympic Games: The First Thousand Years* (New York: Viking Press): 15. The other games honored Apollo, Zeus, and Poseidon. See Finley and Pleket. 1976. *The Olympic Games*: 23–25; Lynn Poole and Gray Poole. 1963. *History of Ancient Olympic Games* (New York: Ivan Obolensky, Inc.); Bruce Kidd. 1984."The Myth of the Ancient Games," in *Five Ring Circus: Money, Power and Politics at the Olympic Games*, ed. Alan Tomlinson and Garry Whannel (London: Pluto Press): 73; Francis Dealy. 1990. *Win at Any Cost: The Sell Out of College Athletics* (New York: Birch Lane Press): 31–32, 60; and Lawrence Hatab. 1991. "The Greeks and the Meaning of Athletics," in *Rethinking College Athletics*, ed. Judith Andre and David James (Philadelphia, PA: Temple University Press): 32–35.

4   Finley and Pleket. 1976. *The Olympic Games*: 77–78; and University of Pennsylvania Museum of Anthropology and Archeology, "The Real Story of the Ancient Olympic Games," at https://www.penn.museum/sites/olympics/olympicathletes.shtml.

5   Tony Perrotet. 2004. *The Naked Olympics* (New York: Random House, 2004): 53.

6   Finley and Pleket. 1976. *The Olympic Games*: 70–71; Dealy. 1990. *Win at Any Cost*: 60; and Hatab. 1991. "The Greeks and the Meaning of Athletics": 31–35.

7   Hatab. 1991. "The Greeks and the Meaning of Athletics": 35; Richard Mandell. 1972. *The Nazi Olympics* (New York: Ballantine Books): 4–5; Poole and Poole. 1963. *History of Ancient Olympic Games*: 24–25, 33; and Kidd. 1984. "The Myth of the Ancient Games": 72–80.

8   "The Battle of Waterloo was won on the playing fields of Eton." See Mandell. 1972. *The Nazi Olympics*: 8–9.

9   Mandell. 1972. *The Nazi Olympics*: 12–13. Mass gymnastics survive to this day, as in the Czech *Sokol* movement.

10 Mandell. 1972. *The Nazi Olympics*: 12–24; Alan Tomlinson. 1984. "De Coubertin and the Modern Olympics," in *Five Ring Circus: Money, Power and Politics at the Olympic Games*, ed. Alan Tomlinson and Garry Whannel (London: Pluto Press): 88–90; and David C. Young. 1996. *The Modern Olympics: A Struggle for Revival* (Baltimore, MD: Johns Hopkins University Press): 24–80.

11 Perrotet. 2004. *The Naked Olympics*: 160.

12 Young. 1996. *The Modern Olympics: A Struggle for Revival*.

13 Robert Baade and Victor Matheson. 2016. "Going for the Gold: The Economics of the Olympics," *Journal of Economic Perspectives*, 30(2), April: 201–218.

14 Baade and Matheson. 2016. "Going for the Gold: The Economics of the Olympics": 215.

15 The Organization for Economic Cooperation and Development (OECD) is an intergovernmental organization of 35 member countries. The group is comprised of the most

highly developed countries in the world, and membership in this group serves as a de facto dividing line between the world's rich and poor countries.

16   Somewhat ominously for the sport, this seminal match ended in a 0–0 tie.

17   The Parisian origin of the organization explains the French name of FIFA, the Fédération Internationale de Football Association.

18   Soccer continued to be played in the Olympics but it featured only amateur players. When the Olympics began to include professional players in other sports, FIFA resisted inclusion of professional players in order to maintain the supremacy of the World Cup. Since 1992, the Olympics men's soccer tournament has featured only teams of players under the age of 23, although professionals are allowed and each team is permitted to include up to three over-age players.

19   Sports Illustrated. 2017. "Super Bowl Commercials: How Much Does a Spot Cost in 2017?" January 26, at https://www.si.com/nfl/2017/01/26/super-bowl-commercial-cost-2017.

20   Jeffrey Humphreys. 1994. "The Economic Impact of Hosting Super Bowl XXVIII on Georgia," *Georgia Business and Economic Conditions*, May–June: 18–21.

21   Humphreys. 1994. "The Economic Impact of Hosting Super Bowl XXVIII on Georgia."

22   Victor Matheson. 2008. "Mega-Events: The Effect of the World's Biggest Sporting Events on Local, Regional, and National Economies," in *The Business of Sports*, vol. 1, ed. Dennis Howard and Brad Humphreys (Westport, CT: Praeger): 81–99.

23   Boulder Daily Camera. 2007. "Democratic Convention an Economic Boon," January 12.

24   Bianca Prieto. 2014. "Super Bowl Week Gets Underway: N.Y./N.J. to See Some 400,000 Tourists," *Denver Post*, January 27.

25   Candyce Stapen. 2014. "Super Bowl Hotel Rates Drop Close to Game Day," *USA Today*, January 29. It seems that New York has no shortage of consultants who took the White Queen to heart when she told Alice that each day everyone should believe "six impossible things before breakfast." Lewis Carroll. 1972. "Through the Looking Glass," in *The Annotated Alice* (New York: Meridian Books).

26   Matheson. 2008. "Mega-Events."

27   Jessica Smetana. 2017. "Super Bowl 2017 Tickets: Why Fans Can't Go to the Game," *SB Nation*, February 3, at http://www.sbnation.com/nfl/2017/2/3/14498480/2017-super-bowl-tickets-prices-patriots-falcons.

28   Quoted in Houston Mitchell. 2015. "Yogi Berra Dies at 90: Here Are Some of His Greatest Quotes," *Los Angeles Times*, September 22.

29   Robert Baade and Victor Matheson. 2016. "Going for the Gold: The Economics of the Olympics."

30   Michael A. Leeds. 2008. "Do Good Olympics Make Good Neighbors?" *Contemporary Economic Policy*, 26(3), July: 460–467.

31   ESPN. 2007. "Casino Exec: All-Star Game Wasn't Good for Business," May 4, at http://sports.espn.go.com/nba/news/story?id=2859699.

32   Thomas Peeters, Victor Matheson, and Stefan Szymanski. 2014. "Tourism and the 2010 World Cup: Lessons for Developing Countries," *Journal of African Economies*, 23(2), January: 290–320.

33   Stan Du Plessis and Wolfgang Maennig. 2010. "The 2010 FIFA World Cup High Frequency Data Economics: Effects on International Tourism and Awareness for South Africa," *Development Southern Africa*, 28(3), September: 349–365.

34   Robert Baumann, Victor Matheson, and Chihiro Muroi. 2009. "Bowling in Hawaii: Examining the Effectiveness of Sports-Based Tourism Strategies," *Journal of Sports Economics*, 10(1), February: 107–123.

35   Lauren Heller and E. Frank Stephenson. "If You Host It Will They Come? The Effect of the Super Bowl on Host City Hotel Occupancy," Working Paper, April 2017.

36   *Orlando Sentinel*, "Cruise Ships Supply City's Super Bowl Room Service," February 3, 2005.

37   More precisely, it looks at the holding period return, the value of owning the stock over a given period of time. For more on event analysis and its application to sports, see Eva Marikova Leeds and Michael A. Leeds. 2012. "Event Analysis," in *The Oxford*

Handbook of Sports Economics, vol. 2, ed. Stephen Shmanske and Leo Kahane, (Oxford: Oxford University Press).

38 Gabrielle Berman, Robert Brooks, and Sinclair Davidson. 2000. "The Sydney Olympic Games Announcement and Australian Stock Market Reaction," *Applied Economics Letters,* 7(12), December: 781–784; Nikolaos Veraros, Evangelia Kasimati, and Peter Dawson. 2004. "The 2004 Olympic Games Announcement and Its Effect on the Athens and Milan Stock Exchanges," *Applied Economics Letters,* 11(12), October: 749–753; and Michael Leeds, John Mirikitani, and Danna Tang. 2009. "Rational Exuberance? An Event Analysis of the 2008 Olympic Announcement," *International Journal of Sport Finance,* 4(1), February: 5–15.

39 Robert Baumann and Victor Matheson. 2017. "Mega-Events and Tourism: The Case of Brazil," *Contemporary Economic Policy,* in press.

40 Jack Lang. 2015. "Mane Garrincha Stadium in Brasilia Being Used as a BUS DEPOT Less Than a Year After 2014 World Cup," *The Mirror,* March 7, at http://www.mirror.co.uk/sport/football/news/mane-garrincha-stadium-brasilia-being-5289603.

41 Sky Sports. 2015. "Olympic Stadium Costs Soar Ahead of West Ham Move," June 19, at http://www.skysports.com/football/news/11685/9890173/olympic-stadium-costs-soar-ahead-of-west-ham-move.

42 James Giesecke and John Madden. 2011. "Modelling the Economic Impacts of the Sydney Olympics in Retrospect—Game Over for the Bonanza Story?" *Economic Papers,* 30(2), June: 218–232.

43 Andrew Zimbalist. 2015. *Circus Maximus: The Economic Gamble Behind Hosting the Olympics and the World Cup* (Washington, DC: Brookings Institution Press).

44 Robert Baade and Victor Matheson. 2016. "Going for the Gold: The Economics of the Olympics."

45 Andrew Rose and Mark Spiegel. 2011. "The Olympic Effect," *Economic Journal,* 121(553): 652–677.

46 Wolfgang Maennig and Felix Richter. 2012. "Exports and Olympics Games: Is There a Signal Effect?" *Journal of Sports Economics,* 13(6): 635–641.

47 Jon Teigland. 1999. "Mega-Events and Impacts on Tourism; the Predictions and Realities of the Lillehammer Olympics," *Impact Assessment and Project Appraisal,* 17(4): 305–317.

48 Robert Baade and Victor Matheson. 2016. "Going for the Gold: The Economics of the Olympics."

49 Mike Kaszuba and Rochelle Olson. 2014. "NFL Had a Long, Pricey and Secret Super Bowl Wish List for Minneapolis," *Star Tribune,* June 9.

50 Mary Jordan and Kevin Sullivan. 1999. "Nagano Burned Documents Tracing '98 Olympics Bid," *Washington Post Foreign Service,* January 21: A1.

51 Bent Flyvbjerg and Allison Stewart. 2012. "Olympic Proportions: Cost and Cost Overrun at the Olympics 1960–2012," Saïd Business School, Working Paper, University of Oxford.

52 BBC. 2013. "London 2012: Olympics and Paralympics 528 Million under Budget," July 19, at http://www.bbc.com/sport/o/olympics/20041426.

53 Andrew Zimbalist. 2015. *Circus Maximus.*

54 Alissa Walker. 2014. "How L.A.'s 1984 Summer Olympics Became the Most Successful Games Ever," *Gizmodo.com,* February 6, at http://gizmodo.com/how-l-a-s-1984-summer-olympics-became-the-most-success-1516228102.

55 Robert Baade and Victor Matheson. 2016. "Going for the Gold: The Economics of the Olympics."

56 BBC. 2017. "Qatar Spending $500m a Week on World Cup Infrastructure Projects," February 8, at http://www.bbc.com/news/world-middle-east-38905510.

57 Chris Dempsey and Andrew Zimbalist. 2017. *No Boston Olympics: How and Why Smart Cities Are Passing on the Torch* (Lebanon, NH: ForeEdge Publishers).

58 Paul Dolan, Georgios Kavetsos, Christian Krekel, Dimitris Mavridis, Robert Metcalfe, Claudia Senik, Stefan Szymanski, and Nicolas R. Ziebart. 2016. "The Host with the Most? The Effects of the Olympic Games on Happiness," Centre for Economic Performance Discussion Paper No. 1441.

59   Richard Thaler. 1988. "The Winner's Curse," *Journal of Economic Perspectives*, 2(1),
     Winter: 191–202. For an application to sports, see James Cassing and Richard Douglas.
     1980. "Implications of the Auction Mechanism in Baseball's Free Agent Draft," *Southern Economic Journal,* 47(1), July: 110–121.
60   Since cities have much greater access to capital than individuals do, we ignore the
     question of the city's ability to pay.
61   Cathy Harasta. 2002. "Romney Shows His Mettle," *Dallas Morning News*, February 17.

Part Four

THE LABOR ECONOMICS OF SPORTS

9

AN INTRODUCTION TO LABOR MARKETS IN PROFESSIONAL SPORTS

After my fourth season I asked for $43,000 and General Manager Ed Barrow told me,
"Young man, do you realize Lou Gehrig, a 16-year-man, is playing for only $44,000?"
I said, Mr. Barrow, there is only one answer to that—Mr. Gehrig is terribly underpaid.
—Yankees outfielder Joe DiMaggio[1]

Introduction

Joe Louis and Oscar de la Hoya were among the best—perhaps *the* best—fighters in the history of boxing. Joe Louis was heavyweight champion for 12 years (1937–1949) and successfully defended his title 25 times (still a record for the heavyweight division). Louis was so dominant that people took to calling his opponents "The Bum of the Month Club." De la Hoya won an Olympic gold medal in the 1992 Barcelona Olympics and went on to win 10 titles in 6 different weight classes.[2]

In addition to sharing glorious careers, both staged less-than-glorious comebacks. Louis re-entered the ring almost two years after retiring but lost a title fight to Ezzard Charles in 1950. In 1951, Louis's career finally ended when he was knocked out by future champion Rocky Marciano. De la Hoya's comeback, also after almost two years away from fighting, met with initial success, when he won the middleweight title in 2006. However, de la Hoya then lost two of his next three fights before retiring in 2009.

While Louis and de la Hoya both attempted comebacks, their motivations for doing so could not have been more different. Louis started fighting again out of poverty. In his 12 years as heavyweight champion, Louis was paid $800,000 (roughly $11 million in 2016 dollars), a large sum to most people at the time, but small change by today's standards for heavyweight champions.[3] Moreover, mismanagement of Louis's funds and tax problems with the IRS left him with almost nothing to live on after retirement. With no skills other than his fading boxing talents, Louis had no choice but to fight again.[4]

De la Hoya had no such money worries. His nickname, "Golden Boy," might have referred to his prodigious skills, but it could just as easily have applied to his extraordinary earnings.[5] De la Hoya earned over $600 million in his career and earned more than twice the value of Joe Louis's lifetime earnings for just one fight (about $23 million for a 2007 loss to Floyd Mayweather). He has also parlayed his success in the ring into a variety of business ventures, most notably Golden Boy Enterprises, whose activities have ranged from promoting boxers to real estate development to a 25 percent stake in the Houston Dynamo soccer team.[6]

The motivation for Joe Louis's attempted comeback is clear. His savings were so low that he could not afford to stop fighting. Oscar de la Hoya had no such monetary worries, but he also could not afford to turn down the offer to return to the ring. The monetary rewards for fighting were too high for him to turn down.

The salaries paid to professional athletes in all sports have risen greatly in recent decades. In 2015–2016, the average *weekly* earnings in the NBA were over 1.5 times the average *annual* earnings of non-athletes in the United States. In this chapter, we analyze the forces that have caused the incomes of professional athletes to reach such levels. This analysis will also place the earnings of professional athletes in perspective and show that, in some cases, professional athletes are underpaid for what they do.

Learning Objectives

- Understand the basic model of wage determination in labor markets, and see how athletes' investment in skills affects their pay.
- Grasp why the rewards to professional athletes are often highly skewed, with a few superstars making huge sums while most others make much less.
- Learn how providing incentives to exert effort can sometimes backfire.

Figure 9.1
Average Player Salaries in the Major Leagues Since 1991

The average salaries of athletes in MLB, and all four major North American leagues, have risen significantly since 1991.

Source: MLB data from "Player Salaries," *USAToday.com,* at https://www.usatoday.com/sports/mlb/salaries/, viewed March 12, 2017. Other data can be reached from that site.

9.1   An Overview of Labor Supply and Labor Demand

As noted in the introduction, Oscar de la Hoya earned more for one fight than Joe Louis earned during his entire career. In general, the salaries paid to professional athletes in the four major North American sports were not always as high as they are now. Figure 9.1 shows that, over the last 25 years, the average salary of a MLB player has more than quintupled from about $850,000 to about $4.4 million. To put this in perspective, the average MLB salary was approximately 36 times per capita GDP in 1991. By 2016, it was almost 84 times per capita GDP. Salaries in the other major team sports in North America show similar growth. Such high salaries are not limited to North America. The average salary of the

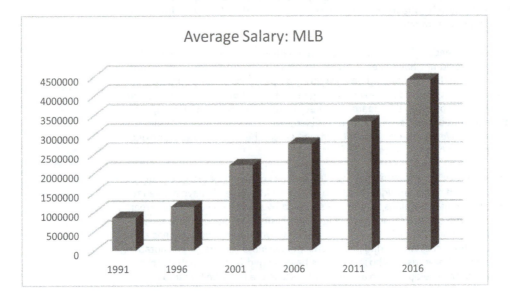

Real Madrid soccer team was more than € 5.6 million in 2016, over 200 times the average personal income in Spain.

In this section, we discuss both sides of the labor market. On the supply side, individual players offer their services to professional sports teams in order to maximize their utility. Teams demand labor in order to maximize profits. Although we know from Chapter 3 that some owners may benefit from fielding a bad team, in this chapter we assume that team quality and profits are directly related. The better the team, the greater the profits.

We begin our analysis by using the basic tools of supply and demand. The supply and demand model does a good job of explaining the broad forces that affect the employment and pay of professional athletes, but it relies on the assumption that the labor market is perfectly competitive. While this assumption might apply to players who are free agents, it does not apply in a great many cases. We shall explore the impact of labor market imperfections, specifically the monopsony power of teams and the countervailing power of player unions, in Chapter 10.

Labor Supply

As Figure 9.2a shows, a worker's labor supply curve resembles a firm's product supply curve.[7] There are, however, several major differences. One difference lies in the units of measurement. The horizontal axis of a product supply curve refers to the amount of output the firm provides and is typically measured in physical units (e.g., the number of shoes or automobiles), and the vertical axis denotes the price per unit of the firm's output. In labor markets, the quantity axis refers to the hours of work that a person is willing to provide. The vertical axis is the price per unit of time. Economists generally use the worker's hourly pay, the **wage**, as the unit price of a worker's time.[8] An upward-sloping labor supply curve indicates that a worker responds to higher wages by offering to work more hours.

In professional sports, we cannot use hours as the unit of labor because almost all athletes contract for a fixed amount of time, be it a football season, a tennis tour, or a boxing match. Figure 9.2b modifies the standard labor supply curve to

Figure 9.2
Individual and Market Labor Supply Curves for Workers and Boxers

The labor supply curve slopes upward, just like the supply curve for a good or service.

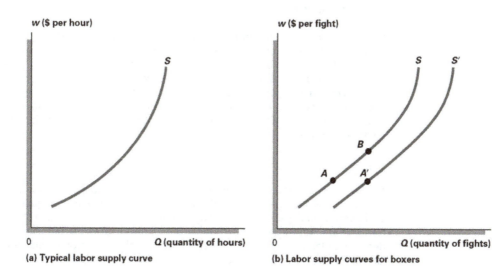

(a) Typical labor supply curve

(b) Labor supply curves for boxers

reflect this fact. The horizontal axis now measures the quantity of fights a boxer has over the course of his career, and the vertical axis measures the boxer's earnings per fight (which, for simplicity, we assume to be uniform). In team sports, the quantity of labor provided by a player is typically set for a given season.[9] The price variable is thus the amount paid per season, or salary. The quantity variable depends on what we want to evaluate. If we analyze the labor market in a given season, the quantity variable refers to the number of players employed in that season. Alternatively, if we look at a typical player's career, the quantity variable refers to the number of seasons that player plays.

Returning to our boxing example, moving from point A to point B shows that a boxer takes on more fights as his pay increases, as was the case for Oscar de la Hoya. By this reasoning, the lower pay that Joe Louis received should have led him to fight less. However, as noted earlier, lower pay was not the only problem facing Louis. After retiring, Louis learned that his manager had mishandled his funds and that he owed the IRS hundreds of thousands of dollars in back taxes. The lower savings—and hence the lower income that Louis would have received in retirement—meant that Louis had to fight more to maintain his standard of living. His labor supply curve shifted right to S' increasing his quantity of fights from point A to point A'.

To see why the labor supply curve looks and shifts the way it does in Figure 9.2b, we must recognize that people choose how much to work based on the benefits and costs of an hour of leisure. Think of leisure as a good that a worker can "purchase" by choosing to not work. The opportunity cost of one more hour of leisure is one hour's worth of earnings. Thus, the cost of leisure equals the wage rate. When wages are low, the opportunity cost of leisure is low.

As wages increase, workers experience an income effect and a substitution effect. The substitution effect captures the increased cost of leisure as wages rise: workers sacrifice higher earnings when they "purchase" leisure. Thus, as wages rise, the substitution effect leads workers to work more. The income effect reflects the increased purchasing power that comes from higher wages. If leisure is a normal good, then workers buy more leisure—and work less—as their income rises. In this case, the income effect counteracts, rather than reinforces, the substitution effect.

In general, the substitution effect is stronger than the income effect, so higher wages lead workers to supply more labor, and the labor supply curve slopes upward.[10] When non-labor income and the value of one's assets fall—as happened to many people's home values when the housing bubble burst in 2007—the demand for all normal goods and services, including leisure time, falls. A decline in the demand for leisure is equivalent to an increase in the supply of labor. Thus, Joe Louis's tax troubles led him to fight more frequently than he otherwise would have.

Labor Demand

Much of the debate among sports fans regarding athletes' salaries stems from a failure to understand the demand for labor. Many armchair quarterbacks spend Sunday afternoons yelling at their televisions, complaining about overpaid athletes. If these same fans understood the factors underlying the demand for labor, they would realize that many highly paid professional athletes are underpaid.

Marginal Revenue Product

We begin our analysis by assuming that firms produce a single output using two inputs, capital (K) and labor (L). We also assume that the firm is operating in the short run, so capital is fixed, and the firm can alter output (Q) only by changing the labor input. Finally, we assume that all markets are perfectly competitive, so firms cannot affect the market price of their output. Firms maximize profit by choosing L to maximize the difference between revenue and cost. This occurs where the marginal revenue from employing one more worker equals the marginal cost of employing that worker.

Ignoring all employment costs except for a worker's pay, the marginal cost of one more hour of labor is the worker's wage, w. The benefit of adding a worker is the extra revenue that worker generates. Economists call the extra revenue produced by an additional worker the **marginal revenue product of labor** (MRP_L). Since marginal revenue equals price in a competitive market, MRP_L is simply the price per unit of output times the additional output produced:

$$MRP_L = MR * MP_L = p * \left(\frac{\Delta Q}{\Delta L} \right).$$

For example, if adding a worker increases output by 20 units per hour, which can be sold for $5 each, the value of that worker to the firm is $100 per hour. A profit-maximizing firm hires just enough workers so that the marginal cost of labor, w, equals the marginal benefit, MRP_L. Because competitive firms are price takers and, as pointed out in Chapter 2, the marginal product of labor falls as the labor input rises, the demand curve is downward-sloping. Figure 9.3 shows the relationship between MRP_L and labor demand.

The labor demand curve in Figure 9.3b starts at L_0, where the MP_L curve is at its peak. At any point to the left of L_0, each additional worker produces more than the one before.[11] Because of the law of diminishing marginal returns, the more workers the firm hires from L_0 on, the less successive workers add to output, and the less the firm is willing to pay them. Suppose the wage, w_1, equals the MRP_L at the employment level L_1. If the wage falls to w_2, the revenue generated by the last worker exceeds his cost to the firm, and the firm responds by hiring more workers until $w = MRP_L$ is restored. If we relabel the vertical axis with

Figure 9.3
The Labor Demand Curve

The downward-sloping MRP_L curve (a) yields a downward-sloping demand for labor curve (b).

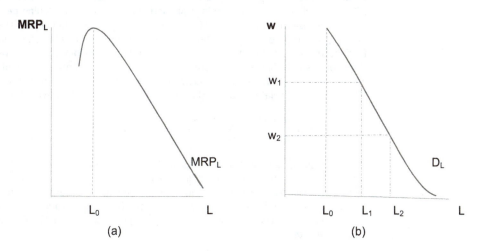

(a)   (b)

the wage, the curve shows that the unit price of labor and the quantity of labor demanded by the firm are negatively related, just like the demand curve for a good or service.

Measuring a Player's Performance

While the theory behind a player's value is quite simple, determining what he or she is worth can be very complex. In part, this is because players do not operate in a vacuum. Peyton Manning retired in 2016 as one of the top quarterbacks in NFL history and a two-time Super Bowl champion. His father, Archie Manning, owns the worst record among starting quarterbacks in NFL history and threw 48 more interceptions than touchdowns.[12] This does not, however, necessarily imply that Peyton was much better than his father. A quarterback's performance depends on an offensive line that gives him time to throw, receivers who can reliably get open and catch the ball, a defense that does not give up a lot of points, forcing the offense into obvious passing situations, and a coaching staff that exploits the quarterback's strengths and hides his weaknesses. In each case, Peyton had better support than his father.

The interdependence of players on one another helps to explain why some standard metrics of performance are surprisingly unstable. For example, in the NHL, save percentage and goals-against average seem obvious ways to evaluate a goalie.[13] However, the correlations of these measures across the 2014–2015 and 2015–2016 seasons are only 0.17 and 0.23, respectively.[14] Some of this is doubtlessly due to "regression to the mean," a goalie's coming back from an unusually bad year or returning to form after an unusually good one. However, it could also be due to his playing behind different defensemen, playing under a coach with a different philosophy, or even playing on a larger or smaller surface.

The attempt to separate a player's performance from the conditions under which he plays, the growing sophistication of video technology, and the introduction of "big data" analyses have led to a burgeoning literature in **sports analytics**, the development and use of advanced statistics to measure a player's "true" performance.

In baseball, for example, analysts have turned away from Earned Run Average (ERA: runs allowed per nine innings pitched) as a measure of pitching performance because the ERA can reflect the fielding ability of the other eight players. Instead, they have developed defense-independent pitching statistics, or DIPS. DIPS focus on outcomes that have nothing to do with fielding, such as walks (BB—for bases on balls), home runs (HR), and strikeouts (K) relative to innings pitched (IP). Among the most popular DIPS is fielding independent pitching (FIP), which is calculated in a way that makes it comparable to a pitcher's ERA:

$$FIP = 3.10 + \frac{13*HR + 3*BB - 2*K}{IP}.$$

By this measure, Clayton Kershaw was MILB's best pitcher in 2016, with a FIP of 1.91; a figure that roughly equaled his ERA (1.69). Max Scherzer, who won the Cy Young Award as the National League's best pitcher, benefited from superior fielding, as seen by the larger difference between his FIP (3.36) and ERA (2.96). For more on advanced analytics in a variety of sports, see the textbook's companion website.

Labor Market Equilibrium

Recall from Chapter 2 that market demand (supply) is the horizontal sum of all individual demand (supply) curves. The same principle applies to labor markets. Figure 9.4 shows the market supply (S_L) and market demand (D_L) of players to a sports league. As was true for the product markets described in Chapters 2 and 3, the equilibrium quantity of labor (L^e) and the equilibrium level of compensation (w^e) are given by the intersection of the supply and demand curves.

Figure 9.5 shows what happens to pay when market conditions change. When basketball became much more popular in the 1980s thanks to the arrival of charismatic stars, such as Magic Johnson, Larry Bird, and Michael Jordan, the demand to see professional basketball both in person and on TV rose. This, in turn, increased the value of each player's contribution to the product provided by the NBA, and the marginal revenue product of all NBA players rose. The increase was not due to higher productivity. Instead, it was due to the rise in the marginal revenue that resulted from greater fan interest. A higher MR_{win} led to a higher MRP, which, in turn, caused the demand for labor to shift to the right and led to higher pay. Declining economic conditions in 2008 reduced the demand for tickets to NBA games. This, in turn, caused the MRP of players in the NBA to decline, and salaries in the NBA for the 2009–2010 season fell slightly.

The number of teams also affects the overall demand for players. The number of teams can vary with the entry of rival leagues or with the expansion or contraction of a given league. Increasing the number of teams shifts the demand for labor from D_L to D_L' in Figure 9.5 and causes the equilibrium quantity of labor to rise to L' and the equilibrium level of pay to rise to w'. The impact of the number of teams explains why players' associations oppose any form of contraction. In 2004, for

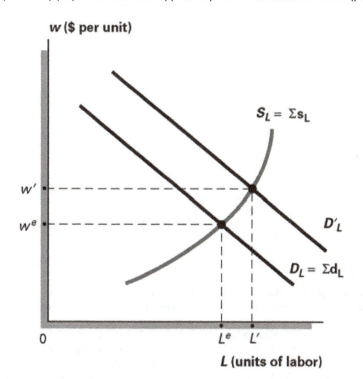

Figure 9.4
The Equilibrium Wage and Quantity in the Labor Market

The equilibrium levels of pay and employment in a labor market are set by the intersection of the labor supply and labor demand curves.

Figure 9.5
Wages Increase in the NBA
Due to Increases in Demand

Between 1978 and 2008,
the demand for professional
basketball increased markedly. It
then fell between 2008 and 2009.

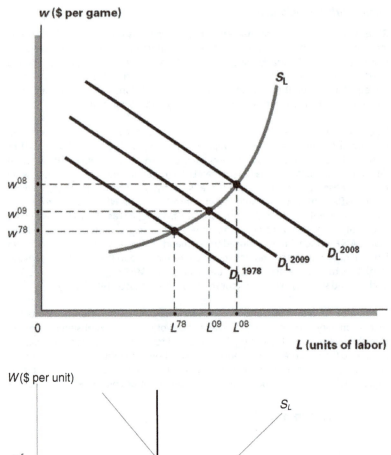

Figure 9.6
The Effect of Roster Limits

With no roster limit, teams
employ L^e players. A roster limit
of L^r reduces employment and
increases pay.

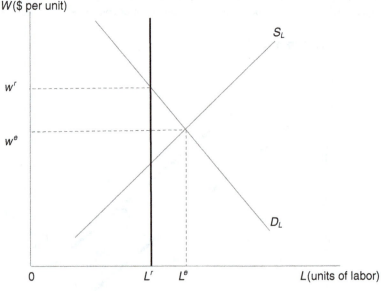

example, baseball players in Japan staged their only strike, a two-day protest of the proposed merger of the Kintetsu Buffaloes and the Orix Blue Wave.[15]

Finally, the number of jobs available is determined partly by roster size. Roster limits are negotiated by team owners and the players' associations. In Figure 9.6, the equilibrium employment level is L^e, but there is a binding roster limit, shown by the vertical line at L^r. The limit reduces total employment falls and increases salaries.

Human Capital and Player Compensation

Workers can increase their *MRP* and their pay by investing in their stock of skills, what economists call their **human capital**. According to Nobel laureate Gary Becker, who developed the theory of human capital in the 1960s, a person who invests in human capital resembles a business that invests in physical capital. When a firm purchases a drill press, it makes a one-time expenditure in return for an expected stream of benefits over the life of the equipment. Similarly, a student who spends four years studying economics in college, or a hockey player who spends four years developing his skills in the minor leagues, endures an up-front cost to acquire skills that he can use for his entire career.[16]

Although an athlete's physical abilities wear out, or **depreciate**, with age, many skills, such as a quarterback's recognition of defensive formations, may increase throughout his or her career. An important difference between human and phys-ical capital is that a firm can generally transfer physical capital to another firm by selling the asset. Human capital, however, is embodied in the individual, who cannot sell his skills to another player.

General and Specific Skills

Human capital theory divides investment into **general** and **specific** training. General training increases the worker's productivity regardless of the setting. For example, learning to read increases one's productivity no matter where one works. General training in hockey includes learning the rules of the game, how to pass or shoot the puck accurately, and how to check (stop) an opposing player. The more a hockey player can master these skills, the more valuable she is to all teams.

Specific training increases a worker's *MRP* in a particular context. At the extreme, it applies only at the firm that provides the training. For example, learning the plays in a team's playbook helps a player only while she is part of that team. Training often provides a mix of both general and specific skills.

Becker concluded that the type of training a worker receives determines who pays for it. When a player receives specific training, he is more valuable to his current team than to other teams. This allows the team to capture much of the return to the training it provides because it must pay the player only enough to prevent him from moving to another team. The ability to recoup their invest-ment leads firms to provide specific training to their workers at no cost.[17]

When a worker receives general training, his productivity rises at all firms. If the team has no way to restrict player mobility, such as with the reserve clause, it is unwilling to pay for the training. Suppose, for example, the Toronto Maple Leafs of the NHL pay for a player's training costs by hiring coaches and providing train-ing facilities while the player plays for the Maple Leafs' minor league team. With no restrictions in place, the player could leave the Leafs for another team when his contract expires, taking his human capital with him. The Maple Leafs would have paid for the training without receiving the benefit of the player's increased productivity. Because all teams recognize this potential loss of investment, they force players to pay for general training in the form of low minor league salaries.

Teams cite their reluctance to invest in the skills of players who may soon leave for another team as one of the main flaws of free agency. They claim that the lack of investment leads to a decline in the quality of play and a resulting decline in fan interest. They use this argument to justify many of the restrictions they place on player mobility, which we discuss in Chapter 10.

9.2 Rank-Order Tournaments and Superstar Effects

If players receive their *MRP*, then a player who is slightly more productive than another player receives a slightly higher reward. Sometimes, however, small differences in performance translate into huge differences in compensation. For example, Roger Federer won the 2017 Men's Singles Championship at the Australian Open in a grueling five-set match with Rafael Nadal that lasted more than three-and-a-half hours. Winning such a tight match brought Federer $3.7 million, while Nadal received only a little over half that amount ($1.9 million). The difference in prize money seems even more drastic considering that a player who was eliminated in the second round earned just $30,000 more than a player who was eliminated in the first round.[18] The return to winning a match increases dramatically as a player advances through the tournament. Similar conclusions hold for golf, bowling, and most other individual sports.

In such cases, *relative* productivity rather than *absolute* productivity matters. Roger Federer would have received the same prize regardless of his margin of victory. Winning is all that counts.[19] Because the order of finish is the only performance criterion, such contests are known as **rank-order tournaments**.

Organizers of the tournament want to provide an exciting contest at which all players try hard. Ideally they, like any employer, would base a player's reward on her *MRP*. The advantage of this policy is that it provides the appropriate incentives. Performing a little better brings a payoff that is a little higher; performing much better brings a much higher payoff. Unfortunately, an athlete's (or employee's) *MRP* can be very difficult and expensive to measure. In all sports, the quality of a performance depends on a long list of factors that have nothing to do with individual ability, such as the nature of the playing surface, the weather conditions, or the ability of the opponent.[20] If the organizers cannot account for all these factors, they cannot provide a reward based on the players' *MRP*s and must devise a new prize structure that provides the appropriate incentives. Fortunately, relative performance is more readily measured. A prize structure in which the increase in reward grows as a player moves up the leaderboard gives athletes a powerful incentive to do their best. The highly uneven distribution of the purse appeals to the most basic of economic tenets: self-interest.[21]

Tournaments and Effort

We can start by assuming that contestants maximize the difference between the benefit of winning prize money and the cost of effort. Figure 9.7 shows how a player determines her optimal level of effort in a tournament. If effort is costly and rises with the degree of effort, then the marginal cost curve is positive and upward-sloping. Finally, if increasing effort adds more to costs at higher levels of effort, the marginal cost curve becomes steeper at greater levels of effort. For example, moving from E_0 to E_1 adds little to the cost of effort, but moving from E_2 to E_3 adds a great deal.

Because the tournament's organizers (reflecting the desires of fans and advertisers) want to see the competitors play hard, they must set prizes that increase steeply as players move to the top of the rankings. Figure 9.8 shows why.

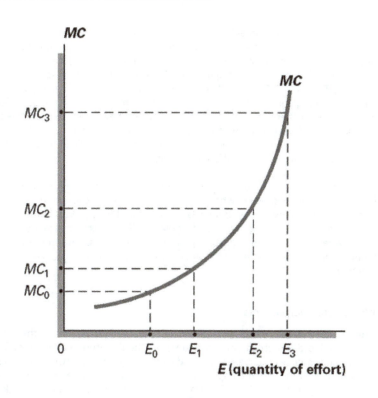

Figure 9.7
The Increasing Marginal Cost of Effort

Because providing greater effort means working harder, the marginal cost of effort slopes upward.

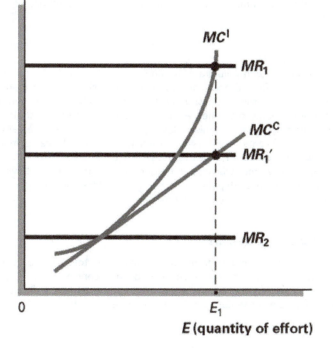

Figure 9.8
Creating the Incentive for a High Level of Effort in a Tournament

Increasing the reward for additional effort increases the optimal level of effort by a player in a tournament.

In a contest with one winner and one loser, such as the finals of a tennis tournament, and with contestants who are roughly equal in ability, the difference between winning and losing may come down to random factors, such as playing conditions.[22] The increasing marginal cost of effort is MC^I. A player sets her level of effort, E_1, where MR, her additional revenue from moving up one position, equals the marginal cost of advancing one position. By setting a large difference between first and second prize, MR_1, the players have a greater incentive to expend more effort than if the difference were small, MR_2. If the marginal cost of effort is linear, as shown by the line MC^C, the organizers can elicit the same level of effort with a much smaller difference in prizes, MR'_1.

One of the first empirical tests of this theory was performed by Ronald Ehrenberg and Michael Bognanno, who studied the response of PGA golfers to differences in prize money.[23] They found that, just as the theory predicts, incentives matter. Particularly in the last round of play, golfers shot significantly lower scores when they had the opportunity to earn larger prizes. Later research has found similar incentive effects in a variety of sports, including distance running and tennis.[24]

Women and Tournaments

There is some evidence that women respond differently from men to the pressure of rank-order tournaments. In a survey of the literature on gender differences in preferences, Rachel Croson and Uri Gneezy note that women do not perform as well as men in competitive situations and are more reluctant than men to engage in competition. This claim is supported by a variety of controlled experiments. In one, Uri Gneezy and Aldo Rustichini had Israeli fourth-graders run in timed non-competitive settings and then in head-to-head competitions. They found that girls ran slower in the head-to-head competition, while boys ran faster.[25]

Studies that analyze the performance of athletes in actual competition, as opposed to analyzing experimental settings, generally provide mixed results. Two studies from tennis illustrate this ambiguity. M. Daniele Paserman uses stroke-level data from Grand Slam tournaments to show that women make more unforced errors in crucial situations than men do but that the difference does not affect game outcomes, as men hit fewer unreturnable shots ("winners"). Lauren Banko, Eva Marikova Leeds, and Michael Leeds use data from non-Grand Slam events, in which women and men both play three-set matches. They show that women who lose the first set are just as likely as men to win the match. However, women who lose in straight sets lose the second set by a wider margin than men do. Both papers thus find gender differences but do not find that these differences affect the outcome.[26]

The Economics of Superstars

Superstar effects resemble the impact of rank-order tournaments, but they arise naturally from the market rather than from an incentive policy.[27] Superstar effects refer to differences in income that are disproportionate to differences in performance. They arise naturally from the desire, in certain situations, to be the best.

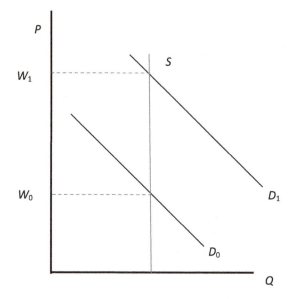

Figure 9.9
Minor Differences in
Performance Can Lead to
Large Shifts in Demand

The demand for an average
surgeon is D_0, but the demand for
a slightly better surgeon is much
greater (D_1).

Figure 9.9 shows the situation facing two brain surgeons. If both surgeons are equally skilled, they both receive the same pay, w_0. Suppose, however, one brain surgeon is slightly better than the other. The demand for his services is much greater because of the small difference in ability, as few people are willing to risk a negative outcome to save a few dollars. As a result, the better surgeon's pay rises to w_1, much more than his greater productivity would appear to justify.

Sports and other forms of entertainment are particularly subject to superstar effects, as people want to see the best soccer player or the best singer. Improvements in technology and transportation have contributed to the superstar effects. A century ago, one could hear Enrico Caruso or watch Babe Ruth only by traveling to the Metropolitan Opera or a Yankees game to experience them in person. Otherwise, one had to settle for the best athlete or entertainer in one's hometown. Today, however, we do not have to settle for the best singer or soccer player in Scranton when we can see Beyoncé on YouTube or Lionel Messi on ESPN.

Tournaments, Superstars, and the Distribution of Income

Because the financial rewards for individual victories are so heavily weighted in favor of top performers, the distribution of income in individual sports is highly skewed. For example, through July, the top three prize winners on the 2016 ATP tennis tour (Novak Djokovic, Andy Murray, and Stan Wawrinka) accounted for roughly 28.5 percent of the total winnings of the top 50 players. As in Chapter 5, we can illustrate the inequality on the men's tennis tour with a Lorenz curve. The horizontal axis in Figure 9.10 shows the cumulative percentage of the population (each player accounts for 2 percent of the population). The vertical axis shows

Figure 9.10
The Lorenz Curve for
the ATP's Top 50 Money
Winners in 2016

Unequal earnings cause the
Lorenz curve to sag below the
line denoting equal earnings by
all players.

Source: Associated Press. 2016.
"ATP Money Leaders," *Federal
News Radio,* September 12, at
http://federalnewsradio.com/
sports-news/2016/09/atp-money-
leaders/, viewed March 16, 2017.

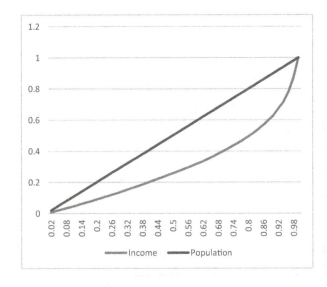

Table 9.1 The Five Highest-Paid Celebrities and Athletes in the *Forbes* 2016 "Celebrity 100"

Rank	Occupation	Earnings (in millions)
Taylor Swift	Musician	$170
One Direction	Musicians	$110
James Patterson	Author	$95
Dr. Phil McGraw	Personality	$88
Cristiano Ronaldo	Soccer Player	$88

Source: Forbes.com. "The World's Highest-Paid Celebrities," at https://www.forbes.com/
celebrities/list/#tab:overall, viewed March 14, 2017.

the cumulative percentage of earnings. The Lorenz curve sags below the straight
line, as the bottom 6 percent of (the 3 lowest) money winners account for about
1.7 percent of total winnings (point *A*), less than one-tenth of the top 6 percent's
winnings.

The salary structure in team sports is highly uneven as well. On the 2016–2017
Cleveland Cavaliers, LeBron James alone accounted for almost one-third of the
team's "cap space" (pay counted toward the salary cap). James, Kevin Love, and
Kyrie Irving combined to take up almost three-fourths of the space. These athletes' extraordinary abilities vastly increase the demand to see games in which
they play. Fans' desire to see the very best players causes the demand for their
services, and hence their earnings, to be much greater than those of players of
only slightly lesser ability.

While many athletes benefit from superstar effects, others benefit even more.
Table 9.1 lists the five highest-paid celebrities from *Forbes* magazine's "Celebrity 100." Only one athlete, Real Madrid's Cristiano Ronaldo, is among them, and
only one other athlete—fittingly, FC Barcelona's Lionel Messi—is among the top
10. LeBron James is the highest-ranked American athlete at #11. No female athlete made the top 100 in 2016.

9.3 The Dangers of Tournaments and Superstar Effects

While tournaments can provide athletes with an incentive to increase their effort, a large spread in rewards can have negative effects on their behavior in both individual and team sports. When teammates compete for individual rewards, the result can be selfish play, which undermines the cooperation that teams need to succeed.

The negative impact of pursuing individual goals on team performance has led economists to question the value of wide spreads in salaries among teammates. Several studies of MLB teams find that, all else equal, teams with higher salary spreads have worse records.[28] Interestingly, a study of baseball in Japan, a country where incomes are much more equal than in the US, by Takuma Kamada and Hajime Katayama finds that higher spreads improve team performance.[29]

In extreme cases, a tournament can lead to outright sabotage. The most famous such case might be that of Tonya Harding, a former national champion figure skater who admitted to "hindering prosecution" in the plot to injure fellow skater Nancy Kerrigan prior to the 1994 Winter Olympics. Harding's ex-husband and an accomplice confessed to attacking Kerrigan at the US Figure Skating Championships prior to the 1994 Winter Olympics and claimed that Harding herself was involved in planning it.[30] The motivation for the attack was to remove Kerrigan as the preeminent US woman figure skater, providing Harding with a "ticket to fame and fortune."[31]

Pay Disparity and Externalities: The Case of NASCAR

The reward scheme used in NASCAR is an interesting exception to both the standard model of wage determination and the highly nonlinear rewards used in golf and tennis. Although stock car racing satisfies the basic conditions for a rank-order tournament, the per-race reward structure is nearly horizontal. Figure 9.11 shows that the prize money for the 2015 PGA Championship decreases

Figure 9.11
Comparing the Rewards in the 2015 PGA Championship and the 2015 Daytona 500

The reward structure in NASCAR is far flatter than for the PGA.

Sources: Mark Sandritter. 2015. "2015 PGA Championship Prize Money: Jason Day Takes Home $1.8 Million Payout," *SBNation*, August 16, at https://www.sbnation.com/golf/2015/8/16/9162723/pga-championship-2015-purse-prize-money-payout-jason-day; Chris Estrada. 2015. "Unofficial Results, Winnings, and Race Stats—57th Daytona 500," *NBC Sports*, February 22, at http://nascar.nbcsports.com/2015/02/22/unofficial-results-winnings-and-race-stats-57th-daytona-500/.

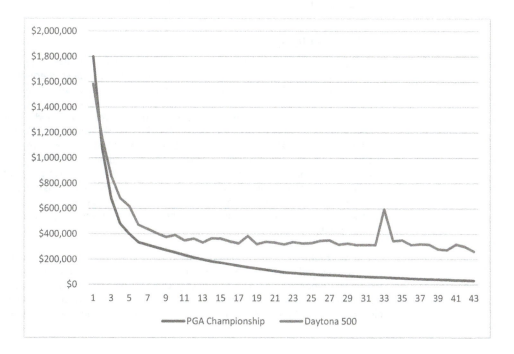

much more rapidly than for the Daytona 500 NASCAR race. Winning the PGA was worth substantially more than winning Daytona (about $1.8 million versus $1.6 million), but finishing second at Daytona was worth almost $80,000 over second place at the PGA, and 20th place at Daytona paid more than twice as much as a 20th-place finish at the PGA. The differing reward patterns raise questions about the payouts. First, are NASCAR's incentives large enough to influence driver effort? Second, why are NASCAR's payouts so different from other sports?

To address the first question, Brad Humphreys and Bernd Frick have estimated the effect of changes in the prize structure. Using a sample of over 1,000 races, they show that a larger spread between prizes yields a faster average speed in the race.[32] Thus, while the increases in payouts are relatively modest, they do appear to generate an incentive to drive faster.

To see why race organizers set such flat payouts, we must consider two unique features of racing. In racing, drivers all compete on the same track at the same time, so tournament-style wages that lead to highly aggressive driving may have catastrophic results.[33] A win-at-all-cost strategy in auto racing could cause a severe accident that harms other drivers. An aggressive strategy in golf might lead a player to hit the ball repeatedly into a water hazard, embarrassing but hardly dangerous. In addition, because stock cars are covered with advertisements, being on the track—and on camera—for a long time becomes very important to race sponsors. Thus, NASCAR has developed complex payoffs that include payments from sponsors, year-end prize money, and a wide variety of bonuses that drivers can win during races. Season championship points also give drivers a powerful incentive to remain on the track for the entire race rather than risk crashing in an attempt to earn points that may lead to a large end-of-season prize. Given that the spread of payouts is much less extreme than those of golf or tennis yet large enough to influence drivers' behavior, NASCAR officials seem to have set these payouts at levels that create exciting racing while being mindful of potential risks.

The Danger of Trying Too Hard

The disproportionate rewards that accompany even small differences in performance sometimes induce coaches, trainers, and athletes to push themselves and others too hard. Perhaps the most disturbing example of such behavior comes from a surprising yet familiar source. Imagine a country in which selected children are put to work full-time. School, friends, a normal childhood are all denied them as they perform hours of backbreaking work. Some are subjected to physical, emotional, even sexual abuse at the hands of their overseers, or even their own parents. By the time they reach adulthood, some of them are physically or emotionally broken by the arduous demands of their supervisors. Unable to form normal relationships with their peers, some take solace in drugs and others in self-abusive behavior. The country is the United States, and the children are the ones we cheer on at events such as the Olympics, Wimbledon, and NCAA championships.[34]

These youths are victims of a reward system in which first place counts for everything and second place for next-to-nothing. Adolescent girls take to the ice for the Olympic figure skating championship with greater individual rewards at stake than for any single event except, perhaps, a heavyweight boxing championship.[35] A gold medalist may get TV specials and starring roles in skating exhibitions. Her name will be entered in record books, and fans will remember her performance fondly for years to come. In contrast, all but a few relatives and friends will soon forget the performance of the fourth-place finisher.

The highly skewed reward structure induces young girls to work extremely long hours, sometimes more than 45 hours per week. Their coaches and gyms, which stand to benefit from the publicity these girls bring them, would be violating child labor laws if they paid the girls for their efforts. The long hours of training can bring permanent physical and psychological damage.

Hoping to please their parents and coaches and yearning for a chance to stand on the Olympic podium, young gymnasts suffer through severe injuries that they do not allow to heal for fear of missing their chance at an Olympic medal. One elite coach discouraged girls from having casts put on fractured limbs because "he feared it would hurt their muscle tone."[36] Some take an array of "laxatives, thyroid pills, and diuretics to lose the weight brought on by puberty."[37] The girls' obsession with weight can become so serious that they develop eating disorders. Surveys show that almost a third of female college athletes—and up to two-thirds of female gymnasts—admit to some sort of eating disorder. One young gymnast, Christy Henrich, starved herself to death. The eating disorders can have long-term effects, leading to menstrual dysfunction and osteoporosis.[38]

Performance-Enhancing Drugs

In 2016, performance-enhancing drugs took over the sports pages and then moved beyond them. After finding evidence of widespread doping that involved Russian Olympic and government officials, the IOC banned 118 Russian athletes from the 2016 Summer Olympics. The investigation eventually implicated roughly 1,000 Russian athletes in 30 sports. Events then took a bizarre and sinister turn. US intelligence agencies report that Russian ruler, Vladimir Putin, was convinced that the banning of Russian athletes was an American plot. In retaliation, he directed Russian agents to embarrass former Secretary of State Hillary Clinton by hacking her 2016 US Presidential campaign and making what they found public. The hacking could well have done more than embarrass Clinton, perhaps swinging the close election to Donald Trump.[39] All this over a few medals!

The use and danger of performance-enhancing drugs (PEDs) are not new. The first documented doping-related fatality came during a bicycle race in 1879. At first, doping was strictly an individual decision. As sport became increasingly politicized, doping became a state policy.

During the Cold War, athletic contests became propaganda campaigns in which the Soviet bloc and Western democracies used Olympic medal counts to demonstrate the superiority of their economic and political systems.[40] Chafing in the shadow of West Germany's economic growth and success in international soccer, East Germany used Olympic sports as a public relations tool.

The fall of the Berlin Wall in 1989 and the resulting publication of state secrets showed the high cost of East German Olympic success. Physical disabilities, birth defects, even a change in sexual identity were all attributed to the "vitamins" that unsuspecting East German girls were given as part of their training regimen. In the United States, some estimates show that as many as 1 million high school students have used anabolic steroids, a popular PED. Researchers claim that the use of steroids causes heart and liver damage, violent mood swings ("roid rage"), and psychological dependency.[41]

Some regard PEDs as just another way to seek an edge, no different from a swimmer using a specially designed swimsuit or a bicyclist using a new material to lighten her bike. Some even say that PEDs are a way for athletes who cannot afford personal trainers and expensive equipment to level the playing field. They also point out that the dangers of using PEDs may be no worse than those of participating in some sports, such as American football.[42] Still, most fans—and all international sports organizations—view PEDs as qualitatively different from other ways of improving one's performance.

PED use is not limited to elite athletes. Brad Humphreys and Jane Ruseski use data collected by the Youth Risk Behavior Surveillance System, a nationwide survey of high school-age students, to study steroid use among US youths from 1991 to 2005. They find that boys (an average of about 5.4 percent) are much more likely than girls to use steroids (2.8 percent). Steroid usage was greater among multi-sport athletes, particularly among those in the higher grades, and was negatively related to parental education and income. Finally, they find that steroid use was positively related to risky behavior in general, such as the use of other, "recreational" drugs.[43]

The dangers of PEDs have not deterred athletes from using them. Some insight into the mindset of elite athletes can be found in a survey of almost 200 of them. The survey confronted the athletes with a hypothetical situation:

You are offered a banned performance-enhancing substance that comes with two guarantees:
1   You will not be caught.
2   You will win every competition you enter for the next five years, and then you will die from the side effects of the substances.
More than half the athletes surveyed said they would accept such an offer.[44]

Such attitudes among athletes have led economists to model PED use as a Prisoner's Dilemma.[45] Figure 9.12 provides a simple model of PED use. It begins with the simplifying assumption that we have only two athletes, Mark and Sam, each of whom chooses to use PEDs or not use them. Using PEDs improves performance and gives each player an advantage if the other does not use them. Consistent with the above survey, Mark and Sam are willing to risk their health if they can dominate their sport.

Figure 9.12
PED Use: A Prisoner's Dilemma

		Mark	
		Doesn't use PEDs	*Uses PEDs*
Sam	*Doesn't use PEDs*	(2,2) No advantage/No harm	(5,0) Mark wins/Sam loses
	Uses PEDs	(0,5) Mark loses/Sam wins	(1,1) No advantage/harm

The payoffs (expressed as units of happiness) in the upper left entry occur when neither athlete takes PEDs, while the payoffs in the lower right occur when both do. In both situations, neither Sam nor Mark has an advantage over the other. The only difference is that both athletes risk their health if they take PEDs. As a result, the payoffs in the upper left square are superior to the outcomes in the lower right square. In the off-diagonal cells, the athlete taking PEDs wins (by setting a world record, winning the home run title, or becoming world champion) and the other loses. Given the preferences described above, taking PEDs is a dominant strategy. The result is a Prisoner's Dilemma in which Mark and Sam risk their health but gain no advantage.

Many professional sports have experienced embarrassing scandals involving PEDs. One well-known scandal involves the Bay Area Laboratory Co-Operative (BALCO), whose founder, Victor Conte, served a short prison sentence after pleading guilty to steroid distribution and money laundering in June 2005. When the government seized BALCO's records, it found evidence that many well-known athletes, including MLB's all-time home run champion Barry Bonds, had used steroids, human growth hormones, and other PEDs. Although it may never be clear whether Bonds knowingly used PEDs, the allegations made Bonds' pursuit of Hank Aaron's home run title an embarrassing episode.[46] The legacies of such baseball stars as Roger Clemens, Mark McGwire, Rafael Palmeiro, Manny Ramirez, Alex Rodriguez, and Sammy Sosa have also been tainted by PED usage.

No other sport has been as severely damaged by PEDs as cycling. From 1996 through 2010, only one winner of the Tour de France, the world's premier bicycle race, did not use PEDs. Tests have implicated no Tour de France winner since 2011, but Team Sky, the team of 2016 champion Chris Froome, has been implicated in a doping scandal that is still unfolding.[47] Whatever the eventual outcome of Froome's case, the sport continues to be tarnished by its association with PEDs. In addition, cyclists may have found a safer alternative to PEDs. They may now be "doping" their bikes. CBS News has reported that 12 riders in the 2015 Tour de France used bicycles with hidden motors.[48]

How often, under what circumstances, and for which substances to test athletes are matters of collective bargaining in most professional sports, including the four major team sports in North America. While it may seem simple to insist that any player can be tested at any time for any substance, the player associations that represent all players in collective bargaining worry about invasions of privacy, inconvenience, and, perhaps most frightening, the negative consequences of a false positive test. Nevertheless, with each successive agreement, owners and the players have agreed to test for more substances, often with increased penalties for violations. In 2016 alone, MLB suspended 14 players and the NFL suspended 19 players for PED use.[49]

The ongoing scandals reveal how widespread the incentive to cheat has become, and how difficult it is for sports leagues and international anti-doping agencies to keep up with the development of new and increasingly sophisticated PEDs. Perhaps nothing reflects the times as well as the fact that FIDE, the World Chess Federation, now requires that participants in international chess tournaments undergo drug testing after their matches.[50]

Biographical Sketch

Scott Boras
(1952–)

> *Talking to Boras about baseball executives is like talking to a lion about red meat.*
>
> —Matt Taibbi[51]

While star baseball players like Bryce Harper and Max Scherzer would be millionaires no matter who represented them, they, and dozens of other baseball players, believe they have benefited significantly from having Scott Boras for an agent. In securing huge paydays for his clients, Boras has earned the universal scorn of owners, who, in the words of one reporter, regard Boras as "Shiva, god of destruction, sent to Earth to wreck all that is holy," but he has proven so successful and so popular with players that few teams can afford to ignore him.

As a young man, Boras did not seem destined to become an agent. In fact, it looked like he might be a baseball player instead. Boras grew up on a farm in northern California and played baseball at the University of the Pacific, eventually becoming team captain. He was not, however, the stereotypical "jock," majoring in chemistry and taking PhD-level classes in industrial pharmacology. This sometimes forced Boras to schedule private labs, some of which lasted until midnight, after baseball practice.

Boras was good enough to sign a contract with the St. Louis Cardinals in 1974, but he did not abandon his graduate studies, sometimes offering his coaches beer to proctor his exams. A series of knee injuries ended Boras's hopes of making the major leagues, and he left baseball in 1978. At the same time, he began studying for a law degree at Pacific's McGeorge School of Law. After graduating from law school, Boras continued to use his background in chemistry, defending drug companies against class-action suits for a large law firm in Chicago, hardly the type of work one would expect of a man who would soon take on the moguls of baseball.

In 1985, Boras helped Bill Caudill, a former minor league teammate, negotiate a contract with the Toronto Blue Jays. The result, a five-year, $7 million contract that made Caudill the second-highest-paid relief pitcher in baseball, caught the baseball world's attention and led Boras to represent players full-time.

Boras has negotiated contracts currently worth $2.2 billion, which will bring his company, Boras Corp., over $132 million in commissions. He has achieved these results by adopting tactics that neutralize or reverse the traditional monopsony power of MLB owners. He has, for example, used the fact that he can speak with multiple teams while the teams are legally forbidden from speaking to each other about player negotiations. Boras used this advantage in 2000 to convince the Texas Rangers that other teams were interested in Alex Rodriguez. The Rangers increased their offer even though no other team was willing to pay more. The result was a contract whose monetary value was greater than the sum the Rangers' owners had paid for the entire team.

Boras has also used the draft to obtain leverage for his clients. Traditionally, the draft has been a source of monopsony power for teams, as they have exclusive rights to negotiate with the players they draft. Boras, however, convinced Tim Belcher, a top draft choice of the Minnesota Twins, to return to college rather than sign with the Twins (Belcher could do so after signing with Boras because his college—Mount Vernon Nazarene—belonged to the NAIA and not the NCAA). He later convinced J. D. Drew, the first overall choice of the 1997 draft, to play with the St. Paul Saints, an independent minor league team, rather than sign with the Philadelphia Phillies. Both Belcher and Drew signed much more lucrative contracts with different teams a year later.

At times, Boras's techniques have backfired. His tactics in negotiating a new contract for Alex Rodriguez were so aggressive—he announced that Rodriguez would opt out of the remaining three years of his contract during game 4 of the 2007 World Series—that Rodriguez eventually dropped him as an agent. In addition, many of the contracts Boras has negotiated have resulted in compensation far greater than the players' value. For example, Barry Zito, for whom Boras had negotiated a $119 million contract with the San Francisco Giants, won 63 games and lost 80 and posted a 4.62 ERA over seven undistinguished years with the team, hardly fit statistics for a player Boras described as "one of the best left-handed pitchers of all time."[52]

Sources: Ben McGrath. 2009. "The Extortionist," *The New Yorker,* October 29, at http://www.newyorker.com/reporting/2007/10/29/071029fa_fact_mcgrath; Bob Nightengale. 2006. "Boras Is Baseball's Bigger Deal Man," *USA Today,* November 14, at http://www.usatoday.com/sports/baseball/2006-11-14-boras-cover_x.htm; Matt Taibbi. 2009. "The Devil's Doorstep: A Visit with Scott Boras," *Men's Journal,* February 23, at http://www.mensjournal.com/the-devil%E2%80%99s-doorstep; and Jason Belzer. 2016. "The World's Most Powerful Sports Agents," *Forbes.com,* September 21, at https://www.forbes.com/sites/jasonbelzer/2016/09/21/the-worlds-most-powerful-sports-agents-2016/, viewed March 16, 2017.

Summary

In this chapter, we examined how labor markets work in professional sports. The forces of labor supply and labor demand do a good job of explaining why the salaries of professional athletes have grown so much over the last several decades. Increasing demand by fans for a sport translates into higher demand for labor by teams. Athletes can increase their own earnings by investing in human capital. To the degree that the skills they acquire are general skills, athletes must pay for the training by accepting lower salaries.

The distribution of income in professional sports is highly skewed toward those with the most talent. Tournament organizers and teams provide disproportionate rewards to get players to provide more effort. Reward systems based on rank-order tournaments and superstar effects pose some dangers, as they can lead to poor teamwork, sabotaging one's opponents, and carrying effort to unhealthy extremes. The unhealthy extremes include levels of practice that lead to permanent disability later in life or to the abuse of performance-enhancing drugs.

Discussion Questions

1   Has the recent focus on measuring individual performance harmed professional sports?
2   Should baseball and football follow the example of the IOC and expunge records set by players who have used PEDs?
3   If PEDs do not cause irreparable harm to an athlete's health, should they be permitted?
4   Are winner-take-all (or winner-take-most) contests a good reward mechanism? Would you want to take part in them at your workplace?

Problems

9.1   Suppose that the market demand for baseball players is perfectly inelastic (vertical) at 750 players. If the market supply increases due to an increase in the number of available international players, show using a graph how wages will change as a result.
9.2   Use a labor supply and labor demand graph to show why salaries in the NBA went down during the Great Recession. Explain why the curves moved the way they did.
9.3   Use a graph similar to Figure 9.5 to show the effect on league salaries of:
    a. An increase in the number of players available
    b. A decrease in television revenues due to fan preferences for drama shows
    c. A minimum salary set above the equilibrium level.
9.4   Show what would have happened to the Lorenz curve in Figure 9.10 if Novak Djokovic, Andy Murray, and Stan Wawrinka had all lost in the first round of the US Open in 2016.
9.5   Some observers claim that free agency has reduced the quality of play in professional sports. Use the model of human capital accumulation to explain why this might be so.
9.6   In the late 1930s and early 1940s, Joe Louis handily defeated a series of opponents who came to be known as the "Bum of the Month Club." Use what you know about rank-order tournaments to explain how this came about.
9.7   Using a graph, show what happens to player effort in a tournament if players find effort more distasteful (the marginal cost-of-effort curve shifts upward).
9.8   Use supply and demand curves to explain how the development of the interstate highway system, which allowed fans to travel much greater distances to watch ballgames, increased pay disparities between major league and minor league baseball players.

9.9   Show how the Prisoner's Dilemma led to massive doping in international track and field. What can authorities do to prevent doping from becoming a dominant strategy?

9.10 Use the supply and demand model to explain why top athletes are paid less than top celebrities.

APPENDIX 9A

Using Indifference Curves to Model the Labor–Leisure Choice

Like all decisions in economics, the decision to work is one of choosing among alternatives. In the simple labor–leisure choice model, a person chooses between working for pay and consuming leisure.[53] Labor economists typically assume that people gain utility from the goods and services they consume (X) and leisure (Z), both of which are normal goods:

$$U = u(X, Z)$$

We can illustrate the utility function using indifference curves, as shown in Figure 9A.1. Each curve represents a specific level of utility, and utility increases as we move away from the origin (i.e., $U_2 > U_1$). The slope of an indifference curve, also called the **marginal rate of substitution**, represents the rate at which the person is willing to exchange one good for the other, holding utility constant. The negative slope of an indifference curve implies a trade-off: To hold utility constant, a person must receive more of one good if she receives less of

Figure 9A.1
Indifference Curves

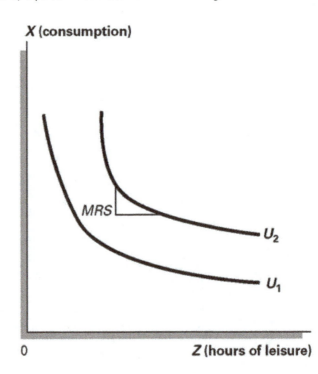

the other. The convex shape of the indifference curves reflects the diminishing marginal utility associated with consuming more of any single commodity.

Consumption is limited by an **income constraint** and a **time constraint**. A person's income consists of her earnings from working h hours at wage w, and exogenous income V, which consists of all non-labor income such as dividends, inheritances, and so on:

$$X = wh + V$$

The time constraint reflects the fact that there are only so many hours in a day (T) that can be allocated to either work or leisure:

$$T = h + Z$$

In Figure 9A.2, the time constraint mandates that a person cannot spend less than zero hours working and more than T hours at leisure (and vice versa). Because many people receive some income even if they do not work, the budget constraint begins from a point $\$V$ directly above T. The constraint has a slope equal to $-w$ since the person must give up $\$w$ for every hour of leisure he or she consumes.

We can combine a person's utility function with her budget constraint to determine her utility-maximizing choice. Suppose a local golf pro, Arnold, can earn income by giving golf lessons for $20 per hour. In addition, he receives $100 per day in dividend income.[54] His constraints are:

$$X = 20h + 100$$
$$24 = h + Z$$

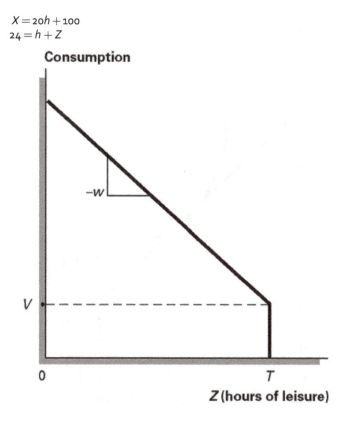

Consumption

$-w$

V

0

T

Z **(hours of leisure)**

Figure 9A.2
The Income and Time
Constraints

Arnold can teach all the lessons he wants, but each hour that he spends teach-ing requires that he give up one hour of leisure. As such, the opportunity cost of consuming an extra hour of leisure is $20. Arnold's utility-maximizing solution is shown in Figure 9A.3. He maximizes his utility by teaching 8 hours per day and consuming 16 hours of leisure. His total daily income is $260, and his utility level is U_2. At the utility-maximizing point, S, the marginal rate of substitution (the slope of the indifference curve), equals the wage rate, the slope of the bud-get constraint:

$$MRS = w$$

If Arnold had a strong preference for leisure, we could illustrate his preferences with the dashed indifference curve U_1. In this example, Arnold does not want to work at all. The indifference curve U_1 touches the budget line at Z, which means that $h = 0$, and Arnold devotes all his time to leisure.

We can derive Arnold's labor supply curve by varying his wage. Figure 9A.4 shows Arnold's initial optimal point from Figure 9A.3. When Arnold's wage rate falls to $10 per hour, his budget line becomes flatter (ZB') and his utility level falls to U_1 at point R. At the new, lower wage, Arnold works 6 hours per day and consumes 18 hours per day of leisure. His total income is now $160 per day. Arnold responds to an increase in his wage to $30 per hour, which shifts the budget line to ZB'', by choosing the consumption–leisure combination labeled T on the indifference curve U_3. Again Arnold decides to work 6 hours per day, giving him an income of $280, and he consumes 18 hours per day of leisure.

Figure 9A.3
Individual Utility-
Maximizing Curves

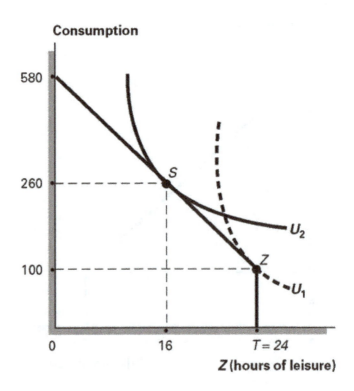

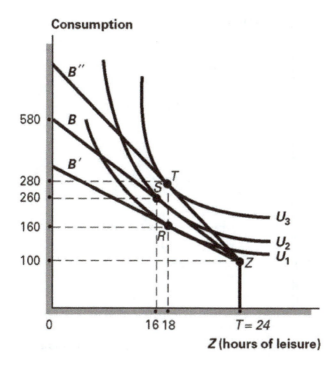

Consumption

Figure 9A.4
Changes in Labor Supply
Due to Wage Changes

Like any supply curve, a labor supply curve shows the quantity (of hours in this case) that Arnold supplies at various prices. In Figure 9A.5, points R', S', and T' correspond to the tangencies R, S, and T in Figure 9A.4. The line ll that connects these points is Arnold's labor supply curve. The difference between this supply curve and a typical product supply curve is that it bends backward at wages above $20. To see why, we must look further into the labor–leisure decision.

Labor supply curves sometimes bend backward because of the *income* and *substitution effects*. The substitution effect causes a person to shift his or her consumption away from goods that have become more expensive. Because the opportunity cost of leisure is the wage, when Arnold's wage increases from R' to S', the cost of leisure rises, which will lead him to consume less leisure and work more.

If leisure is a normal good, an increase in income causes the demand for leisure to rise. When Arnold's wage rises, his income rises as well, which increases his demand for leisure, leading him to work fewer hours. In effect, he "buys" leisure time with his increased earning power. In this case, the income and substitution effects work in opposite directions. Whether Arnold's labor supply curve slopes upward or curves backward depends on which effect is stronger. If the substitution effect is larger, Arnold works more as his wage increases. If the income effect is larger, he works less. Figure 9A.5 shows that Arnold's substitution effect dominates at wages below $20 per hour, but his income effect dominates at wages above $20 per hour.

Because of the intense level of training and dedication required in professional sports, players or coaches sometimes walk away from the game despite still being able to compete at the highest level. Dick Vermeil, coach of the 2000 Super Bowl champion St. Louis Rams, had become a classic case of burnout almost two decades earlier. While coaching the Philadelphia Eagles from 1976 to 1983, Vermeil

Figure 9A.5
The Individual Labor
Supply Curve

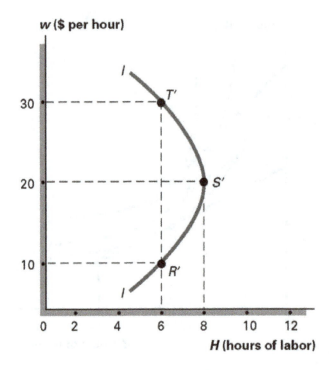

worked so many hours that he noticed a growth spurt of his second oldest son only while watching game film with his assistant coaches and seeing his son standing on the sidelines.[55] He left coaching at the end of the 1982–1983 season after working himself to the point of physical exhaustion. Although he worked after that as a broadcaster and motivational speaker, he did not return to coaching again until 1997, when he took over as head coach of the Rams. For Vermeil, a change in his preferences away from work toward leisure led him to leave the game.

We can also use the labor–leisure model to show how an increase in wealth affects the decision to work. Consider the example of Oscar de la Hoya described at the start of the chapter. In the case of de la Hoya and other highly paid athletes, the vertical portion of the income constraint becomes very large over time due to endorsement and accumulated past income. As the exogenous income segment increases, so does the income effect, because a person can achieve greater and greater utility levels without working, as shown in Figure 9A.6.

9A.1   The Labor–Leisure Model When Hours Are Fixed

The labor supply model assumes that a person can choose the number of hours that he or she would like to work. However, most people cannot choose the number of hours they work. The same is true in sports. Athletes may have to play a longer or a shorter season than they would optimally choose. For example, many WNBA players feel the season is too short. We illustrate the effects of the short season on the utility-maximization problem in Figure 9A.7 by imposing another constraint, fixing hours (or games in this case) along the vertical line set at Z_o. In this example, a WNBA player maximizes her utility on U_1 by playing 40 games. She is constrained however to play only a 34-game season and consume more leisure than she would like, reducing her utility to U_o.[56] While some leisure is a good thing, when a person consumes very large quantities of it, the marginal utility received from the last hour becomes very small.

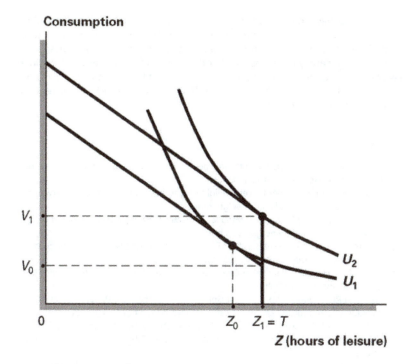

Consumption

V_1

V_0

U_2

U_1

0

Z_0 $Z_1 = T$

Z (hours of leisure)

Figure 9A.6
Increases in Wealth That
Result in No Labor Supplied

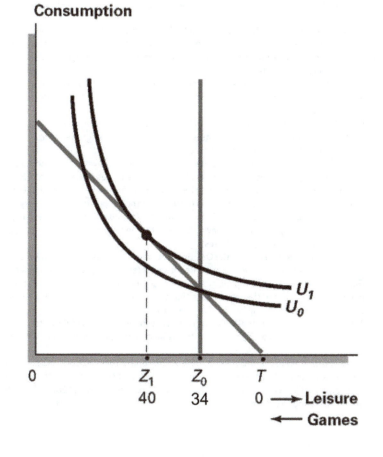

Consumption

U_1

U_0

0

Z_1 Z_0 T

40   34   0 ⟶ **Leisure**

⟵ **Games**

Figure 9A.7
Labor Supply When Players
Cannot Choose the Number
of Games

Athletes who play individual sports typically do not face such stringent quantity constraints. For example, a professional golfer with a newborn child may take several weeks away from the tour.[57] For athletes involved in team sports, part-time play is generally not an option. For them, when family needs dictate time away from the game, retirement may be the only option. Adam LaRoche cited family when he abruptly retired from baseball in 2016, and NASCAR driver Carl Edwards said the same in early 2017.

Notes

1   "Cot's Baseball Contracts," at http://legacy.baseballprospectus.com/compensation/cots/2005/02/. Accessed October 17, 2017.
2   De la Hoya won the super flyweight, lightweight, light welterweight, welterweight, junior middleweight, and middleweight titles.
3   "Joe Louis (Barrow)," *Arlington National Cemetery Website*, July 27, 2009, at http://www.arlingtoncemetery.net/joelouis.htm.
4   See, for example, Chris Mead. 1985. "Triumphs and Trials," *SIVault*, September 23, at https://www.si.com/vault/issue/43501/78/2.
5   It is probably no coincidence that *Golden Boy* is also the title of a play (later made into a musical) about a prizefighter.
6   Tom Van Riper. 2009. "Boxing's Last Golden Boy?" *Forbes.com*, January 15, at http://www.forbes.com/2009/01/14/boxing-oscar-de-la-hoya-biz-sports_cx_tvr_0115delahoya.html; and Simone Walker. 2009. "De la Hoya—Boxing's Future Is Golden," *SportsPro*, October 13, at http://www.sportspromedia.com/notes_and_insights/de_la_hoya_-_boxings_future_is_golden/.
7   For a more complete treatment of the labor supply curve and the labor–leisure choice model, see Appendix 9A.
8   Using the wage can significantly understate the unit price of labor, as it ignores many other factors, such as taxes and fringe benefits. Still, it is a useful first approximation.
9   While the number of minutes or innings played may vary, the players make themselves available for the full season.
10 At high wages, the income effect could become stronger than the substitution effect. If so, higher wages reduce the number of hours worked, leading to a "backward-bending" labor supply curve.
11 If $w = MRP_L$ at a point to the left of L_0 in Figure 9.3a, it adds more to revenue than to cost by moving to L_0. Those with a strong math background might recognize this as violating the second order condition for a maximum.
12 Archie Manning's record (35-101-3) is the worst for quarterbacks with at least 100 starts.
13 A goalie's save percentage is the number of saves a goalie makes (plays that prevent the puck from going into the net) divided by the number of shots on goal (shots that either resulted in a score or would have done so if the goalie had not stopped them). Goals-against average is the number of goals a goalie allows divided by the number of games he plays.
14 For more on these problems see Devid Berri and Martin Schmidt. 2010. *Stumbling on Wins* (Upper Saddle River, NJ: FT Press).
15 The two teams merged to form the Orix Buffaloes, but the owners agreed to keep the number of teams at 12 by admitting the Rakuten Golden Eagles as an expansion team.
16 Gary Becker. 1993. *Human Capital*, 3rd ed. (Chicago, IL: University of Chicago Press).
17 If neither the player nor the team is sure that the training will improve skills and pay, there is an incentive for the two to share the costs of training.
18 Totalsportek2. 2017. "Australian Open Tennis 2017 Prize Money," *Total Sportek*, January 26, at http://www.totalsportek.com/tennis/australian-open-prize-money/, viewed March 14, 2017.
19 Two men were being chased by a grizzly bear when one of them stopped and began to put on track shoes. The other stopped and said, "You don't think track shoes are going to help you outrun a grizzly, do you?" The first man looked up and replied, "It's not the grizzly I'm trying to outrun."

20 In one famous example, the course of the 1960 World Series was changed when a ground ball to the Yankee shortstop hit a pebble, took an unexpected bounce, and sustained a key Pirates rally in the seventh and deciding game.

21 This theory was first proposed in Edward Lazear and Sherwin Rosen. 1981. "Rank Order Tournaments as Optimum Labor Contracts," *Journal of Political Economy*, 89(5), October: 841–864.

22 If the contestants are not equal in ability, the resulting tournament may be poor entertainment. If the weaker opponent knows he or she has no chance to win, there is no incentive to try.

23 Ronald G. Ehrenberg and Michael L. Bognanno. 1990. "Do Tournaments Have Incentive Effects?" *Journal of Political Economy*, 98(6), December: 1307–1324.

24 See for example, Bernd Frick and Joachim Prinz. 2007. "Pay and Performance in Professional Road Running: The Case of City Marathons," *International Journal of Sport Finance*, 2(1), February: 25–35; and Uwe Sunde. 2009. "Heterogeneity and Performance in Tournaments: A Test for Incentive Effects Using Professional Tennis Data," *Applied Economics*, 41(25–27), November-December: 3199–3208.

25 Rachel Croson and Uri Gneezy. 2009. "Gender Differences in Preferences," *Journal of Economic Literature* 47(2), Summer: 1–27; and Uri Gneezy and Aldo Rustichini. 2004. "Gender and Competition at a Young Age," *American Economic Review*, 94(2), May: 377–381.

26 M. Daniele Paserman. 2010. "Gender Differences in Performance in Competitive Environments? Evidence from Professional Tennis Players." *IZA Discussion Paper 2834*; Lauren Banko, Eva Marikova Leeds, and Michael A. Leeds. 2016. "Gender Differences in Response to Setbacks: Evidence from Professional Tennis," *Social Science Quarterly*, 97(2), June: 161–176.

27 For a detailed description of the nonlinear returns to ability, see Sherwin Rosen. 1981. "The Economics of Superstars," *American Economic Review*, 71(5), December: 845–858.

28 See, for example, Craig A. Depken II. 2000. "Wage Disparity and Team Productivity: Evidence from Major League Baseball," *Economics Letters*, 61(1), April: 87–92; R. Todd Jewel and David Molina. 2004. "Productive Efficiency and Salary Distribution: The Case of U.S. Major League Baseball," *Scottish Journal of Political Economy*, 51(1), February: 127–142; Christopher Annala and Jason Winfree. 2011. "Salary Distribution and Team Performance in Major League Baseball," *Sport Management Review*, 14(2), May: 167–175.

29 Takuma Kamada and Hajime Katayama. 2014. "Team Performance and Within-Team Salary Disparity: An Analysis of Nippon Professional Baseball," *Economics Bulletin*, 34(1): 144–151.

30 Sonja Steptoe and E.M. Swift. 1994. "A Done Deal," *Sports Illustrated*, March 28: 32–36.

31 E.M. Swift. 1994. "Anatomy of a Plot: The Kerrigan Assault," *Sports Illustrated*, February 14: 28–38.

32 Bernd Frick and Brad Humphreys, "Prize Structure and Performance: Evidence from NASCAR," University of Alberta Working Paper, at https://www.researchgate.net/publication/254448375_Prize_Structure_and_Performance_Evidence_from_NASCAR.

33 This argument is based on Peter von Allmen. 2000. "Is the Reward System in NASCAR Efficient?" *Journal of Sports Economics*, 2(1), February: 62–79.

34 Joan Ryan. 1995. *Little Girls in Pretty Boxes* (New York: Doubleday), catalogs the horrors confronting many young female gymnasts and figure skaters.

35 Ryan. 1995. *Little Girls in Pretty Boxes*: 193.

36 Merrell Noden. 1994. "Dying to Win," *Sports Illustrated*, August 8: 52–59.

37 Robert Frank and Phillip Cook. 1995. *The Winner-Take-All Society* (New York: The Free Press): 132.

38 See Susan Gilbert. 1996. "The Smallest Olympians Face the Biggest Risks," *New York Times*, July 28: E4; Noden. 1994. "Dying to Win": 52–59; Ryan. 1995. *Little Girls in Pretty Boxes*: 17–54; Ian Tofler, Barri Katz Stryer, Lyle J. Micheli, and Lisa Herman. 1996. "Physical and Emotional Problems of Elite Female Gymnasts," *New England Journal of Medicine*, 335(4), July 25: 281–283.

39 See, for example, Rebecca R. Ruiz. 2016. "Olympic Officials Set Russia's Roster; More Than 100 Are Barred for Doping," *New York Times*, August 4, at https://www.nytimes.com/2016/08/05/sports/olympics/rio-russians-barred-doping.html, viewed August 4,

2016; and Chris Chavez. 2017. "Intelligence Report: Russia's Olympic Doping Scandal Linked to Election Interference," *Sports Illustrated,* January 6, at http://www.si.com/olympics/2017/01/06/us-intelligence-agency-russia-hackers-dnc-wada-doping-scandal, viewed March 15, 2017.

40 See, for example, David Maraniss. 2008. *Rome 1960: The Olympics That Changed the World* (New York: Simon and Schuster).

41 See Aleksander Berentsen. 2002. "The Economics of Doping," *European Journal of Political Economy,* 18(1), March: 109–127; Steven Ungerleider. 2001. *Faust's Gold: Inside the East German Doping Machine* (New York: Thomas Dunne Books); and Jane Weaver. 2005. "Steroid Addiction a Risk for Young Athletes," *MSNBC,* April 5, at http://www.msnbc.msn.com/id/7348758.

42 For a nice summary, see David van Mill. 2015. "Why Are We So Opposed to Performance-Enhancing Drugs in Sport?" *The Conversation,* August 27, at http://theconversation.com/why-are-we-so-opposed-to-performance-enhancing-drugs-in-sport-46528, viewed March 15, 2017.

43 Brad Humphreys and Jane Ruseski. 2011. "Socio-Economic Determinants of Adolescent Use of Performance Enhancing Drugs: Evidence from the YRBSS," *The Journal of Socio-Economics,* 40(2), April: 208–216.

44 Michael Bamberger and Don Yaeger. 1997. "Over the Edge," *Sports Illustrated,* April 14: 61–70.

45 For more detailed treatments of doping as a Prisoner's Dilemma, see Berentsen. 2002. "The Economics of Doping"; and Kjetil K. Haugen. 2004. "The Performance Enhancing Drug Game," *Journal of Sports Economics,* 5(1), February: 67–86.

46 Aaron declined the offer to attend games at which Bonds might break his record. See also Mark Fainaru-Wade and Lance Williams. 2006. *Game of Shadows: Barry Bonds, BALCO, and the Steroids Scandal That Rocked Professional Sports* (New York: Gotham Books).

47 Tom Cary. 2017. "British Cycling Told to Sort Out Mess or Lose £26m as Backlash Intensifies," *The Telegraph,* March 2, at http://www.telegraph.co.uk/cycling/2017/03/02/team-sky-british-cycling-fire-missing-medical-records-latest/, viewed April 5, 2017.

48 Agence France-Presse. 2017. "CBS News: 12 Riders Used Motorized Bikes in the 2015 Tour," *VeloNews,* January 30, at http://www.velonews.com/2017/01/news/cbs-news-12-riders-used-motorized-bikes-in-the-2015-tour_429741, viewed March 15, 2017.

49 "MLB Fines and Suspensions." 2017. *Spotrac,* at http://www.spotrac.com/mlb/fines-suspensions/, viewed March 16, 2017; "NFL Fines and Suspensions." 2017. *Spotrac,* at http://www.spotrac.com/nfl/fines-suspensions/, viewed March 16, 2017.

50 Vassiliy Ivanchuk, the third-ranking chess player in the world, was in danger of receiving a two-year suspension from international competition after he refused to submit to a drug test after the 2008 Dresden Chess Olympiad. A FIDE panel ruled that he had misunderstood the request because of language difficulties and the fact that he was distraught after a loss.

51 Matt Taibbi. 2009. "The Devil's Doorstep: A Visit with Scott Boras," *Men's Journal,* February 23, at http://archive.li/NmdpD.

52 Quoted in Bob Nightengale. 2006. "Boras Is Baseball's Bigger Deal Man," *USA Today,* November 14, at http://www.usatoday.com/sports/baseball/2006-11-14-boras-cover_x.htm.

53 More sophisticated models would allow for additional activities, such as child care, housework, and other "home production."

54 We could alter the model by assuming that Arnold needs to devote a portion of each day to personal needs such as sleeping and eating, but the framework would be the same. With such an allowance, T would shift to the left by the amount of personal time, p, per period ($T - p = h + Z$).

55 Gary Smith. 1983. "A New Life," *Sports Illustrated,* March 28: 60–67.

56 For purposes of this example, we ignore the possibility that WNBA players can spend the off-season playing in other countries.

57 The LPGA now maintains a day care center that travels with the tour, allowing golfers to keep their small children with them rather than being forced to choose between playing and staying home.

10

LABOR MARKET IMPERFECTIONS

The squabbling within baseball, the finger-pointing, the tendency to see economic issues as moral ones . . . all of these are contributing to our joint fall from grace.
—FAY VINCENT, FORMER MLB COMMISSIONER IN 1991

We can move forward to resolve the . . . issue through consensus rather than confrontation, which is the approach I would like to take to each and every problem confronting the game today.
—BUD SELIG, FORMER MLB COMMISSIONER IN 1992[1]

Introduction

As we saw in Chapter 9, the salaries paid to professional athletes grew significantly in the second half of the 20th century. They have, however, grown more rapidly in some sports than in others. For example, in 1980 the average salaries in MLB and the NFL were virtually identical. By 2015, the average salary in MLB was about twice that in the NFL.[2] The faster growth of salaries in baseball is surprising for two reasons. First, revenues in football have grown more rapidly than in baseball. Rising revenues should increase the *MRP* of players and their salaries. Second, the disparity grew at a time when NFL players finally became free agents in large numbers following the 1992 antitrust ruling against the NFL.

Much of this puzzling disparity stems from the relative power of the sports' player associations. The Major League Baseball Players Association (MLBPA) has been far more adept at preventing owners from restricting players' salaries than has the National Football League Players Association (NFLPA). MLB remains the only major North American sports league that has no salary cap on either teams or individual players.

In this chapter, we examine how professional sports leagues have exerted monopsony power over their players. We then show how the different sports unions have exerted countervailing monopoly power by controlling the labor input.

Learning Objectives

- Understand how leagues exert monopsony power on players.
- Grasp how unions serve as a countervailing force on teams' monopsony power and how they have increased player income.
- See how free agency changed the economic relationship between players and teams and what teams have done to limit its impact.
- Appreciate the inefficiency of strikes, why strikes occur despite their contradicting basic economic logic, and why professional sports are particularly susceptible to strikes.

10.1 The Monopsony Power of Sports Leagues

The labor markets in all the major North American sports deviate from the assumptions of the competitive model. In this section, we take a close look at the reserve clause and the monopsony power it gave owners. We go on to explain the advent of free agency in professional sports and the degree to which it has boosted the salaries of players. We also describe how leagues have attempted to limit the access to free agency and have used other mechanisms to slow the salary growth of players who have earned free agent status.

The Economics of Monopsony

A monopsony is the sole buyer of a good or service. Firms that sell goods or services in a monopsony can sell them to only one buyer. In a monopsony labor market, workers can sell their services only to the monopsony employer. The impact of a monopsony is the mirror image of that of a monopoly. While a monopolist uses its market power to drive up the price it charges consumers, a monopsonist uses its market power to drive down the prices it pays producers or workers. A monopsonist and a monopolist are identical in one respect. Both maximize profits by restricting the quantity of transactions relative to a perfectly competitive industry. The lower output and consumption impose a deadweight loss on society.

Figure 10.1 shows that, since the monopsonist is the only buyer in a market, its supply curve is the market supply curve (just as the monopolist's demand curve is the market demand curve). Because the supply curve is

Figure 10.1
Employment and Wage Level for a Monopsonist

Monopsony results in lower wages $(w_m < w_c)$ and employment $(L_m < L_c)$ as well as a deadweight loss.

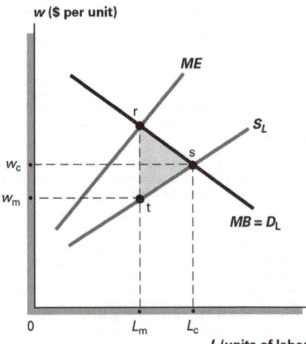

upward-sloping, the monopsonist can buy more only if it is willing and able to pay a higher price. Since a monopsonist usually cannot tell exactly how much each seller is willing to charge, it generally cannot price discriminate and must pay a higher price for all the items it buys—not just for the additional items. The cost of buying a little more, the **marginal expenditure** (ME), is thus greater than the cost of the additional purchases because the monopsonist must spend more on both the marginal unit and all preceding units. As a result, the monopsonist's **marginal expenditure curve** lies above the supply curve (just as the monopolist's marginal revenue curve lies below the demand curve). For example, suppose a monopsonist could hire 10 workers if it paid $10 per hour, for a total expenditure of $100. If it must pay $11 per hour to hire 11 workers, its total expenditure rises to $121, and the marginal expenditure is $21, much more than the $11 wage.

In Figure 10.1, the demand curve shows the monopsonist's marginal benefit. In a labor market, this is the firm's marginal revenue product (MRP_L)—or labor demand—curve. The monopsonist hires workers until MRP_L equals ME. Just as the monopolist determines the price it charges by looking up to the demand curve, the monopsonist determines the price it pays by looking down to the supply curve. Thus, the monopsony price in Figure 10.1 is w_m, not the competitive wage w_c. In the graph, the ME curve cuts the MRP_L curve at point R, and the monopsony level of employment is L_m. If the labor market were competitive, firms would hire L_c workers, which is where the marginal revenue from the last worker equals the competitive wage (w_c). Thus, monopsony results in lower wages and lower employment than in a competitive market. It also results in a deadweight loss (the area rst). Monopsony power was once a cornerstone of professional sports for all players, regardless of their tenure in the league.

The Impact of Rival Leagues

Just as a firm's monopoly power can be undermined by the entry of competing producers, its monopsony power can be undermined by the entry of competing employers. Salary increases caused by competition from rival leagues have occurred in all major US sports leagues. The appearance of the American League as a rival to the National League in 1901 caused the salaries of baseball players to rise sharply. The fear of higher salaries attending the entry of the Federal League led Connie Mack to sell off the star players from a powerful Philadelphia Athletics baseball club in 1915, from which it took the A's over a decade to recover.

Since its merger with the American Football League in 1969, the NFL has faced several rival leagues. The most serious challenges were posed by the World Football League, in 1974 and 1975, and the United States Football League (USFL), from 1983 through 1985. Between 1982 and 1986, the average salary in the NFL almost doubled as a direct result of the USFL's attempt to lure away players.

Similar "wars" drove up salaries when the ABA challenged the NBA in the 1960s and 1970s, and when the WHA opposed the NHL in the 1970s. Between 1970 and 1976, when the WHA actively competed against the NHL for players, salaries in the NHL more than tripled. One study found that the pay in the NHL rose so much that players received more than their marginal revenue product.[3]

International soccer is particularly susceptible to the impact of rival leagues, as each country has its own league or set of leagues.[4] This makes it particularly difficult for any one league to limit the salaries it pays. If Serie A in Italy tries to limit salaries, players can go to the EPL in England or the Bundes-liga in Germany. Even continent-wide confederations have limited power. If UEFA tries to limit salaries throughout Europe, players could easily flee to MLS in the United States or China's Super League. Monopsony power is thus much less an issue for international soccer than it is for the North American sports leagues.

The Reserve Clause

As noted in Chapter 4, we can trace the formation of the National League in baseball to its exerting monopsony power over players through the reserve clause. Prior to the reserve clause, professional baseball players moved freely from team to team, sometimes jumping contracts in the middle of the season.[5] This changed in 1876. Envious of the success of the Boston Red Stockings, William Hulbert, the financial backer of the Chicago White Stockings, lured away four of Boston's star players (and one from Philadelphia) late in the 1875 season. In a remarkable display of chutzpah, Hulbert then appealed to the other backers to create a new system that would, among other things, stop the bidding war for players. This *coup d'état* overthrew baseball's existing structure, the National Association of Professional Base Ball Players. The name of the new organization, the National League of Professional Baseball Clubs, was highly significant. Prior to Hulbert's coup, players' associations had run baseball. Now the clubs, and their owners, reigned supreme, and the players occupied a secondary position.[6]

Just how secondary became apparent in 1887, when the owners unveiled what had been an implicit "gentlemen's agreement" for the previous decade. With the formation of the National League, each owner had reserved the rights to five players' services for as long as he wanted them.[7] By 1889, teams were reserving their entire roster and had written the following "reserve clause" into the standard player's contract:

> if, prior to March 1, . . . the player and the club have not agreed upon the terms of such contract [for the next playing season], then on or before ten days after said March 1, the club shall have the right to renew this contract for the period of one year on the same terms except that the amount payable to the player shall be such as the club shall fix in said notice.[8]

On the surface, the clause seems innocuous. It restricted a player to his team for the length of the contract plus, if the team renewed the existing contract, one additional year of service. The catch lies in the owners' interpreting the right to "renew this contract . . . on the same terms" as renewing all the terms of the contract, including the reserve clause, thus binding the player to the team for yet another year. Using this recursive system, a team could prevent a player from selling his services for as long as it wanted to keep him. Leagues in other sports saw the value of the reserve clause in keeping down costs and copied this clause almost word for word in their own standard contracts.

With no other employer able to bid away the services of their players, teams drove down players' salaries to levels that just kept them in the sport. While players today can afford to support small entourages, even the stars of an earlier time had to hold second jobs. Imagine walking into an appliance store and buying a washing machine from Clayton Kershaw. In 1951, you could have done just that from Jackie Robinson.[9]

The monopsony power conferred on owners by the reserve clause left major league baseball players in an extremely weak position. In an effort to improve their bargaining power, players formed the Major League Baseball Players Association (MLBPA) in 1953. In 1968, the MLBPA negotiated its first collective bargaining agreement (CBA) with the league. Players in the other major leagues have formed similar associations—the National Basketball Players Association (NBPA), the National Hockey League Players Association (NHLPA), and the National Football League Players Association (NFLPA)—all of which are unique forms of unions. A **union** is an organization of workers who agree to act collectively to improve their wages, benefits, and working conditions. In the next section, we show how unions can counteract the monopsony power of team owners.

10.2   Unions in Professional Sports

Unions have played a steadily decreasing role in the private sector of the US economy. In 2015, only 11.1 percent of all employed wage and salary workers were union members, less than half their representation in the early 1980s.[10] American unions have been in steady decline since the early 1950s, when they represented about one-third of the US labor force. Globalization, technological advances, and demographic changes of the workforce (particularly the growing participation of women) have all contributed to the decline. In contrast, union representation in the major sports leagues remains at or near 100 percent. In this section, we examine the impact that unions have had on the labor market for professional athletes.

A Brief Introduction to the Economics of Unions

Unions typically fall into one of two categories: craft unions and industrial unions. **Craft unions** are by far the older of the two. Their origins date back to the medieval guilds, groups of skilled artisans who joined together to prevent others from entering their city to undercut their prices. Modern craft unions consist of workers who share a common skill. For example, it is easy to guess what the members of the International Brotherhood of Electrical Workers do or what task the members of the Screen Actors Guild perform.

Industrial unions are much younger than craft unions. Workers formed these unions in response to the harsh conditions they confronted with the rise of large employers in the 19th century. Partly because they opposed the entrenched interests of their employers, organizers of industrial unions faced greater hostility than did organizers of craft unions. Industrial unions take their names from the types of output they produce, such as the United Auto Workers or the United Steel Workers. Unlike craft unions, industrial unions represent arrays of workers who perform very different tasks.

The different organizational structures of the two types of unions cause them to use different tactics on behalf of their members.[11] Craft unions increase wages by limiting access to the union and to skills. Firms do not hire workers in a craft union. Instead, the union assigns workers to employers through a (literal or figurative) hiring hall. In effect, they make the labor supply curve vertical at the restricted size of the labor pool, as seen in Figure 10.2a. The result is a union wage $\left(w^u\right)$ that exceeds the competitive wage.

Industrial unions represent workers with many different skills. As a result, they leave hiring and firing to the employer. Like craft unions, industrial unions push up wages, but they do so through collective bargaining. In **collective bargaining,** unions meet with employers to produce an agreement that may specify pay, employment levels, and other working conditions. Roster size, for example, is determined by collective bargaining between owners and players' associations. Industrial unions induce employers to accept their demands by engaging in or threatening to engage in strikes. A **strike** occurs when workers act together to remove the labor input from the production process. A **lockout** occurs when the management of the firm does not permit the labor input to operate. The need to stage or threaten a damaging strike means that industrial unions derive their strength from being inclusive. The union cannot succeed unless the firms' employees remain loyal to the union during a strike. This contrasts with craft unions, whose power comes from being exclusive and keeping out competing workers. Figure 10.2b shows that industrial unions seek to push wages above the competitive level.[12]

Opponents of unions assert that unions create inefficiency in the economy. They say that unions limit employment and production, thereby harming the economy. Higher wages mean higher costs of production, which puts domestic producers at a competitive disadvantage and encourages producers to relocate abroad.

Union supporters counter that unions, particularly industrial unions, often operate in industries where monopsonies already restrict employment and create deadweight loss. In such situations, unions can be a countervailing force against the monopsony power of employers, forcing employers to pay workers their marginal revenue product and—perhaps—making the labor market more closely resemble a competitive market.

Unions can also provide an important outlet for workers that improves efficiency. Unions formalize grievance procedures by workers, giving them a way to express their concerns to employers and allowing employers to respond to the needs of their workforce, thereby reducing conflict in the workplace. The recent concussion controversy is an example of the role a union can play in protecting workers. With good reason, players do not always trust their teams to prioritize player safety. However, players' emphasis on "toughness" and fear for their jobs often make them reluctant to call attention to injuries. Unions can play an important role here, pushing for rules—such as the NFL's concussion protocol—to protect players when no one player or team is willing to do so.[13] By protecting workers and preventing conflict, unions increase the MRP_L and shift the demand for labor to the right. The higher MRP_L increases the equilibrium level of employment and justifies the higher wage that union workers receive.

Figure 10.3 shows what happens when a monopoly union confronts a monopsony employer, a situation called **bilateral monopoly.** In this case, the wage falls into an indeterminate range between the union wage and the monopsony wage. In Figure 10.3, the union wants to set the quantity of labor employed at the level where the marginal revenue of adding a union employee (MR) intersects the supply of labor (S). The monopoly wage, w^u, is determined by looking up from this intersection to the demand curve for labor. The monopsonist wants to set the quantity of labor where the marginal expense on the last worker (ME) equals the marginal revenue product $(MRP = D)$ of the last worker. The monopsony wage w^m comes from looking down to the supply curve of labor. Unless one side can impose its will on the other, the precise settlement lies somewhere between w^u and w^m in Figure 10.3 and depends on the bargaining strength of the two sides.

In 1950, Nobel laureate John Nash developed a model to solve this type of bargaining problem, which continues to be the basis for much of the work on bargaining. One of Nash's central findings was that a group's bargaining power stems from its ability to walk away from the bargaining table. Nash called the

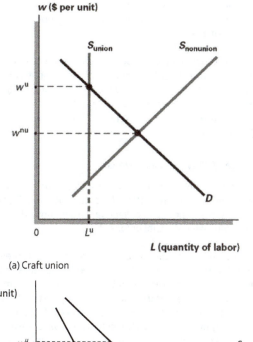

(a) Craft union

Figure 10.2
Effect of Unions on Wages

Craft and industrial unions both
cause wages to rise, but they do
so in different ways.

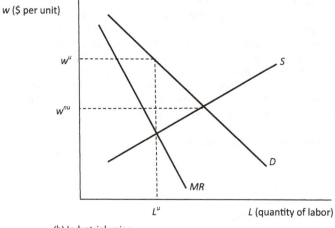

(b) Industrial union

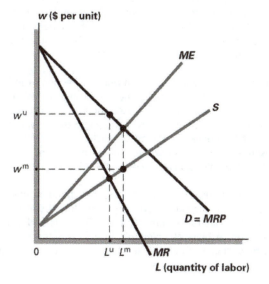

Figure 10.3
Bilateral Monopoly

In a bilateral monopoly, the wage
lies somewhere between the
monopsony wage and the union
wage. The outcome depends on
the two sides' bargaining power.

value of each side's alternative activity its **threat point**. The more valuable the threat point for either side, the greater its bargaining power and the more favorable a solution it can achieve.

If, for example, the employer has a readily available source of labor (perhaps due to high unemployment rates), the benefits of permanently dissolving its relationship with the union may be very high. All else equal, this allows the firm to drive a harder bargain and reach a lower wage settlement. Alternatively, if union workers have high-paying jobs awaiting them elsewhere, their threat point and the resulting wage both rise.

The Unique Role of Player Associations

Professional sports unions do not readily fit into any of the categories outlined above. On one hand, they represent workers with similar skills, like craft unions. On the other hand, they engage in collective bargaining with employers who do the hiring and firing, like industrial unions.

Sports unions are unlike all other unions in two ways. First, they do not engage in wage negotiations. Instead, they bargain over the general framework within which individual players and their agents negotiate with teams.[14] Second, the major sports unions and the leagues with which they negotiate sometimes advocate positions that differ from those of other unions or firms. For example, in the aftermath of the 1998–1999 lockout, the NBA imposed a fixed salary scale on players over the objections of the union, which advocated a free market. These stances are diametrically opposed to those taken by most firms and unions. Typically, unions push for salary scales, and firms want salaries to be set by the market. In this case, the employers were advocating a mechanism that would save them from their own undisciplined spending.

For decades, all four players' associations strove for free agency so their players could receive competitive wages. In Section 10.3, we describe how the player associations accomplished that goal and how the leagues have tried to maintain their economic power.

Professional Associations

Individual sports, such as tennis or golf, also have associations that represent the interests of the players. These unions differ from those in the team sports in several important ways. This section examines the unique aspects of the unions representing men and women tennis players. It also points out some differences in the goals of the men's and women's unions.

In 1968, the first year of "open" tennis, in which professionals and amateurs could both compete, the prize for winning the men's singles at Wimbledon was only £2,000. By 2016, the prize had risen to £2,000,000, an increase of 999 percent. The prizes in women's tennis rose even more spectacularly, growing from £750 to equality with the men at £2,000,000.[15] Much of the increase can be attributed to the presence of two organizations, the Association of Tennis Professionals (ATP) and the Women's Tennis Association (WTA).

These two associations differ significantly from the associations we have discussed thus far. First, they are relatively young. Until the late 1960s, the Grand Slam events—the Australian, French, and US Opens and Wimbledon—were known as Championships (Wimbledon's official name is the "All England Lawn Tennis Championship") and were restricted to amateurs. The participants were largely well-to-do men and women who played tennis for a few years before going on to what they regarded as their adult lives.[16] When these tournaments welcomed professional players, a wider array of people sought to make a living by playing tennis.[17] While recognition by the Grand Slam tournaments conferred prestige on professional tennis, even today only a few tennis players would be able to make a living on their winnings from that handful of major events. The players needed a body that would represent their interests to venues and sponsors that wanted to hold professional tournaments. Unfortunately, the tournament committees at the time had been created by and for amateur players and were either inexperienced at dealing with professionals or openly hostile toward them. To fill this void, the men formed the ATP in 1972 and the women formed the WTA a year later.

Unlike the unions we have encountered so far, the ATP and WTA closely resemble craft unions. Like craft unions, the ATP and WTA define who is and is not a qualified employee. As we saw in Figure 10.2, craft unions increase the pay of their members by restricting the supply curve of labor. Like firms that come to a hiring hall to obtain labor, venues that wish to establish tournaments obtain different classes of labor by applying to the unions for a tournament of a given status. Higher-status tournaments with higher payments and better benefits receive higher-quality players. Because they sanction the events in which players take part, the ATP and WTA have become synonymous with the men's and women's professional tennis tours.

Like other unions in team sports, the ATP and WTA do not specify how much tournaments pay specific players. They do, however, establish the reward structure of the tournaments, so all players know what they will earn from a particular performance. They also negotiate all aspects of the "working conditions" of each tournament, from the types of hotel rooms the players occupy, to the uniforms of the "ballpersons" to the nature of the bathroom facilities in the locker rooms. The ATP and WTA rulebooks, which specify these regulations, are themselves significant. They take the place of the collective bargaining agreements that the major North American team sports negotiate. The difference stems from the fact that the ATP and WTA do not engage in negotiations with a single management group. Instead, they set rules for sponsors who wish to stage a tournament, much like construction unions (a typical craft union) set rules for developers who wish to construct offices or apartment buildings.

Also unlike most other unions, the ATP and WTA are strictly segregated by gender. In part, this is because men and women do not play against one another (except in mixed doubles). In fact, except for the Grand Slams and a few other similar events, men and women do not even compete in the same venues. Moreover, the needs of women who play tennis professionally differ significantly from the needs of men. The WTA, for example, specifies how long a woman may retain her status on the tour after having a child, while the ATP rulebook makes no mention of paternity leave.[18]

10.3   Free Agency

Baseball players initially felt honored by being subject to the reserve clause because it formally recognized them as the top players on the team. Once the impact of the reserve clause on salaries became clear, players in all leagues vehemently opposed it. Rather than face a monopsony employer as depicted in Figure 10.1, they used collective action to advocate for the more favorable outcome in Figure 10.3. Eventually, the unions in all four sports overturned the reserve clause. Three unions did so through the court system, and, as we will see, one union outmaneuvered the owners.

The Advent of Free Agency

Football players were the first to achieve free agency, though they were the last to take advantage of it. The Supreme Court's 1957 *Radovich v. National Football League* concluded that football—unlike baseball—was interstate commerce and therefore was subject to the antitrust laws. The decision categorically rejected NFL teams' right to reserve players.

Despite this resounding court victory, players had to wait another 35 years for true free agency. At first, NFL team owners responded by entering into an informal "gentlemen's agreement" not to pursue each other's players. When this broke down in the early 1960s, NFL commissioner Pete Rozelle unilaterally imposed the "Rozelle rule," which stated:

> Whenever a player, becoming a free agent in such manner thereafter signed a contract with a different club in the league, then unless mutually satisfactory arrangements have been concluded between the two League clubs, the Commissioner may name and then award to the former club one or more players from the Active, Reserve, or Selection List (including future selection choices of the acquiring club as the Commissioner in his sole discretion deems fair and equitable); any such decisions by the Commissioner shall be final and conclusive.[19]

The Rozelle rule thus recognized the players' right to free agency in theory but killed it in practice. The rule turned signing a free agent into a trade in which the team had no control over the players it would lose. A form of the Rozelle rule survived until 1992, when a US District Court ruled in *McNeil et al. v. National Football League* that the rule violated antitrust laws.[20]

The reserve clauses in professional hockey and basketball were both overturned as the result of competition from rival leagues. In 1972, the World Hockey Association (WHA) sued the NHL for violating antitrust laws when the NHL tried to block players from jumping to the WHA. The resulting ruling (*Philadelphia World Hockey Club v. Philadelphia Hockey Club*) struck down the NHL's reserve clause.

In the NBA, the players, rather than a rival league, brought an antitrust lawsuit. Oscar Robertson, a star player and president of the National Basketball Players Association (NBPA), sued the league (*Robertson v. NBA*) in response to the NBA's attempt to end a costly war with the rival American Basketball Association through a partial merger. Faced with an unfavorable court ruling and the prospect of continued rivalry with the ABA, the NBA dropped its appeal of the Robertson case in 1976 and agreed to phase in free agency.

Unlike players in other sports, baseball players could not gain free agency through the courts. The 1922 Supreme Court's *Federal Baseball* decision gave MLB a blanket exemption from antitrust laws. Even though subsequent rulings recognized the absurdity of the *Federal Baseball* decision, the high court repeatedly upheld the monopsony power of baseball teams (e.g., *Toolson v. New York Yankees* in 1953, and *Flood v. Kuhn* in 1971).

The MLBPA was able to overthrow the reserve clause by outsmarting the owners rather than by suing them. Prior to 1970, players filed all their grievances with the Commissioner, who typically sided with the owners. In the 1970 contract negotiations, Marvin Miller, the MLBPA's Executive Director, got the owners to replace the Commissioner with a three-person panel, with one member appointed by the owners, one member appointed by the union, and one member drawn from a mutually agreed-upon list. The owners agreed to a panel after Miller assured them that it would deal only with trifling monetary matters. Then-Commissioner Bowie Kuhn would have the final say in all overarching matters that affected the integrity of the game. By couching its challenge to the reserve clause as a financial matter, the MLBPA was able to force the issue of free agency into the hands of an outside arbitrator, who ruled in favor of the players (and who was promptly dismissed by the owners).[21]

Forms of Free Agency

While the idea of **free agency**—the right of a player to sign with any team that offers him a contract—is universal, each sports league restricts when and how a player becomes a free agent. The collective bargaining agreements contain long lists of qualifications and exceptions that establish the rules for free agency.[22] Before we focus on the economic implications of the restrictions of free agency, we summarize its various forms.

Some sports have two different levels of free agency. Most fans who discuss free agents are actually thinking of unrestricted free agents. An **unrestricted free agent** is a player with no strings attached; he is free to sign with any team that makes him an offer.

In MLB, a player can become an unrestricted free agent after six years of service at the major league level. In the NHL, most players become unrestricted free agents based on the *27 or 7 rule*. A player becomes an unrestricted free agent once he has reached age 27 or has given 7 years of service and his contract has expired. In the NBA, players can become unrestricted free agents after four years if they are not first-round draft picks, or if they are first-round picks and their team does not extend a qualifying offer. NFL players become unrestricted free agents following their fourth year of service if their contract has expired.

Restricted free agents are free to solicit offers from other teams but not to sign with them. If the player signs an offer sheet with another team, his original team has the **right of first refusal**, meaning it can retain the player by matching the other team's offer. To become a restricted free agent, a player must first receive a qualifying offer from his original team. Players who do not receive a qualifying offer immediately become unrestricted free agents.

While restricted free agency allows players to "test the market" to see how much their services are worth to other teams, it does not allow them to decide where they will play. In addition, the fact that the original team can match any offers may reduce the size or number of offers a restricted free agent receives. We discuss some of the empirical findings on this topic later in the chapter.

In the NFL, a player with three years of experience can become a restricted free agent if his contract has expired. In the NBA, a first-round draft pick can become a restricted free agent after his fourth year. Players who were not first-round picks can become restricted free agents when their initial contracts expire. The

NHL has a dizzying array of criteria related to a player's age and level of experience. For example, a player whose contract has expired, who first signed a contract when he was 18–21 years old, and who has three years of experience can become a restricted free agent. The experience requirement is shorter for players who signed their initial contracts when they were older. The MLB player agreement does not include restricted free agent status, though MLB and the NHL have an important intermediate step between reserved status and unrestricted free agency known as salary arbitration.

The Franchise Tag

In most sports, being called a "franchise player" would be a source of pride. It would designate a player as more than a star—as the very foundation of his team's success. In the NFL, however, few if any players care for the title, as it brings a restriction on salary.

The NFL instituted the "franchise tag" in 1993 as a way to limit the movement of free agents.[23] There are three kinds of tags. Most "franchise players" receive the **non-exclusive franchise tag**. This player receives a 1-year contract that pays him at least the average salary of the five highest-paid players at his position over the last five years or 120 percent of his salary in the previous year, whichever is greater. The player may negotiate with other teams, but the team that tags him retains the right of first refusal on any offer sheet he receives. If the team chooses not to match the salary offer, it receives two additional draft choices as compensation.

The **exclusive franchise tag** has been used only twice since 2012 (for Drew Brees in 2012 and Von Miller in 2016). This player does not have the right to seek offers from other teams. In return, the team must pay him the average of the top five salaries at his position in the current year or 120 percent of his previous salary, whichever is greater.

Finally, the **transition tag** guarantees a player the average of the ten highest-paid players at his position. It is a non-exclusive offer, so players may sign offer sheets from other teams. The original team receives no compensation if it chooses not to match the outside offer. A team may tag only one player per year. Teams can cancel the tag, but they may not then tag a different player. A player may refuse the designation and become an unrestricted free agent after sitting out one year.

At first glance, the franchise tag seems to favor players, as it guarantees them one of the highest salaries in the league. It can, however, significantly reduce the salaries of top players. Although the limit is for only one year, the chance that a player could be injured or see his performance decline means that the player's future salary could be severely reduced as well. Finally, restricting the salaries of the top players allows the NFL to reduce the pay scale for players throughout the league. It is little wonder that players have come to resent the franchise tag and sometimes threaten to sit out a season rather than accept its limitations.

Salary Arbitration

Before players become free agents, teams can exert monopsony power, confronting them with the "take it or leave it" offer depicted in Figure 10.1. MLB and NHL players, however, can pass through an intermediate stage. Players in these two sports can submit disputes to salary arbitration. **Arbitration** occurs when parties to a dispute submit proposals to an **arbitrator**, a neutral third party who then suggests or imposes a resolution. Both baseball and hockey have **binding arbitration**, in which both sides commit to accepting the arbitrator's ruling. Outside the sports world, binding arbitration is particularly popular in the public sector. Fearing the consequences of a strike by police or firefighters, municipal officials often offer binding arbitration in exchange for the unions' accepting laws that prohibit them from striking.

Arbitration in the NHL Salary arbitration is open to NHL players who are eligible for restricted free agency. The players who file for arbitration and the teams for which they play both submit proposals based on such factors as the performance of the player, his contribution to the overall performance of the team, and the performance and pay of comparable players. The arbitrator has 48 hours to choose one of the proposals or to impose a decision of their own. One study shows that arbitration rulings in the NHL are roughly equivalent to what statistical analysis predicts the players will be worth to their teams.[24] Thus, arbitration aids efficiency in the NHL by imposing a resolution that players and teams would otherwise have trouble achieving.

Arbitration in the MLB MLB uses a different process, known as final offer arbitration. In **final offer arbitration (FOA)**, arbitrators cannot impose their own solutions; they must choose one of the two proposals submitted to them. The goal of FOA is to prevent the two parties from becoming addicted to arbitration. Arbitration addiction often results from the incentives facing the parties to binding arbitration. Arbitrators, who are generally well-compensated, do not wish to jeopardize their employment by appearing prejudiced toward one side or the other. As a result, they have an incentive to "split the difference" of the offers put in front of them. If the two parties to the negotiation recognize this tendency, they have little reason to compromise, as moderating their stance would lead the arbitrator to impose a less favorable ruling.[25] FOA reverses this incentive. Each party now wants to convince the arbitrator that its proposal is the more reasonable one. This forces the two sides to moderate their positions. Ideally, the two positions will move so close together that the two sides reach an agreement without recourse to arbitration. With few exceptions, FOA is open to all players with three to six years of major league experience. The criteria for FOA judgments are very similar to those used in hockey.

The results of the 2016 FOA proceedings support this view.[26] In 2016, 183 players were eligible for arbitration, but only 34 filed salary proposals. Of these, 30 settled their cases before reaching arbitration, with players winning 3 of the 4 cases that went to arbitration. Even in these 4 cases, FOA brought players and teams together, as the average disparity in the 4 sets of proposals was "only" $350,000, about 11.9 percent of the salary proposed by the team. In fact, Sean Dolinar shows that the differences in cases that went to FOA were far smaller than the differences in cases that were settled before arbitration. This makes sense because, when the proposals are so close together, there is very little for either side to lose in seeking arbitration. The cases that did not go to FOA all settled close to the midpoint of the proposals.

FOA has had a significant impact on player salaries. Former MLBPA Executive Director Marvin Miller went so far as to say that FOA has done more for player salaries than free agency. The evidence from recent history suggests that Miller might be correct in his assessment. In 2016, the 34 players who exchanged figures with their clubs received average raises of close to $3 million per year, an average raise of over 200 percent.

Measuring Monopsony Power

Despite the advent of free agency and salary arbitration, teams still exert a degree of monopsony power, particularly over players who have little experience. Economists measure the degree to which teams exploit their monopsony power by comparing the estimated value of a player (as measured by his MRP) with his wage.

There are two difficulties in determining whether a player is paid his marginal revenue product (MRP). First, we do not observe a player's MRP and instead must infer it from performance data and information about the city in which he plays. Second, in an era of multi-year contracts, a player's salary rarely reflects his MRP in any given year. Most studies get around these problems by using a methodology first proposed by Anthony Krautmann.[27] Krautmann starts by assuming that, in a competitive labor market, workers are paid their marginal revenue product. He then asserts that, in the context of professional sports, this relationship holds only for newly signed free agents. He then estimates the equation:

$$w_{it} = \beta_o + \beta_1 Perf_{it-1} + \beta_2 Z_{it} + \varepsilon_{it}$$

where $Perf_{it-1}$ is a vector of performance measures for free agent i in year $t-1$, Z_{it} is a set of control variables including variables pertaining to the size of the market in which the team plays in year t, w_{it} is player i's salary in year t, and ε_{it} is a random error term. This change transforms an equation in which the key variable is unobservable (MRP) into one in which the key variable is readily observable (w_{it}). Applying the resulting estimated coefficients to data for players who are not free agents allows us to compute an estimated MRP that can be compared to their wage to see whether the "restricted" players also receive salaries that equal their marginal revenue products. Using this methodology, Krautmann found that monopsony power allowed MLB teams to pay players only 25 percent of their value.

More recently, Krautmann, von Allmen, and Berri have compared the degree of monopsony power exercised by teams in baseball, basketball, and football. They find that considerable monopsony power remains, particularly for players with the least amount of experience. These players, whom they call "apprentices," are not eligible for arbitration or restricted free agency. They find that, on average, apprentices receive 66 percent of their MRP in the NBA, 50 percent of their MRP in the NFL, and only 19 percent of their MRP in MLB. "Journeyman" players, who are eligible for arbitration in baseball or restricted free agency in football,[28] did much better. In the NFL, they received 77 percent of their MRP. The impact of arbitration, or at least the threat of arbitration, was strongly felt in MLB, as journeyman players received 86 percent of their MRP. These results are supported by Humphreys and Pyun, who find that teams' ability to exploit monopsony power has remained largely unchanged for all players short of free agency since 2001.[29]

Salary Caps

Team owners claim that salary caps support competitive balance and stabilize the league by providing "cost certainty." Players denounce them as a way to push down salaries. Whatever the true motivation, all four North American sports leagues advocate caps, and three—the NHL, NBA, and NFL—now have them. MLB owners have repeatedly failed to impose one. In Chapter 5, we showed how salary caps affect competitive balance. Here we examine their impact on team payrolls.

The Salary Cap in the NBA

The NBA was the first league to impose a salary cap on its players. Unlike the reserve clause, the salary cap arose out of weakness rather than strength. During the 1970s, the salary war with the ABA and free agency pushed payrolls in the NBA to 70 percent of the league's gross revenues.[30] Prior to the 1984–1985 season, desperate team owners convinced the players to accept a salary cap as part of a revenue-sharing agreement that guaranteed players a percentage of league revenues. NBA owners credit the cap with saving the league in the 1980s.

Team owners were so convinced of the value of the cap that they locked out players in 1998–1999 and again in 2011 to tighten it. In 1999, the owners supplemented the payroll cap with a cap on individual salaries and imposed an escrow tax on salaries. The individual cap sets a salary scale for players based on their years of experience. In 2011, the owners reduced the players' share of revenues from 57 percent of basketball-related income (BRI) to between 49 and 51 percent.[31]

In a new 7-year agreement reached in late 2016, the NBA kept its players' share at 51 percent, though it allows more league revenue to be counted as BRI. Moreover, recent increases in TV revenue have allowed salaries to soar. In 2015–2016, team payrolls had to be less than $70 million, and the salaries of individual players with five years of experience could not exceed $14.75 million. In 2016–2017, maximum team payrolls were slightly over $94 million, with fifth-year player salaries limited to $16.41 million.[32]

The escrow tax enables the NBA to deal with two problems it faces. The first problem is common to all salary caps in that teams must set salaries before league revenue, and hence BRI, is fully determined. The second problem arises from the many exceptions to the NBA's cap, which allow team payrolls to exceed the official limit. The escrow tax has teams set aside 10 percent of each player's salary. If player salaries and benefits—regardless of the exceptions mentioned in Chapter 5—exceed 51 percent of BRI, then the funds in escrow are remitted to the league until the players receive only 51 percent of BRI. Otherwise, players receive the funds held in escrow at the end of the season.

The Salary Cap in the NHL

NHL owners felt so strongly about a salary cap that they locked out their players for the entire 2004–2005 season to get it and for much of the 2012–2013 season to tighten it. The current CBA guarantees players 50 percent of "hockey-related" revenue. In 2016–2017, this translated to a maximum payroll of $73 million per team.

Unlike the NBA, the NHL has a hard cap, which includes all salaries, signing bonuses, and performance bonuses. Individual salaries can be no more than 20 percent of the total payroll and may change by no more than 35 percent from year to year and by no more than 50 percent over the life of a player's contract. The NHL also has an escrow account to ensure that teams stay below the cap. The NHL's escrow rate, which can vary over the course of the season, was set at 15.5 percent of players' salaries at the start of the 2016–2017 season.

The Salary Cap in the NFL

The NFL negotiated a salary cap in 1994 with the National Football League Players Association (NFLPA) in response to the 1992 court ruling that had granted players free agency. Like the NHL, the NFL has a hard cap, in which almost all payments to players count against the cap.

The 2011 CBA, which expires in 2020, grants players varying shares of revenue depending on the source: 55 percent of national media revenue, 45 percent of NFL Ventures revenue, and 40 percent of aggregated local club revenue. Collectively, the clubs must spend 95 percent of the total cap value and, overall, the players' share must average at least 47 percent of revenues over the life of the agreement.[33]

Three factors complicate the NFL's salary cap computations. First, although NFL teams have 53 players on their active rosters, the salary cap applies only to the 51 highest-paid players. Second, the league allows teams to "carryover" unused salary cap space from one year to the next. Hence, a team that has $1 million in unused salary cap space in one year can exceed the league-wide cap by up to $1 million in the following year. Finally, the bonuses a team pays might or might not count toward its salary cap.

Bonuses have become an important part of player contracts in the NFL because football players generally do not have guaranteed contracts. A player who has signed a multiyear contract that is not guaranteed will not be paid if he does not make the team. This has led some teams to cut players with multiyear contracts and then sign them to much lower salaries a few days later. A large signing bonus (which is paid when the player agrees to his contract) or easily obtained incentive bonus can protect a player with a long-term contract by providing a source of guaranteed income. Signing bonuses, roster bonuses (paid if a player makes the team roster), workout bonuses (paid if the player attends off-season team workouts), and any bonus paid for meeting conditions that the player had also satisfied the previous year are all considered *likely to be earned* (LTBE) bonuses and count against the salary cap. However, the NFL allows teams to prorate them over the length of the contract rather than count them at the time they are paid. Thus, for cap purposes, a contract that pays a player $35 million in equal $7 million increments over 5 years is indistinguishable from one that pays the player a $15 million signing bonus and $4 million over 5 years.[34] Bonuses for meeting previously unmet goals (e.g., a running back's running for more yards than he has before) count as *not likely to be earned* (NLTBE) and do not count against the cap.

The Impact of Salary Caps

For all the importance placed on salary caps, they do not always limit what teams actually pay in a given year. Payroll data from *USA Today* indicate that the caps are more effective in some leagues than in others. In 2016, only 2 of the 32 NFL teams (the Minnesota Vikings and New York Jets) exceeded the cap of $128 million. NHL teams are not bound by the cap in the playoffs, perhaps when they are most important. The challenges brought about due to the soft cap in the NBA were most notable, as 21 of 30 NBA teams had payrolls over $94 million, and 16 teams had payrolls over $100 million.

In addition to lowering payrolls, salary caps have equalized spending by teams. Figure 10.4 illustrates the payrolls of the teams in the four major North American sports. The graph shows that the payrolls of teams in the three leagues that have salary caps are far more equal than the payrolls in MLB.

Even discounting the Los Angeles Dodgers, whose 2016 payroll exceeded that of the Boston Red Sox (third-highest in MLB) by almost the total amount of the Tampa Bay Rays' payroll, MLB has far greater variation than any other league. The highest NFL payroll would only rank tenth on the list of MLB payrolls despite the fact that MLB rosters are less than half as large as NFL rosters.

Not all the compression in the leagues with salary caps necessarily comes from lower payrolls. By guaranteeing players a share of league revenue, salary caps also set minimum payroll levels for each team. The minimum payroll provision in the NFL has an uncertain impact, as there is no penalty for failing to pay the

Figure 10.4
Payrolls for Teams in the Four Major Leagues

Source: MLB, NBA, NFL, and NHL salary data can be found at "USA Today Salaries Data Base," *USAToday.com,* at http://usatoday30.usatoday.com/sports/salaries/index.htm, viewed January 18, 2017.

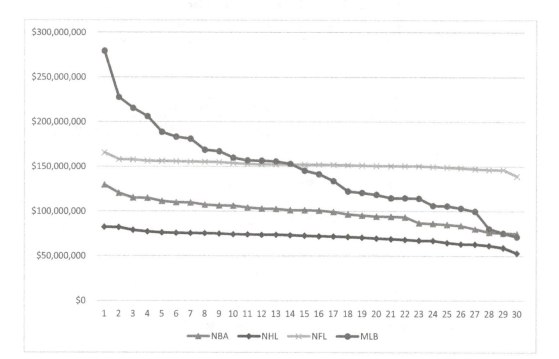

minimum. All a team has to do is increase its spending until it reaches the minimum.[35] Still, there does seem to be some compression at the bottom, as the lowest MLB payroll would rank last in every sport but the NHL, where it would rank 18th.

Luxury or Competitive Balance Taxes

In Chapter 5, we discussed the impact of luxury taxes on competitive balance. We revisit them here because they were implemented through collective bargaining and tend to reduce overall payrolls. The current MLB CBA set threshold levels for 2017 and 2018 at $195 million and $197 million, respectively. First-time violators of the threshold must pay a tax of 20 percent. The penalty increases to 30 percent and then 50 percent for teams that exceed the threshold the second and third (or more) times. There is also a surtax based on both the frequency and degree by which a team exceeds the threshold, which can add up to 45 percent to the tax rate. Teams over the threshold also lose picks in MLB's amateur draft and face restrictions on signing international players.[36] Tax revenue is not redistributed to untaxed teams. Instead, over 50 percent of the revenue is devoted to player benefits, the remainder going equally to MLB's Industry Growth Fund and to defraying teams' obligations to the MLB Players Benefit Plan.[37]

The NBA's luxury tax differs from the MLB tax in that up to half the tax revenues can be redistributed to the untaxed clubs, with the remainder used for unspecified "league purposes." The luxury tax threshold for the 2016–2017 season was $113.3 million. Teams exceeding this limit had to pay $1.50 for every dollar over the cap for the first $5 million and up to $3.25 for every dollar over the cap for all salaries in excess of $15 million above the cap.[38]

10.4 Conflict and Compromise in Collective Bargaining

Compared to the rest of the economy, labor relations in professional sports have been very contentious.[39] From 1972 through 1994, every renewal of the collective bargaining agreement in MLB was accompanied by a strike or lockout. As Table 10.1

Table 10.1 Labor Unrest in Professional Sports Since 1980

Year	MLB	NBA	NFL	NHL
1981	50-day strike			
1982			57-day strike	
1985	2-day strike			
1987			24-day strike	
1989	32-day lockout			
1992				10-day strike
1994–1995	232-day strike			103-day lockout
1998–1999		191-day lockout		
2004–2005				301-day lockout
2011		149-day lockout	132-day lockout	
2012–2013				119-day lockout

shows, each of the four major North American sports has experienced a work stoppage since 1980. Most recently, the NHL suffered a protracted work stoppage in 2012–2013. The lockout shortened the regular season to just 48 games.

At first glance, labor conflict seems inconsistent with the economic assumption that workers and firms behave rationally. Like wars and lawsuits, strikes and lockouts seem to waste resources. For example, the NHL's 301-day lockout in 2004–2005 is widely credited with the imposition of a salary cap. The settlement came, however, only after the cancellation of the entire season and the attendant loss of team revenue and player salaries. Both team owners and players would have been better off if they had agreed to implement a salary cap at the beginning of the season and avoided the loss of income.

In 2004, NHL owners entered negotiations determined to install a salary cap, while the players were equally determined to avoid one. Thus, in the words of Paul Staudohar, "the dispute was more about each side's philosophical approach than numbers."[40] As we have seen, when the parties disagree over broad issues, they are less flexible in their positions and more uncertain about the implications of their positions. Seeking to avoid a strike during the postseason, when the players' leverage would be greatest, the owners locked out the players at the start of the 2004–2005 season. With neither side willing to budge, the standoff resulted in the cancellation of the season.

Economic Theory and Labor Conflict

Economists reconcile strikes with rational behavior by acknowledging the role played by uncertainty. Uncertainty affects negotiations in one of two ways. If one side is overly pessimistic—either because it underestimates its own bargaining power or because it overstates the power of its opposition—it may settle for a less favorable agreement than it could have reached. If the participant errs on the side of optimism—overestimating its own bargaining power or understating the power of its opposition—conflict may result. Unduly optimistic perceptions of reality can prevent one or both parties from making the necessary concessions in time to prevent conflict. Uncertainty might be aggravated by a mistrust of the other side. If one party has reason to mistrust its counterpart, then it runs the risk of disregarding a truthful position.

If both labor and management know exactly how far they can push the other side, they can typically reach a settlement without resorting to conflict. Figure 10.5 illustrates how this might come about. In the figure, the union wants to push wages higher, while the employer wants to drive wages lower. Unless labor and the employer are better off separating permanently, each side will be willing to accept a range of wages or salaries that is also acceptable to the other side. We have labeled this range of wages the **contract zone**.

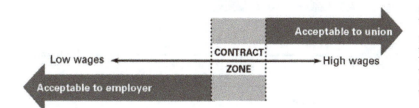

Figure 10.5
The Contract Zone

Unions try to find the highest wage that is acceptable to the firm. The firm tries to find the lowest wage that is acceptable to the union. The overlap of acceptable wages is the contract zone.

The position of the contract zone depends on the two sides' threat points. If the union's alternative opportunities improve, then its threat point corresponds to a higher wage, and the lower end of the contract zone rises, as shown in Figure 10.6a. If the firm has better alternatives, the upper end of the contract zone moves to a lower wage, as shown in Figure 10.6b.

The settlement depends on the bargaining strength of the two parties. A problem arises when workers, firms, or both do not know how far they can push the other side—or even how far they are willing to go themselves. When they are overly pessimistic, they are likely to concede too much and reach an unfavorable settlement.[41] When they are overly optimistic, neither side proposes a settlement in the contract zone, and conflict results, as illustrated in Figure 10.6c.

Figure 10.6
(a) Contract Zone with Powerful Union, (b) Contract Zone with Powerful Employer, (c) Mistaken Perceptions about the Contract Zone

The contract zone shifts left or right depending on the bargaining strengths of the union and the firm. If the firm mistakenly believes the union will accept a wage below the contract zone (or the union believes the firm will accept a higher wage), conflict might result.

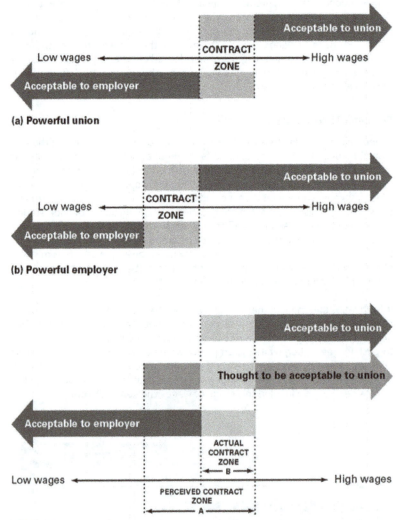

Labor Conflict and Professional Sports

Because sports leagues and unions negotiate broad frameworks rather than dollars and cents issues, such as wages and salaries, they face greater uncertainty and greater risk of conflict than other sectors of the economy. Most unions are legally prohibited from negotiating over "basic entrepreneurial decisions," which are the responsibility of management. Entrepreneurial decisions, such as revenue sharing and league expansion or contraction, however, are often at the heart of negotiations in professional sports.[42] For example, the NFLPA staged two strikes in the 1980s in an attempt to get the NFL to agree to free agency, which would have revolutionized the way in which salaries were determined. The high stakes involved led both sides to take more extreme positions than they otherwise would have. They also caused both sides to be less certain about the implications of their bargaining positions than would have been the case if they had been haggling over whether starting quarterbacks should be paid $5 million or $6 million per year.

The MLBPA often faced a unique source of uncertainty. Because baseball teams rely so heavily on local revenue, the owners often disagreed among themselves on the goals and strategies in their negotiations with the union. Big-market teams, such as the Yankees and Dodgers, were reluctant to implement changes designed to level the financial playing field. The big-market teams also lost much more gate and media revenue from a labor stoppage. As a result, they were eager to avoid prolonged conflict. Small-market teams, such as the Kansas City Royals or Milwaukee Brewers, had very different incentives. They pushed for limits to the financial advantages of big-market teams and were willing to endure long work stoppages to implement such limits. The conflicting goals of the teams made it hard for MLB ownership to present a coherent bargaining position, which made it hard for the union to know where the other side stood.[43] The relative peace in MLB since the strike of 1994–1995 is due in part to the harmony that former MLB Commissioner Bud Selig instilled among the owners.

Strikes are particularly likely if the parties do not trust one another. Unfortunately, mistrust has been a frequent feature of labor relations in professional sports. Jerry McMorris, the former owner of the Colorado Rockies, once said of baseball's negotiations, "I never would have believed the level of mistrust and lack of confidence in each other. . . . It made it very difficult for people to compromise or experiment."[44]

The mistrust is sometimes well-founded. For example, the NHL's 103-day work stoppage in 1994–1995 was due in part to the ill-will created by one man: Alan Eagleson. As director of the NHLPA since its inception in 1967, Eagleson was supposed to represent the interests of the players. However, he frequently pursued other interests at the expense of the players he supposedly represented. While director of the NHLPA, Eagleson was an agent for many players and favored them over players who had other agents. Even players who had him as an agent were often not well-represented. Eagleson ensured that Bobby Orr, the great Boston Bruins player, went to the Chicago Blackhawks as a free agent by failing to convey the Bruins' final offer (which included part-ownership of the team) to Orr. Most serious was Eagleson's role as director of a foundation that staged international hockey exhibitions, such as the Canada Cup series. Eagleson convinced NHL players to participate in these exhibitions without pay by assuring them that a percentage of revenue had been earmarked for the NHLPA pension fund. However, a 1989 investigation showed that the owners used the Canada Cup funds to replace their own contributions, all with Eagleson's knowledge and approval. The NHLPA successfully sued the NHL for $50 million, and Eagleson, who resigned under fire from the NHLPA in 1992, was imprisoned for fraud and mail fraud.[45]

Negotiations between NHL players and owners in the mid-1990s were doomed from the beginning. First, the two sides were negotiating large, defining issues, such as the creation of a salary cap. Second, both sides faced increased uncertainty due to the recent naming of Gary Bettman as NHL Commissioner and Bob Goodenow as Executive Director of the NHLPA. Finally, the players entered the negotiations bitter over their betrayal by Eagleson and mistrustful of owners who had misallocated their pension funds. The two sides were unable to reach an agreement, and the 1994–1995 season began without a contract in place. Fearful that the players would strike on the eve of the playoffs, when their leverage would be greatest (and when they had held a 10-day strike in 1992), the owners staged a preemptive lockout.

Biographical Sketch

Marvin Miller
(1917–2012)

> Man, don't the owners know that there's going to be a whole generation of ballplayers' sons who grow up with the middle name Marvin?
> —New York Yankees pitcher Rudy May[46]

When reporters first asked Marvin Miller why he had gone from being chief economist of the United Steelworkers (USW), one of the nation's foremost unions, to heading a ragtag players' association that did not even have a permanent office, he had a simple response for them: "'I grew up in Brooklyn,' I said, 'not far from Ebbets Field.' . . . Heads nodded. No further explanation was required."[47] Further explanation *is* required, however, of a man who almost single-handedly overthrew the powers of one of the most powerful monopsonies in America and transformed the face of professional sports. In so doing, Marvin Miller evolved from a man who might be the subject of an occasional dissertation on the history of unions to one of the towering figures in professional sports.

Miller did grow up in the shadow of Ebbets Field, the son of a storekeeper and a teacher in the New York public school system. He got his first taste of labor relations during World War II when he worked at the National War

Labor Board, which adjudicated union–management disputes as part of labor's pledge not to impede the war effort by going on strike.

After the war, Miller worked at a variety of jobs with little clear direction when, in 1950, Otis Brubaker, the research director at the United Steelworkers and an acquaintance from the National War Labor Board, asked Miller to join his staff at the USW. Miller found a home at the USW and worked his way up to become the USW's chief economist and assistant to the union's president, David J. McDonald. Ironically, Miller's most notable accomplishment at USW was to create a "productivity sharing plan" at Kaiser Steel that became a model for promoting good union–management relations and preventing conflict.

In 1965, however, I.W. Abel defeated McDonald in a hotly contested union election that centered on McDonald's reliance on "technicians," such as Miller, rather than elected officials. With his future at USW uncertain, Miller was intrigued when several player representatives approached him about becoming the first full-time executive director of the Major League Baseball Players Association.

The road to becoming director was not smooth, as the player representatives voted to retain their part-time director, Robert W. Cannon, instead. When Cannon attached additional conditions to becoming full-time director, refusing, for example, to move from his office in Milwaukee to New York, the players turned to Miller as their second choice. Even then, Miller's selection was far from certain, as he had to secure the approval of the full membership. Egged on by owners who viewed him as a rabble-rousing union boss, the players were skeptical. The Cleveland Indians' manager, Birdie Tebbetts, openly asked Miller, "How can the players be sure you're not a Communist?" After a rocky start—Miller was voted down by the players at the Arizona spring training facilities 102–17 before being approved overwhelmingly by the players at the Florida camps—Miller quickly earned the players' approval and then their fierce devotion.

Miller viewed the MLBPA as a way to practice principles of democratic unionism that would have been hard to implement in a huge union such as the USW. He won the players' confidence not by using the sophisticated arguments that Ed Garvey used with the football players or by intimidating the players like Alan Eagleson did in hockey, but by listening. He made a point of meeting every player during spring training and meeting every team's player representative at least four times a year. These meetings, moreover, were not intended to rubber-stamp prearranged positions. They were often lengthy, untidy affairs with players arguing with Miller and each other at great length. The one rule that Miller imposed was that the players had to leave the meeting unified. "'Anything less than 100 percent is unacceptable,' was his unshakable motto."[48] The result was a union that managed to do what many thought impossible—overturn the reserve clause when it lacked any legal standing to do so.

Sources: James Dworkin. 1981. *Owners versus Players: Baseball and Collective Bargaining* (Boston, MA: Auburn House); Charles Korr. 1991. "Marvin Miller and the New Unionism in Baseball," in *The Business of Professional Sports,* ed. Paul Staudohar and James Mangan (Urbana: University of Illinois Press): 115–134; Miller. 1991. *A Whole Different Ballgame*; and Helyar. 1994. *Lords of the Realm.*

Summary

Labor markets in the four major North American sports leagues were marked by significant monopsony power for most of the 20th century. As the sole buyer, a monopsony can drive down the price it pays. The reserve clause, the main source of monopsony power, bound players to the team that held their contract for as long as the team wanted them.

By 1976, all four major North American sports had discarded the reserve clause and had adopted some form of free agency. Leagues have tried to limit the impact of free agency in a number of ways, including revenue sharing, salary caps, luxury taxes, and the reverse-order draft. Salary caps in particular have proven effective at limiting player salaries and reducing the differences in team payrolls.

Unions in professional sports provide a counterbalance to the monopsony power of leagues. Unlike unions elsewhere in the economy, unions in professional sports have proven remarkably successful at organizing their workforce. Player associations in team sports have elements of both craft and industrial unions. In some ways, such as the determination of individual salaries, they resemble neither. Some sports unions have been more successful than others at promoting their members' interests. Tennis unions more closely resemble craft unions, as they more closely set individual rewards. The sports industry has experienced far more labor conflict than have other labor markets. Economists have difficulty explaining conflict, as it seems to defy rational behavior. When one accounts for uncertainty, however, one can explain strikes as a mistake by one or both of the negotiating parties. When one or both sides in negotiation overestimate their own bargaining power or underestimate the power of the opposition, it may fail to make or accept a proposal in the contract zone.

Discussion Questions

1 Are professional athletes exploited today?
2 Are salary caps good for professional sports? Would you want to have a salary cap in your job? If your answers differ, how do you justify the different answers?
3 Are unions good or bad for professional sports?
4 Should the government step in when there is a strike or lockout in professional sports?

Problems

10.1 Give an economic interpretation of the deadweight loss that accompanies monopsony. What would eliminate this inefficiency?
10.2 Would a craft union or an industrial union be more inclined to argue against the designated hitter? Why?
10.3 Use supply and demand curves to show how the ATP and the WTA increased the prize money offered on the men's and women's professional tennis tours.
10.4 In what way are sports unions like craft unions? In what way are they like industrial unions? In what way do they differ from both?

10.5 Use what you have learned in this chapter to explain why "journeymen" in MLB earn 86 percent of their *MRP* while "apprentices" earn only 19 percent.

10.6 MLB has adopted final offer arbitration because it fears that regular binding arbitration is addictive. In what way can binding arbitration be addictive? Why isn't FOA addictive?

10.7 Explain how each of the following would affect the salaries in the NBA:
   a. The Chinese government creates a new basketball league to rival the NBA.
   b. A change in the tax laws reduces the profitability of owning a sports franchise.

10.8 How has the luxury tax discouraged the New York Yankees from signing free agents to high salaries?

10.9 What would happen to the contract zone between MLB and the MLBPA if Congress repealed MLB's exemption from the antitrust laws?

10.10 Suppose the NBPA had staged a strike at the depths of the Great Recession in 2009. What would economic conditions have done to the contract zones of the NBA and the NBPA?

Notes

1 Vincent quoted in *Cot's Baseball Contracts*, http://legacy.baseballprospectus.com/compensation/cots/2005/02/. Accessed October 17, 2017; Selig quoted in Andrew Zimbalist. 2013. *In the Best Interests of Baseball?* (Lincoln, NE: University of Nebraska Press): 135.

2 The average MLB salary was about $68,000 higher in 1980 and about $2 million higher in 2015. See Michael J. Haupert. 2015. "The Economic History of Major League Baseball," at https://eh.net/encyclopedia/the-economic-history-of-major-league-baseball/, viewed January 19, 2017; United Press International. 1982. "Average N.F.L. Salary Is $90,102, Survey Says," *New York Times*, January 29, at http://www.nytimes.com/1982/01/29/sports/average-nfl-salary-is-90102-survey-says.html, viewed May 25, 2012; Tom Gerencer. 2016. "How Much Money Do NFL Players Make?" *Money Nation*, January 5, at http://moneynation.com/how-much-money-do-nfl-players-make/, viewed December 18, 2016.

3 J.C.H. Jones and W.D. Walsh. 1987. "The World Hockey Association and Player Exploitation in the National Hockey League," *Quarterly Review of Economics and Business*, 27(2) Summer: 87–101.

4 See, for example, Stephen F. Ross. 2004. "Player Restraints and Competition Law throughout the World," *Marquette Sports Law Review*, 15(1), Fall: 49–62.

5 One of the institutional weaknesses of the Negro Leagues was the teams' inability to maintain stable rosters. The Pittsburgh Pirates got their name for allegedly "pirating away" two players from the Philadelphia Athletics of the American Association in 1891. See Harold Seymour. 1960. *Baseball: The Early Years* (New York: Oxford University Press): 251.

6 Seymour. 1960. *Baseball: The Early Years*: 80.

7 Perhaps not surprisingly, this was exactly the number that Hulbert had signed away in 1875.

8 Quoted from James Quirk and Rodney Fort. 1992. *Pay Dirt* (Princeton, NJ: Princeton University Press): 185.

9 John Helyar. 1994. *Lords of the Realm* (New York: Villard Books): 12.

10   Bureau of Labor Statistics. 2016. "Economic News Release: Union Members Summary," January 28, 6, https://www.bls.gov/news.release/union2.nro.htm, viewed December 18, 2016.

11   While workers and unions negotiate over many aspects of the job, we simplify the analysis by focusing solely on wages.

12   The NFLPA had difficulty maintaining unity during a strike due, in part, to racial divisions among players. See Cynthia Gramm and John Schnell. 1994. "Difficult Choices: Crossing the Picket Line during the 1987 National Football League Strike," *Journal of Labor Economics*, 12(1), January: 41–71.

13   SI Wire. 2016. "Drew Brees Says Concussion Safety Has to Be Driven by NFLPA," *Sports Illustrated*, October 4, at https://www.si.com/nfl/2016/10/05/drew-brees-saints-concussion-safety-peter-king-podcast#, viewed April 8, 2017.

14   The NFLPA has reserved the right to conduct salary negotiations in its collective bargaining agreement, but it has never exercised this right. See Paul Staudohar. 1996. *Playing for Dollars: Labor Relations and the Sports Business* (Ithaca, NY: ILR Press): 67.

15   Figures from "The Championships, Wimbledon: Prize Money per Programme," *Wimbledon.com*, at http://www.wimbledon.com/pdf/Wimbledon_Prize_Money_2016.pdf, viewed January 19, 2017.

16   See E. Digby Baltzell. 1995. *Sporting Gentlemen: Men's Tennis from the Age of Honor to the Cult of the Superstar* (New York: The Free Press), for an entertaining, if opinionated, history of men's tennis.

17   By the 1960s, tournaments were offering so many benefits and side payments that detractors called the players "shamateurs." See Baltzell. 1995. *Sporting Gentlemen*: 335–336.

18   ATP World Tour, "The 2017 ATP Official Rulebook," at http://www.atpworldtour.com/en/corporate/rulebook; and WTA. 2017. "2017 WTA Official Rulebook," at http://www.wtatennis.com/sites/default/files/rules2017.pdf, viewed October 18, 2017.

19   Quoted from the standard player contract in James Dworkin. 1981. *Owners versus Players: Baseball and Collective Bargaining* (Boston, MA: Auburn House): 250.

20   See, for example, Staudohar. 1996. *Playing for Dollars*: 82–83.

21   For a complete account, see Helyar. 1994. *Lords of the Realm*.

22   Interested readers can see the actual collective bargaining agreements at the player association websites for each league. These agreements contain complete details on the rules for both unrestricted and restricted free agency.

23   For more on the franchise tag, see Kevin Patra. 2017. "What to Know about NFL Franchise Tag Designations," *Around the NFL*, February 15, at http://www.nfl.com/news/story/0ap3000000785958/article/what-to-know-about-nfl-franchise-tag-designations, viewed April 9, 2017; and Dave DeLuca. 2017. "How the NFL Franchise Tag Works," *SportingNews*, February 27, at http://www.sportingnews.com/nfl/news/how-nfl-franchise-tag-works-exclusive-vs-non-exclusive-transition-difference/1w7mwh36nqnfw1qb7lne9t9kao, viewed April 9, 2017.

24   See James Lambrinos and Thomas D. Ashman. 2007. "Salary Determination in the National Hockey League: Is Arbitration Efficient?" *Journal of Sports Economics*, 8(2), April: 192–201.

25   For more on FOA and the addictive nature of binding arbitration, see Orley Ashenfelter and David Bloom. 1984. "Models of Arbitrator Behavior: Theory and Evidence," *American Economic Review*, 74(1), March: 111–124; David Bloom and Christopher Cavanaugh. 1987. "Negotiator Behavior under Arbitration," *American Economic Review*, 77(2), May: 353–358; and B. Jay Coleman, Kenneth Jennings, and Frank McLaughlin. 1993. "Convergence or Divergence in Final-Offer Arbitration in Professional Baseball," *Industrial Relations*, 32(2), April: 238–247.

26   See MLB Trade Rumors. 2016. "Arbitration Tracker for 2016," *MLB TradeRumors*, at http://www.mlbtraderumors.com/arbtracker2016, viewed December 18, 2016; and Sean Dolinar. 2016. "2016 MLB Arbitration Visualization," *Instagraphs*, January 19, 2016, at http://www.fangraphs.com/blogs/instagraphs/2016-mlb-arbitration-visualization, viewed December 18, 2016.

27 See Anthony Krautmann. 1999. "What's Wrong with Scully-Estimates of a Player's Marginal Revenue Product," *Economic Inquiry*, 37(2), April: 369–381.

28 The authors find that almost no players were restricted free agents in the NBA. See Anthony C. Krautmann, Peter von Allmen, and David Berri. 2009. "The Underpayment of Restricted Players in North American Sports Leagues," *International Journal of Sport Finance*, 4(3), August: 75–93.

29 Brad R. Humphreys and Hyunwoong Pyun. 2017. "Monopsony Exploitation in Professional Sport: Evidence from Major League Baseball Position Players, 2000–2011," *Managerial and Decision Economics*, 38(5), July: 676–688.

30 For a historical discussion of salary caps in the NFL and the NBA, see Staudohar. 1996. *Playing for Dollars*.

31 Scott Cacciola, "N.B.A. and Players' Union Agree to New Labor Deal," *New York Times*, December 14, 2016, at http://www.nytimes.com/2016/12/14/sports/basketball/nba-collective-bargaining-agreement.html.

32 Ken Berger. 2016. "NBA Free Agency Cheat Sheet: Everything You Need to Know," *CBSSports.com*, June 30, at http://www.cbssports.com/nba/news/nba-free-agency-cheat-sheet-everything-you-need-to-know/, viewed January 15, 2016. Rookies drafted in the first round are paid according to a pre-specified rookie salary scale. Under a limited set of performance and seniority criteria, players can earn slightly higher than the specified maximum. See Larry Coon, "Larry Coon's NBA Salary Cap FAQ," http://www.cbafaq.com/, viewed December 20, 2016.

33 The full agreement can be viewed at "Collective Bargaining Agreement," August 4, 2011, at https://nfllabor.files.wordpress.com/2010/01/collective-bargaining-agreement-2011-2020.pdf, viewed January 15, 2017.

34 If a player is released or traded, bonus payments that have not yet been earned are counted in the year in which the player was released. Because such payments go for players who are no longer with the team, they have come to be called "dead money."

35 Sander Philipse. 2015. "Salary Cap Floor Explained: It's Basically Irrelevant," *SB-Nation*, March 13, at http://www.bucsnation.com/2015/3/13/8208069/nfl-salary-cap-floor-explained-its-basically-irrelevant, viewed April 8, 2017.

36 David Schoenfeld. 2016. "Could Teams Actually Pay a 92 Percent Luxury Tax under the New CBA? Yes—and No," *ESPN.com*, December 2, at http://www.espn.com/blog/sweetspot/post/_/id/76736/how-luxury-tax-penalties-would-work-on-baseballs-biggest-payrolls, viewed January 18, 2017; and MLB, "Details of MLB, MLBPA Labor Agreement," *MLB.com*, December 4, 2016, at http://m.mlb.com/news/article/210125462/details-of-mlb-mlbpa-labor-agreement/, viewed January 18, 2017.

37 Rene Rismondo. 2016. "Basic Agreement," *MLBPlayers.com*, June 29, at http://www.mlbplayers.com/ViewArticle.dbml?DB_OEM_ID=34000&ATCLID=211043009.

38 Larry Coon. 2016. "NBA Salary Cap FAQ."

39 For a direct comparison, see James Quirk and Rodney Fort. 1999. *Hardball* (Princeton, NJ: Princeton University Press): 68.

40 Paul Staudohar. 2005. "The Hockey Lockout of 2004–2005," *Monthly Labor Report*, December: 26.

41 See, for example, Beth Hayes. 1984. "Unions and Strikes with Asymmetric Information," *Journal of Labor Economics*, 2(1), January: 57–84; and Michael A. Leeds. 1987. "Bargaining as Search Behavior under Mutual Uncertainty," *Southern Economic Journal*, 53(3), January: 677–684, for two different perspectives on the role uncertainty may play.

42 Robert N. Covington. 2003. "(How Much) Is the Law to Blame for Baseball's Turbulent Labor Relations?" *Journal of Sports Economics*, 4(4), November: 357–361.

43 See Paul Staudohar. 2003. "Why No Baseball Work Stoppage?" *Journal of Sports Economics*, 4(4), November: 362–366; Andrew Zimbalist. 2003. "Labor Relations in Major League Baseball," *Journal of Sports Economics*, 4(4), November: 332–355; and Helyar. 1994. *Lords of the Realm*.

44 Helyar. 1994. *Lords of the Realm*: 602.

45 Jane O'Hara. 1998. "In the Name of Greed," *Maclean's*, January 19: 22–24; Staudohar. 1996. *Playing for Dollars*: 140–141; and Russ Conway. 1997. *Game Misconduct: Alan Eagleson and the Corruption of Hockey* (Buffalo, NY: MacFarlane, Walter, and Ross).

46 Quoted in Helyar. 1994. *Lords of the Realm*: 239.

47 Quoted in Marvin Miller. 1991. *A Whole Different Ballgame: The Sport and Business of Baseball* (Secaucus, NJ: Carol Publishing Group): 11–12.

48 Helyar. 1994. *Lords of the Realm*: 84.

11

DISCRIMINATION

Let the women [soccer players] play in more feminine clothes like they do in volley-ball. They could, for example, have tighter shorts.

—Sepp Blatter, former President of FIFA[1]

I was raised on the beliefs of my father, my uncle, and Dr. Martin Luther King which, in essence, are "Don't do me any favors. Let's agree on what the rules are, and then judge me fairly."

—Arthur Ashe[2]

Introduction

On April 18, 1946, in a minor league game between the Montreal Royals and the Jersey City Little Giants, Jackie Robinson crossed the color line and became the first African American baseball player since the 1880s to be employed by a major league-affiliated team. His first at bat, a ground ball to shortstop, ended more than 50 years of segregated professional baseball in the United States.[3] Almost exactly one year later, on April 15, 1947, he took the field as a Brooklyn Dodger. Over the objections of many fans, players, and owners, the Dodgers' president Branch Rickey had reintegrated baseball. Three months after Robinson broke the color barrier in the National League, Larry Doby became the first black to play in the American League when Bill Veeck signed him to a contract with the Cleveland Indians. Doby suffered the same treatment as Robinson, including endless streams of insults from fans and players, death threats, and segregated hotels and restaurants that often prevented him from staying and eating with his teammates. While baseball's history of discrimination against black players is surely the best-known case of discrimination in sports, it is by no means the only one. As with almost every other walk of life, discrimination has long been a source of concern in virtually every sport. This chapter shows how economists study and measure discrimination, and presents a few instances when those methods have uncovered evidence of discrimination in the sports industry.

Learning Objectives

- Grasp the evidence of the presence or absence of discrimination in professional sports.
- Understand the economic theory of discrimination.
- Describe the different forms of discrimination and how they affect employment and pay.
- Appreciate how gender discrimination differs from racial discrimination.

11.1 Evidence of Discrimination in Sports

This chapter centers on the effects of discrimination, the "unequal treatment of equals" in the sports labor market. The underlying question for all studies in this area is whether people of different demographic groups are evaluated and rewarded solely on the basis of their productivity. Thus, we use human capital theory and productivity data to discuss the existence of, degree of, and changes in discrimination over time.

We look specifically at two aspects of discrimination. The first is *unequal access to work*, whether equally qualified people have equal access to labor markets. For example, if, as Michael Conlin and Patrick Emerson have found, black football players are systematically drafted in lower rounds than whites, they would have unequal access to work. The second aspect is *unequal pay for equal work*, whether equally productive workers in identical positions are paid equally, as when foreign basketball players are paid less than otherwise identical US-born players.

While the overall evidence is mixed, the *Racial and Gender Report Cards*, which are published annually by The Institute for Diversity and Ethics in Sport (TIDES) at the University of Central Florida, find that racial discrimination is no longer a significant factor for professional athletes in the US. (We discuss discrimination at other levels of US sports and in other nations later in the chapter.) The report cards give the NFL and MLB A's for their performance in racial equity, while the NBA and WNBA both receive an A+. Only MLS falls short of a perfect mark, receiving a B+ for 2014 (the most recent report card for MLS covers 2014. TIDES does not issue a report card for the NHL).[4]

This finding, however, is not uniform, as several recent studies conclude that discrimination is still a concern. Chih Hai Yang and Hsuan Yu find that foreign players in the NBA are paid as much as 17.4 percent less than otherwise identical US natives. However, a recent study by Adam Hoffer and Ryan Freidel finds no such gap.[5] Conlin and Emerson studied hiring discrimination in the NFL by comparing when white and black players were drafted to how much they played and found evidence of hiring discrimination against blacks as measured by draft position, though there was no evidence of discriminatory behavior by coaches.[6]

There is also mixed evidence regarding the role race plays in the behavior of coaches and officials. Jesse Schroffel and Christopher Magee show that NBA coaches of both races give more playing time to players of a similar race after controlling for player performance. They found, however, that this effect has decreased over time.[7]

Joseph Price and Justin Wolfers find that the racial make-up of the referee crew affects the number of fouls called on black and white players. Black players are assessed as committing 4–4.5 percent more fouls per 48 minutes than white players. Given the average difference in the racial composition of the teams in a typical game, the probability of victory for the team with more white players rises by about three percentage points as the referee crew changes from all black to all white.

In contrast, two recent studies find little evidence of discrimination by baseball umpires. Jeff Hamrick and John Rasp see no connection between the race of the umpire and that of the pitcher or the batter in the calling of balls and strikes in MLB. Scott Tainsky, Brian Mills, and Jason Winfree find some evidence that umpires are more sympathetic to pitchers of the same race, but the evidence is too weak to conclude that discrimination exists.[8]

11.2 The Economic Theory of Discrimination

Economics is not the only lens through which one can view discrimination. In fact, the economic approach to discrimination is relatively new. Before Gary Becker's groundbreaking book *The Economics of Discrimination* in 1957, economists had generally left the field to other disciplines, such as psychology and sociology.[9] The economic approach to discrimination differs from that of other disciplines because economists focus much more on the outcome of discrimination than on its origin. Economists distinguish between prejudice, which is a feeling or emotion, and discrimination, which is an action.

Becker's theory begins with prejudice in that it rests on the concept of a **taste for discrimination**. Tastes are one of the building blocks of economic theory. As such, economists rarely question them.[10] To see the futility of challenging tastes, ask a friend what his favorite flavor of ice cream is. When he responds, ask him why he chose that flavor (say, peach). He will probably say something like, "Because peach tastes good." Now try asking him why peach tastes better than chocolate chip. Odds are he will shrug his shoulders and say he does not know why, or he will offer a variant on "because it does."

Your friend's inability to explain the reasons behind his tastes does not mean that you cannot alter his actions. If you offer your friend a large enough cash payment along with the chocolate chip ice cream or charge a high enough price for peach ice cream, you might convince him to eat the flavor that he does not most prefer. Becker's central insight was that people can have a taste for discrimination just like they can have a taste for a specific flavor of ice cream. People have a taste for discrimination if they act as if they are willing to pay to associate with one group rather than another. Policymakers can affect those actions by manipulating the price they must pay.

Rather than wrestle with the complexity of the roots and mechanics of prejudice, Becker's theory allows economists to focus directly on behavior. It uses money to measure a person's taste for discrimination, avoiding the challenge of uncovering why someone discriminates. With this definition, testing for the presence of and measuring the results of discrimination are straightforward. In addition, Becker's theory enables analysts to predict how discrimination affects the people who practice it and who are victimized by it.

In labor markets, the payment a discriminator makes to avoid associating with another group can take many forms, such as lower profits, higher prices, or lower wages. We distinguish among these payments because the source of discrimination and the nature of the payment depend on which party (if any) gains and which party loses.

11.3 Different Forms of Discrimination in Professional Sports

This section describes how employers, employees, and consumers discriminate. As people with a taste for discrimination maximize their utility, their willingness to pay to indulge these tastes affects the market in several ways. The degree and nature of this impact depend on the structure in which the individuals and firms operate.[11]

Employer Discrimination

Because it is based on utility maximization, Becker's model takes a broader view of the firm than simple profit maximization. For example, an employer may be willing to sacrifice profits to avoid associating with a group of people that reduces his or her utility. Because a firm's owner may be willing to sacrifice profits to satisfy his taste for discrimination, we can make specific predictions regarding firms that discriminate in competitive, monopoly, or monopsony markets. We discuss these outcomes below in greater detail.

To see how discrimination works in labor markets, consider the experience of European hockey players in the NHL. Although European-born players had played in the NHL since its inception in 1917, most notably Slovak-born Hall of Famer Stan Mikita, no player trained in Europe played in the NHL until 1965, when Swedish star Ulf Sterner played four games for the New York Rangers. As recently as the 2000s, some teams avoided European players. Between 2004 and 2012, the Philadelphia Flyers selected only one European in the player draft.[12]

Several researchers have asked whether European players have been the victims of discrimination by the NHL, particularly by Canadian teams because, in the words of Marc Lavoie, "hockey is seen as a Canadian game."[13] If this were the case, employers might prefer not to associate with "foreign" players. To simplify matters, assume that there are only two groups of players, North American (NA) and European (E). To keep the focus on discrimination, assume for the moment that all players are equally productive. This way, in the absence of discrimination, demand for the two types of players would be equal.

Becker measures the distaste that owners have for E's with a **discrimination coefficient** (d_E). The discrimination coefficient is greater than zero if an owner feels that he pays an emotional (or *psychic*) cost in addition to the wage he pays an E. He acts as if the wage were w for all NA's and $w(1 + d_E)$ for all E's. If NHL owners have a taste for discrimination and prefer hiring North Americans to hiring Europeans, the demand for North Americans (D_{NA}) is greater than that for Europeans (D_E). In Figure 11.1a, we assume that there is an equal supply of each type of player ($S_E = S_{NA}$). The lower demand for Europeans leads employers to hire fewer of them and to pay them lower salaries.

If the supply of North Americans or the taste for discrimination is great enough, then teams will hire no Europeans.[14] That is, there would be unequal access to work. To use an example from other sports, the National and American Leagues in baseball hired no blacks at all between 1890 and 1947. Alternatively, if there were no discrimination at all, we could simply add the two supply curves in Figure 11.1a to arrive at the market supply and add the two (identical) demand curves to get the market demand. Now, players would be hired without regard to race, as in Figure 11.1b.

To make this more concrete, suppose the owner of an NHL club is comparing two players who perform identically on every skill test, play the same position, and have identical past experience. From a productivity standpoint, they are perfect substitutes. Either player would sign a contract for $500,000 per season. However, one player, Eddie, is from Toronto, and the other, Jiri, is from Prague. The owner now separates the prospects into two groups: Eddie is an NA, and Jiri is an E. Because the owner has a taste for discrimination against all E's, his discrimination coefficient is positive, say 0.2. He feels as if he pays Eddie w_{NA} = $500,000 and

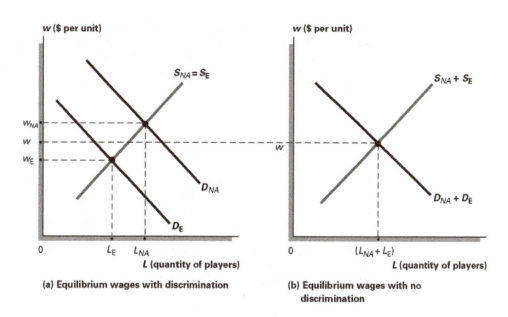

(a) Equilibrium wages with discrimination

(b) Equilibrium wages with no discrimination

pays Jiri w_E = \$500,000(1 + 0.2) = \$600,000. The owner does not actually pay the extra \$100,000, but his desire not to associate with European players makes him feel as though he were paying the extra, psychic cost.

The owner does incur additional costs if the increase in demand for NA's increases their pay above \$500,000. If enough owners have a taste for discrimination against E's, the market for players resembles that shown in Figure 11.1a, and owners with a taste for discrimination pay higher salaries than those without.

In this case, discriminating makes the team owner worse off financially. If his taste for discrimination against E's makes the psychic and monetary wage of E's greater than w_{NA}, he does not hire any E's. He is happier paying w_{NA} to fill his roster with NA's than he is paying a mixed team the competitive rate w. The economic cost of employing only NA's depends on the elasticities of supply and demand. For example, if the supply of NA's is perfectly elastic (a horizontal line), then owners do not have to increase w_{NA} to hire more of them.

Even prejudiced owners employ E's if the players are willing to work for wages that are low enough. In the previous example, a discrimination coefficient of 0.2 means the owner feels that he is paying E's a premium of 20 percent. If the E's are willing to work for 20 percent less than NA's, the owner is willing to hire them. In this case, E's receive unequal pay for equal work.

If players are not homogeneous, the owner may also end up with a mixed team. For simplicity, suppose E's and NA's can be good players (E_g and NA_g) or bad players (E_b and NA_b). If NA_g's are relatively scarce, the team may exhaust the supply of NA_g's and have to choose between the less productive NA_b's and the more productive E_g's. In this case, the owner may maximize his utility by hiring some E_g's.

Discrimination clearly makes E players worse off. E's receive no offers as long as employers feel they pay them more than they pay otherwise equivalent NA's. Even if E's are hired, they receive lower offers than equally productive NA's. NA's

Figure 11.1
(a) Equilibrium Wages with Discrimination;
(b) Equilibrium Wages with No Discrimination

(a) With an equal number of both groups of players but differential demand based on discrimination, wages for European players will be lower than for North American players. (b) If owners have no taste for discrimination and wages, w is the equilibrium wage for all players.

are better off as a group because their chances of making the team, and their pay if they do, both increase. Although owners avoid associating with E's, they pay for the privilege in the form of reduced profits. We stress that owners are worse off *financially*, not worse off overall. Discriminatory owners are maximizing their utility. In this case, utility maximization comes at the cost of reduced profit.

Statistical Discrimination

To this point, we have assumed that there are no systematic differences between E and NA players. However, Leo Kahane, Neil Longley, and Robert Simmons point out that Czech, Slovak, and Russian players are generally better offensive players than North Americans.[15] An NHL team might therefore conclude that any Czech player will be a top goal-scorer but weak on defense. The problem with this reasoning is that group averages are just that. They mask the individual variation *within* groups. Each player should be judged on his own merits, rather than those of the group to which he belongs. The use of group averages to judge individual productivity levels is called **statistical discrimination**.[16] Statistical discrimination differs from ordinary discrimination because it is based on incomplete information (group averages as opposed to individual-level data) rather than on the preferences of people with full information.

While it does not result from prejudice, statistical discrimination can have a very strong impact on a team's hiring practices. Consider, for example, a team that believes that a young Czech player has a 49 percent chance of succeeding in the NHL, while a young North American has a 51 percent chance of success. That team would not seek an almost equal split of Europeans and North Americans. Because the team believes that any one North American is more likely to succeed than any one European, it will hire only North Americans until the pay differential becomes so great that the team is willing to take on players it thinks are worse.

Statistical discrimination is troublesome for two reasons. First, it may be profit-maximizing behavior on the part of firms. Even though assuming that each European player is weaker defensively than each North American is not always accurate, teams may be correct on average if they always use this assumption when choosing players. Thus, they may feel their actions are justified. Second, statistical discrimination can become a self-fulfilling prophecy. If offensive-minded European forwards are drafted and defensive-minded ones are not, over time, league statistics will reflect that Europeans are offensive-minded. Unfortunately, this means that statistical discrimination can persist even if the initial difference in offensive versus defensive ability stemmed from inaccurate perceptions.

Does Anyone Win with Employer Discrimination?

To see if any groups benefit economically from employers' taste for discrimination, consider the case of racial discrimination in Major League Baseball. Blacks were effectively barred from organized baseball from 1888 to 1947 by a "gentlemen's agreement." Many black players who were good enough to play in the major leagues—some of them good enough to be admitted to baseball's Hall of Fame—were confined to the Negro Leagues, which lasted until the late 1950s.[17] These players were certainly worse off.

One group that benefited from discrimination was white players of that era. Because blacks were excluded, more white players played in MLB than would

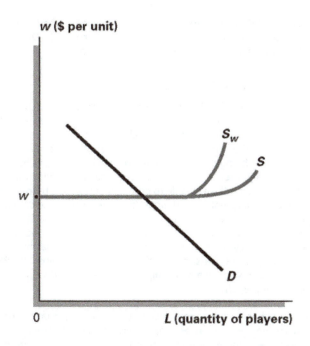

w ($ per unit)

S_w

S

w

D

0

L (quantity of players)

Figure 11.2
Discrimination with a Large
Pool of Players

If the supply of players is large
enough, discrimination by
owners does not reduce wages.
Instead, owners hire only white
players and blacks are excluded
from the market.

have been possible otherwise. To see why, assume that all players are equally productive (homogeneous) and that 30 percent of the available labor force is black. In this case, if there is no discrimination, roughly 30 percent of the players would be black. If there is a very large pool of available labor, the market supply curve (S) of players is a horizontal line, as shown in Figure 11.2, and players receive the market wage (w). In this case, the labor force is so large relative to demand that restricting the market to white players $w/(1-d_j)$ results in the same wage. Because teams have a taste for discrimination, no blacks are hired, and teams employ more whites than if there were no discrimination.

In practice, players vary greatly in ability. If an employer has a taste for discrimination against black players, and the quality of players of both races varies, team owners choose marginal white players over blacks of greater ability to fill out their rosters. In this case, white players of marginal ability benefit from the owners' taste for discrimination. Even with no formal or informal color line, if the decrease in marginal revenue product that results from hiring a less-skilled white player is less than the wage premium, a discriminatory owner would hire the white player.

While white players benefited and black players were hurt by the "color line," one set of beneficiaries may come as a surprise. The color line allowed the largely African American owners of Negro League baseball teams to draw on a pool of captive talent.[18] Because the Negro Leagues could draw on such talented players, attendance at Negro League games was much greater than it would have been with integrated major leagues.

To see the Negro Leagues' reliance on segregation, one need look no further than their demise after MLB ended its color line. As Negro League teams lost increasing numbers of talented players to the major leagues, gate receipts dwindled, teams folded, and a chief source of revenue became the sale of rights to their players to MLB. Salaries for players who remained in the Negro Leagues dropped by about 50 percent, to as low as $200 per month. Despite valiant efforts to keep going, the Negro Leagues folded in 1960.[19]

How Competition Can Eliminate Discrimination

Becker's theory implies that less-discriminatory employers will be more successful than highly discriminatory employers. Suppose, for example, that discriminatory employers are willing to pay blacks $30 per hour and whites $40 per hour. An unprejudiced employer $d = 0$ can enter and undercut any employer who uses white labor by hiring only blacks and paying them $32 per hour. Continued entry by unprejudiced employers increases the wage paid to black workers, driving down the profits available to potential entrants. If there are enough unprejudiced potential employers, their profits will eventually be driven to zero. At that point, any discriminatory employers who continue to pay higher wages to white workers are driven from the market because of their higher costs. They can remain only if they pay white workers the same wage that black workers receive. Although professional sports markets are not perfectly competitive, the pressure to win games and championships is a powerful motivation for owners to overcome their prejudices.

A brief review of baseball's history supports the hypothesis that discriminators sacrifice wins to indulge their tastes. Employers that integrated their teams more quickly generally won more games than those that were slower to integrate. The Dodgers, who led the way to racial integration of the National League, won NL pennants in 1947 and 1949, and five pennants in the 1950s after winning only three in the previous 56 years. The Giants, who were the second-most integrated team, won pennants in 1951 and 1954. Five of the six most successful teams (in terms of winning percentages) in the 1950s were the five teams that integrated most quickly.[20] Only the Yankees stood among the top teams in the 1950s with a relatively low percentage of black players.

In contrast, teams that were slow to integrate saw their performance steadily decline. From 1936 through 1945, the Washington Redskins were one of the NFL's most dominant teams, playing in six NFL Championship Games and winning two. They were also the last NFL team to integrate, not fielding a black player until 1962. From 1946, the year the NFL reintegrated, through 1961, the Redskins had only three winning seasons.[21]

Stefan Szymanski empirically documented the presence of discrimination in a sample of teams from England's Football League over the period 1978 to 1993. Using a multiple regression model that holds team payroll constant, he showed that teams with more black players during this period also won more frequently. Thus, a nondiscriminatory team could "buy" wins more cheaply than a team that wished to hire only white players.[22]

When Markets Are Not Competitive

As in competitive markets, monopsonistic employers with a taste for discrimination feel as if they pay a member of group i the wage $w_i = w(1 + d_i)$. Unlike perfectly competitive firms, discriminatory monopsonies are not driven from the market, as workers have nowhere else to sell their services. Similarly, monopoly employers have no fear that new entrants to the labor market will undercut them by hiring a more productive, less costly workforce. Thus, a prejudiced monopsonist or monopolist who feels as if he is paying $w_i = w(1 + d_i)$ when hiring a member of group i, feels free to act on his prejudices. Conversely, when the market power of a monopolist or monopsonist breaks down, the ability to discriminate often breaks down as well.

Because professional sports leagues exerted both monopsony and monopoly power, they were free to discriminate for much of their history. Challenges to this market power by the government or rival leagues sometimes helped break down racial or ethnic barriers. In 1946, the Los Angeles Rams—having just moved to Los Angeles from Cleveland—were coerced into signing former UCLA star Kenny Washington to secure access to the municipally owned Los Angeles Coliseum.[23] No other NFL team signed a black player until 1948. By then, however, six of eight teams in the rival All-America Football Conference had integrated. Integration received a boost in 1950, when the NFL absorbed three AAFC teams, most notably the Cleveland Browns, who had led the AAFC's integration and dominated the AAFC and then the NFL from 1946 through 1955.[24]

Similarly, the NHL's disdain for European hockey players was undermined by the play of European stars signed by the upstart World Hockey Association in the 1970s. The play of Swedish stars Anders Hedberg and Ulf Nilsson and the Slovak standout Vaclav Nedomansky was simply too good for NHL teams to ignore. European representation in the NHL went from 0 in 1970 to 5.7 percent in 1980 to 20.5 percent in 2000. By the 2015–2016 season, the first in which a majority of NHL players was not Canadian, 26.1 percent of the NHL was European.[25]

Enforcing Discrimination

Prejudiced team owners may face a tradeoff between their desire to avoid members of a particular group and the additional wins and profits members of that group might bring. In a few instances, the lure of wins and profit proved too tempting, and teams attempted to sneak players past the color line by claiming they were Cuban or Native American.[26] Such behavior could have subverted the gentlemen's agreement that excluded African American players through the Prisoner's Dilemma, as seen in Figure 11.3.

For simplicity, assume there are only two teams, the Dodgers and the Phillies, and two strategies, to follow the unofficial ban on African American players or to integrate the team. Given the payoffs listed in the payoff matrix, if the Dodgers

Figure 11.3
The Color Line Breaks Down as a Result of the Prisoner's Dilemma

	Dodgers obey color line	Dodgers integrate
Phillies obey color line	Neither team dominates Color line persists	Dodgers dominate
Phillies integrate	Phillies dominate	Neither team dominates Color line disappears

and Phillies are sufficiently motivated by winning, the dominant strategy will be to integrate.

The color line lasted so long because baseball could avoid the Prisoner's Dilemma. One of Kenesaw Mountain Landis's roles as Baseball Commissioner was to police the color line, pressuring non-compliant teams to release "undesirable" players. Baseball integrated when Landis's successor, Albert ("Happy") Chandler, refused to be a policeman and allowed the Dodgers to employ Jackie Robinson. In 1947, Robinson's rookie year, he was named Rookie of the Year and led the team to the National League Pennant. The Philadelphia Phillies, who integrated in 1957, the last National League team to do so, finished last in 1947. This result corresponds to the upper-right quadrant in Figure 11.3.

Employee Discrimination

Discrimination is not limited to employers. Employees can discriminate against their coworkers. Employees with a taste for discrimination against their coworkers regard the market wage w as $w (1 - d_j)$. As before, d_j represents the coefficient of discrimination.

In the 1880s, a few black baseball players played in the American Association, then a "major" league. The first was Moses Fleetwood Walker, who played for Toledo, along with his brother Weldy, in 1884. Several blacks also played in the International League, which was a minor league. Some white players refused to play for teams that hired blacks. Others played only grudgingly. Cap Anson, a star white player of the time with a well-known dislike for black players, threatened not to play against blacks (though he did play when he learned he would not be paid otherwise) and his opposition prevented the New York Giants from signing black pitcher George Stovey in 1887.[27] Such behavior persisted even though the few blacks who were in the game, such as Fleetwood Walker and Frank Grant, were among the top players in their leagues. It is a sad footnote on baseball history that the feet-first slide originated from attempts by white players to spike Grant, a second baseman; he eventually invented the shinguard to protect himself from their spikes.

Discrimination against blacks continued when the major leagues were reintegrated in 1947. During their first season, Larry Doby and Jackie Robinson were subjected to employee discrimination by players on opposing teams and even by their own teammates. When Doby was introduced to his new team, several players refused to shake his hand. When the other Dodger players learned that Robinson was to begin 1947 with their club, several teammates, including such prominent players as Dixie Walker, Carl Furillo, and Eddie Stanky, circulated a petition opposing the decision. Dodger manager Leo Durocher's response was to call a team meeting at 1:00 am, at which he told his players, in part:

> Boys, I hear that some of you don't want to play with Robinson. Some of you have drawn up a petition. Well you know what you can use that petition for. . . . I'm the manager and I'm paid to win and I'd play an elephant if he could win for me and this fellow Robinson is no elephant. You can't throw him out on the bases and you can't get him out at the plate. This fellow is a great player. He's gonna win pennants. He's gonna put money in your pockets and mine. . . . Unless you wake up, these colored ball players are gonna run you right outa the park. I don't want to see your petition. . . . The meeting is over. Go back to bed.[28]

Ironically, Pee Wee Reese, a Kentucky native and shortstop who ran the risk of losing his position to Robinson, refused to sign.[29]

Early in the 1947 season, both the Philadelphia Phillies and St. Louis Cardinals threatened to strike rather than play against Robinson when he came to town.[30] They relented only when faced with forfeiture and suspensions for not playing. In Robinson's first game in Philadelphia, the Phillies, led by manager Ben Chapman, hurled such savage abuse at Robinson that even those Dodgers who had opposed Robinson rallied around him.

The extent of the economic harm prejudiced workers inflict depends on the nature of the labor market. If players are perfect substitutes for one another and the labor market is competitive, the Becker model predicts that prejudiced players refuse to play on a team that is integrated because they feel as if they are paid only $w(1 - d_j)$ and insist on a wage of $w/(1 - d_j)$ to feel as though they have received the market wage. However, no such offers exist in a market with a perfectly elastic supply of players (horizontal supply curve) at the wage w. White players who refused to play alongside blacks were simply replaced by those who would, as was the case for Dixie Walker, whom the Dodgers traded to Pittsburgh after the 1947 season. If a prejudiced player with a taste for discrimination is traded to an all-white team, he no longer requires a wage premium. Thus, one possible outcome of employee discrimination is segregation. While segregation is usually considered to be employer-driven, in this case, the taste for discrimination by employees creates a segregated market.[31]

As with employer discrimination, the outcome is different when markets are not competitive. If players have different playing abilities, more than one market wage exists, and prejudiced employees may end up as teammates of players they dislike. For example, an owner may be willing to pay the wage differential demanded by a top player with a taste for discrimination because there are no substitutes of equal quality. For instance, a title boxing match must, by definition, include the reigning champion. No black boxer fought for the world heavyweight championship between Jack Johnson's loss of the title in 1915 and Joe Louis's winning the title in 1937. The reason was not a lack of good black boxers. Instead, one could not substitute away from the white champions, and the white champions had such a strong distaste for fighting blacks (such a large d_j) that no match was possible.[32]

If markets cannot be segregated, and players of different groups are perfect substitutes for one another, those with a taste for discrimination are driven from the market. Becker argued that this should eliminate employee discrimination from the market in the long run. Although employer and/or employee discrimination may have significantly depressed salaries of minorities as recently as the mid-1980s, most studies of the NFL, NBA, and MLB find no wage differentials based on race.[33] If Becker's theory is correct, there are two explanations for why this has happened. The competition among teams could have driven out discriminatory owners and players. Alternatively, the utility derived from the economic gains could be so much greater than the utility derived from discriminating that those with a taste for discrimination choose to stay in the market and bear the disutility of playing with groups they do not like.

Consumer Discrimination

Research on salary differentials among black, white, and Latino baseball players indicates that neither race nor ethnic background affects salaries.[34] However, evidence from both baseball and basketball indicates that discrimination still exists among consumers in the sports industry.

Consumers have a taste for discrimination if they prefer not to purchase goods or services from members of a specific group. This was the claim made by George Preston Marshall, the owner of the all-white Washington Redskins, when he said that "Recruiting Southern white players was not prejudice . . . but a business decision." Marshall insisted that he feared offending his Southern white radio and television audience by playing blacks.[35] Even if Marshall was not telling the truth, such a situation could arise. A football fan with a taste for discrimination against black players perceives the price of admission to a game with only white players to be p and the price of admission to a game that includes blacks to be $p(1+d_k)$.

Consumer discrimination can be difficult to isolate in sports because so many factors affect consumer demand, such as the quality of the team or the facility in which it plays.[36] Studies of television ratings can abstract from some confounding factors, such as differences in stadium capacity and the sale of season tickets, which set demand before the composition of the team is set. Even here the evidence is mixed. Mark Kanazawa and Jonas Funk find that Nielsen television ratings of basketball games are higher when white players are on the court more. Some also suggest that the recent influx of players from Europe and Latin America to the NBA reflects the desire of fans to see more white players.[37] Half a world away, Wei-jhan Jane uses pitch-by-pitch ratings for World Baseball Championship games broadcast in Taiwan, to show that consumers tuned in more for Asian batters and pitchers but tuned out when black players were involved. In contrast, Ian Preston and Stefan Szymanski find no evidence that consumers have driven discrimination by professional soccer teams in England, and Eric Aldrich et al. find that Monday Night Football ratings are higher when the game features a black quarterback.[38]

Other researchers have abstracted from other demand factors by analyzing the market for trading cards.[39] The results of these studies are also mixed. Clark Nardinelli and Curtis Simon find that cards for white baseball players are 10–13 percent more expensive than the players' performances justify. Torben Anderson and Sumner La Croix find evidence of discrimination against black players but not Latinos. L.J. Van Scyoc and N.J. Burnett find evidence of consumer discrimination but conclude that it has declined over time. A study of football player cards by Eric Prim et al. finds no evidence when one accounts for the vintage of the card.[40]

Rodney Fort and Andrew Gill posit that some of the disagreement stems from consumers' confusion regarding race. They developed a continuous measure of race by showing people pictures and names of players and asking "how black" and "how Hispanic" the players appeared to be.[41] They find that consumers discriminate more against players who appear to be "more black" or "more Hispanic."

Unfortunately, consumer discrimination differs from other types of discrimination in one important regard: Market forces do not eliminate it over time. If consumers have a taste for discrimination against a particular group, and employers maximize profit, even unprejudiced employers will not hire any members of that group.

Evidence suggests that consumer discrimination continued in the NBA until the early 1990s and that discriminatory consumers were the source of the differential.[42] Lawrence Kahn and Peter Sherer found that blacks in the NBA earned about 20 percent less than equally productive white players in the mid-1980s.[43] A later study by Barton Hamilton found that the average salaries of black and white players had become virtually identical by the 1994–1995 season. However, this was because white players were overrepresented at both ends of the pay distribution. White stars were paid 19 percent more than black stars, while marginal white players displaced marginal black players at the bottom of the pay scale.[44]

Fortunately, US sports fans' taste for discrimination appears to be declining. Andrew Hansen and Torben Anderson find from the results of fan voting for MLB All-Stars that consumer discrimination has declined sharply since the 1970s. Mark Gius and Donn Johnson use salaries of NBA players from the 1995–1996 season to show no evidence of discrimination, contradicting Hamilton's findings from just one year earlier.[45]

While consumer discrimination appears to be on the wane in the US, it is alive and well in international soccer. Black players have been subjected to "monkey chants" and been pelted with bananas in stadiums throughout Europe. Games have been played before empty stadiums from Bergamo, Italy (home of Atalanta, B.C.) to Urawa, Japan (home of the Urawa Reds) because of the racist behavior of home fans. A BBC program advised fans to stay away from the 2012 European Championships after a visit to matches in Poland and Ukraine, the co-hosts of Euro 2012, which documented "Nazi salutes from the terraces, black players being taunted with monkey chants, rampant anti-Semitism and a vicious assault on a group of Asian students." Ironically, even Africa is not immune to racist attitudes, as a recent candidate for the presidency of the Football Association of Zambia was attacked for being Asian despite being born and raised in Zambia.[46]

In a recent paper, Peter von Allmen, Michael Leeds, and Julian Malakorn test for the presence of discrimination against Europeans in the NHL. To do this, they use a sample of skaters (i.e., not goaltenders) from the 2010–2011 and 2011–2012 seasons. To capture the impact of national origin on salary, they regress the natural logarithm of salary on several performance measures from the previous year, and dummy variables indicating whether the player was born in Quebec, elsewhere in North America, or in Europe. To align pay and performance, they restrict the sample to players who were in the first year of a new contract. The performance measures include goals scored, plus/minus (the number of goals scored minus the number of goals allowed while the player is on the ice), "hits" (physical contact that separates an opposing player from the puck), and time spent on the ice while the team is at a man advantage or disadvantage. They find no evidence of discrimination against European players. In fact, they find that European players are paid more than otherwise identical North Americans, which they attribute to the increased bargaining power resulting from European players' greater willingness to play in European leagues.

Positional Discrimination or Hiring Discrimination[47]

Even if professional leagues offer equal access overall, they might not allow minorities equal access to all positions. For example, since about two-thirds of the players in the NFL are black, one would expect about two-thirds of the players at each position and two-thirds of the coaches to be black. As it turns out, these expectations are not realized.

Table 11.1 Racial and Ethnic Breakdown of MLB Players in 2015 at Selected Positions (%)

	Total	Pitchers	Catchers	Infield	Outfield
White	58.8	69.0	51.6	58.4	51.4
African American	8.3	3.1	0.0	7.9	25.4
Latino	29.3	25.4	45.3	32.6	19.7
Asian	3.6	2.2	3.1	0.5	2.1

Source: Richard E. Lapchick, Nikki Bowey, and Ray Matthew. 2015. "2015 Racial and Gender Report Card: Major League Baseball," *The Institute for Diversity and Ethics in Sport,* April 15, at http://www.tidesport.org/mlb-rgrc.html, viewed December 2, 2016.

Historically, positional discrimination, also known as **stacking,** has been an issue in both the NFL and MLB. Even today, whites dominate at some positions while blacks dominate at others. Economists call the systematic steering of minorities to specific positions on the field and within the coaching ranks **role discrimination**. For example, if coaches assume that black players lack the strong arm and quick reactions needed to be a quarterback, then they discourage young black players from investing in the skills required to play quarterback.[48]

In 2014, 81 percent of NFL quarterbacks were white, as were 75 percent of the centers and 55 percent of the tight ends. At the opposite end of the spectrum, 86 percent of the running backs, 91 percent of wide receivers, 78.9 percent of the safeties, and 99.4 percent of the cornerbacks were black. In general, white players are more likely to be found on offense than on defense.[49]

David Berri and Robert Simmons find evidence of discrimination against black quarterbacks in the NFL.[50] They note that about two-thirds of the players in the NFL between 2000 and 2006 were black, but 73 percent of the quarterbacks who attempted 100 or more passes were white. They also find racial differences in salary. They construct a performance measure of quarterbacks that includes both running and passing productivity and show that, controlling for this measure, black quarterbacks at the upper half of the salary scale are paid less than equally productive white quarterbacks. Thus, while salaries and playing opportunities have increased, Berri and Simmons conclude that a racial divide persists at the quarterback position.

Table 11.1 shows the racial and ethnic breakdown of MLB for 2015. It shows that Latinos made up 29.3 percent of the league overall, but almost half of all catchers are Hispanic, while less than 20 percent of outfielders were. In contrast, blacks comprised only 8.3 percent of MLB—the second-lowest figure since records were kept—but are a quarter of all outfielders (and *no* catchers!). Whites were much more likely to be pitchers. Thus, while all groups have the chance to play in the major leagues, positional segregation remains a concern.

Discrimination in Coaching and Administrative Ranks

Unequal access to professional sports is not limited to players. Table 11.2 shows that, compared to players, whites are disproportionately represented among owners, coaches, and assistant coaches.

Research by Janice Madden shows that between 1990 and 2001, minority head coaches in the NFL were significantly more successful than their white

Table 11.2 Percentage of Whites at Different Levels of Professional Sports Leagues (%)

League	Players	Owners	Head Coaches	Assistants
MLB	58.8	98.0	93.3	63.0
MLS	51.1	93.3	89.5	83.3
NFL	28.6	—[a]	81.3	62.1
NBA	23.3	95.0	66.7	59.2
WNBA	24.3	82.1	75.0	50.0

[a]Not reported.

Source: Race and Gender Report Cards.

counterparts, raising the question of whether black coaches must perform better to keep their jobs. By 2003, the NFL had become so alarmed at the lack of black head coaches that it adopted the "Rooney Rule." Named for Dan Rooney, then-owner of the Pittsburgh Steelers and head of the NFL's diversity committee, the rule requires teams to interview minority candidates for head coaching and other senior administrative openings. In a later study, Madden and Matthew Ruther find that the performance differential disappeared in the years after the Rooney Rule was implemented, though research by Benjamin and John Solow and Todd Walker disputes this finding. Studies of the NBA find that race plays no role in the performance or dismissal of head coaches.[51]

We do not report the representation of women because, for all leagues except the WNBA, women had until very recently not appeared at all in the coaching ranks. To the extent that women own teams in the men's leagues, they are largely the wives, widows, or daughters of men who purchased the team. The absence of women suggests that they may be the victims of role discrimination, which is a form of statistical discrimination. For example, if, on average, women do not know as much as men about sports, they could be systematically discouraged from pursuing roles as team officials. The problem is that uncertainty causes employers to attribute the characteristics of the average person in the group to each member of the group. If discrimination occurs early in the application screening process, the women applying may never get the opportunity to reveal their skills. This might explain why, despite receiving high marks for racial policy, MLB, MLS, and the NFL all receive C+ grades or worse on the *Race and Gender Report Card* for gender policy. Not surprisingly, the WNBA receives an A+, while the NBA, which has traditionally had ties with the WNBA, gets a B+.

In the WNBA, women are 35.9 percent of the owners, 50 percent of the coaches, and 45 percent of the assistant coaches. This openness also extends to race and ethnicity. Table 11.2 shows that, while whites are still disproportionately represented at all levels, the imbalance is consistently smaller than for other leagues.

Hiring records at the collegiate level resemble those at the professional level, as coaching and administrative positions are largely held by white men. This is true even for sports that are dominated by black athletes. According to the *2014 Racial and Gender Report Card: College Sport*, blacks make up 57.6 percent of all Division I men's basketball players, but only 22.0 percent of the coaches are black. Perhaps more surprising, men also dominate the coaching ranks of women's sports. In Division I women's sports, only 38.8 percent of the head coaches are women.[52]

11.4   Gender Equity

In March 2016, five members of the US Women's National Soccer Team (USWNT)—Carli Lloyd, Alex Morgan, Megan Rapinoe, Rebecca Sauerbrunn, and Hope Solo—filed a formal complaint with the Equal Employment Opportunity Commission, accusing the US Soccer Federation of discrimination against members of the women's national team. To justify their claims, they pointed to disparities in both performance and pay.

Since winning the initial Women's World Cup tournament in 1991, the USWNT has won two additional championships—most recently in 2015—and has never finished lower than third. Until their disappointing performance at Rio in 2016, the USWNT had never received less than a silver Olympic medal, winning gold in 1996, 2004, 2008, and 2012. In contrast, the US Men's team has never matched its third-place finish in the initial World Cup in 1930. The men's Olympic performance is no better. They last saw the podium in the 1904 Summer Olympics, where US teams finished both second *and* third.[53]

When it comes to compensation, however, the US women run a distant second behind the men. Table 11.3 shows that the US men earned more for finishing 15th in the 2014 men's World Cup competition than the US women did for winning the women's World Cup in 2015. How can one explain such a disparity except by appealing to discrimination?

While there is no question about the USWNT's performance and their popularity in the US, World Cup figures tell a more complex story. In 2015, US women took home 12 percent of the total prize pool of $15 million. For their quarterfinal finish, the US men took home only 1.6 percent of the total prize pool. In fact, the winning German men's team took home a smaller percentage (6.6 percent) than the US women did. However, the prize pool for the men's World Cup, $576 million, dwarfed the women's prize money. The difference in prize money can be traced directly to the difference in sponsorship: $529 million to $17 million.[54]

It is much harder to test for sex discrimination than for racial discrimination in sports because women and men rarely compete together. Differences in venues, times, and conditions make it much harder to isolate the role played by gender. The only professional sports in which men and women routinely compete against one another are mixed doubles in tennis—a somewhat contrived

Table 11.3 Performance and Rewards for Men's and Women's Soccer Teams

Achievement	Women	Men
Make the World Cup roster[a]	$15,000	$76,000
Qualify for World Cup	$345,000	$2.5 million
Reach round of 16	$0	$3.6 million
Finish third	$480,000	$1.25 million
Finish second	$780,000	$6.25 million
Win championship	$1.8 million	$9.3 million

[a]Rewards for making the roster are per player. All other payments are for the team as a whole.

Source: Laura Santhanam. 2016. "Data: How Does the US Women's Soccer Team Pay Compare to the Men?" *PBS NewsHour: The Rundown,* March 31, at http://www.pbs.org/newshour/rundown/data-how-does-the-u-s-womens-soccer-team-pay-compare-to-the-men/.

event at major tournaments—auto racing, and as jockeys in horse racing. Some Olympic competition, such as equestrian events, pairs ice skating and ice dancing are also mixed gender sports. Among the few studies comparing direct competition between men and women, Margaret Ray and Paul Grimes showed that, holding performance and experience constant, female jockeys get fewer racing opportunities and consequently have lower winnings than similarly qualified men.[55]

Tennis provides a striking example of how players can raise both awareness and earnings. When "Open tennis" first allowed professionals to participate in the 1970s, men's prize money was approximately ten times that of women. In November 1972, the Women's US Open champion, Billie Jean King, threatened to lead a boycott of the 1973 Open unless the prize money was equalized. Her protest succeeded, and prize money was soon equalized. Gender differences in prize money persisted, with Wimbledon not awarding equal prizes until 2007. As noted, prize differences by themselves are not sufficient for most economists to conclude that discrimination exists. Even today, some claim that men should be paid more because (at least in Grand Slam tournaments) men play longer matches and because, allegedly, men's tennis is more popular. This latter claim is demonstrably false. For example, women's matches for the 2013 and 2014 US Opens garnered higher TV ratings than men's matches, and the 2015 women's US Open sold out more quickly than the men's tournament.[56]

What Is a Woman?

To provide separate but equal athletic opportunities, sports authorities, from high schools to the International Olympic Committee, must first define gender. This task might seem simple, but it has proven so complex that the IOC essentially gave up trying to do so before the 2016 Rio Games. The reason is that, while most people clearly fall into one gender or the other, a surprisingly large number are not so easy to categorize.

The first Olympic gender controversy came in the 1936 Berlin Games, when Helen Stephens of the US was accused of being a man after she upset the favored Stella Walsh of Poland.[57] At first, the IOC tried to resolve this by directly examining women's anatomies. It soon became clear that direct examination was not always effective because as many as 1 in 1,500 people are born with "atypical genitalia." Thus, in 1968, chromosome tests replaced the so-called "nude parades." These, too, proved inadequate, as the authorities discovered that anatomy sometimes does not match genetics.

In 1985, officials from the International Association of Athletic Federations (IAAF), the body that oversees track and field competition, informed Spanish hurdler Maria José Martínez-Patiño that they considered her to be a man. This came as a huge surprise to Martínez-Patiño, who believed herself to be a woman and who was, at the time, engaged to a man. However, the IAAF-mandated tests showed that she did not have XX chromosomes in her 23 pairs, and that she had testes (which were internal and had never been detected). She also produced levels of testosterone that were consistent with being a man. Martínez-Patiño's body could not process the testosterone, so it could not affect her physique, and she had developed as a woman. Still, denied her "certificate of femininity," Martínez-Patiño's career as a hurdler came to an end.

In 2000, the IAAF and IOC replaced chromosome tests with measurements of testosterone. This test was challenged by lawyers representing Dutee Chand, a runner from India whose gender had been challenged on this basis. In 2015, the Court of Arbitration of Sports struck down this test, claiming that the IAAF and IOC had not proven that Chand had an advantage that surpassed other natural advantages, such as height (Chand is only five feet tall). It gave the IAAF and IOC until 2017 to provide a scientific basis for this test. Until then, one's gender in international competition is based, as it was when women first entered sport, on self-identification.

Biographical Sketch

Branch Rickey
(1881–1965)

> *The greatest proof of Rickey's genius was that you always knew what he was doing—except when he was doing it to you.*
>
> —*Bill Veeck*[58]

Even if Branch Rickey had never broken baseball's color line, he would still be remembered as one of baseball's greatest innovators. In fact, by the time Rickey joined the Dodgers at the age of 62, he had already experienced a full career in baseball.

Born in 1881, Wesley Branch Rickey was raised in a staunch Methodist family. A budding baseball career ended one day in 1903 when he refused to play on a Sunday. For the rest of his life—except for a special war bonds drive during World War II—Rickey never attended a ballgame on a Sunday, though some were quick to point out that did not stop him from calling the ballpark to check on the day's gate receipts.

Rickey's preoccupation with money probably stemmed from an impoverished upbringing. Rickey was so poor that he had to delay going to college for several years after he graduated from high school. He later recalled that when he finally went to Ohio Wesleyan University, "During my first term . . . I had only one pair of pants, and nobody saw me wear anything else."[59]

Rickey's frugality followed him when he took a front office job with the St. Louis Cardinals, which had hired him away from their cross-town rivals, the Browns, in 1916. Frustrated that his scouts would frequently identify talented minor league players only to lose them to wealthier teams such as the New York Giants, Rickey began to buy minor league teams to keep

---

players within the fold. This was the beginning of baseball's "farm system." The Cardinals' system became so extensive and so laden with talent (including Hall of Famers Dizzy Dean, Joe Medwick, and Stan Musial) that the Cardinals displaced the Giants as the National League's dominant team in the 1930s. Rickey's spending on the team, however, eventually ran afoul of the team's ownership, and in 1943, at the age of 62, he headed east to Brooklyn to become president and 25 percent owner of the Dodgers.

While rebuilding the Dodgers' farm system in the early and mid-1940s, Rickey introduced several innovations that are now taken for granted. He was the first to use a pitching machine and to have players practice their slides in sliding pits. Inspired by Dwight Eisenhower's account of preparations for D-Day, Rickey borrowed the philosophy to create "Dodgertown," in Vero Beach, Florida. Dodgertown was a vast complex, where the entire Dodger system, minor leaguers and major leaguers alike, could receive instruction at one time.

Rickey became a well-known figure to New York sportswriters, who dubbed him "The Mahatma" because they saw Rickey in John Gunther's description of Mohandas "Mahatma" Gandhi as "a combination of God, your father, and Tammany Hall."[60] His double-talk was so renowned that his office in Brooklyn became known as "The House of Winds." Rickey *was* silent about one thing: his plan to break baseball's color line.

Rickey took great care to find the right player to integrate the major leagues. With a stealth that befitted a Cold War spy novel, Dodger scouts fanned the nation, ostensibly looking to recruit players for a new Negro League team to be called the "Brooklyn Brown Dodgers." Ruling out established stars such as Satchel Paige or Buck O'Neil as being too old to establish careers in a new league and young stars such as Roy Campanella or Don Newcombe as too inexperienced to withstand the pressures of being the first player to cross the color line, Rickey settled on Jackie Robinson, a rising star with the Kansas City Monarchs.

On October 23, 1945, the Brooklyn Dodgers revealed that they had signed Robinson to a contract with their top farm club, the Montreal Royals. Rickey carefully chose both the signing date and the ball club to which he assigned Robinson. The date was early enough that other players would know that they were likely to play with a black ballplayer and could arrange for a trade if they objected to doing so. The Montreal club was far enough out of the limelight and from America's heated racial atmosphere to allow Robinson a chance at a normal environment. (Even so, he recalled being close to a nervous breakdown by the end of the season.)

Soon after signing Robinson, Rickey had to withstand pressure from other owners—among them the legendary Connie Mack—who called to complain that he was ruining the game; they arranged a vote on the Dodgers' move in which Rickey cast the only approving ballot. Far from being discouraged at the attitudes of the other owners, Rickey soon signed the second, third, fourth, and fifth black baseball players to contracts.

Rickey also had to deal with on-the-field problems. At first he had to reassure the manager in Montreal, a Mississippian named Clay Hopper, who asked, "Mister Rickey, tell me—do you really think a nigra's a human being?"[61] Rickey was so reassuring and Robinson's play and demeanor so exemplary that Hopper eventually became one of Robinson's biggest backers. After Robinson's outstanding year in Montreal, Rickey then had to convince the Dodgers' manager, Leo Durocher, and the team's Mississippi-born broadcaster, Red Barber, to support his move.

In 1950, Walter O'Malley, who also owned 25 percent of the Dodgers and was Rickey's rival for control of the club, gained control of another 25 percent of the Dodgers and forced Rickey out as president. Rickey quickly landed a position as vice president and general manager of the Pittsburgh Pirates, where he built the foundation of a team that won the 1960 World Series (including stealing a young prospect named Roberto Clemente from the Dodger organization).

Rickey continued to affect baseball well into the 1960s. His attempt to create a rival Continental League forced the National League into its first expansion of the century, and led the National League to replace the departed Dodgers and Giants with the New York Mets. In 1963, Rickey returned to the Cardinals as a consultant. He helped oversee the 1964 Cardinals as they appeared in and won the World Series, their first win since the 1946 team, which Rickey also built. Branch Rickey died in 1965, after spending almost 70 years in baseball and living long enough to share the podium at the Baseball Hall of Fame induction of his good friend, Jackie Robinson.

Sources: John Helyar. 1994. *Lords of the Realm* (New York: Ballantine Books); Harvey Frommer. 1982. *Rickey and Robinson* (New York: Macmillan); and Bill Veeck. 1996. *The Hustler's Handbook* (Durham, NC: Baseball America Classic Books).

Summary

This chapter introduced economic theories of discrimination and used them to describe how the tastes and preferences of employers, employees, and consumers can affect wages of athletes. Evidence shows that, although discrimination was overt in the 1940s, it has diminished over time. Examples from MLB and the NFL support the hypothesis that discriminators suffer lower profits and/or lower success rates, as measured in wins. Economists regard discrimination as the indulgence of a distaste for employing, working with, or making a purchase involving members of a specific race, ethnicity, or gender. Discrimination can result from the behavior of employers, employees, and customers. Each form of discrimination affects the athletes and teams involved. There is conflicting evidence regarding the continuing existence of unequal access or unequal pay due to race or ethnicity in professional sports. Positional discrimination still exists in professional sports on the playing field, in the coaching ranks, and in the front office. Measuring gender discrimination in sports is harder than measuring racial discrimination because it is difficult to hold all else equal. The need to provide separate competition for women has forced governing bodies to determine how to draw a line between the sexes.

Discussion Questions

1 The NBA forced Donald Sterling to sell his stake in the Los Angeles Clippers because he made disparaging remarks about blacks, but the NFL still has a team called the Redskins. Did the NBA go too far, or has the NFL not gone far enough in combatting discrimination?

2 The International Olympic Committee now allows athletes to self-identify as male or female. What do you think of this policy?

3 Should professional sports be pressured to field teams that reflect the population of the US? Would you advocate the same policy for General Motors?

4 Suppose George Preston Marshall had been telling the truth and that integrating the Redskins would have severely damaged the team financially. What should the government do in such a case?

Problems

11.1 Suppose that the competitive wage in independent league baseball is $20,000 per season. One team owner has a taste for discrimination against all nonwhite players. Her coefficient of discrimination against (white) Hispanics is 0.20, and her coefficient of discrimination against blacks is 0.18. What would she consider the salaries of members of these two groups to be? If the supply of players were perfectly elastic, what would happen to the representation of blacks, Hispanics, and white non-Hispanics on the team?

11.2 An NFL running back comes to you, claiming that black running backs are the victims of racial discrimination by teams. Devise an econometric model that would test his claim. What finding would prove (or disprove) his claim?

11.3 Under what circumstances would market forces fail to eliminate discrimination?

11.4 Why was the NFL able to exclude black players in the 1930s? Why did this color line collapse so quickly in the early 1950s?

11.5 Use Becker's model of discrimination to explain why the sponsors of Formula 1 racing teams who discriminate will likely experience lower profits for doing so.

11.6 A professional sports team refuses to hire women as executives because it feels their family duties do not allow them to devote adequate time to the team. Is this discrimination? Justify your answer.

11.7 Using supply and demand graphs, show how positional segregation can occur even if only the players (including potential future players) believe that such discrimination exists.

11.8 In 2016, the British Open awarded about $8.5 million in prize money, while the British Women's Open awarded only $3 million. Is this evidence of gender discrimination in golf? Why or why not?

11.9 Use what you know about the Prisoner's Dilemma to explain why the English Premier League teams such as Arsenal have so many foreign players even when, as a group, the Premier League teams agree that they want to limit the number of foreign-born players.

11.10 Draw a set of indifference curves (as described in Appendix 9A) depicting a franchise owner with a taste for discrimination against Europeans. Put the number of Europeans on the vertical axis and the number of North Americans on the horizontal axis.

Notes

1   Will Tidey. 2013. "Sepp Blatter's Most Embarrassing Outbursts," *Bleacher Report*, May 31, at http://bleacherreport.com/articles/1657592-sepp-blatters-most-embarrassing-outbursts/page/2, viewed November 27, 2016.
2   Francis Dealy. 1990. *Win at Any Cost: The Sell Out of College Athletics* (New York: Birch Lane Press): 101.
3   He hit a home run later in the same game. From Robert Peterson. 1970. *Only the Ball Was White: A History of Legendary Black Players and All-Black Professional Teams* (New York: Gramercy Books): 194.
4   Richard Lapchick et al., "The 2014 Racial and Gender Report Card: Major League Soccer"; "The 2015 Racial and Gender Report Card: The National Football League"; "The 2015 Racial and Gender Report Card: Major League Baseball"; "The 2015 Racial and Gender Report Card: National Basketball Association"; and "The 2015 Racial and Gender Report Card: The Women's National Basketball Association," *The Institute for Diversity and Ethics in Sport (TIDES)*, all reports can be accessed through the TIDES home page, at http://www.tidesport.org/, viewed November 25, 2015.
5   Chih-Hai Yang and Hsuan-Y Lin, "Is There Salary Discrimination by Nationality in the NBA?: Foreign Talent or Foreign Market," *Journal of Sports Economics*, 13(1), February 2012: 53–75. The authors also found some evidence of discrimination against white players, though they note that the observed wage difference may be a function of playing time rather than discrimination. Adam Hoffer and Ryan Freidel, "Does Salary Discrimination Persist for Foreign Players in the NBA?" *Applied Economics Letters*, 21(1), February 2014: 1–5.
6   Michael Conlin and Patrick M. Emerson. 2006. "Discrimination in Hiring versus Retention and Promotion: An Empirical Analysis of Within-Firm Treatment of Players in the NFL," *Journal of Law, Economics & Organization*, 22(1), April: 115–136.
7   Jesse L. Schroffel and Christopher S.P. Magee. 2012. "Own-Race Bias among NBA Coaches," *Journal of Sports Economics* 13(2), April: 130–151.
8   Joseph Price and Justin Wolfers. 2010. "Racial Discrimination among NBA Referees," *Quarterly Journal of Economics*, 125(4), November: 1859–1887; Jeff Hamrick and John Rasp. 2015. "The Connection between Race and Called Strikes and Balls," *Journal of Sports Economics*, 16(7), October: 714–734; Scott Tainsky, Brian M. Mills, and Jason A. Winfree. 2015. "Further Examination of Potential Discrimination among MLB Umpires," *Journal of Sports Economics*, 16(4), May: 353–374.
9   Gary S. Becker. 1971. *The Economics of Discrimination*, 2nd ed. (Chicago, IL: University of Chicago Press).
10 A classic treatment of tastes and how economists regard them can be found in George Stigler and Gary Becker. 1977. "De Gustibus Non Est Disputandum," *American Economic Review*, 67(1), March: 76–90.
11 Material in this section is based on Becker. 1971. *The Economics of Discrimination*.
12 International Ice Hockey Federation, "Story #70: Swede Ulf Sterner—The First European in the NHL," *The IIHF 100-Year Anniversary*, at http://www.iihf.com/iihf-home/the-iihf/100-year-anniversary/100-top-stories/story-70/, viewed November 27, 2016; Alex Appleyard. 2016. "The Flyers' European Renaissance," *Philadelphia Sons of Penn*, October 18, at http://sonsofpenn.com/flyers/the-flyers-european-renaissance/, viewed November 27, 2016.
13 Marc Lavoie. 2000. "The Location of Pay Discrimination in the National Hockey League," *Journal of Sports Economics*, 1(4), November: 401–411. Other studies include Claude Vincent and Byron Eastman. 2009. "Determinants of Pay in the NHL: A Quantile Regression Approach," *Journal of Sports Economics*, 10(3), June: 256–277; Leo Kahane, Neil Longley, and Robert Simmons. 2013. "The Effects of Coworker Heterogeneity on Firm-Level Output: Assessing the Impacts of Cultural and Language Diversity in the National Hockey League," *Review of Economics and Statistics*, 95(1), March: 302–314; Kevin Mongeon. 2015. "A Market Test for Ethnic Discrimination in the National Hockey League: A Game-Level Panel Data Approach," *Journal of Sports Economics*, 15(5), June: 460–481; and Peter von Allmen, Michael Leeds, and Julian

Malakorn. 2015. "Victims or Beneficiaries? Wage Premia and National Origin in the National Hockey League," *Journal of Sports Management,* 29(6), November: 633–641.

14 For an application of this to French-speaking Canadians, see Michael A. Curme and Greg M. Dougherty, "Competition and Pay for National Hockey League Players Born in Quebec," *Journal of Sports Economics,* 5(2), May 2004: 186–205.

15 Kahane, Longley, and Simmons. 2013. "The Effects of Coworker Heterogeneity on Firm-Level Output": 309.

16 In the case of ethnicity, players are not able to switch groups. In some cases, however, employees may be able to switch from a less preferred group to a more preferred group in an attempt to signal to potential employers that they are highly productive. For example, a college degree may signal to employers that a person is highly productive. Employers want potential employees to send this signal if it is costly to find out the truth about whether they are highly productive. For a detailed explanation of signaling, see Michael A. Spence. 1973. "Job Market Signaling," *Quarterly Journal of Economics,* 87(3), August: 355–374.

17 For an excellent history of the Negro Leagues, see Peterson. 1970. *Only the Ball Was White.*

18 While the word *Negro* is no longer used to describe African Americans, historians and economists still use the term *Negro Leagues* to describe the collection of all-black teams that competed in the era when baseball was segregated.

19 Peterson. 1970. *Only the Ball Was White* : 203–204.

20 These teams were the Brooklyn (Los Angeles) Dodgers (0.592), Cleveland Indians (0.588), Boston (Milwaukee) Braves (0.554), Chicago White Sox (0.550), and New York (San Francisco) Giants (0.532).

21 Thomas G. Smith. 2011. *Showdown: JFK and the Integration of the Washington Redskins* (Boston, MA: Beacon Press): 140. The NFL had black players from its inception until 1933.

22 Stefan Szymanski. 2000. "A Market Test for Discrimination in the English Professional Soccer Leagues," *Journal of Political Economy,* 108(3), June: 590–603.

23 Michael MacCambridge. 2004. *America's Game: The Epic Story of How Pro Football Captured a Nation* (New York: Random House): 16–20.

24 The Browns won all four AAFC championships (1946–1949) and played in the NFL Championship Game each of their first six years in the league, winning three.

25 Frank Seravalli. 2015. "Canadians Do Not Make Up the Majority of NHL Players This Season," *TSN,* October 22, at http://www.tsn.ca/canadians-do-not-make-up-the-majority-of-nhl-players-this-season-1.380861, viewed November 28, 2016.

26 See, for example, Adrian Burgos. 2007. *Playing America's Game* (Berkeley: University of California Press): 83.

27 Peterson. 1970. *Only the Ball Was White*: 28.

28 From Roger Kahn. 1993. *The Era: 1947–1957* (New York: Ticknor and Fields): 36.

29 Ken Burns. 1994. *Baseball* miniseries, PBS, "Bottom of the Sixth" episode. The movie 42 gives an accurate depiction of the relationship between Robinson and his teammates.

30 Peterson. 1970. *Only the Ball Was White*: 199. Neither strike occurred after the league threatened suspensions.

31 Becker. 1971. *The Economics of Discrimination*: 56.

32 See David Margolick. 2005. *Beyond Glory: Joe Louis vs. Max Schmeling, and a World on the Brink* (New York: Alfred A. Knopf): 11.

33 Orn B. Bodvarsson. 1999. "A Test of Employer Discrimination in the NBA," *Contemporary Economic Policy,* 17(2), April: 243–256, cites several studies that find no evidence of employer discrimination. Jeffrey A. Jenkins. 1996. "A Reexamination of Salary Determination in Professional Basketball," *Social Science Quarterly,* 77(3), September: 594–608 finds no significant differences in NBA salaries by race. Lawrence M. Kahn. 1992. "The Effects of Race on Professional Football Players' Compensation," *Industrial Labor Relations Review,* 45(2), January: 295–310, finds that as early as 1989, racial differences between blacks and whites were no more than 4 percent.

34 For more study results and discussion on this point, see Lawrence M. Kahn. 1991. "Discrimination in Professional Sports: A Survey of the Literature," *ILR Review*, 44(3), April: 395–418.

35 Smith. 2011. *Showdown*: 153.

36 Interestingly, one study finds that the race of a team's players can affect the quality of the stadium in which they play. See Orn B. Bodvarsson and Brad R. Humphreys. 2013. "Labor Market Discrimination and Capital: The Effects of Fan Discrimination on Stadium and Arena Construction," *Contemporary Economic Policy*, 31(3), July: 604–617.

37 Dan McGraw. 2003. "The Foreign Invasion of the American Game," *The Village Voice Online*, May 28–June 3, at https://www.villagevoice.com/2003/05/27/the-foreign-invasion-of-the-american-game/; Mark T. Kanazawa and Jonas P. Funk. 2001. "Racial Discrimination in Professional Basketball: Evidence from Nielsen Ratings," *Economic Inquiry*, 39(4), October: 599–608.

38 Ian Preston and Stefan Szymanski. 2000. "Racial Discrimination in English Football," *Scottish Journal of Political Economy*, 47(4), September: 342–363; Eric M. Aldrich, Peter S. Arcidiacono, and Joseph L. Vigdor. 2005. "Do People Value Racial Diversity? Evidence from Nielsen Ratings," *The B.E. Journal of Economic Analysis and Policy*, 5(1), Article 4: 1–22; Wen-jhan Jane. 2015. "Customer Discrimination and Outcome Uncertainty in the World Baseball Classic: The Case of the Taiwanese Television Audience," in *The Sports Business in the Pacific Rim*, ed. Young Hoon Lee and Rodney Fort (Heidelberg: Springer): 103–122.

39 For a different approach to consumer discrimination, see Daraius Irani. 1996. "Estimating Consumer Discrimination Using Panel Data: 1972–1991," in *Baseball Economics: Current Research*, ed. John Fizel, Elizabeth Gustafson, and Lawrence Hadley (Westport, CT: Praeger).

40 See Clark Nardinelli and Curtis Simon. 1990. "Customer Discrimination in the Market for Memorabilia: The Case of Baseball," *Quarterly Journal of Economics*, 105(3), August: 575–595; Torben Anderson and Sumner J. La Croix. 1991. "Customer Discrimination in Major League Baseball," *Economic Inquiry*, 29(4), October: 665–677; L.J. Van Scyoc and N.J. Burnett. 2013. "How Times Have Changed: Racial Discrimination in the Market for Sports Memorabilia (Baseball Cards)," *Applied Economics Letters*, 20(7–9), June: 875–878; and Eric Primm, Nicole Leeper Piquero, Robert M. Regoli, and Alex R. Piquero. 2010. "The Role of Race in Football Card Prices," *Social Science Quarterly*, 91(1), March: 129–142.

41 Rodney Fort and Andrew Gill. 2000. "Race and Ethnicity Assessment in Baseball Card Markets," *Journal of Sports Economics*, 1(1), February: 21–38.

42 Lawrence M. Kahn and Peter Sherer. 1988. "Racial Differences in Professional Basketball Players' Compensation," *Journal of Labor Economics*, 6(1), January: 40–61; and Barton H. Hamilton. 1997. "Racial Discrimination and Professional Basketball Salaries in the 1990s," *Applied Economics*, 29(3), March: 287–296.

43 Kahn and Sherer. 1988. "Racial Differences in Professional Basketball Players' Compensation": 51.

44 Hamilton. 1997. "Racial Discrimination and Professional Basketball Salaries in the 1990s."

45 Andrew F. Hanssen and Torben Anderson. 1999. "Has Discrimination Lessened over Time? A Test Using Baseball's All-Star Vote," *Economic Inquiry*, 37(2), April: 326–352; Mark Gius and Donn Johnson. 1998. "An Empirical Investigation of Wage Discrimination in Professional Basketball," *Applied Economics Letters*, 5(11), November: 703–705.

46 BBC. 2014. "Atalanta Is Fined over Banana Incident in Italy's Serie A," *Sport: Football*, May 12, at http://www.bbc.com/sport/football/27374486, viewed December 1, 2016; BBC. 2014. "Urawa Reds Play to Empty Stadium after Fans Banned for Racist Banner," *Sport: Football*, March 23, at http://www.bbc.com/sport/football/26704368, viewed December 1, 2016; BBC. 2012. "Sol Campbell Warns Fans to Stay Away from Euro 2012," *News*, May 28, at http://www.bbc.com/news/uk-18192375, viewed December 1, 2016; BBC. 2008. "Faz Presidency Marred by Racial Abuse," *News*, February 25, at http://news.bbc.co.uk/sport2/hi/football/africa/7262763.stm, viewed December 1, 2016.

47 Data in this section, unless otherwise noted, are from Richard E. Lapchick et al. 2015. "The 2015 Racial and Gender Report Cards," *The Institute for Ethics and Diversity in Sport*, at http://tidesport.org.

48 The same argument is frequently used to explain why women are overrepresented in certain occupations and underrepresented in others.

49 Despite these highly lopsided percentages, Lapchick et al. state in "The 2011 Racial and Gender Report Card: National Football League" that stacking is much less of a concern than it has been historically because blacks now appear to have broken down the barrier at the quarterback position.

50 David J. Berri and Rob Simmons. 2009. "Race and the Evaluation of Signal Callers in the National Football League," *Journal of Sports Economics*, 10(1), February: 23–43.

51 Janice Fanning Madden. 2004. "Differences in the Success of NFL Coaches by Race, 1990–2002: Evidence of Last Hire, First Fire," *Journal of Sports Economics*, 5(1), February: 6–19; Janice Fanning Madden and Matthew Ruther. 2011. "Has the NFL's Rooney Rule Efforts 'Leveled the Field' for African American Head Coach Candidates?" *Journal of Sports Economics*, 12(2), April: 127–142; Benjamin L. Solow, John L. Solow, and Todd B. Walker. 2011. "Moving on Up: The Rooney Rule and Minority Hiring in the NFL," *Labour Economics*, 18(3), June: 332–337; Lawrence M. Kahn. 2006. "Race, Performance, Pay, and Retention among National Basketball Association Head Coaches," *Journal of Sports Economics*, 7(2), May: 119–149; and Rodney Fort, Young Hoon Lee, and David Berri. 2008. "Race, Technical Efficiency, and Retention: The Case of NBA Coaches," *International Journal of Sport Finance*, 3(2), May: 84–97.

52 Richard Lapchick and DaWon Baker. 2015. "The 2015 Racial and Gender Report Card: College Sport," *The Institute for Diversity in Sport*, March 3, at http://www.tidesport.org/college-sport.html, viewed December 3, 2016.

53 The 1904 Games were held in St. Louis in conjunction with the World's Fair. Perhaps because of the high travel costs, most of the participants in these Games were American.

54 Laura Santhanam. 2016. "Data: How Does the US Women's Soccer Team Pay Compare to the Men?" *PBS NewsHour: The Rundown*, March 31, at http://www.pbs.org/newshour/rundown/data-how-does-the-u-s-womens-soccer-team-pay-compare-to-the-men/, viewed April 22, 2016; Shane Ferro. 2015. "Here's Why It's Fair That Female Athletes Make Less Than Men," *Business Insider: UK*, July 7, at http://uk.businessinsider.com/womens-small-soccer-salaries-are-fair-2015-7?IR=T, viewed April 22, 2016; Mike Shields. 2015. "Women's World Cup Draws Strong Advertiser Demand for Fox Sports," *Wall Street Journal*, June 5, at http://blogs.wsj.com/cmo/2015/06/05/womens-world-cup-draws-strong-advertiser-demand-for-fox-sports/, viewed April 22, 2016; Andrew Das. 2016. "Pay Disparity in US Soccer? It's Complicated," *New York Times*, April 21, at https://www.nytimes.com/2016/04/22/sports/soccer/usmnt-uswnt-soccer-equal-pay.html, viewed April 22, 2016.

55 Margaret A. Ray and Paul W. Grimes. 1993. "Jockeying for Position: Winnings and Gender Discrimination on the Thoroughbred Track," *Social Science Quarterly*, 74(1), March: 46–61. So far, there has been no systematic study of gender discrimination in auto racing.

56 Kerry Close. 2016. "5 Reasons Why Tennis Should Keep Paying Men and Women Equally," *Everyday Money*, March 22, at http://time.com/money/4265912/equal-pay-tennis-djokovic-williams/, viewed December 3, 2016.

57 Ironically, in an autopsy four decades later, Walsh was found to have "ambiguous genitalia." Most of the material presented here comes from Ruth Padawer. 2016. "The Humiliating Practice of Sex-Testing Female Athletes," *New York Times*, June 28, at https://www.nytimes.com/2016/07/03/magazine/the-humiliating-practice-of-sex-testing-female-athletes.html, viewed June 28, 2016; and Christie Aschwanden. 2016. "The Olympics Are Still Struggling to Define Gender," *FiveThirtyEight*, June 28, at http://fivethirtyeight.com/features/the-olympics-are-still-struggling-to-define-gender/, viewed June 30, 2016.

58 Bill Veeck, with Ed Linn. 1996. *The Hustler's Handbook* (Durham, NC: Baseball America Classic Books): 100.

59   Harvey Frommer. 1982. *Rickey and Robinson* (New York: Macmillan): 38.
60   From Harvey Frommer. 1982. *Rickey and Robinson*: 87. Tammany Hall was where New York City's notorious political machine had been headquartered, so that any political boss in New York was dubbed "a Tammany Hall politician."
61   Harvey Frommer. 1982. *Rickey and Robinson*: 120.

Part Five

SPORTS IN THE NOT-FOR-PROFIT SECTOR

THE ECONOMICS OF INTERCOLLEGIATE SPORTS

Give me six weeks and I can put any school in the country on probation.
—BRENT CLARK, FORMER NCAA INVESTIGATOR[1]

Introduction

At first glance, a chapter on intercollegiate athletics seems like a departure from the rest of the book. After all, colleges and the NCAA spend considerable time, money, and energy reminding the public that they are not profit-making entities and that intercollegiate athletics is an amateur undertaking. In fact, though, an analysis of intercollegiate athletics contains elements of all the preceding chapters.

Questions of how one can—and whether one should—maximize profits are as relevant for an athletic director as they are for a team owner. As in professional sports, colleges can increase profits by exercising monopoly and monopsony power. Unlike the Cleveland Browns, the Ohio State football team is not going to move to Baltimore if Johns Hopkins University builds it a new stadium, but college administrators are keenly aware that spillovers from athletics may benefit the university even if the teams fail to turn a profit.

What most distinguishes intercollegiate sports from professional sports is the fact that colleges do not pay their athletes, contending instead that a college scholarship is adequate compensation. Recent court cases have successfully challenged this notion, opening the door to whether and how college athletes should be paid. While gender-based discrimination—and the role of Title IX in combatting it—has received more attention in recent years, racial discrimination has also played a large, sad role in college athletics. Because we encounter most of the same issues in intercollegiate sports and professional sports, this chapter forms a microcosm of the book as a whole.

Learning Objectives

- Appreciate the history and structure of the NCAA.
- Explain whether athletic departments are a profit center for colleges by examining their revenues and costs.
- Understand the ways that sports teams may affect other aspects of a university, such as alumni donations or applications.
- Describe the peculiar "labor market" in college sports in which athletes are not paid but many receive payment-in-kind through athletic scholarships.

12.1   The NCAA

One cannot discuss intercollegiate sports without understanding the role played by the National Collegiate Athletic Association (NCAA). Trying to do so would be like analyzing the behavior of the 32 professional football teams without acknowledging the presence of the National Football League. Because it performs many of the same functions as the NFL or other professional sports leagues, we begin this chapter with a brief history of the NCAA and an explanation of its structure.

A Brief History of the NCAA

The origins of the NCAA are bound up with the development of football in America. As football grew in popularity in the second half of the 19th century, students formed sports clubs independent of—at times in defiance of—the faculty and administration. Most administrators were disdainful toward the growing popularity of football. The size of football squads may have been determined by such hostility, as the Yale Football Association, which set many of the early rules of football, limited teams to 11 players because it feared that the faculty would not allow more students to leave campus for away games.[2] Because football teams (and all other athletic clubs) were student-run organizations, individual colleges often developed their own set of rules. The lack of consistent rules sometimes forced schools into comical situations. For example, a game between Harvard and McGill in Montreal was played under Harvard's rules for one half and McGill's rules for the other.[3] The transaction costs of negotiating rules on a game-by-game basis discouraged the spread of football and made it difficult to enforce any one set of rules, resulting in an alarmingly violent game.[4]

Events came to a head after the 1905 season, during which 18 students were killed and 159 suffered serious injuries. In the wake of this carnage, President Theodore Roosevelt warned representatives of Harvard, Yale, and Princeton— three major football powers of the time—that they had to regulate the game or see it outlawed. In response, representatives of 13 colleges met to adopt a set of rules and to establish an enforcement mechanism. Within a year, the Intercollegiate Athletic Association of the United States—renamed the National Collegiate Athletic Association in 1910—established a common set of rules.

For several years, the NCAA was primarily concerned with standardizing rules in football and other intercollegiate sports. Soon, however, it turned its attention to behavior off the field, passing numerous resolutions intended to discourage the professionalization of college sports. One can argue whether the NCAA's adherence to amateurism represented a high-minded stand in defense of the academic integrity of its members, or an attempt to guarantee its members a cheap labor force. One cannot deny, however, that the NCAA was coordinating the actions of its membership far beyond its initial mandate.

The challenge for the NCAA was that the rules it imposed often conflicted with individual teams' incentives to produce wins. In 1948, the NCAA learned the consequences of being unable to enforce the rules it imposed when it passed the **Sanity Code**, a set of principles designed to govern the behavior of member schools. However, seven schools—which came to be known as the "seven sinners"—announced that they would not abide by the Sanity Code's prohibition of athletic scholarships.[5] When the NCAA's membership failed to muster the two-thirds majority it needed to expel the seven sinners, the NCAA appeared destined for irrelevance.

Ironically, the NCAA was saved in the early 1950s by one of the worst scandals in the history of collegiate athletics. In the postwar era, college basketball surged in popularity. At the height of the boom, the sport was rocked by a series of point-shaving scandals. Point-shaving enables unscrupulous gamblers to beat point spreads, the expected margin of victory that is set by bookmakers. Gamblers entice players to shave points by paying them to win by a smaller margin than bookies predict and then bet that the team will not cover the point spread.

The scandals destroyed the basketball programs of several schools in the New York area in 1952, including that of former national champion City College of New York.[6] It also implicated several members of the national champion University of Kentucky basketball squad. The ensuing investigation revealed that the Kentucky coach, Adolph Rupp, had associated with Ed Curd, a gambler with links to organized crime (and who may have abetted the point shaving), and that Rupp had flagrantly violated NCAA regulations regarding payments to athletes.

Unable to enforce its own guidelines, the NCAA was powerless to take action against Kentucky. However, the Southeastern Conference (SEC), to which Kentucky belonged, was so embarrassed by Kentucky's actions that its commissioner suspended Kentucky from the SEC for the ensuing year. With no serious rival in the SEC, Kentucky retorted that it would simply play other schools.

At this point, the NCAA saw an opportunity to use a new weapon at its disposal—the boycott. In an earlier dispute with the University of Pennsylvania, which had insisted on an independent TV contract, the NCAA had threatened to get its member schools to boycott Penn games, giving Penn nothing to televise. The NCAA now tried the same tactic with Kentucky, urging its member schools to honor the boycott. Rather than fight the boycott, Kentucky's faculty representatives accepted their punishment.[7]

The realization that it had an effective threat mechanism gave the NCAA a new lease on life. By convincing Kentucky to suspend its basketball program (not, as is popularly believed, closing it down), the NCAA demonstrated that it could punish cheaters. Schools now accept lesser punishments in part because of the fear that failure to do so will result in the "death penalty."[8]

The Structure of the NCAA

The NCAA has continually redefined intercollegiate athletics by dividing schools into smaller, more homogeneous subgroups. When it was first formed, all members were equal partners.[9] In 1973, the schools split into Divisions I, II, and III. The main distinction between the divisions was in the rules governing recruiting and financial aid. Division III schools are typically small, private colleges that offer no athletic scholarships. Division II schools consist of private colleges and smaller state universities and offer some athletic scholarships. Division I consisted of the big-time football powers, but even this distinction failed to capture substantial differences among the most powerful athletic programs.

In 1978, under pressure from the largest Division I football powers, the NCAA split Division I into Division I-A, later renamed the Football Bowl Subdivision (FBS), and Division I-AA, later called the Football Championship Subdivision (FCS). This distinction among Division I schools exists solely for football. Most of the criteria for FBS status relate to the school's commitment to big-time athletics. They must, for example, have at least 16 varsity sports (including football), offer at least 200 athletic scholarships (or spend at least $4 million on scholarships), and have an average home attendance at their football games of at least 15,000 over a rolling 2-year period.[10] The creation of the Bowl Championship Series (BCS) coalition, undertaken by the most powerful conferences and TV networks, created yet another subdivision, albeit one outside the NCAA's jurisdiction.

The advent of the College Football Playoff has changed the way the FBS selects a champion, but it has left the participants largely unchanged. As we will see, participation in the playoff and the most lucrative bowl games is dominated by the Power 5 conferences: the Atlantic Coast Conference (ACC), the Big 12, the Big Ten, the Pacific 12 (PAC-12), and the Southeastern Conference (SEC). All other Division I schools, with the notable exception of Notre Dame, must scramble for what is left over.

The appearance of smaller, more elite groups within the NCAA resembles the changes that have occurred in British soccer. The Football Association (FA) was established in 1863, with all soccer clubs as equal members. After 25 years, the top clubs formed a more select group within the FA known as the Football League (FL). Almost 100 years later, the best clubs in the FL split off to form the Premier League. In both British soccer and American football, the optimal size of the association changed as the market for the product changed.

12.2 The Costs and Benefits of Big-Time College Sports

A persistent bone of contention in intercollegiate athletics is the extent to which major university athletics programs can or should be a profit center. This question presents a unique challenge to American universities. After all, universities seldom debate the profitability of their physics or economics departments. This is also a peculiarly American problem, as athletics plays a much bigger role in US colleges than in schools elsewhere.

The debate over the role of athletics in the broader mission of the university shows the discomfort that many feel with the role it plays in academe. At schools with unprofitable athletics departments, faculty members often complain that athletics drain resources away from "more deserving" activities. At schools with highly profitable athletics departments, the faculty often complain that the profits show the misplaced values of the institution.

It is hard to say what the goal of college athletics departments is—or even whether they have a specific goal. Unlike professional sports teams, athletics departments are embedded in a larger university and take account of spillovers, such as increased applications or alumni donations that affect the larger (university) community.

For now, we ignore such broader considerations and focus on what the late Myles Brand, former President of the NCAA, called the "collegiate model." According to the collegiate model, a college's athletic department "has an obligation to conduct its revenue-generating activities in a productive and sound business-like manner." When it comes to costs—particularly labor costs—however, "athletics must follow its non-profit mission" and rigorously defend the amateur status of its labor force.[11] This section examines the revenues and costs of university athletic programs and the extent to which they are profitable.

The Revenue from Intercollegiate Athletics

At most universities, the bulk of an athletics department's revenue comes from football and, to a lesser extent, men's basketball. This is particularly true for schools in the Power 5 conferences, which dominate college football and basketball both athletically and financially. At schools in the Football Bowl Subdivision (FBS)—the 128 schools that participated in bowls and now are eligible for the College Football Playoff—revenue from football typically dwarfs even that from men's basketball. Table 12.1 shows *Forbes*'s estimates of the revenue and imputed market value of the 20 most valuable football programs in 2015.

From the table, we see that, unlike the NFL, the distribution of revenue and the market value of programs in college football are highly unequal. Five of the top 10 (and 9 of the top 20) universities are from the SEC, but only 3 schools from the ACC and Big 12 conferences combined are in the top 20.

Table 12.1 Market Value and Revenue for the 20 Most Valuable Football Programs

University	Conference	Revenue[a]	Imputed Market Value
University of Texas	Big 12	121	152
University of Notre Dame	Independent	86	127
University of Tennessee	Southeastern Conference (SEC)	94	121
Louisiana State University	SEC	86	111
University of Michigan	Big Ten	88	105
University of Georgia	SEC	76	102
Ohio State University	Big Ten	84	100
University of Alabama	SEC	97	99
University of Oklahoma	Big 12	79	96
Auburn University	SEC	87	89
Penn State University	Big Ten	71	81
University of Arkansas	SEC	66	80
University of Washington	Pacific-12 (PAC-12)	67	78
University of Oregon	PAC-12	61	75
University of Florida	SEC	75	72
Texas A&M University	SEC	65	72
Florida State University	Atlantic Coast Conference (ACC)	70	70
University of South Carolina	SEC	60	69
Michigan State University	Big Ten	59	67
University of Southern California	PAC-12	60	66

[a] All figures in millions of dollars.

Source: Chris Smith. 2015. "College Football's Most Valuable Teams 2015: Texas, Notre Dame and . . . Tennessee?" *Forbes.com*, December 22, at https://www.forbes.com/sites/chrissmith/2015/12/22/college-footballs-most-valuable-teams-2015-texas-notre-dame-and-tennessee/, viewed February 5, 2017.

Gate and Venue Revenue

As was true for professional teams, gate revenue used to be the single most important source of income for college sports, but it has steadily declined in importance (though not in dollar value), as revenue from television and other sources has risen. In 2014–2015, athletic departments in the Power 5 conferences derived a little over one-fifth of their revenue from ticket sales—almost all of it from football and men's basketball.[12]

Although college sports teams do not threaten to move in search of better stadium deals, venues have become important sources of income. Like their professional counterparts, an increasing number of schools have sold the naming rights of their athletics facilities. The $4.1 million that Alaska Airlines pays the University of Washington and the $2 million that State Farm Insurance pays the University of Illinois annually to put their names on the football stadium and basketball arena, respectively, rival the revenues received by many professional franchises.[13]

Luxury boxes and club seating have also become standard features of stadiums and arenas for FBS schools. Of the programs listed in Table 12.1, only the University of Southern California does not have luxury suites in its stadium (though it provides "field suites" in either end zone). The University of Texas and the University of Alabama both have over 100 suites.[14]

Conference Distributions of Television Revenue

With notable exceptions—such as Notre Dame, whose football program belongs to no conference and has a separate television deal with NBC—colleges do not receive the bulk of their broadcast revenue directly from televising their basketball or football games. Instead, they receive distributions from their conferences or the NCAA. Table 12.2 shows the television contracts for the six largest conferences in 2016–2017.

As with TV revenue in the major professional sports, broadcast revenue from football has an equalizing influence on revenues within the conferences. Vanderbilt University, for example, receives as much revenue as the University of Alabama from the SEC's contracts with ESPN and CBS, even if it rarely

Table 12.2 Power 5 Conference Broadcast Revenue for Football

Conference	Revenue per School[a]	Term[b] (expiration)	Network
ACC	16.0	15 (2027)	ESPN
Big Ten	30.7	6 (2022); 25 (2032)	ABC/ESPN; Fox; Big Ten Network
Big 12	20.0	13 (2025)	Fox; ABC/ESPN
Pac-12	20.2	12 (2024)	Fox; ABC/ESPN
SEC	17.1	15 (2024)	ESPN; CBS

[a]In millions of dollars per year.
[b]In years.

Sources: Matt Peloquin. 2012. "2012 NCAA Television Revenue by Conference," *CollegeSportsInfo. com,* May 10, at http://collegesportsinfo.com/2012/05/10/2012-ncaa-television-revenue-by-conference/; Kristi Dosh. 2016. "New Deals with Fox, ESPN, and CBS Nearly Triple Big Ten TV Revenue," *Forbes.com,* June 20, at http://www.forbes.com/sites/kristidosh/2016/06/20/new-deals-with-fox-espn-and-cbs-nearly-triple-big-ten-television-revenue/.

receives national TV exposure, while Alabama is on TV nearly every week. However, broadcast revenue is a major source of *inequality* among conferences. For example, the total broadcast revenue in 2016–2017 for Conference-USA will be $2.8 million. That is about one-tenth what each Big Ten school will receive.[15]

The Revenue from Bowl Games

Broadcast rights come mostly from broadcasting regularly scheduled college football games. College football's postseason, particularly the bowl games played by the sport's top programs, have become a major source of revenue—and inequality. Table 12.3 shows the payments made by the "New Year's Six" bowl games. The Rose, Sugar, Orange, and Cotton Bowls games are the four oldest bowl games and have traditionally been the most prestigious.[16] Since the Power 5 conferences began the College Football Playoff (CFP) in 2015, these four bowl games, along with the Peach and Fiesta Bowls, have rotated the playoff semi-finals, with the other games featuring the top-ranked non-playoff teams. The payoffs of these bowl games, shown in Table 12.3, reflect their lofty status. Most of the other 34 bowl games pay far less. For example, the 2016 Miami Beach Bowl had a payout of only $100,000. Placing teams in the "New Year's Six" bowls has thus become vitally important to conferences, though—as we shall see—playing in a bowl is not so lucrative to the teams that participate in them.

Because the college football playoff is run by the conferences and not the NCAA, all the bowl revenue goes directly to the conferences, the bulk of it to the Power 5 conferences. Table 12.4 shows that revenue from the 2016–2017 bowl season ranged from $132.5 million for the Big Ten to $88.5 million for the ACC. The ACC's payout was still greater than the combined payments to the other five conferences—the Group of 5—that make up the remainder of the FBS schools.[17] Because the bulk of the revenue generated by the Bowl system goes to teams in the Power 5 conferences, these conferences have a clear incentive not to cede control of the CFP, and the revenue it generates, to the NCAA.

While Alabama and Clemson played for the national championship in 2017, the big winners might have been schools like the University of Virginia, which went 2–10 and did not play in a bowl game. Because the bowls pay money to

Table 12.3 Selected Bowl Payouts in 2016–2017

Name	Location	Payout per Team[a]
Rose Bowl presented by Northwestern Mutual	Pasadena, CA	$40,000,000
Allstate Sugar Bowl	New Orleans, LA	$40,000,000
Capital One Orange Bowl	Miami Gardens, FL	$27,500,000
PlayStation Fiesta Bowl	Glendale, AZ	$6,000,000
Chick-fil-A Peach Bowl	Atlanta, GA	$6,000,000
Goodyear Cotton Bowl Classic	Arlington, TX	$4,000,000

[a]Each bowl participant shares this payout with the other members of its conference. In the ACC and SEC, the payout is not shared equally.

Source: "2016-17 Bowl Money," *ACC Football Rx*, at http://accfootballrx.blogspot. com/2016/12/2016-17-bowl-money.html, viewed February 12, 2017; and Kristi Dosh. 2016. "College Football Payouts by Conference for 2016-17," *Forbes.com*, December 31, at http://www.forbes.com/sites/kristidosh/2016/12/31/college-football-playoff-payouts-by-conference-for-2016-17/, viewed February 12, 2017.

Table 12.4 Bowl Payouts by Conference

Conference	Total Payout (in millions)
Big 10	$132.5
Pac-12	$101.0
Southeastern Conference	$101.0
Big 12	$95.0
Atlantic Coast Conference	$88.5
Group of 5 Conferences	$83.5
Notre Dame (Independent)	$2.83

Source: Kristi Dosh. 2016. "College Football Payouts by Conference."

the participating conferences and the conferences split the proceeds roughly equally among schools, not going to a bowl game can be more profitable than going to one. Although schools receive a subsidy to transport the team to the bowl game, they frequently must guarantee the sale of tens of thousands of tickets. The cost of unsold tickets plus bonuses that a school must often pay to coaches and athletic directors can significantly reduce the net payout to a bowl participant. By one estimate, the University of Florida made a net profit of just $47,000 for winning the 2009 national championship game, and many teams—particularly those that play in the lesser bowl games with low payouts—actually lose tens, even hundreds of thousands of dollars from participating in postseason games.[18]

The NCAA Basketball Tournament

Unlike the CFP, the "March Madness" basketball tournament is run by the NCAA. The NCAA's 14-year, $10.8 billion television contract with CBS and Turner (signed in 2010) provides it with almost 90 percent of its annual revenue. The NCAA distributes roughly 60 percent of this total to member schools, mostly according to the number of scholarships a school provides or the number of sports that it sponsors.[19] Because these distributions are based on the number of teams and athletes and not their performance, a small school like Holy Cross, which offers many sports but rarely competes for national titles, receives a similar payout to much larger schools, such as Ohio State, which has the same number of teams and participants but generally plays at a much higher level. Thus, a large portion of the NCAA's annual revenues is relatively evenly split among Division I schools.

A smaller portion of the distribution is based on team performance. In 2016, the NCAA committed to paying about $100 million to conferences based on their member schools' progress in the men's basketball tournament. The payments are made over a 6-year rolling period, with each tournament game in which a team plays (except for the finals) paying $265,791 to the school's conference. Hence, the University of North Carolina's (UNC's) 2017 championship run will bring the ACC about $1.32 million per year for the next 6 years.[20]

UNC was not the only ACC team to play in the NCAA tournament. Eight ACC schools played a total of 16 games (not counting UNC's finals victory), guaranteeing the conference $4.25 million per year for the next 6 years. In contrast, the Ivy League gets only $265,791 per year, from Princeton's first-round loss.

The NCAA tournament thus brings far more revenue to powerful conferences, whose teams are more likely to qualify for the tournament and more likely to advance in it.

Subsidies

As one might expect, "big-time" programs generate much more revenue than lesser programs. The average annual revenue of a Power 5 athletic department is $103.2 million, while that of a department in a Group of 5 conference is $33.0 million. However, athletic departments do not necessarily generate all the revenue they receive. Some schools charge substantial "student athletic fees" that have nothing to do with student access to the weight room or swimming pool and are sent directly to the school's athletic department. Revenues can also include transfers to the athletic department from the university's central administration or direct allocations by the state government.[21]

Subsidies for Power 5 conferences are generally fairly small.[22] The median subsidy in 2014–2015 was $2.7 million, roughly 2.8 percent of total athletic budget. There was, however, considerable variation across schools. Many athletic departments, including six in the SEC, received no subsidy. Five schools received subsidies of over $10 million. Rutgers received the highest subsidy, $23.8 million, over one-third of its total athletic revenue.

Subsidies for the Group of 5 conferences dwarf those of the Power 5. The median subsidy for these schools was $19.2 million, almost two-thirds of their athletic budgets. Over four-fifths of the athletic revenues at Eastern Michigan and Florida International universities come from subsidies.

The Cost of Intercollegiate Athletics

FBS athletic departments may resemble professional sports teams in some ways, but they are unique in one key respect: they do not pay their athletes. Scholarship athletes receive little more than tuition and room and board. Despite their access to an ample supply of cheap labor, universities have been accused of engaging in an athletics arms race, with athletic budgets steadily rising, even as the rest of their budgets are being cut.[23] We now turn our attention to the costs facing athletic departments and the origins of the alleged arms race.

Scholarships

While athletic departments pay their athletes no salaries, Charles Clotfelter reports that athletes at FBS schools represent 14 percent of the average athletic department's budget because universities mark scholarships as a cost to their athletic departments.[24] However, there is good reason to believe that this figure significantly overstates the true cost of scholarships.

In standard economics, an item's price reflects its opportunity cost. For example, spending $50 at a baseball game sacrifices $50 that could have been spent at a concert. The monetary value of a scholarship, however, does not necessarily represent the opportunity cost it imposes.[25]

There are two ways that awarding a basketball player a $40,000 scholarship could impose an opportunity cost of $40,000: if she would have paid full tuition to attend the university in the absence of a scholarship or if the university is operating at full capacity so that admitting the athlete displaces another student who would have paid $40,000. It is highly unlikely that either of the above scenarios holds. The athlete probably would have gone elsewhere had she not received the scholarship, and universities seldom operate so close to capacity that they cannot admit another student (though that might be the case for student housing). It is far more likely that an athlete displaces another student who would have received some form of financial aid from the institution as well. It is even possible that athletes who receive a partial scholarship represent a net gain to the university, as the university receives the tuition fees not covered by the scholarship, which it would not have received otherwise. In sum, the true cost of athletic scholarships is well below the face value of the scholarships.

Coaches' Salaries

Not all the labor supplied to athletic departments is unpaid. Michigan football coach Jim Harbaugh was paid over $9 million for the 2016 football season. Kentucky's basketball coach John Calipari was not far behind, with a salary of $7.1 million. It comes as no surprise that, in 2016, the highest-paid government employee in 27 states was the state university's football coach, and that a basketball coach was the highest-paid employee in 12 others.[26] The high salaries paid to football and basketball coaches are not new. A 1929 report by the Carnegie Foundation for the Advancement of Teaching found that "on average football coaches at large institutions earned more than the highest-paid full professor on campus."[27]

Revenue data from the US Department of Education and salary data from *USA Today* show that the median head coach's salary in 2016 was almost 5.8 percent of the team's total revenue. If head coaches in the NFL received a similar percentage of their team's revenue, then their median salary would be $18.5 million. This is more than double what the *highest*-paid NFL coach (Sean Payton—$8 million) earned in 2016.

Head coaches are not alone in receiving high salaries. *USA Today* reports that 12 *assistant* coaches had salaries of at least $1 million.[28] The growth in salaries has been accompanied by a growth in staff. Between 2004 and 2014, the University of Michigan added 77 non-coaching positions to its athletic department, and its payments to administrators and staff rose by 89 percent. Over the same time period, the administrative and staff payroll for the University of Mississippi's football program rose by over 900 percent.[29]

Capital Expenditures

An athletics arms race is also evident in expenditure on facilities. Spending on college football stadiums resembles that of NFL teams, with recent remodeling of Notre Dame Stadium and Kyle Field at Texas A&M costing close to half a billion dollars each.[30] The spending does not stop with stadiums. In 2014, 48 schools in the Power 5 conferences combined to spend over $772 million on other athletic facilities. Clemson is currently building a $55 million complex for its football players, complete with beach volleyball, miniature golf, and a bowling alley. At Oregon, Phil Knight, the founder of Nike, spent from $95 to $140 million (estimates vary) on the Hatfield-Dowlin Complex, whose amenities sound like those of a luxury hotel:

> The individually ventilated lockers came from Germany; the wood for the floor in the weight room came from Brazil; and the lounge chairs in the players' barber shop came from Italy.[31]

Table 12.5 Mean Revenues, Expenditures, Subsidies, and Profits for FBS Athletic Departments

Conference	Revenue[a]	Expenditure	Subsidy	Profit	Net Profit[b]
ACC	$90.4	$87.8	$7.9	$2.7	−$5.2
Big 12	$103.3	$98.5	$2.7	$4.8	$2.1
Big Ten	$108.5	$106.6	$4.7	$1.9	−$2.8
PAC-12	$81.3	$82.8	$7.2	−$1.5	−$8.7
Southeastern	$122.5	$105.6	$1.3	$16.9	$15.6
Group of 5	$33.0	$32.8	$19.2	$0.1	−$19.1

[a]All figures in millions. Data are from 2015–16.

[b]Net Profit = Profit − Subsidy.

Source: Berkowitz et al., "NCAA Finances," *USAToday.com*, at http://sports.usatoday.com/ncaa/finances/, viewed February 15, 2017.

Do Colleges Make a Profit from Athletics?

Like professional sports teams, universities can report either profits or losses, depending on what numbers they use. Table 12.5 shows the average revenue, expenditure, subsidy, and profits with and without subsidies for public universities in each Power 5 conference as well as overall averages for the Group of 5 conferences. They show that subsidies can make the difference between profit and loss.

If one counts subsidies as revenue, 84.6 percent of the public schools in Power 5 conferences have profitable athletic departments. Without the subsidies, the figure drops by half to 42.3 percent. Every school in the PAC-12 conference and all ACC schools except Florida State report a loss without subsidies. The greatest losses occurred at Rutgers University, which lost $23.8 million. Again, the financial picture is far worse for Group of 5 schools. Counting the subsidies as revenue, 65.4 percent of these schools have profitable athletic departments. Without the subsidies, every athletic department loses money. The losses range from $4 million for the University of Louisiana-Monroe to $28.6 million for San Diego State University.

Rutgers University's subsidy of almost $24 million to cover the losses of its athletic department seems like a huge sum, but it is important to put such numbers in context. The universities that house FBS athletic departments are enormous enterprises. With an overall budget of about $3.8 billion, Rutgers' athletic subsidy comes to 0.6 percent of the university's overall budget. Its total athletic budget is less than 1.9 percent of the overall budget. Once again, sports garner more attention than their economic impact justifies.

12.3 Monopoly Power in College Athletics

The NCAA is not the only regulatory body in intercollegiate athletics—for example, the National Association of Intercollegiate Athletics (NAIA) oversees almost 250 colleges—but it is by far the largest (with almost 1,300 schools) and the most prestigious organization of its kind in the United States. Despite its prominence, the NCAA's precise role and goals are the subject of debate. Supporters of the NCAA regard it as the guardian of integrity in collegiate athletics. Its foes see it as a money-grubbing cartel that ruthlessly exercises both monopoly and monopsony power. In fact, there are elements of truth to both viewpoints. Former Executive Director Walter Byers described his job as "keeping intercollegiate sports clean while generating millions of dollars each year as income for the colleges."[32] In this section, we explore how the NCAA resembles and differs from the classic monopoly model.

The NCAA and Optimal Cartel Behavior

The NCAA is neither a monopoly nor a monopsony in the classic sense. Instead, it is a collection of schools that have come together, for good or ill, to regulate intercollegiate athletics. This regulation consists of coordinating schools' activities so as to fix the market price, assign output levels to their members, divide revenue, and erect barriers to entry by outside producers, all classic cartel activities. One example of the NCAA's predatory behavior came in the wake of Title IX, legislation that vastly expanded funding for women's sports. After first opposing Title IX because it might drain resources away from men's sports, the NCAA changed course and sought to extend its authority to cover women's sports. The only problem was that an oversight body already existed, the Association of Intercollegiate Athletics for Women (AIAW). In the early 1980s, the NCAA used its power over men's sports to coerce member schools to switch their affiliation from the AIAW to the NCAA. The NCAA also used its control over men's sports to guarantee superior media access for those schools that participated in NCAA-sanctioned events. By 1982, the AIAW had folded.

While the NCAA acts like a cartel, it differs from a standard cartel in that it was not formed to monopolize a market. Recall from the beginning of this chapter that colleges and universities founded the organization that evolved into the NCAA under duress. While their initial goal was to formulate rules of play on the football field, they quickly moved into regulating behavior off the field as well, eventually morphing into a multimillion-dollar organization that carefully protects its financial interests to the point of trademarking the phrase "Final Four."[33] This evolution into a collusive structure has led economists to call the NCAA an **incidental cartel**.

Dividing Cartel Profits

The simple model of monopoly behavior is inadequate for analyzing how cartels behave. Because a cartel consists of multiple firms (schools in this case) instead of just one, cartels must choose the best output level and allocate that output (and accompanying revenue) among its members. To see how a cartel operates, consider a cartel with only two members (the general conclusions hold for a cartel of any size).

The problem facing a cartel with two members is identical to that facing a monopoly that allocates output between two plants. If the plants are identical, the decision is easy: have each plant produce half the output. This also divides revenue equally between the two members of the cartel.

Generally, however, the firms in a cartel are not identical. Figure 12.1 shows the marginal cost curves for two heterogeneous firms, A and B. Since the marginal cost curve for Firm A lies below that for Firm B, it is cheaper for Firm A to increase its output a little bit than it is for Firm B if both firms are producing the same level of output. Given the marginal cost curves for the individual firms, we can construct the marginal cost curve for the cartel by computing the horizontal sum, just as we computed the market supply curve from individual supply curves in

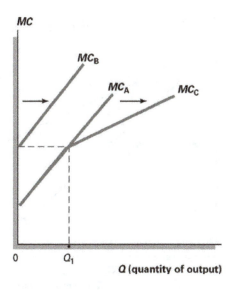

Figure 12.1
Cartels and Marginal Cost

The cartel's *MC* curve is the horizontal sum of the individual *MC* curves.

Chapter 2. At low levels of output, the cartel's marginal cost curve coincides with the marginal cost curve for Firm A alone (MC_A) since Firm B cannot produce at such low marginal cost. When Firm A reaches output level Q_1, the cost of increasing its output by one unit is the same as Firm B's cost of producing its first unit of output. Starting at Q_1, both firms produce, and the cartel's marginal cost curve (MC_C) lies to the right of the individual firms' curves.

If consumers do not care whether they buy from Firm A or Firm B, there is a single market demand curve for their output. With a single demand curve, the two firms also face a common marginal revenue curve, as seen in Figure 12.2. The optimal level of output for the cartel occurs where the cartel's marginal cost curve (MC_C) meets the marginal revenue curve (MR). The overall output of the cartel is Q_C^*, where $MR^* = MC_C^*$.

The division of output that maximizes overall profit allocates production according to the individual firms' marginal costs so that $MC_A = MC_B = MR^*$. In Figure 12.2, this occurs at Q_A^* for Firm A and Q_B^* for Firm B, because the marginal cost curve for the cartel is the horizontal sum of the individual marginal cost curves, $Q_A^* + Q_B^* = Q_C^*$. A cartel therefore allocates the lion's share of output and profit to its most efficient members. In the case of intercollegiate sports, the allocation of bowl appearances and broadcast revenue is consistent with a cartel's allocating output and profit according to the efficient output of high-quality football. The division into Division I, II, and III and the ensuing subdivision of Division I into smaller and smaller components effectively states that the University of Washington (an FBS school) is more efficient at producing top-level football than Youngstown State University (an FCS school), and that both are far more efficient than Johns Hopkins University (a Division III football program).

Prisoner's Dilemma: How Rational Actions Lead to Irrational Outcomes

As with many of the NCAA's anticompetitive actions, its restraint of trade in television began innocently. At a party in 1950, Dick Romney, the commissioner of the Mountain States Conference (now the Western Athletic Conference), approached University of Michigan coach Fritz Crisler, who was helping negotiate

Figure 12.2
Optimal Division of Output by a Cartel

The cartel sets the optimal level of output, Q_C^*, by setting marginal revenue (MR) equal to the sum of the marginal cost curves (MC_C) Firm A produces Q_A^* and firm B produces Q_B^*.

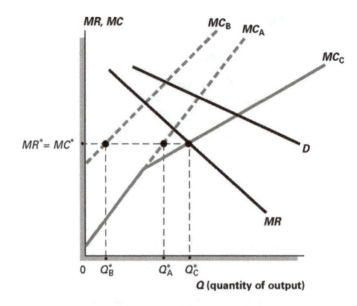

an NCAA-wide television contract. Romney half-seriously asked whether the powerful schools such as Michigan would set aside some TV appearances for lesser programs. To Romney's surprise, Crisler agreed and helped push through a limit on the number of games that each school could have on the network broadcast.[34]

As football became increasingly lucrative, the more powerful schools forgot Crisler's spirit of fairness and sought to increase their control over the flow of money. In 1976, 61 of the largest football powers in the NCAA formed the College Football Association (CFA), whose sole purpose was to lobby for greater control of television appearances and revenue. The NCAA responded in 1978 by splitting Division I, which consisted of the largest schools, into Divisions I-A and I-AA.

The new arrangement increased the share of income flowing to the Division I-A programs, though not enough to satisfy them. In 1982, two CFA members, the University of Georgia and Oklahoma University, brought an antitrust suit against the NCAA. A federal district court ruled against the NCAA in stinging terms, finding it to be in clear violation of Section 1 of the Sherman Antitrust Act.[35] In 1984, the Supreme Court upheld the initial ruling, saying that the NCAA had failed to meet the rule of reason.[36]

The ruling led to the flood of college games that we now see on television every fall. Much to the surprise of the schools involved, their greater exposure did not bring an immediate increase in revenue. In their haste to increase their TV exposure, the members of the CFA forgot that demand curves slope down. With more games on TV, the ratings for a typical broadcast fell by one-fourth, and the fees schools could charge for broadcast rights plummeted. Four years after the decision, broadcast rights fees were only half what they had been. Oklahoma, one of the plaintiffs in the case, saw its average revenue for a regional or national broadcast fall from over $425,000 the year before the Supreme Court ruling to less than $190,000 the season after.[37]

Table 12.6 College Football Broadcasts as a Prisoner's Dilemma

	Miami Televises Many Games	Miami Limits Appearances
FSU Televises Many Games	Miami gets $5 million, FSU gets $5 million	Miami gets $3 million, FSU gets $20 million
FSU Limits Appearances	Miami gets $20 million, FSU gets $3 million	Miami gets $10 million, FSU gets $10 million

We can model the breakdown of the NCAA's cartel power over TV broadcasts as a two-player game that results in a Prisoner's Dilemma. For simplicity, consider only two "players," Florida State University (FSU) and the University of Miami, and assume that each has two possible strategies: limiting its broadcasts in accordance with the cartel, or abandoning the cartel and broadcasting many games. Table 12.6 shows the payoff matrix for FSU and Miami.

Unlimited broadcasts are clearly a dominant strategy, as each school finds it optimal to broadcast many games regardless of what the other school does. While broadcasting many games is optimal for each individual school, it leaves Miami and FSU worse off than they could be.

Academic Standards: A Key to Academic Integrity or Exercise of Monopoly Power?

One of the NCAA's most contentious policies is the academic standards it sets for student-athletes. This should come as no surprise, as standards are a double-edged sword in many areas. Doctors, lawyers, accountants, and many other professionals must meet them before they are allowed to work. Professional standards protect the public by barring unqualified practitioners or ensuring that capable students receive adequate training. However, they also limit the degree of competition in the market and inflate the pay of workers who meet the standards. Similarly, setting academic standards defends the academic mission of universities, but it also protects the interests of established powers by reducing competition.

The NCAA's Current Academic Standards

The NCAA's current standards are based on both students' readiness for college and their academic progress once they are admitted. Applicants must have completed at least 16 core courses while in high school, 10 of them in the first 3 years, with a grade-point average of at least 2.3 in these courses. To compete as a freshman, they must also satisfy a sliding scale of SAT scores and high school grades. For example, students with a cumulative SAT of 400 must have a grade point average of at least 3.55. To maintain their eligibility, students must complete 40 percent of their work after 2 years of college, 60 percent after 3 years, and 80 percent after 4 years.[38]

Although the SAT–GPA tradeoff gives students who perform poorly on standardized tests a chance to qualify, there is evidence that it has also created a new problem. Pete Thamel of the *New York Times* found that at some prep academies, eligibility, rather than academics, was the primary focus.[39] Students at these academies appear to focus more on basketball than on academics.

Division I institutions must also track the academic progress of current students, and can be penalized if too few athletes are making adequate progress toward graduation.[40] **Academic progress rates** (APR) are calculated by award-ing student-athletes one point for remaining enrolled at the institution and one point for remaining academically eligible. For example, "a men's basket-ball team offering the full complement of 13 scholarships could accumulate a maximum of 52 points (13 ×2 points × 2 semesters) each year. Losing four points would lower its APR from 1,000 to 923 (92.3%)."[41] Scores are calcu-lated and penalties are assessed on a team-by-team basis. If a team's score falls below 930, it is subject to sanctions that increase with repeated violations from a public reprimand (Stage 1) to the loss of scholarships and/or practice time (Stage 2) to being banned from postseason play (Stage 3) to losing mem-bership in Division I (Stage 4). In 2016–2017, 31 teams were sanctioned by the NCAA. Of these, 23 were at Historically Black Colleges and Universities.

This unfortunate result reflects the limited budgets of these universities, which prevent them from providing the extensive tutoring, counseling, and summer courses offered by better-funded schools.[42] Critics of academic standards have also claimed that the standards discriminate against black athletes, as they rely on standardized tests that may not be race-neutral. Research by Joshua Price shows, however, that while the standards reduced the number of black athletes entering Division I programs as freshmen, they did not affect the number of black athletes overall and increased the graduation rates of black athletes.[43]

Academic Standards as a Barrier to Entry

Whatever their benefits, eligibility requirements could also form a barrier to entry, protecting the interests of established programs. Unable to pay students more and unable to admit weaker students, less-established athletic programs find it difficult to compete with traditional powers, which have an advantage recruiting athletes who meet the higher academic standards. E. Woodrow Eckard finds that the restrictions on recruiting imposed by the NCAA worsened competitive bal-ance among the big-time football schools, with conference standings becoming increasingly predictable. He also finds that the Herfindahl-Hirschman Index (HHI) for being ranked in the top 20 rises over time, indicating greater concentration at the top.[44] Craig Depken and Dennis Wilson measure competitive balance with a variant of the HHI that gauges the concentration of "performance points"—effectively the share of possible wins—by each team in a given conference in a given year. They find conflicting evidence regarding the effects of standards and enforcement. They show that increases in enforcement efforts increase competi-tive balance, but harsher penalties for violating those standards decrease it.[45]

Kathleen Carroll and Brad Humphreys examine how competitive balance changed in the wake of the 1984 Supreme Court decision that struck down the NCAA's monopoly over broadcast rights.[46] They hypothesize that dominance of the airwaves might lead to dominance on the gridiron, as it is now possible to see Alabama, Ohio State, or Notre Dame each Saturday during the football season.[47] To test this hypothesis, they examine game-level rather than seasonal data.

Using a sample of every game played by Division I teams between 1977 and 1990, they find that the average margin of victory in the seven years following the Supreme Court ruling that struck down the limits on TV appearances was greater than the average margin of victory in the previous seven years, and that this dif-ference was statistically significant at the 5 percent level. When they separate the sample into conference and non-conference games, they find that the ruling did not affect the average margin of victory in games played within conference but significantly increased the margin in non-conference games. Hence, the ruling does not appear to have affected competitive balance within conferences, but did affect the balance of power among conferences.

Antitrust and College Sports

Not all the antitrust suits in college sports have been directed at the NCAA. One reason the Power 5 schools embraced a playoff system after so many years spent opposing it was the threat of an antitrust suit by the state of Utah. Utah's Attorney General alleged that the Bowl Championship Series had unduly favored schools from the Power 5 conferences when selecting participants, unfairly depriving other universities (particularly the University of Utah) of "a fair and equal chance to compete in championships and share in revenues."[48] Utah stopped pursuing the lawsuit after the NCAA announced the shift to a playoff and, not coincidentally, after Utah joined the PAC-12 Conference, enabling it to share in the revenues it coveted.

Other recent antitrust suits against the NCAA have steadily chipped away at its restrictions on paying college athletes. Ironically, the best-known lawsuit, *O'Bannon v. NCAA*, was ultimately unsuccessful for its plaintiff, though it will likely have long-term consequences. In 2009, Ed O'Bannon, a former star basketball player for UCLA, sued the NCAA for allowing EA Sports to use his image without permission in the lucrative *NCAA Basketball* video game. The NCAA responded that paying O'Bannon would violate the code of amateurism that he had signed when accepting his scholarship.

In 2013, US District Court Judge Claudia Wilken ruled that imposing this code violated antitrust laws. She also ruled that colleges could—but did not have to— place up to $5,000 per year for each athlete appearing in the game into a trust that would be payable when the athlete left college. Two years later, a US Court of Appeals panel reversed the monetary award but let stand the basic ruling against the NCAA. The lawsuit led EA Sports to discontinue its college games, though it may start up again in light of the favorable financial ruling.

O'Bannon's victory without compensation resembles Joe Kapp's meaningless victory over the NFL in 1974.[49] Kapp, a quarterback who led the Minnesota Vikings to Super Bowl IV, won an antitrust suit against the NFL in which he alleged that the NFL's standard player contract illegally restrained trade. Oddly, the court maintained that Kapp had not been harmed by this restraint and did not award him any damages. In 1986, the USFL also won an antitrust judgment against the NFL but was awarded $1 in compensation (trebled, according to antitrust law, to $3).[50]

The NCAA amended its policy on compensating athletes thanks to an antitrust suit brought by Shawne Alston, a former running back at West Virginia University. Alston's suit against the NCAA, the Power 5 and Group of 5 conferences, and the Western Athletic Conference challenged the NCAA's limit on scholarships to levels that did not cover the full cost of attendance. In January 2015, just a few months after Alston brought his suit, the NCAA allowed its membership to fund the full cost of attendance. Alston continued his lawsuit, seeking compensation for students who had already graduated, and, in March 2017, the courts approved a $208.7 million settlement that would provide payment to student-athletes who had competed between the 2009–2010 and 2016–2017 academic years and did not receive aid covering the full cost of attendance.[51]

While the Alston suit attacked the degree of the NCAA's restrictions on athletes, a lawsuit brought against the NCAA and the Power 5 conferences by Jeffrey Kessler on behalf of past and current athletes confronts the NCAA's business model head-on. In the suit, which is currently awaiting trial, Kessler claims that the very existence of limits on payments to athletes violates antitrust law. If successful, the lawsuit would bring an element of free agency to college sports, as student-athletes would be able to sell their services to the highest bidder.[52] This would end college sports—at least as practiced by the Division I powers—as we know it.

12.4   Spillovers from Athletics to the University

The relationship between a college's athletic department and its central administration sometimes resembles that of a professional franchise and a municipal government. A college athletic program can still benefit a university even if it loses money. As with cities, universities view sports more broadly than as a profit center. Public goods and financial spillovers play a major role in motivating large state universities and small liberal arts colleges to support athletic programs.

College Sports as Public Goods

College sports provide a public good to the broader college community, much like professional teams do to cities. College teams give students a sense of identity and belonging that some do not seem to get in the classroom. Frequently, the identification with a state university spills over from students and alumni to the entire population of the state.

The particularly rabid followings that football teams in the Midwest and South enjoy stem in part from the convergence of three historical forces. The first two—the rapid growth of state universities and the spread of football—occurred nationwide in the late 19th and early 20th centuries. The third force was the rise of professional sports in the Northeast. The presence of professional baseball teams—and, later, professional football teams—limited the growth of fan bases for college sports in the Northeast. With no major league teams west of St. Louis or south of Washington, DC, college sports in states like Mississippi or Nebraska had little competition.[53] As a Nebraska fan told the novelist James Michener, "'In this state, if you don't go for football, you're a pariah.'"[54] To the extent that such teams provide entertainment and a sense of identity to the community beyond the college walls, they are worthy of subsidies.

Admissions

Recent studies generally find that success on the gridiron and the basketball court helps colleges attract more and better students. Devin and Jaren Pope find that applications rise by about 3 percent at schools that reach the top 10 in football or the "Sweet 16" in the NCAA men's basketball tournament, and by about 7–8 percent if the team wins the national championship in either sport. They also find that the added applications come from across the spectrum of SAT scores, so the schools can also increase the quality of their incoming class. However, they find that progress through the NCAA tournament has no impact on applicants' class rank or grade point average and only a marginal impact on SAT scores. These results are supported somewhat by Stephen Perez's study of the impact of football and basketball success on admissions at eight California state universities. He finds that a football team win increases local admissions by one-half of one percent, while a basketball victory against a Division I opponent increases admissions by about one-fifth of one percent.

Michael Anderson studied the impact of athletic success on several aspects of success for schools in the Football Bowl Subdivision from 1986 to 2009. He finds that additional wins increase applications, reduce acceptance rates, and increase the SAT scores of students who enroll. The first two effects are greater for schools from the Power 5 than for schools from the Group of 5 conferences, while the impact on SAT scores was smaller for Power 5 schools.[55]

Donations and State Funding

In 2014–2015, donations from proud alumni to their athletic teams averaged about 23 percent of athletic departments' revenue.[56] The level of donations—and their importance in an athletic department's budget—vary widely from school to school and from year to year. The widest variation came at Oklahoma State University, where donations ranged from about $19 million in 2007 to $210 million in 2006. That latter figure made up over 87 percent of Oklahoma State's total athletic revenue for the year. Even more surprisingly, $165 million of that came from a single donation by oil magnate T. Boone Pickens.

Donations by happy alumni and fans can have a broader benefit if they spill over to the rest of the university. Unfortunately, the evidence does not show spillovers. Brad Humphreys and Michael Mondello analyze how "restricted" (i.e., designated toward athletics) and "unrestricted" donations respond to performance by universities' athletic teams for a sample of 320 schools over a 20-year period.[57] They find that restricted giving to public universities rises the year after a college's team appears in a postseason bowl game or the NCAA tournament, but unrestricted giving does not. Unrestricted giving to private schools is also insensitive to athletic performance and rises only in response to performance by the college's basketball team.

Jeffrey Stinson and Dennis Howard use data from the Voluntary Support of Education database to identify donations to a college's athletic department.[58] They find that the percentage of donations going to athletics has steadily risen over time, and that the sensitivity of this percentage to athletic performance is lower for schools with stronger academic reputations.

Anderson's study also analyzes the impact of football success on donations. He finds that one more football win increases alumni donations to athletic funds of BCS schools by about $200,000.[59] However, it does not have a statistically significant impact on non-athletic donations, overall donations, or the percentage of alumni making donations. Anderson finds that football success has no statistically discernible impact on donations at non-BCS schools.

It thus appears likely that there are few if any spillovers from athletics to the rest of the university. The situation facing big-time programs is even more negative. At these schools, donations to athletic departments appear to come at the expense of donations to the academic side of the university.

In addition to soliciting private donations, state universities try to leverage their success on the field into allocations from the state. In the 1940s, Michigan State College (now Michigan State University) President John Hannah campaigned to replace the University of Chicago (which had abandoned big-time sports) in the

Big Ten as a way to build MSU from a small agricultural college to a major university.[60] More recently, the University of Connecticut has used the success of its men's and women's basketball teams to the same effect.[61] Probably the most famous instance of using sports to solicit state funds came when George Lynn Cross, the president of the University of Oklahoma, pleaded for more state funds by stating, "We want to build a university our football team can be proud of."[62]

12.5 The College Sports Labor Market

No issue facing intercollegiate sports is as controversial as that of whether athletes, particularly football and men's basketball players at Division I schools, should be paid. Some believe that "An athlete who does not graduate is grossly underpaid as an entertainer. One who graduates is overpaid."[63] Others believe that colleges exercise monopsony power on a level far exceeding that of professional teams. In this section, we explore the labor market facing college athletes and ask whether they are student-athletes or, in the words of Andrew Zimbalist, "unpaid professionals."[64]

The Value of Athletes to Colleges

If a college rewards an athlete (through a scholarship or a salary) by less than his marginal revenue product, the athlete's contribution to the college's revenue, it can generate considerable economic rent. Robert Brown estimated the *MRP* of premium players by assuming that a professional franchise drafts a player only if it regards that player as having the potential to make the team. He then estimated how the number of players the college teams sent to the professional draft (controlling for overall team quality) affected the teams' revenues. He found that a player with the potential to play in the NFL brought a college football team between $500,000 (for a low-revenue team) and $1.3 million (for a high-revenue team) per year. Using a similar methodology, Erin Lane, Juan Nagel, and Janet Netz find that a star basketball player brings his school between $270,000 and $1.2 million annually.[65]

A truly exceptional player could bring his college much more. Texas A&M has claimed that Heisman trophy-winning quarterback Johnny Manziel brought the university $37 million in media exposure alone in 2012.[66] While few players will ever match Manziel's marketability, even lesser programs benefit handsomely from the $40,000 scholarships they provide star football and men's basketball players.

No other sports match the rents generated by football and men's basketball. Consider, for example, the value of a star in women's basketball, the highest-revenue women's intercollegiate sport. Because women's basketball generates relatively little revenue and women's programs vary widely in their popularity, Brown and Jewell (2013) find that a star player could have a widely varying impact on revenues, from $12,000 to $200,000. Thus, even a star player in other Division I sports may not generate revenue exceeding the value of her or his scholarship. This is a major reason why athletes at lower-division colleges or in "non-revenue" sports do not claim they are exploited.

The Value of College to Athletes

Athletic Scholarships

Today, sports fans across the country eagerly follow sports blogs to learn about the high school students their favorite college has offered a scholarship. They then agonize on "National Signing Day," waiting to see which students have accepted the offer. It is hard to imagine that athletic scholarships were ever a subject of controversy, but, as recently as the late 1950s, many colleges refused to give them.

Penn State offered the first athletic scholarship in 1900. Several schools quickly followed suit, while many others paid money under the table. Still, most schools frowned upon such practices.[67] In 1929, the Carnegie Foundation reported with horror that a "system of recruiting and subsidizing has grown up, under which boys are offered pecuniary and other inducements to enter a particular college." Prior to 1956, the NCAA forbade schools from treating athletes and non-athletes differently when awarding financial aid, though the Carnegie Foundation reported that as many as three-fourths of the NCAA's members disobeyed the rules they helped promulgate.[68]

When the NCAA allowed schools to provide scholarships to athletes regardless of their financial need or academic merit, it justified its action by essentially saying, "everyone is doing it anyway, so we may as well keep everything out in the open where we can regulate it." However, this assessment was not universal. The Big Ten conference tried for several years to hold athletes and nonathletes to the same standard for financial aid. Other schools questioned the sincerity of the Big Ten's stance and pointed out that, while the Big Ten schools did not give athletic scholarships, they did provide ample compensation for questionable on-campus employment.[69]

The advent of grants-in-aid for athletes may have eliminated hypocrisy in recruiting, but it created several philosophical and legal problems for colleges. Schools now had to reconcile themselves to providing financial assistance to students for participating in activities that often forced them to miss classes.

More importantly, schools had placed themselves in the position of being considered the athletes' employers. This relationship left colleges open to claims for workers' compensation insurance by athletes who were injured "on the job." NCAA Executive Director Walter Byers first coined the term *student-athlete* in an attempt to avoid such claims. In a Kafkaesque twist, athletes who wish to receive an athletic scholarship must now sign an agreement that explicitly rejects the notion that they are being paid for their athletic performance.[70]

The NCAA has recently acknowledged, however, that these payments often do not cover the full cost of attending college. Joe Nocera and Ben Strauss claim that "more than 80 percent of top-level college athletes on full scholarship lived below the poverty line." All-American basketball player Shabazz Napier's confession, that he and his University of Connecticut teammates sometimes went to bed hungry because they could not afford food, poignantly corroborated this claim.[71]

In 2015, motivated by the bad publicity accompanying Napier's claim as well as the lawsuit by Alston, the NCAA allowed schools from the Power 5 conferences to supplement their athletic scholarships with school-specific sums intended to capture the "full cost of attendance." The amounts are set by the individual schools and vary widely and unpredictably. For example, in 2015–2016, the University of Southern California provided a supplement of $1,580, while cross-town rival UCLA provided $5,941.[72] The lack of consistency in these supplemental payments could undermine a valuable source of student aid.

College Sports as an Investment

The theory of human capital states that workers invest in such activities as schooling and on-the-job training to increase their future earnings. An increasing number of studies have shown that participation in sport can be an important part of human capital accumulation. Participating in athletics, particularly when young, contributes to both cognitive abilities—formal skills like math and reading—and non-cognitive skills, such as the ability to work with others.[73] These findings support the claim by legendary Notre Dame coach Knute Rockne that "Four years of football . . . breed in the average man more of the ingredients of success in life than almost any academic course he takes." There is, however, a big distance between playing football during recess or after school, and playing linebacker at FBS Notre Dame.

A study by James Long and Steven Caudill suggests that participating in intercollegiate athletics may be a good investment even if it does not lead to a professional career. They find that men who were varsity athletes in college earn more in later life than men who were not. They find no statistically significant differential for women.[74]

The study, however, is hampered by several limitations. First, the data available to Long and Caudill did not permit them to control for either the sport the students played or the schools they attended. The study thus treats tennis players at Swarthmore and football players at Louisville as one and the same. Combining such very different populations could misstate the impact of sports for each. In addition, the young men who participate in athletics might have underlying characteristics (e.g., ambition and self-discipline) that would have enabled them to succeed elsewhere even if they had never played a sport.

Graduation Rates of College Athletes

Partly because it is so difficult to determine the impact of sports on later earnings, researchers and the popular media have focused instead on the graduation rates of varsity athletes. Graduation rates are also imperfect measures of success, as they do not account for many differences between athletes and non-athletes. For example, unlike many non-athletes, scholarship athletes are all full-time students, which increases their likelihood of graduating within six years.

There are also concerns regarding the statistics themselves. The metric used by the NCAA, the Graduation Success Rate (GSR), differs from the Federal Graduation Rate (FGR), the metric that the Department of Education applies to non-athletes. The FGR counts students who transfer from one school to another or who drop out for any reason while in good standing as non-graduates, while the GSR excludes such students from its calculations. Advocates of the GSR claim that doing so gives a more accurate picture of the decisions of college athletes. Opponents see it as a way to inflate the academic performance of athletes.[75] Whatever the case, the two statistics are not directly comparable.

The College Sport Research Institute tries to compare apples with apples using an adjusted FGR that counts only full-time students.[76] It finds significant gaps in the graduation rates of the two populations. Football players in the Power 5 conferences have a graduation rate that is 18.4 percentage points below that of non-athletes, while players in the Group of 5 conferences have an average gap of 11.9 percentage points. Even more alarming, the gap for black players (25.2 percentage points) is almost 5 times as large as the gap for white players (5.1 percentage points).

The gap is even greater for men's basketball players, averaging 32.6 percentage points in the Power 5 conferences and 18.3 percentage points in the Group of 5. While the racial differential is not so stark as in football, the gap for black players is almost 10 percentage points greater than for white players. Women's basketball players face a smaller graduation gap than men do (11.1 percentage points), with Power 5 players having a larger gap than Group of 5 players (17.1 points versus 8.2 points). The racial gap for women is not statistically significant. The smaller gap for women could have many different sources. It could reflect innate differences between the sexes, greater attention to academic preparation by coaches of women's sports, or greater professional opportunities for men who leave early. To date, the economics literature has provided no explanation for the gender differences in graduation rates.

Tables 12.7 and 12.8 show that the GSRs for women are higher than for men even at the most successful basketball programs. More than half the women's basketball teams that reached the Sweet 16 in the 2015 NCAA tournament had GSRs of at least 90 percent, of which 5 had GSRs of 100 percent. On the men's side, only 3 schools had GSRs of at least 90 percent, with 2 having perfect GSRs. Of the men's Final Four teams in 2015, only eventual champion Duke had a GSR higher than 90, while three of the women's teams had GSRs over 90, including eventual champion UConn and runner-up Notre Dame.

Table 12.7 Graduation Success Rates (GSRs) for Men's 2015 Sweet 16 Teams

School[a]	GSR
Duke	100
Notre Dame	100
Gonzaga	91
University of Kentucky	89
West Virginia University	89
Xavier University	89
University of North Carolina	88
University of Utah	88
University of Arizona	82
North Carolina State University	80
University of Oklahoma	77
Michigan State University	73
Wichita State University	64
UCLA	60
University of Louisville	58
University of Wisconsin	40

Source: The Institute for Diversity and Ethics in Sport. 2015. "Keeping Score When It Counts: Analyzing the Academic Performance of the 2015 NCAA Women's and Men's Sweet 16 Teams," March 25, at http://nebula.wsimg.com/a726d64c2544c7fe98d458088e1e7ce4?AccessKeyId=DA C3A56D8FB782449D2A&disposition=0&alloworigin=1.

Table 12.8 Graduation Success Rates (GSRs) for Women's 2015 Sweet 16 Teams

School[a]	GSR
Dayton	100
University of Connecticut	100
University of Tennessee	100
Duke	100
Notre Dame	100
Stanford	93
Arizona State	93
Gonzaga	92
Iowa	92
Maryland	92
University of Texas	90
Louisville	89
University of South Carolina	83
Florida State	83
Baylor University	60
University of North Carolina	59

Source: The Institute for Diversity and Ethics in Sport. 2015. "Keeping Score When It Counts: Analyzing the Academic Performance of the 2015 NCAA Women's and Men's Sweet 16 Teams," March 25, at http://nebula.wsimg.com/a726d64c2544c7fe98d458088e1e7ce4?AccessKeyId=DA C3A56D8FB782449D2A&disposition=0&alloworigin=1.

There are a variety of reasons for the low graduation rates of football and men's basketball players. A major contributor is their lack of preparation for college relative to non-athletes. Dean Purdy, Stanley Eitzen, and Rick Hufnagel's case study of students at Colorado State University from 1970 through 1980 showed that athletes there had lower SAT scores and lower high school grades and class rank than other Colorado State students. The shortfall in preparation was particularly large for male athletes, black athletes, and members of the football and men's basketball teams. A study of FBS football programs by Lee Sigelman found similar gaps at many other schools. The average entering student had SAT scores 165 points higher than the average entering student with a football scholarship, and teams with larger gaps in SAT scores generally had better records.[77]

The poor performance of male athletes is not restricted to big-time programs. Studies by William Bowen and Sarah Levin and by Elizabeth Aries, Danielle McCarthy, Peter Salovey, and Mahzarin Banaji of schools in the Ivy League and other elite colleges found similar patterns. At these schools, young men who were recruited to play football, basketball, or ice hockey had SAT scores that averaged 119 to 165 points below non-athletes'. The two studies differ over whether student-athletes underperform relative to their SAT scores. Bowen and Levin found that three-quarters of recruited male athletes ranked in the bottom third of their class. Consistent with Table 12.8, there was no evidence of similar problems for female athletes. Aries et al. found no evidence of academic underperformance.[78]

Table 12.9 The Probability of Signing with a Professional Team

Student-Athletes	Men's Basketball	Women's Basketball	Football	Baseball	Men's Ice Hockey	Men's Soccer
Percent High School to NCAA	3.5%	3.9%	6.7%	7.0%	11.3%	5.7%
Percent NCAA to Professional	1.1%	0.9%	1.6%	9.7%	6.6%	1.4%
Percent High School to Professional	0.04%	0.04%	0.11%	0.68%	0.75%	0.08%

Source: NCAA. 2016. "Estimated Probability of Competing in Professional Athletics," April 25, at http://www.ncaa.org/about/resources/research/estimated-probability-competing-professional-athletics, viewed March 3, 2017.

In some cases, low graduation rates may be a sign of success rather than failure. After all, it makes much more sense for a basketball player at Kentucky, which regularly sends players to the NBA after one year, to focus on his prospects as a basketball player than for a player at Dartmouth. Lawrence DeBrock, Wallace Hendricks, and Roger Koenker hypothesize that some student-athletes choose a specific college as part of their broader career choice. It is therefore as surprising for a football player from a football power such as Clemson to fail to make the NFL as it is for a premed student at a small liberal arts college to fail to get into medical school.[79]

Unfortunately, if one judges success by the likelihood of making the professional ranks, then playing intercollegiate sports as a scholarship athlete is a good investment only for a select few. Table 12.9 shows that investing in a career in professional athletics brings a very high payoff to a lucky few and nothing to the vast majority. Other than baseball and hockey, which have extensive minor league systems, the chances of an NCAA senior athlete's being drafted by a major league team—let alone having a professional career—are less than 2 percent. While the NCAA does not break down these figures by division, even if a Division I basketball player was five times as likely to be drafted, his chances of being selected, let alone playing, are still barely 1 in 20.

12.6 Discrimination and College Sports

For over half a century after the shameful *Plessy v. Ferguson* Supreme Court ruling, the doctrine of "separate but equal" was used to ensure that African Americans received substandard educations and inadequate access to public services. Intercollegiate sports were only one aspect of this unfortunate chapter in American history. Ironically, soon after racial barriers finally crumbled, the provision of separate-but-equal access became a hallmark of attempts to expand opportunities for women under Title IX. In this section, we discuss how the forms of discrimination described in Chapter 11 manifest themselves in intercollegiate sports.

Racial Discrimination

Before Jackie Robinson played an inning for the Dodgers, he was a star athlete at UCLA, earning varsity letters in four different sports (baseball, basketball, football, and track) between 1939 and 1941.[80] African Americans have been a part of college football, and college sports in general, almost since Rutgers and Princeton first faced off in 1869. The first record of a black varsity athlete came in 1888, when William Henry Lewis, who went on to become Assistant Attorney General under President Taft, played football for Amherst.[81]

The early years of college football saw several outstanding black players, such as Fritz Pollard, who became the first African American All-American in 1916 and later became the first African American to play in the NFL, and Paul Robeson, the internationally acclaimed actor and opera singer, who was an All-American at Rutgers in 1917 and 1918. However, most black athletes were not recruited by the largely white universities and instead played at Historically Black Colleges and Universities like Grambling or Jackson State University. The University of Michigan had its first black athlete (George Jewett) in 1890—and its second (Willis Ward) in 1932. Notre Dame had no black athletes—or black students of any kind—until after World War II. The Southeastern Conference did not integrate until 1966.[82]

Most Southern football teams, like their student bodies, were all-white until the 1960s. These schools often imposed their prejudices on others by refusing to play integrated teams unless the black players sat out. No integrated team played in a Southern state until Harvard visited the University of Virginia in 1947; a few months later, Penn State became the first integrated team to play in a New Year's Day Bowl game in the Deep South, when it played Southern Methodist University to a 13–13 tie in the 1948 Cotton Bowl.[83]

Similar to the professional teams that integrated in response to competitive pressure, Southern schools began to recruit African American athletes when the cost of discriminating became too great. The 1970 matchup between the University of Southern California (USC) and the University of Alabama demonstrated this cost to Alabama football fans. This game, the first played by an integrated team in Alabama, resulted in a 42–21 rout by USC. Alabama coach Paul (Bear) Bryant used this result as a way to smooth the way for the freshman Wilbur Jackson to join the varsity the following year and to recruit other African American players in later years.[84] The strategy worked, as the team quickly resumed its winning ways after integrating, while schools that lagged, like the University of Mississippi, took decades to return to glory. One Alabama fan's response to Bryant's claim that African Americans would eventually play for Alabama shows how competitive pressure undermined prejudice: "Well, I hope there're some Negro linebackers available. We need linebackers."[85]

Title IX and Gender Discrimination

Title IX is the most important measure ever undertaken to promote gender equity in sports in the United States. It has completely changed the face of scholastic and collegiate opportunities for women. Many even ascribe the success of US women Olympians and the US Women's World Cup soccer team directly to Title IX. It has not, however, been universally praised. Some claim that Title IX has denied opportunities to as many people as it has helped.

Title IX began as a seemingly innocuous sentence in the 1972 Educational Amendments to the 1964 Civil Rights Act. It reads:

> No Person in the United States shall, on the basis of sex, be excluded from participation in, be denied the benefits of, or be subjected to discrimination under any educational program or activity receiving federal financial assistance.[86]

At first, the nature of the programs and the types of schools covered by Title IX were unclear. In 1975, the Department of Health, Education, and Welfare clarified who could benefit from Title IX by establishing three areas of regulatory jurisdiction: financial aid; other benefits and opportunities; and participation in athletics. In the 1984 *Grove City College* decision, the Supreme Court broadened the coverage of Title IX by ruling that "federal assistance" applied to financial aid as well as direct funding. However, it also narrowed the coverage by applying it only to programs in which federal funding applied. Hence, if no students on the women's basketball team received federally funded financial aid, Title IX did not apply. This narrow interpretation was overruled a few years later by the 1987 Civil Rights Restoration Act, which applied government jurisdiction to the entire institution.[87]

Congress established compliance guidelines for athletics in a 1979 amendment to the original legislation. Schools can comply in one of three ways: proportionality, program expansion, or accommodating the interests and abilities of the student body.

Proportionality means that the percentage of women who participate in sports at a university approximates the percentage of female undergraduates enrolled at the school. For example, if women make up 55 percent of a school's undergraduate enrollment, approximately 55 percent of the athletes participating on the school's teams should be women. The Office of Civil Rights of the Department of Education, which oversees the enforcement of Title IX, uses a ± 5 percentage point rule in its interpretation of this test (e.g., if a school's enrollment is 55 percent female and 50 percent of women are on school teams, the school is in compliance).

Proportionality has generally been difficult for many schools to achieve for two primary reasons. First, football has the largest roster of any NCAA-sanctioned sport, and no single women's sport comes close to balancing the 105-man maximum roster size and 85 potential scholarships offered by football. Second, the student bodies at the nation's colleges and universities are disproportionately female. Women have outnumbered men at US institutions of higher education since 1979 and currently comprise 57% of all college students. Even if a typical school had an equal number of male and female athletes, it would still likely be out of proportionality due to the makeup of the student body.[88]

A school does not have to achieve proportionality if it can demonstrate that it has made progress in increasing opportunities for women. Throughout the 1990s and 2000s, many schools satisfied their Title IX requirements by adding women's teams in sports like soccer, hockey, or rowing. For example, between 1995 and 2008, the number of Division I women's soccer teams rose from 175 to 310.[89] Alternatively, colleges can satisfy Title IX if they can show that they have fully accommodated the interests and abilities of the underrepresented sex. Each of these criteria leaves room for interpretation. Perhaps because it is a numerical measure and thus more easily verified than "expansion" or "interests and abilities," challenges to schools' compliance with Title IX have generally been based on the proportionality standard.

Like most legislation, Title IX has had both intended and unintended effects. Unless a program generates enough revenue to support itself, it can exist only if the university increases its funding or if another program is cut. The balanced-budget approach to changes in athletic funding has greatly contributed to the controversy over the implementation of Title IX guidelines, as men's sports have at times paid the ultimate price—cancellation of their program—in order to accommodate new women's programs. According to Christina Hoff Sommers, colleges have eliminated almost 60 percent of their wrestling teams since Title IX was enacted in 1972.[90] Among Division I schools, 54 percent of the schools that dropped men's teams cited gender equity as a "great or very great" influence on their decisions.[91]

Proponents of Title IX counter that such claims distract supporters of non-money men's sports, such as wrestling or swimming, from the true drain on funds: football and men's basketball. They assert that, for many colleges, these sports are a drain on resources rather than profit centers that support other sports. Moreover, the sheer size of these programs dwarfs the expenditure on any other sport, taking up over three-fourths of all expenditure on Division I sports. Even at Division III schools, football and basketball take up about 40 percent of athletic budgets. To put this in perspective, when Rutgers shut down its men's tennis program, it was costing the university about $175,000. This was roughly what it cost the university to house its football team in hotels for one season—for home games.[92]

Whatever its impact on men's sports, Title IX has clearly increased the number of women who take part in athletics. The participation in sports by high school girls (also covered by Title IX) increased from 294,000 in 1971 to over 3.3 million in 2015–2016.[93] About 200,000 women now participate in intercollegiate sports. That compares with less than 32,000 in 1972.[94]

Unfortunately, as the number of girls and women participating in sports has risen, the number of female head coaches has fallen steadily since the passage of Title IX. This decline may reflect a rational decision by women based on the extraordinary time demands required to work as a head coach. Alternatively, it could result from discrimination by mostly male athletic directors who see an increasing number of men willing to coach women's sports, or from the increased interest in coaching women's sports among male coaches. Research has not yet determined which of these factors dominates, though it has shown that women make equally good coaches.[95]

Biographical Sketch

Sonny Vaccaro
(1939–)

I can honestly say without Sonny there would not be an Air Jordan. . .
                                                                   —*Josh Peter*[96]

Growing up in Trafford, a small town outside of Pittsburgh, John Paul Vincent (Sonny) Vaccaro grew up with dreams of being a football player. When injuries ended that dream, he began teaching special education in Trafford, though he did not do so for long. At the age of 24, Vaccaro used contacts he had made while a student at Youngstown State University to create the Dapper Dan Roundball Classic, a high school basketball camp in Pittsburgh.

In 1977, a misguided idea led to Vaccaro's biggest break. Convinced that he had a revolutionary design for a basketball shoe, Vaccaro pitched his creation to the executives at Nike. Nike, then known as a running shoe company, was looking to break into the mass market by targeting high school basketball players. The executives, led by Nike founder Phil Knight, laughed at Vaccaro's design but were impressed by his contacts with college coaches.

Vaccaro bragged that he could help Nike break into the college basketball market by taking the then-unheard-of step of paying coaches to use their shoes. Knight hired him but says in *Shoe Dog*, his autobiography, "I fully expected . . . Vaccaro to fail." To Knight's astonishment, "One month later [Nike Marketing Director Rob] Strasser was standing in my office beaming. And shouting. And ticking off names."[97]

Universities quickly saw the monetary value of aligning themselves with shoe brands, and soon took the decisions—and money—out of the hands of the coaches. This relationship has left college presidents feeling deeply ambivalent, objecting to their schools' becoming an advertising medium for shoe companies but deeply attached to the money it brings. Indeed, today schools at all levels use the fact that they are an "Adidas school" or a "Nike school" as part of their recruiting. For Vaccaro, however, the best was yet to come.

The origin of the Air Jordan brand remains, after more than 30 years, the subject of considerable debate. Vaccaro claims that the deal would never have happened without him. Nike founder Phil Knight says that Vaccaro played only a supporting role. Michael Jordan himself gives yet another version, in which former Olympic assistant coach George Raveling plays a key role.

It is clear that, until signing with Nike, Michael Jordan was "an Adidas guy" who had never worn Nike shoes. In 1984, at Vaccaro's urging, Nike offered Jordan $250,000—its entire endorsement budget for the year—to endorse their "Air" shoe. Their offer was half of what Adidas offered, but it contained two key features: a percentage of all future sales and a chance to opt out of the deal after 3 years if sales did not reach $3 million. Sales quickly topped $130 million and have continued to climb. In 2014, more than a decade after Michael Jordan retired from basketball, Jordan-brand US shoe sales totaled $2.6 billion for 58 percent of the domestic basketball shoe market.

The money and the notoriety from the Air Jordan deal greatly enhanced Vaccaro's influence, but it also created controversy. Vaccaro's influence over college, and even high school players, made him *persona non grata* with the NCAA, which opposed what it saw as Vaccaro's professionaliza-tion of high school and college athletes. It saw his showering teenag-ers with shoes and equipment as corrupting and was appalled when he advised players to leave college early, or even—before the NBA prohib-ited the practice—bypass college entirely.

In 2007, Vaccaro had what might be termed a revelation. His dealings with shoe companies, schools, coaches, and players had convinced him that everyone was getting rich from college athletics, except for the college athletes. Feeling that he could not speak out on behalf of the players while making money from them, Vaccaro resigned from Reebok, for whom he was then working, and became a full-time advocate for college athletes.

Vaccaro has spent the last decade crisscrossing the country with his wife Pam, attacking what he sees as an inherently corrupt system. He has also remained a consummate dealmaker. It was Vaccaro who put Ed O'Bannon in touch with Michael Hausfeld, the lead attorney in his lawsuit against the NCAA. Eventually, Vaccaro became an informal consultant on the case, lining up players to testify against the NCAA.

Sonny Vaccaro has always courted controversy. Some "quite literally hold him responsible for destroying American basketball." Others view him as a passionate, if quixotic, champion of exploited youths. Perhaps the best picture of Vaccaro comes from his own words: "Look, I play by the rules. . . . What I'm saying is for God's sake, go change the rules."

Sources: Faruq Gbadamosi. 2015. "The Economics of Nike's Air Jordan Brand," *The Market Mogul,* September 19, at http://themarketmogul.com/the-economics-of-nikes-air-jordan-brand/; Phil Knight. 2016. *Shoe Dog* (New York: Scribner); Joe Nocera and Ben Strauss. 2016. *Indentured: The Inside Story of the Rebellion against the NCAA* (New York: Penguin); Joe Nocera and Ben Strauss. 2016. "A Reformed 'Sneaker Pimp' Takes on the NCAA," *New York Times,* February 12, at https://www.nytimes.com/2016/02/14/sports/ncaabasketball/a-reformed-sneaker-pimp-takes-on-the-ncaa.html; Josh Peter. 2015. "Error Jordan: Key Figures Still Argue over Who Was Responsible for Nike Deal," *USA Today,* September 30; Jason Zengerle. 2008. "The Pivot," *The New Republic,* July 9: 24–32.

Summary

This chapter uses the tools we have introduced over the preceding 11 chapters to analyze the behavior of the NCAA, its member schools, and the athletes who participate in collegiate sports. The structure of this chapter thus parallels the structure of the book. It covers the revenues and costs of college sports, the role of monopoly, spillovers into the wider (college) community, and the labor market.

Intercollegiate athletics bring a number of benefits and costs to a university. As with professional sports, ticket sales and television revenues are important revenue sources. Venue revenues from luxury boxes and club seating have also become increasingly important. Unlike professional sports, many of these pay-ments are filtered through the NCAA and conferences. The results often level revenues within college sports conferences—which at the highest level can be divided into the Power 5 and Group of 5 conferences—but exacerbate differences between them. While athletes are not paid, their scholarships are counted—perhaps incorrectly—as a major expense. College coaches and athletic directors are very well paid, earning more—relative to the revenue stream—than their professional counterparts. Whether a college profits from athletics depends on how one defines revenues and costs.

Many view the NCAA as a monopoly in its dealings with TV networks and as a monopsony in its dealings with the athletes. The model of an efficient monopoly helps to explain why TV coverage, bowl appearances, and the revenue they generate have been increasingly concentrated in a small number of schools. As is the case with cartels in general, the NCAA has been attacked by its own members, an example of the Prisoner's Dilemma. Antitrust lawsuits have also challenged the NCAA's restrictions, particularly on payments to athletes.

Even if a college does not profit financially, it might want to support athletics due to the other benefits that they bring. The number and quality of applications to a school are positively related to the success of its football and (men's) basketball teams. Alumni donations also rise with athletic success, though the impact appears to be largely limited to giving to the athletic department.

Although student-athletes are not paid, they can use their time in college to invest in academic and athletic skills. Evidence suggests that student-athletes in football and men's basketball do not have the same academic preparation as non-athletes, and that male athletes in general underperform academically at both major sports powers and academically oriented institutions. Women show no such ill-effects.

As in professional leagues, discrimination based on race and gender has long been a part of college sports. For many years, African American athletes had limited access to schools other than Historically Black Colleges and Universities. Today, Title IX has increased opportunities for women, though its impact on men's sports remains controversial.

Discussion Questions

1   Should the NCAA be exempt from the antitrust laws? Why or why not?
2   Should college athletes be paid? If not, why not? If so, how can one design a system that neither bankrupts most colleges nor discriminates against women?
3   Does the athletic department at your college make a profit? Does it profit even when transfers—such as student fees—are deducted? If it lost money, what—if anything—should be done?
4   If your college were invited to the New Mexico Bowl, would you favor accepting the bid? Why or why not?
5   Are head football and basketball coaches worth the money they are paid?

Problems

12.1 If college sports are a public good, what can you say about the amount of it a university will supply? What can the university's administration do to resolve this problem?
12.2 Use the model of efficient cartel operation to explain why the University of Wisconsin receives a greater portion of bowl revenue than Utah State University.

12.3   What makes an incidental cartel different from other cartels? Why was the NCAA an incidental cartel?

12.4   Use human capital theory to explain why colleges might not pay students their full marginal product.

12.5   Use economic theory to explain why almost all the Southeastern Conference's football and basketball teams integrated within a few years of one another.

12.6   Use game theory to describe how an effort by two universities to recruit a top basketball player might result in both committing NCAA recruiting violations.

12.7   What unselfish and selfish motives might be behind the attempts by some schools to set academic standards for student-athletes?

12.8   Use supply and demand analysis to show and describe the dramatic increase in men who coach women's basketball teams.

12.9   How might failing to graduate from college be an optimal investment in one's human capital?

12.10 Use human capital theory to explain why graduation rates for women's basketball players are so much higher than those of men's basketball players.

Notes

1   Quoted in Joe Nocera and Ben Strauss. 2016. *Indentured: The Inside Story of the Rebellion against the NCAA* (New York: Penguin): 19.

2   Ronald Smith. 1988. *Sports and Freedom: The Rise of Big-Time College Athletics* (New York: Oxford University Press): 73–77.

3   See Eric Leifer. 1995. *Making the Majors: The Transformation of Team Sports in America* (Cambridge, MA: Harvard University Press): 40–42.

4   The most serious early attempt, the Intercollegiate Football Association, ended in failure in 1894 after 18 years.

5   The seven sinners were Boston College, the Citadel, the University of Maryland, the University of Virginia, Virginia Military Institute, Virginia Polytechnic Institute, and Villanova University.

6   City College of New York is the only school ever to win the NCAA championship and the National Invitational Tournament (then the more prestigious event) in the same year. More recent point-shaving scandals have damaged programs from Boston College to Arizona State.

7   See Murray Sperber. 1998. *Onward to Victory: The Crises That Shaped College Sports* (New York: Henry Holt and Co.): 330–343; Paul Lawrence. 1987. *Unsportsmanlike Conduct: The National Collegiate Athletic Association and the Business of College Football* (New York: Praeger): 52–53; and Walter Byers with Charles Hammer. 1995. *Unsportsmanlike Conduct: Exploiting College Athletes* (Ann Arbor: University of Michigan Press): 55–61. See Andrew Zimbalist. 1999. *Unpaid Professionals* (Princeton, NJ: Princeton University Press): 90–93 for an account of the NCAA's dispute with Penn.

8   The most prominent impositions of the death penalty came against the football program at Southern Methodist University, which suspended its football program for the 1987 and 1988 seasons, and the basketball program at the University of Southwest Louisiana (now UL-Lafayette) in 1973–1974 and 1974–1975.

9   For a good history of the subdivisions, see Joseph Crowley. 2006. *In the Arena: The NCAA's First Century* (Indianapolis, IN: NCAA).

10 NCAA. 2014. "Football Bowl Subdivision–Membership Requirements," December 8, 2014, at https://www.ncaa.org/sites/default/files/Football%20Bowl%20Subqa%20 12%208%2014.pdf, viewed April 12, 2017.

11 See Nocera and Strauss. 2016. *Indentured: The Inside Story of the Rebellion against the NCAA*: 128.

12 Data from Steve Berkowitz, Christopher Schnaars, Jodi Upton, Mark Hannan, Michael Stern, Justin Meyer, et al., "NCAA Finances," *USAToday.com*, at http://sports.usatoday.com/ncaa/finances/, viewed January 23, 2017.

13 Adam Jude. 2015. "UW, Alaska Airlines Agree to Naming-Rights Deal for Husky Stadium's Field," *The Seattle Times*, September 2, at http://www.seattletimes.com/sports/uw-husky-football/uw-alaska-airlines-agree-to-naming-rights-deal-for-husky-stadium/, viewed March 12, 2017.

14 "Premium Seating and Hospitality – Football," *TexasSports.com*, at http://www.texassports.com/sports/2013/7/29/tickets_0729135534.aspx, viewed October 19, 2017; Scott Latta. 2006. "Game-Day Inside Peek: Skyboxes Provide Alabama's Most Luxurious Look," *Alabama Crimson Tide*, November 17, at http://www.rolltide.com/news/2006/11/17/Game_Day_Inside_Peek_Skyboxes_Provide_Alabama_s_Most_Luxurious_Look.aspx; "Notre Dame Fighting Irish Premium Seating," *Premium Seating*, at http://www.premiumseating.com/notre-dame-fighting-irish-football-luxury-suites, viewed February 11, 2017.

15 Harry Minium. 2016. "Conference USA TV Revenue to Plummet to $2.8 Million Per Year," *The Virginian-Pilot*, June 7, at http://pilotonline.com/sports/college/old-dominion/football/conference-usa-tv-revenue-to-plummet-to-million-per-year/article_1dd435cb-800e-574d-be6d-0afa42d957e7.html, viewed February 5, 2017. Although it shares the revenue for national and regional broadcasts, the Big 12 allows Texas and Oklahoma to keep the revenue for their separate sports networks.

16 The Rose Bowl was first played in 1902 and has been an annual event since 1916. The Sugar and Orange Bowls were first played in 1935, while the Cotton Bowl debuted in 1937.

17 The Group of 5 consists of the American Athletic Conference, Conference-USA, the Mid-American Conference, the Mountain West Conference, and the Sun Belt Conference.

18 Dan Wetzel, Josh Peter, and Jeff Passan. 2010. *Death to the BCS* (New York: Gotham Books).

19 Mark Schlabach. 2011. "NCAA: Where Does the Money Go?" *ESPN.com*, July 12, at http://espn.go.com/college-sports/story/_/id/6756472/following-ncaa-money.

20 Darren Rovell. 2016. "ACC on Track to Shatter Record for Money Earned in NCAA Tournament," *ESPN.com*, March 26, at http://www.espn.com/mens-college-basketball/story/_/id/15071018/atlantic-coast-conference-set-shatter-record-money-earned-ncaa-men-basketball-tournament, viewed January 25, 2017.

21 For more on how these figures are computed, see USA Today Sports. 2016. "Methodology for NCAA Athletic Department Database," *USAToday.com*, April 14, at http://sports.usatoday.com/2016/04/14/methodology-for-ncaa-athletic-department-revenue-database/, viewed February 15, 2017.

22 Figures are for public universities only. Berkowitz et al., "NCAA Finances," *USAToday.com*, at http://sports.usatoday.com/ncaa/finances/, viewed February 15, 2017.

23 See, for example, Robert Litan, Jonathan Orszag, and Peter Orszag. 2003. "The Empirical Effects of College Athletics: An Interim Report," Sebago Associates, at http://www.sc.edu/faculty/PDF/baseline.pdf; and Adam Hoffer, Brad R. Humphreys, Donald J. Lacombe, and Jane E. Ruseski. 2015. "Trends in NCAA Athletic Spending: Arms Race or Rising Tide?" *Journal of Sports Economics*, 16(6), August: 576–596.

24 Charles T. Clotfelter. 2011. *Big-Time Sports in American Universities* (Cambridge: Cambridge University Press): 96. Clotfelter notes that some state universities do not charge athletics departments the added cost of scholarships for out-of-state students. Clotfelter. 2011. *Big-Time Sports in American Universities*: 107.

25 For a good discussion of the slipperiness of scholarship costs, see Victor Matheson, Debra O'Connor, and Joseph Herberger. 2012. "The Bottom Line: Accounting for Revenues and Expenditures in Intercollegiate Athletics," *International Journal of Sport Finance*, 7(1), February: 30–45.

26 Charlotte Gibson, Jim Keller, and Sachin Dave Chandan. 2017. "Who's the Highest-Paid Public Employee in Every State?" *ESPN.com*, March 30, at http://www.espn.com/

espn/feature/story/_/id/19019077/highest-paid-us-employees-dominated-college-football-college-basketball-coaches, viewed March 30, 2017.

27   Charles Clotfelter, *Big-Time Sports in American Colleges,* 2011: 105.

28   USA Today. "NCAA Salaries," *USAToday.com,* at http://sports.usatoday.com/ncaa/salaries/, viewed February 12, 2017.

29   Will Hobson and Steven Rich. 2015. "As College Sports Revenues Spike, Coaches Aren't the Only Ones Cashing In," *Washington Post,* December 29, at https://www.washingtonpost.com/sports/as-college-sports-revenues-spike-coaches-arent-only-ones-cashing-in/2015/12/29/bbdb924e-ae15-11e5-9ab0-884d1cc4b33e_story.html, viewed March 12, 2016.

30   Don Muret. 2015. "Football Becomes Classroom at Notre Dame," *SportsBusiness Daily,* January 12, at http://www.sportsbusinessdaily.com/Journal/Issues/2015/01/12/In-Depth/Notre-Dame.aspx, viewed February 11, 2017.

31   Hobson and Rich. 2015. "As College Sports Revenues Spike."

32   Byers. 1995. *Unsportsmanlike Conduct*: 5.

33   See Nocera and Strauss. 2016. *Indentured: The Inside Story of the Rebellion against the NCAA*: 27.

34   Anecdote related in Byers. 1995. *Unsportsmanlike Conduct*: 81–82. Schools were limited to three appearances over a two-year period. Each of 12 football conferences also had to be represented over this period.

35   Quoted in Murray Sperber. 1990. *College Sports Inc.* (New York: Henry Holt and Co.): 51.

36   See Eric Seiken. 1996. "The NCAA and the Courts: College Football on Television," in *Sports and the Law*, ed. Charles Quirk (New York: Garland): 56–62; and Sperber. 1990. *College Sports Inc.*: 51–52.

37   Sperber. 1990. *College Sports Inc.*: 52; Francis Dealy. 1990. *Win at Any Cost: The Sell Out of College Athletics* (New York: Birch Lane Press): 150; and Roger Noll. 1992. "The Economics of Intercollegiate Sports," in *Rethinking College Athletics,* ed. Judith Andre and David James (Philadelphia, PA: Temple University Press): 202.

38   See NCAA, "Play Division I Sports," *NCAA.org,* at http://www.ncaa.org/student-athletes/play-division-i-sports, viewed February 19, 2017.

39   Pete Thamel. 2006. "Schools Where the Only Real Test Is Basketball," *New York Times,* February 25, at http://www.nytimes.com/2006/02/25/sports/ncaabasketball/25preps.html, viewed August 22, 2006.

40   For institutions that do not offer scholarships to athletes, the measure applies to recruited athletes. See Welch Suggs. 2005. "New Grades on Academic Progress Show Widespread Failings among Top NCAA Teams," *The Chronicle of Higher Education,* March 1, at http://www.chronicle.com/article/New-Grades-on-Academic/119610, viewed October 19, 2017.

41   Steve Wieberg. 2005. "Academic Progress Rates Analyzed," *USA Today,* March 1, at http://www.usatoday.com/sports/college/2005-03-01-apr-analysis_x.htm, viewed August 6, 2006.

42   See NCAA. 2016. "Division I Student-Athletes Still Making Gains in APR," *NCAA. org,* April 20, at http://www.ncaa.org/about/resources/media-center/news/division-i-student-athletes-still-making-gains-apr, viewed February 18, 2017; and Gerald S. Gurney and Richard M. Southall. 2012. "College Sports' Bait and Switch," *ESPN.com,* August 9, at http://www.espn.com/college-sports/story/_/id/8248046/college-sports-programs-find-multitude-ways-game-ncaa-apr, viewed February 5, 2017.

43   Joshua Price. 2010. "The Effects of Higher Admission Standards on NCAA Student-Athletes: An Analysis of Proposition 16," *Journal of Sports Economics,* 11(4), August: 363–382. Price also details the controversy surrounding the adoption of Proposition 16's standards.

44   E. Woodrow Eckard. 1998. "The NCAA Cartel and Competitive Balance in College Football," *Review of Industrial Organization,* 13(3), June: 347–369.

45   Craig A. Depken II and Dennis P. Wilson. 2006. "NCAA Enforcement and Competitive Balance in College Football," *Southern Economic Journal,* 72(4), April: 826–845.

46 Kathleen Carroll and Brad R. Humphreys. 2016. "Opportunistic Behavior in a Cartel Setting: Effects of the 1984 Supreme Court Decision on College Television Broadcasts," *Journal of Sports Economics,* 17(6), June: 601–628.

47 In the wake of Notre Dame's contract with NBC, some took to calling the network the "Notredame Broadcasting Corporation."

48 Jeff Finley. 2012. "Utah A.G. Drops Antitrust Investigation of College Football's BCS System for Now," *Deseret News,* October 27, at http://www.deseretnews.com/article/865565434/Utah-AG-drops-antitrust-investigation-of-college-footballs-BCS-system--for-now.html, viewed April 14, 2017.

49 Associated Press. 2016. "Supreme Court Rejects NCAA Appeal of Ed O'Bannon Case," *Los Angeles Times,* October 3, at http://www.latimes.com/sports/sportsnow/la-sp-supreme-court-ed-obannon-20161003-snap-story.html, viewed April 14, 2017; and Michael McCann. 2016. "In Denying O'Bannon Case, Supreme Court Leaves Future of Amateurism in Limbo," *Sports Illustrated,* October 3, at https://www.si.com/college-basketball/2016/10/03/ed-obannon-ncaa-lawsuit-supreme-court, viewed April 14, 2017.

50 See Anonymous. 1981. "Kapp Victory Seems Empty," *New York Times,* August 4, at http://www.nytimes.com/1981/08/04/sports/kapp-victory-seems-empty.html, viewed April 14, 2017; and Jim Byrne. 1986. *The $1 League: The Rise and fall of the USFL* (New York: Prentice Hall).

51 ESPN.com. 2017. "NCAA Agrees to Historic $209 Million Settlement over Scholarship Shortages," *ESPN.com,* February 4, at http://www.espn.com/college-sports/story/_/id/18616780/ncaa-agrees-historic-209m-settlement-scholarship-shortages, viewed April 14, 2017; and Justin Sievert. 2015. "The Forgotten Antitrust Case: How an NCAA Loss in Alston Could Impact College Athletics," *SportingNews,* November 4, at http://www.sportingnews.com/ncaa-football/news/ncaa-antitrust-case-shawne-alston-effects-college-athletics/1uro6chmw5naj106n15opblfmy, viewed April 15, 2017.

52 Zac Ellis. 2014. "What Does the Kessler Antitrust Lawsuit vs. The NCAA Mean? Michael McCann Explains," *Sports Illustrated,* March 17, at https://www.si.com/college-football/campus-union/2014/03/17/ncaa-antitrust-lawsuit-jeffrey-kessler#, viewed April 13, 2017; and Tom Farrey. 2014. "Jeffrey Kessler Files against NCAA," *ESPN.com,* March 18, at http://www.espn.com/college-sports/story/_/id/10620388/anti-trust-claim-filed-jeffrey-kessler-challenges-ncaa-amateur-model, viewed April 15, 2017.

53 See Charles T. Clotfelter. 2011. *Big-Time Sports in American Universities*: 46–51.

54 James Michener. 1976. *Sports in America* (New York: Random House): 221.

55 Devin Pope and Jaren Pope. 2009. "The Impact of College Sports Success on the Quantity and Quality of Student Applications," *Southern Economic Journal,* 75(3), January: 750–780; Stephen J. Perez. 2012. "Does Intercollegiate Athletics Draw Local Students to a University?" *Journal of Sports Economics,* 13(2), April: 198–206; Michael L. Anderson. 2017. "The Benefits of College Athletic Success: An Application of the Propensity Score Design," *Review of Economics and Statistics,* 99(1), March: 119–134.

56 Data from Berkowitz et al., "NCAA Finances," *USAToday.com,* at http://sports.usatoday.com/ncaa/finances/, viewed January 23, 2017. Ironically, poor investments dissipated most of Pickens' contribution. See Ann Zimmerman and Leslie Scism. 2012. "Boone Calls the Plays as Largess Complicates Life at Alma Mater," *Wall Street Journal,* July 7, at https://www.wsj.com/articles/SB10001424052702304782404577488592793245510, viewed February 21, 2017.

57 Brad Humphreys and Michael Mondello. 2007. "Intercollegiate Athletic Success and Donations at NCAA Division I Institutions," *Journal of Sport Management,* 21(2), April: 265–280.

58 Jeffrey Stinson and Dennis Howard. 2007. "Athletic Success and Private Giving to Athletic and Academic Programs at NCAA Institutions," *Journal of Sport Management,* 21(2), April: 235–264.

59 Because the Big East was a major football conference for the period Anderson studies, he refers to the Power 5 plus the Big East as "Bowl Championship Series" (BCS) conferences.

60   Beth Shapiro. 1983. "John Hannah and the Growth of Big-Time Intercollegiate Athletics at Michigan State University," *Journal of Sports History*, 10(3), Winter: 26–40.

61   Charles T. Clotfelter. 2011. *Big-Time Athletics at American Universities*: 126.

62   J. Robert Byrom. 2009. "ESPN Names Oklahoma Most Prestigious Program during AP/BCS Eras," *USC Trojans*, January 23, at http://bleacherreport.com/articles/114758-espn-names-ou-most-prestigious-school-during-apbcs-eras. At the time, Oklahoma was in the midst of a 47-game winning streak.

63   Martin Kane. 1972. "Scorecard," *SI Vault*, August 14, at https://www.si.com/vault/1972/08/14/613127/scorecard.

64   Zimbalist. 1999. *Unpaid Professionals*.

65   Robert Brown. 2011. "Estimates of a College Football Player's Rents," *Journal of Sports Economics*, 12(2), April: 200–212; Erin Lane, Juan Nagel, and Janet S. Netz. 2014. "Alternative Approaches to Measuring MRP: Are All Men's College Basketball Players Exploited?" *Journal of Sports Economics*, 14(3), June: 237–262.

66   Jason Cook. 2013. "End of Football Season Brought $37 Million in Media Exposure for Texas A&M," *Texas A&M Today*, January 12, at http://today.tamu.edu/2013/01/18/study-end-of-football-season-produced-37-million-in-media-exposure-for-texas-am/, viewed February 9, 2017.

67   Smith. 1988. *Sports and Freedom*: 171. In the 1880s, Yale supposedly had a secret $100,000 fund to pay its athletes. See Dealy. 1990. *Win at Any Cost*: 69; and Zimbalist. 1999. *Unpaid Professionals*: 7.

68   Quote from Allen Guttman. 1991. "The Anomaly of Intercollegiate Athletics," in *Rethinking College Athletics*, ed. Judith Andre and David James (Philadelphia, PA: Temple University Press): 20. See also Zimbalist. 1999. *Unpaid Professionals*: 8.

69   See, for example, Byers. 1995. *Unsportsmanlike Conduct*: 67–72; and Sperber. 1998. *Onward to Victory*: 177–185 and 227–242.

70   Zimbalist. 1999. *Unpaid Professionals*: 37; and Byers. 1999. *Unsportsmanlike Conduct*: 67–70.

71   Nocera and Strauss. 2016. *Indentured: The Inside Story of the Rebellion against the NCAA*: 66; Ryan Grenoble. 2014. "UConn Basketball Player Speaks of 'Hungry Nights,' Going to Bed 'Starving,'" *Huffington Post*, April 7, at http://www.huffingtonpost.com/2014/04/07/shabazz-napier-hungry-uconn-basketball_n_5106132.html, viewed March 5, 2017.

72   Jon Solomon. 2015. "CBS Sports 2015-16 FBS College Football Cost of Attendance Database," *CBSSports.com*, August 20, at http://www.cbssports.com/college-football/news/2015-16-cbs-sports-fbs-college-football-cost-of-attendance-database/, viewed March 5, 2017.

73   For a useful summary of this literature, see Michael A. Leeds. 2015. "Youth Sports and the Accumulation of Human Capital," *IZA World of Labor*, February, at http://wol.iza.org/articles/youth-sports-and-accumulation-of-human-capital/long, viewed March 4, 2017.

74   James Long and Steven Caudill. 1991. "The Impact of Participation in Intercollegiate Athletics on Income and Graduation," *Review of Economics and Statistics*, 73(3), August: 525–531. See also Zimbalist. 1999. *Unpaid Professionals:* 51.

75   For a skeptical view of the GSR, see Nocera and Strauss. 2016. *Indentured: The Inside Story of the Rebellion against the NCAA*: 126.

76   Richard M. Southall, Mark S. Nagel, Allen Wallace, and Megan Sexton. 2016. *2016 Adjusted Graduation Gap Report: NCAA FBS Football*, October 19, at http://csri-sc.org/wp-content/uploads/2016/10/2016-Football-AGG-Report_Publish_Final_10-19-2016.pdf; Richard M. Southall, Mark S. Nagel, and Megan Sexton. 2016. *2016 Adjusted Graduation Gap Report: NCAA Division-I Basketball*, April 6, at http://csri-sc.org/wp-content/uploads/2013/09/2016-Basketball-AGG-Report_Final.pdf.

77   See, for example, Dean Purdy, Stanley Eitzen, and Rick Hufnagel. 1985. "Are Athletes Also Students? The Educational Attainment of College Athletes," in *Sport and Higher Education*, ed. Donald Chu, Jeffrey Segrave, and Beverly Becker (Champaign, IL: Human Kinetics Publishers): 221–234; and Lee Sigelman. 1995. "It's Academic—or Is It? Admissions Standards and Big-Time Football," *Social Science Quarterly*, 76(2): 247–261.

78   William Bowen and Sarah Levin. 2003. *Reclaiming the Game: College Sports and Educational Values* (Princeton, NJ: Princeton University Press); Elizabeth Aries, Danielle McCarthy, Peter Salovey, and Mahzarin Banaji. 2004. "A Comparison of Athletes and Non-Athletes at Highly-Selective Colleges: Academic Performance and Personal Development," *Research in Higher Education,* 45(6), September: 577–602.

79   Lawrence DeBrock, Wallace Hendricks, and Roger Koenker. 1996. "The Economics of Persistence: Graduation Rates of Athletes as Labor Market Choice," *Journal of Human Resources,* 31(3), Summer: 513–539.

80   Robinson was the first UCLA athlete to accomplish this feat.

81   Lane Demas. 2010. *Integrating the Gridiron: Black Civil Rights and American College Football* (New Brunswick, NJ: Rutgers University Press): 5.

82   Demas. 2010. *Integrating the Gridiron*: 3 and 7.

83   Charles Martin. 1997. "Integrating New Year's Day: The Racial Politics of College Bowl Games in the American South," *Journal of Sport History,* 24(3), Fall: 358–377.

84   At that time, freshmen did not play varsity sports. Jackson went on to be a first-round NFL draft pick. See Darren Everson. 2009. "The Game That Changed Alabama," *Wall Street Journal,* December 4: W6; CBS. 2006. "The Football Game That Broke Racial Barriers," *YouTube,* at https://www.youtube.com/watch?v=CnOpZvEulvY, viewed September 23, 2011.

85   Allen Barra. 2005. *The Last Coach: A Life of Paul "Bear" Bryant* (New York: W.W. Norton): 330.

86   *Title IX Legal Manual,* United States Department of Justice, Civil Rights Division, updated August 6, 2015, at https://www.justice.gov/crt/title-ix.

87   See, for example, Megan Rehberg. 2015. *"Grove City College v. Bell," Law and Higher Education,* at http://caselaw.findlaw.com/us-supreme-court/465/555.html, viewed April 16, 2017.

88   Nick Anderson. 2014. "The Gender Factor in College Admissions: Do Men or Women Have an Edge?" *Washington Post,* March 26, at https://www.washingtonpost.com/local/education/the-gender-factor-in-college-admissions/2014/03/26/4996e988-b4e6-11e3-8020-b2d790b3c9e1_story.html?utm_term=.2c0148c84b8b, viewed April 11, 2017.

89   NCAA. 2016. "NCAA Sports Sponsorship and Participation Rates Report," at http://www.ncaapublications.com/productdownloads/PR1516.pdf.

90   Christina Hoff Sommers. 2014. "Title IX: How a Good Law Went Terribly Wrong," *Time,* June 23, at http://time.com/2912420/titleix-anniversary/, viewed March 5, 2017.

91   "'Open to All': Title IX at Thirty," Report of the Secretary of Education's Commission on Opportunity in Athletics, February 28, 2003, at https://www2.ed.gov/about/bdscomm/list/athletics/title9report.pdf: 19.

92   Kate Fagan and Luke Cyphers. 2012. "Five Myths about Title IX," *ESPNW.com,* April 29, at http://www.espn.com/espnw/title-ix/article/7729603/five-myths-title-ix, viewed March 5, 2017.

93   NFHS News. 2016. "High School Sports Participation Increases for 27th Consecutive Year," *National Federation of State High School Associations,* September 12, at https://www.nfhs.org/articles/high-school-sports-participation-increases-for-27th-consecutive-year/, viewed March 5, 2017.

94   Brad Wolverton. 2012. "Female Participation in College Sports Reaches All-Time High," *The Chronicle of Higher Education,* January 22, at http://www.chronicle.com/article/Female-Participation-in/130431/, viewed March 8, 2017; National Women's Law Center, "The Battle for Gender Equity in Athletics in Colleges and Universities," *Title IX and Women's Athletic Opportunity,* at http://www.nwlc.org/sites/default/files/pdfs/2011_8_battle_in_college_athletics_final.pdf, viewed March 8, 2017.

95   Peter von Allmen. 2013. "Coaching Women and Women Coaching: Pay Differentials in the Title IX Era," in *Handbook on the Economics of Women in Sports,* ed. Eva Marikova Leeds and Michael A. Leeds (Cheltenham, UK: Edward Elgar): 269–289.

96   Josh Peter. 2015. "Error Jordan: Key Figures Still Argue over Who Was Responsible for Nike Deal," *USA Today,* September 30

97   Phil Knight. 2016. *Shoe Dog* (New York: Scribner): 309.

REFERENCES

"2016 NFL Attendance Data," *Pro Football Reference*, at http://www.pro-football-reference.com/years/2016/attendance.htm.

"2016-17 Bowl Money," *ACC Football Rx*, at http://accfootballrx.blogspot.com/2016/12/2016-17-bowl-money.html.

"2017–2021 Basic Agreement," at http://www.mlbplayers.com/pdf9/5450407.pdf.

Abrams, Roger. 1998. *Legal Bases: Baseball and the Law.* Philadelphia, PA: Temple University Press.

Agence France-Presse. 2017. "CBS News: 12 Riders Used Motorized Bikes in the 2015 Tour," *VeloNews*, January 30, at http://www.velonews.com/2017/01/news/cbs-news-12-riders-used-motorized-bikes-in-the-2015-tour_429741.

Aldrich, Eric M, Peter S. Arcidiacono, and Joseph L. Vigdor. 2005. "Do People Value Racial Diversity? Evidence from Nielsen Ratings," *The B.E. Journal of Economic Analysis and Policy*, 5(1), Article 4: 1–22.

Allmers, Swatje, and Wolfgang Maennig. 2009. "Economic Impacts of the FIFA Soccer World Cups in France 1998, Germany 2006, and Outlook for South Africa 2010," *Eastern Economic Journal*, 35(4): 500–519.

Amar, Harshit. 2015. "La Liga Suspended: The Strange Case of TV Rights," *Footballtarget.com*, November 5, at http://www.footballtarget.com/la-liga-strange-case-tv-rights/.

Anderson, Michael L. 2017. "The Benefits of College Athletic Success: An Application of the Propensity Score Design," *Review of Economics and Statistics*, 99(1), March: 119–134.

Anderson, Nick. 2014. "The Gender Factor in College Admissions: Do Men or Women Have an Edge?" *Washington Post*, March 26, at https://www.washingtonpost.com/local/education/the-gender-factor-in-college-admissions/2014/03/26/4996e988-b4e6-11e3-8020-b2d790b3c9e1_story.html?utm_term=.2c0148c84b8b.

Anderson, Torben, and Sumner J. La Croix. 1991. "Customer Discrimination in Major League Baseball," *Economic Inquiry*, 29(4), October: 665–677.

Andreff, Wladimir, and Paul Staudohar. 2002. "European and US Sports Business Models," in *Transatlantic Sport: The Comparative Economics of North American and European Sport*, ed. Carlos Pestana Barros, Muradali Ibrahimo, and Stefan Szymanski. Cheltenham: Edward Elgar: 23–49.

Annala, Christopher, and Jason Winfree. 2011. "Salary Distribution and Team Performance in Major League Baseball," *Sport Management Review*, 14(2), May: 167–175.

"Annual Lobbying by the National Football League," *OpenSecrets.org*, January 25, 2017, at https://www.opensecrets.org/lobby/clientsum.php?id=D000027847.

Anonymous, "MLB Executives: Alan H. (Bud) Selig," at http://mlb.mlb.com/mlb/official_info/about_mlb/executives.jsp?bio=selig_bud.

Anonymous. 1981. "Kapp Victory Seems Empty," *New York Times*, August 4, at http://www.nytimes.com/1981/08/04/sports/kapp-victory-seems-empty.html?pagewanted=all.

Appleyard, Alex. 2016. "The Flyers' European Renaissance," *Philadelphia Sons of Penn*, October 18, at http://sonsofpenn.com/flyers/the-flyers-european-renaissance/.

Aries, Elizabeth, Danielle McCarthy, Peter Salovey, and Mahzarin Banaji. 2004. "A Comparison of Athletes and Non-Athletes at Highly-Selective Colleges: Academic Performance and Personal Development," *Research in Higher Education*, 45(6), September: 577–602.

Aschwanden, Christie. 2016. "The Olympics Are Still Struggling to Define Gender," *FiveThirtyEight*, June 28, at http://fivethirtyeight.com/features/the-olympics-are-still-struggling-to-define-gender/.

Ashenfelter, Orley, and David Bloom. 1984. "Models of Arbitrator Behavior: Theory and Evidence," *American Economic Review*, 74(1), March: 111–124.

Associated Press. 2000. "Soldier Field Referendum Rejected," December 29.

Associated Press. 2002. "Commissioner Spent $1.2 Million on Lobbying in 2001," *ESPN.com*, May 15.

Associated Press. 2005. "Saints' Home Games: 4 at LSU, 3 in Alamodome," September 12, at http://sports.espn.go.com/nfl/news/story?id=2159595.

Associated Press. 2006. "A Look at Spending on Recent Winter Olympics," October 2, at http://wintergames.ap.org/article/look-spending-recent-winter-olympics.

Associated Press. 2013. "Deloitte: Qatar to Spend $200 Billion for World Cup," *USA Today*, July 9, at http://www.usatoday.com/story/sports/soccer/2013/07/09/deloitte-qatar-to-spend-200-billion-world-cup/2501815/.

Associated Press. 2015. "NFL Teams That Use Variable or Dynamic Ticket Pricing," *ESPN.com*, July 11, at http://www.espn.com/espn/wire?id=13237217&section=nfl.

Associated Press. 2016. "ATP Money Leaders," *Federal News Radio*, September 12, at http://federalnewsradio.com/sports-news/2016/09/atp-money-leaders/.

Associated Press. 2016. "Supreme Court Rejects NCAA Appeal of Ed O'Bannon Case," *Los Angeles Times*, October 3, at http://www.latimes.com/sports/sportsnow/la-sp-supreme-court-ed-obannon-20161003-snap-story.html.

Associated Press. 2017. "Russia Increases 2018 World Cup Budget by $325 Million," February 6, at http://www.espnfc.com/fifa-world-cup/story/3055194/russia-increases-2018-world-cup-budget-by-$325-million.

ATP World Tour, "The 2017 ATP Official Rulebook," at http://www.atpworldtour.com/en/corporate/rulebook.

Austrian, Ziona, and Mark Rosentraub. 1997. "Cleveland's Gateway to the Future," in *Sports, Jobs, and Taxes*, ed. Roger G. Noll and Andrew Zimbalist. Washington, DC: Brookings Institution Press: 355–384.

Aynsworth, Hugh. 2004. "Owner of Dallas Cowboys Seeks $1 Billion in Tax Funds," *Washington Times*, February 2, at http://www.washingtontimes.com/national/20040202-120350-8901r.htm.

Baade, Robert, Robert Baumann, and Victor Matheson. 2008. "Selling the Game: Estimating the Economic Impact of Professional Sports through Taxable Sales," *Southern Economic Journal*, 74(3), January: 794–810.

Baade, Robert, Robert Baumann, and Victor Matheson. 2010. "Slippery Slope: Assessing the Economic Impact of the 2002 Winter Olympic Games in Salt Lake City, Utah," *Region et Développement*, 31: 81–91.

Baade, Robert, and Richard Dye. 1988. "Sports Stadiums and Area Development: A Critical Review," *Economic Development Quarterly*, 2(3), August: 265–275.

Baade, Robert, and Victor Matheson. 2002. "Bidding for the Olympics: Fool's Gold?" in *Transatlantic Sport: The Comparative Economics of North American and European Sport*, ed. Carlos Pestana Barros, Muradali Ibrahimo, and Stefan Szymanski. Cheltenham, UK: Edward Elgar: 127–151.

Baade, Robert, and Victor Matheson. 2006. "Have Public Finance Principles Been Shut Out of Financing New Stadiums for the NFL?" *Public Finance and Management*, 6(3): 284–320.

Baade, Robert, and Victor Matheson. 2006. "Padding Required: Assessing the Economic Impact of the Super Bowl," *European Sports Management Quarterly*, 6(4): 353–374.

Baade, Robert, and Victor Matheson. 2013. "Financing Professional Sports Facilities," in *Financing Economic Development in the 21st Century*, ed. Sammis White and Zenia Kotval. New York: M.E. Sharpe Publishers.

Baade, Robert, and Victor Matheson. 2016. "Going for the Gold: The Economics of the Olympics," *Journal of Economic Perspectives*, 30(2), April: 201–218.

Baade, Robert, and Allen Sanderson. 1997. "The Employment Effect of Teams and Sports Facilities," in *Sports, Jobs, and Taxes: The Economic Impact of Sports Teams and*

Stadiums, ed. Roger G. Noll and Andrew Zimbalist. Washington, DC: Brookings Institution Press: 92–118.

Badenhausen, Kurt. 2011. "The NFL Signs TV Deal Worth $27 Billion," *Forbes.com*, December 14, at https://www.forbes.com/sites/kurtbadenhausen/2011/12/14/the-nfl-signs-tv-deals-worth-26-billion/.

Badenhausen, Kurt. 2016. "Warriors, Chase Tie-Up Ranks among Biggest Stadium Naming Deals Ever," *Forbes.com*, January 28, at http://www.forbes.com/sites/kurtbadenhausen/2016/01/28/warriors-chase-tie-up-joins-ranks-of-biggest-stadium-naming-rights-deals/.

Badenhausen, Kurt, and Michael Ozanian. 2009. "The Business of Baseball," *Forbes.com*, April 22, at http://www.forbes.com/lists/2009/33/baseball-values-09_New-York-Yankees_334613.html.

Badenhausen, Kurt, Michael Ozanian, and Christina Settimi. 2010. "The Business of Baseball," *Forbes.com*, April 7, at http://www.forbes.com/lists/2010/33/baseball-valuations-10_New-York-Yankees_334613.html.

Badenhausen, Kurt, Michael Ozanian, and Christina Settimi. 2011. "MLB Team Values," *Forbes.com*, March 22, at http://www.forbes.com/lists/2011/33/baseball-valuations-11_land.html.

Baker, William. 1982. *Sports in the Western World*. Totowa, NJ: Rowman & Littlefield.

Ballotpedia. "Largest Cities in the United States by Population," at https://ballotpedia.org/Largest_cities_in_the_United_States_ by population.

Baltzell, F. Digby. 1995. *Sporting Gentlemen: Men's Tennis from the Age of Honor to the Cult of the Superstar*. New York: The Free Press.

Bamberger, Michael, and Don Yaeger. 1997. "Over the Edge," *Sports Illustrated*, April 14: 61–70.

Banko, Lauren, Eva Marikova Leeds, and Michael A. Leeds. 2016. "Gender Differences in Response to Setbacks: Evidence from Professional Tennis," *Social Science Quarterly*, 97(2), June: 161–176.

Baroncelli, Alessandro, and Umberto Lago. 2006. "Italian Football," *Journal of Sports Economics*, 7(1), February: 13–28.

Barra, Allen. 2000. "In Anti-trust We Trust," *Salon Magazine*, May 19, at http://www.salon.com/news/feature/2000/05/19/antitrust/index.html.

Barra, Allen. 2005. *The Last Coach: A Life of Paul "Bear" Bryant*. New York: W.W. Norton.

Barry, Dave. 1999. *Dave Barry Turns Fifty*. New York: Random House.

Bartlett, Donald, and James Steele. 2001. "Snow Job," *Sports Illustrated*, December 10: 79–97.

Baseball Almanac, at http://www.baseball-almanac.com.

Baseball Almanac, "President George W. Bush Baseball Related Quotations," at http://www.baseball-almanac.com/prz_qgwb.shtml.

Baumann, Robert, Bryan Engelhardt, and Victor Matheson. 2012. "Employment Effects of the 2002 Winter Olympics in Salt Lake City, Utah," *Journal of Economics and Statistics*, 232(3), May: 308–317.

Baumann, Robert, and Victor Matheson. 2017. "Mega-Events and Tourism: The Case of Brazil," *Contemporary Economic Policy*, in press.

Baumann, Robert, Victor Matheson, and Chihiro Muroi. 2009. "Bowling in Hawaii: Examining the Effectiveness of Sports-Based Tourism Strategies," *Journal of Sports Economics*, 10(1), February: 107–123.

BBC. 2008. "Faz Presidency Marred by Racial Abuse," February 25, at http://news.bbc.co.uk/sport2/hi/football/africa/7262763.stm.

BBC. 2012. "Sol Campbell Warns Fans to Stay Away from Euro 2012," May 28, at http://www.bbc.com/news/uk-18192375.

BBC. 2013. "London 2012: Olympics and Paralympics 528 Million under Budget," July 19, at http://www.bbc.com/sport/0/olympics/20041426.

BBC. 2014. "Urawa Reds Play to Empty Stadium after Fans Banned for Racist Banner," March 23, at http://www.bbc.com/sport/football/26704368.

BBC. 2014. "Atalanta Is Fined over Banana Incident in Italy's Serie A," May 12, at http://www.bbc.com/sport/football/27374486.

BBC. 2017. "Qatar Spending $500m a Week on World Cup Infrastructure Projects," February 8, at http://www.bbc.com/news/world-middle-east-38905510.

Becker, Gary. 1971. *The Economics of Discrimination*, 2nd ed. Chicago, IL: University of Chicago Press.

Becker, Gary. 1983. "A Theory of Competition among Pressure Groups for Political Influence," *Quarterly Journal of Economics*, 97(3), August: 371–400.

Becker, Gary. 1993. *Human Capital*, 3rd ed. Chicago, IL: University of Chicago Press.

Beckett Baseball Card Price Guide, 2016.

Belson, Ken. 2009. "Tickets Cost Too Much? Check Back Tomorrow," *New York Times*, May 18: D-2.

Belson, Ken. 2011. "New Sponsor on WNBA Uniforms," *New York Times*, August 22, at http://www.nytimes.com/2011/08/22/sports/basketball/wnba-makes-sponsorship-deal-with-boost-mobile.html.

Belzer, Jason. 2016. "The World's Most Powerful Sports Agents," *Forbes*, September 21, at https://www.forbes.com/sites/jasonbelzer/2016/09/21/the-worlds-most-powerful-sports-agents-2016/.

Berentsen, Aleksander. 2002. "The Economics of Doping," *European Journal of Political Economy*, 18(1), March: 109–127.

Berger, Ken. 2016. "NBA Free Agency Cheat Sheet: Everything You Need to Know," *CBSSports.com*, June 30, at http://www.cbssports.com/nba/news/nba-free-agency-cheat-sheet-everything-you-need-to-know/.

Berkowitz, Steve, Christopher Schnaars, Jodi Upton, Mark Hannan, Michael Stern, Justin Meyer, et al., "NCAA Finances," *USAToday.com*, at http://sports.usatoday.com/ncaa/finances/.

Berman, Gabrielle, Robert Brooks, and Sinclair Davidson. 2000. "The Sydney Olympic Games Announcement and Australian Stock Market Reaction," *Applied Economics Letters*, 7(12), December: 781–784.

Berri, David, Stacey Brook, Bernd Frick, Aju Fenn, and Roberto Vicente-Mayoral. 2005. "The Short Supply of Tall People: Explaining Competitive Imbalance in the National Basketball Association," *Journal of Economic Issues*, 39(4), December: 1029–1041.

Berri, David J., and Martin B. Schmidt. 2010. *Stumbling on Wins*. Upper Saddle River, NJ: FT Press.

Berri, David J., Martin B. Schmidt, and Stacey L. Brook. 2006. *The Wages of Wins: Taking Measure of the Many Myths in Modern Sport*. Stanford, CA: Stanford University Press.

Berri, David J., and Rob Simmons. 2009. "Race and the Evaluation of Signal Callers in the National Football League," *Journal of Sports Economics*, 10(1), February: 23–43.

Betzold, Michael, and Ethan Casey. 1992. *Queen of Diamonds: The Tiger Stadium Story*. West Bloomfield, MI: Northfield Publishing.

Birger, Jon. 2009. "Baseball Battles the Slump," *CNNMoney.com*, February 19, at http://money.cnn.com/2009/02/18/magazines/fortune/birger_baseball.fortune/index.htm.

Bloom, David, and Christopher Cavanaugh. 1987. "Negotiator Behavior under Arbitration," *American Economic Review*, 77(2), May: 353–358.

Blum, Ronald. 2016. "Dodgers, Latin American Players Losers in MLB Labor Deal," *Associated Press*, December 1, at http://bigstory.ap.org/91335e2ae60d440d9a72ee1ed3caa14d.

Bodvarsson, Orn B. 1999. "A Test of Employer Discrimination in the NBA," *Contemporary Economic Policy*, 17(2), April: 243–256.

Bodvarsson, Orn B., and Brad R. Humphreys. 2013. "Labor Market Discrimination and Capital: The Effects of Fan Discrimination on Stadium and Arena Construction," *Contemporary Economic Policy*, 31(3), July: 604–617.

Boniface, Daniel. 2016. "MLS Player Salaries 2016 Released by Major League Soccer Players Union," *The Denver Post: The Terrace*, May 19, at http://blogs.denverpost.com/rapids/2016/05/19/mls-player-salaries-2016-released-major-league-soccer-players-union/27671/.

Borland, Jeffrey, and Robert MacDonald. 2003. "Demand for Sport," *Oxford Review of Economic Policy*, 19(4): 478–502.

Boulder Daily Camera. 2007. "Democratic Convention an Economic Boon," January 12.

Bowen, William, and Sarah Levin. 2003. *Reclaiming the Game: College Sports and Educational Values.* Princeton, NJ: Princeton University Press.

Brooke, James. 2002. "Legacy of World Cup May Be the Stadiums Left Behind," *New York Times,* June 2, at http://www.nytimes.com/2002/06/02/sports/soccer-legacy-of-world-cup-may-be-the-stadiums-left-behind.html.

Brown, Robert W., and R. Todd Jewell. 2013. "Revenues and Subsidies in Collegiate Sports: An Analysis of NCAA Division I Women's Basketball," in *Handbook on the Economics of Women in Sports,* ed. Eva Marikova Leeds and Michael A. Leeds. Cheltenham: Edward Elgar.

Brown, Maury. 2016. "2016 MLB Advanced Media Revenues Projected to Reach $1.1–$1.2 Billion," *Forbes.com,* March, at https://www.forbes.com/sites/maurybrown/2016/03/03/mlb-advanced-media-projected-revenues-to-be-1-1-1-2-billion-in-2016/.

Brown, Maury. 2016. "How Major League Baseball Continues Massive Growth with the Addition of BAMTech Europe," *Forbes.com,* November 1, at http://www.forbes.com/sites/maurybrown/2016/11/01/how-major-league-baseball-continues-massive-growth-with-addition-of-bamtech-europe/.

Brown, Robert. 2011. "Estimates of a College Football Player's Rents," *Journal of Sports Economics,* 12(2), April: 200–212.

Brustein, Joshua. 2010. "Star Pitchers in a Duel? Tickets Will Cost More," *New York Times,* June 27, at http://www.nytimes.com/2010/06/28/technology/28tickets.html.

Buchanan, James. 1965. "An Economic Theory of Clubs," *Economica,* 32(125), February: 1–14.

Buraimo, Babatunde. 2008. "Stadium Attendance and Television Audience Demand in English League Football," *Managerial and Decision Economics,* 29(6): 513–523.

Buraimo, Babatunde, and Rob Simmons. 2008. "Do Sports Fans Really Value Uncertainty of Outcome? Evidence from the English Premier League," *International Journal of Sport Finance,* 3(3), August: 146–155.

Bureau of Labor Statistics. 2016. "Economic News Release: Union Members Summary," January 28, at http://www.bls.gov/news.release/union2.nro.htm.

Burgos, Adrian. 2007. *Playing America's Game.* Berkeley: University of California Press.

Burk, Robert. 1994. *Never Just a Game: Players, Owners, and American Baseball to 1920.* Chapel Hill: University of North Carolina Press.

Burns, Ken. 1994. *Baseball* (film). PBS Video.

BusinessWeek, "Company Overview of Giants Stadium LLC," *BusinessWeek.com,* at http://investing.businessweek.com/research/stocks/private/snapshot.asp?privcapId=36320464.

Byers, Walter, with Charles Hammer. 1995. *Unsportsmanlike Conduct: Exploiting College Athletes.* Ann Arbor: University of Michigan Press.

Byrne, Jim. 1986. *The $1 League: The Rise and Fall of the USFL.* New York: Prentice Hall.

Byrom, J. Robert. 2009. "ESPN Names Oklahoma Most Prestigious Program during AP/BCS Eras," *USC Trojans,* January 23, at http://bleacherreport.com/articles/114758-espn-names-ou-most-prestigous-school-during-apbcs-eras.

Cacciola, Scott. 2016. "NBA and Players' Union Agree to New Labor Deal," *New York Times,* December 14, at http://www.nytimes.com/2016/12/14/sports/basketball/nba-collective-bargaining-agreement.html.

Cagan, Joanna, and Neil deMause. 1998. *Field of Schemes.* Monroe, ME: Common Courage Press.

Campbell, Tim. 2012. "Jets Will Not Need NHL's Revenue-Sharing," *Winnipeg Free Press,* April 25, at http://www.winnipegfreepress.com/breakingnews/Jets-will-not-need-NHLs-revenue-sharing--146445605.html.

Canadian Broadcasting Corporation. 2005. "Montreal Says No to 'Big Owe'," October 8, at http://www.cbc.ca/news/canada/montreal-says-no-to-big-owe-1.569446.

Canellos, Peter S. 1997. "In City with Short Memory, Astrodome May Become History," *Milwaukee Journal-Sentinel,* July 27: 26A.

Card, David, and Gordon B. Dahl. 2011. "Family Violence and Football: The Effect of Unexpected Emotional Cues on Violent Behavior," *Quarterly Journal of Economics,* 126(1), February: 103–143.

Carlino, Gerald, and N. Edward Coulson. 2004. "Compensating Differentials and the Social Benefit of the NFL," *Journal of Urban Economics,* 56(1), July: 25–50.

Carroll, Kathleen, and Brad R. Humphreys. 2016. "Opportunistic Behavior in a Cartel Setting: Effects of the 1984 Supreme Court Decision on College Television Broadcasts,"
Journal of Sports Economics, 17(6), June: 601–628.

Carroll, Lewis. 1972. "Through the Looking Glass," in *The Annotated Alice.* New York: Meridian Books.

Cary, Tom. 2017. "British Cycling Told to Sort Out Mess or Lose £26m as Backlash Intensifies," *The Telegraph,* March 2, at http://www.telegraph.co.uk/cycling/2017/03/02/
team-sky-british-cycling-fire-missing-medical-records-latest/.

Cassing, James, and Richard Douglas. 1980. "Implications of the Auction Mechanism in
Baseball's Free Agent Draft," *Southern Economic Journal,* 47(1), July: 110–121.

Cayleff, Susan. 1995. *Babe: The Life and Legend of Babe Didrickson Zaharias.* Urbana: University of Illinois Press.

CBS. 2006. "The Football Game That Broke Racial Barriers," *YouTube,* at https://www.
youtube.com/watch?v=CnOpZvEulvY.

Center for Public Integrity. 2000. "How George W. Bush Scored Big with the Texas Rangers," January 18, at https://www.publicintegrity.org/2000/01/18/3313/how-
george-w-bush-scored-big-texas-rangers.

Chapman, Steve. 2003. "A Stadium Deal That Is Hard to Bear," *Chicago Tribune,* September 14.

Chavez, Chris. 2017. "Intelligence Report: Russia's Olympic Doping Scandal Linked to Election Interference," *Sports Illustrated,* January 6, at http://ww.si.com/olympics/
2017/01/06/us-intelligence-agency-russia-hackers-dnc-wada-doping-scandal.

Chema, Thomas. 1996. "When Professional Sports Justify the Subsidy," *Journal of Urban
Affairs,* 18(1), February: 19–22.

Chiari, Mike. 2015. "NHL Salary Cap Announced for 2015-16 Season," *Bleacher Report,*
June 23, at http://bleacherreport.com/articles/2504174-nhl-salary-cap-announced-
for-2015-16-season.

Clapp, Christopher M., and Jahn K. Hakes. 2005. "How Long a Honeymoon? The Effect of
New Stadiums on Attendance in Major League Baseball," *Journal of Sports Economics,*
6(3), August: 237–263.

Close, Kerry. 2016. "5 Reasons Why Tennis Should Keep Paying Men and Women Equally,"
Everyday Money, March 22, at http://time.com/money/4265912/equal-pay-tennis-
djokovic-williams/.

Clotfelter, Charles T. 2011. *Big-Time Sports in American Universities.* Cambridge: Cambridge
University Press.

Coase, Ronald. 1960. "The Problem of Social Cost," *Journal of Law and Economics,* 3(1),
October: 1–44.

Coates, Dennis. 2007. "Stadiums and Arenas: Economic Development or Economic Redistribution?" *Contemporary Economic Policy,* 25(4), October: 565–577.

Coates, Dennis, and Craig Depken. 2010. "Mega-Events: Is Baylor Football to Waco What
the Super Bowl Is to Houston?" *Journal of Sports Economics,* 12(6): 599–620.

Coates, Dennis, and Brad R. Humphreys. 2003. "The Effect of Professional Sports on Earnings and Employment in U.S. Cities," *Regional Science and Urban Economics,* 33(2),
March: 175–198.

Coates, Dennis, and Brad R. Humphreys. 2003. "Professional Sports Facilities, Franchises,
and Urban Economic Development," *Public Finance and Management,* 3(3), September: 335–357.

Coates, Dennis, Brad R. Humphreys, and Li Zhou. 2014. "Reference-Dependent Preferences,
Loss Aversion, and Live Game Attendance," *Economic Inquiry,* 52(3), July: 959–973.

Cobb, Nathan. 1986. "Baseball Border War: In Milford, Conn. Geography Brings Sox and
Mets Fans Cheek to Jowl," *Boston Globe,* October 20: 8.

Coleman, B. Jay, Kenneth Jennings, and Frank McLaughlin. 1993. "Convergence or Divergence in Final-Offer Arbitration in Professional Baseball," *Industrial Relations,* 32(2),
April: 238–247.

"Collective Bargaining Agreement." 2011, August 4, at https://nfllabor.files.wordpress.
com/2010/01/collective-bargaining-agreement-2011-2020.pdf.

Condor, Bob. 2011. "NHL, NBC Sign Record-Setting 10-Year TV Deal," *NHL.com*, April 19, at https://www.nhl.com/news/nhl-nbc-sign-record-setting-10-year-tv-deal/c-560238.

Conlin, Michael, and Patrick M. Emerson. 2006. "Discrimination in Hiring versus Retention and Promotion: An Empirical Analysis of Within-Firm Treatment of Players in the NFL," *Journal of Law, Economics & Organization*, 22(1), April: 115–136.

Conway, Russ. 1997. *Game Misconduct: Alan Eagleson and the Corruption of Hockey.* Buffalo, NY: MacFarlane, Walter, and Ross.

Cook, Jason. 2013. "End of Football Season Brought $37 Million in Media Exposure for Texas A&M," *Texas A&M Today*, January 12, at http://today.tamu.edu/2013/01/18/study-end-of-football-season-produced-37-million-in-media-exposure-for-texas-am/.

Coon, Larry. "NBA Salary Cap FAQ," at http://www.cbafaq.com.

Corbett, Peter. 2015. "Report: Super Bowl Lifted Valley Economy by $720 Million," *Arizona Republic*, June 23.

Corbitt, Craig, and Jan Yi. "*American Needle, Inc. v. National Football League, et al.*: Amicus Curiae Brief of Economists in Support of Petitioner," at http://people.stern.nyu.edu/wgreene/entertainmentandmedia/AmericanNeedleEconomists.pdf.

Cot's Baseball Contracts, at http://legacy.baseballprospectus.com/compensation/cots/2005/02/.

Covington, Robert N. 2003. "How Much Is the Law to Blame for Baseball's Turbulent Labor Relations?" *Journal of Sports Economics*, 4(4), November: 357–361.

Croson, Rachel, and Uri Gneezy. 2009. "Gender Differences in Preferences." *Journal of Economic Literature*, 47(2), Summer: 1–27.

Crowley, Joseph. 2006. *In the Arena: The NCAA's First Century.* Indianapolis: NCAA.

Cubs.com. "Six Game Pack," at http://chicago.cubs.mlb.com/chc/ticketing/sixpacks.jsp.

Curme, Michael A., and Greg M. Dougherty. 2004. "Competition and Pay for National Hockey League Players Born in Quebec," *Journal of Sports Economics*, 5(2), May: 186–205.

Danielson, Michael. 1997. *Home Team: Professional Sport and the American Metropolis.* Princeton, NJ: Princeton University Press.

Das, Andrew. 2016. "Pay Disparity in US Soccer? It's Complicated," *New York Times*, April 21, at http://www.nytimes.com/2016/04/22/sports/soccer/usmnt-uswnt-soccer-equal-pay.html.

Dealy, Francis. 1990. *Win at Any Cost: The Sell Out of College Athletics.* New York: Birch Lane Press.

DeBrock, Lawrence, Wallace Hendricks, and Roger Koenker. 1996. "The Economics of Persistence: Graduation Rates of Athletes as Labor Market Choice," *Journal of Human Resources*, 31(3), Summer: 513–539.

Delaney, Kevin. 2003. *Public Dollars, Private Stadiums.* New Brunswick, NJ: Rutgers University Press.

Deloitte Sports Business Group. June 2016. "Annual Review of Football Finance 2016," ed. Dan Jones, at https://www2.deloitte.com/content/dam/Deloitte/uk/Documents/sports-business-group/deloitte-uk-annual-review-of-football-finance-2016.pdf.

DeLuca, Dave. 2017. "How the NFL Franchise Tag Works," *SportingNews*, February 27, at http://www.sportingnews.com/nfl/news/how-nfl-franchise-tag-works-exclusive-vs-non-exclusive-transition-difference/1w7mwh36nqnfw1qb7lne9tgkao.

Demas, Lane. 2010. *Integrating the Gridiron: Black Civil Rights and American College Football.* New Brunswick, NJ: Rutgers University Press.

Dempsey, Chris, and Andrew Zimbalist. 2017. *No Boston Olympics: How and Why Smart Cities Are Passing on the Torch.* Lebanon, NH: ForeEdge Publishers.

Depken, Craig A. II. 1999. "Free-Agency and the Competitiveness of Major League Baseball," *Review of Industrial Organization*, 14(3), May: 205–217.

Depken, Craig A. II. 2000. "Wage Disparity and Team Productivity: Evidence from Major League Baseball," *Economics Letters*, 61(1), April: 87–92.

Depken, Craig A. II, and Dennis P. Wilson. 2006. "NCAA Enforcement and Competitive Balance in College Football," *Southern Economic Journal*, 72(4), April: 826–845.

Deutsche Welle. 2006. "World Cup to Boost German Economy," January 2, at http://www.dw.com/en/world-cup-to-boost-german-economy/a-1842332.

Dickey, Glenn. 1991. *Just Win, Baby: Al Davis and His Raiders.* New York: Harcourt, Brace, Jovanovich.

Dolan, Paul, Georgios Kavetsos, Christian Krekel, Dimitris Mavridis, Robert Metcalfe, Claudia Senik, Stefan Szymanski, and Nicolas R. Ziebart. 2016. "The Host with the Most? The Effects of the Olympic Games on Happiness," Centre for Economic Performance Discussion Paper No. 1441.

Dolinar, Sean. 2016. "2016 MLB Arbitration Visualization," *Instagraphs,* January 19, at http://www.fangraphs.com/blogs/instagraphs/2016-mlb-arbitration-visualization.

Dorian, P. Owen, Michael Ryan, and Clayton R. Weatherston. 2007. "Measuring Competitive Balance in Professional Team Sports Using the Herfindahl-Hirschman Index," *Journal of Industrial Organization,* 31(4), December: 289–302.

Dosh, Kristi. 2016. "College Football Payouts by Conference for 2016-17," *Forbes.com,* December 31, at http://www.forbes.com/sites/kristidosh/2016/12/31/college-football-playoff-payouts-by-conference-for-2016-17/.

Dosh, Kristi. 2016. "New Deals with Fox, ESPN, and CBS Nearly Triple Big Ten TV Revenue," *Forbes.com,* June 20, at https://www.forbes.com/sites/kristidosh/2016/06/20/new-deals-with-fox-espn-and-cbs-nearly-triple-big-ten-television-revenue/.

Downie, Andrew. 2012. "Soccer-Brazil World Cup Stadiums on Track, but Costs Soar," *Reuters,* April 3, at http://www.reuters.com/article/2012/04/03/soccer-world-brazil-idUSL2E8F2GG820120403.

Drellich, Evan. 2016. "MLB Changes Market Rank Formula in Revenue Sharing," *The Boston Herald,* December 3, at http://www.bostonherald.com/sports/red_sox/clubhouse_insider/2016/12/mlb_changes_market_rank_formula_in_revenue_sharing.

Du Plessis, Stan, and Wolfgang Maennig. 2010. "The 2010 FIFA World Cup High Frequency Data Economics: Effects on International Tourism and Awareness for South Africa," *Development Southern Africa,* 28(3), September: 349–365.

Dubas-Fisher, David. 2016. "How Much Should Chelsea Season Tickets Cost Based on the Rate of Inflation?" *getwestlondon,* February 9, at http://www.getwestlondon.co.uk/sport/football/football-news/how-much-should-chelsea-season-10864543.

Dworkin, James. 1981. *Owners versus Players: Baseball and Collective Bargaining.* Boston, MA: Auburn House.

Ebert, Graydon. "MLSE Buy," *Offside: A Sports Law Blog,* at http://offsidesportsblog.blogspot.com/p/mlse-buy.html.

Eckard, E. Woodrow. 1998. "The NCAA Cartel and Competitive Balance in College Football," *Review of Industrial Organization,* 13(3), June: 347–369.

Eckard, E. Woodrow. 2003. "The ANOVA-Based Competitive Balance Measure: A Defense," *Journal of Sports Economics,* 4(1), February: 74–80.

Economy, Peter. "Mark Cuban: 19 Inspiring Power Quotes for Success," *Inc.com,* at http://www.inc.com/peter-economy/mark-cuban-19-inspiring-power-quotes-for-success.html.

Ehrenberg, Ronald G., and Michael Bognanno. 1990. "Do Tournaments Have Incentive Effects?" *Journal of Political Economy,* 98(6), December: 1307–1324.

El-Hodiri, Mohamed, and James Quirk. 1971. "An Economic Model of a Professional Sports League," *Journal of Political Economy,* 79(6), November–December: 1302–1319.

Ellis, Zac. 2014. "What Does the Kessler Antitrust Lawsuit vs. The NCAA Mean? Michael McCann Explains," *Sports Illustrated,* March 17, at https://www.si.com/college-football/campus-union/2014/03/17/ncaa-antitrust-lawsuit-jeffrey-kessler#.

ESPN. 2007. "Casino Exec: All-Star Game Wasn't Good for Business," *ESPN.com,* May 4, at http://sports.espn.go.com/nba/news/story?id=2859699.

ESPN. 2012. "MLB Completes New TV Deals," *ESPN.com,* October 2, at http://www.espn.com/mlb/story/_/id/8453054/major-league-baseball-completes-eight-year-deal-fox-turner-sports.

ESPN. 2016. "NBA Extends Television Deals," *ESPN.com,* February 14, at http://www.espn.com/nba/story/_/id/11652297/nba-extends-television-deals-espn-tnt.

ESPN. 2017. "NCAA Agrees to Historic $209 Million Settlement over Scholarship Shortages," *ESPN.com,* February 4, at http://www.espn.com/college-sports/story/_/id/18616780/ncaa-agrees-historic-209m-settlement-scholarship-shortages.

Estrada, Chris. 2015. "Unofficial Results, Winnings, and Race Stats – 57th Daytona 500," *NBCSports*, February 22, at http://nascar.nbcsports.com/2015/02/22/unofficial-results-winnings-and-race-stats-57th-daytona-500/.

Euchner, Charles. 1993. *Playing the Field*. Baltimore, MD: Johns Hopkins University Press.

Everson, Darren. 2009. "The Game That Changed Alabama," *Wall Street Journal*, December 4: W6.

Fagan, Kate, and Luke Cyphers. 2012. "Five Myths about Title IX," *ESPNW.com*, April 29, at http://www.espn.com/espnw/title-ix/article/7729603/five-myths-title-ix.

Fainaru-Wade, Mark, and Lance Williams. 2006. *Game of Shadows: Barry Bonds, BALCO, and the Steroids Scandal That Rocked Professional Sports*. New York: Gotham Books.

Farber, Michael. 1995. "Giant Sucking Sound," *Sports Illustrated*, March 20: 104.

Farhi, Paul. 2014. "Did the Winter Olympics in Sochi Really Cost $50 Billion? A Closer Look at That Figure," *Washington Post*, February 10.

Farrar, Doug. 2010. "The NFL Loses American Needle: What It Means," *Shutdown Corner/ Yahoo! Sports*, May 24, at http://sports.yahoo.com/nfl/blog/shutdown_corner/post/The-NFL-loses-American-Needle-What-it-means?urn=nfl,243282.

Farrey, Tom. 2014. "Jeffrey Kessler Files against NCAA," *ESPN.com*, March 18, at http://www.espn.com/college-sports/story/_/id/10620388/anti-trust-claim-filed-jeffrey-kessler-challenges-ncaa-amateur-model.

Feddersen, Arne, and Wolfgang Maennig. 2012. "Sectoral Labour Market Effects of the 2006 FIFA World Cup," *Labour Economics*, 19(6): 860–869.

Feddersen, Arne, and Wolfgang Maennig. 2013. "Mega-Events and Sectoral Employment: The Case of the 1996 Olympic Games," *Contemporary Economic Policy*, 31(3): 580–603.

Feldman, Louis. 2001. "Financing the Colosseum," *Biblical Archaeology Review*, 27(4), July/August, at https://members.bib-arch.org/biblical-archaeology-review/27/4/1.

Feloni, Richard. 2015. "How Mark Cuban Turned the Dallas Mavericks Franchise around by Treating It Like a Startup," *Business Insider*, April 21, at http://www.businessinsider.com/how-mark-cuban-turned-around-dallas-mavericks-2015-4.

Ferretti, Christine. 2015. "John Oliver Challenges Funding of New Red Wings Arena," *The Detroit News*, July 13.

Ferro, Shane. 2015. "Here's Why It's Fair That Female Athletes Make Less Than Men," *Business Insider: UK*, July 7, at http://uk.businessinsider.com/womens-small-soccer-salaries-are-fair-2015-7?IR=T.

Finley, Jeff. 2012. "Utah A.G. Drops Investigation of College Football's BCS System for Now," *Deseret News*, October 27, at http://www.deseretnews.com/article/865565434/Utah-AG-drops-antitrust-investigation-of-college-footballs-BCS-system--for-now.html.

Finley, Moses, and H.W. Pleket. 1976. *The Olympic Games: The First Thousand Years*. New York: Viking Press.

Flohr, Andrew. 2015. "The Gentrification of Oracle Arena," *SBNation*, December 22, at https://www.goldenstateofmind.com/2015/12/22/9775912/NBA-ticket-prices-2015-golden-state-warriors-christmas.

Flyvbjerg, Bent, and Allison Stewart. 2012. "Olympic Proportions: Cost and Cost Overrun at the Olympics 1960–2012," Saïd Business School, Working Paper, University of Oxford.

Foer, Franklin. 2004. *How Soccer Explains the World: An Unlikely Theory of Globalization*. New York: HarperCollins.

Forbes.com. 2014. "DirecTV Extends Its Deal with NFL for $12 Billion," October 8, at https://www.forbes.com/sites/greatspeculations/2014/10/08/directv-extends-its-deal-with-nfl-for-12-billion/#f6de4c1639b8.

Forbes.com. "The Business of Baseball: 2016 Ranking," at http://www.forbes.com/mlb-valuations/list/, accessed December 10, 2016.

Forbes.com. "The Business of Basketball: 2016 Ranking," at http://www.forbes.com/nba-valuations/list/, accessed December 10, 2016.

Forbes.com. "The Business of Football: 2016 Ranking," at http://www.forbes.com/nfl-valuations/list/, accessed December 10, 2016.

Forbes.com. "The Business of Hockey: 2016 Ranking," at http://www.forbes.com/nhl-valuations/list/, accessed December 10, 2016.

Forbes.com. "The Business of Soccer: 2016 Ranking," at http://www.forbes.com/soccer-valuations/list/, accessed December 10, 2016.

Forbes.com. "#204 Mark Cuban," at http://www.forbes.com/profile/mark-cuban/, accessed May 27, 2017.

Forbes.com. "Dallas Mavericks," at http://www.forbes.com/teams/dallas-mavericks/, accessed February 2017.

Forbes.com. "The World's Highest-Paid Celebrities," at https://www.forbes.com/celebrities/list/#tab:overall, accessed April 15, 2017.

Forsyth, Jennifer S. 2009. "American Needle Throws Downfield in NFL Licensing Dispute," *Law Blog: The Wall Street Journal*, September 18, at http://blogs.wsj.com/law/2009/09/18/american-needle-throws-downfield-in-nfl-licensing-dispute/.

Fort, Rodney, and Andrew Gill. 2000. "Race and Ethnicity Assessment in Baseball Card Markets," *Journal of Sports Economics*, 1(1), February: 21–38.

Fort, Rodney, Young Hoon Lee, and David Berri. 2008. "Race, Technical Efficiency, and Retention: The Case of NBA Coaches," *International Journal of Sport Finance*, 3(2), May: 84–97.

Fort, Rodney, and Robert Rosenman. 1999. "Streak Management," in *Sports Economics: Current Research*, ed. J. Fizel, E. Gustafson, and L. Hadley. Westport, CT: Praeger.

Fortune.com. "Fortune 500," at http://beta.fortune.com/fortune500/list/.

Frank, Robert, and Philip Cook. 1995. *The Winner-Take-All Society*. New York: The Free Press.

Frick, Bernd, and Brad Humphreys. "Prize Structure and Performance: Evidence from NAS-CAR," University of Alberta Working Paper, at https://www.researchgate.net/publication/254448375_Prize_Structure_and_Performance_Evidence_from_NASCAR.

Frick, Bernd, and Joachim Prinz. 2007. "Pay and Performance in Professional Road Running: The Case of City Marathons," *International Journal of Sport Finance*, 2(1), February: 25–35.

Frommer, Harvey. 1982. *Rickey and Robinson*. New York: Macmillan.

Gaines, Cork. 2014. "A Luxury Suite at the New 49ers Stadium Will Cost You $60,000," *Business Insider*, October 22, at http://www.businessinsider.com/49ers-stadium-suites-nfl-2014-10.

Gayer, Ted, Austin J. Drukker, and Alexander K. Gold. 2016. "Tax-Exempt Municipal Bonds and the Financing of Professional Sports Stadiums," Economic Studies at Brookings, September.

Gbadamosi, Faruq. 2015. "The Economics of Nike's Air Jordan Brand," *The Market Mogul*, September 19, at http://themarketmogul.com/the-economics-of-nikes-air-jordan-brand/.

Gerencer, Tom. 2016. "How Much Money Do NFL Players Make?" *Money Nation*, January 5, at http://moneynation.com/how-much-money-do-nfl-players-make/.

Gerrard, Bill. 2007. "Is the *Moneyball* Approach Transferrable to Complex Invasion Sports?" *International Journal of Sport Finance*, 2(4), November: 214–230.

Gibson, Charlotte, Jim Keller, and Sachin Dave Chandan. 2017. "Who's the Highest-Paid Public Employee in Every State?" *ESPN.com*, March 30, at http://www.espn.com/espn/feature/story/_/id/19019077/highest-paid-us-employees-dominated-college-football-college-basketball-coaches.

Giesecke, James, and John Madden. 2011. "Modelling the Economic Impacts of the Sydney Olympics in Retrospect—Game Over for the Bonanza Story?" *Economic Papers*, 30(2), June: 218–232.

Gilbert, Susan. 1996. "The Smallest Olympians Face the Biggest Risks," *New York Times*, July 28: E4.

Gitter, Seth, and Thomas Rhoads. 2014. "Stadium Construction and Minor League Baseball Attendance," *Contemporary Economic Policy*, 32(1), January: 144–154.

Gius, Mark, and Donn Johnson. 1998. "An Empirical Investigation of Wage Discrimination in Professional Basketball," *Applied Economics Letters*, 5(11), November: 703–705.

Gneezy, Uri, and Aldo Rustichini. 2004. "Gender and Competition at a Young Age," *American Economic Review*, 94(2), May: 377–381.

375

Gramm, Cynthia, and John Schnell. 1994. "Difficult Choices: Crossing the Picket Line during the 1987 National Football League Strike," *Journal of Labor Economics,* 12(1), January: 41–71.

Gregory, Sean, and Steve Goldberg. 2009. "Daytona Drag: NASCAR Tries to Outrace the Recession," *Time,* February 12, at www.time.com/time/business/article/0,8599,1879136,00.html.

Grenoble, Ryan. 2014. "UConn Basketball Player Speaks of 'Hungry Nights,' Going to Bed 'Starving,'" *Huffington Post,* April 7, at http://www.huffingtonpost.com/2014/04/07/shabazz-napier-hungry-uconn-basketball_n_5106132.html.

Groothuis, Peter, Bruce Johnson, and John Whitehead. 2004. "Public Funding of Professional Sports Stadiums: Public Choice or Civic Pride?" *Eastern Economic Journal,* 30(4), Fall: 515–526.

Gurney, Gerald S., and Richard M. Southall. 2012. "College Sports' Bait and Switch," *ESPN.com,* August 9, at http://www.espn.com/college-sports/story/_/id/8248046/college-sports-programs-find-multitude-ways-game-ncaa-apr.

Guttman, Allen. 1991. "The Anomaly of Intercollegiate Athletics," in *Rethinking College Athletics,* ed. Judith Andre and David James. Philadelphia, PA: Temple University Press: 17–30.

Hakes, Jahn, and Christopher Clapp. 2006. "The Edifice Complex: The Economics of Public Subsidization of Major League Baseball Facilities," *The International Journal of Sport Finance,* 1(2): 77–95.

Hakes, Jahn, and Raymond Sauer. 2006. "An Economic Evaluation of the *Moneyball* Hypothesis," *Journal of Economic Perspectives,* 20(3), Summer: 173–185.

Hamilton, Barton H. 1997. "Racial Discrimination and Professional Basketball Salaries in the 1990s," *Applied Economics,* 29(3), March: 287–296.

Hamilton, Bruce, and Peter Kahn. 1997. "Baltimore's Camden Yards Ballparks," in *Sports, Jobs, and Taxes,* ed. Roger G. Noll and Andrew Zimbalist. Washington, DC: Brookings Institution Press: 245–281.

Hamrick, Jeff, and John Rasp. 2015. "The Connection between Race and Called Strikes and Balls," *Journal of Sports Economics,* 16(7), October: 714–734.

Hanssen, Andrew F., and Torben Anderson. 1999. "Has Discrimination Lessened over Time? A Test Using Baseball's All-Star Vote," *Economic Inquiry,* 37(2), April: 326–352.

Harasta, Cathy. 2002. "Romney Shows His Mettle," *Dallas Morning News,* February 17.

Harris, David. 1986. *The League: The Rise and Decline of the NFL.* New York: Bantam Books.

Harris, Nick. 2015. "Club by Club Guide to the Premier League's Financial Health: Find Out What State Your Club Is in with Our Graphic," *Daily Mail,* March 28, at http://www.dailymail.co.uk/sport/football/article-3016432/Club-club-guide-Premier-League-s-financial-health.html.

Hatab, Lawrence. 1991. "The Greeks and the Meaning of Athletics," in *Rethinking College Athletics,* ed. Judith Andre and David James. Philadelphia, PA: Temple University Press: 31–42.

Haugen, Kjetil K. 2004. "The Performance Enhancing Drug Game," *Journal of Sports Economics,* 5(1), February: 67–86.

Haupert, Michael J. 2015. "The Economic History of Major League Baseball," at https://eh.net/encyclopedia/the-economic-history-of-major-league-baseball/.

Hayes, Beth. 1984. "Unions and Strikes with Asymmetric Information," *Journal of Labor Economics,* 2(1), January: 57–84.

Heintel, Robert. 1996. "The Need for an Alternative to Antitrust Regulation of the National Football League," *Case Western Reserve Law Review,* 46(4), Summer: 1033–1069.

Helgeson, Baird, and Jennifer Brooks. 2012. "After Years of Dealing and Debate, Vikings Get Their Biggest Win," *Minnesota Star-Tribune,* May 11, at http://www.startribune.com/politics/statelocal/150960525.html.

Heller, Lauren, and E. Frank Stephenson. 2017. "If You Host It Will They Come? The Effect of the Super Bowl on Host City Hotel Occupancy," Working Paper, April.

Helyar, John. 1994. *Lords of the Realm.* New York: Villard Books.

Hepp, Christopher. 1999. "Near Fabled Park, Ambience a Lure," *Philadelphia Inquirer,* September 29: A1, A6.

Hobson, Will, and Steven Rich. 2015. "As College Sports Revenues Spike, Coaches Aren't the Only Ones Cashing In," *Washington Post,* December 29, at https://www.washingtonpost.com/sports/as-college-sports-revenues-spike-coaches-arent-only-ones-cashing-in/2015/12/29/bbdb924e-ae15-11e5-9ab0-884d1cc4b33e_story.html?utm_term=.f833819885c8.

Hoffer, Adam, and Ryan Freidel. 2014. "Does Salary Discrimination Persist for Foreign Players in the NBA?" *Applied Economics Letters,* 21(1), February: 1–5.

Hoffer, Adam, Brad R. Humphreys, Donald J. Lacombe, and Jane E. Ruseski. 2015. "Trends in NCAA Athletic Spending: Arms Race or Rising Tide?" *Journal of Sports Economics,* 16(6), August: 576–596.

Hotchkiss, Julie, Robert Moore, and Stephanie Zobay. 2003. "Impact of the 1996 Summer Olympic Games on Employment and Wages in Georgia," *Southern Economic Journal,* 69(3): 691–704.

Humphreys, Brad. 2002. "Alternative Measures of Competitive Balance," *Journal of Sports Economics,* 3(2), May: 133–148.

Humphreys, Brad. 2003. "The ANOVA-Based Competitive Balance Measure: A Reply," *Journal of Sports Economics,* 4(1), February: 81–82.

Humphreys, Brad, and Xia Feng. 2012. "The Impact of Sports Facilities on Housing Values: Evidence from Census Block Group Data," *City, Culture and Society,* 3(3), September: 189–200.

Humphreys, Brad, and Michael Mondello. 2007. "Intercollegiate Athletic Success and Donations at NCAA Division I Institutions," *Journal of Sport Management,* 21(2), April: 265–280.

Humphreys, Brad, and Hyunwoong Pyun. 2017. "Monopsony Exploitation in Professional Sport: Evidence from Major League Baseball Position Players, 2000–2011," *Managerial and Decision Economics,* 38(5), July: 676–688.

Humphreys, Brad, and Jane Ruseski. 2011. "Socio-Economic Determinants of Adolescent Use of Performance Enhancing Drugs: Evidence from the YRBSS," *The Journal of Socio-Economics,* 40(2), April: 208–216.

Humphreys, Jeffrey. 1994. "The Economic Impact of Hosting Super Bowl XXVIII on Georgia," *Georgia Business and Economic Conditions,* May–June: 18–21.

Humphreys, Jeffrey, and M. Plummer. 1995. *The Economic Impact on the State of Georgia of Hosting the 1996 Summer Olympic Games.* Athens: Selig Center for Economic Growth, University of Georgia.

IEGSR. 2015. "Sponsorship Spending on MLB Totals $778 Million in 2015 Season," *Sponsorship.com,* November 9, at http://www.sponsorship.com/iegsr/2015/11/09/Sponsorship-Spending-On-MLB-Totals-$778-Million-In.aspx.

International Ice Hockey Federation, "Swede Ulf Sterner – The First European in the NHL," *The IIHF 100-Year Anniversary, Ice Hockey Federation,* at http://www.iihf.com/iihf-home/the-iihf/100-year-anniversary/100-top-stories/story-70/.

International Olympic Committee. 2010. "Factsheet: Legacies of the Games, Update—January 2010," at http://www.olympic.org/Documents/Reference_documents_Factsheets/Legacy.pdf.

Irani, Daraius. 1996. "Estimating Consumer Discrimination Using Panel Data: 1972–1991," in *Baseball Economics: Current Research,* ed. John Fizel, Elizabeth Gustafson, and Lawrence Hadley. Westport, CT: Praeger.

Ivins, Molly, and Lou Dubose. 2000. *Shrub: The Short but Happy Political Life of George W. Bush.* New York: Vintage Books.

Jane, Wen-jhan. 2015. "Customer Discrimination and Outcome Uncertainty in the World Baseball Classic: The Case of the Taiwanese Television Audience," in *The Sports Business in the Pacific Rim,* ed. Young Hoon Lee and Rodney Fort. Heidelberg: Springer: 103–122.

Jansen, Steve. 2017. "The Super Bowl May Bring a $500 Million Boost to Houston, or None at All," *Houston Press,* January 31, at http://www.houstonpress.com/news/the-super-bowl-may-bring-a-500-million-boost-to-houston-or-none-at-all-9156999.

"Japan's Earthquake and Tsunami Hit Parts Supplies," *Motor Trend,* June 2011, at http://www.motortrend.com/features/auto_news/2011/1106_japan_earthquake_tsunami_hit_parts_supplies/viewall.html.

Jenkins, Jeffrey A. 1996. "A Reexamination of Salary Determination in Professional Basket-ball," *Social Science Quarterly*, 77(3), September: 594–608.

Jewel, Todd R., and David Molina. 2004. "Productive Efficiency and Salary Distribution: The Case of U.S. Major League Baseball," *Scottish Journal of Political Economy*, 51(1), Feb-ruary: 127–142.

"Joe Louis (Barrow)," *Arlington National Cemetery Website*, July 27, 2009, at http://www.arlingtoncemetery.net/joelouis.htm.

Johnson, Bruce K., and John C. Whitehead. 2012. "Contingent Valuation of Sports," in *The Oxford Handbook of Sports Economics*, ed. Stephen Shmanske and Leo Kahane. Oxford: Oxford University Press.

Johnson, John. 1996. "When a Professional Sport Is Not a Business: Baseball's Infamous Antitrust Exemption," in *Sports and the Law*, ed. Charles Quirk. New York: Garland: 149–165.

Jones, J.C.H., and William D. Walsh. 1987. "The World Hockey Association and Player Exploitation in the National Hockey League," *Quarterly Review of Economics and Busi-ness*, 27(2), Summer: 87–101.

Jones, Richard, and Don Walker. 2000. "Packer Boss Warns of Move if Stadium Doesn't Get Upgrade," *Milwaukee Sentinel Journal*, March 1.

Jordan, Mary, and Kevin Sullivan. 1999. "Nagano Burned Documents Tracing '98 Olympics Bid," *Washington Post Foreign Service*, January 21: A1.

Jude, Adam. 2015. "UW, Alaska Airlines Agree to Naming-Rights Deal for Husky Stadium's Field," *The Seattle Times*, September 2, at http://www.seattletimes.com/sports/uw-husky-football/uw-alaska-airlines-agree-to-naming-rights-deal-for-husky-stadium/.

Justia US Supreme Court. *United States v. International Boxing Club*. 348 U.S. 236 (1955), at https://supreme.justia.com/cases/federal/us/348/236/case.html#241.

Kahane, Leo, Neil Longley, and Robert Simmons. 2013. "The Effects of Coworker Heterogeneity on Firm-Level Output: Assessing the Impacts of Cultural and Language Diversity in the National Hockey League," *Review of Economics and Statistics*, 95(1), March: 302–314.

Kahn, Lawrence M. 1991. "Discrimination in Professional Sports: A Survey of the Litera-ture," *ILR Review*, 44(3), April: 395–418.

Kahn, Lawrence M. 1992. "The Effects of Race on Professional Football Players' Compensa-tion," *Industrial Labor Relations Review*, 45(2), January: 295–310.

Kahn, Lawrence M. 2006. "Race, Performance, Pay, and Retention among National Basket-ball Association Head Coaches," *Journal of Sports Economics*, 7(2), May: 119–149.

Kahn, Lawrence M., and Peter Sherer. 1988. "Racial Differences in Professional Basketball Players' Compensation," *Journal of Labor Economics*, 6(1), January: 40–61.

Kahn, Roger. 1993. *The Era: 1947–1957*. New York: Ticknor and Fields.

Kahneman, Daniel. 2011. *Thinking Fast and Slow*. New York: Farrar, Straus and Giroux.

Kamada, Takuma, and Hajime Katayama. 2014. "Team Performance and Within-Team Sal-ary Disparity: An Analysis of Nippon Professional Baseball," *Economics Bulletin*, 34(1): 144–151.

Kanazawa, Mark T., and Jonas P. Funk. 2001. "Racial Discrimination in Professional Basket-ball: Evidence from Nielsen Ratings," *Economics Inquiry*, 39(4), October: 599–608.

Kane, Martin. 1972. "Scorecard," *SIVault*, August 14, at https://www.si.com/vault/1972/08/14/613127/scorecard.

Kaplan, Daniel. 2015. "Dynamic Ticket Pricing Makes Successful Debut in NFL," *Street and Smith's Sports Business Journal*, October 26, at http://www.sportsbusinessdaily.com/Journal/Issues/2015/10/26/Leagues-and-Governing-Bodies/NFL-dynamic.aspx.

Kaszuba, Mike, and Rochelle Olson. 2014. "NFL Had a Long, Pricey and Secret Super Bowl Wish List for Minneapolis," *Star Tribune*, June 9.

Kidd, Bruce. 1984. "The Myth of the Ancient Games," in *Five Ring Circus: Money, Power and Politics at the Olympic Games*, ed. Alan Tomlinson and Garry Whannel. London: Pluto Press: 71–83.

Kindelain, Katie. 2012. "Kentucky Students Riot after NCAA Championship Win," *ABCNews.com*, April 3, at http://abcnews.go.com/blogs/headlines/2012/04/kentucky-students-riot-after-ncaa-championship-win.

Kinsella, W.P. 1999. *Shoeless Joe*. New York: Mariner Books.

Klein, Christopher. 2016. "College Football's Most Lopsided Game." *History in the Headlines*, October 7, at http://www.history.com/news/college-footballs-most-lopsided-game.

Klein, Eugene. 1987. *First Down and a Billion: The Funny Business of Pro Football*. New York: Morrow.

Knight, Phil. 2016. *Shoe Dog*. New York: Scribner.

Knoblauch, Austin. 2016. "NFL Salary Cap Set at $155.27 Million for 2016," *NFL.com*, February 26, at http://www.nfl.com/news/story/0ap3000000639226/article/nfl-salary-cap-set-at-15527-million-for-2016.

Knowles, Glenn, Keith Sherony, and Mike Haupert. 1992. "The Demand for Major League Baseball: A Test of the Uncertainty of Outcome Hypothesis," *American Economist*, 36(2), Fall: 72–80.

Komisarchik, Mayya, and Aju Fenn. 2010. "Trends in Stadium and Arena Construction, 1995-2015," Colorado College Working Paper, April 5, 2010.

Koren, James Rufus, and Roger Vincent. 2017. "How Much Could the Rams and Chargers Make in Their New Stadium? We Ran the Numbers," *Los Angeles Times*, February 11, at http://www.latimes.com/business/la-fi-rams-chargers-revenue-20170211-story.html.

Korr, Charles. 1991. "Marvin Miller and the New Unionism in Baseball," in *The Business of Professional Sports*, ed. Paul Staudohar and James Mangan. Urbana: University of Illinois Press: 115–134.

Krautmann, Anthony. 1999. "What's Wrong with Scully-Estimates of a Player's Marginal Revenue Product," *Economic Inquiry*, 37(2), April: 369–381.

Krautmann, Anthony C., and David C. Berri. 2007. "Can We Find It in the Concessions: Understanding Price Elasticity in Professional Sports," *Journal of Sports Economics*, 8(2), May: 183–191.

Krautmann, Anthony C., Peter von Allmen, and David Berri. 2009. "The Underpayment of Restricted Players in North American Sports Leagues," *International Journal of Sport Finance*, 4(3), August: 75–93.

Kuklick, Bruce. 1991. *To Everything a Season: Shibe Park and Urban Philadelphia, 1909–1976*. Princeton, NJ: Princeton University Press.

La Franco, Robert. 1997. "Profits on Ice," *Forbes*, May 5: 86–89.

Lambrinos, James, and Thomas D. Ashman. 2007. "Salary Determination in the National Hockey League: Is Arbitration Efficient?" *Journal of Sports Economics*, 8(2), April: 192–201.

Lane, Erin, Juan Nagel, and Janet S. Netz. 2014. "Alternative Approaches to Measuring MRP: Are All Men's College Basketball Players Exploited?" *Journal of Sports Economics*, 14(3), June: 237–262.

Lang, Jack. 2015. "Mane Garrincha Stadium in Brasilia Being Used as a BUS DEPOT Less than a Year after 2014 World Cup," *The Mirror*, March 7, at http://www.mirror.co.uk/sport/football/news/mane-garrincha-stadium-brasilia-being-5289603.

Lapchick, Richard E., and DaWon Baker. 2015. "The 2015 Racial and Gender Report Card: College Sport," *The Institute for Ethics and Diversity in Sport*, at http://www.tidesport.org/college-sport.html.

Lapchick, Richard E., Nikki Bowey, and Ray Matthew. 2015. "2015 Racial and Gender Report Card: Major League Baseball," *The Institute for Diversity and Ethics in Sport*, April 15, at http://www.tidesport.org/mlb-rgrc.html.

Lapchick, Richard E., Juan Dominguez, Lizzie Haldane, Erika Loomer, and Jonathan Pelts. 2014. "The 2014 Racial and Gender Report Card: Major League Soccer," *The Institute for Ethics and Diversity in Sport*, at http://www.tidesport.org/mls-rgrc.html.

Lapchick, Richard E., and Angelica Guiao. 2015. "The 2015 Racial and Gender Report Card: National Basketball Association," *The Institute for Ethics and Diversity in Sport*, at http://www.tidesport.org/racial-and-gender-report-cards.html.

Lapchick, Richard E., and Natalie Nelson. 2015. "The 2015 Racial and Gender Report Card: Women's National Basketball Association," *The Institute for Ethics and Diversity in Sport*, at http://www.tidesport.org/wnba-rgrc.html.

Lapchick, Richard E., and Leroy Robinson. 2015. "The 2015 Racial and Gender Report Card: National Football League," *The Institute for Ethics and Diversity in Sport*, at http://www.tidesport.org/nfl-rgrc.html.

Lapchick, Richard E., and Diego Salas. 2015. "The 2015 Racial and Gender Report Card: Major League Baseball," *The Institute for Ethics and Diversity in Sport,* at http://www. tidesport.org/mlb-rgrc.html.

Latta, Scott. 2006. "Game-Day Inside Peek: Skyboxes Provide Alabama's Most Luxurious Look," *Alabama Crimson Tide*, November 17, at http://www.rolltide.com/news/ 2006/11/17/Game_Day_Inside_Peek_Skyboxes_Provide_Alabama_s_Most_Luxurious_ Look.aspx.

Lavoie, Marc. 2000. "The Location of Pay Discrimination in the National Hockey League," *Journal of Sports Economics*, 1(4), November: 401–411.

Lawrence, Paul. 1987. *Unsportsmanlike Conduct: The National Collegiate Athletic Association and the Business of College Football.* New York: Praeger.

Lazear, Edward, and Sherwin Rosen. 1981. "Rank Order Tournaments as Optimum Labor Contracts," *Journal of Political Economy*, 89(5), October: 841–864.

Leadley, John C., and Zenon X. Zygmont. 2005. "When Is the Honeymoon Over? Major League Baseball Attendance 1970–2000," *Journal of Sport Management*, 19(3), July: 278–299.

Leadley, John C., and Zenon X. Zygmont. 2005. "When Is the Honeymoon Over? National Basketball Association Attendance 1971–2000," *Journal of Sports Economics*, 6(2), May: 203–221.

Leadley, John C., and Zenon X. Zygmont. 2006. "When Is the Honeymoon Over? National Hockey League Attendance 1970–2003," *Canadian Public Policy*, 32(2), June: 213–232.

Leeds, Eva Marikova, and Michael A. Leeds. 2012. "Event Analysis," in *The Oxford Handbook of Sports Economics,* vol. 2, ed. Stephen Shmanske and Leo Kahane. Oxford: Oxford University Press.

Leeds, Eva Marikova, Michael A. Leeds, and Irina Pistolet. 2007. "A Stadium by Any Other Name," *Journal of Sports Economics*, 8(6), December: 581–595.

Leeds, Michael A. 1987. "Bargaining as Search Behavior under Mutual Uncertainty," *Southern Economic Journal*, 53(3), January: 677–684.

Leeds, Michael A. 2008. "Salary Caps and Luxury Taxes in Professional Sports Leagues," in *The Business of Sports,* vol. 2, ed. Brad R. Humphreys and Dennis R. Howard. Westport, CT: Praeger: 181–206.

Leeds, Michael A. 2008. "Do Good Olympics Make Good Neighbors?" *Contemporary Economic Policy*, 26(3), July: 460–467.

Leeds, Michael A. 2015. "Youth Sports and the Accumulation of Human Capital," *IZA World of Labor*, February, at http://wol.iza.org/articles/youth-sports-and-accumulation-of-human-capital/long.

Leeds, Michael, John Mirikitani, and Danna Tang. 2009. "Rational Exuberance? An Event Analysis of the 2008 Olympic Announcement," *International Journal of Sport Finance*, 4(1), February: 5–15.

Legal Information Institute. Cornell University Law School, at https://www.law.cornell.edu/ uscode/text/15/1.

Leifer, Eric. 1995. *Making the Majors: The Transformation of Team Sports in America.* Cambridge, MA: Harvard University Press.

Lewis, Michael. 2003. *Moneyball: The Art of Winning an Unfair Game.* New York: W.W. Norton.

Lewis, Michael. 2006. *The Blind Side: Evolution of a Game.* New York: W.W. Norton.

Litan, Robert, Jonathan Orszag, and Peter Orszag. 2003. "The Empirical Effects of College Athletics: An Interim Report," Sebago Associates, at http://www.sc.edu/faculty/PDF/ baseline.pdf.

Lombardo, John. 2012. "Inside NBA's Revenue Sharing: How Complex Plan Will Shift $140 Million to Needy Teams," *Street and Smith's Sports Business Journal*, January 23, at http://www.sportsbusinessdaily.com/Journal/Issues/2012/01/23/Leagues-and-Governing-Bodies/NBA-revenue.aspx.

Long, James, and Steven Caudill. 1991. "The Impact of Participation in Intercollegiate Athletics on Income and Graduation," *Review of Economics and Statistics*, 73(3), August: 525–531.

Long, Judith Grant. 2004. "Public Funding for Major League Sports Facilities Data Series: A History of Public Funding, 1890 to 2005," Edward J. Bloustein School of Planning and Public Policy, Center for Urban Policy Research Working Paper Series.

Long, Judith Grant. 2012. *Public/Private Partnerships for Major League Sports Facilities*. New York: Routledge Research in Sport Business and Management.

Longman, Jere. 1998. "Nagano 1998: Seven Days to Go—High Costs and High Expectations," *New York Times*, January 30.

Lorge, Barry. 1990. "Kroc Wanted to Give Padres to City," *San Diego Union-Tribune*, July 29: H1.

MacCambridge, Michael. 2004. *America's Game: The Epic Story of How Pro Football Captured a Nation*. New York: Random House.

Madden, Janice Fanning. 2004. "Differences in the Success of NFL Coaches by Race, 1990–2002: Evidence of Last Hire, First Fire," *Journal of Sports Economics*, 5(1), February: 6–19.

Madden, Janice Fanning, and Matthew Ruther. 2011. "Has the NFL's Rooney Rule Efforts 'Leveled the Field' for African American Head Coach Candidates?" *Journal of Sports Economics*, 12(2), April: 127–142.

Maennig, Wolfgang, and Felix Richter. 2012. "Exports and Olympics Games: Is There a Signal Effect?" *Journal of Sports Economics*, 13(6): 635–641.

Major League Soccer, at www.mlssoccer.com.

Mandell, Richard. 1972. *The Nazi Olympics*. New York: Ballantine Books.

Maraniss, David. 2008. *Rome 1960: The Olympics That Changed the World*. New York: Simon and Schuster.

Margolick, David. 2005. *Beyond Glory: Joe Louis vs. Max Schmeling, and a World on the Brink*. New York: Alfred A. Knopf.

"Mark Cuban," *Bio.com*, at http://www.biography.com/people/mark-cuban-562656.

"Mark Cuban Won't Sell the Mavericks for Any Amount of Money," *SI.com*, June 30, 2016, at http://www.si.com/nba/2016/06/30/mark-cuban-dallas-mavericks-wont-sell-any-amount.

"Mark's Bio," at http://markcubancompanies.com/about.html.

Martin, Charles. 1997. "Integrating New Year's Day: The Racial Politics of College Bowl Games in the American South," *Journal of Sport History*, 24(3), Fall: 358–377.

Matheson, Victor. 2006. "Professional Sports," in *Encyclopedia of American Business History*, ed. Charles Geisst. New York: Facts on File: 403–408.

Matheson, Victor. 2008. "Mega-Events: The Effect of the World's Biggest Sporting Events on Local, Regional, and National Economies," in *The Business of Sports*, vol. 1, ed. Dennis Howard and Brad Humphreys. Westport, CT: Praeger: 81–99.

Matheson, Victor, Debra O'Connor, and Joseph Herberger. 2012. "The Bottom Line: Accounting for Revenues and Expenditures in Intercollegiate Athletics," *International Journal of Sport Finance*, 7(1), February: 30–45.

Mathews, Karen. 2006. "Yankees Break Ground on New $1 Billion Stadium," *USAToday.com*, August 16, at http://www.usatoday.com/sports/baseball/al/yankees/2006-08-16-stadium-groundbreaking_x.htm.

McCann, Michael. 2016. "In Denying O'Bannon Case, Supreme Court Leaves Future of Amateurism in Limbo," *Sports Illustrated*, October 3, at https://www.si.com/college-basketball/2016/10/03/ed-obannon-ncaa-lawsuit-supreme-court.

McGrath, Ben. 2009. "The Extortionist," *The New Yorker*, October 29, at http://www.newyorker.com/reporting/2007/10/29/071029fa_fact_mcgrath.

McGraw, Dan. 2003. "The Foreign Invasion of the American Game," *The Village Voice*, May 28–June 3, at https://www.villagevoice.com/2003/05/27/the-foreign-invasion-of-the-american-game/.

McManimon, Kevin. 2006. "The House That Debt Built: Will the IRS Allow Cities to Finance Construction of Stadiums on a Tax-Exempt Basis?" *McManimon and Scotland, LLC*, May 29, at http://www.mandslaw.com/articles/the-house-that-debt-built-will-the-irs-allow-cities-to-finance-construction-of-stadiums-on-a-tax-exempt-basis/.

Mead, Chris. 1985. "Triumphs and Trials," *SIVault*, September 23, at https://www.si.com/vault/issue/43501/78/2.

Meyer, Joe. 2009. "The Roman Colosseum," March 10, at http://www.synthreal.com/Colosseum.htm.

Michener, James. 1976. *Sports in America*. New York: Random House.

Mickle, Tripp, and Terry Lefton. 2009. "Several Leagues Later, Debate on Single Entity Model Still Lively," *SportsBusinessJournal.com*, June 8, at http://www.sportsbusinessjournal.com/article59720.

Miller, James. 1990. *The Baseball Business: Pursuing Pennants and Profits in Baltimore*. Chapel Hill: University of North Carolina Press.

Miller, Marvin. 1991. *A Whole Different Ballgame: The Sport and Business of Baseball*. Secaucus, NJ: Carol Publishing Group.

Minium, Harry. 2016. "Conference USA TV Revenue to Plummet to $2.8 Million Per Year," *The Virginian-Pilot*, June 7, at http://pilotonline.com/sports/college/old-dominion/football/conference-usa-tv-revenue-to-plummet-to-million-per-year/article_1dd435cb-800e-574d-be6d-0afa42d957e7.html.

Mitchell, Houston. 2015. "Yogi Berra Dies at 90: Here Are Some of His Greatest Quotes," *Los Angeles Times*, September 22.

MLB. 2016. "Details of MLB, MLBPA Labor Agreement," *MLB.com*, December 4, at http://m.mlb.com/news/article/210125462/details-of-mlb-mlbpa-labor-agreement/.

MLB, "2012-2016 MLB, MLBPA Basic Agreement," at https://ipmall.law.unh.edu/sites/default/files/hosted_resources/SportsEntLaw_Institute/2012MLB_MLBPA_CBA.pdf.

"MLB Attendance Report—2011," *ESPN.com*, at http://www.espn.com/mlb/attendance/_/year/2011.

"MLB Attendance Report—2016," *ESPN.com*, at http://www.espn.com/mlb/attendance/_/year/2016.

MLB.com, "Standings," at http://mlb.mlb.com/mlb/standings/index.jsp?tcid=mm_mlb_standings#19960929.

MLB.com, "World Series History: Championships by Club," at http://mlb.mlb.com/mlb/history/postseason/mlb_ws.jsp?feature=club_champs.

"MLB Confidential: The Financial Documents MLB Doesn't Want You to See, Part 1," *Deadspin*, August 23, 2010, at http://deadspin.com/5615096.

"MLB Confidential Part 2: Seattle Mariners," *Deadspin*, August 23, 2010, at http://deadspin.com/5619509.

"MLB Fines and Suspensions." 2017. *Spotrac*, at http://www.spotrac.com/mlb/fines-suspensions/.

"MLB Standings—2011," *ESPN.com*, at http://www.espn.com/mlb/standings/_/seasontype/2/season/2011.

MLB Trade Rumors. 2016. "Arbitration Tracker for 2016," *MLB TradeRumors*, at http://www.mlbtraderumors.com/arbtracker2016.

Money & Company. 2011. "Yankee Stadium's Troubled Tax-Free Financing," *LATimes.com*, June 17, at http://latimesblogs.latimes.com/money_co/2011/06/yankee-stadiums-troubled-tax-free-financing-.html.

Mongeon, Kevin. 2015. "A Market Test for Ethnic Discrimination in the National Hockey League: A Game-Level Panel Data Approach," *Journal of Sports Economics*, 15(5), June: 460–481.

Morgan, Jon. 1997. *Glory for Sale: Fans, Dollars, and the New NFL*. Baltimore, MD: Bancroft Press.

Munsey, Paul, and Corey Suppes. 2017. "Ballparks," at http://www.ballparks.com.

Muret, Don. 2015. "Football Becomes Classroom at Notre Dame," *SportsBusiness Daily*, January 12, at http://www.sportsbusinessdaily.com/Journal/Issues/2015/01/12/In-Depth/Notre-Dame.aspx.

Nack, William. 1999. "This Old House," *Sports Illustrated*, June 7: 100–116.

Nardinelli, Clark, and Curtis Simon. 1990. "Customer Discrimination in the Market for Memorabilia: The Case of Baseball," *Quarterly Journal of Economics*, 105(3), August: 575–595.

National Sports Law Institute, "Sports Facilities Reports," *Marquette University Law School*, at http://law.marquette.edu/national-sports-law-institute/sports-facility-reports.

National Women's Law Center, "The Battle for Gender Equity in Athletics in Colleges and Universities," *Title IX and Women's Athletic Opportunity*, at http://www.nwlc.org/sites/default/files/pdfs/2011_8_battle_in_college_athletics_final.pdf.

NBA.com. 2015. "Salary Cap for 2015-16 Season Jumps to $70 Million," July 8, at http://www.nba.com/2015/news/07/08/nba-salary-cap-2016-official-release/.

"NBA Attendance Report 2015-16," *ESPN.com*, at http://www.espn.com/nba/attendance/_/year/2016.

NCAA. 2014. "Football Bowl Subdivision – Membership Requirements," *NCAA.org*, December 8, at https://www.ncaa.org/sites/default/files/Football%20Bowl%20Subqa%2012%208%2014.pdf.

NCAA. 2016. "Division I Student-Athletes Still Making Gains in APR," *NCAA.org*, April 20, at http://www.ncaa.org/about/resources/media-center/news/division-i-student-athletes-still-making-gains-apr.

NCAA. 2016. "Estimated Probability of Competing in Professional Athletics," April 25, at http://www.ncaa.org/about/resources/research/estimated-probability-competing-professional-athletics.

NCAA. 2016. "NCAA Sports Sponsorship and Participation Rates Report," at http://www.ncaapublications.com/productdownloads/PR1516.pdf.

NCAA. "Play Division I Sports," *NCAA.org*, at http://www.ncaa.org/student-athletes/play-division-i-sports.

Neale, Walter C. 1964. "The Peculiar Economics of Professional Sports," *Quarterly Journal of Economics*, 78(1), February: 1–14.

"New York Yankees Attendance Data," *Baseball Almanac*, at http://www.baseball-almanac.com/teams/yankatte.shtml.

NFHS News. 2016. "High School Sports Participation Increases for 27th Consecutive Year," *National Federation of State High School Associations*, September 12, at https://www.nfhs.org/articles/high-school-sports-participation-increases-for-27th-consecutive-year/.

"NFL Fines and Suspensions." 2017. *Spotrac*, at http://www.spotrac.com/nfl/fines-suspensions/.

"NHL Attendance Report 2015-16," *ESPN.com*, at http://www.espn.com/nhl/attendance/_J year/2016.

NHLPA. "Collective Bargaining Agreement between National Hockey League and National Hockey League Players' Association," Article 49, at http://cdn.agilitycms.com/nhlpacom/PDF/NHL_NHLPA_2013_CBA.pdf.

Nightengale, Bob. 2006. "Boras Is Baseball's Bigger Deal Man," *USA Today*, November 14, at http://www.usatoday.com/sports/baseball/2006-11-14-boras-cover_x.htm.

Nocera, Joe, and Ben Strauss. 2016. *Indentured: The Inside Story of the Rebellion against the NCAA*. New York: Penguin.

Nocera, Joe, and Ben Strauss. 2016. "A Reformed 'Sneaker Pimp' Takes on the NCAA," *New York Times*, February 12, at https://www.nytimes.com/2016/02/14/sports/ncaabasketball/a-reformed-sneaker-pimp-takes-on-the-ncaa.html.

Noden, Merrell. 1994. "Dying to Win," *Sports Illustrated*, August 8: 52–59.

Noll, Roger. 1974. "Attendance and Price Setting," in *Government and the Sports Business*, ed. Roger Noll. Washington, DC: Brookings Institution.

Noll, Roger. 1992. "The Economics of Intercollegiate Sports," in *Rethinking College Athletics*, ed. Judith Andre and David James. Philadelphia, PA: Temple University Press: 197–209.

Noll, Roger G. 2003. "The Organization of Sports Leagues," *Oxford Review of Economic Policy*, 19(4), Winter: 530–551.

Noll, Roger G., and Andrew Zimbalist. 1997. "Build the Stadium—Create the Jobs!" In *Sports, Jobs, and Taxes*, ed. Roger G. Noll and Andrew Zimbalist. Washington, DC: Brookings Institution Press: 1–54.

Noll, Roger G., and Andrew Zimbalist. 1997. "The Economic Impact of Sports Teams and Facilities," in *Sports, Jobs, and Taxes*, ed. Roger G. Noll and Andrew Zimbalist. Washington, DC: Brookings Institution Press: 55–91.

"Notre Dame Fighting Irish Premium Seating," *Premium Seating*, at http://www.premium-seating.com/notre-dame-fighting-irish-football-luxury-suites.

O'Hara, Jane. 1998. "In the Name of Greed," *Maclean's*, January 19: 22–24.

"'Open to All': Title IX at Thirty," Report of the Secretary of Education's Commission on Opportunity in Athletics, February 28, 2003, at https://www2.ed.gov/about/bdscomm/list/athletics/title9report.pdf: 19.

Orlando Sentinel. 2005. "Cruise Ships Supply City's Super Bowl Room Service," February 3.

Ozanian, Mike. 2016. "The NFL's Most Valuable Teams 2016," *Forbes.com*, September 14, at https://www.forbes.com/sites/mikeozanian/2016/09/14/the-nfls-most-valuable-teams-2016/.

Pace, Levi. 2006. "Economic Impact of the 2002 Olympic Winter Games," Policy Brief: 07-25-2006, at http://gardner.utah.edu/_documents/publications/econ-dev/olympics-econ-impact.pdf.

Padawer, Ruth. 2016. "The Humiliating Practice of Sex-Testing Female Athletes," *New York Times*, June 28, at https://www.nytimes.com/2016/07/03/magazine/the-humiliating-practice-of-sex-testing-female-athletes.html.

Pallotta, Frank, and Brian Stelter. 2016. "NFL Makes Enormous 'Thursday Night Football' Deal with NBC and CBS," *CNN.com*, February 1, at http://money.cnn.com/2016/02/01/media/thursday-night-football-nbc-cbs-deal/.

Parrish, Paula. 2002. "Leap of Faith: Mitt Romney Embraces Challenges, and This Might Be His Biggest One," *Rocky Mountain News*, February 4: 8S.

Paserman, M. Daniele. 2010. "Gender Differences in Performance in Competitive Environments? Evidence from Professional Tennis Players," *IZA Discussion Paper 2834*.

Patra, Kevin. 2017. "What to Know about NFL Franchise Tag Designations," *Around the NFL*, February 15, at http://www.nfl.com/news/story/0ap3000000785958/article/what-to-know-about-nfl-franchise-tag-designations.

Peeters, Thomas, Victor Matheson, and Stefan Szymanski. 2014. "Tourism and the 2010 World Cup: Lessons for Developing Countries," *Journal of African Economies*, 23(2), January: 290–320.

Peeters, Thomas, and Stefan Szymanski. 2014. "European Football," *Economic Policy*, 29(78), April: 343–390.

Peloquin, Matt. 2012. "2012 NCAA Television Revenue by Conference," *CollegeSportsInfo.com*, May 10, at http://collegesportsinfo.com/2012/05/10/2012-ncaa-television-revenue-by-conference/.

Perez, A.J. 2016. "The Chicago Cubs' Billy Goat Curse Explained," *USA Today Sports*, October 25, at http://www.usatoday.com/story/sports/mlb/2016/10/25/chicago-cubs-billy-goat-curse-explained/92715898/.

Perez, Matt. 2016. "Where MLB Receives Its Revenue," *Camden Depot*, January 26, at http://camdendepot.blogspot.com/2016/01/where-mlb-receives-its-revenue.html.

Perez, Stephen J. 2012. "Does Intercollegiate Athletics Draw Local Students to a University?" *Journal of Sports Economics*, 13(2), April: 198–206.

Perrotet, Tony. 2004. *The Naked Olympics*. New York: Random House.

Peter, Josh. 2015. "Error Jordan: Key Figures Still Argue over Who Was Responsible for Nike Deal," *USA Today*, September 30.

Peter, Josh. 2015. "Hosting a Super Bowl a Huge Economic Plum, and Costly," *USA Today*, January 25, at https://www.usatoday.com/story/sports/nfl/2015/01/25/super-bowl-host-cities-economic-impact/22324109/.

Peterson, Robert. 1970. *Only the Ball Was White: A History of Legendary Black Players and All-Black Professional Teams*. New York: Gramercy Books.

Philipse, Sander. 2015. "Salary Cap Floor Explained: It's Basically Irrelevant," *SB-Nation*, March 13, at http://www.bucsnation.com/2015/3/13/8208069/nfl-salary-cap-floor-explained-its-basically-irrelevant.

Poole, Lynn, and Gray Poole. 1963. *History of Ancient Olympic Games*. New York: Ivan Obolensky, Inc.

Pope, Devin, and Jaren Pope. 2009. "The Impact of College Sports Success on the Quantity and Quality of Student Applications," *Southern Economic Journal*, 75(3), January: 750–780.

Porter, Philip. 1999. "Mega-Sporting Events as Municipal Investments: A Critique of Impact Analysis," in *Sports Economics: Current Research*, ed. John Fizel, Elizabeth Gustafson, and Larry Hadley. Westport, CT: Praeger.

Porter, Philip, and Deborah Fletcher. 2008. "The Economic Impact of the Olympic Games: Ex Ante Predictions and Ex Post Reality," *Journal of Sport Management*, 22(4): 470–486.

Posner, Richard. 1975. "The Social Costs of Monopoly and Regulation," *Journal of Political Economy,* 83(4), August: 807–827.

Powell-Morse, Andrew. 2013. "Mark Cuban: King of NBA Fines," *Bleacher Report.com,* April 25, at http://bleacherreport.com/articles/1614812-mark-cuban-king-of-nba-fines.

"Premier League 2015/16 Attendance," *Worldfootball.net,* at http://www.worldfootball.net/attendance/eng-premier-league-2015-2016/1/.

"Premium Seating and Hospitality – Football," *TexasSports.com,* at http://www.texassports.com/sports/2013/7/29/tickets_0729135534.aspx.

Preston, Ian, and Stefan Szymanski. 2000. "Racial Discrimination in English Football," *Scottish Journal of Political Economy,* 47(4), September: 342–363.

Preuss, Holger. 2004. *Economics of the Olympic Games.* London: Edward Elgar.

"Price Better," *Qcue,* at http://www.qcue.com/#price-better.

Price, Dwain. 2015. "Fifteen Years Ago, Mark Cuban Came to Mavericks' Rescue," *Star Telegram,* January 3, at http://www.star-telegram.com/sports/nba/dallas-mavericks/article5390883.html.

Price, Joseph, Brian Soebbing, David Berri, and Brad Humphreys. 2010. "Tournament Incentives, League Policy, and NBA Team Performance Revisited," *Journal of Sports Economics,* 11(2), April: 117–135.

Price, Joseph, and Justin Wolfers. 2010. "Racial Discrimination among NBA Referees," *Quarterly Journal of Economics,* 125(4), November: 1859–1887.

Price, Joshua. 2010. "The Effects of Higher Admission Standards on NCAA Student-Athletes: An Analysis of Proposition 16," *Journal of Sports Economics,* 11(4), August: 363–382.

Prieto, Bianca. 2014. "Super Bowl Week Gets Underway: N.Y./N.J. to See Some 400,000 Tourists," *Denver Post,* January 27.

Primm, Eric, Nicole Leeper Piquero, Robert M. Regoli, and Alex R. Piquero. 2010. "The Role of Race in Football Card Prices," *Social Science Quarterly,* 91(1), March: 129–142.

Purdy, Dean D., Stanley Eitzen, and Rick Hufnagel. 1985. "Are Athletes Also Students? The Educational Attainment of College Athletes," in *Sport and Higher Education,* ed. Donald Chu, Jeffrey Segrave, and Beverly Becker. Champaign, IL: Human Kinetics Publishers: 221–234.

Quinn, Kevin, Paul B. Bursik, Christopher Borick, and Lisa Raethz. 2003. "Do New Digs Mean More Wins? The Relationship Between a New Venue and a Professional Sports Team's Success," *Journal of Sports Economics,* 4(3), August: 167–182.

Quirk, James, and Rodney Fort. 1992. *Pay Dirt.* Princeton, NJ: Princeton University Press.

Quirk, James, and Rodney Fort. 1999. *Hardball.* Princeton, NJ: Princeton University Press.

Randle, Jeff. 2003. "Chelsea Owner Seeks 'Fun and Trophies,'" *BBC News,* July 3, at http://news.bbc.co.uk/2/hi/business/3039750.stm.

Rascher, Daniel A. 2008. "Franchise Relocation, Expansions, and Mergers in Professional Sports Leagues," in *The Business of Sports Volume 2: Economic Perspectives on Sport,* ed. B.H. Humphreys and D.R. Howard. Westport, CT: Praeger.

Rascher, Daniel A., Chad D. McEvoy, Mark S. Nagel, and Matthew T. Brown. 2007. "Variable Ticket Pricing in Major League Baseball," *Journal of Sport Management,* 21(3), July: 407–437.

Ray, Edgar W. 1980. *The Grand Huckster: Houston's Judge Roy Hofheinz, Genius of the Astrodome.* Memphis: Memphis State University Press.

Ray, Margaret A., and Paul W. Grimes. 1993. "Jockeying for Position: Winnings and Gender Discrimination on the Thoroughbred Track," *Social Science Quarterly,* 74(1), March: 46–61.

"Record Six Teams to Pay Luxury Tax, Led by Dodgers," *USA Today,* December 16, 2016, at http://www.usatoday.com/story/sports/mlb/2016/12/16/apnewsbreak-record-6-mlb-teams-to-pay-luxury-tax/95536006/.

Rehberg, Megan. 2015. "*Grove City College v. Bell,*" *Law and Higher Education,* at http://caselaw.findlaw.com/us-supreme-court/465/555.html

Ribowsky, Mark. 1991. *Slick: The Silver and Black Life of Al Davis.* New York: Macmillan.

Rice, Lewis. 2002. "Games Saver," *Harvard Law Bulletin,* Spring, at https://today.law.harvard.edu/feature/games-saver/.

Rios, Edwin. 2016. "These Are the Actual Costs of the Rio Olympics," *Mother Jones*, August 5, at http://www.motherjones.com/media/2016/08/true-cost-rio-summer-olympics-zika.

Rishe, Patrick. 2012. "The Best and Worst NFL Teams Regarding Drafting Proficiency," *Forbes.com*, April 25, at http://www.forbes.com/sites/prishe/2012/04/25/the-best-and-worst-nfl-teams-in-drafting-collegiate-talent/.

Rishe, Patrick. 2012. "Dynamic Pricing: The Future of Ticket Pricing in Sports," *Forbes.com*, January 6, at https://www.forbes.com/sites/prishe/2012/01/06/dynamic-pricing-the-future-of-ticket-pricing-in-sports/.

Rismondo, Rene. 2016. "Basic Agreement," *MLBPlayers.com*, June 29, at http://www.mlbplayers.com/ViewArticle.dbml?DB_OEM_ID=34000&ATCLID=211043009.

Roberts, Gary R. 1992. "Antitrust Issues in Professional Sports," in *Law of Professional and Amateur Sports*, ed. Gary Uberstine. Deerfield, IL: Clark, Boardman, and Callaghan: 19-1–19-45.

Roberts, Gary R. 1997. "*Brown v. Pro Football, Inc.*: The Supreme Court Gets It Right for the Wrong Reasons," *Antitrust Bulletin*, 42(3), Fall: 595–639.

Roberts, Gary R., Stephen F. Ross, and Robert A. Baade. 1996. "Should Congress Stop the Bidding War for Sports Franchises?" Hearing before the Subcommittee on Antitrust, Business Rights, and Competition, Senate Committee on the Judiciary, August 1. "Academics," *Heartland Policy*, vol. 4 (November 29), at https://www.heartland.org/_template-assets/documents/publications/3924.pdf.

Romney, Mitt, and Timothy Robinson. 2004. *Turnaround: Crisis, Leadership, and the Olympic Games.* Washington, DC: Regnery Publishing.

Rose, Andrew, and Mark Spiegel. 2011. "The Olympic Effect," *Economic Journal*, 121(553): 652–677.

Rosen, Dan. 2013. "NHL, Rogers Announce Landmark 12-Year Deal," *NHL.com*, November 26, at https://www.nhl.com/news/nhl-rogers-announce-landmark-12-year-deal/c-693152.

Rosen, Harvey, and Ted Gayer. 2014. *Public Finance.* New York: McGraw-Hill.

Rosen, Sherwin. 1981. "The Economics of Superstars," *American Economic Review*, 71(5), December: 845–858.

Rosentraub, Mark. 1997. *Major League Losers.* New York: Basic Books.

Rosentraub, Mark. 1997. "Stadiums and Urban Space," in *Sports, Jobs, and Taxes*, ed. Roger G. Noll and Andrew Zimbalist. Washington, DC: Brookings Institution Press: 178–207.

Ross, Stephen F. 2004. "Player Restraints and Competition Law throughout the World," *Marquette Sports Law Review*, 15(1), Fall: 49–62.

Rottenberg, Simon. 1956. "The Baseball Players' Labor Market," *Journal of Political Economy*, 64(3), June: 242–258.

Rovell, Darren. 2016. "ACC on Track to Shatter Record for Money Earned in NCAA Tournament," *ESPN.com*, March 26, at http://www.espn.com/mens-college-basketball/story/_/id/15071018/atlantic-coast-conference-set-shatter-record-money-earned-ncaa-men-basketball-tournament.

Ruiz, Rebecca R. 2016. "Olympic Officials Set Russia's Roster; More Than 100 Are Barred for Doping," *New York Times*, August 4, at https://www.nytimes.com/2016/08/05/sports/olympics/rio-russians-barred-doping.html.

Ryan, Joan. 1995. *Little Girls in Pretty Boxes.* New York: Doubleday.

Saffer, Paul. 2015. "How Each Nation Has Done in Champions League," *UEFA.com*, September 10, at http://www.uefa.com/uefachampionsleague/news/newsid=2275207.html.

Sandomir, Richard. 2009. "Yankees Slash the Price of Top Tickets," *New York Times*, April 28, at www.nytimes.com/2009/04/29/sports/baseball/29tickets.html.

Sandritter, Mark. 2015. "2015 PGA Championship Prize Money: Jason Day Takes Home $1.8 Million Payout," *SBNation*, August 16, at https://www.sbnation.com/golf/2015/8/16/9162723/pga-championship-2015-purse-prize-money-payout-jason-day.

San Jose Redevelopment Agency. 2009. "Economic Impact Analysis: Proposed Major League Ballpark in San Jose, CA," September 22, at http://www.sjredevelopment.org/ballpark/meetings/092409/SanJosePresentation092109.pdf.

Santhanam, Laura. 2016. "Data: How Does the US Women's Soccer Team Pay Compare to the Men?" *PBS NewsHour: The Rundown,* March 31, at http://www.pbs.org/newshour/rundown/data-how-does-the-u-s-womens-soccer-team-pay-compare-to-the-men/.

Scahill, Edward. 1990. "Did Babe Ruth Have a Comparative Advantage as a Pitcher?" *Journal of Economic Education,* 21(4), Fall: 402–410.

Schlabach, Mark. 2011. "NCAA: Where Does the Money Go?" *ESPN.com,* July 12, at http://espn.go.com/college-sports/story/_/id/6756472/following-ncaa-money.

Schmidt, Martin B., and David J. Berri. 2002. "Competitive Balance and Market Size in Major League Baseball," *Review of Industrial Organization,* 21(1), August: 41–54.

Schoenfeld, David. 2016. "Could Teams Actually Pay a 92 Percent Luxury Tax under the New CBA? Yes – and No," *ESPN.com,* December 2, at http://www.espn.com/blog/sweetspot/post/_/id/76736/how-luxury-tax-penalties-would-work-on-baseballs-biggest-payrolls.

Schroffel, Jesse L., and Christopher S.P. Magee. 2012. "Own-Race Bias among NBA Coaches," *Journal of Sports Economics,* 13(2), April: 130–151.

Scully, Gerald W. 1989. *The Business of Major League Baseball.* Chicago, IL: University of Chicago Press.

Scully, Gerald W. 1995. *The Market Structure of Sports.* Chicago, IL: University of Chicago Press.

Seattle Times. 2011. "Safeco Field Taxes: In with a Bang, Out with a Whimper," *The Seattle Times,* October 11, at https://www.seattletimes.com/opinion/safeco-field-taxes-in-with-a-bang-out-with-a-whimper/.

Seiken, Eric. 1996. "The NCAA and the Courts: College Football on Television," in *Sports and the Law,* ed. Charles Quirk. New York: Garland: 56–62.

Seldon, Arthur. 1987. "Public Choice and the Choices of the Public," in *Democracy and Public Choice,* ed. Charles Rowley. London: Basil Blackwell: 122–134.

Seravalli, Frank. 2015. "Canadians Do Not Make Up the Majority of NHL Players This Season," *TSN,* October 22, at http://www.tsn.ca/canadians-do-not-make-up-the-majority-of-nhl-players-this-season-1.380861.

Seymour, Harold. 1960. *Baseball: The Early Years.* New York: Oxford University Press.

Seymour, Harold. 1971. *Baseball: The Golden Age.* New York: Oxford University Press.

Shapiro, Beth. 1983. "John Hannah and the Growth of Big-Time Intercollegiate Athletics at Michigan State University," *Journal of Sports History,* 10(3), Winter: 26–40.

Shields, Mike. 2015. "Women's World Cup Draws Strong Advertiser Demand for Fox Sports," *Wall Street Journal,* June 5, at http://blogs.wsj.com/cmo/2015/06/05/womens-world-cup-draws-strong-advertiser-demand-for-fox-sports/.

Shingler, Ronald J. 1988. "Antitrust Law and the Sports League Relocation Rules," *Golden State University Law Review,* 18(1), article 5, at http://digitalcommons.law.ggu.edu/ggulrev/vol18/iss1/5.

SI Wire. 2016. "Drew Brees Says Concussion Safety Has to Be Driven by NFLPA," *Sports Illustrated,* October 4, at https://www.si.com/nfl/2016/10/05/drew-brees-saints-concussion-safety-peter-king-podcast#.

Siegfried, John, and Andrew Zimbalist. 2000. "The Economics of Sports Facilities and Their Construction," *Journal of Economic Perspectives,* 14(3), Summer: 95–114.

Siegfried, John, and Andrew Zimbalist. 2002. "A Note on the Local Economic Impact of Sports Expenditures," *Journal of Sports Economics,* 3(4), November: 361–366.

Sievert, Justin. 2015. "The Forgotten Antitrust Case: How an NCAA Loss Could Impact College Athletics," *SportingNews,* November 4, at http://www.sportingnews.com/ncaa-football/news/ncaa-antitrust-case-shawne-alston-effects-college-athletics/1uro6chmw5naj106n150pblfmy.

Sigelman, Lee. 1995. "It's Academic—or Is It? Admissions Standards and Big-Time Football," *Social Science Quarterly,* 76(2): 247–261.

Simmons, Bill. 2009. "Welcome to the No Benjamins Association," *Grantland.com,* February 27, at http://grantland.com/features/welcome-to-the-no-benjamins-association/.

Sirak, Ron. 2008. "LPGA Facing Economic Realities," *Golf Digest,* November 18, at http://www.golfdigest.com/golf-tours-news/2008-11/20081119sirak.

Sky Sports. 2015. "Olympic Stadium Costs Soar Ahead of West Ham Move," June 19, at http://www.skysports.com/football/news/11685/9890173/olympic-stadium-costs-soar-ahead-of-west-ham-move.

Smetana, Jessica. 2017. "Super Bowl 2017 Tickets: Why Fans Can't Go to the Game," *SB Nation*, February 3, at http://www.sbnation.com/nfl/2017/2/3/14498480/2017-super-bowl-tickets-prices-patriots-falcons.

Smith, Chris. 2015. "College Football's Most Valuable Teams 2015: Texas, Notre Dame and . . . Tennessee?" *Forbes.com*, December 22, at https://www.forbes.com/sites/chrissmith/2015/12/22/college-footballs-most-valuable-teams-2015-texas-notre-dame-and-tennessee/.

Smith, Chris. 2016. "Major League Soccer's Most Valuable Teams 2016: New York, Orlando Thrive in First Seasons," *Forbes.com*, September 7, at https://www.forbes.com/sites/chrissmith/2016/09/07/major-league-soccers-most-valuable-teams-2016-new-york-orlando-thrive-in-first-seasons/.

Smith, Chris. 2016. "The Most Valuable Sponsorship Deals in Soccer," *Forbes.com*, May 11, athttp://www.forbes.com/sites/chrissmith/2016/05/11/the-most-valuable-sponsorship-deals-in-soccer/

Smith, Gary. 1983. "A New Life," *Sports Illustrated,* March 28: 60–67.

Smith, Ronald. 1988. *Sports and Freedom: The Rise of Big-Time College Athletics.* New York: Oxford University Press.

Smith, Thomas G. 2011. *Showdown: JFK and the Integration of the Washington Redskins.* Boston, MA: Beacon Press: 140.

Solomon, Jon. 2015. "CBS Sports 2015-16 FBS College Football Cost of Attendance Database," *CBSSports.com*, August 20, at http://www.cbssports.com/college-football/news/2015-16-cbs-sports-fbs-college-football-cost-of-attendance-database/.

Solow, Benjamin L., John L. Solow, and Todd B. Walker. 2011. "Moving on Up: The Rooney Rule and Minority Hiring in the NFL," *Labour Economics,* 18(3), June: 332–337.

Solow, John L., and Anthony C. Krautmann. 2007. "Leveling the Playing Field or Just Lowering Salaries? The Effects of Redistribution in Baseball," *Southern Economic Journal,* 73(4): 947–958.

Sommers, Christina Hoff. 2014. "Title IX: How a Good Law Went Terribly Wrong," *Time*, June 23, at http://time.com/2912420/titleix-anniversary/.

Southall, Richard M., Mark S. Nagel, and Megan Sexton. 2016. *2016 Adjusted Graduation Gap Report: NCAA Division-I Basketball*, April 6, at http://csri-sc.org/wp-content/uploads/2013/09/2016-Basketball-AGG-Report_Final.pdf.

Southall, Richard M., Mark S. Nagel, Allen Wallace, and Megan Sexton. 2016. *2016 Adjusted Graduation Gap Report: NCAA FBS Football*, October 19, at http://csri-sc.org/wp-content/uploads/2016/10/2016-Football-AGG-Report_Publish_Final_10-19-2016.pdf.

Spence, A. Michael. 1973. "Job Market Signaling," *Quarterly Journal of Economics,* 87(3), August: 355–374.

Sperber, Murray. 1990. *College Sports Inc.* New York: Henry Holt and Co.

Sperber, Murray. 1998. *Onward to Victory: The Crises That Shaped College Sports.* New York: Henry Holt.

Sports Illustrated. 2017. "Super Bowl Commercials: How Much Does a Spot Cost in 2017?" January 26, at https://www.si.com/nfl/2017/01/26/super-bowl-commercial-cost-2017/.

Staff Writer. 2016. "Sabres Announce New Dynamic Ticket Pricing Structure," *NHL.com*, August 24, at https://www.nhl.com/sabres/news/sabres-announce-new-dynamic-ticket-pricing-structure/c-891524.

"Standings," *MLB.com*, at http://mlb.mlb.com/mlb/standings/index.jsp#20161002.

Stapen, Candyce. 2014. "Super Bowl Hotel Rates Drop Close to Game Day," *USA Today*, January 29.

Stark, Jason. 2011. "How the New CBA Changes Baseball," *ESPN.com: Baseball*, November 22, at http://espn.go.com/espn/print?id=7270203&type=story.

Statista.com. 2016. "NFL League and Team Sponsorship Revenue Worldwide 2010 to 2016 (in Million U.S. Dollars)," at https://www.statista.com/statistics/456355/nfl-league-team-sponsorship-revenue-worldwide/.

Statista.com. 2016. "NHL League and Team Sponsorship Revenue Worldwide 2011 to 2016 (in Million U.S. Dollars)," at https://www.statista.com/statistics/456365/nhl-league-team-sponsorship-spending-worldwide/.

Statista.com. 2017. "National Basketball Association (League and Teams) Sponsorship Revenue from 2010 to 2017 (in Million U.S. Dollars)," at https://www.statista.com/statistics/380270/nba-sponsorship-revenue/.

Staudohar, Paul. 1996. *Playing for Dollars: Labor Relations and the Sports Business.* Ithaca, NY: ILR Press.

Staudohar, Paul. 2003. "Why No Baseball Work Stoppage?" *Journal of Sports Economics,* 4(4), November: 362–366.

Staudohar, Paul. 2005. "The Hockey Lockout of 2004–2005," *Monthly Labor Report,* December: 23–29.

Steptoe, Sonja, and E.M. Swift. 1994. "A Done Deal," *Sports Illustrated,* March 28: 32–36.

Stigler, George, and Gary Becker. 1977. "De Gustibus Non Est Disputandum," *American Economic Review,* 67(1), March: 76–90.

Stinson, Jeffrey, and Dennis Howard. 2007. "Athletic Success and Private Giving to Athletic and Academic Programs at NCAA Institutions," *Journal of Sport Management,* 21(2), April: 235–264.

Stratmann, Thomas. 1997. "Logrolling," in *Perspectives on Public Choice: A Handbook,* ed. Dennis Mueller. Cambridge, UK: Cambridge University Press: 322–341.

Suggs, Welch. 2005. "New Grades on Academic Progress Show Widespread Failings among Top NCAA Teams," *The Chronicle of Higher Education,* March 1, at http://www.chronicle.com/article/New-Grades-on-Academic/119610.

Sullivan, Neil J. 1987. *The Dodgers Move West.* New York: Oxford University Press.

"Summary of Major League Baseball Players Association – Major League Baseball Labor Agreement," at http://mlb.mlb.com/mlb/downloads/2011_CBA.pdf.

Sunde, Uwe. 2009. "Heterogeneity and Performance in Tournaments: A Test for Incentive Effects Using Professional Tennis Data," *Applied Economics,* 41(25–27), November–December: 3199–3208.

Swift, E.M. 1994. "Anatomy of a Plot: The Kerrigan Assault," *Sports Illustrated,* February 14: 28–38.

Swindell, David, and Mark Rosentraub. 1998. "Who Benefits from the Presence of Professional Sports Teams? The Implications for Public Funding of Stadiums and Arenas," *Public Administration Review,* 58(1), January/February: 11–20.

Szymanski, Stefan. 2000. "A Market Test for Discrimination in the English Professional Soccer Leagues," *Journal of Political Economy,* 108(3), June: 590–603.

Szymanski, Stefan, and Andrew Zimbalist. 2005. *National Pastime: How Americans Play Baseball and the Rest of the World Plays Soccer.* Washington, DC: Brookings Institution Press.

Tagaris, Karolina. 2014. "Ten Years on, Athens 2004 Gives Greece Little to Cheer," *Reuters,* August 7, at http://uk.reuters.com/article/2014/08/07/uk-olympics-greece-idUKKBN0G70Y220140807.

Taibbi, Matt. 2009. "The Devil's Doorstep: A Visit with Scott Boras," *Men's Journal,* February 23, at http://archive.li/NmdpD.

Tainsky, Scott, Brian M. Mills, and Jason A. Winfree. 2015. "Further Examination of Potential Discrimination among MLB Umpires," *Journal of Sports Economics,* 16(4), May: 353–374.

Tannenwald, Jonathan. 2015. "MLS, U.S. Soccer Officially Announce New TV Deal with ESPN, Fox, Univision," December 13, at http://www.philly.com/philly/blogs/thegoalkeeper/Live-MLS-US-Soccer-officially-announce-new-TV-deal-with-ESPN-Fox-Univision.html.

Taylor, Beck A., and Justin G. Trogdon. 2002. "Losing to Win: Tournament Incentives in the National Basketball Association," *Journal of Labor Economics,* 20(1), January: 23–41.

"Team Marketing Report – NFL 2016," at https://www.teammarketing.com/public/uploadedPDFs/NFL_FCI_2016.pdf.

Teigland, Jon. 1999. "Mega-Events and Impacts on Tourism; the Predictions and Realities of the Lillehammer Olympics," *Impact Assessment and Project Appraisal,* 17(4): 305–317.

Teammarketing.com, at https://www.teammarketing.com/public/uploadedPDFs/NBA-FCI-2015-16.pdf; https://www.teammarketing.com/public/uploadedPDFs/MLB_FCI_2016.pdf; https://www.teammarketing.com/public/uploadedPDFs/NFL_FCI_2016.pdf; https://www.teammarketing.com/public/uploadedPDFs/nhl%20fci%2015.pdf.

Thaler, Richard. 1988. "The Winner's Curse," *Journal of Economic Perspectives,* 2(1), Winter: 191–202.

Thamel, Pete. 2006. "Schools Where the Only Real Test Is Basketball," *New York Times,* February 25, at http://www.nytimes.com/2006/02/25/sports/ncaabasketball/25preps.html.

"The Championships, Wimbledon: Prize Money per Programme," *Wimbledon.com,* at http://www.wimbledon.com/pdf/Wimbledon_Prize_Money_2016.pdf.

The Institute for Diversity and Ethics in Sport. 2015. "Keeping Score When It Counts: Analyzing the Academic Performance of the 2015 NCAA Women's and Men's Sweet 16 Teams," March 25, at http://nebula.wsimg.com/a726d64c2544c7fe98d458088e1e7ce4?AccessKeyId=DAC3A56D8FB782449D2A&disposition=0&alloworigin=1.

Thornley, Stew. 2000. *Land of the Giants: New York's Polo Grounds.* Philadelphia, PA: Temple University Press.

Tidey, Will. 2013. "Sepp Blatter's Most Embarrassing Outbursts," *Bleacher Report,* May 31, at http://bleacherreport.com/articles/1657592-sepp-blatters-most-embarrassing-outbursts/page/2.

Title IX Legal Manual, United States Department of Justice, Civil Rights Division, updated August 6, 2015, at https://www.justice.gov/crt/title-ix.

Tofler, Ian, Barri Katz Stryer, Lyle J. Micheli, and Lisa Herman. 1996. "Physical and Emotional Problems of Elite Female Gymnasts," *New England Journal of Medicine,* 335(4), July 25: 281–283.

Tollison, Robert. 1997. "Rent Seeking," in *Perspectives on Public Choice: A Handbook,* ed. Dennis Mueller. Cambridge, UK: Cambridge University Press: 506–525.

Tomlinson, Alan. 1984. "De Coubertin and the Modern Olympics," in *Five Ring Circus: Money, Power and Politics at the Olympic Games,* ed. Alan Tomlinson and Garry Whannel. London: Pluto Press: 84–97.

Totalsportek2. 2016. "German Bundesliga New TV Rights Money Distribution System," June 9, at http://www.totalsportek.com/money/bundesliga-tv-rights/.

Totalsportek2. 2016. "Italian Serie A TV Rights & Prize Money Distribution for 2016 (Explained)," February 17, at http://www.totalsportek.com/football/italian-serie-a-tv-rights-money-distribution/.

Totalsportek2. 2017. "Australian Open Tennis 2017 Prize Money," *Total Sportek,* January 26, at http://www.totalsportek.com/tennis/australian-open-prize-money/.

Totalsportek2. 2017. "Premier League Player Salaries of 20 Clubs (Wage Bills 2016-17)," January 20, at http://www.totalsportek.com/money/english-premier-league-wage-bills-club-by-club/.

Tottenham Hotspur. "Match Day Prices 2017/2018," at http://www.tottenhamhotspur.com/tickets/ticket-prices/.

Trumpbour, Robert. 2007. *The New Cathedrals.* Syracuse, NY: Syracuse University Press.

Tu, Charles. 2005. "How Does a New Stadium Affect Housing Values? The Case of FedEx Field," *Land Economics,* 81(3), August: 379–395.

UEFA.com. 2015. "Financial Fair Play: All You Need to Know," June 30, at http://www.uefa.com/community/news/newsid=2064391.html.

UEFA.com. 2016. "2015/16 Champions League Revenue Distribution," November 1, at http://www.uefa.com/uefachampionsleague/news/newsid=2418253.html.

UEFA.com. 2016. "2015/16 Europa League Revenue Distribution," November 1, at http://www.uefa.com/uefaeuropaleague/news/newsid=2418259.html.

UEFA.com. "Regulations of the UEFA Champions League 2015-2018 Cycle," at http://www.uefa.com/MultimediaFiles/Download/Regulations/uefaorg/Regulations/02/35/87/89/2358789_DOWNLOAD.pdf.

Ungerleider, Steven. 2001. *Faust's Gold: Inside the East German Doping Machine.* New York: Thomas Dunne Books.

United Press International. 1982. "Average N.F.L. Salary Is $90,102, Survey Says," *New York Times,* January 29, at http://www.nytimes.com/1982/01/29/sports/average-nfl-salary-is-90102-survey-says.html.

"United States Consumer Price Index for All Urban Consumers (CPI-U) 1970 – 2016," at http://www.dlt.ri.gov/lmi/pdf/cpi.pdf.

University of Pennsylvania Museum of Anthropology and Archeology. 1996. "The Real Story of the Ancient Olympic Games," at https://www.penn.museum/sites/olympics/olympicathletes.shtml.

US Department of Commerce, "Table CA1-3: Personal Income Summary," *Regional Data: GDP & Personal Income,* at http://www.bea.gov/iTable/iTable.cfm?reqid=70&step=1&isuri=1&acrdn=5.

US Youth Soccer, "Key Statistics," at http://www.usyouthsoccer.org/media_kit/keystatistics/.

USA Today, "NCAA Salaries," *USAToday.com,* at http://sports.usatoday.com/ncaa/salaries/.

USA Today, "Player Salaries," *USAToday.com,* at https://www.usatoday.com/sports/mlb/salaries/.

"USA Today Salaries Data Base," *USAToday.com,* at http://usatoday30.usatoday.com/sports/salaries/index.htm.

USA Today Sports. 2016. "Methodology for NCAA Athletic Department Database," *USAToday.com,* April 14, at http://sports.usatoday.com/2016/04/14/methodology-for-ncaa-athletic-department-revenue-database/.

van Mill, David. 2015. "Why Are We So Opposed to Performance-Enhancing Drugs in Sport?" *The Conversation,* August 27, at http://theconversation.com/why-are-we-so-opposed-to-performance-enhancing-drugs-in-sport-46528.

Van Riper, Tom. 2009. "Boxing's Last Golden Boy?" *Forbes.com,* January 15, at https://www.forbes.com/2009/01/14/boxing-oscar-de-la-hoya-biz-sports_cx_tvr_0115delahoya.html.

Van Riper, Tom. 2010. "The NFL Vs. American Needle," *Forbes.com,* January 7, at http://www.forbes.com/2010/01/06/american-needle-supreme-court-business-sports-nfl.html.

Van Scyoc, L.J., and N.J. Burnett. 2013. "How Times Have Changed: Racial Discrimination in the Market for Sports Memorabilia (Baseball Cards)," *Applied Economics Letters,* 20(7–9), June: 875–878.

Van Wynsberghe, Rob. 2011. "Olympic Games Impact (OGI) Study for the 2010 Olympic and Paralympic Winter Games Games-time Report," at http://cfss.sites.olt.ubc.ca/files/2011/10/The-Olympic-Games-Impact-Study-Games-time-Report-2011-11-21.pdf.

Veeck, Bill. 1962. *Veeck as in Wreck.* Chicago, IL: University of Chicago Press.

Veeck, Bill, with Ed Linn. 1996. *The Hustler's Handbook.* Durham, NC: Baseball America Classic Books.

Veraros, Nikolaos, Evangelia Kasimati, and Peter Dawson. 2004. "The 2004 Olympic Games Announcement and Its Effect on the Athens and Milan Stock Exchanges," *Applied Economics Letters,* 11(12), October: 749–753.

Vincent, Claude, and Byron Eastman. 2009. "Determinants of Pay in the NHL: A Quantile Regression Approach," *Journal of Sports Economics,* 10(3), June: 256–277.

Voigt, Kevin. 2010. "Is There a World Cup Economic Bounce?" *CNN.com,* June 11, at http://edition.cnn.com/2010/BUSINESS/06/11/business.bounce.world.cup/index.html.

von Allmen, Peter. 2000. "Is the Reward System in NASCAR Efficient?" *Journal of Sports Economics,* 2(1), February: 62–79.

von Allmen, Peter. 2012. "Multiplier Effects and Local Economic Impact," in *The Oxford Handbook of Sports Economics,* vol. 2, ed. Stephen Shmanske and Leo Kahane. Oxford: Oxford University Press.

von Allmen, Peter. 2013. "Coaching Women and Women Coaching: Pay Differentials in the Title IX Era," in *Handbook on the Economics of Women in Sports,* ed. Eva Marikova Leeds and Michael A. Leeds (Cheltenham, UK: Edward Elgar): 269–289.

von Allmen, Peter, Michael Leeds, and Julian Malakorn. 2015. "Victims or Beneficiaries? Wage Premia and National Origin in the National Hockey League," *Journal of Sports Management,* 29(6), November: 633–641.

Vrooman, John. 1997. "Franchise Free Agency in Professional Sports Leagues," *Southern Journal of Economics,* 64(1), July: 191–219.

Vrooman, John. 2009. "Theory of the Perfect Game: Competitive Balance in Monopoly Sports," *Review of Industrial Organization,* 34(5): 5–44.

Waldron, Travis. 2016. "St. Louis Taxpayers Aren't Finished Paying for the Stadium the Rams Abandoned," *Huffington Post,* January 13, at http://www.huffingtonpost.com/entry/rams-los-angeles-st-louis-taxpayers_us_5696955ee4b0778f46f7c330.

Walker, Alissa. 2014. "How L.A.'s 1984 Summer Olympics Became the Most Successful Games Ever," *Gizmodo.com,* February 6, at http://gizmodo.com/how-l-a-s-1984-summer-olympics-became-the-most-success-1516228102.

Walker, Simone. 2009. "De la Hoya – Boxing's Future Is Golden," *SportsPro,* October 13, at http://www.sportspromedia.com/notes_and_insights/de_la_hoya_-_boxings_future_is_golden/.

Wall Street Journal. 2017. "Russia's 2018 World Cup Stadiums," October 2, at https://graphics.wsj.com/embeddable-carousel/?slug=russia-world-cup-2018.

Ward, Geoffrey, and Kenneth Burns. 1994. *Baseball: An Illustrated History.* New York: Alfred A. Knopf.

Weaver, Jane. 2005. "Steroid Addiction a Risk for Young Athletes," *MSNBC,* April 5, at http://www.msnbc.msn.com/id/7348758.

Westcott, Rich. 1996. *Philadelphia's Old Ballparks.* Philadelphia, PA: Temple University Press.

Wetzel, Dan, Josh Peter, and Jeff Passan. 2010. *Death to the BCS.* New York: Gotham Books.

Wieberg, Steve. 2005. "Academic Progress Rates Analyzed," *USA Today,* at http://www.usatoday.com/sports/college/2005-03-01-apr-analysis_x.htm.

Will, George F. 1998. *Bunts.* New York: Scribner.

Winfree, Jason, Jill McCluskey, Ron Mittelhammer, and Rodney Fort. 2004. "Location and Attendance in Major League Baseball," *Applied Economics,* 36(19), October: 2117–2124.

Wolverton, Brad. 2012. "Female Participation in College Sports Reaches All-Time High," *The Chronicle of Higher Education,* January 22, at http://www.chronicle.com/article/Female-Participation-in/130431/.

Wong, Glenn. 2010. *Essentials of Sports Law,* 4th ed. Santa Barbara, CA: Praeger.

World Population Review. "Toronto Population 2016," at http://worldpopulationreview.com/world-cities/toronto-population/.

WTA. 2017. "2017 WTA Official Rulebook," at http://www.wtatennis.com/sites/default/files/rules2017.pdf.

Yang, Chih-Hai, and Hsuan-Y Lin. 2012. "Is There Salary Discrimination by Nationality in the NBA?: Foreign Talent or Foreign Market," *Journal of Sports Economics,* 13(1), February: 53–75.

Young, David. 1996. *The Modern Olympics: A Struggle for Revival.* Baltimore, MD: Johns Hopkins University Press.

Zengerle, Jason. 2008. "The Pivot," *The New Republic,* July 9: 24–32.

Zimbalist, Andrew. 1992. *Baseball and Billions.* New York: Basic Books.

Zimbalist, Andrew. 1999. *Unpaid Professionals.* Princeton, NJ: Princeton University Press.

Zimbalist, Andrew. 2003. "Labor Relations in Major League Baseball," *Journal of Sports Economics,* 4(4), November: 332–355.

Zimbalist, Andrew. 2003. *May the Best Team Win: Baseball Economics and Public Policy.* Washington, DC: Brookings Institution Press.

Zimbalist, Andrew. 2003. "Sport as Business," *Oxford Review of Economic Policy,* 19(4): 503–511.

Zimbalist, Andrew. 2012. Personal Communication.

Zimbalist, Andrew. 2013. *In the Best Interests of Baseball? Governing the National Pastime.* Lincoln, NE: University of Nebraska Press.

Zimbalist, Andrew. 2015. *Circus Maximus: The Economic Gamble behind Hosting the Olympics and the World Cup.* Washington, DC: Brookings Institution Press.

Zimmerman, Ann, and Leslie Scism. 2012. "Boone Calls the Plays as Largess Complicates Life at Alma Mater," *Wall Street Journal,* July 7, at https://www.wsj.com/articles/SB100 01424052702304782404577488592793245510.

Zimmerman, Dennis. 1997. "Subsidizing Stadiums: Who Benefits, Who Pays?" in *Sports, Jobs, and Taxes,* ed. Roger G. Noll and Andrew Zimbalist. Washington, DC: Brookings Institution Press: 119–147.

INDEX